HVAC DUCT CONSTRUCTION STANDARDS

METAL AND FLEXIBLE

ANSI/SMACNA 006-2020

**SHEET METAL AND AIR CONDITIONING CONTRACTORS'
NATIONAL ASSOCIATION, INC.
www.smacna.org**

HVAC DUCT CONSTRUCTION STANDARDS

METAL AND FLEXIBLE

FOURTH EDITION – 2020

**SHEET METAL AND AIR CONDITIONING CONTRACTORS'
NATIONAL ASSOCIATION, INC.**
4201 Lafayette Center Drive
Chantilly, VA 20151 – 1219
www.smacna.org

HVAC
DUCT CONSTRUCTION
STANDARDS
METAL AND FLEXIBLE

COPYRIGHT © SMACNA 2005
All Rights Reserved
by

**SHEET METAL AND AIR CONDITIONING CONTRACTORS'
NATIONAL ASSOCIATION, INC.**

4201 Lafayette Center Drive
Chantilly, VA 20151–1209

Printed in the U.S.A.

FIRST EDITION – 1985
SECOND EDITION – 1995
THIRD EDITION – 2005
FOURTH EDITION – 2020

Except as allowed in the Notice to Users and in certain licensing contracts, no part of this book may be reproduced, stored in a retrievable system, or transmitted, in any form or by any means, electronic, mechanical, photocopying, recording, or otherwise, without the prior written permission of the publisher.

FOREWORD

Building on a history of duct construction standards nearly 100 years old the Fourth Edition of SMACNA's HVAC Duct Construction Standards Metal and Flexible represents the state of the art in sheet metal duct fabrication and installation

The advances in fabrication and installation are made possible by many in the industry providing suggestions for improvement based on knowledge, experience and research. Special thanks is given to those who volunteered their time and efforts towards developing this edition and previous editions of this long running standard. Although standardization intrinsically involves selection, no intention of discrimination against the use of any product or method that would serve a designer's need equally or better exists.

SHEET METAL AND AIR CONDITIONING CONTRACTORS'
NATIONAL ASSOCIATION, INC.

HVAC DUCT CONSTRUCTION TASK FORCE

Richard C. Mertz *Chair*
H.T. Lyons, Inc.
Allentown, PA

Steven Benkovsky
Triple S Air Systems, Inc.
Ronkonkoma, NY

Roy Jensen
MechOne
Colorado Springs, CO

Eric Porras
ACCO Engineered Systems
Glendale, CA

Mark Bengard
Murphy Company
Saint Louis, MO

Matt Dejong
Environmental Mechanical Contractors
Olathe, KS

Jerry Manta
F.E. Moran, Inc.
Northbrook, IL

Kevin Richison
The Brandt Companies, LLC
Carrollton, TX

Richard Freeman
Stromberg Sheet Metal Works, Inc.
Beltsville, MD

Mark Terzigni *Staff Liaison*
SMACNA
Chantilly, VA

FORMER COMMITTEE MEMBERS AND OTHER CONTRIBUTORS TO THE FOURTH EDITION

Roy Jensen, *Chairman 2005–2006*
MechOne
Colorado Springs, Colorado

Douglas Ahlberg
Arctic Sheet Metal, Inc.
Portland, Oregon

Chris Combe
Superior Air Handling Corporation
Clearfield, Utah

Mark Edhammer
Southland Industries
San Jose, California

Roy Ricci
McCusker–Gill, Inc.
Hingham, Massachusetts

Jerry Robinson
Stromberg Sheet Metal Works, Inc.
Beltsville, Maryland

Robert J. Wasilewski, *Staff Liaison*
SMACNA, Inc.
Chantilly, Virginia

Eli P. Howard, III, *Staff Liaison*
SMACNA, Inc.
Chantilly, Virginia

Michael Mamayek*, *Chairman 1992 – 1993*
Illingworth Corporation
Milwaukee, WI

Andrew J. Boniface*, *Chairman 1989 – 1991*
Bonland Industries
Wayne, NJ

H. Andrew Kimmel*, *Chairman 1988*
E.W. Ensroth Co.
Warren, MI

Robert S. Deeds*, *Chairman 1986 – 1987*
METCO, Inc.
Salt Lake City, UT

Norman T.R. Heathorn*
N.B. Heathorn, Inc.
Oakland, CA

Gerald D. Hermanson*
Hermanson Corporation
Renton, WA

iv   HVAC Duct Construction Standards Metal and Flexible • Fourth Edition

George J. Thomas, Jr.*
Thomas Roofing & Sheet Metal Co., Inc.
Atlantic City, NJ

Guillermo ("Bill") Navas, *Staff*
SMACNA
Chantilly, VA

Ronald Rodgers, *Chairman*
J.B. Rodgers Mechanical Contractors
Phoenix, AZ

Seymore Cohen
Knecht, Inc.
Camden, NJ

Dick Hoffa
Corn States Metal Fabricators, Inc.
West Des Moine, IA

Ronald Palmerick
AABCO Sheet Metal
Brooklyn, NY

Les Santeler
Climatemp, Inc.
Chicago, IL

John H. Stratton, *Staff*
SMACNA
Chantilly, VA

NOTICE TO USERS OF THIS PUBLICATION

1. DISCLAIMER OF WARRANTIES

a) The Sheet Metal and Air Conditioning Contractors' National Association ("SMACNA") provides its product for informational purposes.

b) The product contains "Data" which is believed by SMACNA to be accurate and correct but the data, including all information, ideas and expressions therein, is provided strictly "AS IS," with all faults. SMACNA makes no warranty either express or implied regarding the Data and SMACNA EXPRESSLY DISCLAIMS ANY IMPLIED WARRANTIES OF MERCHANTABILITY OR FITNESS FOR PARTICULAR PURPOSE.

c) By using the data contained in the product user accepts the Data "AS IS" and assumes all risk of loss, harm or injury that may result from its use. User acknowledges that the Data is complex, subject to faults and requires verification by competent professionals, and that modification of parts of the Data by user may impact the results or other parts of the Data.

d) IN NO EVENT SHALL SMACNA BE LIABLE TO USER, OR ANY OTHER PERSON, FOR ANY INDIRECT, SPECIAL OR CONSEQUENTIAL DAMAGES ARISING, DIRECTLY OR INDIRECTLY, OUT OF OR RELATED TO USER'S USE OF SMACNA'S PRODUCT OR MODIFICATION OF DATA THEREIN. This limitation of liability applies even if SMACNA has been advised of the possibility of such damages. IN NO EVENT SHALL SMACNA'S LIABILITY EXCEED THE AMOUNT PAID BY USER FOR ACCESS TO SMACNA'S PRODUCT OR $1,000.00, WHICHEVER IS GREATER, REGARDLESS OF LEGAL THEORY.

e) User by its use of SMACNA's product acknowledges and accepts the foregoing limitation of liability and disclaimer of warranty and agrees to indemnify and hold harmless SMACNA from and against all injuries, claims, loss or damage arising, directly or indirectly, out of user's access to or use of SMACNA's product or the Data contained therein.

2. ACCEPTANCE

This document or publication is prepared for voluntary acceptance and use within the limitations of application defined herein, and otherwise as those adopting it or applying it deem appropriate. It is not a safety standard. Its application for a specific project is contingent on a designer or other authority defining a specific use. SMACNA has no power or authority to police or enforce compliance with the contents of this document or publication and it has no role in any representations by other parties that specific components are, in fact, in compliance with it.

3. AMENDMENTS

The Association may, from time to time, issue formal interpretations or interim amendments, which can be of significance between successive editions.

4. PROPRIETARY PRODUCTS

SMACNA encourages technological development in the interest of improving the industry for the public benefit. SMACNA does not, however, endorse individual manufacturers or products.

5. FORMAL INTERPRETATION

a) A formal interpretation of the literal text herein or the intent of the technical committee or task force associated with the document or publication is obtainable only on the basis of written petition, addressed to the Technical Resources Department and sent to the Association's national office in Chantilly, Virginia. In the event that the petitioner has a substantive disagreement with the interpretation, an appeal may be filed with the Technical Resources Committee, which has technical oversight responsibility. The request must pertain to a specifically identified portion of the document that does not involve published text which provides the requested information. In considering such requests, the Association will not review or judge products or components as being in compliance with the document or publication. Oral and written interpretations otherwise obtained from anyone affiliated with the Association are unofficial. This procedure does not prevent any committee or task force chairman, member of the committee or task force, or staff liaison from expressing an opinion on a provision within the document, provided that such person clearly states that the opinion is personal and does not represent an official act of the Association in any way, and it should not be relied on as such. The Board of Directors of SMACNA shall have final authority for interpretation of this standard with such rules or procedures as they may adopt for processing same.

b) SMACNA disclaims any liability for any personal injury, property damage, or other damage of any nature whatsoever, whether special, indirect, consequential or compensatory, direct or indirectly resulting from the publication, use of, or reliance upon this document. SMACNA makes no guaranty or warranty as to the accuracy or completeness of any information published herein.

6. APPLICATION

a) Any standards contained in this publication were developed using reliable engineering principles and research plus consultation with, and information obtained from, manufacturers, users, testing laboratories, and others having specialized experience. They are subject to revision as further experience and investigation may show is necessary or desirable. Construction and products which comply with these Standards will not necessarily be acceptable if, when examined and tested, they are found to have other features which impair the result contemplated by these requirements. The Sheet Metal and Air Conditioning Contractors' National Association and other contributors assume no responsibility and accept no liability for the application of the principles or techniques contained in this publication. Authorities considering adoption of any standards contained herein should review all federal, state, local, and contract regulations applicable to specific installations.

b) In issuing and making this document available, SMACNA is not undertaking to render professional or other services for or on behalf of any person or entity. SMACNA is <u>not</u> undertaking to perform any duty owed to any person or entity to someone else. Any person or organization using this document should rely on his, her or its own judgement or, as appropriate, seek the advice of a competent professional in determining the exercise of reasonable care in any given circumstance.

7. REPRINT PERMISSION

Non-exclusive, royalty-free permission is granted to government and private sector specifying authorities to reproduce *only* any construction details found herein in their specifications and contract drawings prepared for receipt of bids on new construction and renovation work within the United States and its territories, provided that the material copied is unaltered in substance and that the reproducer assumes all liability for the specific application, including errors in reproduction.

8. THE SMACNA LOGO

The SMACNA logo is registered as a membership identification mark. The Association prescribes acceptable use of the logo and expressly forbids the use of it to represent anything other than possession of membership. Possession of membership and use of the logo in no way constitutes or reflects SMACNA approval of any product, method, or component. Furthermore, compliance of any such item with standards published or recognized by SMACNA is not indicated by presence of the logo.

THIS PAGE INTENTIONALLY LEFT BLANK

MODEL PROJECT SPECIFICATION

DUCT CONSTRUCTION

Ductwork and supports shall conform to the *HVAC Duct Construction Standards, Metal and Flexible*, FOURTH EDITION *2020*. Where fittings of configurations not shown in the HVAC-DCS are shown on the contract drawings, they shall be constructed as though they were therein.

DUCT DIMENSIONS

Duct dimensions shown in the contract drawings are for airflow area. When ducts are acoustically lined, their dimensions shall be increased as necessary.

DUCT PRESSURE CLASS

Duct pressure classes are to be identified on the contract drawings.

Schedule the pressure classes here by fan system number, or portion thereof, if they are not shown on the drawings.

See Section 1.4.

DUCT SEAL CLASS

Ducts shall be sealed as specified in the *HVAC-DCS*.

DUCT LEAKAGE CLASS

Consult the HVAC-Air Duct Leakage Test Manual and select appropriate allowable leakage. If field leak tests are required, appropriate test pressure and clear scope of testing must be specified.

DUCT LINER

Metal nosing shall be used on leading edges of each piece of lined duct when the velocity exceeds 4000 fpm (20.3 m/s) otherwise, it shall be used on the leading edge of any lined duct section that is preceded by unlined duct.

NOTES FOR SPECIFIER

See duct liner test and references in the HVAC-DCS and specify the material, thickness, density and performance characteristics desired.

FLEXIBLE DUCT AND CONNECTOR

Where the specifications for connecting and supporting these in the HVAC-DCS are more stringent or restrictive, they shall supersede.

VIBRATION ISOLATION CONNECTORS

Flexible isolation connectors shall not exceed 10 in. in length in direction of airflow and shall be made of flame-retardant fabric having a flame spread rating not over 25 and a smoke developed rating not over 50.

Consult the applicable codes, The U.L. Fire Resistance Directory, references in the HVAC-DCS, the Air Duct Council's Flexible Air Duct Performance and Installation Standards and identify the products and performance characteristics desired.

PROPRIETARY PRODUCTS

Description of products from a proprietary or single source manufacturer shall be submitted for approval along with substantiation of fitness for the service conditions that are proposed but not already identified in the project specifications.

PENETRATIONS

All wall penetrations that require special-purpose dampers (fire, smoke, etc.) shall be shown in the contract drawings.

Consult the SMACNA Fire, Smoke, and Radiation Damper Guide and local codes for obligations to show the location of each barrier penetration protection device on contract drawing. Review the commentary in Section 2.3 of these standards for obligation to show all air volume control devices on the contract drawings when they are not specified to be integral with HVAC units or air terminal units. Also specify the size and location of all access doors and access panels to be used in ductwork.

LIST OF SIGNIFICANT CHANGES FROM THE THIRD EDITION

1. Added information on spray and aerosolized duct sealants

2. Added tables for spiral flat oval duct for positive and negative pressure applications

3. Added options for internal supports for spiral flat oval duct

4. Updated liner requirements to include non-fiberglass liner types

5. Added information for lined round duct

6. Added details for hangers to better illustrate where hangers are required

7. Updated requirements for flex duct hanger spacing and hanger width.

8. Added information for spiral fittings

Although no changes were made to the root tables for rectangular duct a few inconsistencies were fixed in the tables specifically addressing T25a/b (TDC/TDF). Corrections included gage, reinforcement size, and number of tie rods required.

Also, minor corrections and clarifications were made to the round tables as well.

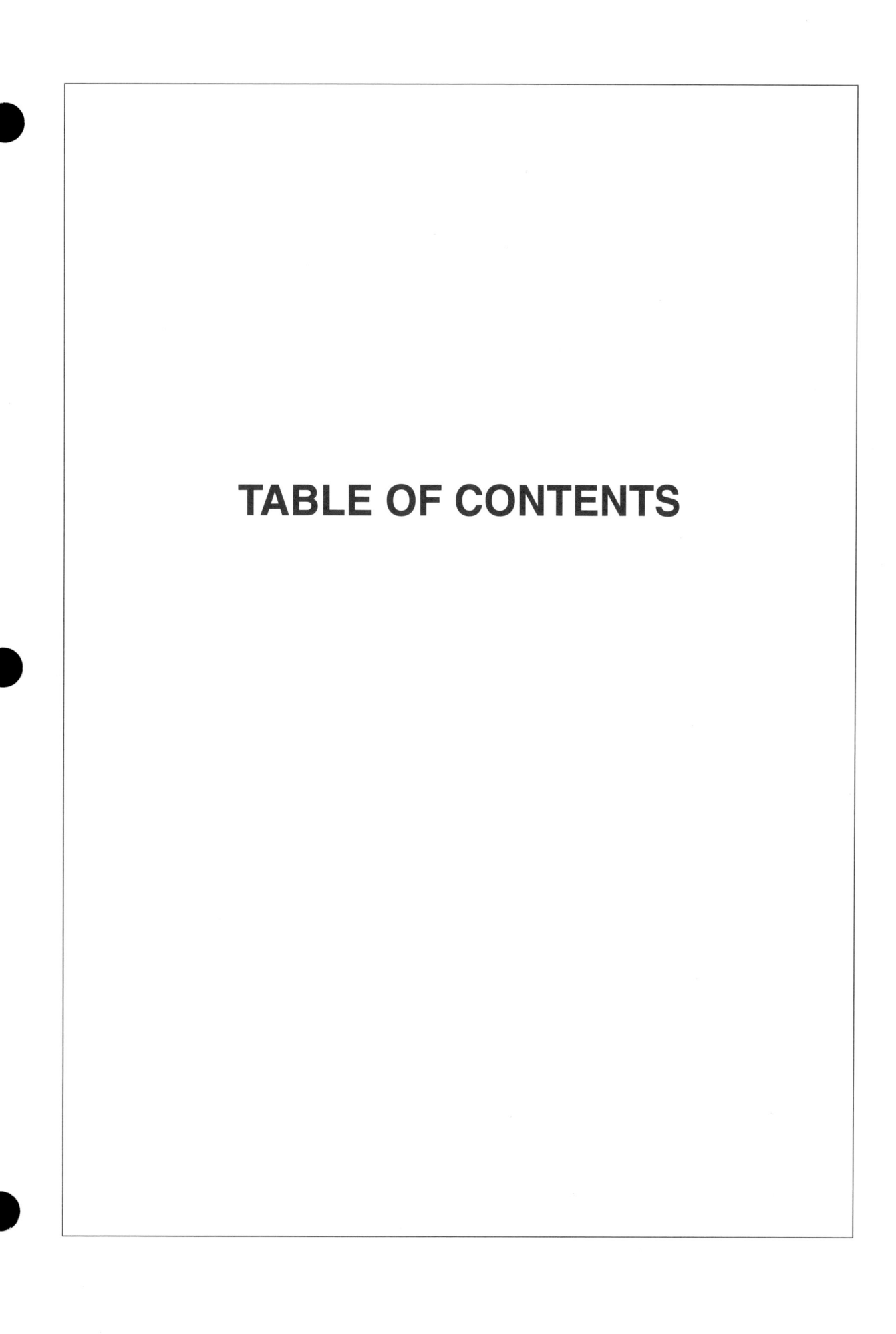

TABLE OF CONTENTS

TABLE OF CONTENTS

FOREWORD iii

HVAC DUCT CONSTRUCTION TASK FORCE iv

NOTICE TO USERS OF THIS PUBLICATION vi

MODEL PROJECT SPECIFICATION ix

LIST OF MAJOR CHANGES FROM THE THIRD EDITION x

TABLE OF CONTENTS xi

CHAPTER 1   ENGINEERING AND DESIGN .... Page

    1.1   INTRODUCTION 1.1
    1.2   INFORMATION REQUIRED FOR DUCT CONSTRUCTION 1.1
    1.3   MODEL SPECIFICATIONS 1.1
    1.4   DUCT SEALING 1.11
    1.5   INTRODUCTION TO BASIC CONSTRUCTION 1.13
    1.6   DEPENDENT VARIABLES 1.18

CHAPTER 2   RECTANGULAR DUCT CONSTRUCTION

    2.1   INTRODUCTION TO THE RECTANGULAR DUCT CONSTRUCTION SCHEDULES.. 2.1
    2.2   RECTANGULAR DUCT REINFORCEMENT 2.4
    2.3   LONGITUDINAL SEAMS FOR RECTANGULAR DUCT 2.11
    2.4   TRANSVERSE JOINTS FOR RECTANGULAR DUCT 2.73
    2.5   TIE ROD INSTALLATIONS 2.80
    2.6   COMMENTARY 2.81
    2.7   MIDPANEL TIE ROD APPLICATIONS 2.97
    2.8   MIDPANEL TIE ROD (MPT) USE GUIDE 2.97
    2.9   MIDPANEL TIE ROD SELECTIONS 2.98
    2.10   COMMENTARY ON ALUMINUM DUCT 2.123

CHAPTER 3   ROUND, OVAL AND FLEXIBLE DUCT

    3.1   ROUND DUCT CONSTRUCTION STANDARDS 3.1
    3.2   COMMENTARY 3.2
    3.3   FLAT OVAL DUCT CONSTRUCTION STANDARDS 3.27
    3.4   COMMENTARY 3.27
    3.5   FLEXIBLE DUCT INSTALLATION STANDARDS 3.48
    3.6   SPECIFICATION FOR JOINING AND ATTACHING FLEXIBLE DUCT 3.48
    3.7   SPECIFICATION FOR SUPPORTING FLEXIBLE DUCT 3.48
    3.8   COMMENTARY 3.54

CHAPTER 4   FITTINGS AND OTHER CONSTRUCTION

    4.1   REQUIREMENTS 4.1

CHAPTER 5   HANGERS AND SUPPORTS

    5.1   HANGING AND SUPPORTING SYSTEMS 5.1
    5.2   COMMENTARY 5.1

CHAPTER 6   EXTERIOR COMPONENTS .... Page

    6.1   INTRODUCTION 6.1
    6.2   ROOFTOP EQUIPMENT INSTALLATION 6.5
    6.3   COMMENTARY 6.5

CHAPTER 7   ACCESSORIES

    7.1   VOLUME DAMPERS 7.5
    7.2   NOTES FOR FIGURES 7–4 AND 7–5 .... 7.5
    7.3   COMMENTARY 7.5
    7.4   INSTALLATION STANDARDS FOR RECTANGULAR DUCTS USING FLEXIBLE LINER 7.14
    7.5   COMMENTARY 7.15
    7.6   INSTALLATION STANDARDS FOR SINGLE WALL, ROUND DUCT INSULATION DUCT LINERS 7.16
    7.7   SINGLE WALL ROUND APPLICATIONS REQUIRING ADDITIONAL SUPPORT OR MECHANICAL FASTENING 7.16
    7.8   SINGLE WALL ROUND APPLICATIONS REQUIRING NOSINGS 7.17
    7.9   COMMENTARY 7.18

CHAPTER 8   DOUBLE-WALL DUCT CONSTRUCTION

    8.1   INSTALLATION STANDARDS COMMENTARY 8.1

CHAPTER 9   EQUIPMENT AND CASINGS

    9.1   CASING AND PLENUM CONSTRUCTION STANDARDS 9.1
    9.2   COMMENTARY 9.24
    9.3   CASING ARRANGEMENT 9.24

CHAPTER 10   SPECIALTY SYSTEMS

    10.1   HOODS 10.2
    10.2   UNDERGROUND DUCT CONSTRUCTION STANDARDS 10.4
    10.3   COMMENTARY 10.7

CHAPTER 11   FUNCTIONAL CRITERIA

    11.1   FUNCTIONAL CRITERIA FOR DUCTS 11.1
    11.2   RECTANGULAR DUCTS 11.1
    11.3   COMMENTARY 11.2
    11.4   PROCEDURE FOR RATING DUCT CONSTRUCTION METHODS RELATIVE TO THE SMACNA CONSTRUCTION TABLES 11.8
    11.5   NOTES ON SPECIMEN TESTING 11.9
    11.6   SOUND AND VIBRATION 11.10

APPENDIX A

TABLES

		Page
1–1	Standard Duct Sealing Requirements	1.11
1–2	Pressure Classification for Ductwork	1.17

> Due to the large number of tables in Chapter 2 the list of tables has been place immediately after the Chapter 2 title page.

1–3	Static Pressure	1.18
3–1	Mitered Elbows	3.1
3–2	Angle Ring Size	3.6
3–2M	Angle Ring Size	3.7
3–3	Ring Attachment Schedule	3.6
3–3M	Ring Attachment Schedule	3.7
3–4	Companion Flange Joints Used As Reinforcement	3.6
3–4M	Companion Flange Joints Used As Reinforcement	3.7
3–5	Round Duct Gage Unreinforced Positive Pressure To 10 in. wg	3.8
3–5M	Round Duct Gage Unreinforced Positive Pressure To 10 in. wg	3.9
3–6	Min. Required Gage for Longitudinal Seam Duct Under Neg. Pressure	3.10
3–6M	Min. Required Gage for Longitudinal Seam Duct Under Neg. Pressure	3.11
3–7	Min. Required Gage for Longitudinal Seam Duct Under Neg. Pressure	3.12
3–7M	Min. Required Gage for Longitudinal Seam Duct Under Neg. Pressure	3.13
3–8	Min. Required Gage for Longitudinal Seam Duct Under Neg. Pressure	3.14
3–8M	Min. Required Gage for Longitudinal Seam Duct Under Neg. Pressure	3.15
3–9	Min. Required Gage for Longitudinal Seam Duct Under Neg. Pressure	3.16
3–9M	Min. Required Gage for Longitudinal Seam Duct Under Neg. Pressure	3.17
3–10	Min. Required Gage for Spiral Seam Duct Under Neg. Pressure	3.18
3–10M	Min. Required Gage for Spiral Seam Duct Under Neg. Pressure	3.19
3–11	Min. Required Gage for Spiral Seam Duct Under Neg. Pressure	3.20
3–11M	Min. Required Gage for Spiral Seam Duct Under Neg. Pressure	3.21
3–12	Min. Required Gage for Spiral Seam Duct Under Neg. Pressure	3.22
3–12M	Min. Required Gage for Spiral Seam Duct Under Neg. Pressure	3.23
3–13	Min. Required Gage for Spiral Seam Duct Under Neg. Pressure	3.24
3–13M	Min. Required Gage for Spiral Seam Duct Under Neg. Pressure	3.25
3–14	Aluminum Round Duct Gage Schedule	3.26
3–14M	Aluminum Round Duct Gage Schedule	3.26
3-15	Longitudinal Seam Flat Oval Duct Gage Positive Pressure to 10 in. wg	3.28
3-15M	Longitudinal Seam Flat Oval Duct Gage Positive Pressure to 2500 Pa	3.28
3-16	Spiral Flat Oval Reinforcement Table	3.30
3-16M	Spiral Flat Oval Reinforcement Table	3.31
3-17	Spiral Flat Oval Reinforcement Table	3.32
3-17M	Spiral Flat Oval Reinforcement Table	3.33
3-18	Spiral Flat Oval Reinforcement Table	3.34
3-18M	Spiral Flat Oval Reinforcement Table	3.35
3-19	Spiral Flat Oval Reinforcement Table	3.36
3-19M	Spiral Flat Oval Reinforcement Table	3.37
3-20	Spiral Flat Oval Reinforcement Table	3.38
3-20M	Spiral Flat Oval Reinforcement Table	3.39
3-21	Spiral Flat Oval Reinforcement Table	3.40
3-21M	Spiral Flat Oval Reinforcement Table	3.41
3-22	Spiral Flat Oval Reinforcement Table	3.42
3-22M	Spiral Flat Oval Reinforcement Table	3.43
5–1	Rectangular Duct Hangers Minimum Size	5.7
5–1M	Rectangular Duct Hangers Minimum Size	5.8

HVAC Duct Construction Standards Metal and Flexible • Fourth Edition

5–2	Minimum Hanger Sizes for Round Duct	5.9
5–3	Allowable Loads in Pounds for Trapeze Bars	5.11
5–3M	Allowable Loads in Pounds for Trapeze Bars	5.12
5–4	Channel (Strut) Used as Trapeze	5.13
9–1	Alternate Casing Panels	9.6
9–1	Alternate Casing Panels (Continued)	9.7
9–2	Plenum and Casing Access Doors – 2 in. wg	9.22
9–2M	Plenum and Casing Access Doors – 500 Pa	9.22
'A'	Minimum Threshold Velocities at Various Internal Static Pressures	11.11
'B'	Relative Vibration of Various Ducts	11.15

FIGURES   Page

1–1	Duct Pressure Classification	1.16
1–2	Dependent Variables	1.19
1–3	Symbols For HVAC Systems (I–P)	1.20
1–3M	Symbols For HVAC Systems (SI)	1.21

> Due to the large number of figures in Chapter 2 the list of figures has been place immediately after the Chapter 2 title page.

3–1	Round Duct Transverse Joints	3.3
3–1	Round Duct Transverse Joints (Continued)	3.4
3–2	Round Duct Longitudinal Seams	3.5
3–3	Round Duct Reinforcement	3.6
3–4	Round Duct Elbows	3.44
3–5	90° Tees And Laterals	3.45
3–6	Conical Tees	3.46
3–7	Flat Oval Ducts	3.47
3–8	Types Of Flexible Duct	3.50
3–9	Typical Accessories	3.51
3–10	Flexible Duct Supports	3.52
3–11	Flexible Duct Supports	3.53
4–1	Typical Supply Or Return Duct	4.2
4–2	Rectangular Elbows	4.3
4–2	Rectangular Elbows (Continued)	4.4
4–3	Vanes And Vane Runners	4.5
4–4	Vane Support In Elbows	4.6
4–5	Divided Flow Branches	4.7
4–6	Branch Connection	4.8
4–7	Offsets And Transitions	4.9
4–8	Obstructions	4.10
4–9	Telescope Connection	4.11
4–10	Construction Of Short Radius Vanes	4.14
5–1	Hanger Attachments To Structures	5.3
5–2	Upper Attachment Devices – Typical	5.4
5–3	Alternative Joist Attachments	5.5
5–4	Upper Attachments – Typical	5.6
5–5	Lower Hanger Attachments	5.10
5–6	Trapeze Load Diagram	5.14
5–7	Large Duct Support	5.15
5–8	Riser Supports – From Floor	5.16
5–8M	Riser Supports – From Floor	5.17
5–9	Supports From Wall	5.18

5–9M	Supports From Wall.	5.19
5–10	Riser Support – From Floor.	5.20
5–11	Typical HVAC Unit Suspension	5.21
5–12	Elbow Supports.	5.22
5–13	Branch Supports	5.23
6–1	Louvers And Screens	6.2
6–1M	Louvers And Screens	6.3
6–2	Louver Free Area Calculation	6.4
6–3	Rooftop Duct Installation.	6.6
6–4	Equipment And Duct Support Flashing.	6.7
6–5	Rectangular Gooseneck	6.8
6–6	Intake Or Exhaust Ventilators	6.9
6–7	Large Intake Or Exhaust Ventilators	6.10
7–1	Remote Heating And Cooling Coil Installations	7.1
7–2	Duct Access Doors And Panels	7.2
7–2M	Duct Access Doors And Panels	7.3
7–3	Access Doors – Round Duct.	7.4
7–4	Volume Dampers – Single Blade Type	7.6
7–5	Multiblade Volume Dampers	7.7
7–6	Grille And Register Connections.	7.8
7–7	Ceiling Diffuser Branch Ducts	7.9
7–8	Flexible Connections At Fan	7.10
7–9	Alternative Flex Connector Details	7.11
7–10	Typical HVAC Unit Connections	7.12
7–11	Flexible Duct Liner Installation	7.13
7–12	Liner Fasteners	7.19
7–13	Optional Hat Section	7.20
7–14	Duct Liner Interruption	7.21
8–1	Fire Damper Installation In Double–Wall Duct	8.2
8–2	Double–Wall Round Duct	8.3
8–3	Rectangular Double–Wall Duct.	8.4
8–4	Flat Oval Double–Wall Duct	8.5
8–5	Double–Wall Duct Fitting.	8.6
8–6	Double–Wall Duct Fitting.	8.7
8–7	Double–Wall Duct Sleeve	8.8
8–8	Double–Wall Duct Joint.	8.9
8–9	Double–Wall Duct Tie Rod Installation	8.10
8–10	Double–Wall Duct – Van Stone Joint.	8.11
8–11	Double–Wall Duct – Dampers.	8.12
8–12	Double–Wall Duct With Flange Connections.	8.13
8–13	Double–Wall Duct – Flange Connection	8.14
8–14	Double–Wall Duct Details	8.15
8–15	Double–Wall Duct Access Doors	8.16
9–1	Built–Up Standing Seam Casing.	9.2
9–1M	Built–Up Standing Seam Casing.	9.3
9–2	Standing Seam Casings	9.4
9–3	Alternate Casing Construction	9.5
9–4	Over 2 in. wg Casing Arrangement.	9.8
9–5	Over 2 in. wg Pressure Apparatus Casing	9.9
9–5M	Over 2 in. wg Pressure Apparatus Casing	9.10
9–6	Inside Seam Casing – 6 ft wg (1500 Pa) Max.	9.11
9–7	Double Wall Casing.	9.12
9–8	Alternate Casing Construction Using TDC or TDF Flanges	9.13
9–9	Alternate Casing Construction Using TDC or TDFF Flanges	9.14
9–10	Corner Closures (Using TDC or TDF).	9.15

9–11	Double Wall Casing Details	9.16
9–11M	Double Wall Casing Details	9.16
9–11	Double Wall Casing Details (Continued)	9.17
9–11M	Double Wall Casing Details (Continued)	9.17
9–12	Curb Detail	9.18
9–13	Casing Eliminators And Drain Pans	9.19
9–14	Pipe Penetrations Of Casings	9.20
9–15	Casing Access Doors – 2 in. wg. (500 Pa)	9.21
9–16	Casing Access Doors – 3–10 in. wg (750–2500 Pa)	9.23
10–1	Linear Diffuser Plenum	10.1
10–2	Dishwasher Vapor Exhaust	10.3
10–3	Typical Underslab Duct	10.5
10–4	Anchors For Duct Encasement	10.6
10–5	Security Duct Barrier Detail	10.8
10–6	Alternative Security Barrier Detail	10.9
11–1	Models For Functional Standards	11.3
11–2	Test Duct Configuration	11.4
11–3	Deflection And Leakage Measurement	11.5
11–4	Test Apparatus	11.13
11–4M	Test Apparatus	11.14
11–5	Oscillograph Traces	11.17

CHARTS .... Page

4–1	Number of Short Radius Vanes	4.12
4–1M	Number of Short Radius Vanes	4.13

CHAPTER 1

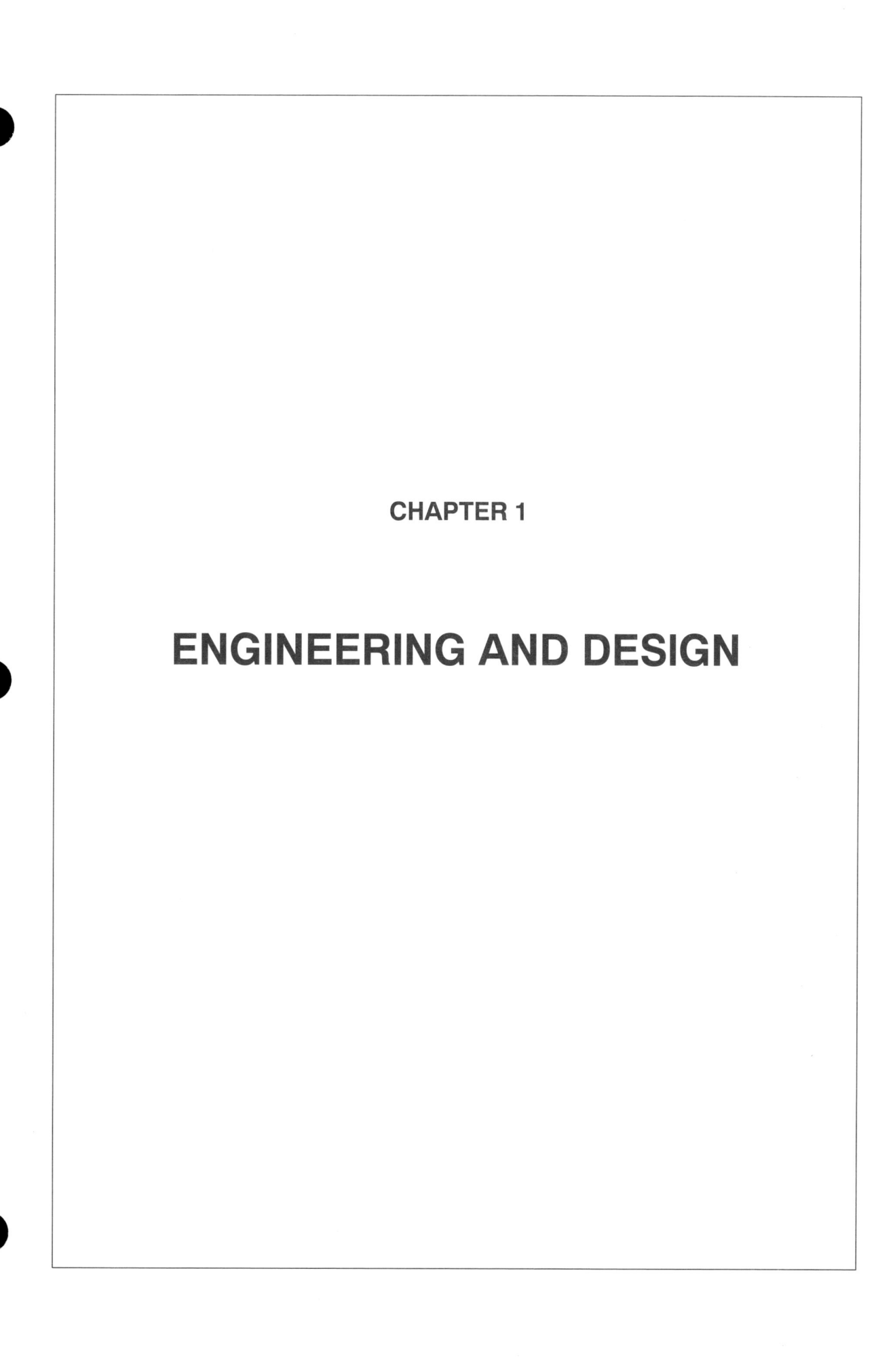

ENGINEERING AND DESIGN

CHAPTER 1　　ENGINEERING AND DESIGN

1.1　INTRODUCTION

This chapter is intended to provide the design professional an understanding of the concepts involved in HVAC duct construction and guidance as to the required elements which are necessary in project plans and specifications to allow the fabricating and installing contractor to provide a duct system which meets the requirements of those plans and specifications.

1.2　INFORMATION REQUIRED FOR DUCT CONSTRUCTION

Various types of information are required in project plans and specifications in order for the fabricating and installing contractor to provide the duct system performance intended by the system designer. Among those are:

1. A comprehensive duct layout indicating sizes, design airflows, pressure class, and routing of the duct system.

2. The types of fittings to be used based on the designer's calculations of fitting losses (*i.e.*, square versus 45 degrees entry taps, conical versus straight taps, etc.).

3. Use of turning vanes or splitter vanes.

4. Location of access doors.

5. Location and type of control and balancing dampers.

6. Location and types of diffusers.

7. Requirements for duct insulation.

8. Location and types of any fire protection device including fire dampers, smoke dampers, combination fire/smoke dampers, and ceiling dampers. Building codes require this information to be shown on the design documents submitted for building permit.

NOTE: UL 555 (Fire Dampers) and UL 555S (Smoke Dampers) now indicate three velocity ratings and three pressure ratings for dynamic Fire, Smoke and Combination Fire/Smoke Dampers. It is recommended that a schedule of these dampers be included with equipment schedules in order to insure that the correct damper is used.

9. Details of offsets required to route ductwork around obstructions (columns, beams, etc.).

1.3　MODEL SPECIFICATIONS

Specification sections designated with an S are obligatory.

1.3.1　Duct Construction and Installation Standards

S1.0　General Requirements

S1.1　These construction and installation specifications and illustrations include:

  a.　Single-prescriptive method requirements,

  b.　Optional alternatives, and

  c.　Performance requirements for specific items that are different in detail from the generalized illustrations.

S1.2　These standards are not meant to exclude any products or methods that can be demonstrated to be equivalent in performance for the application. Substitutions based on sponsor demonstrated adequacy and approval of the regulating authority are recognized.

S1.3　These requirements presume that the designers have prepared contract drawings showing the size and location of ductwork, including permissible fitting configurations. Where area change, direction change, divided flow, or united flow fittings other than those illustrated here are shown on the contract drawings, are not of proprietary manufacture, and are defined with friction loss coefficients in either the SMACNA *HVAC Systems Duct Design* manual or the *ASHRAE Handbook - Fundamentals* chapter on duct design, such fittings shall be fabricated with materials, assembly techniques, and sealing provisions given here.

S1.4　EACH DUCT SYSTEM SHALL BE CONSTRUCTED FOR THE SPECIFIC DUCT PRESSURE CLASSIFICATIONS SHOWN ON THE CONTRACT DRAWINGS. WHERE NO PRESSURE CLASSES ARE SPECIFIED BY THE DESIGNER, THE 1 IN. WG (250 Pa) PRESSURE CLASS IS THE BASIS OF COMPLIANCE WITH THESE STANDARDS, REGARDLESS OF VELOCITY IN THE DUCT, EXCEPT WHEN THE DUCT IS VARIABLE VOL-

HVAC Duct Construction Standards Metal and Flexible • Fourth Edition

UME: ALL VARIABLE VOLUME DUCT UPSTREAM OF VAV BOXES HAS A 2 IN. WG (500 Pa) BASIS OF COMPLIANCE WHEN THE DESIGNER DOES NOT GIVE A PRESSURE CLASS.

S1.5 No specification or illustration in this manual obliges a contractor to supply any volume control dampers, fire dampers, smoke dampers, or fittings that are not shown on contract drawings.

S1.6 Where dimensions, sizes, and arrangements of elements of duct assembly and support systems are not provided in these standards the contractor shall select configurations suitable for the service.

S1.7 The contractor shall follow the application recommendations of the manufacturer of all hardware and accessory items and select them to be consistent with the duct classification and services.

S1.8 Unless otherwise specified steel sheet and strip used for duct and connectors shall be G-60 coated galvanized steel of lockforming grade conforming to ASTM A653 and A924 standards. Minimum yield strength for steel sheet and reinforcements is 30,000 psi (207 kPa).

S1.9 Where sealing is required in Table 1-1 or in other tables or illustrations in this manual, it means the following:

a. The use of adhesives, gaskets, tape systems, or combinations of these to close openings in the surface of the ductwork and field-erected plenums and casings through which air leakage would occur or the use of continuous welds.

b. The prudent selection and application of sealing methods by fabricators and installers, giving due consideration to the designated pressure class, pressure mode (positive or negative), chemical compatibility of the closure system, potential movement of mating parts, workmanship, amount and type of handling, cleanliness of surfaces, product shelf life, curing time, and manufacturer-identified exposure limitations.

c. That these provisions apply to duct connections to equipment and to apparatus but are not for equipment and apparatus.

d. That where distinctions are made between seams and joints, a seam is defined as joining of two longitudinally (in the direction of airflow) oriented edges of duct surface material occurring between two joints. Helical (spiral) lock seams are exempt from sealant requirements. All other duct wall connections are deemed to be joints. Joints include but are not limited to girth joints, branch and sub-branch intersections, so-called duct collar tap-ins, fitting subsections, louver and air terminal connections to ducts, access door and access panel frames and jambs, and duct, plenum, and casing abutments to building structures.

e. Unless otherwise specified by the designer, that sealing requirements do not contain provisions to:

1. Resist chemical attack;

2. Be dielectrically isolated;

3. Be waterproof, weatherproof, or ultraviolet ray resistant;

4. Withstand temperatures higher than 120°F (48°C) or lower than 40°F (4.4°C);

5. Contain radionuclides or serve in other safety-related construction;

6. Be electrically grounded;

7. Maintain leakage integrity at pressures in excess of their duct classification;

8. Be underground below the water table;

9. Be submerged in liquid;

10. Withstand continuous vibration visible to the naked eye;

11. Be totally leak-free within an encapsulating vapor barrier; and

12. Create closure in portions of the building structure used as ducts,

such as ceiling plenums, shafts, or pressurized compartments.

f. The requirements to seal apply to both positive and negative pressure modes of operation.

g. Externally insulated ducts located outside of buildings shall be sealed before being insulated, as though they were inside. If air leak sites in ducts located outside of buildings are exposed to weather, they shall receive exterior duct sealant. An exterior duct sealant is defined as a sealant that is marketed specifically as forming a positive air- and watertight seal, bonding well to the metal involved, remaining flexible with metal movement, and having a service temperature range of -30°F (-34°C) to 175°F (79°C). If exposed to direct sunlight, it shall also be ultraviolet ray- and ozone-resistant or shall, after curing, be painted with a compatible coating that provides such resistance. The term sealant is not limited to adhesives or mastics but includes tapes and combinations of open-weave fabric or absorbent strips and mastics.

1.3.2 Rectangular Duct Reinforcement

S1.10 Unless otherwise specified or allowed, rectangular ductwork shall be constructed in accordance with Tables 2-1 through 2-33 and details associated with them.

S1.11 The duct gage tables are based on G-60 coated galvanized steel of lockforming grade conforming to ASTM Standards A653 and A924. Uncoated steel, prepainted steel, steel with metal coating such as aluminum or aluminum-zinc compounds, and stainless steel may be used if a minimum corresponding base metal thickness and material strength is provided. Lockforming grades of such material must be used.

The use of alternative materials requires specification or approval by a designer. The surface conditions, hardness, ductility, corrosion resistance, and other characteristics of these materials must be judged acceptable by the designer for the planned service.

Specifications that refer to use of material that is two gages heavier mean two numbers separated in a series that uses both odd and even number progression; *e.g.*, 18 is two gages heavier than 20 on Appendix pages A.1, A.2 and A.3.

S1.12 Unless otherwise specified, reinforcement may be uncoated steel or galvanized steel.

S1.13 A reinforcement code classification (letter and EI index) higher than indicated must be substituted when the tables do not provide the specific construction details for a lower classification. A higher rated construction member may also be substituted for convenience.

S1.14 Joint spacing on unreinforced ducts is unlimited. On ducts that require reinforcement, joint spacing is unrestricted except that the joint itself must qualify for the minimum reinforcement code associated with the reinforcement spacing. Exceptions can be made for T21, T22, T24 and T25 transverse joints provided the connections are mechanically fastened or welded and the joint is not credited towards the reinforcement requirements.

S1.15 Duct sides that are 19 in. (483 mm) and over and are 20 gage (1.00 mm) or less, with more than 10 square feet (0.93 square m) of unbraced panel area, shall be crossbroken or beaded as indicated in Figure 2-10 unless they are lined or externally insulated. Ducts that are of heavier gage, smaller dimensions, and smaller panel area and those that are lined or externally insulated are not required to have crossbreaking or beading.

S1.16 Fittings shall be reinforced like sections of straight duct. On size change fittings, the greater fitting dimension determines the duct gage. Where fitting curvature or internal member attachments provide equivalent rigidity, such features may be credited as reinforcement.

S1.17 Duct wall thickness, joints, seams, and reinforcements must be coordinated to provide proper assembly.

S1.18 Other construction that meets the functional criteria in Chapter 11 or is as serviceable as that produced by the construction tables may be provided.

1.3.3 Tie Rod Installations

S1.19 Internal ties shall be one of the methods shown in Figures 2-5 and 2-6. The restraining member and its connections shall be capable of sustaining a load equal to 75 percent of the

HVAC Duct Construction Standards Metal and Flexible • Fourth Edition

duct construction pressure class load applied as 5.2 pounds per square foot per inch of water gage (101.63 kg per square meter per kPa) over an area equal to the width of the duct times the reinforcement interval. When more than one tie rod is used at a crossection of the duct, the design load may be proportionately reduced. For Tables 2-1 through 2-7, duct sizes over 20 in. (508 mm) have tie rod construction alternatives in many instances.

S1.19.1 Intermediate Reinforcement and Joint Tie Rod Loads

The steel tie rod design load Tables 2-34 and 2-34M give the load for both positive and negative pressure service on ducts of 48 in. (1200 mm) through 120 in. (3000 mm) at each pressure class.

S1.19.2 Tie Rod Alternatives

A tie rod may be attached to any intermediate angle, channel, or zee by Figure 2-5 (A), (B), (C), or (F). When one of these backs up a joint, the attachment options are the same. The attachment of a tie rod member that reinforces a joint is allowed for joints T-3, T-6a, T-8a, T-14, T-16, T-21, T-24, and T-25.

The attachment of tie rods or tie straps as in Figure 2-6 by welding, bolting, riveting, or screwing within one inch (25 mm) of each side of joints T-15, T-21, and the T-24 and T-25 series. Each tie rod may be sized for one half of the load in Tables 2-34 and 2-34M.

S1.19.3 Only one tie rod is required for joint T-22. Only one tie rod is required on negative pressure for joints T-15, T-21, T-24, T-25 using Figure 2-5(G). On 18 gage (1.31 mm) duct with 2 in. wg (500 Pa) positive pressure a single tie rod for T-21, the pocket side of T-15 or pinned flanges of T-24 and T-25 is accepted as G rating up to 96 in. (2400 mm).

S1.19.4 For positive pressure service, several alternatives are available for compliance with Tables 2-34 and 2-34M. Partially or fully threaded tie rod from Tables 2-35 and 2-35M may be used by size readout or the allowable load data may be used for sizing calculations at 150 percent of the loads in Tables 2-34 and 2-34M. One half inch (12.7 mm) ridgid conduit (RC) may be used. Thinwall (EMT) conduit may be used with these size and load limits applying for Tables 2-34 and 2-34M: 900 lbs (400 kg) for ½ in. (12.1 mm); 1340 lbs (600 kg) for ¾ in. (19.1 mm); 1980 lbs (900 kg) for 1 in. (25 mm). 1 in. × ¼ in. (25 × 3 mm) strap may be used provided that weld stress does not exceed 13,600 psi (93,772 kPa) and that any bolts are sized per Tables 2-35 and 2-35M as minimums.

S1.19.5 For negative pressure rods, tubing, pipe, or angles are alternatives. The selection steps are as follows:

Step 1: Find the design load for the pressure class and duct width in Table 2-34.

Step 2A: For rods, from Table 2-36 for the length to be used, select a size to meet the load from Table 2-34 or calculate the size needed to limit the compression stress to that associated with a maximum length to radius of gyration ratio (L/r_g) or;

Step 2B: For rigid conduit (RC), select from Table 2-37 the smallest size of the length that satisfies the load from Table 2-34 or;

Step 2C: For EMT conduit, select from Table 2-38 the smallest size for the length that satisfies the load from Table 2-34 or;

Step 2D: For pipe, select from Table 2-39 the smallest size for the length that satisfies the load from Table 2-34 or;

Step 2E: For angles, select from Table 2-40 the smallest size for the length that satisfies the load from Table 2-34.

S1.20 Holes made in the duct wall for tie rod passage shall be of minimum size and shall be sealed in accordance with the provisions of S1.8 and S1.9. Except as limited by joint specifications and certain mandatory uses, tie rod alternatives are indicated in Tables 2-1 through 2-7 for reinforcement sizes listed to the right of duct wall thickness. G denotes the size with tie rod on 22 gage in H-22G nomenclature.

S1.21 Tie rods shall be galvanized steel. All internal ties, whether of rod, tube, pipe, or angle shall

be of material having the same nature and corrosion resistance as the duct wall material. Concealed components shall not be subject to nor cause galvanic corrosion. Tie straps, used on positive pressure only, shall be 1 in. × ⅛ in. (25 × 3.2 mm) minimum galvanized steel and the smallest edge shall face the airflow.

S1.22　When the internal ties are integrated with supports such as those in Figure 5-9, they shall be selected to be suitable for additional duty.

S1.23　Up to 120 in. (3048 mm) width ties shall be spaced at even intervals of duct width not exceeding 60 in. (1524 mm). The use of ties does not void the need to attach reinforcements to the duct wall, however, when ties occur outside the duct, as on two-sided or four-sided reinforcements at positive 4 in. wg (1000 Pa) and over, the attachment within two inches of the corner is not required. Refer to Figure 2-13.

S1.24　Ties shall be attached so that they will not loosen or detach for the selected duct pressure service class nor for an occasional 50 percent over pressure temporary condition. For positive pressure, threaded inserts placed in pipes and tubes shall be secure at 200 percent of Table 2-34 design load.

S1.25　When ties occur in two directions in the same vicinity, they shall either be prevented from contacting or be permanently fastened together.

S1.26　Refer to Figures 2-5, 2-6, 2-13, and 5-9 for basic tie rod application details on medium and large size ducts.

S1.27　Ties may be structural components of the duct and used as part of the suspension system for ducts over 96 in. (2438 mm) in width, provided that the hanger load is directly transmitted to a trapeze or duct reinforcement member beneath the duct.

S1.28　The construction of ducts of widths greater than 120 in. (30,488 mm) involves the use of tie rods on joints and intermediate reinforcement at intervals not exceeding 60 in. (1.5 m) for 6 in. wg (1500 Pa) or less. For 10 in. wg (2500 Pa) the maximum interval is 48 in. (1.2 m), *see* Figure 2-14 for construction schedules.

S1.29　Rectangular aluminum duct construction using ASTM Standard B 209 alloy sheet and the adaptations of the steel duct construction tables set forth in Tables 2-50 to 2-52 is acceptable for pressure classes not exceeding 3 in. wg (750 Pa).

S1.30　For Tables 2-1, 2-2, 2-3, and 2-4, use equivalent sheet thickness from Table 2-50.

S1.31　For Tables 2-31, 2-32, and 2-33, a connector not using angles or bar stock must have its thickness increased per Table 2-50 and its dimensions increased per Table 2-51.

S1.32　For Tables 2-31, 2-32 and 2-33, a connector using angles or bar stock must have its aluminum thickness increased per Table 2-50 and must use either aluminum stock or galvanized stock from Table 2-51.

S1.33　For Table 2-29, use only galvanized steel members in Table 2-52 or the equivalent aluminum members. Use either galvanized steel members of dimensions given or aluminum members having both thickness and dimension conforming to Table 2-52. Other suitable aluminum shapes having a moment of inertia three times that of steel may be used.

S1.34　Add fasteners as necessary to carry loadings.

S1.35　Consider the need for dielectric isolation by zinc chromate paint, asphalt impregnated paper, bituminous paint, or other method.

S1.36　Follow construction details for steel construction standards unless they are superseded by data on this page or by other considerations pertinent to aluminum. Use a lock-forming grade of sheet material.

1.3.4　Transverse Joints for Rectangular Duct

S1.37　Transverse joints shall be selected and used that are consistent with the static pressure class, applicable sealing requirements, materials involved, duct support intervals, and other provisions for proper assembly of ductwork outlined in the construction standards. The precise type, size, location, and material of fastenings used in joint assemblies are

HVAC Duct Construction Standards Metal and Flexible • Fourth Edition

sometimes left open to prudent judgment for the specific service. Notching, bending, folding, and fit-up tolerances shall be appropriate for the composite assembly. When there is a choice of materials and methods, do not use such latitude as to create a deficiency in the integrity of the ductwork.

S1.38 *See* S2.1 and S2.2. Where the text and illustrations in sections 1 through 5 indicate certain sealing provisions independent of the provisions in paragraphs S2.1 and S2.2, they apply regardless of exemptions from sealing shown in Table 1.1.

S1.39 Where bar or angle stock is incorporated in a joint, it shall be secured. Where intermediate type reinforcements are used as supplements for joints, they shall be attached to the duct wall within 3 in. (76 mm) of the joint by weld, bolt, screw, or blind rivet fastening within 2 in. (51 mm) of duct corners and at intervals not exceeding 12 in. (305 mm). Exception: where the ends are tied to members on adjacent sides, the fastening to the duct within 2 in. (51 mm) may be omitted in consideration of the end restraint.

S1.40 Fasteners used on steel duct shall be steel. They may be zinc or cadmium coated. Standard or self-drilling sheet metal screws may be used as appropriate. Blind rivets using pull-through mandrels are not permitted unless the holes are sealed to reduce air leakage. Fastenings shall not project into duct interiors more than ¾ in. (20 mm). Where only bolts or welds are specified, other types of fastening are not allowed. Clinching or similar techniques are permitted on sheet metal to sheet metal applications. Consult equipment manufacturer for adjustments to type and quantity of clinches required.

1.3.5 Longitudinal Seams for Rectangular Duct

S1.41 Seams shall be selected for the material, pressure classification, and other construction detail appropriate for the service.

S1.42 Seams shall be formed and assembled with proper dimension and proportion for tight and secure fit up. Notching shall be minimal and consistent with transverse joint make-up needs.

S1.43 Although they are not illustrated here, seams may be of butt weld, corner weld, plug weld or spot weld design. They may also be of the spiral lockseam type.

S1.44 Solder for watertight seam closure, when specified, should conform to ASTM Standard B32 or Federal Specification QQ-S-571.

1.3.6 Installation Standards for Rectangular Ducts Using Flexible Liner

S2.0. Flexible duct liner of the specified material, thickness, and density shall be furnished and installed where shown on the contract drawings.

S2.1. Unless otherwise indicated, the net free area of the duct dimensions given on the contract drawings shall be maintained. The duct dimensions shall be increased as necessary to compensate for liner thickness.

S2.2. The liner surface designated to be exposed shall face the airstream.

S2.3. Each layer of duct liner shall be attached with sufficient adhesive at the liner contact surface area to ensure proper adhesion.

S2.4. All transversely oriented edges of liner not receiving metal nosing shall be coated with adhesive. Liner shall be neatly butted without gaps at transverse joints and shall be coated with adhesive at such joints before butting.

S2.5. Liner shall be folded and compressed in the corners of rectangular duct sections or shall be cut and fit to ensure butted edge overlapping. Longitudinal joints in the duct liner shall not occur except at the corners of ducts, unless the size of the duct and standard liner product dimensions make them necessary.

S2.6. Ducts with interior widths of 8 in. (203 mm) or less do not require mechanical fasteners in addition to adhesive.

S2.7. Except as noted in S2.6, mechanical fasteners shall be located with respect to interior dimensions and regardless of airflow direction as in the accompanying table and in Figure 7-11.

Velocity	Transversely Around Perimeter	Longitudinally
2500 fpm (12.7 mps) and less	At 4 in. (102 mm) from longitudinal liner edges, at 6 in. (152 mm) from folded corners and at intervals not exceeding 12 in. (305 mm)	At 3 in. (76 mm) from transverse joints and at intervals not exceeding 18 in. (457 mm)
2500 fpm (12.7 mps) to 6000 fpm (30.5 mps)	At 4 in. (102 mm) from longintudinal liner edges, at 6 in. (152 mm) from folded corners and at intervals not exceeding 6 in. (152 mm)	At 3 in. (76 mm) from transverse joints and at intervals not exceeding 16 in. (406 mm)

S2.8. Longitudinal joints in liners shall be coated with adhesive when velocities over 2500 fpm (12.7 mps) are anticipated.

S2.9. Metal nosings that are either channel or zee profile or are integrally formed from the duct wall shall be securely installed over transversely oriented liner edges facing the airstream, at fan discharge and at any interval of lined duct preceded by unlined duct. In addition, where velocities exceed 4000 fpm (20.3 mps), metal nosing shall be used on upstream edges of liner at every transverse joint.

S2.10. Where dampers, turning vane assemblies, or other devices are placed inside lined ducts or fittings, the installation must not damage the liner or cause erosion of the liner. The use of metal hat sections or other buildout means is optional; when used, buildouts shall be secured to the duct wall with bolts, screws, rivets, or welds.

S2.11. Liners shall also be installed with mechanical fastening devices that:

    a. Are spaced in accordance with Figure 7-11,

    b. When installed, are as corrosion resistant as G-60 coated galvanized steel,

    c. Will not adversely affect the fire resistance classification of liner and adhesives,

    d. Do not damage the liner when applied as recommended by the manufacturer,

    e. Do not cause leakage in the duct,

    f. Do not project more than nominally into the airstream,

    g. Will indefinitely sustain a 50 lb (22.7 Kg) tensile dead load test perpendicular to the duct wall,

    h. Are the correct length specified for the liner thickness used, and

    i. Are installed with pins perpendicular to the duct wall.

1.3.7 Round Duct Construction Standards

S3.0. Round ducts shall be constructed in accordance with Tables 3-5 through 3-14 in S3.0 and S3.1. Table 3-5 is based on G-60 coated galvanized steel of ASTM Standards A653 and A924 grades. Uncoated, polyvinyl coated, aluminum alloy coated or aluminum-zinc alloy coated steel or stainless steel may be used if a minimum corresponding base metal thickness and material strength is provided. Lockforming quality is required. The use of an alternative material requires specification or approval by a designer.

S3.1. Fittings with a longitudinal seam shall have a wall thickness not less than that specified for longitudinal-seam straight duct in Tables 3-5 and 3-14. Spirally constructed fittings must have a gage corresponding to spiral construction and reinforcement per Tables 3-5 and 3-14. The diameter of fittings shall be appropriate for mating with sections of the straight duct, equipment, and air terminals to which they connect.

S3.2. Sleeves, collars, and fittings to connect a round duct to a rectangular duct or to flexible ducts shall conform to S3.1 unless a different practice is supported by test data or affidavits confirming suitability for the service, *see* Figures 4-6 and 7-7 and pages 3-29 through 3-39.

S3.3. Nothing in this specification is meant to imply that the designer cannot, by project specification, designate acceptable construction methods.

S3.4. The use of a saddle or a direct connection of a branch into a larger duct is acceptable.

HVAC Duct Construction Standards Metal and Flexible • Fourth Edition

Where they are used, the diameter of the branch shall not exceed two-thirds of the diameter of the main and protrusions into the interior of the main, are not allowed. Direct connection of a branch into a main shall include mechanical attachment sufficient to maintain the integrity of the assembly. All saddle fittings shall be sealed at all pressures.

S3.5. Where other limitations are not stated, mitered elbows shall be based on the velocity of flow and shall be constructed to comply with Table 3-1.

S3.6. The illustration of 90 degrees elbow in Figure 3-4 does not preclude shapes of less than 90 degrees.

S3.7. Figure 4-7 is applicable for in-line offsets.

S3.8. Volume damper construction is provided in Figures 7-4 and 7-5.

S3.9. Ducts shall be suspended in accordance with Chapter 5. Additional supports shall be added if necessary to control deflection of ducts or to maintain their alignment at branch intersections. The support system shall not cause out-of-round shape.

S3.10. The requirements of Table 1-1 for sealing are applicable.

1.3.8 Flat Oval Duct Construction Standards

S3.11 Flat oval duct shall be provided where shown and as shown on the contract drawings.

S3.12 Minimum wall thickness for longitudinal seam flat oval duct shall be as indicated in Table 3–15.

S3.13 Reinforcement for flat sides of longitudinal flat oval duct shall be of the same size and spacing interval as specified for rectangular duct or shall be provided to limit wall deflection to ¾ in. (19 mm) and reinforcement deflection to ¼ in. (6.4 mm).

S3.14 Minimum duct wall thickness and reinforcement spacing, type, and size for flat sides of spiral flat oval duct shall be selected from tables 3-16 through 3-22M and are suitable for negative pressure applications.

S3.15 Unless otherwise specified, joints and seams shall be similar to those indicated for round duct.

S3.16 Fittings used in conjunction with longitudinal seam duct shall conform to the thickness schedules in Table 3–15, shall conform to the seam, joint, and connection arrangements permitted for round duct, and shall be reinforced to conform to S3.13.

S3.17 Fittings used in conjunction with spiral seam flat oval duct will be fabricated by a gage that is two gages thicker (one even gage) than the duct provided the reinforcement size, type and spacing are maintained.

S3.16 The duct construction shall be capable of withstanding a pressure 50 percent greater than that of the assigned pressure class without structural failure or permanent deformation.

S3.17 Duct wall deflection at atmospheric pressure, with reinforcements and connections in place, shall not exceed ¼ in. (6.4mm) on widths of 36 in. (914 mm) or less or ½ win. (13 mm) on greater widths, *see* criteria in Chapter 11.

1.3.9 Flexible Duct Installation Standards

S3.19. Unless otherwise designated, the term "flexible air duct" is used for all ducts classified by UL as either flexible air ducts or connectors.

S3.20. These provisions apply to ducts used for indoor comfort heating, ventilating, and air conditioning service. They do not apply to service for conveying particulates, corrosive fumes and vapors, high temperature air, corrosive or contaminated atmosphere, etc.

S3.21. It is presumed that project specifications define the specific materials, pressure limits, velocity limits, friction rate, thermal conductivity, acoustical ratings, and other attributes.

S3.22. When ducts must conform to NFPA Standard 90A or 90B, flexible ducts must be tested in accordance with Underwriters Laboratories UL Standard for Safety, Factory-Made Air Ducts and Air Connectors, UL 181, and must be installed in accordance with the conditions of their UL listing. Separate installation limitations for flexible connectors and flexible ducts are identified in NFPA Standard 90A and 90B.

1.8   HVAC Duct Construction Standards Metal and Flexible • Fourth Edition

By UL Standard 181, a flexible connector is defined as a flexible air duct not having certain flame penetration, puncture, and impact tests.

S3.23. The minimum length of flexible duct should be used.

S3.24. Bends shall be made with not less than one duct diameter centerline radius. Ducts should extend a few inches beyond the end of a sheet metal connection before bending. Ducts should not be compressed.

S3.25. Ducts shall be located away from hot equipment such as furnaces and steam pipes to avoid excess temperature exposure.

S3.26. Illustrations of accessories, sleeves, and collars are representative of classes of items. The use of components not precisely identical to these is acceptable.

S3.27. If the application guidelines dictated by the flexible duct manufacturer are more stringent than the specifications in this manual, those of the manufacturer shall govern.

1.3.9 Specification for Joining and Attaching Flexible Duct

S3.28. The provisions for sealing ducts specified on Table 1-1 apply. Adhesives shall be chemically compatible with materials they contact.

S3.29. The ends of ducts shall be trimmed square before installation.

S3.30. Collars to which flexible duct is attached shall be a minimum of 2 in. (51 mm) in length. Sleeves used for joining two sections of flexible duct shall be a minimum of 4 in. (102 mm) in length.

S3.31. Collars and sleeves shall be inserted into flexible duct a minimum of 1 in. (25 mm) before fastening.

S3.32. Metallic flexible duct shall be attached with at least three #8 sheet metal screws equally spaced around the duct's circumference. Ducts larger than 12 in. (305 mm) in diameter shall have at least five #8 sheet metal screws. Screws shall be located at least ½ in. (13 mm) from the duct end.

S3.33. Non metallic flexible duct shall be secured to the sleeve or collar with a draw band. If the duct collar exceeds 12 in. (305 mm) in diameter the draw band must be positioned behind a bead on the metal collar.

S3.34. Insulation and vapor barriers on flexible ducts shall be fitted over the core connection and shall also be secured with a draw band.

1.3.10 Specification for Supporting Flexible Duct

S3.35. Flexible duct shall be supported at the manufacturer's recommended intervals but at least every 4 ft (1.2 m). Maximum permissible sag is a ½ in. per foot (41.7 mm/m) of spacing between supports. A connection to another duct or to equipment is considered a support point.

S3.36. Hanger or saddle material in contact with the flexible duct shall be wide enough so that it does not reduce the internal diameter of the duct when the supported section rests on the hanger or saddle material. In no case will the material contacting the flexible duct be less than 1 ½ in. (38 mm) wide. Narrower hanger material may be used in conjunction with a sheet metal saddle that meets this specification. This saddle must cover one-half the circumference of the outside diameter of the flexible duct and fit neatly around the lower half of the duct's outer circumference.

S3.37. Pre-installed suspension systems that are integral to the flexible duct are acceptable for hanging when the manufacturer's recommended procedures are followed.

S3.38. Hangers shall be adequately attached to the building structure.

S3.39. To avoid tearing the vapor barrier, do not support the entire weight of the flexible duct on any one hanger during installation. Avoid contacting the flexible duct with sharp edges of the hanger material. Damage to the vapor barrier may be repaired with approved tape. If the internal core is penetrated, replace the flexible duct or treat the tear as a connection.

S3.40. Terminal devices connected to flexible duct shall be supported independently of the flexible duct.

HVAC Duct Construction Standards Metal and Flexible • Fourth Edition

1.3.11 Underground Duct Construction Standards

S3.41. This installation standard is applicable to ducts placed in or beneath concrete floors or in areas free from vehicle traffic.

S3.42. Materials shall conform to the project specifications.

S3.43. Ducts shall be located as shown on the contract drawings.

S3.44. The duct contractor shall provide:

a. Proper assembly of the duct, including connections and sealing as prescribed;

b. Verification of the undamaged condition of the duct before enclosure with fill or encasement;

c. Anchorage for the duct, if any;

d. Notices of requirements for successive placements of fill, if any;

e. Precautions against use of powered vibrators in placing concrete on or around ducts;

f. Witnessing of backfill or encasement; and

g. Temporary protection of openings in ducts.

1.3.12 Hanging and Support Systems

S4.0. Rigid round, rectangular, and flat oval metal ducts shall be installed with support systems indicated in Tables 5-1 to 5-5 and Figures 5-1 to 5-10. They shall be installed as required to maintain alignment. Horizontal ducts shall have a support within 2 ft (0.61 m) of each elbow and within 4 ft (1.2 m) of each branch intersection. Upper attachments to structures shall have an allowable load not more than one-fourth of the failure (proof test) load but are not limited to the specific methods shown here.

1.3.13 Casing and Plenum Construction Standards

S6.0. Unless details are shown otherwise on contract drawings, provide casings and plenums of the designated pressure classification as required by this standard.

S6.1. Submit details selected from the illustrated alternatives for approval of the contracting authority. When equivalent construction is proposed as substitution, clearly identify the substitution. Use construction appropriate for the pressure classification.

S6.2. All casing on the suction side of the fan shall be of 2 in. wg (500 Pa) pressure classification. Casing on fan discharge shall be of the designated pressure class.

S6.3. All joints, seams, connections, and abutments to the building structure shall be sealed with suitable compounds or gaskets.

S6.4. Drains shall have water seals not less than 2 in. wg (500 Pa) greater than the maximum operating pressure in the chamber.

S6.5. Pipe penetrations shall be sealed to prevent air leakage and condensation movement through the seal.

S6.6. Casing material shall be of the same commercial grades as for ducts except that G-90 coated galvanized steel shall be used in all chambers with moisture present.

S6.7. Metal drain pans shall be of G-90 coated galvanized steel.

S6.8. All welds on casing interiors shall be painted.

S6.9. Close-off or safing sheets and strips shall be of G90 galvanized steel of thickness not less than that of the duct widths and shall be securely attached. They shall not be used for structural support of equipment.

S6.10. Casings and plenums shall be constructed to withstand 133 percent of the rated pressure without structural failure. Wall and roof deflections at the rated pressure shall not exceed ⅛ in. per foot (0.97 mm/m) of width.

1.4 DUCT SEALING

Seal Class	Sealing Requirements	Applicable Static Pressure Construction Class
A	Class A: All Transverse joints, longitudinal seams, and duct wall penetrations	4 in. wg and up (1000 Pa)
B	Class B: All Transverse joints and longitudinal seams only	3 in. wg (750 Pa)
C	Class C: Transverse joints only	2 in. wg (500 Pa)
In addition to the above, any variable air volume systems duct of 1 in. (250 Pa) and ½ in. wg (125 PA) construction class that is upstream of the VAV boxes shall meet Seal Class C.		

Table 1–1 Standard Duct Sealing Requirements

1.4.1 Duct Sealing

Ducts must be sufficiently airtight to ensure economical and quiet performance of the system. It must be recognized that airtightness in ducts cannot, and need not, be absolute (as it must be in a water piping system). Codes normally require that ducts be reasonably airtight. Concerns for energy conservation, humidity control, space temperature control, room air movement, ventilation, maintenance, etc., necessitate regulating leakage by prescriptive measures in construction standards. Leakage is largely a function of static pressure and the amount of leakage in a system is significantly related to system size. Adequate airtightness can normally be ensured by a) selecting a static pressure, construction class suitable for the operating condition, and b) sealing the ductwork properly.

The designer is responsible for determining the pressure class or classes required for duct construction and for evaluating the amount of sealing necessary to achieve system performance objectives. It is recommended that all duct constructed for the 1 in. (250 Pa) and ½ in. (125 Pa) pressure class meet Seal Class C. However, because designers sometimes deem leakage in unsealed ducts not to have adverse effects, the sealing of all ducts in the 1 in. (250 Pa) and ½ in. (125 Pa) pressure class is not required by this construction manual. Designers occasionally exempt the following from sealing requirements: small systems, residential occupancies, ducts located directly in the zones they serve, ducts that have short runs from volume control boxes to diffusers, certain return air ceiling plenum applications, etc. When Seal Class C is to apply to all 1 in. (250 Pa) and ½ in. (125 Pa) pressure class duct, the designer must require this in the project specification. The designer should review the *HVAC Air Duct Leakage Test* Manual for estimated and practical leakage allowances.

Seven pressure classes exist [½ in. (125 Pa), 1 in. (250 Pa), 2 in. (500 Pa), 3 in. (750 Pa), 4 in. (1000 Pa), 6 in. (1500 Pa) and 10 in. wg (2500 Pa)]. If the designer does not designate pressure class for duct construction on the contract drawings, the basis of compliance with the SMACNA *HVAC Duct Construction Standards* is as follows: 2 in. wg (500 Pa) for all ducts between the supply fan and variable volume control boxes and 1 in. wg (250 Pa) for all other ducts of any application.

Some sealants can adversely affect the release function of breakaway connections to fire dampers; consult the damper manufacturer for installation restrictions.

1.4.2 Leakage Tests

There is no need to verify leakage control by field testing when adequate methods of assembly and sealing are used. Leakage tests are an added expense in system installation. It is not recommended that duct systems constructed to 3 in. wg (750 Pa) class or lower be tested because this is generally not cost effective. For duct systems constructed to 4 in. wg (1000 Pa) class and higher, the designer must determine if any justification for testing exists. If it does, the contract documents must clearly designate the portions of the system(s) to be tested and the appropriate test methods. Energy conservation standards text on leakage control generally requires tests only for pressures in excess of 3 in. wg (750 Pa) and ductwork located outside the building envelope.

The *HVAC Air Duct Leakage Test* Manual provides practical and detailed procedures for conducting leakage tests.

Apparent differences of about ten percent between fan delivery and sum of airflow measurements at terminals do not necessarily mean poor sealing and excess leakage. Potential accuracy of flow measurements should be evaluated.

Otherwise, open access doors, unmade connections, missing end caps, or other oversights contribute to such discrepancies.

HVAC Duct Construction Standards Metal and Flexible • Fourth Edition

Schools, shopping centers, airports, and other buildings may use exposed ductwork. Selecting sealing systems for such ducts may involve more attention to the final appearance of the duct system than with ducts in concealed spaces. It may also be prudent to leave the duct unsealed.

The contractor should carefully select construction details consistent with sealing requirements, the direction of the air pressure, and familiar sealing methods. The cost of restoring systems not receiving the required sealing or not being properly sealed can greatly exceed the modest cost of a proper application. Contractors using slip and drive connection systems must control connector length and notch depth on rectangular duct ends to facilitate sealing. Failure to do so will compromise seal effectiveness. Round duct joints are normally easier to seal than other types. However, with proper attention to joint selection, workmanship, and sealant application, almost any joint can achieve low leakage. Applying sealant in a spiral lockseam can result in poor seam closure and less than satisfactory control. No single sealant is the best for all applications. Selecting the most appropriate sealant depends primarily on the basic joint design and on application conditions such as joint position, clearances, direction of air pressure in service, etc.

The listing of certain duct products by recognized test laboratories may be based on the use of a particular joint sealing product. Such a component listing only reflects laboratory test performance and does not necessarily mean that the closure method can routinely be successful for the contractor or that it will withstand in-service operation of the system on a long-term basis.

1.4.3 Liquids

Many manufacturers produce liquid sealants specifically for ducts. They have the consistency of heavy syrup and can be applied either by brush or with a cartridge gun or powered pump. Liquid sealants normally contain 30 to 60 percent volatile solvents; therefore, they shrink considerably when drying. They are recommended for slip-type joints where the sealant fills a small space between the overlapping pieces of metal. Where metal clearances exceed $1/16_{[??]}$ in. (1.6 mm), several applications may be necessary to fill the voids caused by shrinkage or runout of the sealant. These sealants are normally brushed on to round slip joints and pumped into rectangular slip joints.

1.4.4 Mastics

Heavy mastic sealants are more suitable as fillets, in grooves, or between flanges. Mastics must have excellent adhesion and elasticity. Although not marketed specifically for ductwork, high quality curtain wall sealants have been used for this application. Oil-based caulking and glazing compounds should not be used.

1.4.5 Gaskets

Durable materials such as soft elastomer butyl or extruded forms of sealants should be used in flanged joints. For ease of application, gaskets should have adhesive backing or otherwise be tacky enough to adhere to the metal during joint assembly. The choice of open cell or closed cell rubber gaskets depends on the amount and frequency of compression and on the elastic memory.

1.4.6 Tapes

Nothing in this standard is intended to unconditionally prohibit the use of pressure sensitive tapes. Several such closures are listed as components of systems complying with UL Standard 181 tests. There are no industry recognized performance standards that set forth peel adhesion, shear adhesion, tensile strength, temperature limits, accelerated aging, etc., which are quality control characteristics specifically correlated with metal duct construction service. However, the SMACNA *Fibrous Glass Duct Construction Standards* illustrate the closure of a fibrous duct to metal duct with a tape system. The variety of advertised products is very broad. Some test results for tapes are published in the product directories of the Pressure Sensitive Tape Council located in Chicago, IL.

The shelf life of tapes may be difficult to identify. It may be only six months or one year. Although initial adhesion may appear satisfactory, the aging characteristics of these tapes in service is questionable. They tend to lose adhesion progressively at edges or from exposures to air pressure, flexure, the drying effects at the holes or cracks being sealed, etc. The tape's adhesive may be chemically incompatible with the substrate, as is apparently the case with certain nonmetal flexible ducts. Application over uncured sealant may have failures related to the release of volatile solvents. Sea air may have different effects on rubber, acrylic, silicone-based (or other) adhesives.

Tapes of a gum-like consistency with one or two removable waxed liners have become popular for some applications. They are generally known as the peel and seal variety and have been used between flanges and on the exterior of ducts. Such tapes are typically of thicknesses several times that of tapes traditionally known as the pressure sensitive type. Some may have mesh reinforcement. Others may have metal or nonmetal backing on one surface.

1.4.7 Heat Applied Materials

Hot melt and thermally activated sealants are less widely known but are used for ductwork. The hot melt type is normally a shop application. Thermally activated types use heat to either shrink-fit closures or to expand compounds within joint systems.

1.4.8 Mastic and Embedded Fabric

There are several combinations of woven fabrics (fibrous glass mesh, gauze, canvas, etc.) and sealing compounds (including lagging adhesive) that appear better suited for creating and maintaining effective seals than sealant alone. Glass fabric and mastic (GFM) used for fibrous glass duct appears to adhere well to galvanized steel.

1.4.9 Aerosol Based Sealants

Aerosolized sealants are small droplets of sealant that are suspended in the air. These are dispersed into the duct and adhere to the edges of openings reducing the size of the opening and thereby reducing leakage. Currently the method for applying these sealants simultaneously measures leakage. This method of application may not directly meet the requirements for seal class, which dictates where sealant is applied, however it can meet the associated leakage class. When these products are used an acceptable leakage class must be determined in lieu of meeting a specific seal class.

1.4.10 Spray Sealants

Spray sealants are similar to liquid sealants however these products are sprayed onto the duct, joints, and seams. These products can be sprayed internally or externally and can be applied to specific locations thereby meeting seal class requirements.

1.4.11 Surface Preparation

Surfaces to receive sealant should be clean, meaning free from oil, dust, dirt, rust, moisture, ice crystals, and other substances that inhibit or prevent bonding. Solvent cleaning is an additional expense. Surface primers are now available, but their additional cost may not result in measurable long-term benefits.

1.4.12 Sealant Strength

No sealant system is recognized as a substitute for mechanical attachments. Structural grade adhesive systems are being developed to replace spot welded and soldered connections of metals. They have lap shear strengths of 1000 to 5000 psi (6895 to 34,475 KPa) or more. SMACNA is not able to comprehensively define their characteristics at this time; however, authorities are encouraged to monitor their development progress and consider their use.

1.4.13 Shelf Life

The installer is cautioned to verify that the shelf life has not been exceeded.

1.4.14 Safety Considerations

Sealant systems may be flammable in the wet, partially cured, or cured state.

USE LIQUIDS AND MASTICS IN WELL VENTILATED AREAS AND OBSERVE PRINTED PRECAUTIONS OF MANUFACTURERS.

The contractor should carefully consider the effects of loss of seal and fire potential when welding on or near sealed connections. NFPA Standard 90A requires adhesives to have a flame spread rating not over 25 and a smoke developed rating not over 50.

1.5 INTRODUCTION TO BASIC CONSTRUCTION

1.5.1 Duct System Design

A duct system is an assembly whose primary function is to convey air between specified points. Systems should be designed using accepted engineering practice and data such as that in the SMACNA *HVAC Systems Duct Design* manual or other credible sources. A duct system may contain ducts under positive and negative pressure. Air velocities will vary within the system. At coils and filters, the velocity may vary from below 1000 fpm (5.08 m/s) to over 3000 fpm (15.24 m/s). Velocity in duct mains and branches can be at constant or varying levels. With the many available systems sizing methods (*e.g.*, equal friction, static regain, velocity reduction, total pressure) and system types, performance cannot be economically optimized unless the designer selects construction details appropriate for the given pressure and velocity.

Generally speaking, duct strength, deflection, and leakage are more functions of pressure than of velocity. In conventional systems, noise, vibration, and friction loss are more related to velocity than to pressure.

Because total pressure is less downstream than upstream, a duct construction pressure classification equal to the fan outlet pressure (or to the fan total

HVAC Duct Construction Standards Metal and Flexible • Fourth Edition

static pressure rating) cannot economically be imposed on the entire duct system.

Pressure in ducts near room air terminals is nearly always below ½ in. water gage (125 Pa).

For a clear interpretation of requirements for ducts and for economical attainment of performance objectives, it is ESSENTIAL THAT CONTRACT PLANS IDENTIFY THE PORTION OF EACH DUCT SYSTEM TO BE CONSTRUCTED FOR A PARTICULAR PRESSURE CLASSIFICATION OR THAT THE ENTIRE SYSTEM BE ASSIGNED A PRESSURE CLASSIFICATION.

1.5.2 General Performance Requirements for All Air Ducts

In fulfilling the function of moving air, the duct assembly must satisfy certain fundamental performance criteria. Elements of the assembly are sheets, reinforcements, seams, and joints. Theoretical and practical limits for the following criteria must be considered for the duct assembly and its elements.

1. Dimensional stability (shape deformation and strength).

2. Containment of the air being conveyed (leakage control).

3. Vibration (fatigue and appearance).

4. Noise (generation, transmission, or attenuation).

5. Exposure (to damage, weather, temperature extremes, flexure cycles, wind, corrosive atmospheres, biological contamination, flow interruption or reversal, underground or other encasement conditions, combustion, or other in-service conditions).

6. Support (alignment and position retention).

7. Seismic restraint.

8. Thermal conductivity (heat gain or loss and condensation control).

In establishing limitations for these factors, consideration must be given to effects of the pressure differential across the duct wall, airflow friction losses, air velocities, infiltration or exfiltration, as well as the inherent strength characteristics of the duct components. Construction methods that economically achieve the predicted and desired performance must be determined and specified. To the extent that functional requirements for ducts are not identified by test or rating criteria, the construction details here represent acceptable practice in the industry except in special service conditions. Where other construction details are needed to meet the special needs of a particular system design, the designer should comply with appropriate construction standards.

1.5.3 Pressure–Velocity Classification

The terms "low" and "high" as applied to velocity and pressure are vague and are no longer used. The designer must select a numerical static pressure class or classes which satisfy the requirements of the particular system. Table 1-2 defines operating pressure in relation to duct pressure class.

1.5.4 Scope

The construction described in this manual is related to heating, cooling, ventilating, and air conditioning systems.

Although some detail and discussion of hood exhaust and dishwasher exhaust is included, systems carrying particulate, corrosive fumes, or flammable vapors or systems serving industrial processes are not covered. Duct systems for residences are not ordinarily subject to the provisions in this document. NFPA Standard 90B, the SMACNA *Residential Comfort System Installation Standards Manual* and local codes normally have provisions for construction of ducts with different details and service than those shown here.

1.5.5 Reinforcement Arrangements

The basic elements of duct construction consist of duct wall(s), transverse joints, and reinforcements at, or between, joints and supports. All of these form an integrated combination for each pressure class and duct size. Each size in a pressure class has a minimum duct wall thickness and a minimum specification for joints, reinforcements, etc. An element from a higher pressure class or larger duct size may be substituted in a construction of a lower pressure class or smaller duct size. This is generally acceptable because the substituted element will exceed the minimum requirements. However, using some over designed elements does not justify underdesigning other elements in the composite assembly unless the overall resulting construction can be shown to meet the minimum standards.

1.14   HVAC Duct Construction Standards Metal and Flexible • Fourth Edition

For example, substituting a stronger reinforcement member does not necessarily permit a larger reinforcement interval; the minimum requirements for each element in the system must continue to be met. For certain duct widths and reinforcement intervals, duct wall deflection is not affected by the strength and rigidity of joints or reinforcements.

The designer must apply construction standards appropriate for the requirements and scope of each project. Fabricators and installers must select features from the joint, seam, reinforcement, and support options that will result in a composite assembly that will conform to the performance criteria identified in this manual. Experience in construction is valuable; no book can provide all the detail and knowledge necessary to select, fabricate, and install a workable assembly. Careless selection and poor workmanship weaken construction integrity. However, the contractor's obligation to make suitable selections does not mean the contractor must make up for the designer who writes a negligent specification.

SAMPLE SITUATION WITH A TERMINAL REQUIRING .15" (37 Pa) STATIC,
A BRANCH DAMPER REQUIRING .15" (37 Pa) STATIC, DUCT DESIGNED FOR .1" LOSS/100 FT
(25 Pa/30 m) AND FITTING LOSSES EQUAL TO STRAIGHT DUCT LOSS THE
CIRCUIT CAN BE 100 L.F. (30 m) LONG BEFORE 1/2" (125 Pa) LOSS IS EXCEEDED.

TYPICAL – .15 (37 Pa) NEGATIVE STATIC BEHIND TERMINALS

(125 Pa) ⟨1/2 | 1⟩ (250 Pa)

TO ROOF

VD   VD   VD   VD

3/4" (187 Pa) STATIC

(125 Pa)   ⟨1/2⟩   ⟨1/2 | 1⟩ (125 Pa)

(250 Pa)

V.D.

AIR HDLG UNIT EXTERNAL STATIC IS 1.5"W.G.
(375 Pa) FAN STATIC IS 3"W.G. (750 Pa)

R.A. FAN ⟨1⟩ (250 Pa)

–.2" (50 Pa) STATIC   –.7" (174 Pa) STATIC   –1.5" (378 Pa) STATIC   +1 1/2" (375 Pa) STATIC   3/4" P.D. (187 Pa) SOUND TRAP   +3/4" (187 Pa) STATIC

ATM   F   H C   C C   ST

LOUVER   ELIM   (500 Pa) ⟨2 | 1⟩ (250 Pa)

THE NUMBER ASSIGNS PRESSURE CLASS
WHICH WILL ACCOMODATE MAXIMUM
OPERATING PRESSURE IN THE DUCT SUBSECTION.
THE SYMBOL CONTINUES THE ASSIGNMENT
UNTIL THE DUCT TERMINATES OR ANOTHER
SYMBOL APPEARS.

MEANS 1" (250 Pa) WG CLASS

(500 Pa) ⟨2 | 1⟩ (250 Pa)

OR 3" (750 Pa)
4" (1000 Pa)
6" (1500 Pa)

(500 Pa) ⟨2⟩

(250 Pa) ⟨1⟩   ⟨1/2⟩ (125 Pa)

TERMINAL UNIT (BOX)

(500 Pa) ⟨2^N⟩

"N" SUPERSCRIPT
IS USED TO CLARIFY
NEGATIVE PRESSURE
DUCT ON CERTAIN LESS
OBVIOUS APPLICATIONS.

VARIABLE VOLUME UNITS, MIXING BOXES,
ETC. REQUIRE A MINIMUM OPERATING
PRESSURE, BUT THE DUCT SHOULD BE
ASSIGNED A CLASS FOR THE MAXIMUM
OPERATING PRESSURE THAT MAY OCCUR.

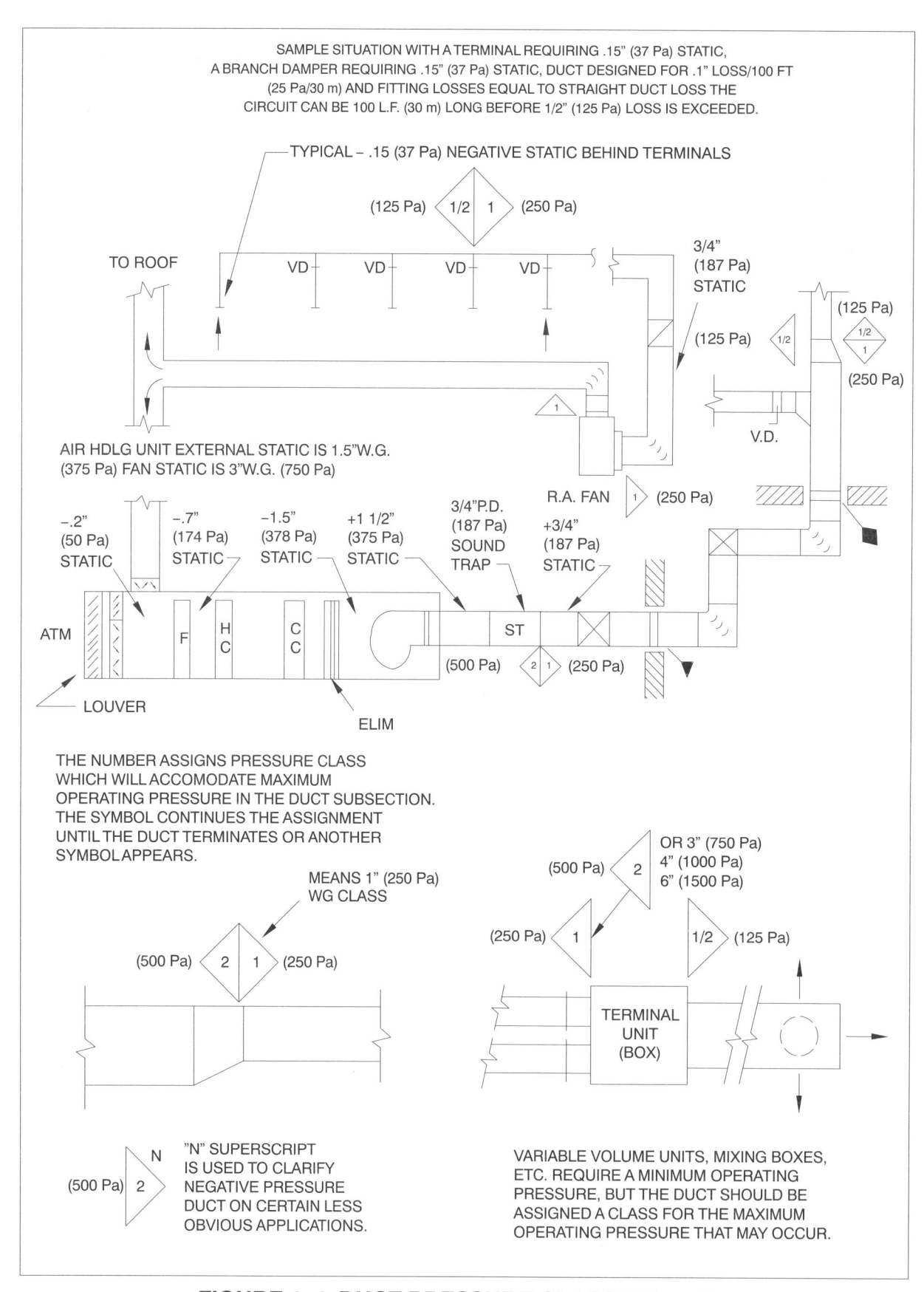

FIGURE 1-1 DUCT PRESSURE CLASSIFICATION

Static Pressure Class [in. wg (Pa)]	+1/2 in.	−1/2 in.	+1 in.	−1 in.	+2 in.	−2 in.	+3 in.	−3 in.	+4 in.	−4 in.	+6 in.	−6 in.	+10 in.	−10 in.
Rectangular Style	A	A	STD	STD	STV	A	A	A	A	A	A	A	A	A
Round Style					STV	STD			A	A			A	A
Flat Oval Style			STD		STV		A		A		A		A	
Flexible Style	A	A	STD	STD	STV		A		A		A			

Table 1–2 Pressure Classification for Ductwork

NOTES:

a. "STD" denotes standard (nonvariable volume) air duct construction requirements (regardless of actual velocity level) for compliance with this document for all cases in which the designer does not designate the pressure classification for the duct system independent of fan static rating. "STV" denotes the standard construction classification for variable volume ducts for compliance with this document when the designer does not designate a class for this application, *see* S1.4 on page 1.1.

b. "A" denotes other pressure classes for which construction or installation details are given in this document and are AVAILABLE for designation in contract documents prepared by designers.

c. *See* Section 1.4 for sealing requirements related to duct pressure class.

d. The pressure class number in Tables 1-2 and 1-3 denotes construction suitable for a maximum level not less than the maximum operating pressure in the portion of the system receiving the classification from the designer.

e. Designer selection of duct construction pressure class is acknowledgment of acceptable design velocity level and pressure level including any overpressure or underpressure conditions that may occur during normal and special modes of operation.

f. The designation of a pressure class pertains to straight duct and duct fittings except for equipment and special components inserted into the ductwork system; such items are governed by separate specifications in the contract documents.

Text references for ducts:

1. Rectangular 2.1
2. Round 3.1
3. Flat oval 3.27
4. Flexible 3.33
5. Duct liner 7.14

PRECAUTIONS:

a. The construction is, as indicated elsewhere in this manual, qualified by freedom from structural failure; however, accidental overpressure that could occur must be provided for at the design stage by overpressure relief (such as fail safe features, replaceable relief panels, controlled failure points, etc.)

b. Field tests (if ever used) to test structural adequacy should not exceed 125 percent of rated pressure. The assignment of a pressure class number less than the numerical value of the anticipated operating pressure involves risk.

c. Leakage test pressure should not exceed duct pressure class level.

d. Short-cycle pressure changes in duct systems can cause temporary noise. This is normally acceptable at system start-up and shutdown. To reduce or eliminate this noise, the designer must specify shorter-interval bracing, diagonal bracing, lagging, or other control means.

| Duct Pressure Class || Operating Pressure |
in. wg	Pa	
½	125	Up to ½ in. wg
1	250	Over ½ in. up to 1 in. wg
2	500	Over 1 in. up to 2 in. wg
3	750	Over 2 in. up to 3 in. wg
4	1000	Over 3 in. up to 4 in. wg
6	1500	Over 4 in. up to 6 in. wg
10	2500	Over 6 in. up to 10 in. wg

Table 1-3 Static Pressure

1.6 DEPENDENT VARIABLES

Figure 1-2 depicts the interrelationship between the elements of any duct construction. The pressure class tables in Chapter 2 provide the prescriptive requirements for a specific size of duct at a specific pressure class. The fabricating contractor has several options for a given duct size and pressure. The choice of reinforcement size and spacing and sheet thickness generally is governed by the type of sheet metal fabrication equipment that the contractor is using. Depending on the equipment available in an individual sheet metal shop, the variables in Figure 1-2 will be different. THE CONTRACTOR IS THE APPROPRIATE ENTITY TO DETERMINE HIS CHOICE AND ARRANGEMENT OF THE VARIABLES. THE DESIGNER SHOULD NOT ATTEMPT TO SPECIFY OR REGULATE THESE VARIABLES IN THE CONTRACT DOCUMENTS. SPECIFYING ANY OF THE VARIABLES COULD PLACE SOME CONTRACTORS AT A SIGNIFICANT DISADVANTAGE IN THEIR ABILITY TO FABRICATE THE DUCT SYSTEM IN THE MOST ECONOMICAL WAY.

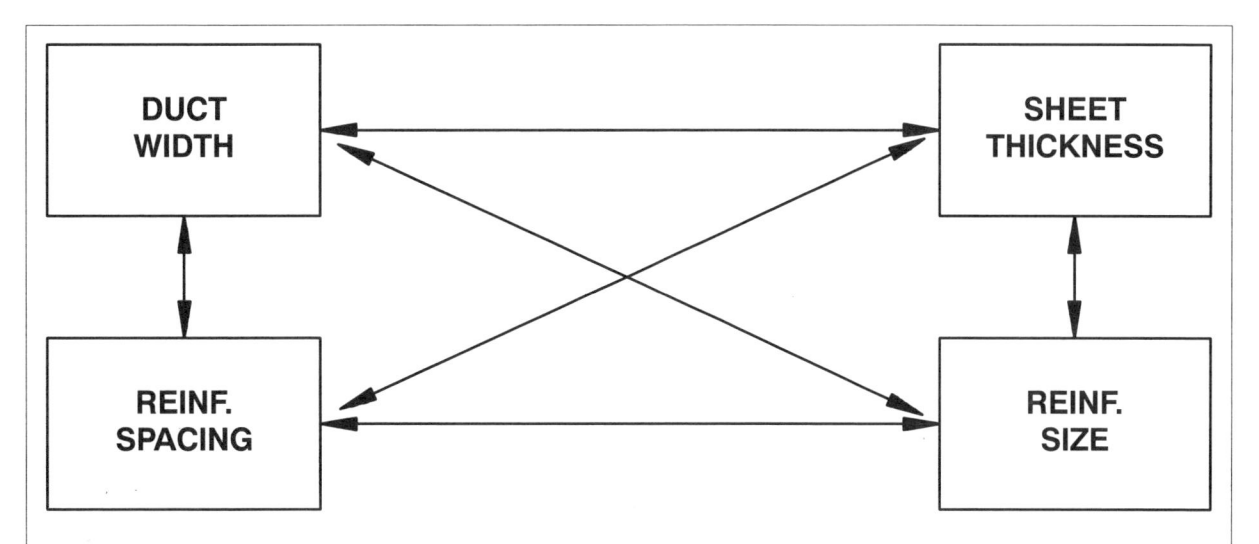

```
┌─────────────┐                    ┌─────────────┐
│    DUCT     │◄──────────────────►│   SHEET     │
│   WIDTH     │◄──┐            ┌──►│  THICKNESS  │
└──────┬──────┘   └──┐      ┌──┘   └──────┬──────┘
       │             └──┐┌──┘             │
       ▼                ><                ▼
┌─────────────┐      ┌──┘└──┐      ┌─────────────┐
│   REINF.    │◄────┘        └────►│   REINF.    │
│  SPACING    │◄──────────────────►│    SIZE     │
└─────────────┘                    └─────────────┘
```

RELATIONSHIPS:

a. For each pressure level and a constant duct size, the thicker the sheet the more distant the reinforcement spacing; the thinner the sheet the closer the reinforcement spacing.

b. For a given sheet thickness and constant duct size, reinforcement size, and reinforcement spacing, reduce with pressure reduction and increase with pressure increase.

c. The larger a duct at a given pressure, the larger the reinforcement and the closer the reinforcement spacing on a selected gage.

d. For each combination of sheet thickness, pressure, and duct width, a maximum reinforcement spacing occurs beyond which sheet deflection is not controlled by reinforcement size nor reinforcement position.

Maximum Deflection		Maximum Test Pressure
Joint and Reinf. 1/4 in. on 48 in.W. on W/200 on 49 – 120 in.	Sheet: 3/8 in. on 12 in. Dn. 1/2 in. on 13 – 18 in. 5/8 in. on 19 – 24 in. 3/4 in. on 25 – 84 in. 1 in. on 85 – 120 in.	Lab: Class Rating + 50% Field: Class Rating + 25%
Tolerance: +7.75%	Tolerance: +10%	

Maximum Deflection		Maximum Test Pressure
Joint and Reinf. 6.4 mm on 1200 mm W. on W/200 on 1201 – 3000 mm	Sheet: 9.53 mm on 300 mm Dn. 12.7 mm on 301 – 450 mm 15.9 mm on 451 – 600 mm 19.0 mm on 601 – 2100 mm 25 mm on 2101 – 3000 mm	Lab: Class Rating + 50% Field: Class Rating + 25%
Tolerance: +7.75%	Tolerance: +10%	

FIGURE 1–2 DEPENDENT VARIABLES

SYMBOL MEANING	SYMBOL	SYMBOL MEANING	SYMBOL
POINT OF CHANGE IN DUCT CONSTRUCTION (BY STATIC PRESSURE CLASS)		SUPPLY GRILLE (SG)	20 x 12 SG / 700 CFM
DUCT (1ST FIGURE, SIDE SHOWN 2ND FIGURE, SIDE NOT SHOWN)	20 x 12	RETURN (RG) OR EXHAUST (EG) GRILLE (NOTE AT FLR OR CLG)	20 x 12 RG / 700 CFM
ACOUSTICAL LINING DUCT DIMENSIONS FOR NET FREE AREA		SUPPLY REGISTER (SR) (A GRILLE + INTEGRAL VOL. CONTROL)	20 x 12 SR / 700 CFM
DIRECTION OF FLOW		EXHAUST OR RETURN AIR INLET CEILING (INDICATE TYPE)	20 x 12 GR / 700 CFM
DUCT SECTION (SUPPLY)	S 30 x 12	SUPPLY OUTLET. CEILING, ROUND (TYPE AS SPECIFIED) INDICATE FLOW DIRECTION	20 / 700 CFM
DUCT SECTION (EXHAUST OR RETURN)	E OR R 20 x 12	SUPPLY OUTLET. CEILING, SQUARE (TYPE AS SPECIFIED) INDICATE FLOW DIRECTION	12 x 12 / 700 CFM
INCLINED RISE (R) OR DROP (D) ARROW IN DIRECTION OF AIR FLOW	R	TERMINAL UNIT. (GIVE TYPE AND OR SCHEDULE)	T.U.
TRANSITIONS: GIVE SIZES. NOTE F.O.T. FLAT ON TOP OR F.O.B. FLAT ON BOTTOM IF APPLICABLE		COMBINATION DIFFUSER AND LIGHT FIXTURE	
STANDARD BRANCH FOR SUPPLY & RETURN (NO SPLITTER) 45° INLET	S R	DOOR GRILLE	DG 12 x 6
WYE JUNCTION		SOUND TRAP	ST
VOLUME DAMPER MANUAL OPERATION	VD	FAN & MOTOR WITH BELT GUARD & FLEXIBLE CONNECTIONS	
AUTOMATIC DAMPERS MOTOR OPERATED	SEC MOD	VENTILATING UNIT (TYPE AS SPECIFIED)	
ACCESS DOOR (AD) ACCESS PANEL (AP)	AP AD	UNIT HEATER (DOWNBLAST)	
FIRE DAMPER: SHOW ◄ VERTICAL POS. SHOW ◆ HORIZ. POS.	FD AD	UNIT HEATER (HORIZONTAL)	
SMOKE DAMPER	AD S	UNIT HEATER (CENTRIFUGAL FAN) PLAN	
HEAT STOP – CEILING DAMPER – RADIATION DAMPER –		THERMOSTAT	T
TURNING VANES (TYPE AS SPECIFIED)		POWER OR GRAVITY ROOF VENTILATOR – EXHAUST (ERV)	
FLEXIBLE DUCT FLEXIBLE CONNECTION		POWER OR GRAVITY ROOF VENTILATOR – INTAKE (SRV)	
GOOSENECK HOOD (COWL)		POWER OR GRAVITY ROOF VENTILATOR – LOUVERED	
BACK DRAFT DAMPER	BDD	LOUVERS & SCREEN	36 H x 24 L

FIGURE 1–3 SYMBOLS FOR HVAC SYSTEMS (I–P)

SYMBOL MEANING	SYMBOL	SYMBOL MEANING	SYMBOL
POINT OF CHANGE IN DUCT CONSTRUCTION (BY STATIC PRESSURE CLASS)		SUPPLY GRILLE (SG)	508 x 305 SG / 330 LPS
DUCT (1ST FIGURE, SIDE SHOWN 2ND FIGURE, SIDE NOT SHOWN)	508 x 305	RETURN (RG) OR EXHAUST (EG) GRILLE (NOTE AT FLR OR CLG)	508 x 305 RG / 330 LPS
ACOUSTICAL LINING DUCT DIMENSIONS FOR NET FREE AREA		SUPPLY REGISTER (SR) (A GRILLE + INTEGRAL VOL. CONTROL)	508 x 305 SR / 330 LPS
DIRECTION OF FLOW		EXHAUST OR RETURN AIR INLET CEILING (INDICATE TYPE)	508 x 305 GR / 330 LPS
DUCT SECTION (SUPPLY)	S 762 x 305	SUPPLY OUTLET. CEILING, ROUND (TYPE AS SPECIFIED) INDICATE FLOW DIRECTION	508 / 330 LPS
DUCT SECTION (EXHAUST OR RETURN)	E OR R 762 x 305	SUPPLY OUTLET. CEILING, SQUARE (TYPE AS SPECIFIED) INDICATE FLOW DIRECTION	508 / 330 LPS
INCLINED RISE (R) OR DROP (D) ARROW IN DIRECTION OF AIR FLOW	R	TERMINAL UNIT. (GIVE TYPE AND OR SCHEDULE)	T.U.
TRANSITIONS: GIVE SIZES. NOTE F.O.T. FLAT ON TOP OR F.O.B. FLAT ON BOTTOM IF APPLICABLE		COMBINATION DIFFUSER AND LIGHT FIXTURE	
STANDARD BRANCH FOR SUPPLY & RETURN (NO SPLITTER) 45° INLET	S R	DOOR GRILLE	DG 305 x 152
WYE JUNCTION		SOUND TRAP	ST
VOLUME DAMPER MANUAL OPERATION	VD	FAN & MOTOR WITH BELT GUARD & FLEXIBLE CONNECTIONS	
AUTOMATIC DAMPERS MOTOR OPERATED	SEC MOD	VENTILATING UNIT (TYPE AS SPECIFIED)	
ACCESS DOOR (AD) ACCESS PANEL (AP)	AP AD	UNIT HEATER (DOWNBLAST)	
FIRE DAMPER: SHOW ◀ VERTICAL POS. SHOW ◆ HORIZ. POS.	FD AD	UNIT HEATER (HORIZONTAL)	
SMOKE DAMPER ⟨S⟩	AD S	UNIT HEATER (CENTRIFUGAL FAN) PLAN	
HEAT STOP – ▶◀ CEILING DAMPER – ⟨C⟩ RADIATION DAMPER – ⟨R⟩		THERMOSTAT	T
TURNING VANES (TYPE AS SPECIFIED)		POWER OR GRAVITY ROOF VENTILATOR – EXHAUST (ERV)	
FLEXIBLE DUCT FLEXIBLE CONNECTION		POWER OR GRAVITY ROOF VENTILATOR – INTAKE (SRV)	
GOOSENECK HOOD (COWL)		POWER OR GRAVITY ROOF VENTILATOR – LOUVERED	
BACK DRAFT DAMPER	BDD	LOUVERS & SCREEN	914 H x 610 L

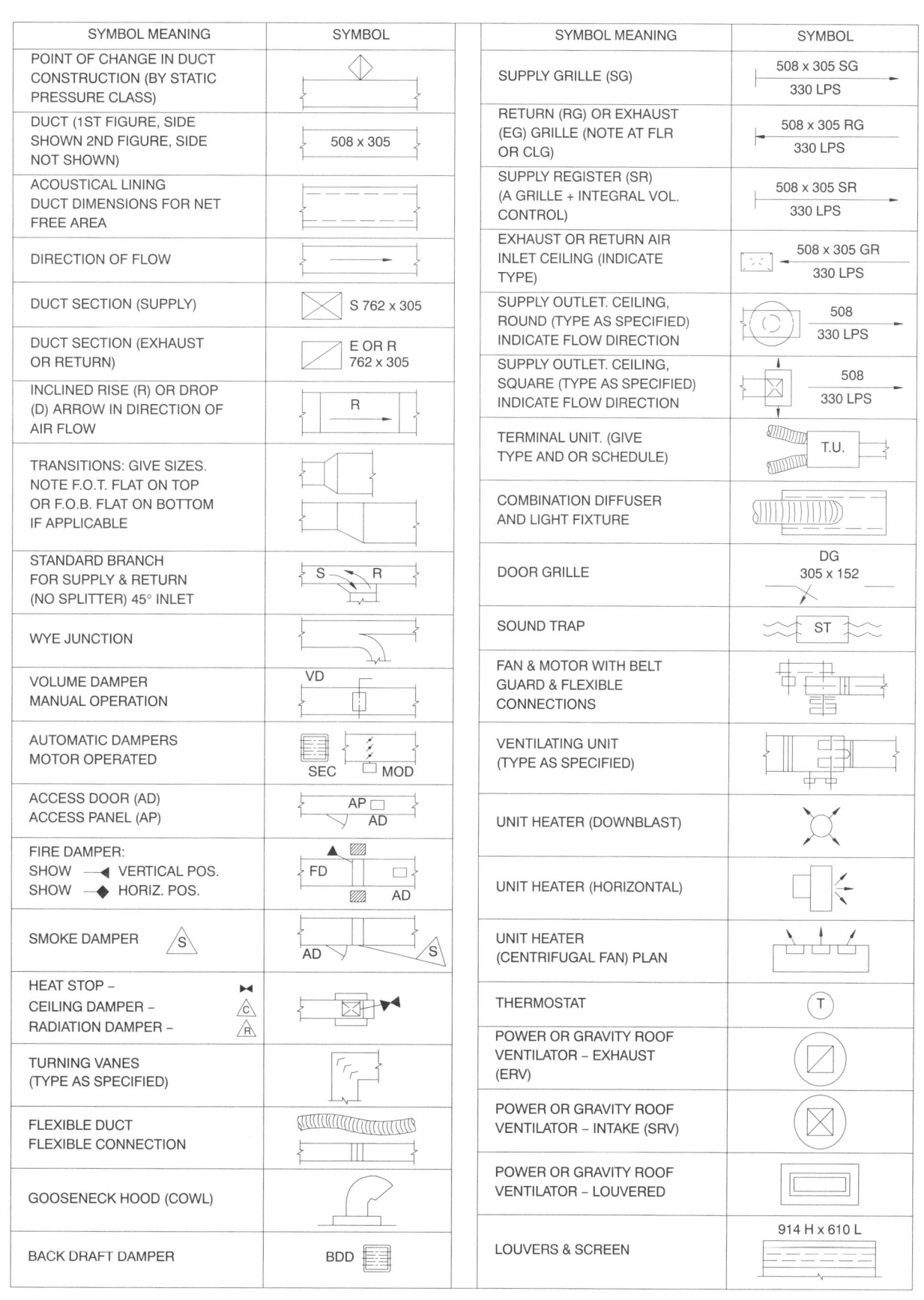

FIGURE 1–3M SYMBOLS FOR HVAC SYSTEMS (SI)

THIS PAGE INTENTIONALLY LEFT BLANK

CHAPTER 2

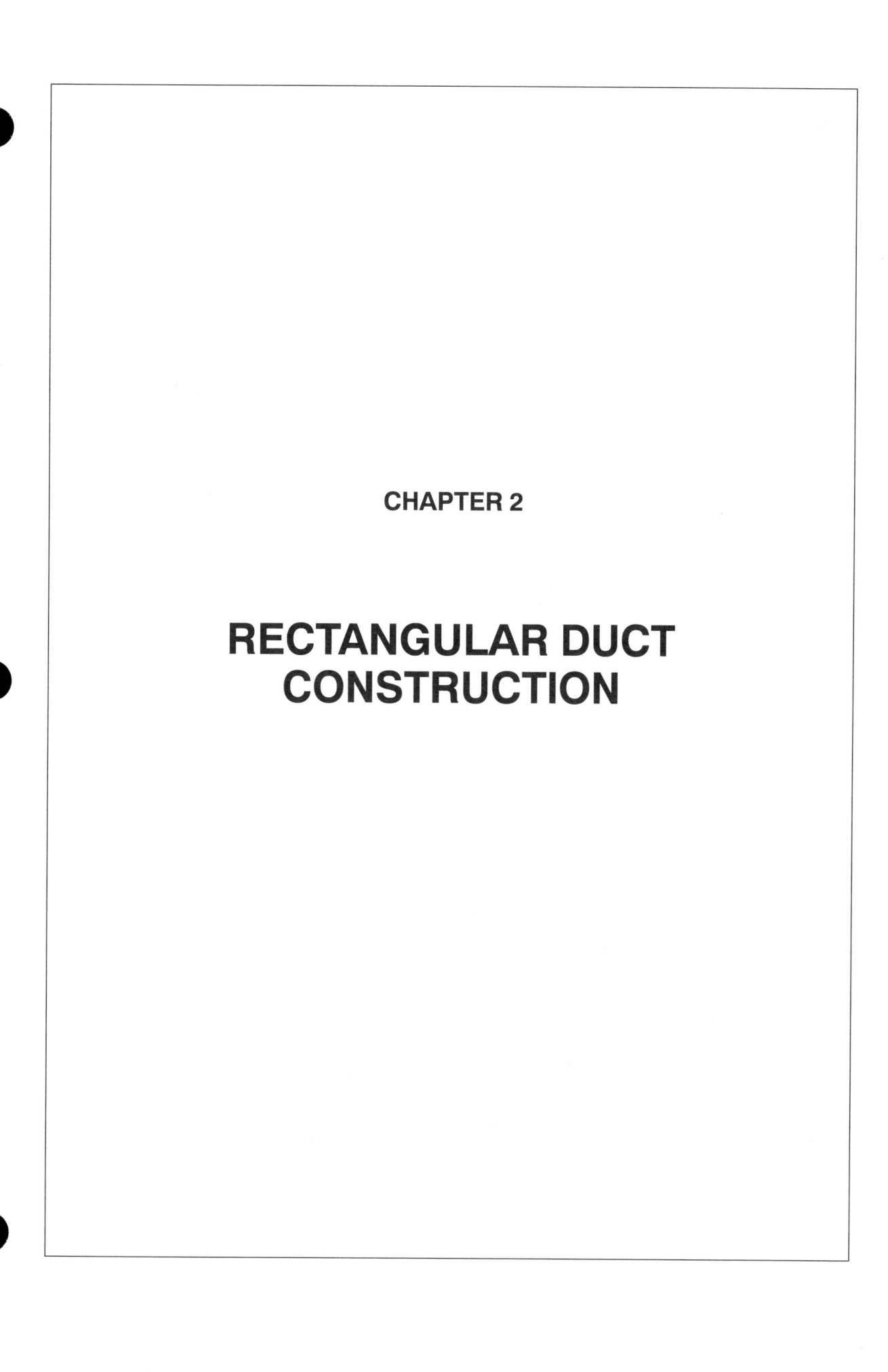

RECTANGULAR DUCT CONSTRUCTION

TABLES

		Page
2–1	Rectangular Duct Reinforcement	2.14
2–1M	Rectangular Duct Reinforcement	2.15
2–2	Rectangular Duct Reinforcement	2.16
2–2M	Rectangular Duct Reinforcement	2.17
2–3	Rectangular Duct Reinforcement	2.18
2–3M	Rectangular Duct Reinforcement	2.19
2–4	Rectangular Duct Reinforcement	2.20
2–4M	Rectangular Duct Reinforcement	2.21
2–5	Rectangular Duct Reinforcement	2.22
2–5M	Rectangular Duct Reinforcement	2.23
2–6	Rectangular Duct Reinforcement	2.24
2–6M	Rectangular Duct Reinforcement	2.25
2–7	Rectangular Duct Reinforcement	2.26
2–7M	Rectangular Duct Reinforcement	2.27
2–8	4 ft Coil/Sheet Stock/T25a/T25b (TDC/TDF) Duct Reinforcement	2.28
2–8M	4 ft Coil/Sheet Stock/T25a/T25b (TDC/TDF) Duct Reinforcement	2.29
2–9	4 ft Coil/Sheet Stock/T25a/T25b (TDC/TDF) Duct Reinforcement	2.30
2–9M	4 ft Coil/Sheet Stock/T25a/T25b (TDC/TDF) Duct Reinforcement	2.31
2–10	4 ft Coil/Sheet Stock/T25a/T25b (TDC/TDF) Duct Reinforcement	2.32
2–10M	4 ft Coil/Sheet Stock/T25a/T25b (TDC/TDF) Duct Reinforcement	2.33
2–11	4 ft Coil/Sheet Stock/T25a/T25b (TDC/TDF) Duct Reinforcement	2.34
2–11M	4 ft Coil/Sheet Stock/T25a/T25b (TDC/TDF) Duct Reinforcement	2.35
2–12	4 ft Coil/Sheet Stock/T25a/T25b (TDC/TDF) Duct Reinforcement	2.36
2–12M	4 ft Coil/Sheet Stock/T25a/T25b (TDC/TDF) Duct Reinforcement	2.37
2–13	4 ft Coil/Sheet Stock/T25a/T25b (TDC/TDF) Duct Reinforcement	2.38
2–13M	4 ft Coil/Sheet Stock/T25a/T25b (TDC/TDF) Duct Reinforcement	2.39
2–14	4 ft Coil/Sheet Stock/T25a/T25b (TDC/TDF) Duct Reinforcement	2.40
2–14M	4 ft Coil/Sheet Stock/T25a/T25b (TDC/TDF) Duct Reinforcement	2.41
2–15	5 ft Coil/Sheet Stock/T25a/T25b (TDC/TDF) Duct Reinforcement	2.42
2–15M	5 ft Coil/Sheet Stock/T25a/T25b (TDC/TDF) Duct Reinforcement	2.43
2–16	5 ft Coil/Sheet Stock/T25a/T25b (TDC/TDF) Duct Reinforcement	2.44
2–16M	5 ft Coil/Sheet Stock/T25a/T25b (TDC/TDF) Duct Reinforcement	2.45
2–17	5 ft Coil/Sheet Stock/T25a/T25b (TDC/TDF) Duct Reinforcement	2.46
2–17M	5 ft Coil/Sheet Stock/T25a/T25b (TDC/TDF) Duct Reinforcement	2.47
2–18	5 ft Coil/Sheet Stock/T25a/T25b (TDC/TDF) Duct Reinforcement	2.48
2–18M	5 ft Coil/Sheet Stock/T25a/T25b (TDC/TDF) Duct Reinforcement	2.49
2–19	5 ft Coil/Sheet Stock/T25a/T25b (TDC/TDF) Duct Reinforcement	2.50
2–19M	5 ft Coil/Sheet Stock/T25a/T25b (TDC/TDF) Duct Reinforcement	2.51
2–20	5 ft Coil/Sheet Stock/T25a/T25b (TDC/TDF) Duct Reinforcement	2.52
2–20M	5 ft Coil/Sheet Stock/T25a/T25b (TDC/TDF) Duct Reinforcement	2.53
2–21	5 ft Coil/Sheet Stock/T25a/T25b (TDC/TDF) Duct Reinforcement	2.54
2–21M	5 ft Coil/Sheet Stock/T25a/T25b (TDC/TDF) Duct Reinforcement	2.55
2–22	6 ft Coil/Sheet Stock/T25a/T25b (TDC/TDF) Duct Reinforcement	2.56
2–22M	6 ft Coil/Sheet Stock/T25a/T25b (TDC/TDF) Duct Reinforcement	2.57
2–23	6 ft Coil/Sheet Stock/T25a/T25b (TDC/TDF) Duct Reinforcement	2.58
2–23M	6 ft Coil/Sheet Stock/T25a/T25b (TDC/TDF) Duct Reinforcement	2.59
2–24	6 ft Coil/Sheet Stock/T25a/T25b (TDC/TDF) Duct Reinforcement	2.60
2–24M	6 ft Coil/Sheet Stock/T25a/T25b (TDC/TDF) Duct Reinforcement	2.61
2–25	6 ft Coil/Sheet Stock/T25a/T25b (TDC/TDF) Duct Reinforcement	2.62
2–25M	6 ft Coil/Sheet Stock/T25a/T25b (TDC/TDF) Duct Reinforcement	2.63
2–26	6 ft Coil/Sheet Stock/T25a/T25b (TDC/TDF) Duct Reinforcement	2.64
2–26M	6 ft Coil/Sheet Stock/T25a/T25b (TDC/TDF) Duct Reinforcement	2.65

2–27	6 ft Coil/Sheet Stock/T25a/T25b (TDC/TDF) Duct Reinforcement	2.66
2–27M	6 ft Coil/Sheet Stock/T25a/T25b (TDC/TDF) Duct Reinforcement	2.67
2–28	6 ft Coil/Sheet Stock/T25a/T25b (TDC/TDF) Duct Reinforcement	2.68
2–28M	6 ft Coil/Sheet Stock/T25a/T25b (TDC/TDF) Duct Reinforcement	2.69
2–29	Intermediate Reinforcement	2.70
2–29M	Intermediate Reinforcement	2.71
2–30	Framing Channel	2.72
2–30M	Framing Channel	2.72
2–31	Transverse Joint Reinforcement	2.74
2–31M	Transverse Joint Reinforcement	2.75
2–32	Transverse Joint Reinforcement	2.76
2–32M	Transverse Joint Reinforcement	2.77
2–33	Transverse Joint Reinforcement	2.78
2–33M	Transverse Joint Reinforcement	2.79
2–34	Internal Tie Rod Design Load in Pounds	2.84
2–34M	Internal Tie Rod Design Load in Pounds	2.85
2–35	Internal Tie Rod Size (+) Pressure	2.86
2–35M	Internal Tie Rod Size (+) Pressure	2.87
2–36	Internal Tie Rod Size (−) Pressure	2.88
2–36M	Internal Tie Rod Size (−) Pressure	2.88
2–37	Internal RC Conduit Size (−) Pressure	2.89
2–37M	Internal RC Conduit Size (−) Pressure	2.90
2–38	Internal EMT Conduit Size (−) Pressure	2.91
2–38M	Internal EMT Conduit Size (−) Pressure	2.92
2–39	Steel Pipe Size (−) Pressure	2.93
2–39M	Steel Pipe Size (−) Pressure	2.94
2–40	Allowable Load for Angles as Columns with Maximum Unbraced Length L	2.95
2–40M	Allowable Load for Angles as Columns with Maximum Unbraced Length L	2.96
2–41	Midpanel Tie Rod (MPT) Schedule (RS)	2.100
2–41M	Midpanel Tie Rod (MPT) Schedule (RS)	2.101
2–42	Internal Midpanel Tie Rod (MPT) Size (Dia.)	2.102
2–42M	Internal Midpanel Tie Rod (MPT) Size (Dia.)	2.102
2–43	Internal Midpanel Tie Rod (MPT) Size (Dia.)	2.103
2–43M	Internal Midpanel Tie Rod (MPT) Size (Dia.)	2.103
2–44	Internal Midpanel Tie Rod (MPT) Size (Dia.)	2.104
2–44M	Internal Midpanel Tie Rod (MPT) Size (Dia.)	2.104
2–45	Internal Midpanel Tie Rod (MPT) Size (Dia.)	2.105
2–45M	Internal Midpanel Tie Rod (MPT) Size (Dia.)	2.105
2–46	Midpanel Tie Rod (MPT) Design Load in Pounds	2.106
2–46M	Midpanel Tie Rod (MPT) Design Load in Pounds	2.107
2–47	Unreinforced Duct (Wall Thickness)	2.108
2–47M	Unreinforced Duct (Wall Thickness)	2.109
2–48	T–1 Flat Drive Accepted as Reinforcement	2.110
2–48M	T–1 Flat Drive Accepted as Reinforcement	2.110
2–49	Large (Over 120 in.) Duct Construction	2.117
2–50	Thickness Adjustments	2.124
2–51	Dimension Adjustments	2.124
2–52	Reinforcements	2.124

FIGURES

		Page
2–1	Rectangular Duct/Transverse Joints	2.6
2–1	Rectangular Duct/Transverse Joints (Continued)	2.7
2–1	Rectangular Duct/Transverse Joints (Continued)	2.8
2–1	Rectangular Duct/Transverse Joints (Continued)	2.9
2–2	Rectangular Duct/Longitudinal Seams	2.10
2–3	Rectangular Duct External Reinforcements	2.12
2–4	Channel (Strut) Used as Duct Reinforcement	2.72
2–5	Tie Rod Attachments	2.82
2–6	Tie Rod Attachments	2.83
2–7	Tie Rod Arrangements	2.98
2–8	Inside Standing Seam – Longitudinal – 2 in. wg (500 Pa) Maximum	2.111
2–9	Unreinforced Duct	2.112
2–10	Crossbroken And Beaded Duct	2.113
2–11	Duct Reinforced On Two Sides	2.114
2–12	Duct Reinforced On All Sides	2.115
2–13	Reinforcement Attachment	2.116
2–14	Duct Over 120 in. (3048 mm) Wide	2.117
2–15	Corner Closures – Slips And Drives	2.118
2–16	Corner Closures – Flanges	2.119
2–17	Corner Closures – Flanges	2.120
2–18	Corner Closures – Flanges	2.121
2–19	Corner Closures	2.122

CHAPTER 2 — RECTANGULAR DUCT CONSTRUCTION

2.1 INTRODUCTION TO THE RECTANGULAR DUCT CONSTRUCTION SCHEDULES

2.1.1 Rectangular Table Reading Guide

1. Determine pressure class assigned by the designer.

2. Go to the reinforcement schedule for the duct pressure class. Table 2-2 is used in this review.

3. The greater duct dimension determines the gage for all sides. Reinforcement may be different on sides with unequal dimension.

4. The duct side will either qualify for flat type joint connections because the duct wall gage is thick enough to control deflection without needing reinforcement or will require an alphabet letter code reinforcement that is suited for the width, the wall thickness and a maximum spacing interval.

   a. The gage of duct not requiring reinforcement is in column 2, *see* Figure 2-9.

   b. Duct reinforcement options are in columns 3 to 10: Read horizontally right from the greater duct dimension in column 1 and vertically under a reinforcement interval spacing (in columns 3 to 10) of your choice.

   The number in the cell is minimum duct gage; the left letter code is type of joint or intermediate reinforcement, whichever you choose. This applies for joint-to-joint, joint-to-intermediate, or intermediate-to-intermediate intervals. If, for example, you are using 5 ft (1.5 m) joint spacing and do not want to use between-joint reinforcements stay in the 5 ft (1.5 m) column (column 6) until it becomes "Not Designed"; then you go to column 9 to find the joint rating and the intermediate (between-joint) bracing and the potentially lighter gage duct wall permitted with 2½ ft (0.75 m) reinforcement spacing.

5. Having found the gage for the wide side, check column 2 to see if that gage is exempt from reinforcement on the short side. If it is not, find which column (of 3 to 10) this gage is in; there find the maximum spacing in the column heading and the prescribed joint (or reinforcement) size (letter code) listed in the gage.

   If the maximum short side reinforcement spacing thus found exceeds a joint spacing that you are committed to, go to the column with the joint spacing to find the joint size. Even though the duct gage listed at this width-spacing cell may be less, the joint rating cannot be less than at this cell.

6. Beading and crossbreaking are not substitutes for reinforcement. These are not required for any of the following conditions: liner or external insulation is used; width is less than 19 in.; duct pressure class is over 3 in. wg; duct gage is over 20 gage (1.0 mm); unbraced panel area is 10 square feet (0.93 square meters) or less. Otherwise, one or the other must be used.

7. Within the pressure limits given for specific forms, choices for reinforcement are:

   a. Use of flat drive (T-1) as Class A, B, or C per Table 2-48;

   b. Use of any flat connector backed up by a Table 2-29, 2-30 (intermediate type) member;

   c. Use of any appropriately rated joint or inter- mediate member from Tables 2-29 through 2-33;

   d. Downsizing certain joints, joint backup members or intermediates as tie rod options allow.

   In the table, an entry such as H- 18G means that the H reinforcement size may be downsized to a G per Section 2.5 if an internal tie rod is used. This does not apply for joints that require tie rods on both sides of the joint. In some schedules, only the tie rodded construction is given. Kt-18 is an example.

8. You may also use larger reinforcements than specified. In some cases, you must use a larger size than Tables 2-1 to 2-7 call for because some prescribed sizes are observed as minimum.

9. In some cases, a flange is rolled (formed) on the end of a duct section and the minimum gage in the joint rating table will override a lighter gage of the duct wall that is indicated in the Tables 2-1 through 2-7. Then the duct wall must be increased above that needed for

the reinforcement spacing and interval in order to meet the joint requirements.

10. Due to infrequent use, some of the joints in the first edition were omitted. The T numbers of those remaining were not changed for this edition. Authorities can be petitioned to allow use of the omitted joints based on the first edition requirements.

11. Reinforcement requirements are given in rigidity class (both in alphabet letter and EI coding) and also by prescribed sizes. The EI code is modulus of elasticity times the effective moment of inertia times 100,000 (ten to the 5th power).

    The HVAC-DCS Text makes provision for use of equivalent substitutions. Use Chapter 11 to evaluate these.

12. Positive pressure reinforcements for service over 3 in. wg (750 Pa) generally require end ties outside of the duct unless internal tie rods are used, see Figure 2-13. Negative pressure reinforcements attachments to the duct wall are generally at closer intervals than on positive pressure service.

13. For ducts over certain widths only tie rod construction is indicated in order to limit the size of reinforcements. The table entry Kt-16, for example, designates 16 gage duct with K class joints and intermediates having tie rods or straps at intervals not exceeding 60 in. (1524 mm), see Figure 2-14.

    Very large ducts may require internal hangers as shown in Figure 5-7 or may require other internal supports to provide shape retention. Such internal supports should be illustrated on the contract drawings.

The rectangular duct construction standards provide the following options for constructing ducts: a. those unreinforced and joined by flat type connections only, b. those joined by flat type joint connectors backed by a qualified reinforcement, c. those joined by an upright connector that meets reinforcement requirements alone or in conjunction with an incorporated reinforcement, and d. in sizes over 48 in. (1.2 m) width, those using tie rods that permit the use of smaller reinforcements. Not all options exist at all sizes and all static pressure classes. The options are provided to correlate performance with economy and the preference of fabricators and specifiers. SMACNA does not validate equivalency.

The tables can be investigated to suit a preference for each of several features:

a. Look for a preferred duct gage under each reinforcement spacing and find the associated code and maximum duct dimensions.

b. Look for a preferred joint or intermediate reinforcement size in Tables 2-29 to 2-33.

c. Preference for a particular sheet or coil stock size will dictate reinforcement intervals (maximum and subdivisions).

Sometimes, if a project calls for small amounts of ductwork in many size ranges or pressure classes, it may be more economical to select heavier constructions than are required, so that fewer variations are needed.

The duct construction tables define relationships between static pressure, width, wall thickness, reinforcement spacing, and reinforcement strength so that ducts have adequate strength and acceptable deflection limits. The greater dimension of a duct determines the duct gage for all four sides. This applies to reinforced and unreinforced ducts.

The first step in determining construction requirements is to locate the table with the applicable static pressure.

2.1.2 Unreinforced Duct (Fig. 2–8)

Duct sides having a gage listed in the second column of Tables 2-1 to 2-7 do not require reinforcement. These are summarized in Table 2-47. Flat type joints may be used at any spacing. Flat slips and drives must not be less than two gages lower than the duct gage or below 24 gage (0.70 mm).

The T-1 drive slip connection provides sufficient rigidity to be treated as Class A, B, or C reinforcement within the limits of Table 2-48. This gives the appearance of increasing the range of unreinforced duct sizes.

2.1.3 Reinforced Duct (Figs. 2–10, 2–11, 2–12)

In the Reinforcement Spacing columns of Tables 2-1 through 2-7, across from each duct width, each cell shows that duct width's minimum duct gage as a number and its minimum reinforcement grade as a letter. Any cell within a row is an acceptable selection for that duct width. Reinforcement spacings of 10 ft (3.0 m) to 2 ft (0.61 m) are alternative choices. See appendices A.13 to A.16 for discussion of variables that affect choices.

First investigate the duct side with the greater dimension because this side dictates the duct gage. Then find the smaller duct dimension in the first column, and on the same horizontal line, locate the duct gage of the wide side. If the duct gage is in the second column, no reinforcement is required on that side; otherwise, the minimum reinforcement code is the letter listed under the spacing used. The actual duct gage may occur in a column giving allowable spacing greater than will be used. In such a case the minimum reinforcement grade is that associated with the actual spacing.

2.1.4 Transverse Joint and Intermediate Reinforcement (Tables 2-29, 2-30 Fig. 2-12)

The reinforcement spacing in Tables 2-1 to 2-7 denotes distance between two joints or two intermediate reinforcements or from a joint to an intermediate member. Any joint or reinforcement member having a corresponding letter code in Tables 2-29 through 2-33 may be used to comply.

The letter code for reinforcement corresponds to a stiffness index number (EI). This is the modulus of elasticity multiplied by a moment of inertia that is based on the contributing elements of the connector, the reinforcement, the duct wall, or combinations of these. Unless other evidence of adequate strength and rigidity is presented, equivalent construction must meet the EI index associated with the code letter.

In some cases (for example, T-25 joints and standing seams), the metal in the duct counts in the joint qualification. A minimum gage of duct that is heavier than the duct gage shown in Tables 2-1 through 2-7 may be indicated by the joint specifications in Tables 2-32 and 2-33.

Flat slips or drives (or any flat joint shown) may be used at one of the spacing limits, provided that a backup member (of the intermediate type) is used with them; the joint is then rated by the backup member taken from Table 2-29 or 2-30.

Tie rod duct construction described on pages 2.80 through 2.107 is also an alternative. For certain ducts of dimension greater than 48 in. (1.2 m), alternative sizes of reinforcement using tie rods is depicted in the tables. An entry such as H-18G indicates that on 18 ga (1.3 mm) duct, the reinforcement code for either joint or intermediate stiffener is H class, but G class may be substituted if an available tie rod alternative is selected.

For ducts over 120 in. (4.72 m) width, only tie rod construction is indicated in order to limit the size of reinforcements. The table entry Ht-18, for example, designates 18 ga duct with H class joints and intermediates having tie rods or straps at intervals not exceeding 60 in. (1524 mm), *see* Figure 2-14. Very large ducts may require internal hangers as shown in Figure 5-7 or may require other internal supports to provide shape retention. Such internal supports should be illustrated on the contract drawings. Other construction that meets the functional criteria in Chapter 11 may be provided.

2.1.4.1 Sample Uses of Table 2-2 [At 1 in. wg (250 Pa)]

Example 1, 18 in. × 12 in. duct:

If the duct is of 24 ga, the second column shows that reinforcement is not required.

If the duct is of 26 ga, the 12 in. side may be unreinforced, but class B joints are required at 8 ft maximum spacing on the 18 in. sides.

Notice that Table 2-48 allows the T-1 drive slip (alone) to be used on the 18 in. sides at a max spacing of 8 ft if the panel is 26 ga and the pressure is 1 in. wg.

Example 2, 800 mm × 450 mm duct:

The 800 mm side has the following options: If 1.31mm thick steel is used no reinforcement is required. If 1.00 mm thick steel is used, class E joints are required at a max spacing of 3.00 m. If 0.85 mm thick steel is used, class E joints are required at a max spacing of 2.40 m. If 0.70 mm thick steel is used class E joints can be used at a max spacing of 1.80 m or class D joints can be used at a max spacing of 1.5 m. If 0.55 mm thick steel is used class D joints can be used with a max spacing of 1.20 m or class C joints can be used with a max spacing of 0.90 m.

If 0.70 mm thick steel is used then no reinforcement is required on the 450 mm side. If 0.55 mm thick steel is used then class B joints must be used with a max spacing of 2.40 m on the 450 mm side.

Example 3, 54 in. × 30 in. duct, with 5 ft joint spacing preselected:

For 54 in. width, class F is required and the minimum panel thickness is 22 ga. If reinforcement at the mid-span is used the reinforcement spacing changes to 2½ ft and the gage can be reduced to 24. E class joints are required in addition to an E class intermediate reinforcement.

For the 30 in. side: Grade D is required on a minimum panel gage of 26 for 5 ft max spacing. If you did not have the 5 ft joint limitation and it was economical to do so, 18 ga could be used and reinforcement on the 30 in. side would not be required.

Using 18 ga and class H reinforcement would allow the reinforcement spacing to increase to 10 ft on the 54 in. side. Note that an unreinforced option does not exist for a 54 in. width.

Example 4, 72 in. × 72 in. with 5 ft joint spacing and no intermediate reinforcing use 18 ga duct with H rated joints or the option exists to use G rated joints with joint tie rods added (unless the G rating already requires tie rod use).

If intermediate reinforcement is used the reinforcement spacing reduces to 2 ½ ft. The panel gage can be reduced to 24 ga and the reinforcement class is F. So Class F joints must be used as well as class F intermediate reinforcement.

2.2 RECTANGULAR DUCT REINFORCEMENT

S1.10 Unless otherwise specified or allowed, rectangular ductwork shall be constructed in accordance with Tables 2–1 through 2–33 and with details associated with them.

S1.11 The duct gage tables are based on G–60 coated galvanized steel of lockforming grade conforming to ASTM Standards A653 and A924. Uncoated steel, prepainted steel, steel with metal coating such as aluminum or aluminum-zinc compounds, and stainless steel may be used if a minimum corresponding base metal thickness and material strength is provided. Lockforming grades of such material must be used.

The use of alternative materials requires specification or approval by a designer. The surface conditions, hardness, ductility, corrosion resistance, and other characteristics of these materials must be judged acceptable by the designer for the planned service.

Specifications that refer to use of material that is two gages heavier mean two numbers separated in a series that uses both odd and even number progression; *e.g.*, 18 is two gages heavier than 20 on Appendix pages A.1 and A.2.

S1.12 Unless otherwise specified, reinforcement may be uncoated steel or galvanized steel.

S1.13 A reinforcement code classification (letter and EI index) higher than indicated must be substituted when the tables do not provide the specific construction details for a lower classification. A higher rated construction member may also be substituted for convenience.

S1.14 Joint spacing on unreinforced ducts is unlimited. On ducts that require reinforcement, joint spacing is unrestricted except that the joint itself must qualify for the minimum reinforcement code associated with the reinforcement spacing. Exceptions can be made for T21, T22, T24 and T25 transverse joints provided the connections are mechanically fastened or welded and the joint is not credited towards the reinforcement requirements.

S1.15 Duct sides that are 19 in. (483 mm) and over and are 20 ga (1.00 mm) or less, with more than 10 square ft (0.93 square m) of unbraced panel area, shall be crossbroken or beaded as indicated in Figure 2–10 unless they are lined or externally insulated. Ducts that are of heavier gage, smaller dimensions, and smaller panel area and those that are lined or externally insulated are not required to have cross-breaking or beading.

S1.16 Fittings shall be reinforced like sections of straight duct. On size change fittings, the greater fitting dimension determines the duct gage. Where fitting curvature or internal member attachments provide equivalent rigidity, such features may be credited as reinforcement.

S1.17 Duct wall thickness, joints, seams, and reinforcements must be coordinated to provide proper assembly.

S1.18 Other construction that meets the functional criteria in Chapter 11 or is as serviceable as that produced by the construction tables may be provided.

READING GUIDE SUMMARY

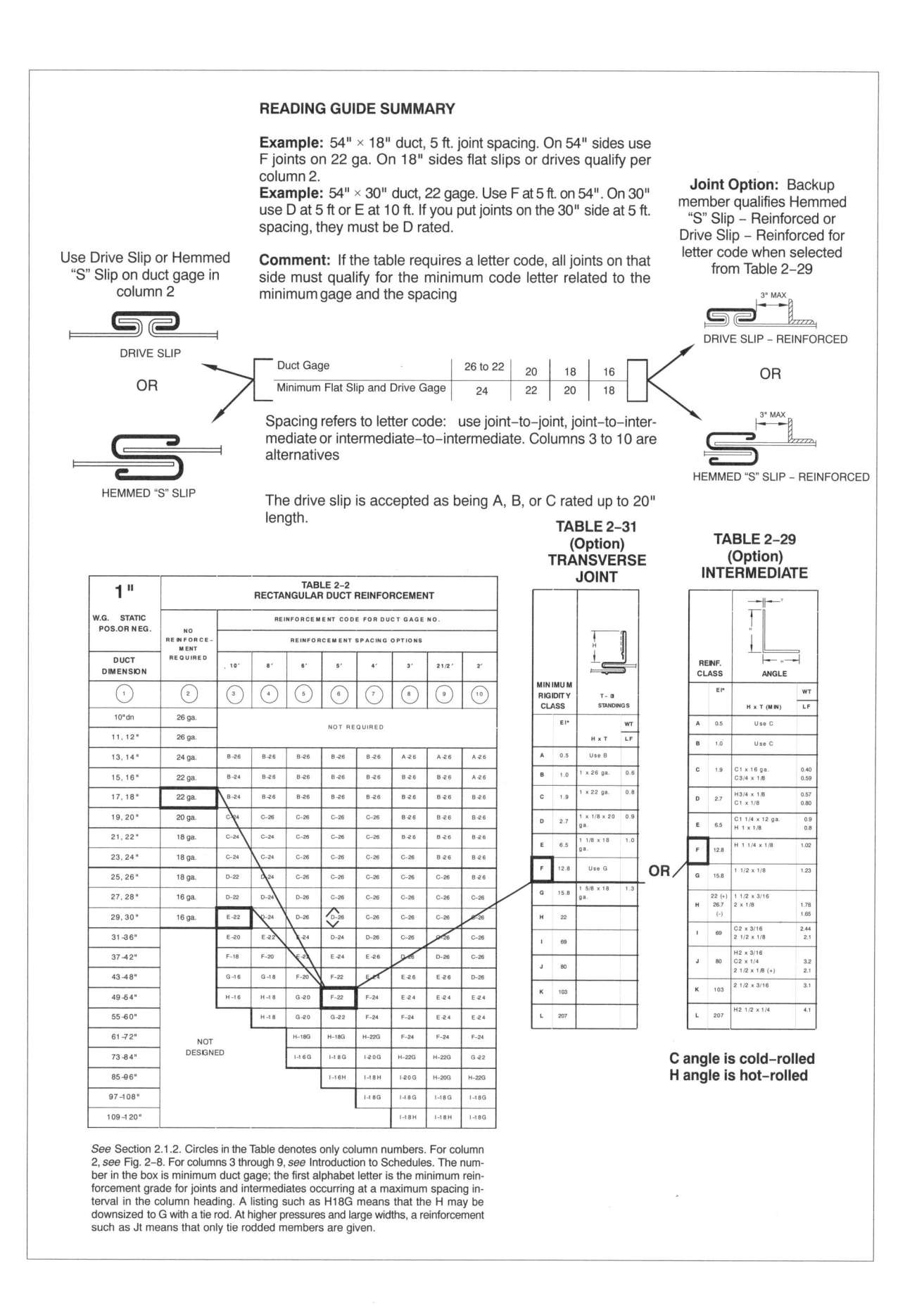

Example: 54" × 18" duct, 5 ft. joint spacing. On 54" sides use F joints on 22 ga. On 18" sides flat slips or drives qualify per column 2.

Example: 54" × 30" duct, 22 gage. Use F at 5 ft. on 54". On 30" use D at 5 ft or E at 10 ft. If you put joints on the 30" side at 5 ft. spacing, they must be D rated.

Comment: If the table requires a letter code, all joints on that side must qualify for the minimum code letter related to the minimum gage and the spacing

Joint Option: Backup member qualifies Hemmed "S" Slip – Reinforced or Drive Slip – Reinforced for letter code when selected from Table 2–29

Use Drive Slip or Hemmed "S" Slip on duct gage in column 2

DRIVE SLIP

OR

HEMMED "S" SLIP

Duct Gage	26 to 22	20	18	16
Minimum Flat Slip and Drive Gage	24	22	20	18

Spacing refers to letter code: use joint-to-joint, joint-to-intermediate or intermediate-to-intermediate. Columns 3 to 10 are alternatives

The drive slip is accepted as being A, B, or C rated up to 20" length.

DRIVE SLIP – REINFORCED

OR

HEMMED "S" SLIP – REINFORCED

TABLE 2-2 RECTANGULAR DUCT REINFORCEMENT

1" W.G. STATIC POS. OR NEG.

DUCT DIMENSION (1)	NO REINFORCEMENT REQUIRED (2)	10' (3)	8' (4)	6' (5)	5' (6)	4' (7)	3' (8)	2½' (9)	2' (10)
10" dn	26 ga.	NOT REQUIRED							
11, 12"	26 ga.								
13, 14"	24 ga.	B-26	B-26	B-26	B-26	B-26	A-26	A-26	A-26
15, 16"	22 ga.	B-24	B-26	B-26	B-26	B-26	B-26	B-26	A-26
17, 18"	22 ga.	B-24	B-26	B-26	B-26	B-26	B-26	B-26	B-26
19, 20"	20 ga.	C-24	C-26	C-26	C-26	C-26	B-26	B-26	B-26
21, 22"	18 ga.	C-24	C-26	C-26	C-26	C-26	B-26	B-26	B-26
23, 24"	18 ga.	C-24	C-24	C-26	C-26	C-26	C-26	B-26	B-26
25, 26"	18 ga.	D-22	D-24	C-26	C-26	C-26	C-26	C-26	B-26
27, 28"	16 ga.	D-22	D-24	C-26	C-26	C-26	C-26	C-26	C-26
29, 30"	16 ga.	E-22	D-24	D-26	D-26	C-26	C-26	C-26	C-26
31-36"		E-20	E-22	E-24	D-24	D-26	C-26	C-26	C-26
37-42"		F-18	F-20	E-22	E-24	E-26	D-26	D-26	C-26
43-48"		G-16	G-18	F-20	F-22	E-24	E-26	E-26	D-26
49-54"		H-16	H-18	G-20	F-22	F-24	E-24	E-24	E-24
55-60"			H-18	G-20	G-22	F-24	F-24	E-24	E-24
61-72"	NOT DESIGNED		H-18G	H-18G	H-22G	F-24	F-24		
73-84"			I-16G	I-18G	I-20G	H-22G	H-22G	G-22	
85-96"				I-16H	I-18H	I-20G	H-20G	H-22G	
97-108"					I-18G	I-18G	I-18G	I-18G	
109-120"						I-18H	I-18H	I-18G	

TABLE 2-31 (Option) TRANSVERSE JOINT

MINIMUM RIGIDITY CLASS	EI*	T-α STANDINGS H x T	WT LF
A	0.5	Use B	
B	1.0	1 x 26 ga.	0.6
C	1.9	1 x 22 ga.	0.8
D	2.7	1 x 1/8 x 20 ga.	0.9
E	6.5	1 1/8 x 18 ga.	1.0
F	12.8	Use G	
G	15.8	1 5/8 x 18 ga.	1.3
H	22		
I	69		
J	80		
K	103		
L	207		

OR

TABLE 2-29 (Option) INTERMEDIATE

REINF. CLASS	EI*	ANGLE H x T (MIN)	WT LF
A	0.5	Use C	
B	1.0	Use C	
C	1.9	C1 x 16 ga. / C3/4 x 1/8	0.40 / 0.59
D	2.7	H3/4 x 1/8 / C1 x 1/8	0.57 / 0.80
E	6.5	C1 1/4 x 12 ga. / H 1 x 1/8	0.9 / 0.8
F	12.8	H 1 1/4 x 1/8	1.02
G	15.8	1 1/2 x 1/8	1.23
H	22 (+) 26.7 (-)	1 1/2 x 3/16 / 2 x 1/8	1.78 / 1.65
I	69	C2 x 3/16 / 2 1/2 x 1/8	2.44 / 2.1
J	80	H2 x 3/16 / C2 x 1/4 / 2 1/2 x 1/8 (+)	3.2 / 2.1
K	103	2 1/2 x 3/16	3.1
L	207	H2 1/2 x 1/4	4.1

C angle is cold-rolled
H angle is hot-rolled

See Section 2.1.2. Circles in the Table denotes only column numbers. For column 2, *see* Fig. 2-8. For columns 3 through 9, *see* Introduction to Schedules. The number in the box is minimum duct gage; the first alphabet letter is the minimum reinforcement grade for joints and intermediates occurring at a maximum spacing interval in the column heading. A listing such as H18G means that the H may be downsized to G with a tie rod. At higher pressures and large widths, a reinforcement such as Jt means that only tie rodded members are given.

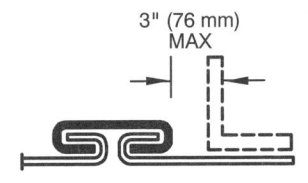

T-1 – DRIVE SLIP
T-3 – REINFORCED (3" (76 mm) MAX)

- Gage no less than two gages less than duct gage
- 24 ga minimum
- Qualification as reinforcement per Table 2-48
- T-3 – Slip Gage as per T-1
  - Any length at 2 in. wg
  - 36 in. maximum length at 3 in. wg
  - 30 in. maximum length at 4 in. wg
  - Not allowed above 4 in. wg

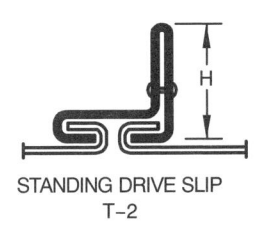

STANDING DRIVE SLIP T-2

- Fasten standing portions within 2 in. of each end and elsewhere at 8 in. spacing or less
- Any length at 2 in. wg
- 36 in. maximum length at 3 in. wg
- 30 in. maximum length at 4 in. wg
- Not allowed above 4 in. wg

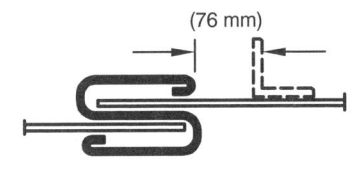

PLAIN "S" SLIP T-5
T-6 HEMMED "S" SLIP (T-6a REINFORCED) (76 mm)

- Not less than two gages less than duct gage
- 24 ga minimum
- When used on all 4 sides, fasten within 2 in. of the corners and at 12 in. maximum intervals
- 2 in. wg maximum pressure

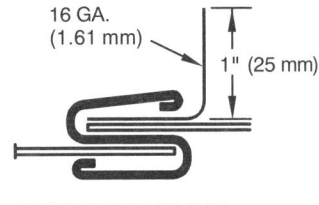

REINFORCED "S" SLIP T-7 (16 GA. (1.61 mm), 1" (25 mm))

- Use slips conforming to T-6
- Use 16 ga angle of 1 in. height into slip pocket
- Fasten with screws at ends
- Angle used only for A, B, or C rigidity class
- 2 in. wg maximum pressure

FIGURE 2-1 RECTANGULAR DUCT/TRANSVERSE JOINTS

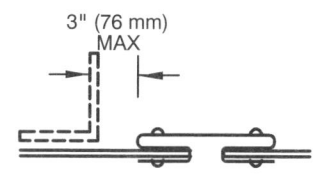

T-8 DOUBLE "S" SLIP
(T-8a REINFORCED)

3" (76 mm) MAX

- 24 ga for 30 inch width or less
- 22 ga over 30 inch width
- Fasten to each section of the duct within 2 in. from corners and at 6 in. maximum intervals
- 5/8 in. minimum tabs to close corners

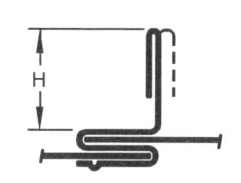

STANDING S
T-10

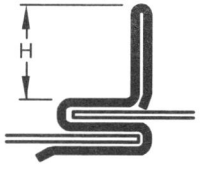

STANDING S (ALT.)
T-11

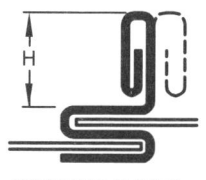

STANDING S (ALT.)
T-12

- When using S on all four sides, fasten slip to duct within 2 in. of the corner and at 12 in. maximum intervals
- Any length at 2 in. wg
- 36 in. maximum length at 3 in. wg
- 30 in. maximum length at 4 in. wg
- Not allowed above 4 in. wg

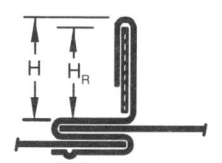

STANDING S
(BAR REINFORCED)
T-13

- Fasten as per Joint T-10
- Standing portion as per T-10 or T-11 to hold Flat Bar
- Fasten bar stock to the connector within 2 in. of the corner and at 12 in. maximum intervals
- Any length at 2 in. wg
- 36 in. maximum length at 3 in. wg
- 30 in. maximum length at 4 in. wg
- Not allowed above 4 in. wg

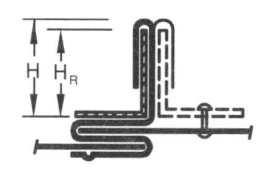

STANDING S
(ANGLE REINFORCED)
T-14

- Fasten as per Joint T-10
- Fasten angle to the connector or duct wall within 2 in. of the corner and at 12 in. maximum intervals
- Any length at 2 in. wg
- 36 in. maximum length at 3 in. wg
- 30 in. maximum length at 4 in. wg
- Not allowed above 4 in. wg

FIGURE 2-1 RECTANGULAR DUCT/TRANSVERSE JOINTS (CONTINUED)

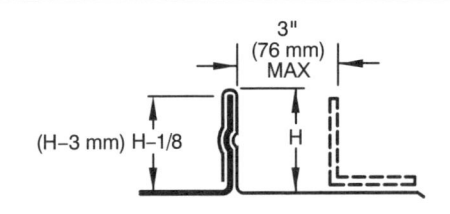

STANDING SEAM
T-15

ANGLE REINFORCED STANDING SEAM
T-16

- Button punch or otherwise fasten within 2 in. of each corner and at 6 in. maximum intervals
- Seal and fold corners
- Stagger joints on adjacent sides if using standing seam on all four sides
- Hammer longitudinal seam at ends of standing seam

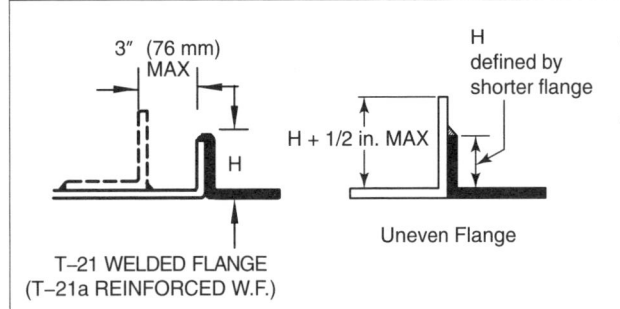

T-21 WELDED FLANGE
(T-21a REINFORCED W.F.)

Uneven Flange

- Use ½ in. minimum flange and continuous end weld
- Flanges larger than ¾ in. must be spot welded, bolted, riveted or screwed to prevent separation (2 in. from ends and at 8 in. maximum intervals)

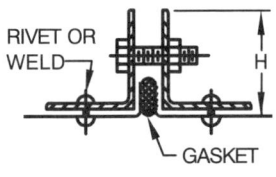

COMPANION ANGLES (CAULK OR GASKET)
T-22

- ⅜ in. minimum flange on duct
- Angles must have welded corners
- Angles must be tack welded, bolted or screwed to the duct wall at 2 in. maximum from the ends and at 12 in. maximum intervals
- Bolt Schedule:
  - ⁵⁄₁₆ minimum diameter at 6 in. maximum spacing at 4 in. wg or lower
  - ⅛ in. angle requires 4 in. maximum spacing at 4 in. wg
  - 4 in. maximum spacing at higher pressures

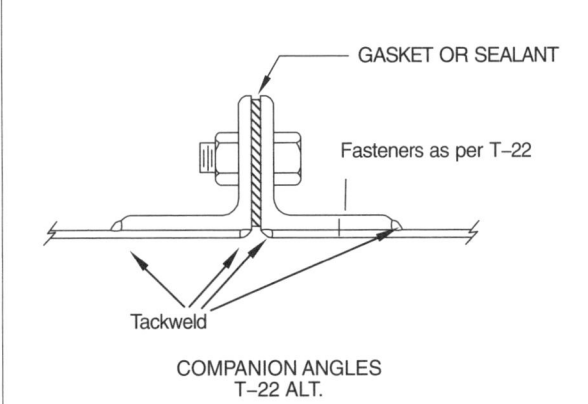

COMPANION ANGLES
T-22 ALT.

- Hold duct back ⅛ in. from vertical face of the angle and tack weld to the flange along the edge of the duct
- Fasten angle to duct as per T-22
- For additional tightness place sealant between the angle and duct or seal the weld
- If the faces of the angles are flush, thick consistency sealant may be used in lieu of gasket
- Use gasket suitable for the specific service and fit it uniformly to avoid protruding into the duct

FIGURE 2-1 RECTANGULAR DUCT/TRANSVERSE JOINTS (CONTINUED)

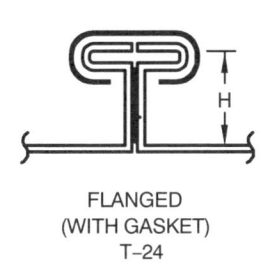

FLANGED (WITH GASKET) T-24

- Assemble per Figure 2-17
- Close corners with minimum 16 ga corner pieces and ⅜ in. bolts min.
- Lock flanges together with 6 in. long clips located within 6 in. of each corner
- Clips spaced at 15 in. maximum for 3 in. wg pressure class or lower
- Clips spaced at 12 in. maximum for 4, 6 and 10 in. wg
- Gasket to be located to form an effective seal

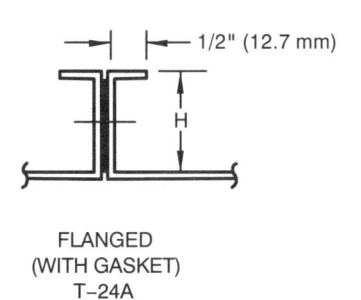

FLANGED (WITH GASKET) T-24A

- Bolt, rivet 1 in. maximum from ends and at 6 in. maximum intervals
- Limited to 2 in. wg pressure class
- *See* Figure 2-17
- Gasket to be located to form an effective seal

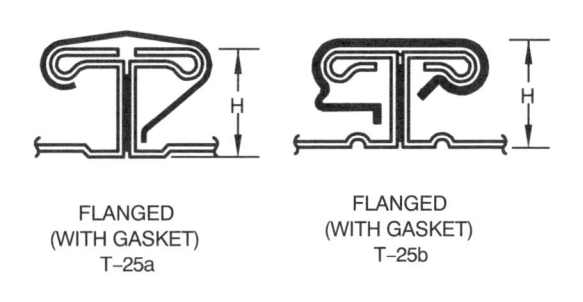

FLANGED (WITH GASKET) T-25a

FLANGED (WITH GASKET) T-25b

- Assemble per Figure 2-18
- Ratings may be adjusted with EI-rated bar stock or members from Tables 2-29 and 2-30
- Supplemental members may be attached to the duct wall on both sides of the joint
- Single members may be used if they are fastened through both mating flanges
- Gasket to be located to form an effective seal

SLIP-ON FLANGE

- Consult manufacturers for ratings established by performance documented to functional criteria in Chapter 11.

FIGURE 2–1 RECTANGULAR DUCT/TRANSVERSE JOINTS (CONTINUED)

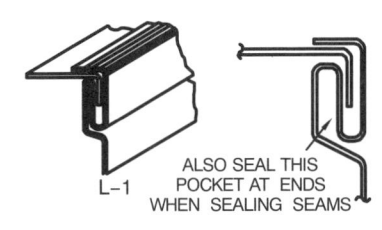

L-1 PITTSBURGH LOCK (ALSO SEAL THIS POCKET AT ENDS WHEN SEALING SEAMS)	• Pocket depth from ¼ in. to ⅝ in. • Use on straight duct and fittings • To ± 10 in. wg
L-2 BUTTON PUNCH SNAP LOCK (2")	• ⅝ in. pocket depth for 20, 22, and 24 ga • ½ in. pocket depth for 24 and 26 ga • To ± 4 in. wg • Screws must be added at the ends of all duct of 4 in. wg and at the ends of 3 in. wg when the duct is over 48 in. width
L-3 GROOVED SEAM ALSO CALLED FLAT LOCK AND PIPE LOCK / **L-6 DOUBLE CORNER SEAM** (SEE L-1 SEALING NOTE.)	• To ± 10 in. wg
L-4 STANDING SEAM (SEE FIG. 2-8 ALSO)	• To ± 10 in. wg • 1 in. seam minimum • May be used on duct interiors • Fasten at 2 in. maximum from ends and at 8 in. maximum intervals
L-5 SINGLE CORNER SEAM	• To ± 10 in. wg • Fasten as per L-4
FLANGED (WITH GASKET) T-25a / **FLANGED (WITH GASKET) T-25b**	• Modify for longitudinal seam application.

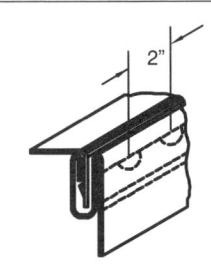

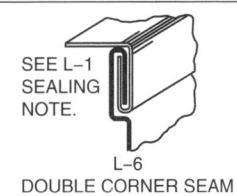

FIGURE 2–2 RECTANGULAR DUCT/LONGITUDINAL SEAMS

2.3 LONGITUDINAL SEAMS FOR RECTANGULAR DUCT

S1.43　Seams shall be selected for the material, pressure classification, and other construction detail appropriate for the service.

S1.44　Seams shall be formed and assembled with proper dimension and proportion for tight and secure fit up. Notching shall be minimal and consistent with transverse joint make-up needs.

S1.45　Although they are not illustrated here, seams may be of butt weld, corner weld, plug weld or spot weld design. They may also be of the spiral lockseam type.

S1.46　Solder for watertight seam closure, when specified, should conform to ASTM Standard B32 or Federal Specification QQ-S-571.

ANGLE

HAT SECTION

CHANNEL OR ZEE

FRAMING CHANNEL

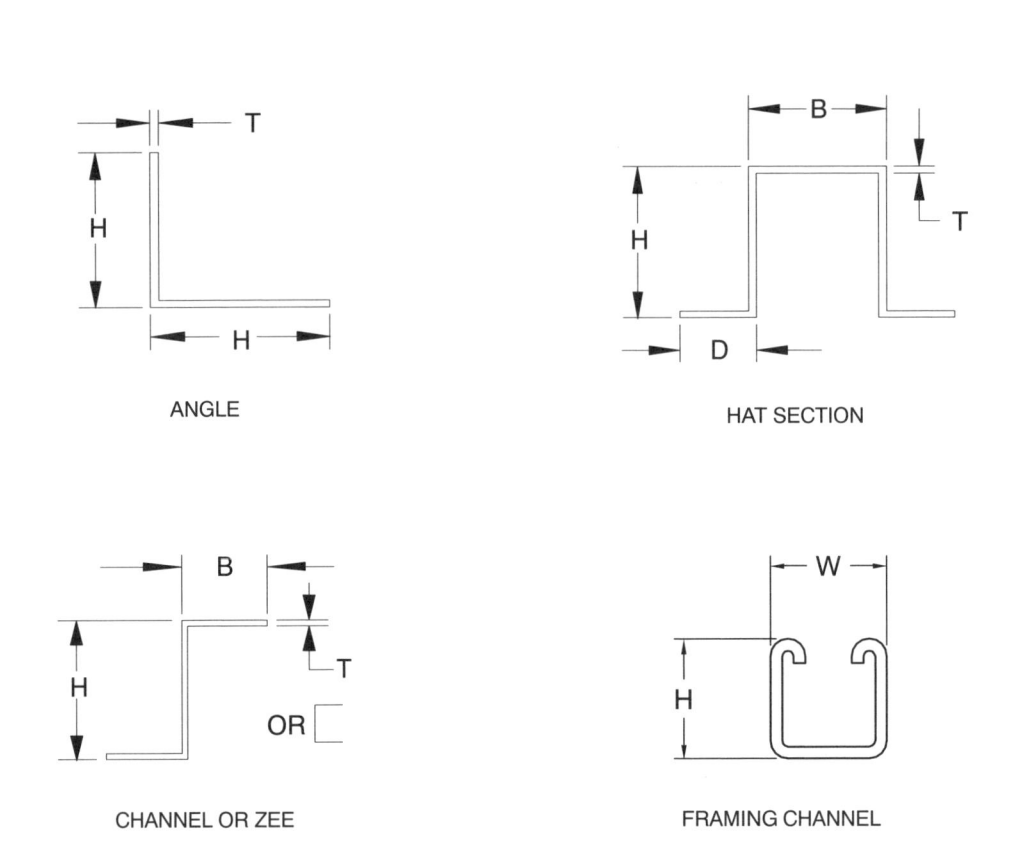

- *SEE* TABLE 2–29 FOR REINFORCEMENT CLASS RATINGS, FOR ANGLES, CHANNELS, OR HAT SECTION.
- *SEE* TABLE 2–30 FOR FRAMING CHANNEL RIGIDITY CLASS EQUIVALENTS.
- REINFORCEMENTS TO BE ATTACHED TO DUCT WALL WITH SCREWS, RIVETS OR WELDS 2 IN. MAX. FROM THE ENDS AND SPACED AT 12 IN. MAX.
- REINFORCEMENTS REQUIRE END TIES AT 4 IN. WG (1000 PA) AND UP, *SEE* FIGURES 2–12, 2–13.

NOTE:

OTHER STRUCTURAL SHAPES MAY BE USED FOR EXTERNAL REINFORCEMENTS WHEN EQUIVALENT EFFECTIVE STIFFENERS RATING (EI) CAN BE DEMONSTRATED.

FIGURE 2–3 RECTANGULAR DUCT EXTERNAL REINFORCEMENTS

NOTES: FOR USE OF PRESSURE CLASS TABLES (Tables 2-1 through 2-7)

a. Circles in the table denote only Column numbers.

b. For Column 2, *see* Figure 2-9.

c. For Columns 3 through 10, *see* Introduction to Schedules.

d. The number in the box is the minimum gage.

e. The letter in the box to the left of the gage is the minimum reinforcement grade for joints and intermediate stiffeners occurring at a maximum spacing interval in the column heading.

f. A letter to the right of the gage gives a tie-rodded reinforcement alternative.

g. A "t" compels the use of tie rods for the reinforcement listing.

h. For beading or cross breaking, *see* Figure 2-10.

½ in. wg Static Pos. or Neg. Duct Dimension (1)	No Reinforcement Required (2)	Reinforcement Code for Duct Gage Number — Reinforcement Spacing Options							
		10 ft (3)	8 ft (4)	6 ft (5)	5 ft (6)	4 ft (7)	3 ft (8)	2½ ft (9)	2 ft (10)
10 in. and under	26 ga.	Not Required							
11 – 12 in.	26 ga.								
13 – 14 in.	26 ga.								
15 – 16 in.	26 ga.								
17 – 18 in.	26 ga.								
19 – 20 in.	24 ga.	B-26	B-26	B-26	B-26	B-26	B-26	A-26	A-26
21 – 22 in.	22 ga.	B-26	B-26	B-26	B-26	B-26	B-26	B-26	A-26
23 – 24 in.	22 ga.	C-26	C-26	C-26	B-26	B-26	B-26	B-26	B-26
25 – 26 in.	20 ga.	C-26	C-26	C-26	C-26	B-26	B-26	B-26	B-26
27 – 28 in.	18 ga.	C-24	C-26	C-26	C-26	C-26	B-26	B-26	B-26
29 – 30 in.	18 ga.	C-24	C-26	C-26	C-26	C-26	B-26	B-26	B-26
31 – 36 in.	18 ga.	D-22	D-24	C-26	C-26	C-26	C-26	C-26	B-26
37 – 42 in.	16 ga.	E-20	E-24	D-24	D-26	C-26	C-26	C-26	C-26
43 – 48 in.	16 ga.	E-20	E-22	E-24	E-26	D-26	D-26	C-26	C-26
49 – 54 in.	Not Designed	F-18	F-20	E-22	E-26	E-26	E-26	D-26	C-26
55 – 60 in.		G-18	F-20	F-22	E-24	E-24	E-26	E-26	D-26
61 – 72 in.		H-16	H-18	F-20	F-22	F-24	E-24	E-24	E-24
73 – 84 in.			I-16G	H-18G	H-22G	G-24	F-24	F-24	F-24
85 – 96 in.			I-16G	I-18G	H-20G	H-22G	G-22	F-22	F-22
97 – 108 in.				I-16G	I-18G	I-18G	H-18G	H-18G	G-18
109 – 120 in.					I-16G	I-16G	I-18G	H-18G	H-18G

Table 2–1 Rectangular Duct Reinforcement

125 Pa Static Pos. or Neg. Duct Dimension (mm)	No Reinforcement Required (mm)	Reinforcement Code for Duct Panel Thickness (mm)							
		Reinforcement Spacing Options							
		3.00 m	2.40 m	1.80 m	1.50 m	1.20 m	0.90 m	0.75 m	0.60 m
①	②	③	④	⑤	⑥	⑦	⑧	⑨	⑩
250 and under	0.55	Not Required							
251 – 300	0.55									
301 – 350	0.55									
351 – 400	0.55									
401 – 450	0.55									
451 – 500	0.70	B-0.55	B-0.55	B-0.55	B-0.55	B-0.55	B-0.55	A-0.55	A-0.55
501 – 550	0.85	B-0.55	B-0.55	B-0.55	B-0.55	B-0.55	B-0.55	B-0.55	A-0.55
551 – 600	0.85	C-0.55	C-0.55	C-0.55	B-0.55	B-0.55	B-0.55	B-0.55	B-0.55
601 – 650	1.00	C-0.55	C-0.55	C-0.55	C-0.55	B-0.55	B-0.55	B-0.55	B-0.55
651 – 700	1.31	C-0.70	C-0.55	C-0.55	C-0.55	C-0.55	B-0.55	B-0.55	B-0.55
701 – 750	1.31	C-0.70	C-0.55	C-0.55	C-0.55	C-0.55	B-0.55	B-0.55	B-0.55
751 – 900	1.31	D-0.85	D-0.70	C-0.55	C-0.55	C-0.55	C-0.55	C-0.55	B-0.55
901 – 1000	1.61	E-1.00	E-0.70	D-0.70	D-0.55	C-0.55	C-0.55	C-0.55	C-0.55
1001 – 1200	1.61	E-1.00	E-0.85	E-0.70	E-0.55	D-0.55	D-0.55	C-0.55	C-0.55
1201 – 1300		F-1.31	F-1.00	E-0.85	E-0.55	E-0.55	E-0.55	D-0.55	C-0.55
1301 – 1500		G-1.31	F-1.00	F-0.85	E-0.70	E-0.70	E-0.55	E-0.55	D-0.55
1501 – 1800		H-1.61	H-1.31	F-1.00	F-0.85	F-0.70	E-0.70	E-0.70	E-0.70
1801 – 2100	Not Designed		I-1.61G	H-1.31G	H-0.85G	G-0.70	F-0.70	F-0.70	F-0.70
2101 – 2400			I-1.61G	I-1.31G	H-1.00G	H-0.85G	G-0.85	F-0.85	F-0.85
2401 – 2700				I-1.61G	I-1.31G	I-1.31G	H-1.31G	H-1.31G	G-1.31
2701 – 3000					I-1.61G	I-1.61G	I-1.31G	H-1.31G	H-1.31G

Table 2–1M Rectangular Duct Reinforcement

1 in. wg Static Pos. or Neg. Duct Dimension	No Reinforcement Required	Reinforcement Code for Duct Gage Number							
		Reinforcement Spacing Options							
		10 ft	8 ft	6 ft	5 ft	4 ft	3 ft	2½ ft	2 ft
①	②	③	④	⑤	⑥	⑦	⑧	⑨	⑩
10 in. and under	26 ga.	Not Required							
11 – 12 in.	26 ga.								
13 – 14 in.	26 ga.								
15 – 16 in.	26 ga.								
17 – 18 in.	24 ga.		B-26	B-26	B-26	B-26	B-26	B-26	B-26
19 – 20 in.	24 ga.		C-26	C-26	C-26	C-26	B-26	B-26	B-26
21 – 22 in.	22 ga.	C-24	C-24	C-26	C-26	C-26	B-26	B-26	B-26
23 – 24 in.	22 ga.	C-24	C-24	C-26	C-26	C-26	C-26	B-26	B-26
25 – 26 in.	20 ga.	D-22	D-24	C-26	C-26	C-26	C-26	C-26	B-26
27 – 28 in.	18 ga.	D-22	D-24	D-26	C-26	C-26	C-26	C-26	C-26
29 – 30 in.	18 ga.	E-22	D-24	D-26	D-26	C-26	C-26	C-26	C-26
31 – 36 in.	18 ga.	E-20	E-22	E-24	D-24	D-26	C-26	C-26	C-26
37 – 42 in.	16 ga.	F-18	F-20	E-22	E-24	E-26	D-26	D-26	C-26
43 – 48 in.	16 ga.	G-18	G-18	F-20	F-22	E-24	E-26	E-26	D-26
49 – 54 in.		H-18	H-18	G-20	F-22	F-24	E-24	E-24	E-24
55 – 60 in.		I-16	H-18	G-20	G-22	F-24	F-24	E-24	E-24
61 – 72 in.			I-16G	H-18G	H-18G	H-22G	F-24	F-24	F-24
73 – 84 in.	Not Designed			I-18G	I-18G	I-20G	H-22G	H-22G	G-22
85 – 96 in.				J-16H	I-18H	I-18H	I-20G	H-20G	H-22G
97 – 108 in.					J-16H	I-18H	I-18G	I-18G	I-18G
109 – 120 in.						J-16H	I-18H	I-18H	I-18G

Table 2–2 Rectangular Duct Reinforcement

250 Pa Static Pos. or Neg. Duct Dimension (mm)	No Reinforcement Required (mm)	Reinforcement Code for Duct Panel Thickness (mm)							
		Reinforcement Spacing Options							
		3.00 m	2.40 m	1.80 m	1.50 m	1.20 m	0.90 m	0.75 m	0.60 m
①	②	③	④	⑤	⑥	⑦	⑧	⑨	⑩
250 and under	0.55	Not Required							
251 – 300	0.55									
301 – 350	0.55									
351 – 400	0.55									
401 – 450	0.70		B-0.55	B-0.55	B-0.55	B-0.55	B-0.55	B-0.55	B-0.55
451 – 500	0.70		C-0.55	C-0.55	C-0.55	C-0.55	B-0.55	B-0.55	B-0.55
501 – 550	0.85	C-0.70	C-0.70	C-0.55	C-0.55	C-0.55	B-0.55	B-0.55	B-0.55
551 – 600	0.85	C-0.70	C-0.70	C-0.55	C-0.55	C-0.55	C-0.55	B-0.55	B-0.55
601 – 650	1.00	D-0.85	D-0.70	C-0.55	C-0.55	C-0.55	C-0.55	C-0.55	B-0.55
651 – 700	1.31	D-0.85	D-0.70	D-0.55	C-0.55	C-0.55	C-0.55	C-0.55	C-0.55
701 – 750	1.31	E-0.85	D-0.70	D-0.55	D-0.55	C-0.55	C-0.55	C-0.55	C-0.55
751 – 900	1.31	E-1.00	E-0.85	E-0.70	D-0.70	D-0.55	C-0.55	C-0.55	C-0.55
901 – 1000	1.61	F-1.31	F-1.00	E-0.85	E-0.70	E-0.55	D-0.55	D-0.55	C-0.55
1001 – 1200	1.61	G-1.31	G-1.31	F-1.00	F-0.85	E-0.70	E-0.55	E-0.55	D-0.55
1201 – 1300		H-1.31	H-1.31	G-1.00	F-0.85	F-0.70	E-0.70	E-0.70	E-0.70
1301 – 1500		I-1.61	H-1.31	G-1.00	G-0.85	F-0.70	F-0.70	E-0.70	E-0.70
1501 – 1800			I-1.61G	H-1.31G	H-1.31G	H-0.85G	F-0.70	F-0.70	F-0.70
1801 – 2100	Not Designed			I-1.31G	I-1.31G	I-1.00G	H-0.85G	H-0.85G	G-0.85
2101 – 2400				J-1.61H	I-1.31H	I-1.31H	I-1.00G	H-1.00G	H-0.85G
2401 – 2700					J-1.61H	I-1.31H	I-1.31H	I-1.31G	I-1.31G
2701 – 3000						J-1.61H	I-1.31H	I-1.31H	I-1.31G

Table 2–2M Rectangular Duct Reinforcement

2 in. wg Static Pos. or Neg. Duct Dimension	No Reinforcement Required	Reinforcement Code for Duct Gage Number							
		Reinforcement Spacing Options							
		10 ft	8 ft	6 ft	5 ft	4 ft	3 ft	2½ ft	2 ft
①	②	③	④	⑤	⑥	⑦	⑧	⑨	⑩
10 in. and under	26 ga.	Not Required							
11 – 12 in.	26 ga.								
13 – 14 in.	24 ga.		B-26	B-26	B-26	B-26	B-26	B-26	B-26
15 – 16 in.	24 ga.		C-26	C-26	C-26	C-26	C-26	B-26	B-26
17 – 18 in.	22 ga.		C-26	C-26	C-26	C-26	C-26	C-26	B-26
19 – 20 in.	20 ga.	C-22	C-24	C-26	C-26	C-26	C-26	C-26	C-26
21 – 22 in.	18 ga.	D-22	D-24	D-26	D-26	C-26	C-26	C-26	C-26
23 – 24 in.	18 ga.	E-22	E-24	D-26	D-26	D-26	C-26	C-26	C-26
25 – 26 in.	18 ga.	E-22	E-22	E-24	D-26	D-26	C-26	C-26	C-26
27 – 28 in.	18 ga.	F-20	E-20	E-22	E-24	D-26	D-26	C-26	C-26
29 – 30 in.	18 ga.	F-20	F-20	E-22	E-24	E-26	D-26	D-26	C-26
31 – 36 in.	16 ga.	G-18	G-20	F-22	F-24	E-24	E-26	D-26	D-26
37 – 42 in.		H-16	H-18	G-20	G-22	F-24	E-24	E-26	E-26
43 – 48 in.			I-18	H-20	H-22	G-22	F-24	F-24	E-24
49 – 54 in.			I-16G	I-18G	H-20G	H-20G	G-24	F-24	F-24
55 – 60 in.				I-18G	I-20G	H-20G	G-22	G-24	F-24
61 – 72 in.	Not Designed			J-16H	J-18H	I-20G	H-22G	H-22G	H-24
73 – 84 in.					J-16H	I-20G	I-20G	I-22G	I-22G
85 – 96 in.						J-18H	I-18H	I-20H	I-22H
97 – 108 in.						K-16I	K-18H	J-18H	I-18H
109 – 120 in.							K-16I	K-18I	J-18I

Table 2–3 Rectangular Duct Reinforcement

500 Pa Static Pos. or Neg. Duct Dimension (mm)	No Reinforcement Required (mm)	Reinforcement Code for Duct Panel Thickness (mm)							
		Reinforcement Spacing Options							
		3.00 m	2.40 m	1.80 m	1.50 m	1.20 m	0.90 m	0.75 m	0.60 m
①	②	③	④	⑤	⑥	⑦	⑧	⑨	⑩
250 and under	0.55	Not Required							
251 – 300	0.55								
301 – 350	0.70		B-0.55	B-0.55	B-0.55	B-0.55	B-0.55	B-0.55	B-0.55
351 – 400	0.70		C-0.55	C-0.55	C-0.55	C-0.55	C-0.55	B-0.55	B-0.55
401 – 450	0.85		C-0.55	C-0.55	C-0.55	C-0.55	C-0.55	C-0.55	B-0.55
451 – 500	1.00	C-0.85	C-0.70	C-0.55	C-0.55	C-0.55	C-0.55	C-0.55	C-0.55
501 – 550	1.31	D-0.85	D-0.70	D-0.55	D-0.55	C-0.55	C-0.55	C-0.55	C-0.55
551 – 600	1.31	E-0.85	E-0.70	D-0.55	D-0.55	D-0.55	C-0.55	C-0.55	C-0.55
601 – 650	1.31	E-0.85	E-0.85	E-0.70	D-0.55	D-0.55	C-0.55	C-0.55	C-0.55
651 – 700	1.31	F-1.00	E-1.00	E-0.85	E-0.70	D-0.55	D-0.55	C-0.55	C-0.55
701 – 750	1.31	F-1.00	F-1.00	E-0.85	E-0.70	E-0.55	D-0.55	D-0.55	C-0.55
751 – 900	1.61	G-1.31	G-1.00	F-0.85	F-0.70	E-0.70	E-0.55	D-0.55	D-0.55
901 – 1000		H-1.61	H-1.31	G-1.00	G-0.85	F-0.70	E-0.70	E-0.55	E-0.55
1001 – 1200			I-1.31	H-1.00	H-0.85	G-0.85	F-0.70	F-0.70	E-0.70
1201 – 1300			I-1.61G	I-1.31G	H-1.00G	H-1.00G	G-0.70	F-0.70	F-0.70
1301 – 1500				I-1.31G	I-1.00G	H-1.00G	G-0.85	G-0.70	F-0.70
1501 – 1800		Not Designed			J-1.61H	J-1.31H	I-1.00G	H-0.85G	H-0.85G	H-0.70
1801 – 2100					J-1.61H	I-1.00G	I-1.00G	I-0.85G	I-0.85G
2101 – 2400						J-1.31H	I-1.31H	I-1.00H	I-0.85H
2401 – 2700						K-1.61I	K-1.31H	J-1.31H	I-1.31H
2701 – 3000							K-1.61I	K-1.31I	J-1.31I

Table 2–3M Rectangular Duct Reinforcement

3 in. wg Static Pos. or Neg. Duct Dimension	No Reinforcement Required	Reinforcement Code for Duct Gage Number Reinforcement Spacing Options							
		10 ft	8 ft	6 ft	5 ft	4 ft	3 ft	2½ ft	2 ft
①	②	③	④	⑤	⑥	⑦	⑧	⑨	⑩
10 in. and under	24 ga.	Not Required		B-26	B-26	B-26	B-26	B-26	B-26
11 – 12 in.	24 ga.			B-26	B-26	B-26	B-26	B-26	B-26
13 – 14 in.	22 ga.			C-24	C-24	C-26	C-26	B-26	B-26
15 – 16 in.	22 ga.			C-24	C-24	C-26	C-26	C-26	C-26
17 – 18 in.	20 ga.		D-24	D-24	C-24	C-26	C-26	C-26	C-26
19 – 20 in.	18 ga.		D-22	D-22	D-24	D-24	C-26	C-26	C-26
21 – 22 in.	18 ga.		E-22	E-22	D-24	D-24	D-26	C-26	C-26
23 – 24 in.	18 ga.		E-20	E-22	E-24	E-24	D-26	D-26	C-26
25 – 26 in.	18 ga.		F-20	E-22	E-24	E-24	D-26	D-26	C-26
27 – 28 in.	18 ga.		F-20	F-20	F-22	E-24	E-26	D-26	D-26
29 – 30 in.	18 ga.		G-20	F-20	F-22	E-24	E-26	E-26	D-26
31 – 36 in.	16 ga.	H-18G	H-18G	H-18G	G-20	F-22	F-24	E-26	E-26
37 – 42 in.	Not Designed		I-16G	H-18G	H-20G	G-22	F-24	F-24	E-26
43 – 48 in.			J-16H	I-18G	I-18G	H-20	G-22	G-24	F-24
49 – 54 in.				J-16H	I-18G	I-18G	H-22G	G-24	G-24
55 – 60 in.				J-16H	I-18G	I-18G	H-20G	H-22G	G-24
61 – 72 in.					J-16I	J-18H	I-20G	I-22G	I-24G
73 – 84 in.					L-16I	K-16H	J-18H	I-20H	I-22G
85 – 96 in.						L-16I	K-18I	J-18I	I-20H
97 – 108 in.							L-16I	L-18I	K-18I
109 – 120 in.							L-16I	L-18I	K-18I

Table 2–4 Rectangular Duct Reinforcement

750 Pa Static Pos. or Neg. Duct Dimension (mm)	No Reinforcement Required (mm)	Reinforcement Code for Duct Panel Thickness (mm)							
		Reinforcement Spacing Options							
		3.00 m	2.40 m	1.80 m	1.50 m	1.20 m	0.90 m	0.75 m	0.60 m
①	②	③	④	⑤	⑥	⑦	⑧	⑨	⑩
250 and under	0.70	Not Required		B-0.55	B-0.55	B-0.55	B-0.55	B-0.55	B-0.55
251 – 300	0.70			B-0.55	B-0.55	B-0.55	B-0.55	B-0.55	B-0.55
301 – 350	0.85			C-0.70	C-0.70	C-0.55	C-0.55	B-0.55	B-0.55
351 – 400	0.85			C-0.70	C-0.70	C-0.55	C-0.55	C-0.55	C-0.55
401 – 450	1.00		D-0.70	D-0.70	C-0.70	C-0.55	C-0.55	C-0.55	C-0.55
451 – 500	1.31		D-0.85	D-0.85	D-0.70	D-0.70	C-0.55	C-0.55	C-0.55
501 – 550	1.31		E-0.85	E-0.85	D-0.70	D-0.70	D-0.55	C-0.55	C-0.55
551 – 600	1.31		E-1.00	E-0.85	E-0.70	E-0.70	D-0.55	D-0.55	C-0.55
601 – 650	1.31		F-1.00	E-0.85	E-0.70	E-0.70	D-0.55	D-0.55	C-0.55
651 – 700	1.31		F-1.00	F-1.00	F-0.85	E-0.70	E-0.55	D-0.55	D-0.55
701 – 750	1.31		G-1.00	F-1.00	F-0.85	E-0.70	E-0.55	E-0.55	D-0.55
751 – 900	1.61	H-1.31G	H-1.31G	H-1.31G	G-1.00	F-0.85	F-0.70	E-0.55	E-0.55
901 – 1000	Not Designed			I-1.61G	H-1.31G	H-1.00G	G-0.85	F-0.70	F-0.70	E-0.55
1001 – 1200				J-1.61H	I-1.31G	I-1.31G	H-1.00	G-0.85	G-0.70	F-0.70
1201 – 1300					J-1.61H	I-1.31G	I-1.31G	H-0.85G	G-0.70	G-0.70
1301 – 1500					J-1.61H	I-1.31G	I-1.31G	H-1.00G	H-0.85G	G-0.70
1501 – 1800						J-1.61I	J-1.31H	I-1.00G	I-0.85G	I-0.70G
1801 – 2100						L-1.61I	K-1.61H	J-1.31H	I-1.00H	I-0.85G
2101 – 2400							L-1.61I	K-1.31I	J-1.31I	I-1.00H
2401 – 2700								L-1.61I	L-1.31I	K-1.31I
2701 – 3000								L-1.61I	L-1.31I	K-1.31I

Table 2–4M Rectangular Duct Reinforcement

4 in. wg Static Pos. or Neg. Duct Dimension	No Reinforcement Required	Reinforcement Code for Duct Gage Number Reinforcement Spacing Options							
		10 ft	8 ft	6 ft	5 ft	4 ft	3 ft	2½ ft	2 ft
①	②	③	④	⑤	⑥	⑦	⑧	⑨	⑩
8 in. and under	24 ga.	Not Required		B-26	B-26	B-26	B-26	B-26	B-26
9 – 10 in.	22 ga.	^^		B-24	B-26	B-26	B-26	B-26	B-26
11 – 12 in.	22 ga.		B-24	C-24	C-26	C-26	C-26	B-26	B-26
13 – 14 in.	20 ga.		C-22	C-22	C-24	C-26	C-26	C-26	C-26
15 – 16 in.	20 ga.		D-22	D-22	C-24	C-26	C-26	C-26	C-26
17 – 18 in.	18 ga.		D-22	D-22	D-24	D-26	C-26	C-26	C-26
19 – 20 in.	18 ga.		E-20	E-22	E-24	D-24	D-26	C-26	C-26
21 – 22 in.	18 ga.		E-20	E-20	E-24	E-24	D-26	D-26	C-26
23 – 24 in.	18 ga.		F-20	F-20	E-22	E-24	E-26	D-26	D-26
25 – 26 in.	16 ga.	G-18	G-18	F-20	F-22	E-24	E-26	E-26	D-26
27 – 28 in.	16 ga.	H-18G	G-18	G-20	F-22	F-24	E-26	E-26	D-26
29 – 30 in.	16 ga.	H-18G	H-18G	G-18	G-22	F-24	E-26	E-26	E-26
31 – 36 in.	Not Designed	J-16H	I-16G	H-18G	H-20	G-22	F-24	F-26	E-26
37 – 42 in.			J-16H	I-16G	I-18G	H-20G	G-22	G-24	F-26
43 – 48 in.				J-16H	I-18G	I-18G	H-22G	H-24G	G-24
49 – 54 in.				J-16H	I-18H	I-18G	I-20G	H-22G	H-24G
55 – 60 in.					J-16I	I-18H	I-20G	I-22G	H-24G
61 – 72 in.						K-16H	J-18H	I-20H	I-22G
73 – 84 in.						K-16I	J-18I	I-20H
85 – 96 in.						L-16I	K-18I	J-20I
97 – 108 in.						L-16I	L-18I	L-18I
109 – 120 in.						L-16I	L-18J	L-18J

Table 2–5 Rectangular Duct Reinforcement

1000 Pa Static Pos. or Neg. Duct Dimension (mm)	No Reinforcement Required (mm)	Reinforcement Code for Duct Panel Thickness (mm) Reinforcement Spacing Options							
		3.00 m	2.40 m	1.80 m	1.50 m	1.20 m	0.90 m	0.75 m	0.60 m
①	②	③	④	⑤	⑥	⑦	⑧	⑨	⑩
200 and under	0.70	Not Required		B-0.55	B-0.55	B-0.55	B-0.55	B-0.55	B-0.55
230 – 250	0.85			B-0.70	B-0.55	B-0.55	B-0.55	B-0.55	B-0.55
251 – 300	0.85		B-0.70	C-0.70	C-0.55	C-0.55	C-0.55	B-0.55	B-0.55
301 – 350	1.00		C-0.85	C-0.85	C-0.70	C-0.55	C-0.55	C-0.55	C-0.55
351 – 400	1.00		D-0.85	D-0.85	C-0.70	C-0.55	C-0.55	C-0.55	C-0.55
401 – 450	1.31		D-0.85	D-0.85	D-0.70	D-0.55	C-0.55	C-0.55	C-0.55
451 – 500	1.31		E-1.00	E-0.85	E-0.70	D-0.70	D-0.55	C-0.55	C-0.55
501 – 550	1.31		E-1.00	E-1.00	E-0.70	E-0.70	D-0.55	D-0.55	C-0.55
551 – 600	1.31		F-1.00	F-1.00	E-0.85	E-0.70	E-0.55	D-0.55	D-0.55
601 – 650	1.61	G-1.31	G-1.31	F-1.00	F-0.85	E-0.70	E-0.55	E-0.55	D-0.55
651 – 700	1.61	H-1.31G	G-1.31	G-1.00	F-0.85	F-0.70	E-0.55	E-0.55	D-0.55
701 – 750	1.61	H-1.31G	H-1.31G	G-1.31	G-0.85	F-0.70	E-0.55	E-0.55	E-0.55
751 – 900		J-1.61H	I-1.61G	H-1.31G	H-1.00	G-0.85	F-0.70	F-0.55	E-0.55
901 – 1000			J-1.61H	I-1.61G	I-1.31G	H-1.00G	G-0.85	G-0.70	F-0.55
1001 – 1200				J-1.61H	I-1.31G	I-1.31G	H-0.85G	H-0.70G	G-0.70
1201 – 1300				J-1.61H	I-1.31H	I-1.31G	I-1.00G	H-0.85G	H-0.70G
1301 – 1500		Not Designed			J-1.61I	I-1.31H	I-1.00G	I-0.85G	H-0.70G
1501 – 1800						K-1.61H	J-1.31H	I-1.00H	I-0.85G
1801 – 2100						K-1.61I	J-1.31I	I-1.00H
2101 – 2400						L-1.61I	K-1.31I	J-1.00I
2401 – 2700						L-1.61I	L-1.31I	L-1.31I
2701 – 3000						L-1.61I	L-1.31I	L-1.31J

Table 2–5M Rectangular Duct Reinforcement

6 in. wg Static Pos. or Neg. Duct Dimension	No Reinforcement Required	Reinforcement Code for Duct Gage Number — Reinforcement Spacing Options							
		10 ft	8 ft	6 ft	5 ft	4 ft	3 ft	2½ ft	2 ft
①	②	③	④	⑤	⑥	⑦	⑧	⑨	⑩
8 in. and under	24 ga.	Not Required				C-26	C-26	B-26	B-26	B-26
9 – 10 in.	22 ga.			B-24	C-24	C-24	B-26	B-26	B-26
11 – 12 in.	20 ga.		C-22	C-22	C-24	C-24	C-26	C-26	C-26
13 – 14 in.	20 ga.		C-22	D-20	D-22	C-24	C-26	C-26	C-26
15 – 16 in.	18 ga.		D-20	D-20	D-22	D-24	D-26	C-26	C-26
17 – 18 in.	18 ga.		E-20	E-20	E-22	E-24	D-26	D-26	C-26
19 – 20 in.	16 ga.	F-18	F-20	F-20	E-22	E-24	D-24	D-26	D-26
21 – 22 in.	16 ga.	F-18	F-18	F-20	F-22	F-24	E-24	E-26	D-26
23 – 24 in.	16 ga.	G-18	G-18	G-20	F-22	F-22	E-24	E-26	E-26
25 – 26 in.		H-16G	H-16G	G-18	G-20	F-22	F-24	E-24	E-24
27 – 28 in.			H-16G	H-18G	H-20G	G-22	F-24	F-24	E-24
29 – 30 in.			I-16G	H-18G	H-18G	G-22	F-24	F-24	E-24
31 – 36 in.				I-16H	I-18H	H-20G	H-22G	G-24	F-24
37 – 42 in.				J-16H	I-16H	I-18G	H-20G	H-22G	G-22
43 – 48 in.					J-16H	I-18H	I-20H	I-22G	I-22G
49 – 54 in.		Not Designed			J-16H	I-18H	I-20G	I-22G
55 – 60 in.					J-16H	J-18H	I-20H	I-22G
61 – 72 in.						K-16I	J-18I	J-20H
73 – 84 in.						L-16J	L-18J	K-18I
85 – 96 in.						It-16	It-16	L-18J
97 – 108 in.						Jt-16	Jt-16	L-18J
109 – 120 in.						Kt-16	Kt-16	Kt-18

Table 2–6 Rectangular Duct Reinforcement

NOTE: t following Reinforcement Class letter code indicates tie rod required.

1500 Pa Static Pos. or Neg. Duct Dimension (mm)	No Reinforcement Required (mm)	Reinforcement Code for Duct Panel Thickness (mm)							
		Reinforcement Spacing Options							
		3.00 m	2.40 m	1.80 m	1.50 m	1.20 m	0.90 m	0.75 m	0.60 m
①	②	③	④	⑤	⑥	⑦	⑧	⑨	⑩
200 and under	0.70	Not Required				C-0.55	C-0.55	B-0.55	B-0.55	B-0.55
230 – 250	1.00			B-0.70	C-0.70	C-0.70	B-0.55	B-0.55	B-0.55
251 – 300	1.00		C-0.85	C-0.85	C-0.70	C-0.70	C-0.55	C-0.55	C-0.55
301 – 350	1.00		C-0.85	D-1.00	D-0.85	C-0.70	C-0.55	C-0.55	C-0.55
351 – 400	1.31		D-1.00	D-1.00	D-0.85	D-0.70	D-0.55	C-0.55	C-0.55
401 – 450	1.31		E-1.00	E-1.00	E-0.85	E-0.70	D-0.55	D-0.55	C-0.55
451 – 500	1.61	F-1.31	F-1.00	F-1.00	E-0.85	E-0.70	D-0.70	D-0.55	D-0.55
501 – 550	1.61	F-1.31	F-1.31	F-1.00	F-0.85	F-0.70	E-0.70	E-0.55	D-0.55
551 – 600	1.61	G-1.31	G-1.31	G-1.00	F-0.85	F-0.85	E-0.70	E-0.55	E-0.55
601 – 650		H-1.61G	H-1.61G	G-1.31	G-1.00	F-0.85	F-0.70	E-0.70	E-0.70
651 – 700		H-1.61G	H-1.31G	H-1.00G	G-0.85	F-0.70	F-0.70	E-0.70	
701 – 750		I-1.61G	H-1.31G	H-1.31G	G-0.85	F-0.70	F-0.70	E-0.70	
751 – 900			I-1.61H	I-1.31H	H-1.00G	H-0.85G	G-0.70	F-0.70	
901 – 1000			J-1.61H	I-1.61H	I-1.31G	H-1.00G	H-0.85G	G-0.85	
1001 – 1200				J-1.61H	I-1.31H	I-1.00H	I-0.85G	I-0.85G	
1201 – 1300		Not Designed			J-1.61H	I-1.31H	I-1.00G	I-0.85G	
1301 – 1500						J-1.61H	J-1.31H	I-1.00H	I-0.85G
1501 – 1800						K-1.61I	J-1.31I	J-1.00H	
1801 – 2100						L-1.61J	L-1.31J	K-1.31I	
2101 – 2400						It-1.61	It-1.61	L-1.31J	
2401 – 2700						Jt-1.61	Jt-1.61	L-1.31J	
2701 – 3000						Kt-1.61	Kt-1.61	Kt-1.31	

Table 2–6M Rectangular Duct Reinforcement

NOTE: t following Reinforcement Class letter code indicates tie rod required.

10 in. wg Static Pos. or Neg. Duct Dimension	No Reinforcement Required	Reinforcement Code for Duct Gage Number Reinforcement Spacing Options							
		10 ft	8 ft	6 ft	5 ft	4 ft	3 ft	2½ ft	2 ft
①	②	③	④	⑤	⑥	⑦	⑧	⑨	⑩
8 in. and under	22 ga.	Not Required			C-24	C-26	C-26	C-26	C-26
9 – 10 in.	20 ga.	^^^			C-22	C-24	C-26	C-26	C-26
11 – 12 in.	18 ga.		C-20	D-20	D-22	D-24	C-26	C-26	C-26
13 – 14 in.	18 ga.		D-20	E-20	E-20	D-22	D-24	D-26	C-26
15 – 16 in.	16 ga.	E-18	E-18	E-18	E-20	E-20	E-24	D-24	D-26
17 – 18 in.	16 ga.	F-18	F-18	F-18	F-20	F-20	E-24	E-24	D-26
19 – 20 in.		G-16	G-18	G-18	G-18	F-20	F-22	E-24	E-24
21 – 22 in.		H-16G	H-18G	H-18G	G-18	G-20	F-22	F-24	E-24
23 – 24 in.		I-16G	I-18G	H-18G	H-18G	H-20G	G-22	F-24	F-24
25 – 26 in.			J-16G	I-16G	H-18G	H-20G	G-22	F-24	F-24
27 – 28 in.				I-16G	I-18G	H-18G	H-22G	G-24	F-24
29 – 30 in.				J-16G	I-18G	I-18G	H-22G	H-24G	G-24
31 – 36 in.		Not Designed			J-16H	I-18H	I-20G	H-22G	H-24G
37 – 42 in.		^^^			J-16I	J-18I	I-18G	I-20H	I-22G
43 – 48 in.		^^^				J-16I	J-18I	I-18H	I-22H
49 – 54 in.		^^^				L-16I	K-18I	J-18H	I-20H
55 – 60 in.		^^^					L-16I	K-18I	J-20I
61 – 72 in.		^^^					L-16I	L-18I	L-18I
73 – 84 in.		^^^						L-16J	L-18J
85 – 96 in.		^^^							Lt-16
97 – 108 in.		^^^							Lt-16
109 – 120 in.		^^^							Lt-16

Table 2–7 Rectangular Duct Reinforcement

NOTE: t following Reinforcement Class letter code indicates tie rod required.

2500 Pa Static Pos. or Neg. Duct Dimension (mm)	No Reinforcement Required (mm)	\multicolumn{8}{c	}{Reinforcement Code for Duct Panel Thickness (mm)}
		\multicolumn{8}{c	}{Reinforcement Spacing Options}
		3.00 m	2.40 m	1.80 m	1.50 m	1.20 m	0.90 m	0.75 m	0.60 m
①	②	③	④	⑤	⑥	⑦	⑧	⑨	⑩
200 and under	0.85 ga.	\multicolumn{3}{c	}{Not Required}	C-0.70	C-0.55	C-0.55	C-0.55	C-0.55
230 – 250	1.00 ga.				C-0.85	C-0.70	C-0.55	C-0.55	C-0.55
251 – 300	1.31 ga.		C-1.00	D-1.00	D-0.85	D-0.70	C-0.55	C-0.55	C-0.55
301 – 350	1.31 ga.		D-1.00	E-1.00	E-1.00	D-0.85	D-0.70	D-0.55	C-0.55
351 – 400	1.61 ga.	E-1.31	E-1.31	E-1.31	E-1.00	E-1.00	E-0.70	D-0.70	D-0.55
401 – 450	1.61 ga.	F-1.31	F-1.31	F-1.31	F-1.00	F-1.00	E-0.70	E-0.70	D-0.55
451 – 500		G-1.61	G-1.31	G-1.31	G-1.31	F-1.00	F-0.85	E-0.70	E-0.70
501 – 550		H-1.61G	H-1.31G	H-1.31G	G-1.31	G-1.00	F-0.85	F-0.70	E-0.70
551 – 600		I-1.61G	I-1.31G	H-1.31G	H-1.31G	H-1.00G	G-0.85	F-0.70	F-0.70
601 – 650			J-1.61G	I-1.61G	H-1.31G	H-1.00G	G-0.85	F-0.70	F-0.70
651 – 700				I-1.61G	I-1.31G	H-1.31G	H-0.85G	G-0.70	F-0.70
701 – 750				J-1.61G	I-1.31G	I-1.31G	H-0.85G	H-0.70G	G-0.70
751 – 900					J-1.61H	I-1.31H	I-1.00G	H-0.85G	H-0.70G
901 – 1000					J-1.61I	J-1.31I	I-1.31G	I-1.00H	I-0.85G
1001 – 1200		\multicolumn{3}{c	}{Not Designed}		J-1.61I	J-1.31I	I-1.31H	I-0.85H
1201 – 1300						L-1.61I	K-1.31I	J-1.31H	I-1.00H
1301 – 1500							L-1.61I	K-1.31I	J-1.00I
1501 – 1800							L-1.61I	L-1.31I	L-1.31I
1801 – 2100								L-1.61J	L-1.31J
2101 – 2400									Lt-1.61
2401 – 2700									Lt-1.61
2701 – 3000									Lt-1.61

Table 2–7M Rectangular Duct Reinforcement

NOTE: t following Reinforcement Class letter code indicates tie rod required.

½ in. wg Static Pos. or Neg. Duct Dimension	4 ft Joints			4 ft Joints w/2 ft Reinf. Spacing				
	Min ga	Joint Reinf.	Alt. Joint Reinf.	Joints/Reinf.			Int. Reinf.	
				Min ga	Joint Reinf.	Alt. Joint Reinf.	Tie Rod	Alt. Reinf.
10 in. and under	26	N/R	N/A					
11 – 12 in.	26	N/R	N/A					
13 – 14 in.	26	N/R	N/A					
15 – 16 in.	26	N/R	N/A					
17 – 18 in.	26	N/R	N/A					
19 – 20 in.	26	N/R	N/A					
21 – 22 in.	26	N/R	N/A	Use 4 ft Joints				
23 – 24 in.	26	N/R	N/A					
25 – 26 in.	26	N/R	N/A					
27 – 28 in.	26	N/R	N/A					
29 – 30 in.	26	N/R	N/A					
31 – 36 in.	26	N/R	N/A					
37 – 42 in.	26	N/R	N/A					
43 – 48 in.	26	N/R	N/A					
49 – 54 in.	24	N/R	N/A	26	N/R	N/R	MPT	C
55 – 60 in.	24	N/R	N/A	26	N/R	N/R	MPT	D
61 – 72 in.	22	N/R	N/A	24	N/R	N/R	MPT	E
73 – 84 in.	22	JTR	(2) C	22	N/R	N/R	MPT	F
	20	N/R	N/A					
85 – 96 in.	22	JTR	(2) E	22	N/R	N/R	MPT	F
97 – 108 in.	18	JTR	(2) G	18	N/R	N/R	✕	G
109 – 120 in.	16	JTR	(2) G	18	N/R	N/R	✕	H

Table 2–8 4 ft Coil/Sheet Stock/T25a/T25b (TDC/TDF) Duct Reinforcement

N/R - Not Required

N/A - Not Applicable

JTR - Joint Tie Rod

MPT - Mid Panel Tie Rod(s) 2 MPT indicates two Mid Panel Tie Rods are required

(2) (X) - Indicates 2 external reinforcements of class (X) to be used in lieu of Joint Tie Rods

125 Pa Static Pos. or Neg. Duct Dimension (mm)	1.20 m Joints			1.20 m Joints w/0.60 m Reinf. Spacing				
^	Min (mm)	Joint Reinf.	Alt. Joint Reinf.	Joints/Reinf.			Int. Reinf.	
^	^	^	^	Min (mm)	Joint Reinf.	Alt. Joint Reinf.	Tie Rod	Alt. Reinf.
250 and under	0.55	N/R	N/A					
251 – 300	0.55	N/R	N/A					
301 – 350	0.55	N/R	N/A					
251 – 400	0.55	N/R	N/A					
401 – 450	0.55	N/R	N/A					
451 – 500	0.55	N/R	N/A					
501 – 550	0.55	N/R	N/A					
551 – 600	0.55	N/R	N/A	Use 1.20 m Joints				
601 – 650	0.55	N/R	N/A					
651 – 700	0.55	N/R	N/A					
701 – 750	0.55	N/R	N/A					
751 – 900	0.55	N/R	N/A					
901 – 1000	0.55	N/R	N/A					
1001 – 1200	0.55	N/R	N/A					
1201 – 1300	0.70	N/R	N/A	0.55	N/R	N/R	MPT	C
1301 – 1500	0.70	N/R	N/A	0.55	N/R	N/R	MPT	D
1501 – 1800	0.85	N/R	N/A	0.70	N/R	N/R	MPT	E
1801 – 2100	0.85	JTR	(2) C	0.85	N/R	N/R	MPT	F
^	1.00	N/R	N/A					
2101 – 2400	0.85	JTR	(2) E	0.85	N/R	N/R	MPT	F
2401 – 2700	1.31	JTR	(2) G	1.31	N/R	N/R	✕	G
2701 – 3000	1.61	JTR	(2) G	1.31	N/R	N/R	✕	H

Table 2–8M 1.20 m Coil/Sheet Stock/T25a/T25b (TDC/TDF) Duct Reinforcement

N/R - Not Required
N/A - Not Applicable
JTR - Joint Tie Rod
MPT - Mid Panel Tie Rod(s) 2 MPT indicates two Mid Panel Tie Rods are required
(2) (X) - Indicates 2 external reinforcements of class (X) to be used in lieu of Joint Tie Rods

1 in. wg Static Pos. or Neg. Duct Dimension	4 ft Joints			4 ft Joints w/2 ft Reinf. Spacing				
^	Min ga	Joint Reinf.	Alt. Joint Reinf.	Joints/Reinf.			Int. Reinf.	
^	^	^	^	Min ga	Joint Reinf.	Alt Joint Reinf.	Tie Rod	Alt. Reinf.
10 in. and under	26	N/R	N/R					
11 – 12 in.	26	N/R	N/R					
13 – 14 in.	26	N/R	N/R					
15 – 16 in.	26	N/R	N/R					
17 – 18 in.	26	N/R	N/R					
19 – 20 in.	26	N/R	N/R	Use 4 ft Joints				
21 – 22 in.	26	N/R	N/R					
23 – 24 in.	26	N/R	N/R					
25 – 26 in.	26	N/R	N/R					
27 – 28 in.	26	N/R	N/R					
29 – 30 in.	26	N/R	N/R					
31 – 36 in.	26	N/R	N/R					
37 – 42 in.	24	N/R	N/R	26	N/R	N/R	MPT	C
43 – 48 in.	24	N/R	N/R	26	N/R	N/R	MPT	D
49 – 54 in.	22	N/R	N/R	24	N/R	N/R	MPT	E
55 – 60 in.	22	N/R	N/R	24	N/R	N/R	MPT	E
61 – 72 in.	22	JTR	(2) E	22	N/R	N/R	MPT	F
73 – 84 in.	20	JTR	(2) H	22	JTR	(2) E	MPT	G
^	^	^	^	20	N/R	N/R	MPT	G
85 – 96 in.	18	JTR	(2) H	20	JTR	(2) E	2 MPT	H
97 – 108 in.	18	JTR	(2) H	18	JTR	(2) H	—	I
109 – 120 in.	16	JTR	(2) H	18	JTR	(2) H	—	I

Table 2–9 4 ft Coil/Sheet Stock/T25a/T25b (TDC/TDF) Duct Reinforcement

N/R - Not Required
N/A - Not Applicable
JTR - Joint Tie Rod
MPT - Mid Panel Tie Rod(s)
(2) (X) - Indicates 2 external reinforcements of class (X) to be used in lieu of Joint Tie Rods

250 Pa Static Pos. or Neg. Duct Dimension (mm)	1.20 m Joints			1.20 m Joints w/0.60 m Reinf. Spacing				
^	^	^	^	Joints/Reinf.			Int. Reinf.	
^	Min (mm)	Joint Reinf.	Alt. Joint Reinf.	Min (mm)	Joint Reinf.	Alt Joint Reinf.	Tie Rod	Alt. Reinf.
250 and under	0.55	N/R	N/R					
251 – 300	0.55	N/R	N/R					
301 – 350	0.55	N/R	N/R					
351 – 400	0.55	N/R	N/R					
401 – 450	0.55	N/R	N/R					
451 – 500	0.55	N/R	N/R					
501 – 550	0.55	N/R	N/R		Use 1.20 m Joints				
551 – 600	0.55	N/R	N/R					
601 – 650	0.55	N/R	N/R					
651 – 700	0.55	N/R	N/R					
701 – 750	0.55	N/R	N/R					
751 – 900	0.55	N/R	N/R					
901 – 1000	0.70	N/R	N/R	0.55	N/R	N/R	MPT	C
1001 – 1200	0.70	N/R	N/R	0.55	N/R	N/R	MPT	D
1201 – 1300	0.85	N/R	N/R	0.70	N/R	N/R	MPT	E
1301 – 1500	0.85	N/R	N/R	0.70	N/R	N/R	MPT	E
1501 – 1800	0.85	JTR	(2) E	0.85	N/R	N/R	MPT	F
1801 – 2100	1.00	JTR	(2) H	0.85	JTR	(2) E	MPT	G
^				1.00	N/R	N/R	MPT	G
2101 – 2400	1.31	JTR	(2) H	0.85	JTR	(2) E	2 MPT	H
2401 – 2700	1.31	JTR	(2) H	1.31	JTR	(2) H	—	I
2701 – 3000	1.61	JTR	(2) H	1.31	JTR	(2) H	—	I

Table 2–9M 1.20 m Coil/Sheet Stock/T25a/T25b (TDC/TDF) Duct Reinforcement

N/R   - Not Required
N/A   - Not Applicable
JTR   - Joint Tie Rod
MPT   - Mid Panel Tie Rod(s)
(2) (X)   - Indicates 2 external reinforcements of class (X) to be used in lieu of Joint Tie Rods

2 in. wg Static Pos. or Neg. Duct Dimension	4 ft Joints			4 ft Joints w/2 ft Reinf. Spacing				
^	^	^	^	Joints/Reinf.			Int. Reinf.	
^	Min ga	Joint Reinf.	Alt. Joint Reinf.	Min ga	Joint Reinf.	Alt. Joint Reinf.	Tie Rod	Alt. Reinf.
10 in. and under	26	N/R	N/A					
11 – 12 in.	26	N/R	N/A					
13 – 14 in.	26	N/R	N/A					
15 – 16 in.	26	N/R	N/A					
17 – 18 in.	26	N/R	N/A	Use 4 ft Joints				
19 – 20 in.	26	N/R	N/A					
21 – 22 in.	26	N/R	N/A					
23 – 24 in.	26	N/R	N/A					
25 – 26 in.	26	N/R	N/A					
27 – 28 in.	26	N/R	N/A					
29 – 30 in.	24	N/R	N/A	26	N/R	N/A	MPT	C
31 – 36 in.	24	N/R	N/A	26	N/R	N/A	MPT	D
37 – 42 in.	22	N/R	N/A	24	N/R	N/A	MPT	E
43 – 48 in.	22	JTR	(2) C	24	N/R	N/A	MPT	E
^	20	N/R	—					
49 – 54 in.	20	JTR	(2) E	22	N/R	N/A	MPT	F
55 – 60 in.	20	JTR	(2) E	22	N/R	N/A	MPT	F
61 – 72 in.	20	JTR	(2) H	20	JTR	(2) E	MPT	H
^	^	^	^	18	N/R	N/A	MPT	H
73 – 84 in.	20	JTR	(2) H	20	JTR	(2) H	2 MPT	I
85 – 96 in.	18	JTR	(2) H	20	JTR	(2) H	2 MPT	I
97 – 108 in.	16	JTR	(2) I	18	JTR	(2) H	✕	I
109 – 120 in.	Not Designed			18	JTR	(2) H	✕	J

Table 2–10   4 ft Coil/Sheet Stock/T25a/T25b (TDC/TDF) Duct Reinforcement

N/R   - Not Required
N/A   - Not Applicable
JTR   - Joint Tie Rod
MPT   - Mid Panel Tie Rod(s)
(2) (X) - Indicates 2 external reinforcements of class (X) to be used in lieu of Joint Tie Rods

500 Pa Static Pos. or Neg. Duct Dimension (mm)	1.20 m Joints			1.20 m Joints w/0.60 m Reinf. Spacing				
^	Min (mm)	Joint Reinf.	Alt. Joint Reinf.	Joints/Reinf.			Int. Reinf.	
^	^	^	^	Min (mm)	Joint Reinf.	Alt. Joint Reinf.	Tie Rod	Alt. Reinf.
250 and under	0.55	N/R	N/A					
251 – 300	0.55	N/R	N/A					
301 – 350	0.55	N/R	N/A					
351 – 400	0.55	N/R	N/A					
401 – 450	0.55	N/R	N/A	Use 1.20 m Joints				
451 – 500	0.55	N/R	N/A					
501 – 550	0.55	N/R	N/A					
551 – 600	0.55	N/R	N/A					
601 – 650	0.55	N/R	N/A					
651 – 700	0.55	N/R	N/A					
701 – 750	0.70	N/R	N/A	0.55	N/R	N/A	MPT	C
751 – 900	0.70	N/R	N/A	0.55	N/R	N/A	MPT	D
901 – 1000	0.85	N/R	N/A	0.70	N/R	N/A	MPT	E
1001 – 1200	0.85	JTR	(2) C	0.70	N/R	N/A	MPT	E
^	1.00	N/R	—					
1201 – 1300	1.00	JTR	(2) E	0.85	N/R	N/A	MPT	F
1301 – 1500	1.00	JTR	(2) E	0.85	N/R	N/A	MPT	F
1501 – 1800	1.00	JTR	(2) H	1.00	JTR	(2) E	MPT	H
^				1.31	N/R	N/A	MPT	H
1801 – 2100	1.00	JTR	(2) H	1.00	JTR	(2) H	2 MPT	I
2101 – 2400	1.31	JTR	(2) H	1.00	JTR	(2) H	2 MPT	I
2401 – 2700	1.61	JTR	(2) I	1.31	JTR	(2) H	✕	I
2701 – 3000	Not Designed			1.31	JTR	(2) H	✕	J

Table 2–10M 1.20 m Coil/Sheet Stock/T25a/T25b (TDC/TDF) Duct Reinforcement

N/R - Not Required
N/A - Not Applicable
JTR - Joint Tie Rod
MPT - Mid Panel Tie Rod(s)
(2) (X) - Indicates 2 external reinforcements of class (X) to be used in lieu of Joint Tie Rods

3 in. wg Static Pos. or Neg. Duct Dimension	4 ft Joints			4 ft Joints w/2 ft Reinf. Spacing				
				Joints/Reinf.			Int. Reinf.	
	Min ga	Joint Reinf.	Alt. Joint Reinf.	Min ga	Joint Reinf.	Alt. Joint Reinf.	Tie Rod	Alt. Reinf.
10 in. and under	26	N/R	N/A	Use 4 ft Joints				
11 – 12 in.	26	N/R	N/A					
13 – 14 in.	26	N/R	N/A					
15 – 16 in.	26	N/R	N/A					
17 – 18 in.	26	N/R	N/A					
19 – 20 in.	24	N/R	N/A	26	N/R	N/A	MPT	C
21 – 22 in.	24	N/R	N/A	26	N/R	N/A	MPT	C
23 – 24 in.	24	N/R	N/A	26	N/R	N/A	MPT	C
25 – 26 in.	24	N/R	N/A	26	N/R	N/A	MPT	C
27 – 28 in.	24	N/R	N/A	26	N/R	N/A	MPT	D
29 – 30 in.	24	N/R	N/A	26	N/R	N/A	MPT	D
31 – 36 in.	22	N/R	N/A	24	N/R	N/A	MPT	E
37 – 42 in.	22	JTR	(2) C	24	N/R	N/A	MPT	E
	20	N/R	N/R					
43 – 48 in.	20	JTR	(2) E	22	N/R	N/A	MPT	F
49 – 54 in.	18	JTR	(2) H	22	JTR	(2) C	MPT	G
				20	N/R	N/R	MPT	G
55 – 60 in.	18	JTR	(2) H	22	JTR	(2) C	MPT	G
				20	N/R	N/R	MPT	G
61 – 72 in.	18	JTR	(2) I	20	JTR	(2) H	MPT	I
73 – 84 in.	16	JTR	(2) I	20	JTR	(2) I	2 MPT	I
85 – 96 in.	16	JTR	(2) L	20	JTR	(2) I	2 MPT	I
97 – 108 in.	Not Designed			18	JTR	(2) J	—	K
109 – 120 in.				18	JTR	(2) J	—	K

Table 2–11   4 ft Coil/Sheet Stock/T25a/T25b (TDC/TDF) Duct Reinforcement

N/R   - Not Required
N/A   - Not Applicable
JTR   - Joint Tie Rod
MPT   - Mid Panel Tie Rod(s)
(2) (X)   - Indicates 2 external reinforcements of class (X) to be used in lieu of Joint Tie Rods

750 Pa Static Pos. or Neg. Duct Dimension (mm)	1.20 m Joints Min (mm)	1.20 m Joints Joint Reinf.	1.20 m Joints Alt. Joint Reinf.	1.20 m Joints w/0.60 m Reinf. Spacing Joints/Reinf. Min (mm)	Joints/Reinf. Joint Reinf.	Joints/Reinf. Alt. Joint Reinf.	Int. Reinf. Tie Rod	Int. Reinf. Alt. Reinf.
250 and under	0.55	N/R	N/A					
251 – 300	0.55	N/R	N/A					
351 – 350	0.55	N/R	N/A	Use 1.20 m Joints				
351 – 400	0.55	N/R	N/A					
401 – 450	0.55	N/R	N/A					
451 – 500	0.70	N/R	N/A	0.55	N/R	N/A	MPT	C
501 – 550	0.70	N/R	N/A	0.55	N/R	N/A	MPT	C
551 – 600	0.70	N/R	N/A	0.55	N/R	N/A	MPT	C
601 – 650	0.70	N/R	N/A	0.55	N/R	N/A	MPT	C
651 – 700	0.70	N/R	N/A	0.55	N/R	N/A	MPT	D
701 – 750	0.70	N/R	N/A	0.55	N/R	N/A	MPT	D
751 – 900	0.85	N/R	N/A	0.70	N/R	N/A	MPT	E
901 – 1000	0.85	JTR	(2) C	0.70	N/R	N/A	MPT	E
901 – 1000	1.00	N/R	N/R					
1001 – 1200	1.00	JTR	(2) E	0.85	N/R	N/A	MPT	F
1201 – 1300	1.31	JTR	(2) H	0.85	JTR	(2) C	MPT	G
1201 – 1300				1.00	N/R	N/R	MPT	G
1301 – 1500	1.31	JTR	(2) H	0.85	JTR	(2) C	MPT	G
1301 – 1500				1.00	N/R	N/R	MPT	G
1501 – 1800	1.31	JTR	(2) I	1.00	JTR	(2) H	MPT	I
1801 – 2100	1.61	JTR	(2) I	1.00	JTR	(2) I	2 MPT	I
2101 – 2400	1.61	JTR	(2) L	1.00	JTR	(2) I	2 MPT	I
2401 – 2700	Not Designed			1.31	JTR	(2) J	—	K
2701 – 3000				1.31	JTR	(2) J	—	K

Table 2–11M 1.20 m Coil/Sheet Stock/T25a/T25b (TDC/TDF) Duct Reinforcement

N/R - Not Required
N/A - Not Applicable
JTR - Joint Tie Rod
MPT - Mid Panel Tie Rod(s)
(2) (X) - Indicates 2 external reinforcements of class (X) to be used in lieu of Joint Tie Rods

4 in. wg Static Pos. or Neg. Duct Dimension	4 ft Joints Min ga	4 ft Joints Joint Reinf.	4 ft Joints Alt. Joint Reinf.	4 ft Joints w/2 ft Reinf. Spacing Joints/Reinf. Min ga	4 ft Joints w/2 ft Reinf. Spacing Joints/Reinf. Joint Reinf.	4 ft Joints w/2 ft Reinf. Spacing Joints/Reinf. Alt. Joint Reinf.	4 ft Joints w/2 ft Reinf. Spacing Int. Reinf. Tie Rod	4 ft Joints w/2 ft Reinf. Spacing Int. Reinf. Alt. Reinf.
8 in. and under	26	N/R	N/A					
9 – 10 in.	26	N/R	N/A					
11 – 12 in.	26	N/R	N/A					
13 – 14 in.	26	N/R	N/A	Use 4 ft Joints				
15 – 16 in.	26	N/R	N/A					
17 – 18 in.	26	N/R	N/A					
19 – 20 in.	24	N/R	N/A	26	N/R	N/A	MPT	C
21 – 22 in.	24	N/R	N/A	26	N/R	N/A	MPT	C
23 – 24 in.	24	N/R	N/A	26	N/R	N/A	MPT	D
25 – 26 in.	24	N/R	N/A	26	N/R	N/A	MPT	D
27 – 28 in.	22	N/R	N/A	26	N/R	N/A	MPT	D
29 – 30 in.	22	N/R	N/A	26	N/R	N/A	MPT	E
31 – 36 in.	22	JTR	(2) C	24	N/R	N/A	MPT	E
31 – 36 in.	20	N/R	N/A					
37 – 42 in.	20	JTR	(2) E	22	N/R	N/A	MPT	F
37 – 42 in.	18	N/R	N/A					
43 – 48 in.	18	JTR	(2) H	20	N/R	N/A	MPT	G
49 – 54 in.	18	JTR	(2) H	20	JTR	(2) E	MPT	H
49 – 54 in.				18	N/R	N/A	MPT	H
55 – 60 in.	18	JTR	(2) H	20	JTR	(2) E	MPT	H
55 – 60 in.				18	N/R	N/A	MPT	H
61 – 72 in.	16	JTR	(2) I	20	JTR	(2) I	MPT	I
73 – 84 in.				18	JTR	(2) H	MPT	I
85 – 96 in.	Not Designed			18	JTR	(2) I	2 MPT	J
97 – 108 in.				18	JTR	(2) K	—	L
109 – 120 in.				18	JTR	(2) K	—	L

Table 2–12 4 ft Coil/Sheet Stock/T25a/T25b (TDC/TDF) Duct Reinforcement

N/R   - Not Required
N/A   - Not Applicable
JTR   - Joint Tie Rod
MPT   - Mid Panel Tie Rod(s)
(2) (X)   - Indicates 2 external reinforcements of class (X) to be used in lieu of Joint Tie Rods

1000 Pa Static Pos. or Neg. Duct Dimension (mm)	1.20 m Joints			1.20 m Joints w/0.60 m Reinf. Spacing			
^	^	^	^	Joints/Reinf.			Int. Reinf.	
^	Min (mm)	Joint Reinf.	Alt. Joint Reinf.	Min (mm)	Joint Reinf.	Alt. Joint Reinf.	Tie Rod	Alt. Reinf.
200 and under	0.55	N/R	N/A	colspan="5" rowspan="6" Use 1.20 m Joints				
230 – 250	0.55	N/R	N/A	^				
251 – 300	0.55	N/R	N/A	^				
301 – 350	0.55	N/R	N/A	^				
351 – 400	0.55	N/R	N/A	^				
401 – 450	0.55	N/R	N/A	^				
451 – 500	0.70	N/R	N/A	0.55	N/R	N/A	MPT	C
501 – 550	0.70	N/R	N/A	0.55	N/R	N/A	MPT	C
551 – 600	0.70	N/R	N/A	0.55	N/R	N/A	MPT	D
601 – 650	0.85	N/R	N/A	0.55	N/R	N/A	MPT	D
651 – 700	0.85	N/R	N/A	0.55	N/R	N/A	MPT	D
701 – 750	0.85	N/R	N/A	0.55	N/R	N/A	MPT	E
751 – 900	0.85	JTR	(2) C	0.70	N/R	N/A	MPT	E
^	1.00	N/R	N/A	^	^	^	^	^
901 – 1000	1.00	JTR	(2) E	0.85	N/R	N/A	MPT	F
^	1.31	N/R	N/A	^	^	^	^	^
1001 – 1200	1.31	JTR	(2) H	1.00	N/R	N/A	MPT	G
1201 – 1300	1.31	JTR	(2) H	1.00	JTR	(2) E	MPT	H
^				1.31	N/R	N/A	MPT	H
1301 – 1500	1.31	JTR	(2) H	1.00	JTR	(2) E	MPT	H
^				1.31	N/R	N/A	MPT	H
1501 – 1800	1.61	JTR	(2) I	1.00	JTR	(2) I	MPT	I
1801 – 2100	colspan="3" rowspan="4" Not Designed			1.31	JTR	(2) H	MPT	I
2101 – 2400	^	^	^	1.31	JTR	(2) I	2 MPT	J
2401 – 2700	^	^	^	1.31	JTR	(2) K	—	L
2701 – 3000	^	^	^	1.31	JTR	(2) K	—	L

Table 2–12M 1.20 m Coil/Sheet Stock/T25a/T25b (TDC/TDF) Duct Reinforcement

N/R - Not Required
N/A - Not Applicable
JTR - Joint Tie Rod
MPT - Mid Panel Tie Rod(s)
(2) (X) - Indicates 2 external reinforcements of class (X) to be used in lieu of Joint Tie Rods

6 in. wg Static Pos. or Neg. Duct Dimension	4 ft Joints			4 ft Joints w/2 ft Reinf. Spacing				
^	Min ga	Joint Reinf.	Alt Joint Reinf.	Joints/Reinf.			Int. Reinf.	
^	^	^	^	Min ga	Joint Reinf.	Alt. Joint Reinf.	Tie Rod	Alt. Reinf.
8 in. and under	26	N/R	N/A	Use 4 ft Joints				
9 – 10 in.	24	N/R	N/A	26	N/R	N/A	MPT	B
11 – 12 in.	24	N/R	N/A	26	N/R	N/A	MPT	C
13 – 14 in.	24	N/R	N/A	26	N/R	N/A	MPT	C
15 – 16 in.	24	N/R	N/A	26	N/R	N/A	MPT	C
17 – 18 in.	24	N/R	N/A	26	N/R	N/A	MPT	C
19 – 20 in.	24	N/R	N/A	26	N/R	N/A	MPT	D
21 – 22 in.	22	N/R	N/A	26	N/R	N/A	MPT	D
23 – 24 in.	22	N/R	N/A	24	N/R	N/A	MPT	E
25 – 26 in.	22	N/R	N/A	24	N/R	N/A	MPT	E
27 – 28 in.	20	N/R	N/A	24	N/R	N/A	MPT	E
29 – 30 in.	20	N/R	N/A	24	N/R	N/A	MPT	F
31 – 36 in.	20	JTR	(2) E	24	N/R	N/A	MPT	F
^	18	N/R	N/A	^	^	^	^	^
37 – 42 in.	18	JTR	(2) H	22	JTR	(2) D	MPT	G
43 – 48 in.	18	JTR	(2) H	20	JTR	(2) H	MPT	I
49 – 54 in.	16	JTR	(2) H	20	JTR	(2) H	MPT	I
55 – 60 in.	16	JTR	(2) H	20	JTR	(2) H	MPT	I
61 – 72 in.	Not Designed			18	JTR	(2) H	MPT	J
73 – 84 in.	^			18	JTR	(2) I	2 MPT	K
85 – 96 in.	^			18	JTR	(2) K	2 MPT	L
97 – 108 in.	^			18	JTR	(2) K	—	L
109 – 120 in.	^			18	JTR	(2) L	—	Kt

Table 2-13 4 ft Coil/Sheet Stock/T25a/T25b (TDC/TDF) Duct Reinforcement

N/R - Not Required
N/A - Not Applicable
JTR - Joint Tie Rod
MPT - Mid Panel Tie Rod(s)
(2) (X) - Indicates 2 external reinforcements of class (X) to be used in lieu of Joint Tie Rods

Note: t following Reinforcement Class letter indicates tie rod required.

1500 Pa Static Pos. or Neg. Duct Dimension (mm)	1.20 m Joints			1.20 m Joints w/0.60 m ft Reinf. Spacing				
^	Min (mm)	Joint Reinf.	Alt Joint Reinf.	Joints/Reinf.			Int. Reinf.	
^	^	^	^	Min (mm)	Joint Reinf.	Alt. Joint Reinf.	Tie Rod	Alt. Reinf.
200 and under	0.55	N/R	N/A	Use 1.20 m Joints			
230 – 250	0.70	N/R	N/A	0.55	N/R	N/A	MPT	B
251 – 300	0.70	N/R	N/A	0.55	N/R	N/A	MPT	C
301 – 350	0.70	N/R	N/A	0.55	N/R	N/A	MPT	C
351 – 400	0.70	N/R	N/A	0.55	N/R	N/A	MPT	C
401 – 450	0.70	N/R	N/A	0.55	N/R	N/A	MPT	C
451 – 500	0.70	N/R	N/A	0.55	N/R	N/A	MPT	D
501 – 550	0.85	N/R	N/A	0.55	N/R	N/A	MPT	D
551 – 600	0.85	N/R	N/A	0.70	N/R	N/A	MPT	E
601 – 650	0.85	N/R	N/A	0.70	N/R	N/A	MPT	E
651 – 700	1.00	N/R	N/A	0.70	N/R	N/A	MPT	E
701 – 750	1.00	N/R	N/A	0.70	N/R	N/A	MPT	F
751 – 900	1.00	JTR	(2) E	0.70	N/R	N/A	MPT	F
^	1.31	N/R	N/A					
901 – 1000	1.31	JTR	(2) H	0.85	JTR	(2) D	MPT	G
1001 – 1200	1.31	JTR	(2) H	1.00	JTR	(2) H	MPT	I
1201 – 1300	1.61	JTR	(2) H	1.00	JTR	(2) H	MPT	I
1301 – 1500	1.61	JTR	(2) H	1.00	JTR	(2) H	MPT	I
1501 – 1800	Not Designed			1.31	JTR	(2) H	MPT	J
1801 – 2100	^ ^ ^	1.31	JTR	(2) I	2 MPT	K
2101 – 2400	^ ^ ^	1.31	JTR	(2) K	2 MPT	L
2401 – 2700	^ ^ ^	1.31	JTR	(2) K	—	L
2701 – 3000	^ ^ ^	1.31	JTR	(2) L	—	Kt

Table 2–13M 1.20 m Coil/Sheet Stock/T25a/T25b (TDC/TDF) Duct Reinforcement

N/R - Not Required
N/A - Not Applicable
JTR - Joint Tie Rod
MPT - Mid Panel Tie Rod(s)
(2) (X) - Indicates 2 external reinforcements of class (X) to be used in lieu of Joint Tie Rods

Note: t following Reinforcement Class letter indicates tie rod required.

10 in. wg Static Pos. or Neg. Duct Dimension	4 ft Joints			4 ft Joints w/2 ft Reinf. Spacing				
^	^	^	^	Joints/Reinf			Int. Reinf.	
^	Min ga	Joint Reinf.	Alt. Joint Reinf.	Min ga	Joint Reinf.	Alt. Joint Reinf.	Tie Rod	Alt. Reinf.
8 in. and under	26	N/R	N/A	Use 4 ft Joints			
9 – 10 in.	24	N/R	N/A	26	N/R	N/A	N/A	C
11 – 12 in.	24	N/R	N/A	26	N/R	N/A	N/A	C
13 – 14 in.	22	N/R	N/A	26	N/R	N/A	N/A	C
15 – 16 in.	20	N/R	N/A	26	N/R	N/A	N/A	D
17 – 18 in.	20	N/R	N/A	26	N/R	N/A	N/A	D
19 – 20 in.	20	N/R	N/A	24	N/R	N/A	N/A	E
21 – 22 in.	20	N/R	N/A	24	N/R	N/A	N/A	E
23 – 24 in.	20	JTR	(2) E	22	N/R	N/A	N/A	F
^	18	N/R	N/A					
25 – 26 in.	20	JTR	(2) E	22	N/R	N/A	N/A	F
^	18	N/R	N/A					
27 – 28 in.	20	JTR	(2) E	22	N/R	N/A	N/A	F
^	18	N/R	N/A					
29 – 30 in.	18	JTR	(2) H	22	JTR	(2) E	N/A	G
^				20	N/R		N/A	G
31 – 36 in.	18	JTR	(2) H	20	JTR	(2) E	N/A	H
37 – 42 in.	18	JTR	(2) H	20	JTR	(2) H	N/A	I
43 – 48 in.	16	JTR	(2) I	20	JTR	(2) H	N/A	I
49 – 54 in.	16	JTR	(2) K	20	JTR	(2) H	N/A	I
55 – 60 in.	Not Designed			18	JTR	(2) I	N/A	J
61 – 72 in.	^		^	18	JTR	(2) L	N/A	L
73 – 84 in.	^		^	18	JTR	(2) L	N/A	L
85 – 96 in.	^		^	16	JTR	(2) L	N/A	Lt
97 – 108 in.	^		^	16	JTR	(2) L	✕	Lt
109 – 120 in.	^		^	16	JTR	(2) L	✕	Lt

Table 2–14   4 ft Coil/Sheet Stock/T25a/T25b (TDC/TDF) Duct Reinforcement

N/R   - Not Required
N/A   - Not Applicable
JTR   - Joint Tie Rod
MPT   - Mid Panel Tie Rod(s)
(2) (X) - Indicates 2 external reinforcements of class (X) to be used in lieu of Joint Tie Rods

Note: t following Reinforcement Class letter indicates tie rod required.

2500 Pa Static Pos. or Neg. Duct Dimension (mm)	1.20 m Joints			1.20 m Joints w/0.60 m Reinf. Spacing				
^	Min (mm)	Joint Reinf.	Alt. Joint Reinf.	Joints/Reinf			Int. Reinf.	
^	^	^	^	Min (mm)	Joint Reinf.	Alt. Joint Reinf.	Tie Rod	Alt. Reinf.
200 and under	0.55	N/R	N/A	Use 1.20 m Joints			
230 – 250	0.70	N/R	N/A	0.55	N/R	N/A	N/A	C
251 – 300	0.70	N/R	N/A	0.55	N/R	N/A	N/A	C
301 – 350	0.85	N/R	N/A	0.55	N/R	N/A	N/A	C
351 – 400	1.00	N/R	N/A	0.55	N/R	N/A	N/A	D
401 – 450	1.00	N/R	N/A	0.55	N/R	N/A	N/A	D
451 – 500	1.00	N/R	N/A	0.70	N/R	N/A	N/A	E
501 – 550	1.00	N/R	N/A	0.70	N/R	N/A	N/A	E
551 – 600	1.00	JTR	(2) E	0.85	N/R	N/A	N/A	F
^	1.31	N/R	N/A					
601 – 650	1.00	JTR	(2) E	0.85	N/R	N/A	N/A	F
^	1.31	N/R	N/A					
651 – 700	1.00	JTR	(2) E	0.85	N/R	N/A	N/A	F
^	1.31	N/R	N/A					
701 – 750	1.31	JTR	(2) H	0.85	JTR	(2) E	N/A	G
^				1.00	N/R		N/A	G
751 – 900	1.31	JTR	(2) H	1.00	JTR	(2) E	N/A	H
901 – 1000	1.31	JTR	(2) H	1.00	JTR	(2) H	N/A	I
1001 – 1200	1.61	JTR	(2) I	1.00	JTR	(2) H	N/A	I
1201 – 1300	1.61	JTR	(2) K	1.00	JTR	(2) H	N/A	I
1301 – 1500	Not Designed			1.31	JTR	(2) I	N/A	J
1501 – 1800	^ ^ ^	1.31	JTR	(2) L	N/A	L
1801 – 2100	^ ^ ^	1.31	JTR	(2) L	N/A	L
2101 – 2400	^ ^ ^	1.61	JTR	(2) L	N/A	Lt
2401 – 2700	^ ^ ^	1.61	JTR	(2) L	✕	Lt
2701 – 3000	^ ^ ^	1.61	JTR	(2) L	✕	Lt

Table 2–14M 1.20 m Coil/Sheet Stock/T25a/T25b (TDC/TDF) Duct Reinforcement

N/R - Not Required
N/A - Not Applicable
JTR - Joint Tie Rod
MPT - Mid Panel Tie Rod(s)
(2) (X) - Indicates 2 external reinforcements of class (X) to be used in lieu of Joint Tie Rods

Note: t following Reinforcement Class letter indicates tie rod required.

½ in. wg Static Pos. or Neg. Duct Dimension	5 ft Joints			5 ft Joints w/2 ½ ft Reinf. Spacing				
^	^	^	^	Joints/Reinf.			Int. Reinf.	
^	Min ga	Joint Reinf.	Alt. Joint Reinf.	Min ga	Joint Reinf.	Alt. Joint Reinf.	Tie Rod	Alt. Reinf.
10 in. and under	26	N/R	N/R					
11 – 12 in.	26	N/R	N/R					
13 – 14 in.	26	N/R	N/R					
15 – 16 in.	26	N/R	N/R					
17 – 18 in.	26	N/R	N/R					
19 – 20 in.	26	N/R	N/R					
21 – 22 in.	26	N/R	N/R			Use 5 ft Joints		
23 – 24 in.	26	N/R	N/R					
25 – 26 in.	26	N/R	N/R					
27 – 28 in.	26	N/R	N/R					
29 – 30 in.	26	N/R	N/R					
31 – 36 in.	26	N/R	N/R					
37 – 42 in.	26	N/R	N/R					
43 – 48 in.	24	N/R	N/R	26	N/R	N/A	MPT	C
49 – 54 in.	24	N/R	N/R	26	N/R	N/A	MPT	D
55 – 60 in.	24	N/R	N/R	24	N/R	N/A		E
61 – 72 in.	22	N/R	N/R	24	N/R	N/A	MPT	E
73 – 84 in.	20	JTR	(2) E	22	N/R	N/A	MPT	F
85 – 96 in.	20	JTR	(2) E	22	N/R	N/A	MPT	F
97 – 108 in.	18	JTR	(2) H	18	N/R	N/A	—	H
109 – 120 in.	16	JTR	(2) H	18	N/R	N/A	—	H

Table 2–15 5 ft Coil/Sheet Stock/T25a/T25b (TDC/TDF) Duct Reinforcement

N/R - Not Required
N/A - Not Applicable
JTR - Joint Tie Rod
MPT - Mid Panel Tie Rod(s)
(2) (X) - Indicates 2 external reinforcements of class (X) to be used in lieu of Joint Tie Rods

125 Pa Static Pos. or Neg. Duct Dimension (mm)	1.50 m Joints			1.50 m Joints w/0.75 m Reinf. Spacing				
^	Min (mm)	Joint Reinf.	Alt. Joint Reinf.	Joints/Reinf.			Int. Reinf.	
^	^	^	^	Min (mm)	Joint Reinf.	Alt. Joint Reinf.	Tie Rod	Alt. Reinf.
250 and under	0.55	N/R	N/R	\multicolumn{5}{c}{Use 1.50 m Joints}				
251 – 300	0.55	N/R	N/R	^				
301 – 350	0.55	N/R	N/R	^				
351 – 400	0.55	N/R	N/R	^				
401 – 450	0.55	N/R	N/R	^				
451 – 500	0.55	N/R	N/R	^				
501 – 550	0.55	N/R	N/R	^				
551 – 600	0.55	N/R	N/R	^				
601 – 650	0.55	N/R	N/R	^				
651 – 700	0.55	N/R	N/R	^				
701 – 750	0.55	N/R	N/R	^				
751 – 900	0.55	N/R	N/R	^				
901 – 1000	0.55	N/R	N/R	^				
1001 – 1200	0.70	N/R	N/R	0.55	N/R	N/A	MPT	C
1201 – 1300	0.70	N/R	N/R	0.55	N/R	N/A	MPT	D
1301 – 1500	0.70	N/R	N/R	0.70	N/R	N/A		E
1501 – 1800	0.85	N/R	N/R	0.70	N/R	N/A	MPT	E
1801 – 2100	1.00	JTR	(2) E	0.85	N/R	N/A	MPT	F
2101 – 2400	1.00	JTR	(2) E	0.85	N/R	N/A	MPT	F
2401 – 2700	1.31	JTR	(2) H	1.31	N/R	N/A	—	H
2701 – 3000	1.61	JTR	(2) H	1.31	N/R	N/A	—	H

Table 2–15M 1.50 m Coil/Sheet Stock/T25a/T25b (TDC/TDF) Duct Reinforcement

N/R - Not Required
N/A - Not Applicable
JTR - Joint Tie Rod
MPT - Mid Panel Tie Rod(s)
(2) (X) - Indicates 2 external reinforcements of class (X) to be used in lieu of Joint Tie Rods

| 1 in. wg Static Pos. or Neg. Duct Dimension | 5 ft Joints ||| 5 ft Joints w/2 ½ ft Reinf. Spacing |||||
| | Min ga | Joint Reinf. | Alt. Joint Reinf. | Joints/Reinf. ||| Int. Reinf. ||
				Min ga	Joint Reinf.	Alt. Joint Reinf.	Tie Rod	Alt. Reinf.
10 in. and under	26	N/R	N/R					
11 – 12 in.	26	N/R	N/R					
13 – 14 in.	26	N/R	N/R					
15 – 16 in.	26	N/R	N/R					
17 – 18 in.	26	N/R	N/R					
19 – 20 in.	26	N/R	N/R	Use 5 ft Joints				
21 – 22 in.	26	N/R	N/R					
23 – 24 in.	26	N/R	N/R					
25 – 26 in.	26	N/R	N/R					
27 – 28 in.	26	N/R	N/R					
29 – 30 in.	26	N/R	N/R					
31 – 36 in.	24	N/R	N/R	26	N/R	N/R	MPT	C
37 – 42 in.	24	N/R	N/R	26	N/R	N/R	MPT	D
43 – 48 in.	22	N/R	N/R	24	N/R	N/R	MPT	E
49 – 54 in.	22	N/R	N/R	24	N/R	N/R	MPT	E
55 – 60 in.	22	JTR	(2) C	24	N/R	N/R	MPT	E
61 – 72 in.	18	N/R	N/R	22	N/R	N/R	MPT	F
73 – 84 in.	18	JTR	(2) H	20	JTR	(2) F	MPT	H
85 – 96 in.	18	JTR	(2) H	20	JTR	(2) E	(2) MPT	H
97 – 108 in.	16	JTR	(2) H	18	JTR	(2) I	—	I
109 – 120 in.	Not Designed			18	JTR	(2) I	—	I

Table 2–16 5 ft Coil/Sheet Stock/T25a/T25b (TDC/TDF) Duct Reinforcement

N/R - Not Required
N/A - Not Applicable
JTR - Joint Tie Rod
MPT - Mid Panel Tie Rod(s)
(2) (X) - Indicates 2 external reinforcements of class (X) to be used in lieu of Joint Tie Rods

250 Pa Static Pos. or Neg. Duct Dimension (mm)	1.50 m Joints			1.50 m Joints w/0.75 m Reinf. Spacing				
^	Min (mm)	Joint Reinf.	Alt. Joint Reinf.	Joints/Reinf.			Int. Reinf.	
^	^	^	^	Min (mm)	Joint Reinf.	Alt. Joint Reinf.	Tie Rod	Alt. Reinf.
250 and under	0.55	N/R	N/R	Use 1.50 m Joints				
251 – 300	0.55	N/R	N/R	^				
301 – 350	0.55	N/R	N/R	^				
351 – 400	0.55	N/R	N/R	^				
401 – 450	0.55	N/R	N/R	^				
451 – 500	0.55	N/R	N/R	^				
501 – 550	0.55	N/R	N/R	^				
551 – 600	0.55	N/R	N/R	^				
601 – 650	0.55	N/R	N/R	^				
651 – 700	0.55	N/R	N/R	^				
701 – 750	0.55	N/R	N/R	^				
751 – 900	0.70	N/R	N/R	0.55	N/R	N/R	MPT	C
901 – 1000	0.70	N/R	N/R	0.55	N/R	N/R	MPT	D
1001 – 1200	0.85	N/R	N/R	0.70	N/R	N/R	MPT	E
1201 – 1300	0.85	N/R	N/R	0.70	N/R	N/R	MPT	E
1301 – 1500	0.85	JTR	(2) C	0.70	N/R	N/R	MPT	E
1501 – 1800	1.31	N/R	N/R	0.70	N/R	N/R	(2) MPT	F
1801 – 2100	1.31	JTR	(2) H	0.85	JTR	(2) F	(2) MPT	H
2101 – 2400	1.31	JTR	(2) H	1.00	JTR	(2) E	(2) MPT	H
2401 – 2700	1.61	JTR	(2) H	1.31	JTR	(2) I	—	I
2701 – 3000	Not Designed			1.31	JTR	(2) I	—	I

Table 2–16M 1.50 m Coil/Sheet Stock/T25a/T25b (TDC/TDF) Duct Reinforcement

N/R - Not Required
N/A - Not Applicable
JTR - Joint Tie Rod
MPT - Mid Panel Tie Rod(s)
(2) (X) - Indicates 2 external reinforcements of class (X) to be used in lieu of Joint Tie Rods

2 in. wg Static Pos. or Neg. Duct Dimension	5 ft Joints			5 ft Joints w/2 ½ ft Reinf. Spacing				
^	Min ga	Joint Reinf.	Alt. Joint Reinf.	Joints/Reinf.			Int. Reinf.	
^	^	^	^	Min ga	Joint Reinf.	Alt. Joint Reinf.	Tie Rod	Alt. Reinf.
10 in. and under	26	N/R	N/R	Use 5 ft Joints					
11 – 12 in.	26	N/R	N/R	^				
13 – 14 in.	26	N/R	N/R	^				
15 – 16 in.	26	N/R	N/R	^				
17 – 18 in.	26	N/R	N/R	^				
19 – 20 in.	26	N/R	N/R	^				
21 – 22 in.	26	N/R	N/R	^				
23 – 24 in.	26	N/R	N/R	^				
25 – 26 in.	26	N/R	N/R	^				
27 – 28 in.	24	N/R	N/R	26	N/R	N/R	MPT	C
29 – 30 in.	24	N/R	N/R	26	N/R	N/R	MPT	D
31 – 36 in.	22	N/R	N/R	26	N/R	N/R	MPT	D
37 – 42 in.	22	JTR	(2) C	24	N/R	N/R	MPT	E
^	20	N/R	N/A	^				
43 – 48 in.	20	JTR	(2) E	22	N/R	N/R	MPT	F
^	18	N/R	N/A	^				
49 – 54 in.	20	JTR	(2) E	22	N/R	N/R	MPT	F
^	18	N/R	N/A	^				
55 – 60 in.	20	JTR	(2) H	22	JTR	(2) C	MPT	G
61 – 72 in.	18	JTR	(2) H	20	JTR	(2) E	MPT	H
73 – 84 in.	16	JTR	(2) H	20	JTR	(2) H	(2) MPT	I
85 – 96 in.	Not Designed			20	JTR	(2) H	(2) MPT	I
97 – 108 in.	^			18	JTR	(2) I	✕	J
109 – 120 in.	^			18	JTR	(2) I	✕	K

Table 2–17 5 ft Coil/Sheet Stock/T25a/T25b (TDC/TDF) Duct Reinforcement

N/R - Not Required
N/A - Not Applicable
JTR - Joint Tie Rod
MPT - Mid Panel Tie Rod(s)
(2) (X) - Indicates 2 external reinforcements of class (X) to be used in lieu of Joint Tie Rods

500 Pa Static Pos. or Neg. Duct Dimension (mm)	1.50 m Joints			1.50 m Joints w/0.75 m Reinf. Spacing				
^	Min (mm)	Joint Reinf.	Alt. Joint Reinf.	Joints/Reinf.			Int. Reinf.	
^	^	^	^	Min (mm)	Joint Reinf.	Alt. Joint Reinf.	Tie Rod	Alt. Reinf.
250 and under	0.55	N/R	N/R					
251 – 300	0.55	N/R	N/R					
301 – 350	0.55	N/R	N/R					
351 – 400	0.55	N/R	N/R					
401 – 450	0.55	N/R	N/R	Use 1.50 m Joints				
451 – 500	0.55	N/R	N/R					
501 – 550	0.55	N/R	N/R					
551 – 600	0.55	N/R	N/R					
601 – 650	0.55	N/R	N/R					
651 – 700	0.70	N/R	N/R	0.55	N/R	N/R	MPT	C
701 – 750	0.70	N/R	N/R	0.55	N/R	N/R	MPT	D
751 – 900	0.85	N/R	N/R	0.55	N/R	N/R	MPT	D
901 – 1000	0.85	JTR	(2) C	0.70	N/R	N/R	MPT	E
^	1.00	N/R	N/A					
1001 – 1200	1.00	JTR	(2) E	0.85	N/R	N/R	MPT	F
^	1.31	N/R	N/A					
1201 – 1300	1.00	JTR	(2) E	0.85	N/R	N/R	MPT	F
^	1.31	N/R	N/A					
1301 – 1500	1.00	JTR	(2) H	0.85	JTR	(2) C	MPT	G
1501 – 1800	1.31	JTR	(2) H	1.00	JTR	(2) E	MPT	H
1801 – 2100	1.61	JTR	(2) H	1.00	JTR	(2) H	(2) MPT	I
2101 – 2400	Not Designed			1.00	JTR	(2) H	(2) MPT	I
2401 – 2700	^	^	^	1.31	JTR	(2) I	—	J
2701 – 3000	^	^	^	1.31	JTR	(2) I	—	K

Table 2–17M 1.50 m Coil/Sheet Stock/T25a/T25b (TDC/TDF) Duct Reinforcement

N/R   - Not Required
N/A   - Not Applicable
JTR   - Joint Tie Rod
MPT   - Mid Panel Tie Rod(s)
(2) (X)   - Indicates 2 external reinforcements of class (X) to be used in lieu of Joint Tie Rods

3 in. wg Static Pos. or Neg. Duct Dimension	5 ft Joints			5 ft Joints w/2 ½ ft Reinf. Spacing				
^	Min ga	Joint Reinf.	Alt. Joint Reinf.	Joints/Reinf.			Int. Reinf.	
^	^	^	^	Min ga	Joint Reinf	Alt. Joint Reinf.	Tie Rod	Alt. Reinf.
10 in. and under	26	N/R	N/R	Use 5 ft Joints				
11 – 12 in.	26	N/R	N/R	^				
13 – 14 in.	24	N/R	N/R	26	N/R	N/A	MPT	B
15 – 16 in.	24	N/R	N/R	26	N/R	N/A	MPT	C
17 – 18 in.	24	N/R	N/R	26	N/R	N/A	MPT	C
19 – 20 in.	24	N/R	N/R	26	N/R	N/A	MPT	C
21 – 22 in.	24	N/R	N/R	26	N/R	N/A	MPT	C
23 – 24 in.	24	N/R	N/R	26	N/R	N/A	MPT	D
25 – 26 in.	24	N/R	N/R	26	N/R	N/A	MPT	D
27 – 28 in.	22	N/R	N/R	26	N/R	N/A	MPT	D
29 – 30 in.	22	N/R	N/R	24	N/R	N/A	MPT	E
31 – 36 in.	20	N/R	N/R	24	N/R	N/A	MPT	E
37 – 42 in.	20	JTR	(2) E	22	N/R	N/A	MPT	F
43 – 48 in.	18	JTR	(2) H	22	JTR	(2) C	MPT	G
49 – 54 in.	18	JTR	(2) H	22	JTR	(2) C	MPT	G
55 – 60 in.	18	JTR	(2) H	20	JTR	(2) E	MPT	H
61 – 72 in.	16	JTR	(2) H	20	JTR	(2) H	2 MPT	I
73 – 84 in.	16	JTR	(2) K	20	JTR	(2) H	2 MPT	I
85 – 96 in.	Not Designed			18	JTR	(2) I	2 MPT	J
97 – 108 in.	^			18	JTR	(2) K		L
109 – 120 in.	^			18	JTR	(2) K		L

Table 2–18 5 ft Coil/Sheet Stock/T25a/T25b (TDC/TDF) Duct Reinforcement

N/R   - Not Required
N/A   - Not Applicable
JTR   - Joint Tie Rod
MPT   - Mid Panel Tie Rod(s)
(2) (X) - Indicates 2 external reinforcements of class (X) to be used in lieu of Joint Tie Rods

750 Pa Static Pos. or Neg. Duct Dimension (mm)	1.50 m Joints			1.50 m Joints w/0.75 m Reinf. Spacing				
^	Min (mm)	Joint Reinf.	Alt. Joint Reinf.	Joints/Reinf.			Int. Reinf.	
^	^	^	^	Min (mm)	Joint Reinf	Alt. Joint Reinf.	Tie Rod	Alt. Reinf.
250 and under	0.55	N/R	N/R	Use 1.50 m Joints			
251 – 300	0.55	N/R	N/R	^			
301 – 350	0.70	N/R	N/R	0.55	N/R	N/A	MPT	B
351 – 400	0.70	N/R	N/R	0.55	N/R	N/A	MPT	C
401 – 450	0.70	N/R	N/R	0.55	N/R	N/A	MPT	C
451 – 500	0.70	N/R	N/R	0.55	N/R	N/A	MPT	C
501 – 550	0.70	N/R	N/R	0.55	N/R	N/A	MPT	C
551 – 600	0.70	N/R	N/R	0.55	N/R	N/A	MPT	D
601 – 650	0.70	N/R	N/R	0.55	N/R	N/A	MPT	D
651 – 700	0.85	N/R	N/R	0.55	N/R	N/A	MPT	D
701 – 750	0.85	N/R	N/R	0.70	N/R	N/A	MPT	E
751 – 900	1.00	N/R	N/R	0.70	N/R	N/A	MPT	E
901 – 1000	1.00	JTR	(2) E	0.85	N/R	N/A	MPT	F
1001 – 1200	1.31	JTR	(2) H	0.85	JTR	(2) C	MPT	G
1201 – 1300	1.31	JTR	(2) H	0.85	JTR	(2) C	MPT	G
1301 – 1500	1.31	JTR	(2) H	1.00	JTR	(2) E	MPT	H
1501 – 1800	1.61	JTR	(2) H	1.00	JTR	(2) H	2 MPT	I
1801 – 2100	1.61	JTR	(2) K	1.00	JTR	(2) H	2 MPT	I
2101 – 2400	Not Designed			1.31	JTR	(2) I	2 MPT	J
2401 – 2700	^			1.31	JTR	(2) K	—	L
2701 – 3000	^			1.31	JTR	(2) K	—	L

Table 2–18M 1.50 m Coil/Sheet Stock/T25a/T25b (TDC/TDF) Duct Reinforcement

N/R   - Not Required

N/A   - Not Applicable

JTR   - Joint Tie Rod

MPT   - Mid Panel Tie Rod(s)

(2) (X)   - Indicates 2 external reinforcements of class (X) to be used in lieu of Joint Tie Rods

4 in. wg Static Pos. or Neg. Duct Dimension	5 ft Joints			5 ft Joints w/2 ½ ft Reinf. Spacing				
^	Min ga	Joint Reinf.	Alt. Joint Reinf.	Joints/Reinf.			Int. Reinf.	
^	^	^	^	Min ga	Joint Reinf.	Alt. Joint Reinf.	Tie Rod	Alt. Reinf.
8 in. and under	26	N/R	N/R	\multicolumn{5}{c}{Use 5 ft Joints}				
9 – 10 in.	26	N/R	N/R	^				
11 – 12 in.	26	N/R	N/R	^				
13 – 14 in.	24	N/R	N/R	26	N/R	N/R	MPT	C
15 – 16 in.	24	N/R	N/R	26	N/R	N/R	MPT	C
17 – 18 in.	24	N/R	N/R	26	N/R	N/R	MPT	C
19 – 20 in.	24	N/R	N/R	26	N/R	N/R	MPT	C
21 – 22 in.	24	N/R	N/R	26	N/R	N/R	MPT	D
23 – 24 in.	22	N/R	N/R	26	N/R	N/R	MPT	D
25 – 26 in.	22	N/R	N/R	24	N/R	N/R	MPT	E
27 – 28 in.	22	N/R	N/R	24	N/R	N/R	MPT	E
29 – 30 in.	20	N/R	N/R	24	N/R	N/R	MPT	E
31 – 36 in.	20	JTR	(2) E	22	N/R	N/R	MPT	F
37 – 42 in.	18	JTR	(2) H	22	JTR	(2) C	MPT	G
^	^	^	^	20	N/R	N/R	MPT	G
43 – 48 in.	18	JTR	(2) H	20	JTR	(2) E	MPT	H
^	^	^	^	18	N/R	N/R	MPT	H
49 – 54 in.	18	JTR	(2) H	20	JTR	(2) E	MPT	H
^	^	^	^	18	N/R	N/R	MPT	H
55 – 60 in.	16	JTR	(2) H	20	JTR	(2) I	MPT	I
61 – 72 in.	\multicolumn{3}{c}{Not Designed}			20	JTR	(2) I	(2) MPT	I
73 – 84 in.	^			18	JTR	(2) I	(2) MPT	J
85 – 96 in.	^			18	JTR	(2) I	(2) MPT	K
97 – 108 in.	^			18	JTR	(2) K	—	L
109 – 120 in.	^			18	JTR	(2) K	—	L

Table 2–19 5 ft Coil/Sheet Stock/T25a/T25b (TDC/TDF) Duct Reinforcement

N/R   - Not Required
N/A   - Not Applicable
JTR   - Joint Tie Rod
MPT   - Mid Panel Tie Rod(s)
(2) (X)   - Indicates 2 external reinforcements of class (X) to be used in lieu of Joint Tie Rods

1000 Pa Static Pos. or Neg. Duct Dimension (mm)	1.50 m Joints				1.50 m Joints w/0.75 m Reinf. Spacing				
^	Min (mm)	Joint Reinf.	Alt. Joint Reinf.		Joints/Reinf.			Int. Reinf.	
^	^	^	^		Min (mm)	Joint Reinf.	Alt. Joint Reinf.	Tie Rod	Alt. Reinf.
200 and under	0.55	N/R	N/R		Use 1.50 m Joints				
230 – 250	0.55	N/R	N/R		^				
251 – 300	0.55	N/R	N/R		^				
301 – 350	0.70	N/R	N/R		0.55	N/R	N/R	MPT	C
351 – 400	0.70	N/R	N/R		0.55	N/R	N/R	MPT	C
401 – 450	0.70	N/R	N/R		0.55	N/R	N/R	MPT	C
451 – 500	0.70	N/R	N/R		0.55	N/R	N/R	MPT	C
501 – 550	0.70	N/R	N/R		0.55	N/R	N/R	MPT	D
551 – 600	0.85	N/R	N/R		0.55	N/R	N/R	MPT	D
601 – 650	0.85	N/R	N/R		0.70	N/R	N/R	MPT	E
651 – 700	0.85	N/R	N/R		0.70	N/R	N/R	MPT	E
701 – 750	1.00	N/R	N/R		0.70	N/R	N/R	MPT	E
751 – 900	1.00	JTR	(2) E		0.85	N/R	N/R	MPT	F
901 – 1000	1.31	JTR	(2) H		0.85	JTR	(2) C	MPT	G
^					1.00	N/R	N/R	MPT	G
1001 – 1200	1.31	JTR	(2) H		1.00	JTR	(2) E	MPT	H
^					1.31	N/R	N/R	MPT	H
1201 – 1300	1.31	JTR	(2) H		1.00	JTR	(2) E	MPT	H
^					1.31	N/R	N/R	MPT	H
1301 – 1500	1.61	JTR	(2) H		1.00	JTR	(2) I	MPT	I
1501 – 1800	Not Designed				1.00	JTR	(2) I	(2) MPT	I
1801 – 2100	^				1.31	JTR	(2) I	(2) MPT	J
2101 – 2400	^				1.31	JTR	(2) I	(2) MPT	K
2401 – 2700	^				1.31	JTR	(2) K		L
2701 – 3000	^				1.31	JTR	(2) K		L

Table 2–19M 1.50 m Coil/Sheet Stock/T25a/T25b (TDC/TDF) Duct Reinforcement

N/R — Not Required
N/A — Not Applicable
JTR — Joint Tie Rod
MPT — Mid Panel Tie Rod(s)
(2) (X) — Indicates 2 external reinforcements of class (X) to be used in lieu of Joint Tie Rods

6 in. wg Static Pos. or Neg. Duct Dimension	5 ft Joints			5 ft Joints w/2 ½ ft Reinf. Spacing				
:::	Min ga	Joint Reinf.	Alt. Joint Reinf.	Joints/Reinf.			Int. Reinf.	
:::	:::	:::	:::	Min ga	Joint Reinf.	Alt. Joint Reinf.	Tie Rod	Alt. Reinf.
8 in. and under	26	N/R	N/A	Use 5 ft Joints			
9 – 10 in.	24	N/R	N/A	26	N/R	N/R	MPT	B
11 – 12 in.	24	N/R	N/A	26	N/R	N/R	MPT	C
13 – 14 in.	22	N/R	N/A	26	N/R	N/R	MPT	C
15 – 16 in.	22	N/R	N/A	26	N/R	N/R	MPT	C
17 – 18 in.	22	N/R	N/A	26	N/R	N/R	MPT	D
19 – 20 in.	22	N/R	N/A	26	N/R	N/R	MPT	D
21 – 22 in.	22	N/R	N/A	24	N/R	N/R	MPT	E
23 – 24 in.	22	N/R	N/A	24	N/R	N/R	MPT	E
25 – 26 in.	20	N/R	N/A	24	N/R	N/R	MPT	E
27 – 28 in.	20	JTR	(2) E	22	N/R	N/R	MPT	F
29 – 30 in.	18	N/R	N/R	22	N/R	N/R	MPT	F
31 – 36 in.	18	JTR	(2) H	20	N/R	N/R	MPT	G
37 – 42 in.	16	JTR	(2) H	20	JTR	(2) E	MPT	H
:::	:::	:::	:::	18	N/R	N/R	MPT	H
43 – 48 in.	16	JTR	(2) H	20	JTR	(2) H	MPT	I
49 – 54 in.	Not Designed			20	JTR	(2) H	MPT	I
55 – 60 in.	:::			20	JTR	(2) H	2 MPT	I
61 – 72 in.	:::			18	JTR	(2) I	MPT	J
73 – 84 in.	:::			18	JTR	(2) K	2 MPT	L
85 – 96 in.	:::			16	JTR	N/A	2 MPT	It
97 – 108 in.	:::			16	JTR	N/A	—	Jt
109 – 120 in.	:::			16	JTR	N/A	—	Kt

Table 2–20 5 ft Coil/Sheet Stock/T25a/T25b (TDC/TDF) Duct Reinforcement

N/R   - Not Required
N/A   - Not Applicable
JTR   - Joint Tie Rod
MPT   - Mid Panel Tie Rod(s)
(2) (X)   - Indicates 2 external reinforcements of class (X) to be used in lieu of Joint Tie Rods

Note: t following Reinforcement Class letter indicates tie rod required.

1500 Pa Static Pos. or Neg. Duct Dimension (mm)	1.50 m Joints			1.50 m Joints w/0.75 m Reinf. Spacing				
:::	Min (mm)	Joint Reinf.	Alt. Joint Reinf.	Joints/Reinf.			Int. Reinf.	
:::	:::	:::	:::	Min (mm)	Joint Reinf.	Alt. Joint Reinf.	Tie Rod	Alt. Reinf.
200 and under	0.55	N/R	N/A	Use 1.50 m Joints			
230 – 250	0.70	N/R	N/A	0.55	N/R	N/R	MPT	B
251 – 300	0.70	N/R	N/A	0.55	N/R	N/R	MPT	C
301 – 350	0.85	N/R	N/A	0.55	N/R	N/R	MPT	C
351 – 400	0.85	N/R	N/A	0.55	N/R	N/R	MPT	C
401 – 450	0.85	N/R	N/A	0.55	N/R	N/R	MPT	D
451 – 500	0.85	N/R	N/A	0.55	N/R	N/R	MPT	D
501 – 550	0.85	N/R	N/A	0.70	N/R	N/R	MPT	E
551 – 600	0.85	N/R	N/A	0.70	N/R	N/R	MPT	E
601 – 650	1.00	N/R	N/A	0.70	N/R	N/R	MPT	E
651 – 700	1.00	JTR	(2) E	0.85	N/R	N/R	MPT	F
701 – 750	1.31	N/R	N/R	0.85	N/R	N/R	MPT	F
751 – 900	1.31	JTR	(2) H	1.00	N/R	N/R	MPT	G
901 – 1000	1.61	JTR	(2) H	1.00	JTR	(2) E	MPT	H
:::				1.31	N/R	N/R	MPT	H
1001 – 1200	1.61	JTR	(2) H	1.00	JTR	(2) H	MPT	I
1201 – 1300	Not Designed			1.00	JTR	(2) H	MPT	I
1301 – 1500	:::			1.00	JTR	(2) H	2 MPT	I
1501 – 1800	:::			1.31	JTR	(2) I	MPT	J
1801 – 2100	:::			1.31	JTR	(2) K	2 MPT	L
2101 – 2400	:::			1.61	JTR	N/A	2 MPT	It
2401 – 2700	:::			1.61	JTR	N/A	✕	Jt
2701 – 3000	:::			1.61	JTR	N/A	✕	Kt

Table 2–20M 1.20 m Coil/Sheet Stock/T25a/T25b (TDC/TDF) Duct Reinforcement

N/R   - Not Required
N/A   - Not Applicable
JTR   - Joint Tie Rod
MPT   - Mid Panel Tie Rod(s)
(2) (X)   - Indicates 2 external reinforcements of class (X) to be used in lieu of Joint Tie Rods

Note: t following Reinforcement Class letter indicates tie rod required.

10 in. wg Static Pos. or Neg. Duct Dimension	5 ft Joints			5 ft Joints w/2 ½ ft Reinf. Spacing				
^	Min ga	Joint Reinf.	Alt. Joint Reinf.	Joints/Reinf.			Int. Reinf.	
^	^	^	^	Min ga	Joint Reinf.	Alt. Joint Reinf.	Tie Rod	Alt. Reinf.
8 in. and under	24	N/R	N/R	26	N/R	N/R	N/A	C
9 – 10 in.	22	N/R	N/R	26	N/R	N/R	N/A	C
11 – 12 in.	22	N/R	N/R	26	N/R	N/R	N/A	C
13 – 14 in.	20	N/R	N/R	26	N/R	N/R	N/A	D
15 – 16 in.	20	N/R	N/R	24	N/R	N/R	N/A	D
17 – 18 in.	20	N/R	N/R	24	N/R	N/R	N/A	E
19 – 20 in.	18	N/R	N/R	24	N/R	N/R	N/A	E
21 – 22 in.	18	N/R	N/R	22	N/R	N/R	N/A	F
23 – 24 in.	18	N/R	N/R	22	N/R	N/R	N/A	F
25 – 26 in.	18	N/R	N/R	22	N/R	N/R	N/A	F
27 – 28 in.	18	JTR	(2) H	22	JTR	(2) C	N/A	G
^	^	^	^	20	N/R	N/R	N/A	G
29 – 30 in.	18	JTR	(2) H	20	JTR	(2) E	N/A	H
^	^	^	^	18	N/R	N/R	N/A	H
31 – 36 in.	16	JTR	(2) I	20	JTR	(2) E	N/A	H
^	^	^	^	18	N/R	N/R	N/A	H
37 – 42 in.	16	JTR	(2) I	20	JTR	(2) H	N/A	I
43 – 48 in.				18	JTR	(2) H	N/A	I
49 – 54 in.				18	JTR	(2) I	N/A	J
55 – 60 in.				18	JTR	(2) I	N/A	K
61 – 72 in.				18	JTR	(2) K	N/A	L
73 – 84 in.				16	JTR	(2) K	N/A	L
85 – 96 in.	Not Designed							
97 – 108 in.	^							
109 – 120 in.	^							

Table 2–21 5 ft Coil/Sheet Stock/T25a/T25b (TDC/TDF) Duct Reinforcement

N/R   - Not Required
N/A   - Not Applicable
JTR   - Joint Tie Rod
MPT - Mid Panel Tie Rod(s)
(2) (X) - Indicates 2 external reinforcements of class (X) to be used in lieu of Joint Tie Rods

2500 Pa Static Pos. or Neg. Duct Dimension (mm)	1.50 m Joints			1.50 m Joints w/0.75 m Reinf. Spacing				
^	Min (mm)	Joint Reinf.	Alt. Joint Reinf.	Joints/Reinf.			Int. Reinf.	
^	^	^	^	Min (mm)	Joint Reinf.	Alt. Joint Reinf.	Tie Rod	Alt. Reinf.
200 and under	0.70	N/R	N/R	0.55	N/R	N/R	N/A	C
230 – 250	0.85	N/R	N/R	0.55	N/R	N/R	N/A	C
251 – 300	0.85	N/R	N/R	0.55	N/R	N/R	N/A	C
301 – 350	1.00	N/R	N/R	0.55	N/R	N/R	N/A	D
351 – 400	1.00	N/R	N/R	0.70	N/R	N/R	N/A	D
401 – 450	1.00	N/R	N/R	0.70	N/R	N/R	N/A	E
451 – 500	1.31	N/R	N/R	0.70	N/R	N/R	N/A	E
501 – 550	1.31	N/R	N/R	0.85	N/R	N/R	N/A	F
551 – 600	1.31	N/R	N/R	0.85	N/R	N/R	N/A	F
601 – 650	1.31	N/R	N/R	0.85	N/R	N/R	N/A	F
651 – 700	1.31	JTR	(2) H	0.85	JTR	(2) C	N/A	G
^				1.00	N/R	N/R	N/A	G
701 – 750	1.31	JTR	(2) H	1.00	JTR	(2) E	N/A	H
^				1.31	N/R	N/R	N/A	H
751 – 900	1.61	JTR	(2) I	1.00	JTR	(2) E	N/A	H
^				1.31	N/R	N/R	N/A	H
901 – 1000	1.61	JTR	(2) I	1.00	JTR	(2) H	N/A	I
1001 – 1200				1.31	JTR	(2) H	N/A	I
1201 – 1300				1.31	JTR	(2) I	N/A	J
1301 – 1500				1.31	JTR	(2) I	N/A	K
1501 – 1800				1.31	JTR	(2) K	N/A	L
1801 – 2100				1.61	JTR	(2) K	N/A	L
2101 – 2400	Not Designed							
2401 – 2700	^							
2701 – 3000	^							

Table 2–21M 1.50 m Coil/Sheet Stock/T25a/T25b (TDC/TDF) Duct Reinforcement

N/R — Not Required
N/A — Not Applicable
JTR — Joint Tie Rod
MPT — Mid Panel Tie Rod(s)
(2) (X) — Indicates 2 external reinforcements of class (X) to be used in lieu of Joint Tie Rods

½ in. wg Static Pos. or Neg. Duct Dimension	6 ft Joints			6 ft Joints w/3 ft Reinf. Spacing				
				Joints/Reinf.			Int. Reinf.	
	Min ga	Joint Reinf.	Alt. Joint Reinf.	Min ga	Joint Reinf.	Alt. Joint Reinf.	Tie Rod	Alt. Reinf.
10 in. and under	26	N/R	N/A					
11 – 12 in.	26	N/R	N/A					
13 – 14 in.	26	N/R	N/A					
15 – 16 in.	26	N/R	N/A					
17 – 18 in.	26	N/R	N/A					
19 – 20 in.	26	N/R	N/A			Use 6 ft Joints		
21 – 22 in.	26	N/R	N/A					
23 – 24 in.	26	N/R	N/A					
25 – 26 in.	26	N/R	N/A					
27 – 28 in.	26	N/R	N/A					
29 – 30 in.	26	N/R	N/A					
31 – 36 in.	26	N/R	N/A					
37 – 42 in.	24	N/R	N/A	26	N/R	N/A	MPT	C
43 – 48 in.	24	N/R	N/A	26	N/R	N/A	MPT	D
49 – 54 in.	22	N/R	N/A	24	N/R	N/A	MPT	E
55 – 60 in.	22	N/R	N/A	24	N/R	N/A	MPT	E
61 – 72 in.	20	N/R	N/A	24	N/R	N/A	MPT	E
73 – 84 in.	20	JTR	(2) E	22	N/R	N/A	MPT	F
	18	N/R	N/A					
85 – 96 in.	18	JTR	(2) H	22	JTR	(2) C	MPT	G
				20	N/R	N/A	MPT	G
97 – 108 in.	16	JTR	(2) H	18	N/R	N/A	✕	H
109 – 120 in.	Not Designed			18	JTR	(2) H	✕	I

Table 2–22 6 ft Coil/Sheet Stock/T25a/T25b (TDC/TDF) Duct Reinforcement

N/R - Not Required
N/A - Not Applicable
JTR - Joint Tie Rod
MPT - Mid Panel Tie Rod(s)
(2) (X) - Indicates 2 external reinforcements of class (X) to be used in lieu of Joint Tie Rods

125 Pa Static Pos. or Neg. Duct Dimension (mm)	1.80 m Joints			1.80 m Joints w/0.90 m Reinf. Spacing				
^^^	Min (mm)	Joint Reinf.	Alt. Joint Reinf.	Joints/Reinf.			Int. Reinf.	
^^^	^^^	^^^	^^^	Min (mm)	Joint Reinf.	Alt. Joint Reinf.	Tie Rod	Alt. Reinf.
250 and under	0.55	N/R	N/A	Use 1.80 m Joints				
251 – 300	0.55	N/R	N/A	^^^				
301 – 350	0.55	N/R	N/A	^^^				
351 – 400	0.55	N/R	N/A	^^^				
401 – 450	0.55	N/R	N/A	^^^				
451 – 500	0.55	N/R	N/A	^^^				
501 – 550	0.55	N/R	N/A	^^^				
551 – 600	0.55	N/R	N/A	^^^				
601 – 650	0.55	N/R	N/A	^^^				
651 – 700	0.55	N/R	N/A	^^^				
701 – 750	0.55	N/R	N/A	^^^				
751 – 900	0.55	N/R	N/A	^^^				
901 – 1000	0.70	N/R	N/A	0.55	N/R	N/A	MPT	C
1001 – 1200	0.70	N/R	N/A	0.55	N/R	N/A	MPT	D
1201 – 1300	0.85	N/R	N/A	0.70	N/R	N/A	MPT	E
1301 – 1500	0.85	N/R	N/A	0.70	N/R	N/A	MPT	E
1501 – 1800	1.00	N/R	N/A	0.70	N/R	N/A	MPT	E
1801 – 2100	1.00	JTR	(2) E	0.85	N/R	N/A	MPT	F
^^^	1.31	N/R	N/A					
2101 – 2400	1.31	JTR	(2) H	0.85	JTR	(2) C	MPT	G
^^^				1.00	N/R	N/A	MPT	G
2401 – 2700	1.61	JTR	(2) H	1.31	N/R	N/A	—	H
2701 – 3000	Not Designed			1.31	JTR	(2) H	—	I

Table 2–22M 1.80 m Coil/Sheet Stock/T25a/T25b (TDC/TDF) Duct Reinforcement

N/R   - Not Required
N/A   - Not Applicable
JTR   - Joint Tie Rod
MPT   - Mid Panel Tie Rod(s)
(2) (X)   - Indicates 2 external reinforcements of class (X) to be used in lieu of Joint Tie Rods

1 in. wg Static Pos. or Neg. Duct Dimension	6 ft Joints			6 ft Joints w/3 ft Reinf. Spacing				
^	Min ga	Joint Reinf.	Alt. Joint Reinf.	Joints/Reinf.			Int. Reinf.	
^	^	^	^	Min ga	Joint Reinf.	Alt. Joint Reinf.	Tie Rod	Alt. Reinf.
10 in. and under	26	N/R	N/A	colspan="5" rowspan="10"	Use 6 ft Joints				
11 – 12 in.	26	N/R	N/A					
13 – 14 in.	26	N/R	N/A					
15 – 16 in.	26	N/R	N/A					
17 – 18 in.	26	N/R	N/A					
19 – 20 in.	26	N/R	N/A					
21 – 22 in.	26	N/R	N/A					
23 – 24 in.	26	N/R	N/A					
25 – 26 in.	26	N/R	N/A					
27 – 28 in.	26	N/R	N/A					
29 – 30 in.	26	N/R	N/A					
31 – 36 in.	24	N/R	N/A	26	N/R	N/A	MPT	C
37 – 42 in.	22	N/R	N/A	26	N/R	N/A	MPT	D
43 – 48 in.	20	N/R	N/A	24	N/R	N/A	MPT	E
49 – 54 in.	20	N/R	N/A	24	N/R	N/A	MPT	E
55 – 60 in.	20	N/R	N/A	22	N/R	N/A	MPT	F
61 – 72 in.	20	JTR	(2) E	22	N/R	N/A	MPT	F
^	18	N/R	N/A					
73 – 84 in.	18	JTR	(2) H	20	JTR	(2) E	MPT	H
^				18	N/R	N/A	MPT	H
85 – 96 in.	16	JTR	(2) H	20	JTR	(2) H	2 MPT	I
97 – 108 in.	colspan="3" rowspan="2"	Not Designed			18	JTR	(2) H	—	I
109 – 120 in.				18	JTR	(2) H	—	I

Table 2–23 6 ft Coil/Sheet Stock/T25a/T25b (TDC/TDF) Duct Reinforcement

N/R - Not Required

N/A - Not Applicable

JTR - Joint Tie Rod

MPT - Mid Panel Tie Rod(s)

(2) (X) - Indicates 2 external reinforcements of class (X) to be used in lieu of Joint Tie Rods

250 Pa Static Pos. or Neg. Duct Dimension (mm)	1.80 m Joints			1.80 m Joints w/0.90 m Reinf. Spacing					
:::	Min (mm)	Joint Reinf.	Alt. Joint Reinf.	Joints/Reinf.			Int. Reinf.	
:::	:::	:::	:::	Min (mm)	Joint Reinf.	Alt. Joint Reinf.	Tie Rod	Alt. Reinf.
250 and under	0.55	N/R	N/A	Use 1.80 m Joints				
251 – 300	0.55	N/R	N/A	^^				
301 – 350	0.55	N/R	N/A	^^				
351 – 400	0.55	N/R	N/A	^^				
401 – 450	0.55	N/R	N/A	^^				
451 – 500	0.55	N/R	N/A	^^				
501 – 550	0.55	N/R	N/A	^^				
551 – 600	0.55	N/R	N/A	^^				
601 – 650	0.55	N/R	N/A	^^				
651 – 700	0.55	N/R	N/A	^^				
701 – 750	0.55	N/R	N/A	^^				
751 – 900	0.70	N/R	N/A	0.55	N/R	N/A	MPT	C
901 – 1000	0.85	N/R	N/A	0.55	N/R	N/A	MPT	D
1001 – 1200	1.00	N/R	N/A	0.70	N/R	N/A	MPT	E
1201 – 1300	1.00	N/R	N/A	0.70	N/R	N/A	MPT	E
1301 – 1500	1.00	N/R	N/A	0.85	N/R	N/A	MPT	F
1501 – 1800	1.00	JTR	(2) E	0.85	N/R	N/A	MPT	F
:::	1.31	N/R	N/A					
1801 – 2100	1.31	JTR	(2) H	1.00	JTR	(2) E	MPT	H
:::				1.31	N/R	N/A	MPT	H
2101 – 2400	1.61	JTR	(2) H	1.00	JTR	(2) H	2 MPT	I
2401 – 2700	Not Designed			1.31	JTR	(2) H	—	I
2701 – 3000	^^			1.31	JTR	(2) H	—	I

Table 2–23M 1.80 m Coil/Sheet Stock/T25a/T25b (TDC/TDF) Duct Reinforcement

N/R - Not Required
N/A - Not Applicable
JTR - Joint Tie Rod
MPT - Mid Panel Tie Rod(s)
(2) (X) - Indicates 2 external reinforcements of class (X) to be used in lieu of Joint Tie Rods

2 in. wg Static Pos. or Neg. Duct Dimension	6 ft Joints			6 ft Joints w/3 ft Reinf. Spacing				
^	Min ga	Joint Reinf.	Alt. Joint Reinf.	Joints/Reinf.			Int. Reinf.	
^	^	^	^	Min ga	Joint Reinf.	Alt. Joint Reinf.	Tie Rod	Alt. Reinf.
10 in. and under	26	N/R	N/A	Use 6 ft Joints				
11 – 12 in.	26	N/R	N/A	^				
13 – 14 in.	26	N/R	N/A	^				
15 – 16 in.	26	N/R	N/A	^				
17 – 18 in.	26	N/R	N/A	^				
19 – 20 in.	26	N/R	N/A	^				
21 – 22 in.	26	N/R	N/A	^				
23 – 24 in.	26	N/R	N/A	^				
25 – 26 in.	24	N/R	N/A	26	N/R	N/A	MPT	C
27 – 28 in.	22	N/R	N/A	26	N/R	N/A	MPT	D
29 – 30 in.	22	N/R	N/A	26	N/R	N/A	MPT	D
31 – 36 in.	22	N/R	N/A	24	N/R	N/A	MPT	E
37 – 42 in.	20	N/R	N/A	24	N/R	N/A	MPT	E
43 – 48 in.	20	JTR	(2) E	22	N/R	N/A	MPT	F
^	18	N/R	N/A					
49 – 54 in.	18	JTR	(2) H	22	JTR	(2) C	2 MPT	G
^				20	N/R	N/A	2 MPT	G
55 – 60 in.	18	JTR	(2) H	22	JTR	(2) C	2 MPT	G
^				20	N/R	N/A	2 MPT	G
61 – 72 in.	16	JTR	(2) H	20	JTR	(2) E	2 MPT	H
73 – 84 in.	Not Designed			20	JTR	(2) H	2 MPT	I
85 – 96 in.	^			18	JTR	(2) H	2 MPT	I
97 – 108 in.	^			18	JTR	(2) I	—	K
109 – 120 in.	^			16	JTR	(2) I	—	K

Table 2–24 6 ft Coil/Sheet Stock/T25a/T25b (TDC/TDF) Duct Reinforcement

N/R — Not Required
N/A — Not Applicable
JTR — Joint Tie Rod
MPT — Mid Panel Tie Rod(s)
(2) (X) — Indicates 2 external reinforcements of class (X) to be used in lieu of Joint Tie Rods

500 Pa Static Pos. or Neg. Duct Dimension (mm)	1.80 m Joints Min (mm)	Joint Reinf.	Alt. Joint Reinf.	1.80 m Joints w/0.90 m Reinf. Spacing Joints/Reinf. Min (mm)	Joint Reinf.	Alt. Joint Reinf.	Int. Reinf. Tie Rod	Alt. Reinf.
250 and under	0.55	N/R	N/A					
251 – 300	0.55	N/R	N/A					
301 – 350	0.55	N/R	N/A					
351 – 400	0.55	N/R	N/A		Use 1.80 m Joints			
401 – 450	0.55	N/R	N/A					
451 – 500	0.55	N/R	N/A					
501 – 550	0.55	N/R	N/A					
551 – 600	0.55	N/R	N/A					
601 – 650	0.70	N/R	N/A	0.55	N/R	N/A	MPT	C
651 – 700	0.85	N/R	N/A	0.55	N/R	N/A	MPT	D
701 – 750	0.85	N/R	N/A	0.55	N/R	N/A	MPT	D
751 – 900	0.85	N/R	N/A	0.70	N/R	N/A	MPT	E
901 – 1000	1.00	N/R	N/A	0.70	N/R	N/A	MPT	E
1001 – 1200	1.00	JTR	(2) E	0.85	N/R	N/A	MPT	F
1001 – 1200	1.31	N/R	N/A					
1201 – 1300	1.31	JTR	(2) H	0.85	JTR	(2) C	2 MPT	G
1201 – 1300				1.00	N/R	N/A	2 MPT	G
1301 – 1500	1.31	JTR	(2) H	0.85	JTR	(2) C	2 MPT	G
1301 – 1500				1.00	N/R	N/A	2 MPT	G
1501 – 1800	1.61	JTR	(2) H	1.00	JTR	(2) E	2 MPT	H
1801 – 2100	Not Designed			1.00	JTR	(2) H	2 MPT	I
2101 – 2400	Not Designed			1.31	JTR	(2) H	2 MPT	I
2401 – 2700	Not Designed			1.31	JTR	(2) I	—	K
2701 – 3000	Not Designed			1.61	JTR	(2) I	—	K

Table 2–24M 1.80 m Coil/Sheet Stock/T25a/T25b (TDC/TDF) Duct Reinforcement

N/R - Not Required
N/A - Not Applicable
JTR - Joint Tie Rod
MPT - Mid Panel Tie Rod(s)
(2) (X) - Indicates 2 external reinforcements of class (X) to be used in lieu of Joint Tie Rods

3 in. wg Static Pos. or Neg. Duct Dimension	6 ft Joints Min ga	6 ft Joints Joint Reinf.	6 ft Joints Alt. Joint Reinf.	6 ft Joints w/3 ft Reinf. Spacing Joints/Reinf. Min ga	6 ft Joints w/3 ft Reinf. Spacing Joints/Reinf. Joint Reinf.	6 ft Joints w/3 ft Reinf. Spacing Joints/Reinf. Alt. Joint Reinf.	6 ft Joints w/3 ft Reinf. Spacing Int. Reinf. Tie Rod	6 ft Joints w/3 ft Reinf. Spacing Int. Reinf. Alt. Reinf.
10 in. and under	26	N/R	N/A	Use 6 ft Joints				
11 – 12 in.	26	N/R	N/A	Use 6 ft Joints				
13 – 14 in.	24	N/R	N/A	26	N/R	N/A	MPT	C
15 – 16 in.	24	N/R	N/A	26	N/R	N/A	MPT	C
17 – 18 in.	24	N/R	N/A	26	N/R	N/A	MPT	C
19 – 20 in.	22	N/R	N/A	26	N/R	N/A	MPT	C
21 – 22 in.	22	N/R	N/A	26	N/R	N/A	MPT	D
23 – 24 in.	22	N/R	N/A	26	N/R	N/A	MPT	D
25 – 26 in.	22	N/R	N/A	26	N/R	N/A	MPT	D
27 – 28 in.	20	N/R	N/A	24	N/R	N/A	MPT	E
29 – 30 in.	20	N/R	N/A	24	N/R	N/A	MPT	E
31 – 36 in.	18	N/R	N/A	22	N/R	N/A	MPT	F
37 – 42 in.	18	N/R	N/A	22	N/R	N/A	MPT	F
43 – 48 in.	18	JTR	(2) H	22	JTR	(2) C	MPT	G
43 – 48 in.				20	N/R	N/A	MPT	G
49 – 54 in.	16	JTR	(2) H	22	JTR	(2) E	2 MPT	H
55 – 60 in.	16	JTR	(2) H	20	JTR	(2) E	2 MPT	H
61 – 72 in.	Not Designed			20	JTR	(2) H	2 MPT	I
73 – 84 in.	Not Designed			18	JTR	(2) H	2 MPT	J
85 – 96 in.	Not Designed			18	JTR	(2) I	2 MPT	K
97 – 108 in.				16	JTR	(2) K	✕	L
109 – 120 in.				16	JTR	(2) K	✕	L

Table 2–25 6 ft Coil/Sheet Stock/T25a/T25b (TDC/TDF) Duct Reinforcement

N/R - Not Required
N/A - Not Applicable
JTR - Joint Tie Rod
MPT - Mid Panel Tie Rod(s)
(2) (X) - Indicates 2 external reinforcements of class (X) to be used in lieu of Joint Tie Rods

750 Pa Static Pos. or Neg. Duct Dimension (mm)	1.80 m Joints			1.80 m Joints w/0.90 m Reinf. Spacing				
:::	Min (mm)	Joint Reinf.	Alt. Joint Reinf.	Joints/Reinf.			Int. Reinf.	
:::	:::	:::	:::	Min (mm)	Joint Reinf.	Alt. Joint Reinf.	Tie Rod	Alt. Reinf.
250 and under	0.55	N/R	N/A	Use 1.80 m Joints				
251 – 300	0.55	N/R	N/A	:::				
301 – 350	0.70	N/R	N/A	0.55	N/R	N/A	MPT	C
351 – 400	0.70	N/R	N/A	0.55	N/R	N/A	MPT	C
401 – 450	0.70	N/R	N/A	0.55	N/R	N/A	MPT	C
451 – 500	0.85	N/R	N/A	0.55	N/R	N/A	MPT	C
501 – 550	0.85	N/R	N/A	0.55	N/R	N/A	MPT	D
551 – 600	0.85	N/R	N/A	0.55	N/R	N/A	MPT	D
601 – 650	0.85	N/R	N/A	0.55	N/R	N/A	MPT	D
651 – 700	1.00	N/R	N/A	0.70	N/R	N/A	MPT	E
701 – 750	1.00	N/R	N/A	0.70	N/R	N/A	MPT	E
751 – 900	1.31	N/R	N/A	0.85	N/R	N/A	MPT	F
901 – 1000	1.31	N/R	N/A	0.85	N/R	N/A	MPT	F
1001 – 1200	1.31	JTR	(2) H	0.85	JTR	(2) C	MPT	G
:::				1.00	N/R	N/A	MPT	G
1201 – 1300	1.61	JTR	(2) H	0.85	JTR	(2) E	2 MPT	H
1301 – 1500	1.61	JTR	(2) H	1.00	JTR	(2) E	2 MPT	H
1501 – 1800	Not Designed			1.00	JTR	(2) H	2 MPT	I
1801 – 2100	:::			1.31	JTR	(2) H	2 MPT	J
2101 – 2400	:::			1.31	JTR	(2) I	2 MPT	K
2401 – 2700	:::			1.61	JTR	(2) K		L
2701 – 3000	:::			1.61	JTR	(2) K		L

Table 2–25M 1.80 m Coil/Sheet Stock/T25a/T25b (TDC/TDF) Duct Reinforcement

N/R - Not Required
N/A - Not Applicable
JTR - Joint Tie Rod
MPT - Mid Panel Tie Rod(s)
(2) (X) - Indicates 2 external reinforcements of class (X) to be used in lieu of Joint Tie Rods

4 in. wg Static Pos. or Neg. Duct Dimension	6 ft Joints			6 ft Joints w/3 ft Reinf. Spacing				
^	Min ga	Joint Reinf.	Alt. Joint Reinf.	Joints/Reinf.			Int. Reinf.	
^	^	^	^	Min ga	Joint Reinf.	Alt. Joint Reinf.	Tie Rod	Alt. Reinf.
8 in. and under	26	N/R	N/A	Use 6 ft Joints					
9 – 10 in.	24	N/R	N/A	26	N/R	N/A	MPT	B
11 – 12 in.	24	N/R	N/A	26	N/R	N/A	MPT	C
13 – 14 in.	22	N/R	N/A	26	N/R	N/A	MPT	C
15 – 16 in.	22	N/R	N/A	26	N/R	N/A	MPT	C
17 – 18 in.	22	N/R	N/A	26	N/R	N/A	MPT	C
19 – 20 in.	22	N/R	N/A	26	N/R	N/A	MPT	D
21 – 22 in.	20	N/R	N/A	26	N/R	N/A	MPT	D
23 – 24 in.	20	N/R	N/A	24	N/R	N/A	MPT	E
25 – 26 in.	20	N/R	N/A	24	N/R	N/A	MPT	E
27 – 28 in.	20	N/R	N/A	24	N/R	N/A	MPT	E
29 – 30 in.	18	N/R	N/A	24	N/R	N/A	MPT	E
31 – 36 in.	18	N/R	N/A	22	N/R	N/A	MPT	F
37 – 42 in.	16	JTR	(2) H	22	JTR	(2) C	MPT	G
^	^	^	^	20	N/R	N/A	MPT	G
43 – 48 in.	16	JTR	(2) H	20	JTR	(2) E	MPT	H
^	^	^	^	18	N/R	N/A	MPT	H
49 – 54 in.	16	JTR	(2) H	20	JTR	(2) H	MPT	I
55 – 60 in.	Not Designed			20	JTR	(2) H	2 MPT	I
61 – 72 in.	^			18	JTR	(2) H	2 MPT	J
73 – 84 in.	^			16	JTR	(2) I	2 MPT	K
85 – 96 in.	^			16	JTR	(2) K	N/A	L
97 – 108 in.	^			16	JTR	(2) K	—	L
109 – 120 in.	^			16	JTR	(2) K	—	L

Table 2-26 6 ft Coil/Sheet Stock/T25a/T25b (TDC/TDF) Duct Reinforcement

N/R - Not Required
N/A - Not Applicable
JTR - Joint Tie Rod
MPT - Mid Panel Tie Rod(s)
(2) (X) - Indicates 2 external reinforcements of class (X) to be used in lieu of Joint Tie Rods

1000 Pa Static Pos. or Neg. Duct Dimension (mm)	1.80 m Joints Min (mm)	1.80 m Joints Joint Reinf.	1.80 m Joints Alt. Joint Reinf.	1.80 m Joints w/0.90 m Reinf. Spacing Joints/Reinf. Min (mm)	Joints/Reinf. Joint Reinf.	Joints/Reinf. Alt. Joint Reinf.	Int. Reinf. Tie Rod	Int. Reinf. Alt. Reinf.
200 and under	0.55	N/R	N/A	Use 1.80 m Joints			
230 – 250	0.70	N/R	N/A	0.55	N/R	N/A	MPT	B
251 – 300	0.70	N/R	N/A	0.55	N/R	N/A	MPT	C
301 – 350	0.85	N/R	N/A	0.55	N/R	N/A	MPT	C
351 – 400	0.85	N/R	N/A	0.55	N/R	N/A	MPT	C
401 – 450	0.85	N/R	N/A	0.55	N/R	N/A	MPT	C
451 – 500	0.85	N/R	N/A	0.55	N/R	N/A	MPT	D
501 – 550	1.00	N/R	N/A	0.55	N/R	N/A	MPT	D
551 – 600	1.00	N/R	N/A	0.70	N/R	N/A	MPT	E
601 – 650	1.00	N/R	N/A	0.70	N/R	N/A	MPT	E
651 – 700	1.00	N/R	N/A	0.70	N/R	N/A	MPT	E
701 – 750	1.31	N/R	N/A	0.70	N/R	N/A	MPT	E
751 – 900	1.31	N/R	N/A	0.85	N/R	N/A	MPT	F
901 – 1000	1.61	JTR	(2) H	0.85	JTR	(2) C	MPT	G
901 – 1000				1.00	N/R	N/A	MPT	G
1001 – 1200	1.61	JTR	(2) H	1.00	JTR	(2) E	MPT	H
1001 – 1200				1.31	N/R	N/A	MPT	H
1201 – 1300	1.61	JTR	(2) H	1.00	JTR	(2) H	MPT	I
1301 – 1500	Not Designed			1.00	JTR	(2) H	2 MPT	I
1501 – 1800	Not Designed			1.31	JTR	(2) H	2 MPT	J
1801 – 2100	Not Designed			1.61	JTR	(2) I	2 MPT	K
2101 – 2400	Not Designed			1.61	JTR	(2) K	N/A	L
2401 – 2700	Not Designed			1.61	JTR	(2) K	—	L
2701 – 3000	Not Designed			1.61	JTR	(2) K	—	L

Table 2–26M 1.80 m Coil/Sheet Stock/T25a/T25b (TDC/TDF) Duct Reinforcement

N/R - Not Required
N/A - Not Applicable
JTR - Joint Tie Rod
MPT - Mid Panel Tie Rod(s)
(2) (X) - Indicates 2 external reinforcements of class (X) to be used in lieu of Joint Tie Rods

6 in. wg Static Pos. or Neg. Duct Dimension	6 ft Joints			6 ft Joints w/3 ft Reinf. Spacing				
^	Min ga	Joint Reinf.	Alt. Joint Reinf.	Joints/Reinf.			Int. Reinf.	
^	^	^	^	Min ga	Joint Reinf.	Alt. Joint Reinf.	Tie Rod	Alt. Reinf.
8 in. and under	24	N/R	N/A	26	N/R	N/A	MPT	B
9 – 10 in.	24	N/R	N/A	26	N/R	N/A	MPT	B
11 – 12 in.	22	N/R	N/A	26	N/R	N/A	MPT	C
13 – 14 in.	20	N/R	N/A	26	N/R	N/A	MPT	C
15 – 16 in.	20	N/R	N/A	26	N/R	N/A	MPT	D
17 – 18 in.	20	N/R	N/A	26	N/R	N/A	MPT	D
19 – 20 in.	20	N/R	N/A	24	N/R	N/A	MPT	D
21 – 22 in.	20	N/R	N/A	24	N/R	N/A	MPT	E
23 – 24 in.	20	N/R	N/A	24	N/R	N/A	MPT	E
25 – 26 in.	18	N/R	N/A	22	N/R	N/A	MPT	F
27 – 28 in.	18	N/R	N/A	22	N/R	N/A	MPT	F
29 – 30 in.	18	N/R	N/A	22	N/R	N/A	MPT	F
31 – 36 in.	16	JTR	(2) H	20	JTR	(2) E	MPT	H
37 – 42 in.	16	JTR	(2) H	20	JTR	(2) E	MPT	H
43 – 48 in.	Not Designed			20	JTR	(2) H	2 MPT	I
49 – 54 in.	^		^	18	JTR	(2) H	MPT	I
55 – 60 in.	^		^	18	JTR	(2) H	2 MPT	J
61 – 72 in.	^		^	16	JTR	(2) I	2 MPT	K
73 – 84 in.	^		^	16	JTR	(2) K	N/A	L
85 – 96 in.	^		^	16	JTR	(2) L	N/A	It
97 – 108 in.	^		^	16	JTR	(2) L	╳	Jt
109 – 120 in.	^		^	16	JTR	(2) L	╳	Kt

Table 2–27 6 ft Coil/Sheet Stock/T25a/T25b (TDC/TDF) Duct Reinforcement

N/R   - Not Required
N/A   - Not Applicable
JTR   - Joint Tie Rod
MPT   - Mid Panel Tie Rod(s)
(2) (X)   - Indicates 2 external reinforcements of class (X) to be used in lieu of Joint Tie Rods

Note: t following Reinforcement Class letter indicates tie rod required.

1500 Pa Static Pos. or Neg. Duct Dimension	1.80 m Joints				1.80 m Joints w/0.90 m Reinf. Spacing				
	Min (mm)	Joint Reinf.	Alt. Joint Reinf.		Joints/Reinf.			Int. Reinf.	
					Min (mm)	Joint Reinf.	Alt. Joint Reinf.	Tie Rod	Alt. Reinf.
200 and under	0.70	N/R	N/A		0.55	N/R	N/A	MPT	B
230 – 250	0.70	N/R	N/A		0.55	N/R	N/A	MPT	B
251 – 300	0.85	N/R	N/A		0.55	N/R	N/A	MPT	C
301 – 350	1.00	N/R	N/A		0.55	N/R	N/A	MPT	C
351 – 400	1.00	N/R	N/A		0.55	N/R	N/A	MPT	D
401 – 450	1.00	N/R	N/A		0.55	N/R	N/A	MPT	D
451 – 500	1.00	N/R	N/A		0.70	N/R	N/A	MPT	D
501 – 550	1.00	N/R	N/A		0.70	N/R	N/A	MPT	E
551 – 600	1.00	N/R	N/A		0.70	N/R	N/A	MPT	E
601 – 650	1.31	N/R	N/A		0.85	N/R	N/A	MPT	F
651 – 700	1.31	N/R	N/A		0.85	N/R	N/A	MPT	F
701 – 750	1.31	N/R	N/A		0.85	N/R	N/A	MPT	F
751 – 900	1.61	JTR	(2) H		1.00	JTR	(2) E	MPT	H
901 – 1000	1.61	JTR	(2) H		1.00	JTR	(2) E	MPT	H
1001 – 1200	Not Designed				1.00	JTR	(2) H	2 MPT	I
1201 – 1300					1.31	JTR	(2) H	MPT	I
1301 – 1500					1.31	JTR	(2) H	2 MPT	J
1501 – 1800					1.61	JTR	(2) I	2 MPT	K
1801 – 2100					1.61	JTR	(2) K	N/A	L
2101 – 2400					1.61	JTR	(2) L	N/A	It
2401 – 2700					1.61	JTR	(2) L	—	Jt
2701 – 3000					1.61	JTR	(2) L	—	Kt

Table 2–27M 1.80 m Coil/Sheet Stock/T25a/T25b (TDC/TDF) Duct Reinforcement

N/R - Not Required
N/A - Not Applicable
JTR - Joint Tie Rod
MPT - Mid Panel Tie Rod(s)
(2) (X) - Indicates 2 external reinforcements of class (X) to be used in lieu of Joint Tie Rods

Note: t following Reinforcement Class letter indicates tie rod required.

10 in. wg Static Pos. or Neg. Duct Dimension	6 ft Joints			6 ft Joints w/3 ft Reinf. Spacing				
				Joints/Reinf.			Int. Reinf.	
	Min ga	Joint Reinf.	Alt. Joint Reinf.	Min ga	Joint Reinf.	Alt. Joint Reinf.	Tie Rod	Alt. Reinf.
8 in. and under	20	N/R	N/A	26	N/R	N/A	N/A	C
9 – 10 in.	20	N/R	N/A	26	N/R	N/A	N/A	C
11 – 12 in.	20	N/R	N/A	26	N/R	N/A	N/A	C
13 – 14 in.	20	N/R	N/A	24	N/R	N/A	N/A	D
15 – 16 in.	18	N/R	N/A	24	N/R	N/A	N/A	E
17 – 18 in.	18	N/R	N/A	24	N/R	N/A	N/A	E
19 – 20 in.	18	N/R	N/A	22	N/R	N/A	N/A	F
21 – 22 in.	18	N/R	N/A	22	JTR	(2) C	N/A	F
23 – 24 in.	18	N/R	N/A	22	JTR	(2) C	N/A	G
				20	N/R	N/A	N/A	G
25 – 26 in.	16	JTR	(2) H	22	JTR	(2) C	N/A	G
				20	N/R	N/A	N/A	G
27 – 28 in.	16	JTR	(2) H	20	JTR	(2) E	N/A	H
				18	N/R	N/A	N/A	H
29 – 30 in.	16	JTR	(2) H	20	JTR	(2) E	N/A	H
				18	N/R	N/A	N/A	H
31 – 36 in.				20	JTR	(2) H	N/A	I
37 – 42 in.				18	JTR	(2) H	N/A	I
43 – 48 in.				18	JTR	(2) I	N/A	J
49 – 54 in.				18	JTR	(2) I	N/A	K
55 – 60 in.				16	JTR	(2) K	N/A	L
61 – 72 in.				16	JTR	(2) K	N/A	L
73 – 84 in.				Not Designed				
85 – 96 in.								
97 – 108 in.								
109 – 120 in.								

Table 2–28 6 ft Coil/Sheet Stock/T25a/T25b (TDC/TDF) Duct Reinforcement

N/R   - Not Required
N/A   - Not Applicable
JTR   - Joint Tie Rod
MPT   - Mid Panel Tie Rod(s)
(2) (X)   - Indicates 2 external reinforcements of class (X) to be used in lieu of Joint Tie Rods

2500 Pa Static Pos. or Neg. Duct Dimension (mm)	1.80 m Joints			1.80 m Joints w/0.90 m Reinf. Spacing				
^	Min (mm)	Joint Reinf.	Alt. Joint Reinf.	Joints/Reinf.			Int. Reinf.	
^	^	^	^	Min (mm)	Joint Reinf.	Alt. Joint Reinf.	Tie Rod	Alt. Reinf.
200 and under	1.00	N/R	N/A	0.55	N/R	N/A	N/A	C
230 – 250	1.00	N/R	N/A	0.55	N/R	N/A	N/A	C
251 – 300	1.00	N/R	N/A	0.55	N/R	N/A	N/A	C
301 – 350	1.00	N/R	N/A	0.70	N/R	N/A	N/A	D
351 – 400	1.31	N/R	N/A	0.70	N/R	N/A	N/A	E
401 – 450	1.31	N/R	N/A	0.70	N/R	N/A	N/A	E
451 – 500	1.31	N/R	N/A	0.85	N/R	N/A	N/A	F
501 – 550	1.31	N/R	N/A	0.85	JTR	(2) C	N/A	F
551 – 600	1.31	N/R	N/A	0.85	JTR	(2) C	N/A	G
^				1.00	N/R	N/A	N/A	G
601 – 650	1.61	JTR	(2) H	0.85	JTR	(2) C	N/A	G
^				1.00	N/R	N/A	N/A	G
651 – 700	1.61	JTR	(2) H	1.00	JTR	(2) E	N/A	H
^				1.31	N/R	N/A	N/A	H
701 – 750	1.61	JTR	(2) H	1.00	JTR	(2) E	N/A	H
^				1.31	N/R	N/A	N/A	H
751 – 900				1.00	JTR	(2) H	N/A	I
901 – 1000				1.31	JTR	(2) H	N/A	I
1001 – 1200				1.31	JTR	(2) I	N/A	J
1201 – 1300				1.31	JTR	(2) I	N/A	K
1301 – 1500				1.61	JTR	(2) K	N/A	L
1501 – 1800				1.61	JTR	(2) K	N/A	L
1801 – 2100	Not Designed							
2101 – 2400	^							
2401 – 2700	^							
2701 – 3000	^							

Table 2–28M 1.80 m Coil/Sheet Stock/T25a/T25b (TDC/TDF) Duct Reinforcement

N/R - Not Required
N/A - Not Applicable
JTR - Joint Tie Rod
MPT - Mid Panel Tie Rod(s)
(2) (X) - Indicates 2 external reinforcements of class (X) to be used in lieu of Joint Tie Rods

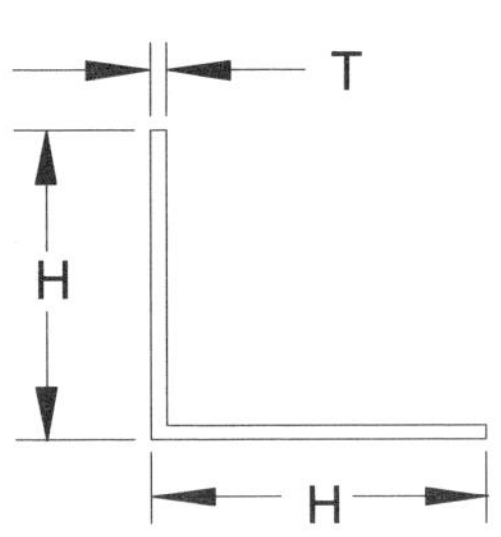

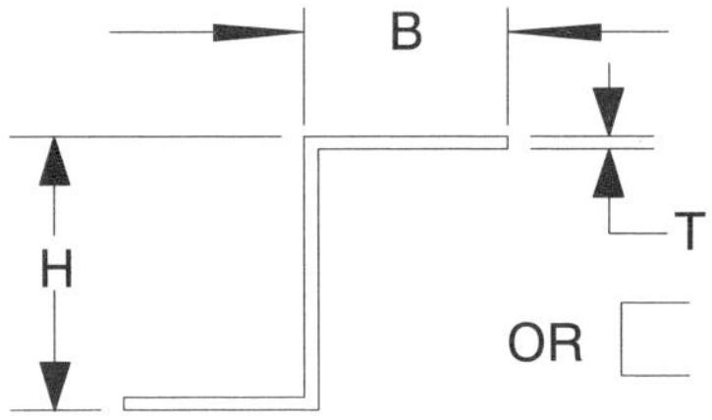

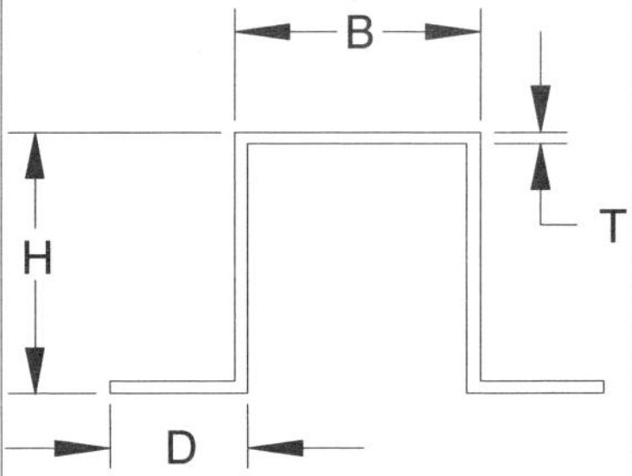

Reinf. Class	EI*	Angle H × T (MIN)	WT/LF	Channel or Zee H × B × T (MIN)	WT/LF	Hat Section H × B × D × T (MIN)	WT/LF
A	0.43	Use C		Use B		Use F	
B	1.0	Use C		¾ × ½ × 20 ga	0.24	Use F	
C	1.9	C 1 × 16 ga C ¾ × ⅛	0.40 0.57	¾ × ½ × 18 ga 1 × ¾ × 20 ga	0.31	Use F	
D	2.7	H ¾ × ⅛ C 1 × ⅛	0.57 0.80	1 × ¾ × 18 ga	0.45	Use F	
E	6.5	C 1 ¼ × 12 ga H 1 × ⅛	0.90	2 × 1 ⅛ × 20 ga	0.60	Use F	
F	12.8	H 1 ¼ × ⅛	1.02	1 ½ × ¾ × 18 ga	0.54	1 ½ × ¾ × ⅝ × 20 ga 1 ½ × 1 ½ × ¾ × 20 ga	0.90 0.83
G	15.8	1 ½ × ⅛	1.23	1 ½ × ¾ × 16 ga	0.66	1 ½ × ¾ × ⅝ × 18 ga	0.80
H	26.4	1 ½ × 3/16 2 × ⅛	1.78 1.65	1 ½ × ¾ × ⅛	1.31	1 ½ × 1 ½ × ¾ × 18 ga 2 × 1 × ¾ × 20 ga	1.08 0.90
I	69	C 2 × 3/16 2 ½ × ⅛	2.44 2.10	2 × 1 ⅛ × 12 ga 3 × 1 ⅛ × 16 ga	1.60 1.05	2 × 1 × ¾ × 16 ga	1.44
J	80	H 2 × 3/16 C 2 × ¼ 2 ½ × ⅛ (+)	2.44 3.20 2.10	2 × 1 ⅛ × ⅛	1.85	2 × 1 × ¾ × 12 ga 2 ½ × 2 × ¾ × 18 ga	2.45 1.53
K	103	2 ½ × 3/16	3.10	3 × 1 ⅛ × 12 ga	2.00	2 ½ × 2 × ¾ × 16 ga 3 × 1 ½ × ¾ × 16 ga	1.88 2.00
L	207	H 2 ½ × ¼	4.10	3 × 1 ⅛ × ⅛	2.29	2 ½ × 2 × ¾ × ⅛ 3 × 1 ½ × ¾ × 12 ga	3.70 3.40

Table 2–29 Intermediate Reinforcement

See Section 2.1.4. *Effective EI is number listed times 10^5 before adjustment for bending moment capacity. C and H denote cold formed and hot rolled ratings; when neither is listed, either may be used. *See* tie rod options elsewhere.

NOTES:

a. (+) indicates positive pressure use only.

b. Hat Section Dimension "B" may be equal to 2 times Dimension "H" with the same reinforcement class rating.

Reinf. Class	EI*	Angle H × T (MIN) (mm)	KG/LM	Channel or Zee H × B × T (MIN) (mm)	KG/LM	Hat Section H × B × D × T (MIN) (mm)	KG/LM
A	0.12	Use C		Use B		Use F	
B	0.29	Use C		19.1 × 12.7 × 1.00	0.36	Use F	
C	0.55	C 25 × 1.61 C 19.1 × 3.2	0.60 0.85	19.1 × 12.7 × 1.31 25 × 19.1 × 1.00	0.46	Use F	
D	0.78	H 19.1 × 3.2 C 25 × 3.2	0.85 1.19	25 × 19.1 × 1.31	0.67	Use F	
E	1.9	C 31.8 × 2.75 H 25 × 3.2	1.34	51 × 28.6 × 1.00	0.89	Use F	
F	3.7	H 31.8 × 3.2	1.52	38.1 × 19.1 × 1.31	0.80	38.1 × 19.1 × 15.9 × 1.00 38.1 × 38.1 × 19.1 × 1.00	1.34 1.24
G	4.5	38.1 × 3.2	1.83	38.1 × 19.1 × 1.61	0.98	38.1 × 19.1 × 15.9 × 1.31	1.19
H	7.6	38.1 × 4.8 51 × 3.2	2.64 2.46	38.1 × 19.1 × 3.2	1.95	38.1 × 38.1 × 19.1 × 1.31 51 × 25 × 19.1 × 1.00	1.61 1.34
I	20	C 51 × 4.8 63.5 × 3.2	3.63 3.13	51 × 28.6 × 2.5 76 × 28.6 × 1.61	2.38 1.56	51 × 25 × 19.1 × 1.61	2.14
J	23	H 51 × 4.8 C 51 × 6.4 63.5 × 3.2 (+)	3.63 4.76 3.13	51 × 28.6 × 3.2	2.75	51 × 25 × 19.1 × 2.5 63.5 × 51 × 19.1 × 1.31	3.65 2.28
K	30	63.5 × 4.8	4.61	76 × 28.6 × 2.5	2.98	63.5 × 51 × 19.1 × 1.61 76 × 38.1 × 19.1 × 1.61	2.80 2.98
L	60	H 63.5 × 6.4	6.10	76 × 28.6 × 3.2	3.40	63.5 × 51 × 19.1 × 3.2 76 × 38.1 × 19.1 × 2.75	5.51 5.06

Table 2–29M Intermediate Reinforcement

See Section 2.1.4. *Effective EI is number listed times 10^5 before adjustment for bending moment capacity. C and H denote cold formed and hot rolled ratings; when neither is listed, either may be used. *See* tie rod options elsewhere.

NOTES:

a. (+) Indicates positive pressure use only.

b. Hat Section Dimension "B" may be equal to 2 times Dimension "H" with the same reinforcement class rating.

FRAMING CHANNEL (STRUT) MAY BE USED AS DUCT REINFORCEMENT AS FOLLOWS:

Channel (Strut)			Reinforcement Class Per Table 2-29
H	**W**	**GA**	
13/16 in.	13/16 in.	19	A, B, C
13/16 in.	1 5/8 in.	14	D
7/8 in.	1 5/8 in.	12	D, E
1 3/8 in.	1 5/8 in.	12	F, G
2 7/16 in.	1 5/8 in.	12	H, I, J
3 1/4 in.	1 5/8 in.	12	K, L

Table 2–30 Framing Channel

NOTE: Framing channels having the same physical dimensions as those listed above, but fabricated from thicker steel may be used at the reinforcement class assigned to the lighter version.

Channel (Strut)			Reinforcement Class Per Table 2-29M
H	**W**	**MM**	
20.6 mm	20.6 mm	1.1	A, B, C
20.6 mm	41.3 mm	1.8	D
22.2 mm	41.3 mm	2.5	D, E
34.9 mm	41.3 mm	2.5	F, G
61.9 mm	41.3 mm	2.5	H, I, J
82.6 mm	41.3 mm	2.5	K, L

Table 2–30M Framing Channel

NOTE: Framing channels having the same physical dimensions as those listed above, but fabricated from thicker steel may be used at the reinforcement class assigned to the lighter version.

Strut with holes or slots may be used. Consult manufacturer's literature to adjust reinforcement class.

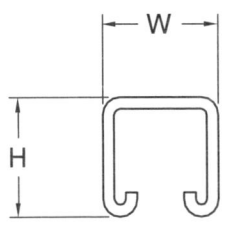

FIGURE 2–4 CHANNEL (STRUT) USED AS DUCT REINFORCEMENT

2.4 TRANSVERSE JOINTS FOR RECTANGULAR DUCT

S1.38 Transverse joints shall be selected and used that are consistent with the static pressure class, applicable sealing requirements, materials involved, duct support intervals, and other provisions for proper assembly of ductwork outlined in the construction standards. The precise type, size, location, and material of fastenings used in joint assemblies are sometimes left open to prudent judgment for the specific service. Notching, bending, folding, and fit-up tolerances shall be appropriate for the composite assembly. When there is a choice of materials and methods, do not use such latitude as to create a deficiency in the integrity of the ductwork.

S1.39 *See* Sections 2.1 and 2.2. Where the text and illustrations in Chapters 2 through 5 indicate certain sealing provisions independent of the provisions in Sections 2.1 and 2.2, they apply regardless of exemptions from sealing shown in Table 1-1.

S1.40 Where bar or angle stock is incorporated in a joint, it shall be secured. Where intermediate type reinforcements are used as supplements for joints, they shall be attached to the duct wall within 3 in. (76 mm) of the joint by weld, bolt, screw, or blind rivet fastening within 2 in. (51 mm) of duct corners and at intervals not exceeding 12 in. (305 mm). Exception: where the ends are tied to members on adjacent sides, the fastening to the duct within 2 in. (51 mm) may be omitted in consideration of the end restraint.

S1.41 Fasteners used on steel duct shall be steel. They may be zinc or cadmium coated. Standard or self-drilling sheet metal screws may be used as appropriate. Blind rivets using pull-through mandrels are not permitted if they leave holes for air leakage. Fastenings shall not project into duct interiors more than ½ in. (13 mm). Where only bolts or welds are specified, other types of fastening are not allowed.

S1.42 Unless otherwise specified, joints shall comply with all of the provisions in Chapter 11 except the commentaries.

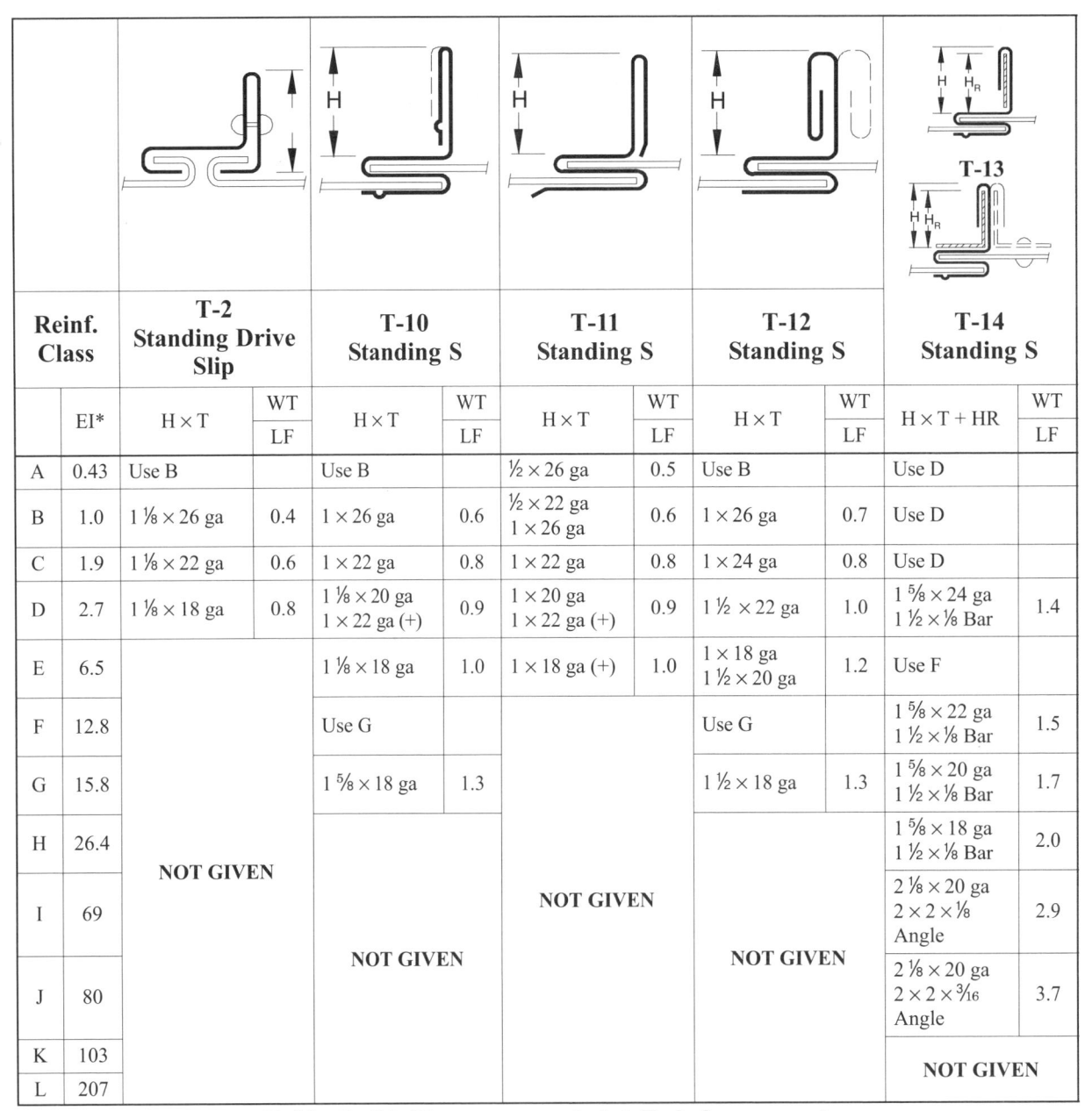

Reinf. Class		T-2 Standing Drive Slip		T-10 Standing S		T-11 Standing S		T-12 Standing S		T-14 Standing S	
	EI*	H × T	WT/LF	H × T	WT/LF	H × T	WT/LF	H × T	WT/LF	H × T + HR	WT/LF
A	0.43	Use B		Use B		½ × 26 ga	0.5	Use B		Use D	
B	1.0	1 ⅛ × 26 ga	0.4	1 × 26 ga	0.6	½ × 22 ga 1 × 26 ga	0.6	1 × 26 ga	0.7	Use D	
C	1.9	1 ⅛ × 22 ga	0.6	1 × 22 ga	0.8	1 × 22 ga	0.8	1 × 24 ga	0.8	Use D	
D	2.7	1 ⅛ × 18 ga	0.8	1 ⅛ × 20 ga 1 × 22 ga (+)	0.9	1 × 20 ga 1 × 22 ga (+)	0.9	1 ½ × 22 ga	1.0	1 ⅝ × 24 ga 1 ½ × ⅛ Bar	1.4
E	6.5			1 ⅛ × 18 ga	1.0	1 × 18 ga (+)	1.0	1 × 18 ga 1 ½ × 20 ga	1.2	Use F	
F	12.8			Use G				Use G		1 ⅝ × 22 ga 1 ½ × ⅛ Bar	1.5
G	15.8			1 ⅝ × 18 ga	1.3			1 ½ × 18 ga	1.3	1 ⅝ × 20 ga 1 ½ × ⅛ Bar	1.7
H	26.4	NOT GIVEN				NOT GIVEN				1 ⅝ × 18 ga 1 ½ × ⅛ Bar	2.0
I	69			NOT GIVEN				NOT GIVEN		2 ⅛ × 20 ga 2 × 2 × ⅛ Angle	2.9
J	80									2 ⅛ × 20 ga 2 × 2 × 3/16 Angle	3.7
K	103									NOT GIVEN	
L	207										

Table 2–31 Transverse Joint Reinforcement

See Section 2.1.4. *Effective EI is number listed times 10^5 before adjustment for bending moment capacity. T-2 and T-10 through T-14 are restricted to 30 in. length at 4 in. wg, to 36 in. length at 3 in. wg and are not recommended for service above 4 in. wg. (+) indicates positive pressure use only.

Reinf. Class	EI*	T-2 Standing Drive Slip H×T (mm)	KG LM	T-10 Standing S H×T (mm)	KG LM	T-11 Standing S H×T (mm)	KG LM	T-12 Standing S H×T (mm)	KG LM	T-14 Standing S H×T + HR (mm)	KG LM
A	0.12	Use B		Use B		12.7 × 0.55	0.74	Use B		Use D	
B	0.29	28.6 × 0.55	0.6	25.x 0.55	0.9	12.7 × 0.85 25 × 0.55	0.9	25 × 0.55	1.0	Use D	
C	0.55	28.6 × 0.85	0.9	25 × 0.85	1.2	25 × 0.85	1.2	25 × 0.70	1.2	Use D	
D	0.78	28.6 × 1.31	1.2	28.6 × 1.00 25 × 0.85 (+)	1.3	25 × 1.00 25 × 0.85 (+)	1.3	Use E	1.5	41.3 × 0.70 38.1 × 3.2 Bar	2.1
E	1.9			28.6 × 1.31	1.5	25 × 1.31 (+)	1.3	25 × 1.31 38.1 × 1.00	1.8	Use F	
F	3.7			Use G				Use G		41.3 × 0.85 38.1 × 3.2 Bar	2.2
G	4.5			41.3 × 1.31	1.9			38.1 × 1.00	1.9	41.3 × 1.00 38.1 × 3.2 Bar	2.6
H	7.6	NOT GIVEN				NOT GIVEN				41.3 × 1.31 38.1 × 3.2 Bar	3.0
I	20									54 × 1.00 51 × 51 × 3.2 Angle	4.3
J	23			NOT GIVEN				NOT GIVEN		54 × 1.00 51 × 51 × 4.76 Angle	5.5
K	30									NOT GIVEN	
L	60										

Table 2–31M Transverse Joint Reinforcement

See Section 2.1.4. *Effective EI is number listed times 10^5 before adjustment for bending moment capacity. T-2 and T-10 through T-14 are restricted to 750 mm length at 1000 Pa, to 914 mm length at 750 Pa and are not recommended for service above 1000 Pa. (+) indicates positive pressure use only.

Reinf. Class	EI*	T-22 Companion Angles H × T	WT / LF	T-24 Flanged T (Nom.)	WT / LF	T-24a Flanged H × T (Nom.)	WT / LF	T-25b Flanged H × T (Nom.)	WT / LF	Slip-On Flange
B	1.0	Use E		Use D		Use D		Use D		
C	1.9	Use E		Use D		Use D		Use D		Consult manufacturers for ratings established by performance documented to functional criteria in Chapter 11. See text S1.18 on page 2.4.
D	2.7	Use E		26 ga	0.5	1 × 22 ga	0.4	26 ga	0.5	
E	6.5	C 1 × 1/8	1.7	24 ga	0.6	Use F		24 ga	0.6	
F	12.8	H 1 × 1/8	1.7	22 ga	0.7	1½ × 20 ga	0.6	22 ga	0.7	
G	15.8	1¼ × 1/8	2.1	22 ga (R) 20 ga	1.0	1½ × 18 ga	0.8	22 ga (R) 20 ga	1.0	
H	26.4	C 1½ × 1/8 (+) H 1½ × 1/8	2.6	18 ga	1.1			18 ga	1.1	
I	69	1½ × ¼	3.7	20 ga (R)	1.0	SEE TIE ROD TEXT		20 ga (R)	1.0	
J	80	1½ × ¼ (+) 2 × 1/8	4.7	18 ga (R)	1.1			18 ga (R)	1.1	
K	103	2 × 3/16	5	18 ga (R)	1.1			18 ga (R)	1.1	
L	207	H 2 × ¼	6.5	18 ga (R)	1.1			18 ga (R)	1.1	

Table 2–32 Transverse Joint Reinforcement

See Section 2.1.4. *Effective EI is number listed times 10^5 before adjustment for bending moment capacity. For T-22, see tie rod downsize options in Tables 2-1 to 2-7; one rod for two angles. (R) means Tie Rodded. Accepted Pressure Mode for T-24a is (+) or (-) 2 in. wg maximum. *See* Figures 2-5 and 2-6 and tie rod text. (+) indicates positive pressure use only.

Reinf. Class		T-22 Companion Angles		T-24 Flanged		T-24a Flanged		T-25b Flanged		Slip-On Flange
Reinf. Class	EI*	H × T (mm)	KG/LM	T (Nom.) (mm)	KG/LM	H × T (Nom.) (mm)	KG/LM	H × T (Nom.) (mm)	KG/LM	
B	0.29	Use E		Use D		Use D		Use D		Consult manufacturers for ratings established by performance documented to functional criteria in Chapter 11. *See* text S1.18 on page 2.4.
C	0.55	Use E		Use D		Use D		Use D		
D	0.78	Use E		0.55	0.7	25 × 0.85	0.6	0.55.	0.7	
E	1.90	25 × 3.2	2.5	0.70	0.9	Use F		0.70.	0.9	
F	3.70	H 25 × 3.2	2.5	0.85	1.0	38.1 × 1.00	0.9	0.85.	1.0	
G	4.50	31.8 × 3.2	3.1	0.85 (R) 1.00	1.5	38.1 × 1.31	1.2	0.85 (R) 1.00	1.5	
H	7.6	C (+) H 38.1 × 3.2	3.9	1.31	1.6			1.31	1.6	
I	20	38.1 × 6.4	5.5	1.00 (R)	1.5	SEE TIE ROD TEXT		1.00 (R)	1.5	
J	23	38.1 × 6.4 (+) 51 × 3.2	7.0	1.31 (R)	1.6			1.31 (R)	1.6	
K	30	51 × 4.8	7.5	1.31 (R)	1.6			1.31 (R)	1.6	
L	60	51 × 6.4	9.7	1.31 (R)	1.6			1.31 (R)	1.6	

Table 2–32M Transverse Joint Reinforcement

See Section 2.1.4. *Effective EI is number listed times 10^5 before adjustment for bending moment capacity. For T-22, see tie rod downsize options in Tables 2-1M to 2-7M; one rod for two angles. (R) means Tie Rodded. Accepted Pressure Mode for T-24a is (+) or (-) 500 Pa maximum. *See* Figures 2-5 and 2-6 and tie rod text. (+) indicates positive pressure use only.

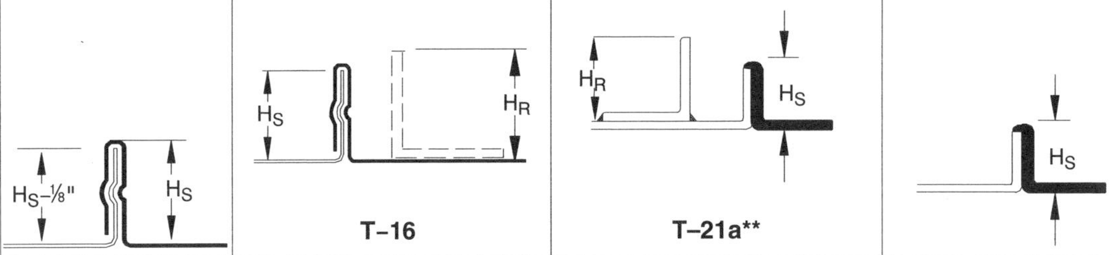

Minimum Rigidity Class	T-15 Standing Seam			Standing Seam or Welded Flange Reinforced						T-21** Welded Flange	
				26 to 22 ga Duct			20 to 16 ga Duct				
	EI*	H_S × T	WT/LF	H_S	Angle H_R × T	WT/LF	H_S	Angle H_R × T	WT/LF	H_S × T	WT/LF
A	0.43	½ × 24 ga	0.2			1.0				½ × 22 ga	0.1
B	1.0	¾ × 24 ga	0.3			1.0				½ × 16 ga	0.2
C	1.9	Use D	0.5			1.0				¾ × 18 ga	0.3
D	2.7	¾ × 16 ga / 1 × 20 ga	0.3	1"	1 × 1 × 16 ga	1.0				1¼ × 18 ga / 1¼ × 22 ga (+)	0.4
E	6.5	1 × 16 ga	0.7	1"	1 × 1 × ⅛ or 1½ × 1½ × 16 ga	1.4	1"	1 × 1 × ⅛	1.0	1¼ × 16 ga / 1½ × 20 ga (+)	0.5
F	12.8	1½ × 18 ga	0.8		Use G	1.8	1¼"	1¼ × 1¼ × 12 ga	1.7	1½ × 16 ga (+)	0.6
G	15.8	1½ × 18 ga(+)	0.8	1½"	1½ × 1½ × ⅛	2.0	1½"	1¼ × 1¼ × ⅛	2.4	See T-21a And Tie Rod Options	
H	26.4	See T-16 And Tie Rod Options		1½"	2 × 2 × ⅛	2.7	1½"	1½ × 1½ × 3/16	2.6		
I	69			1½"	2 × 2 × 3/16		1½"	2 × 2 × ⅛	2.7		
J	80				Use K	3.5	1½"	2 × 2 × 3/16	3.5		
K	103			1½"	2½ × 2½ × 3/16		1½"	2½ × 2½ × 3/16	4.1		
L	207				Not Given						

Table 2–33 Transverse Joint Reinforcement

See Section 2.1.4. *Effective EI is number listed times 10^5 before adjustment for bending moment capacity. *See* tie rod options elsewhere. (+) indicates positive pressure use only. **T21 and T21a welded flange may be limited to a height of 1/2 in. for certain applications. Adjust the EI rating using structural shapes while limiting the flange height.

Minimum Rigidity Class		T-15 Standing Seam		Standing Seam or Welded Flange Reinforced						T-21** Welded Flange	
				0.55 to 0.85 mm Duct			1.00 to 1.61 mm Duct				
	EI*	$H_S \times T$ (mm)	KG/LM	H_S (mm)	Angle $H_R \times T$	KG/LM	H_S	Angle $H_R \times T$	KG/LM	$H_S \times T$ (mm)	KG/LM
A	0.12	12.7 × 0.70	0.3			1.5				12.7 × 0.85	0.1
B	0.29	19.1 × 0.70	0.4			1.5				19.1 × 1.61	0.3
C	0.55	Use D	0.7			1.5				19.1 × 1.31	0.4
D	0.78	19.1 × 1.61 25 × 1.0	0.4	25	25 × 25 × 1.61	1.5				31.8 × 1.31 31.8 × 0.85 (+)	0.6 0.4
E	1.9	25 × 1.61	1.0	25	25 × 3.2	2.1	25	25 × 3.2	2.1	31.8 × 1.61 38.1 × 1.0 (+)	0.7
F	3.7	38.1 × 1.31	1.2		Use G	2.7	31.8	31.8 × 2.8	2.5	38.1 × 1.61 (+)	0.9
G	4.5	38.1 × 1.31 (+)	1.2	38.1	38.1 × 3.2	3.0	38.1	38.1 × 3.2	3.6	See T-21a And Tie Rod Options	
H	7.6	See T-16 And Tie Rod Options		38.1	51 × 3.2	4.0	38.1	38.1 × 4.8	3.9		
I	20			38.1	51 × 4.8		38.1	51 × 3.2	4.0		
J	23				Use K	5.2	38.1	51 × 4.8	5.2		
K	30			38.1	63.5 × 4.8		38.1	63.5 × 4.8	6.1		
L	60				Not Given						

Table 2-33M Transverse Joint Reinforcement

See Section 2.1.4. *Effective EI is number listed times 10^5 before adjustment for bending moment capacity. *See* tie rod options elsewhere. (+) indicates positive pressure use only. **T21 and T21a welded flange may be limited to a height of 13mm for certain applications. Adjust the EI rating using structural shapes while limiting the flange height.

2.5 TIE ROD INSTALLATIONS

S1.19 Internal ties shall be one of the methods shown in Figures 2-5 and 2-6. The restraining member and its connections shall be capable of sustaining a load equal to 75 percent of the duct construction pressure class load applied as 5.2 pounds per square foot per inch of water gage (101.63 kg per square meter per kPa) over an area equal to the width of the duct times the reinforcement interval. When more than one tie rod is used at a crossection of the duct, the design load may be proportionately reduced. For Tables 2-1 through 2-7, duct sizes over 20 in. (508 mm) have tie rod construction alternatives in many instances.

S1.19.1 Intermediate Reinforcement and Joint Tie Rod Loads

The steel tie rod design load Tables 2-34 and 2-34M give the load for both positive and negative pressure service on ducts of 48 in. (1200 mm) through 120 in. (3000 mm) at each pressure class.

S1.19.2 Tie Rod Alternatives

A tie rod may be attached to any intermediate angle, channel, or zee by Figure 2-5 (A), (B), (C), or (F). When one of these backs up a joint, the attachment options are the same. The attachment of a tie rod member that reinforces a joint is allowed for joints T-3, T-6a, T-8a, T-14, T-16, T-21, T-24, and T-25.

The attachment of tie rods or tie straps as in Figure 2-6 by welding, bolting, riveting, or screwing within one inch (25 mm) of each side of joints T-15, T-21, and the T-24 and T-25 series. Each tie rod may be sized for one half of the load in Table 2-34.

S1.19.3 Only one tie rod is required for joint T-22. Only one tie rod is required on negative pressure for joints T-15, T-21, T-24, T-25 using Figure 2-5(G). On 18 ga (1.31 mm) duct with 2 in. wg (500 Pa) positive pressure a single tie rod for T-21, the pocket side of T-15 or pinned flanges of T-24 and T-25 is accepted as G rating up to 96 in. (2400 mm).

S1.19.4 For positive pressure service, several alternatives are available for compliance with Tables 2-34 and 2-34M. Partially or fully threaded tie rod from Tables 2-35 and 2-35M may be used by size readout or the allowable load data may be used for sizing calculations at 150 percent of the loads in Tables 2-34 and 2-34M. One half inch (12.7 mm) RC conduit may be used. Thinwall (EMT) conduit may be used with these size and load limits applying for Tables 2-34 and 2-34M: 900 lbs (400 kg) for ½ in. (12.1 mm); 1340 lbs (600 kg) for ¾ in. (19.1 mm); 1980 lbs (900 kg) for 1 in. (25 mm). 1 in. × ¼ in. (25 × 3 mm) strap may be used provided that weld stress does not exceed 13,600 psi (93772 kPa) and that any bolts are sized per Tables 2-35 and 2-35M as minimums.

S1.19.5 For negative pressure rods, tubing, pipe, or angles are alternatives. The selection steps are as follows:

Step 1: Find the design load for the pressure class and duct width in Table 2-34.

Step 2A: For rods, from Table 2-36 for the length to be used, select a size to meet the load from Table 2-34 or calculate the size needed to limit the compression stress to that associated with a maximum length to radius of gyration ratio (L/r_g) or;

Step 2B: For rigid conduit (RC), select from Table 2-37 the smallest size of the length that satisfies the load from Table 2-34 or;

Step 2C: For EMT conduit, select from Table 2-38 the smallest size for the length that satisfies the load from Table 2-34 or;

Step 2D: For pipe, select from Table 2-39 the smallest size for the length that satisfies the load from Table 2-34 or;

Step 2E: For angles, select from Table 2-40 the smallest size for the length that satisfies the load from Table 2-34.

S1.20 Holes made in the duct wall for tie rod passage shall be of minimum size and shall be sealed in accordance with the provisions of Section 1.4.1. Except as limited by joint specifications and certain mandatory uses, tie rod alternatives are indicated in Tables 2-1 through 2-7 for reinforcement sizes listed to the right of duct wall thickness. G denotes the size with tie rod on 22 ga in H-22G nomenclature.

S1.21 Tie rods shall be galvanized steel. All internal ties, whether of rod, tube, pipe, or angle for shall be of material having the same nature and corrosion resistance as the duct wall material. Concealed components shall not be subject to nor cause galvanic corrosion. Tie straps, used on positive pressure only, shall be 1 in. × 1/8 in. (25 × 3.2 mm) minimum galvanized steel and the smallest edge shall face the airflow.

S1.22 When the internal ties are integrated with supports such as those in Figure 5-9, they shall be selected to be suitable for additional duty.

S1.23 Up to 120 in. (3048 mm) width ties shall be spaced at even intervals of duct width not exceeding 60 in. (1524 mm). The use of ties does not void the need to attach reinforcements to the duct wall, however, when ties occur outside the duct, as on two-sided or four-sided reinforcements at positive 4 in. wg (1000 Pa) and over, the attachment within two in. of the corner is not required. Refer to Figure 2-13.

S1.24 Ties shall be attached so that they will not loosen or detach for the selected duct pressure service class nor for an occasional 50 percent over pressure temporary condition. For positive pressure, threaded inserts placed in pipes and tubes shall be secure at 200 percent of Table 2-34 design load.

S1.25 When ties occur in two directions in the same vicinity, they shall either be prevented from contacting or be permanently fastened together.

S1.26 Refer to Figures 2-5, 2-6, 2-14 and 5-7 for basic tie rod application details on medium and large size ducts.

S1.27 Ties may be structural components of the duct and used as part of the suspension system for ducts over 96 in. (2438 mm) in width, provided that the hanger load is directly transmitted to a trapeze or duct reinforcement member beneath the duct.

S1.28 The construction of ducts of widths greater than 120 in. (3048 mm) involves the use of tie rods on joints and intermediate reinforcement at intervals not exceeding 60 in. (1.5 m) for 6 in. wg (1500 Pa) or less. For 10 in. wg (2500 Pa) the maximum interval is 48 in. (1.2 m). See Figure 2-14 for construction schedules.

2.6 COMMENTARY

Smaller reinforcements than would otherwise be required can be used when a tie rod is placed in the duct so as to lock reinforcements on opposite sides of the duct together to restrain their bending. Ties can be attached to intermediate reinforcements or to joint-backup-reinforcements or to certain joints able to withstand the forces involved. The term "tie rod" applies to a variety of galvanized steel shapes (*i.e.*, rod, pipe, tube, and angles) or to the use of 1 in. × 1/8 in. (25 × 3.2 mm) galvanized steel straps. The duct dimension defines tie rod length. Duct size and weight and operating pressure determine tie rod size, shape and internal geometry. Pipes and angles were not sized for positive pressure because other options seemed more economical; they may be used.

ROD WITH INTERNAL AND
EXTERNAL NUTS

(A)

BOLT OR MACHINE SCREW

TUBING OR CONDUIT
WITH MALE OR FEMALE
THREADED INSERTS

(B)

TUBING
ENCASED ROD

(C)

PIPE, TUBING OR CONDUIT WITHOUT THREADED INSERTS MAY BE BRAZED OR WELDED TO THE DUCT WALL.

IN GENERAL THESE ARE ALTERNATIVES.
FOR SPECIFIC LIMITS SEE TEXT

JOINT — 1" (25 mm) FROM JOINT
WELD
TIE ROD

(D)

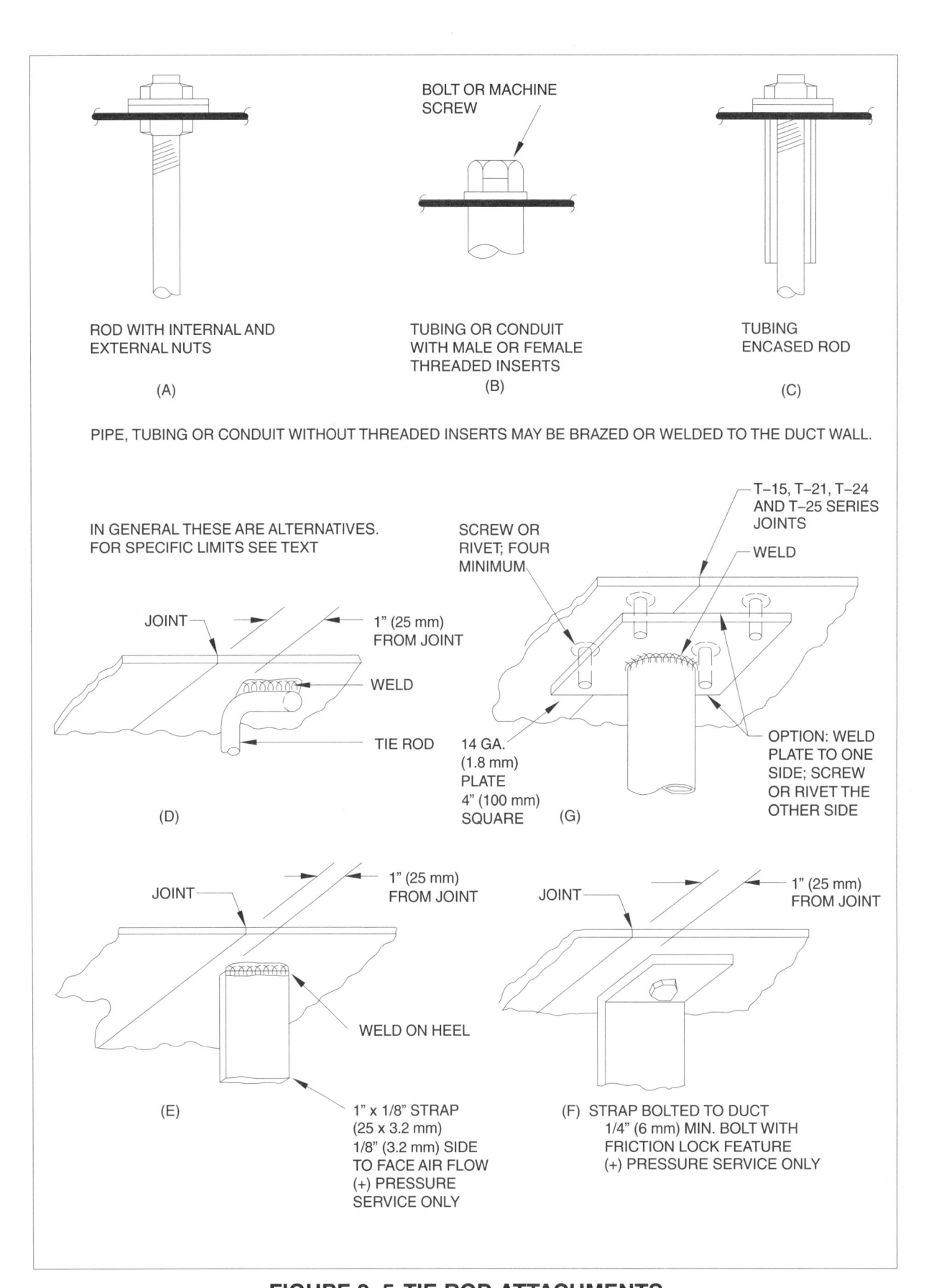

SCREW OR RIVET; FOUR MINIMUM
T–15, T–21, T–24 AND T–25 SERIES JOINTS
WELD
14 GA. (1.8 mm) PLATE 4" (100 mm) SQUARE
OPTION: WELD PLATE TO ONE SIDE; SCREW OR RIVET THE OTHER SIDE

(G)

JOINT — 1" (25 mm) FROM JOINT
WELD ON HEEL

(E)

1" x 1/8" STRAP
(25 x 3.2 mm)
1/8" (3.2 mm) SIDE
TO FACE AIR FLOW
(+) PRESSURE
SERVICE ONLY

JOINT — 1" (25 mm) FROM JOINT

(F) STRAP BOLTED TO DUCT
1/4" (6 mm) MIN. BOLT WITH
FRICTION LOCK FEATURE
(+) PRESSURE SERVICE ONLY

FIGURE 2–5 TIE ROD ATTACHMENTS

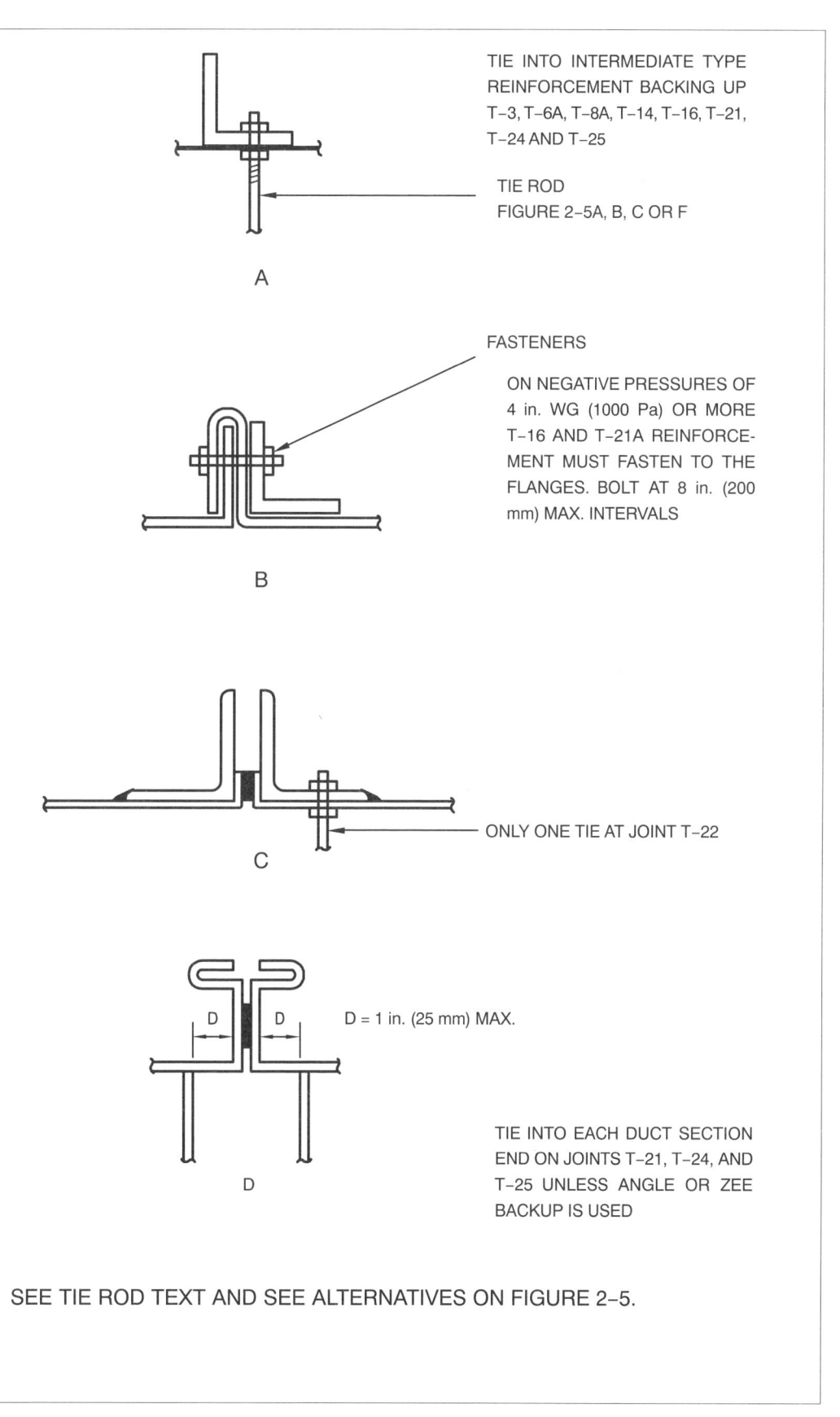

A — TIE INTO INTERMEDIATE TYPE REINFORCEMENT BACKING UP T-3, T-6A, T-8A, T-14, T-16, T-21, T-24 AND T-25

TIE ROD
FIGURE 2-5A, B, C OR F

B — FASTENERS

ON NEGATIVE PRESSURES OF 4 in. WG (1000 Pa) OR MORE T-16 AND T-21A REINFORCEMENT MUST FASTEN TO THE FLANGES. BOLT AT 8 in. (200 mm) MAX. INTERVALS

C — ONLY ONE TIE AT JOINT T-22

D — D = 1 in. (25 mm) MAX.

TIE INTO EACH DUCT SECTION END ON JOINTS T-21, T-24, AND T-25 UNLESS ANGLE OR ZEE BACKUP IS USED

SEE TIE ROD TEXT AND SEE ALTERNATIVES ON FIGURE 2-5.

FIGURE 2-6 TIE ROD ATTACHMENTS

W	RS	½"	1"	2"	3"	4"	6"	10"	RS	½"	1"	2"	3"	4"	6"	10"
		\multicolumn{7}{c}{Static Pressure Class, in. wg}		\multicolumn{7}{c}{Static Pressure Class, in. wg}
48"	6 ft	47	94	188	282	396	564	940	3 ft	24	47	94	141	198	282	470
	5 ft	39	78	156	234	312	486	780	2.5 ft	20	39	78	117	156	234	390
	4 ft	33	62	124	186	250	372	620	2 ft	15	31	62	93	124	186	310
54"	6 ft	53	105	210	315	421	630	1050	3 ft	26	53	105	158	210	316	525
	5 ft	44	88	176	264	351	528	880	2.5 ft	22	44	88	132	176	264	440
	4 ft	35	70	140	210	281	420	700	2 ft	17	35	70	105	140	210	350
60"	6 ft	59	117	234	351	468	702	1170	3 ft	34	59	117	176	234	351	585
	5 ft	49	98	195	294	390	588	980	2.5 ft	25	49	98	147	195	294	490
	4 ft	39	78	156	234	312	468	780	2 ft	20	39	78	167	156	234	390
72"	6 ft	70	140	280	420	560	840	1400	3 ft	35	70	140	210	280	421	700
	5 ft	59	117	234	351	468	702	1170	2.5 ft	30	59	117	177	234	354	590
	4 ft	47	94	188	282	376	564	940	2 ft	23	47	94	142	188	284	470
84"	6 ft	82	164	328	492	656	984	1640	3 ft	41	82	164	264	328	492	820
	5 ft	68	137	274	411	548	822	1370	2.5 ft	34	68	137	205	274	410	680
	4 ft	55	109	218	327	436	654	1090	2 ft	27	55	109	164	218	328	546
96"	6 ft	94	188	366	564	792	1128	1880	3 ft	47	94	188	282	396	564	940
	5 ft	78	156	312	468	624	936	1560	2.5 ft	39	78	156	234	312	468	780
	4 ft	62	125	250	375	500	750	1250	2 ft	31	62	125	187	250	374	620
108"	6 ft	105	211	422	633	844	1266	2110	3 ft	52	105	210	315	420	630	1053
	5 ft	88	176	352	528	704	1056	1760	2.5 ft	44	88	176	264	352	528	880
	4 ft	70	140	280	420	560	840	1400	2 ft	35	70	140	210	288	420	700
120"	6 ft	117	234	468	702	936	1404	2334	3 ft	59	117	234	351	468	702	1170
	5 ft	98	195	390	585	780	1170	1950	2.5 ft	49	98	195	294	390	588	975
	4 ft	78	156	312	468	624	936	1560	2 ft	39	78	156	234	312	468	780

Table 2–34 Internal Tie Rod Design Load in Pounds

See the rod text and Figure 2-7 "W" is width, "RS" is reinforcement spacing. The load basis is 75 percent of the pressure load on an area equal to width times reinforcement spacing. If more than one tie is used, the load is proportional. Applicable for positive and negative pressures. Not all W by RS load conditions listed in Table 2-34 occur in Tables 2-1 through 2-7. Also, loads for widths less than 48 in. may be calculated for Table 2-34.

W mm	RS mm	\multicolumn{7}{c	}{Static Pressure Class, Pa}	RS mm	\multicolumn{7}{c	}{Static Pressure Class, Pa}
		125	250	250	750	1000	1500	2500		125	250	500	750	1000	1500	2500
1200	1.8	21	42	85	128	179	255	426	0.90	10	21	42	64	89	128	213
	1.5	17	35	70	106	141	212	353	0.75	9	17	35	53	70	106	177
	1.2	15	28	56	84	168	168	241	0.60	6	14	28	42	56	84	140
1330	1.8	24	47	95	142	285	285	476	0.90	11	24	47	71	95	142	238
	1.5	20	40	80	119	239	239	399	0.75	10	20	40	59	80	119	199
	1.2	161	31	63	96	190	190	317	0.60	7	15	31	47	63	95	158
1500	1.8	26	53	106	159	212	318	530	0.90	15	26	53	80	106	159	265
	1.5	22	44	88	133	176	266	444	0.75	11	22	44	66	88	133	222
	1.2	17	35	70	106	141	212	353	0.60	9	17	35	75	70	106	177
1800	1.8	31	63	127	190	254	381	635	0.90	15	31	63	140	127	281	317
	1.5	26	53	106	159	212	318	530	0.75	13	26	53	80	106	160	267
	1.2	21	42	95	128	170	264	426	0.60	10	21	42	64	85	128	213
2100	1.8	37	74	148	223	297	446	743	0.90	18	37	74	111	148	223	372
	1.5	30	69	124	186	248	372	621	0.75	15	30	62	93	124	186	308
	1.2	25	49	98	128	197	296	494	0.60	12	25	49	74	98	148	247
2400	1.8	42	85	166	255	359	511	852	0.90	21	42	85	128	179	255	426
	1.5	35	70	141	212	283	424	707	0.75	17	35	70	106	141	212	353
	1.2	28	56	113	170	226	340	567	0.60	14	28	56	84	113	170	281
2700	1.8	47	95	191	287	382	574	975	0.90	23	47	95	142	190	287	477
	1.5	40	80	169	239	319	479	789	0.75	20	40	80	119	147	239	399
	1.2	31	63	127	190	254	381	635	0.60	15	31	63	95	130	190	317
3000	1.8	53	106	212	318	424	636	1058	0.90	26	53	106	159	212	318	530
	1.5	44	88	177	265	353	530	884	0.75	22	44	88	133	177	265	442
	1.2	35	70	141	212	283	424	707	0.60	17	35	70	106	141	212	353

Table 2–34M Internal Tie Rod Design Load in Kilograms

See the rod text and Figure 2-7 "W" is width, "RS" is reinforcement spacing. The load basis is 75 percent of the pressure load on an area equal to width times reinforcement spacing. If more than one tie is used, the load is proportional. Applicable for positive and negative pressures. Not all W by RS load conditions listed in Table 2-34M occur in Tables 2-1M through 2-7M. Also, loads for widths less than 1200 mm may be calculated for Table 2-34M.

		Static Pressure Class, in. wg							Static Pressure Class, in. wg							
W	RS	1/2"	1"	2"	3"	4"	6"	10"	RS	1/2"	1"	2"	3"	4"	6"	10"
	6 ft						5/16	3/8	3 ft							
48"	5 ft							5/16	2.5 ft							
	4 ft							5/16	2 ft							
	6 ft					5/16	5/16	3/8	3 ft							5/16
54"	5 ft					5/16	5/16	3/8	2.5 ft							
	4 ft							5/16	2 ft							
	6 ft						5/16	3/8	3 ft							5/16
60"	5 ft						5/16	3/8	2.5 ft							5/16
	4 ft							5/16	2 ft							
	6 ft					5/16	3/8	7/16	3 ft						5/16	5/16
72"	5 ft						5/16	3/8	2.5 ft							5/16
	4 ft						5/16	3/8	2 ft							
	6 ft				5/16	5/16	3/8	1/2	3 ft						5/16	3/8
84"	5 ft					5/16	3/8	7/16	2.5 ft							5/16
	4 ft						5/16	3/8	2 ft							5/16
	6 ft				5/16	3/8	3/8	1/2	3 ft						5/16	3/8
96"	5 ft					5/16	3/8	7/16	2.5 ft							5/16
	4 ft					5/16	5/16	7/16	2 ft							5/16
	6 ft				5/16	3/8	7/16	5/8	3 ft						5/16	3/8
108"	5 ft				5/16	5/16	3/8	1/2	2.5 ft						5/16	3/8
	4 ft					5/16	3/8	7/16	2 ft							5/16
	6 ft				5/16	3/8	7/16	5/8	3 ft						5/16	3/8
120"	5 ft				5/16	5/16	3/8	1/2	2.5 ft						5/16	3/8
	4 ft					5/16	3/8	7/16	2 ft							5/16

Table 2-35 Internal Tie Rod Size (+) Pressure

NOTES:

1/4 in. diameter is used in all blank cells in the table.

W is width. RS is reinforcement spacing.

Whenever tie rod exceeds 36 in., 3/8 in. diameter is the minimum size.

When duct width is between sizes, selection must be made for the larger W.

Allowable load on galvanized steel rods for Positive Pressure Service:

Dia.	Load (lbs.)	Dia.	Load (lbs)
1/4 in.	480	7/16 in.	1600
5/16 in.	780	1/2 in.	2130
3/8 in.	1170	3/8 in.	3380

This assumes that threaded connections carry the load. If rod(s) are welded to lugs on the duct wall, weld stress must be limited to 13,600 PSI.

W mm	RS mm	\multicolumn{7}{c	}{Static Pressure Class, Pa}	RS mm	\multicolumn{7}{c}{Static Pressure Class, Pa}
		125	250	250	750	1000	1500	2500		125	250	500	750	1000	1500	2500
1200	1.8						7.9	9.5	0.90							
	1.5							7.9	0.75							
	1.2							7.9	0.60							
1350	1.8					7.9	7.9	9.5	0.90							7.9
	1.5						7.9	9.5	0.75							
	1.2							7.9	0.60							
1500	1.8						7.9	9.5	0.90							7.9
	1.5						7.9	9.5	0.75							7.9
	1.2							7.9	0.60							
1800	1.8					7.9	9.5	11.1	0.90						7.9	7.9
	1.5						7.9	9.5	0.75							7.9
	1.2						7.9	9.5	0.60							
2100	1.8				7.9	7.9	9.5	12.7	0.90						7.9	9.5
	1.5					7.9	9.5	11.1	0.75							7.9
	1.2						7.9	9.5	0.60							7.9
2400	1.8				7.9	9.5	9.5	12.7	0.90						7.9	9.5
	1.5					7.9	9.5	11.1	0.75							7.9
	1.2					7.9	7.9	11.1	0.60							7.9
2700	1.8				7.9	9.5	11.1	15.9	0.90						7.9	9.5
	1.5				7.9	7.9	9.5	12.7	0.75						7.9	9.5
	1.2					7.9	9.5	11.1	0.60							7.9
3000	1.8				7.9	9.5	11.1	15.9	0.90						7.9	11.1
	1.5				7.9	7.9	9.5	11.1	0.75						7.9	9.5
	1.2					7.9	9.5	9.5	0.60							7.9

Table 2–35M Internal Tie Rod Size (+) Pressure

NOTES:

6.4 mm diameter is used in all blank cells in the table.

W is width. RS is reinforcement spacing.

Whenever tie rod exceeds 0.90 m, 9.5 mm diameter is the minimum size.

When duct width is between sizes, selection must be made for the larger W.

Allowable load on galvanized steel rods for Positive Pressure Service:

Dia. (mm)	Load (kg)	Dia. (mm)	Load (kg)
6.4	217	11.1	725
7.9	353	12.7	966
9.5	530	15.9	1533

This assumes that threaded connections carry the load. If rod(s) are welded to lugs on the duct wall, weld stress must be limited to 93772kPa.

Rod Spec	L=	≤12 in.	13–18 in.	19–24 in.	25–30 in.	31–36 in.	37–42 in.
5/16 in.–18		125	X				
3/8 in.–16		232	X				
1/2 in.–12		824	330	X			
5/8 in.–11		2143	902	541	X		
3/4 in.–10			2004	1002	X		
7/8 in.–9				1845	1384	1107	X
1 in.–8					2420	1815	1452

Table 2–36 Internal Tie Rod Size (–) Pressure

NOTES:

Rod specification is diameter and threads per inch. Allowable stress (σ_a) in psi for steel rod is:

σ_a	9500	6000	4000	3000	2400
L/r_g	≤100	101–125	126–150	151–175	176–200

The table gives maximum allowable load in pounds; *see* Table 2-34 for assumed loads for various width, pressure, and reinforcement spacing combinations. X means the size is not acceptable at this greater length.

Rod Spec	L=	≤305 (mm)	330-457 (mm)	482-610 (mm)	635-762 (mm)	787-914 (mm)	940-1066 (mm)
7.9–0.71		56	X				
9.5–0.63		105	X				
12.7–0.47		373	149	X			
15.9–0.43		972	409	245	X		
19.1–0.39			909	454	X		
22.2–0.35				836	627	502	X
25–0.31					1097	823	658

Table 2–36M Internal Tie Rod Size (–) Pressure

NOTES:

Rod specification is diameter and threads per mm. Allowable stress (σ_a) in kPa for steel rod is:

σ_a	65502	41370	27580	206685	16548
L/r_g	≤100	101–125	126–150	151–175	176–200

The table gives maximum allowable load in pounds; *see* Table 2-34M for assumed loads for various width, pressure, and reinforcement spacing combinations. X means the size is not acceptable at this greater length.

				Compression Stress Allowed (PSI)							
				9000	8000	7000	6000	5200	4700	4200	3700
		r_g	$L/r_g=$	130	140	150	160	170	180	190	200
Dia.	Type										
½ in.	RC	0.263	LEN.	34 in.	36 in.	38 in.	42 in.	44 in.	46 in.	50 in.	52 in.
			LBS.	2160	1920	1680	1440	1248	1128	1008	888
¾ in.	RC	0.335	LEN.	44 in.	46 in.	50 in.	54 in.	56 in.	60 in.	64 in.	66 in.
			LBS.	2844	2528	2212	1896	1643	1448	1327	1169
1 in.	RC	0.423	LEN.				68 in.	72 in.	76 in.	80 in.	84 in.
			LBS.				2820	2444	2209	1974	1739
1¼ in.	RC	0.542	LEN.							102 in.	108 in.
			LBS.							2680	2361
1½ in.	RC	0.625	LEN.							118 in.	124 in.
			LBS.							3208	2827
2 in.	RC	0.79	LEN.								150 in.
			LBS.								3781

Table 2–37 Internal RC Conduit Size (–) Pressure

NOTES:

The table gives maximum length and maximum load; *see* Table 2-34 for assumed loads. Blank spaces are not economical.

Rigid Conduit (RC) Data				
Dia.	Rigid Conduit			Weight	(+) Pressure lbs Load at 15,000 PSI
	O.D. in.	t in.	A in²	lbs/ft	
½ in.	0.84	0.104	0.240	0.80	3600
¾ in.	1.05	0.107	0.316	1.08	4740
1 in.	1.31	0.126	0.470	1.60	-
1¼ in.	1.66	0.133	0.638	2.08	-
1½ in.	1.90	0.138	0.764	2.54	-
2 in.	2.37	0.146	1.022	3.44	-

				Compression Stress Allowed (kPa)							
				62055	55160	48265	41370	35854	32406	28959	25511
		r_g	L/r_g=	130	140	150	160	170	180	190	200
Dia. (mm)	Type	(mm)									
12.7	RC	6.7	LEN.	863	914	965	1066	1117	1168	1270	1320
			kg.	980	871	762	653	566	511	457	402
19.1	RC	8.5	LEN.	1117	1168	1270	1371	1422	1524	1625	1676
			kg.	1290	1146	1003	860	745	673	602	530
25	RC	10.7	LEN.				1727	1828	1930	2032	2133
			kg.				1279	1108	1002	872	788
31.8	RC	13.8	LEN.							2590	2743
			kg.							1202	1070
38.1	RC	15.9	LEN.							2997	3150
			kg.							1455	1282
50.8	RC	20.1	LEN.								3810
			kg.								1715

Table 2–37M Internal RC Conduit Size (–) Pressure

NOTES:

The table gives maximum length and maximum load; *see* Table 2-34M for assumed loads. Blank spaces are not economical.

Rigid Conduit (RC) Data				
Dia. (mm)	Rigid Conduit			Weight	(+) Pressure kg Load at 103425 kPa
	O.D. (mm)	t (mm)	A mm^2	kg/m	
12.7	21.3	2.6	155	1.19	1633
19.1	26.7	2.7	204	1.61	2150
25	33.3	3.2	303	2.38	–
31.8	42.2	3.4	416	3.1	–
38.1	48.3	3.5	493	3.78	–
50.8	60.2	3.7	659	5.12	–

				Compression Stress Allowed (PSI)							
				9000	8000	7000	6000	5200	4700	4200	3700
		r_g	$L/r_g=$	130	140	150	160	170	180	190	200
Dia.	Type										
½ in.	EMT	0.235	LEN.	30 in.	32 in.	34 in.	36 in.	40 in.	42 in.	44 in.	46 in.
			LBS.	792	704	616	528	458	414	370	325
¾ in.	EMT	0.309	LEN.	40 in.	42 in.	46 in.	48 in.	52 in.	54 in.	58 in.	62 in.
			LBS.	1206	1072	938	804	697	630	563	496
1 in.	EMT	0.371	LEN.	48 in.	52 in.	54 in.	58 in.	62 in.	66 in.	70 in.	74 in.
			LBS.	1782	1584	1386	1188	1030	930	831	732
1¼ in.	EMT	0.511	LEN.	66 in.	72 in.	76 in.	82 in.	86 in.	92 in.	96 in.	102 in.
			LBS.	2655	2360	2065	1770	1534	1386	1239	1091
1½ in.	EMT	0.592	LEN.	76 in.	82 in.	88 in.	94 in.	100 in.	106 in.	112 in.	118 in.
			LBS.	3078	2736	2394	2052	1778	1607	1436	1265
2 in.	EMT	0.754	LEN.		106 in.	112 in.	120 in.	128 in.	136 in.	142 in.	150 in.
			LBS.		3480	3045	2610	2262	2044	1827	1609

Table 2-38 Internal EMT Conduit Size (-) Pressure

NOTES:

The table gives maximum length and maximum load; *see* Table 2-34 for assumed loads. Blank spaces are not economical.

EMT Conduit Data				
Dia.	EMT Conduit			Weight
	O.D. in.	t in.	A in^2	lbs/ft
½ in.	0.71	0.042	0.088	0.29
¾ in.	0.92	0.049	0.134	0.45
1 in.	1.16	0.057	0.198	0.65
1¼ in.	1.51	0.065	0.295	0.96
1½ in.	1.74	0.065	0.342	1.11
2 in.	2.2	0.065	0.435	1.41

				Compression Stress Allowed (kPa)							
				62055	55160	48265	41370	35854	32406	28959	25511
		r_g	$L/r_g=$	130	140	150	160	170	180	190	200
Dia. (mm)	Type	(mm)									
12.7	EMT	5.9	LEN.	762	813	864	914	1016	1067	1118	1168
			kg.	359	319	279	239	207	187	167	147
19.1	EMT	7.8	LEN.	1016	1067	1168	1219	1321	1372	1473	1575
			kg.	547	486	425	364	316	285	255	225
25	EMT	9.4	LEN.	1219	1321	1422	1473	1575	1676	1778	1880
			kg.	808	718	628	538	467	421	377	332
31.8	EMT	12.9	LEN.	1676	1829	1930	2083	2184	2337	2438	2591
			kg.	1204	1070	936	802	695	628	562	494
38.1	EMT	15	LEN.	1930	2083	2235	2388	2540	2692	2845	2997
			kg.	1396	1241	1086	930	806	729	651	573
50.8	EMT	19.1	LEN.		2692	2845	3048	3251	3454	3607	3810
			kg.		1578	1381	1183	1026	927	828	729

Table 2–38M Internal EMT Conduit Size (–) Pressure

NOTES:

The table gives maximum length and maximum load; *see* Table 2-34M for assumed loads. Blank spaces are not economical.

EMT Conduit Data				
Dia. (mm)	EMT Conduit			Weight
	O.D. (mm)	t (mm)	A mm^2	kg/m
12.7	18	1.1	57	0.43
19.1	23.4	1.2	86	0.67
25	29.5	1.4	128	0.97
31.8	38.4	1.7	190	1.4
38.1	44.5	1.7	221	1.7
50.8	55.9	1.7	281	2.1

| Dia. | Schedule | r_g | $L/r_g=$ | Compression Stress Allowed (PSI) |||||||||
| | | | | 10,000 | 9000 | 8000 | 7000 | 6000 | 5200 | 4700 | 4200 | 3700 |
				120	130	140	150	160	170	180	190	200
¼ in.	10S	0.169	LEN.	20	22	24	25	27	29	30	32	34
			LBS.	970	873	776	679	582	504	456	407	359
	40	0.153	LEN.	20	21	23	24	26	28	29	31	33
			LBS.	1250	1125	1000	875	750	650	588	525	462
⅜ in.	10S	0.217	LEN.	26	28	30	32	35	37	39	41	43
			LBS.	1240	1116	992	868	744	645	583	521	459
	40	0.209	LEN.	25	27	29	31	33	35	38	40	42
			LBS.	1670	1503	1336	1169	1002	868	785	701	618
½ in.	10S	0.269	LEN.	32	35	38	40	43	46	48	51	54
			LBS.	1970	1773	1576	1379	1182	1024	926	827	729
	40	0.261	LEN.	31	34	36	39	42	44	47	49	52
			LBS.	2500	2250	2000	1750	1500	1300	1175	1050	925
¾ in.	5S	0.349	LEN.	42	45	49	52	56	59	63	66	70
			LBS.	2010	1809	1608	1407	1206	1045	945	844	744
	10S	0.343	LEN.	41	44	48	51	55	58	61	65	68
			LBS.	2520	2268	2016	1764	1512	1310	1184	1058	932
	40	0.334	LEN.	40	43	47	50	53	57	60	63	67
			LBS.	3340	3006	2672	2338	2004	1737	1570	1402	1236
1 in.	5S	0.443	LEN.	NOT GIVEN			66	71	75	80	84	88
			LBS.				3100	2658	2304	2082	1860	1639
	10S	0.428	LEN.				64	68	73	77	81	85
			LBS.				2996	2568	2225	2010	1798	1585
	40	0.420	LEN.				63	67	71	75	80	84
			LBS.				2940	2520	2184	1974	1764	1554

Table 2–39 Steel Pipe Size (–) Pressure

Lengths (L) is in inches and allowable compression load (LD) is in pounds.

Galvanized steel pipe is of ASTM A53, A106, or A120 grade.

Ends are considered pinned.

Blank spaces in the table are not considered economical selections.

For the load from Table 2-34, select a pipe from Table 2-39 that has load capacity and is within the length limit.

Dia. mm	Schedule	r_g	$L/r_g=$	10,000 / 120	9000 / 130	8000 / 140	7000 / 150	6000 / 160	5200 / 170	4700 / 180	4200 / 190	3700 / 200
6.4	10S	4.3	LEN.	508	559	610	635	686	737	764	813	864
			Kg.	440	396	352	308	264	228	206	184	162
	40	4.1	LEN.	508	533	584	610	660	711	737	787	838
			Kg.	567	510	453	397	340	294	266	238	209
9.5	10S	5.5	LEN.	660	711	762	813	889	940	991	1041	1092
			Kg.	562	506	450	393	337	292	264	236	208
	40	5.3	LEN.	635	686	737	787	838	889	965	1016	1067
			Kg.	757	681	606	530	454	393	356	318	280
12.7	10S	6.8	LEN.	610	889	965	1016	1092	1168	1219	1295	1372
			Kg.	893	804	714	625	536	464	420	375	330
	40	6.6	LEN.	787	864	914	991	1067	1118	1194	1245	1321
			Kg.	1134	1020	907	793	680	589	533	476	419
19.1	5S	8.9	LEN.	1067	1143	1245	1321	1422	1499	1600	1676	1778
			Kg.	911	820	729	638	547	474	442	382	337
	10S	21.8	LEN.	1041	1118	1219	1294	1397	1473	1549	1651	1727
			Kg.	1143	1028	914	800	685	594	537	480	422
	40	8.5	LEN.	1016	1092	1194	1270	1346	1448	1524	1600	1702
			Kg.	1515	1362	1212	1060	909	788	712	636	560
25	5S	11.3	LEN.	NOT GIVEN	NOT GIVEN	NOT GIVEN	1676	1803	1905	2032	2134	2235
			Kg.				1406	1205	1045	944	843	743
	10S	10.9	LEN.				1626	1727	1854	1956	2057	2159
			Kg.				1359	1164	1009	911	815	718
	40	10.7	LEN.				1600	1702	1803	1905	2032	2134
			Kg.				1333	1143	990	895	800	704

Compression Stress Allowed (kPa)

Table 2–39M Steel Pipe Size (–) Pressure

Lengths (L) is in millimeters and allowable compression load (LD) is in kilograms.

Galvanized steel pipe is of ASTM A53, A106, or A120 grade.

Ends are considered pinned.

Blank spaces in the table are not considered economical selections.

For the load from Table 2-34M, select a pipe from Table 2-39M that has load capacity and is within the length limit.

Size	Area in.²	L = 2 ft A7	L = 2 ft A36	L = 4 ft A7	L = 4 ft A36	L = 6 ft A7	L = 6 ft A36	L = 8 ft A7	L = 8 ft A36
2 in. × 1¼ in. × ³⁄₁₆ in.	0.57	13.7	15.2	8.6	8.8	ND		ND	
2 in. × 2 in. × ³⁄₁₆ in.	0.71	16.9	18.6	13.3	14.5	9.7	9.9	6.30	6.30
2½ in. × 2½ in. × ³⁄₁₆ in.	0.90	26.1	29.6	22.5	25.1	17.1	18.6	13.9	14.5
3 in. × 2 in. × ³⁄₁₆ in.	0.90	26.8	29.7	23.9	26.8	21.0	23.2	18.1	19.5
2 in. × 2 in. × ¼ in.	0.93	26.2	29.6	21.4	23.5	16.6	17.4	11.5	11.5
3 in. × 3 in. × ³⁄₁₆ in.	1.09	32.3	36.0	28.7	32.2	25.1	27.6	21.5	23.0
3 in. × 2 in. × ¼ in.	1.19	35.4	39.2	31.4	35.3	27.5	30.3	23.6	25.4
2½ in. × 2½ in. × ¼ in.	1.19	34.4	39.1	29.6	32.9	24.8	26.8	19.9	20.7

Size	Area in.²	L = 10 ft A7	L = 10 ft A36	L = 12 ft A7	L = 12 ft A36	L = 14 ft A7	L = 14 ft A36
2 in. × 2 in. × ³⁄₁₆ in.	0.71	6.1	6.1	ND		ND	
2½ in. × 2½ in. × ³⁄₁₆ in.	0.90	11.3	11.3	8.6	8.6	ND	
3 in. × 2 in. × ³⁄₁₆ in.	0.90	15.2	15.8	12.3	12.1	9.6	9.6
2 in. × 2 in. × ¼ in.	0.93	7.8	7.8	13.8	13.8	ND	
3 in. × 2 in. × ¼ in.	1.19	19.7	20.4	15.3	15.3	12.3	12.3
2½ in. × 2½ in. × ¼ in.	1.19	14.8	14.8	11.1	11.1	ND	
3 in. × 2 in. × ¼ in.	1.31	27.5	29.3	23.4	24.2	ND	

Table 2–40 Allowable Load for Angles as Columns with Maximum Unbraced Length L

NOTES:

Load is in KSi or 1000s of pounds per square inch.

A7 and A36 are grades of steel.

ND means Not Designed.

Divide the load from Table 2-34 by a trial size angle area (in²); divide the result by 1000. If this KSi load is not in excess of one in Table 2-40 for a listed length that is also not exceeded, the size is acceptable. If unacceptable, select a size with a larger area and check again. You may interpolate for lengths between those listed.

Size	Area mm.²	L = 609 A7	L = 609 A36	L = 1219 A7	L = 1219 A36	L = 1829 A7	L = 1829 A36	L = 2438 A7	L = 2438 A36
51 × 31.8 × 4.8	367	94.4	104.8	59.2	60.6	ND	ND	ND	ND
51 × 51 × 4.8	458	136.5	157.8	112.3	123.4	87.5	92.3	61.3	61.3
63.5 × 63.5 × 4.8	580	179.9	204	155.1	173	117.9	128.2	95.8	99.9
76 × 51 × 4.8	600	184.7	204	164.7	184.7	144.7	159.9	124.7	134.4
51 × 51 × 6.4	703	180.6	204	147.5	162	114.4	119.9	79.2	79.2
76 × 76 × 4.8	768	222.7	248.2	197.8	222	173	190.3	148.2	158.5
76 × 51 × 6.4	768	244	201.3	216.5	243.3	189.6	208.9	162.7	175.1
63.5 × 63.5 × 6.4		237.1	269.5	204	226.8	170.9	184.7	137.2	142.7

Size	Area mm.²	L = 3048 A7	L = 3048 A36	L = 3658 A7	L = 3658 A36	L = 4267 A7	L = 4267 A36
51 × 51 × 4.8	458	42	42	ND	ND	ND	ND
63.5 × 63.5 × 4.8	580	77.9	77.9	59.2	59.2	ND	ND
76 × 51 × 4.8	580	104.8	108.9	84.8	83.4	66.1	66.1
51 × 51 × 6.4	600	53.7	53.7	95.1	95.1	ND	ND
76 × 51 × 6.4	703	135.8	140.6	105.4	105.4	84.8	84.8
63.5 × 63.5 × 6.4	768	102	102	76.5	76.5	ND	ND
76 × 63.5 × 6.4	845	189.6	202	161.3	166.8	ND	ND

Table 2–40M Allowable Load for Angles as Columns with Maximum Unbraced Length L

NOTES:

Load is in 1000 kPa or 1000 kilopascal. One KSi equals 6.893 kPa.

A7 and A36 are grades of steel.

ND means Not Designed.

Divide the load from Table 2-34M by a trial size angle area (mm²); divide the result by 1000. If this kPa load is not in excess of one in Table 2-40M for a listed length that is also not exceeded, the size is acceptable. If unacceptable, select a size with a larger area and check again. You may interpolate for lengths between those listed.

2.7 MIDPANEL TIE ROD APPLICATIONS

2.7.1 General Requirements for Midpanel Tie Rod (MPT) Use

1. Tie rods at midpanel are acceptable economical alternatives to external intermediate reinforcements for ducts in the width range through 96 in. (2400 mm) Petitions to local authorities for acceptance under conditions other than that stipulated may be made using DCS Chapter 11, method 2.

2. Except as limited herein, this alternative applies for construction with joint spacing of 6 ft (1.8 meters) or less using transverse joints already qualified as reinforcements (within pressure limits and construction details elsewhere specified in the HVAC-DCS).

3. Internal tie rods at midpanel are not allowed in the following applications:

    a. In ducts outside of buildings when the ducts do not have waterproof external insulation or waterproof and corrosion resistant duct wall penetrations;

    b. In ducts in which condensation or grease would collect except where no wall penetrations occur or the penetration is waterproof;

    c. In underground, in-slab or under-slab ducts;

    d. In fittings on non-parallel duct sides unless they do not penetrate the duct or they use load distributing means such as shims or wedges;

    e. When the air velocity exceeds 2500 fpm (12.7 m/s);

    f. Near centrifugal and axial flow fans where SYSTEM EFFECT FACTORS apply. For more information consult Air Movement and Control Association International (AMCA) publication 201.

4. Where fibrous glass liner particles would be exposed to airflow at a tie rod penetration of the liner, particle erosion shall be protected by use of suitable adhesive coatings, washers or other shielding.

5. MPT materials and attachments shall conform to DCS Section 2.5 and figures referenced therein. Any method shown in Figure 2–5 may be used for MPT. With Table 2–46 (2–46M) loading capacity required as minimum for MPT use, any member may be selected from Tables 2–35 to 2–40 (within the table limits) as a midpanel tie rod, see S1.19.4 and S1.19.5.

6. This does not prequalify MPT use for aluminum ducts nor polyvinyl coated steel ducts. The potential for such use is recognized; however, it requires mutual agreement between a specifying authority and a sponsor on terms of acceptable use.

7. Table 2-41 (2-41M) contains the combination of metal thicknesses, reinforcement spacings and duct widths for which midpanel tie rod (MPT) use is acceptable using one or two tie rods.

8. These schedules are not intended to preempt use of others that satisfy the requirements of DCS specification S1.2 and S1.18.

2.8 MIDPANEL TIE ROD (MPT) USE GUIDE

2.8.1 General Procedure

1. Read the General Requirements for MPT use.

2. Find the pressure, width and reinforcement spacing rating parameters in Column 8, 9 or 10 in Table 2-1 to 2-7.

3. Confirm the duct gage required and the number of tie rods; if the joint rating in Tables 2-32 and 2-33 contains a duct wall thickness that overrides (joints T-24, 24a, 25a, 25b, 15, 16, 21 or 21a may do this), increase the wall thickness as in the case of external-integral reinforcement use. In a few instances, the thickness is greater than the minimum for external reinforcement.

4. Read Note d for Table 2-41 and consider a thickness increase that would allow fewer rods or increased width.

5. Select the optimum wall thickness and number of rods.

6. For positive pressure, select solid steel rods or EMT from Table 2-42. Typical attachments are Figures 2-5(A) and 2-5(B).

7. For negative pressure, identify the rod lengths and select them from Table 2-43, 2-44, 2-45 or use the load from Table 2-46 and the actual length to make selections from Tables 2-36 to 2-40. Typical attachments are Figure 2-5(A), 2-5(B) or by welding.

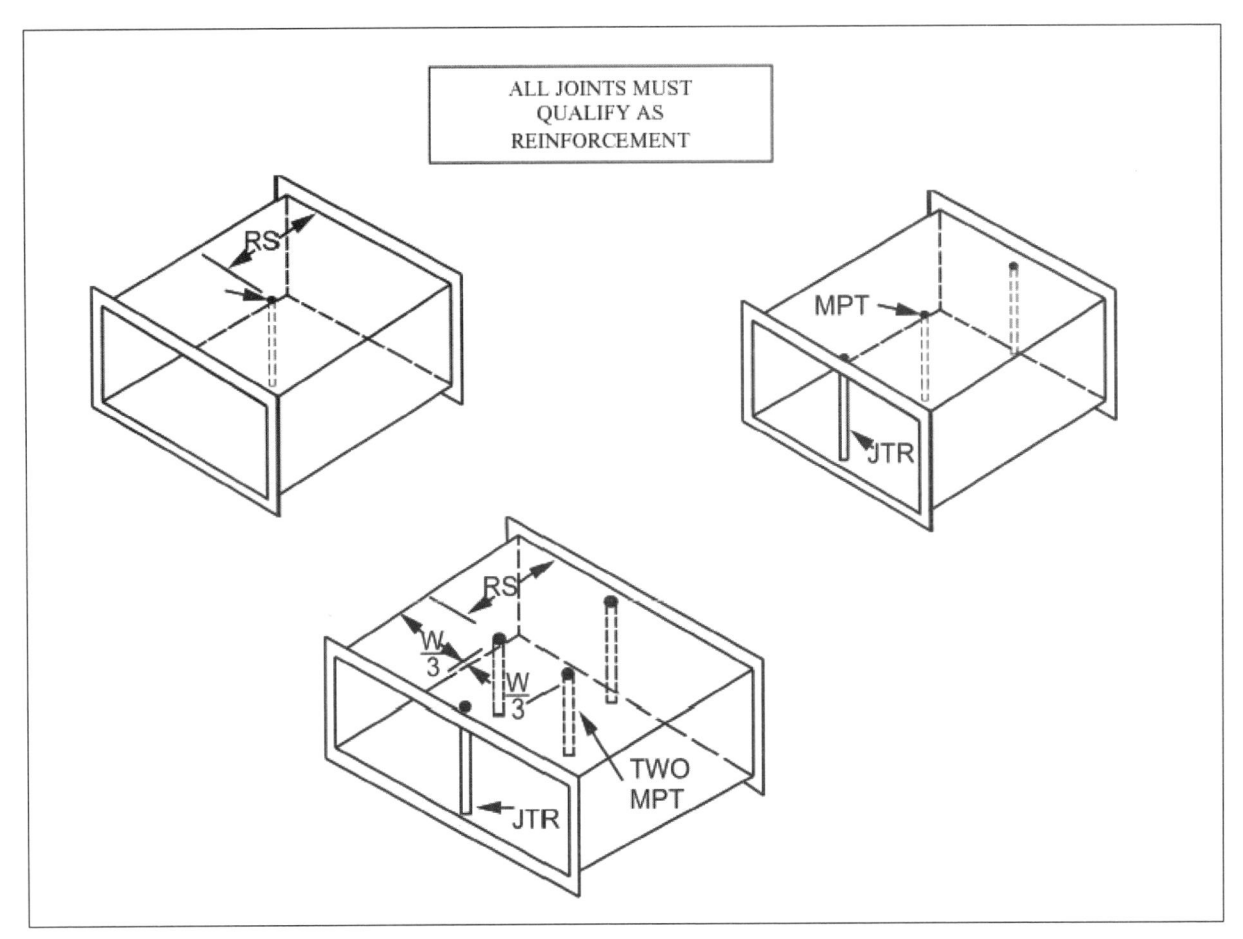

FIGURE 2-7

2.9 MIDPANEL TIE ROD SELECTIONS

Example No. 1:

48 × 18 in. (1200 × 450 mm) duct, 2 in. wg (500 Pa) positive pressure per Table 2-3; 5 ft (1.50 m) joint spacing; T-25a or T-25b joints:

In Table 2-3 for 48 in. (1200 mm) width, Column 6 gives reinforcement for 5 ft (1.50 m) RS (reinforcement spacing) as H-20 and Column 9 for 2 1/2 ft (0.75 m) RS as F-24; these are basic alternatives, but the joint ratings must be checked for duct gage override per text Section 2.1.4 and S1.13 and S1.14.

Therefore, for 5 ft (1.50 m) RS option Table 2-32 shows T-25 joints of H Code requiring 18 ga (1.31 mm) duct wall to satisfy the H joint rating; however, T-25 of 20 ga (1.00 mm) with tie rods at the joints (JTR) is I Code which satisfies both Tables 2-3 and 2-32. No between joint reinforcement is required. On the 18 in. (1.31 mm) wide sides, Column 2 shows that reinforcement is not required.

For 48 in. (1200 mm) width, the alternative of 2-½ ft (0.75 m) RS would only require 24 ga (0.70 mm) duct wall per Table 2-3, Column 9, but the F Code in Table 2-32 requires the use of T-25 of 22 ga (0.85 mm) duct wall, an override upgrade from Table 2-3. No tie rod is required at the joint, but one must be used at mid panel between joints (unless external reinforcement per Table 2-29 and 2-30 is used there). 22 ga (0.85 mm) metal will be used on all four sides; *see* text section 2.1.1 (3). On the 18 in. (1.31 mm) side, T-25 of 22 ga (0.85 mm) is F Code (which exceeds the C Code required in Column 9 of Table 2-3).

The requirements for tie rods at T-25 joints are the same as they would be for external reinforcement systems. The joints must qualify independently according to the reinforcement interval. For the conditions in Example No. 1, rods at T-25 joints are only required for 5 ft (1.50 m) RS intervals. Therefore, the rod size for the joint is selected based on one rod per Fig. 2-5(G) or two rods per Fig. 2-5(D) and the load from Table 2-34. In Table 2-34, the load for 2 in. wg (500 Pa) and 5 ft (1.50 m) RS on 48 in. (1200 mm) width is

156 pounds (70.76 kgs) (for one rod or 78 pounds (35.38 kgs) for each of two). From Table 2-35, ¼ in. (6.4 mm) rod suffices. From S1.19.4, ½ in. (12.7 mm) EMT is adequate.

Example No. 2:

The duct is the same as in Example No. 1 except the pressure is 2 in. wg (500 Pa) negative.

Gage, joint qualification and RS options are as for positive pressure. Tie rod loads in Table 2-34 are also the same.

To select the MPT of EMT, find in Table 2-43 that ½ in. (12.7 mm) diameter EMT is adequate at 2-½ ft (0.75 m) RS up to 46 in. (1168 mm) length. To consider steel rod Table 2-34 gives [at 48 in. (1200 mm) width, 30 in. (750 mm) RS and 2 in. wg (500 Pa)] 104 pounds (47.17 kg).

Then Table 2-36 shows that ½ in. (12.7 mm) steel rod is required for 18 in. (450 mm) length (to avoid buckling with a reasonable safety factor).

Example No. 3:

72 × 54 in. (1800 × 1300 mm) duct at 3 in. wg (750 Pa) negative pressure with 4 ft (1.20 m) joint spacing and 2 ft (0.60 m) RS; use standing S or T-25 joints.

Table 2-4 has I-24G on 72 in. (1800 mm) width and G-24 on 54 in. (1300 mm) width.

Table 2-41 show that on 72 in. (1800 mm) width, two MPT are required on 24 ga (0.70 mm) and 22 ga (0.85 mm) duct; however, Table 2-41 also shows that if the duct was 20 ga (1.00 mm) only one MPT tie rod is required. Both tables show that only one MPT tie rod is required on 54 in. (1300 mm) width.

	RS	16 ga	18 ga	20 ga	22 ga	24 ga	26 ga
±½ in. wg	3 ft				To 96(1)	To 84(1)	To 60(1)
	2 ½ ft				To 96(1)	To 84(1)	To 60(1)
	2 ft				To 96(1)	To 84(1)	To 60(1)
±1 in. wg	3 ft		To 96(1)*	To 84(1)*	To 72(1)*	To 60(1)	To 48(1)
				85-96(2)	73-84(2)	61-72(2)	
	2 ½ in.		To 96(1)*	To 84(1)*	To 72(1)*	To 60(1)	To 48(1)
				85-96(2)	73-84(2)	61-72(2)	
	2 ft		To 96(1)*	To 84(1)*	To 72(1)	To 72(1)	To 48(1)
				85-96(2)	73-96(2)		
±2 in. wg	3 ft		To 84(1)*	To 60(1)*	To 48(1)*	To 42(1)	To 36(1)
			To 96(2)	61-84(2)	49-72(2)	43-54(2)	
	2 ½ ft		To 84(1)*	To 72(1)*	To 60(1)*	To 54(1)	To 42(1)
			85-96(2)	73-96(2)	61-84(2)	55-60(2)	
	2 ft		To 96(1)*	To 72(1)*	To 60(1)	To 60(1)	To 42(1)
				73-96(2)	61-96(2)	61-72(2)	
±3 in. wg	3 ft		To 72(1)*	To 54(1)*	To 48(1)	To 42(1)	To 30(1)
			73-84(2)	55-72(2)	49-54(2)		
	2 ½ ft		To 72(1)*	To 60(1)*	To 54(1)*	To 42(1)	To 36(1)
			To 96(2)	61-84(2)	55-72(2)	43-54(2)	
	2 ft		To 84(1)*	To 72(1)*	To 60(1)*	To 54(1)	To 42(1)
			85-96(2)	73-96(2)	61-84(2)	55-72(2)	
±4 in. wg	3 ft	To 84(2)	To 60(1)*	To 54(1)*	To 48(1)	To 36(1)	To 30(1)
			61-72(2)	55-60(2)			
	2 ½ ft		To 72(1)*	To 60(1)*	To 48(1)	To 48(1)	To 36(1)
			73-96(2)	61-72(2)	49-60(2)		
	2 ft		To 84(1)*	To 60(1)*	To 60(1)	To 48(1)	To 42(1)
			85-96(2)	61-96(2)	61-72(2)	49-60(2)	
±6 in. wg	3 ft	To 72(2)	To 54(1)*	To 42(1)	To 36(1)	N/A	N/A
			55-60(2)	43-60(2)			
	2 ½ ft	To 96(2)	To 72(1)*	To 54(1)	To 48(1)	To 36(1)	N/A
			To 84(2)	55-60(2)			
	2 ft		To 72(1)*	To 60(1)*	To 48(1)	To 36(1)	N/A
			73-96(2)	61-72(2)	49-60(2)		

Table 2-41 Midpanel Tie Rod (MPT) Schedule (RS)

NOTES:

a. Table cells give duct width limit range in inches for use of one (1) and two (2) tie rods at midpanel (MPT) as a substitute for Table 2-29 intermediate reinforcements that would be centrally located between two otherwise qualified transverse joints. Joint spacings greater than six feet are not available for this alternative.

b. N/A refers to a ga not available to RS condition. RS is the Reinforcement Spacing.

c. For some conditions and joint types, the MPT option is contingent on use of tie rods at joints (JTR).

d. In some cases use of the MPT option would require that the gage be increased above those in Tables 2-1 to 2-6. An asterisk in Table 2-41 denotes a one tie rod thickness option when less thickness requires two rods.

	RS (m)	1.61 mm	1.31 mm	1.00 mm	0.85 mm	0.70 mm	0.55 mm
±125 Pa	0.90				To 2400(1)	To 2100(1)	To 1500(1)
	0.75				To 2400(1)	To 2100(1)	To 1500(1)
	0.60				To 2400(1)	To 2100(1)	To 1500(1)
±250 Pa	0.90		To 2400(1)*	To 2100(1)*	To 1800(1)*	To 1500(1)	To 1200(1)
				To 2400(2)	To 2100(2)	To 1800(2)	
	0.75		To 2400(1)*	To 2100(1)*	To 1800(1)*	To 1500(1)	To 1200(1)
				To 2400(2)	To 2100(2)	To 1800(2)	
	0.60		To 2400(1)*	To 2100(1)*	To 1800(1)	To 1800(1)	To 1200(1)
				To 2400(2)	To 2400(2)		
±500 Pa	0.90		To 2100(1)*	To 1500(1)*	To 1200(1)*	To 1000(1)	To 900(1)
			To 2400(2)	To 2100(2)	To 1800(2)	To 1300(2)	
	0.75		To 2100(1)*	To 1800(1)*	To 1500(1)*	To 1300(1)	To 1000(1)
			To 2400(2)	To 2400(2)	To 2100(2)	To 1500(2)	
	0.60		To 2400(1)*	To 1800(1)*	To 1500(1)	To 1500(1)	To 1000(1)
				To 2400(2)	To 2400(2)	To 1800(2)	
±750 Pa	0.90		To 1800(1)*	To 1300(1)*	To 1200(1)	To 1000(1)	To 700(1)
			To 2100(2)	To 1800(2)	To 1300(2)		
	0.75		To 1800(1)*	To 1500(1)*	To 1300(1)*	To 1000(1)	To 900(1)
			To 2400(2)	To 2100(2)	To 1800(2)	To 1300(2)	
	0.60		To 2100(1)*	To 1800(1)*	To 1500(1)*	To 1300(1)	To 1000(1)
			To 2400(2)	To 2400(2)	To 2100(2)	To 1800(2)	
±1000 Pa	0.90	To 2100(2)	To 1500(1)*	To 1300(1)*	To 1200(1)	To 900(1)	To 700(1)
			To 1800(2)	To 1500(2)	To 1500(2)		
	0.75		To 1800(1)*	To 1500(1)*	To 1200(1)	To 1200(1)	To 900(1)
			To 2400(2)	To 1800(2)	To 1500(2)		
	0.60		To 2100(1)*	To 1500(1)*	To 1500(1)	To 1200(1)	To 1000(1)
			To 2400(2)	To 2400(2)	To 1800(2)	To 1800(2)	
±1500 Pa	0.90	To 1800(2)	To 1300(1)*	To 1000(1)	To 900(1)	N/A	N/A
			To 1500(2)				
	0.75	To 2400(2)	To 1800(1)*	To 1300(1)	To 1200(1)	To 900(1)	N/A
				To 1500(2)			
	0.60		To 1800(1)*	To 1500(1)*	To 1200(1)	To 900(1)	N/A
			To 2400(2)	To 1800(2)	To 1500(2)		

Table 2–41M Midpanel Tie Rod (MPT) Schedule (RS)

NOTES:

a. Table cells give duct width limit range in inches for use of one (1) and two (2) tie rods at midpanel (MPT) as a substitute for Table 2-29M intermediate reinforcements that would be centrally located between two otherwise qualified transverse joints. Joint spacings greater than 1.8 m are not available for this alternative.

b. N/A refers to a thickness not available to RS condition. RS is the Reinforcement Spacing.

c. For some conditions and joint types, the MPT option is contingent on use of tie rods at joints (JTR).

d. In some cases use of the MPT option would require that the thickness be increased above those in Tables 2-1M to 2-6M. An asterisk in Table 2-41M denotes a one tie rod thickness option when less thickness requires two rods.

Static (+)	3 in. wg or Less			4 in. wg			6 in. wg		
Duct Dimension	3 ft	2½ ft	2 ft	3 ft	2½ ft	2 ft	3 ft	2½ ft	2 ft
①	⑧	⑨	⑩	⑧	⑨	⑩	⑧	⑨	⑩
37-60 in.	¼ in. Diameter Steel Rod						¼ in.	¼ in.	¼ in.
61-72 in.	^						⁵⁄₁₆ in.	¼ in.	¼ in.
73-84 in.	^						⁵⁄₁₆ in.	⁵⁄₁₆ in.	¼ in.
85-96 in.				⁵⁄₁₆ in.			⁵⁄₁₆ in.	⁵⁄₁₆ in.	⁵⁄₁₆ in.
37-96 in.	½ in. Diameter EMT								

Table 2–42 Internal Midpanel Tie Rod (MPT) Size (Dia.)

NOTES:

a. Midpanel means the use of tie rods in lieu of external Table 2-29 intermediate reinforcements that would be centrally located between two otherwise qualified transverse joints. Joint spacings greater than six feet are not available for this alternative.

b. Whenever steel rod length exceeds 36 in., ⅜ in. diameter is minimum, whether one or two rods are specified.

c. These preselected commonly used types of rod do not preclude use of other types.

Static (+)	750 Pa or Less			1000 Pa			1500 Pa		
Duct Dimension (mm)	0.90 m	0.75 m	0.60 m	0.90 m	0.75 m	0.60 m	0.90 m	0.75 m	0.60 m
①	⑧	⑨	⑩	⑧	⑨	⑩	⑧	⑨	⑩
901-1500	6.4 mm Diameter Steel Rod						6.4 mm	6.4 mm	6.4 mm
1501-1800	^						7.9 mm	6.4 mm	6.4 mm
1801-2100	^						7.9 mm	7.9 mm	6.4 mm
2101-2400				7.9 mm			7.9 mm	7.9 mm	7.9 mm
901-2400	12.7 mm Diameter EMT								

Table 2–42M Internal Midpanel Tie Rod (MPT) Size (Dia.)

NOTES:

a. Midpanel means the use of tie rods in lieu of external Table 2-29M intermediate reinforcements that would be centrally located between two otherwise qualified transverse joints. Joint spacings greater than 1.8 m are not available for this alternative.

b. Whenever steel rod length exceeds 900mm, 9.5 mm diameter is minimum, whether one or two rods are specified.

c. These preselected commonly used types of rod do not preclude use of other types.

½ to 3 in. wg Negative Pressure				
EMT Size and Length for Duct Width (W)		Rod Spacing Between Qualified Joints		
^	^	3 ft RS	2 ½ ft RS	2 ft RS
^	Max. L, in.	Duct Width (W)		
½ in. Dia.	46	to 83 in.	to 96 in.	to 96 in.
^	42	84 - 96	—	—
¾ in. Dia.	62	to 96 in.	to 96 in.	to 96 in.
1.0 in. Dia.	74	to 96 in.	to 96 in.	to 96 in.
1 ¼ in. Dia.	96	to 96 in.	to 96 in.	to 96 in.

Table 2–43 Internal Midpanel Tie Rod (MPT) Size (Dia.)

125 to 750 Pa Negative Pressure				
EMT Size and Length for Duct Width (W)		Rod Spacing Between Qualified Joints		
^	^	0.90 m RS	0.75 m RS	0.60 m RS
^	Max. L, mm	Duct Width (W)		
12.7 mm Dia.	1168	to 2108 mm	to 2438 mm	to 2438 mm
^	1067	2134 - 2438 mm	—	—
19.1 mm Dia.	1575	to 2438 mm	to 2438 mm	to 2438 mm
25 mm Dia.	1880	to 2438 mm	to 2438 mm	to 2438 mm
31.8 mm Dia.	2400	to 2438 mm	to 2438 mm	to 2438 mm

Table 2–43M Internal Midpanel Tie Rod (MPT) Size (Dia.)

4 in. wg Negative Pressure				
EMT Size and Length for Duct Width (W)		Rod Spacing Between Qualified Joints		
^	^	3 ft RS	2 ½ ft RS	2 ft RS
^	Max. L, in.	Duct Width (W)		
½ in. Dia.	47	to 62 in.	to 72 in.	to 90 in.
^	44	63 - 72	73 - 84	to 96 in.
^	42	73 - 78	85 - 96	–
^	38	79 - 84	–	–
^	36	85 - 96	–	–
¾ in. Dia.	62	to 62 in.	to 60 in.	to 96 in.
^	58	63 - 72	61 - 78	–
^	54	73 - 80	79 - 96	–
^	50	81 - 88	–	–
^	48	89 - 96	–	–
1.0 in. Dia.	74	to 96 in.		
1 ¼ in. Dia.	96	to 96 in.		

Table 2-44 Internal Midpanel Tie Rod (MPT) Size (Dia.)

1000 Pa Negative Pressure				
EMT Size and Length for Duct Width (W)		Rod Spacing Between Qualified Joints		
^	^	0.90 m RS	0.75 m RS	0.60 m RS
^	Max. L, mm	Duct Width (W)		
12.7 mm Dia.	1194	to 1575 mm	to 1829 mm	to 2286 mm
^	1118	1600 - 1829	1854 - 2134	to 2438 mm
^	1067	1854 - 1981	2159 - 2438	–
^	965	2007 - 2137	–	–
^	914	2159 - 2438	–	–
19.1 mm Dia.	1575	to 1575 mm	to 1524 mm	to 2438 mm
^	1473	1600 - 1829	1549 - 1981	–
^	1372	1854 - 2032	2007 - 2438	–
^	1270	2057 - 2235	–	–
^	1219	2261 - 2438	–	–
25 mm Dia.	1880	to 2438 mm		
31.8 mm Dia.	2438	to 2438 mm		

Table 2-44M Internal Midpanel Tie Rod (MPT) Size (Dia.)

6 in. wg Negative Pressure			
EMT Size and Length for Duct Width (W)		Rod Spacing Between Qualified Joints		
		3 ft RS	2 ½ ft RS	2 ft RS
	Max. L, in.	Duct Width (W)		
½ in. Dia.	47	to 40 in.	to 50 in.	to 62 in.
	44	41 - 47	51 - 56	63 - 70
	42	48 - 52	57 - 62	71 - 78
	38	53 - 58	63 - 70	79 - 86
	36	59 - 66	71 - 80	87 - 96
¾ in. Dia.	62	to 62 in.	to 76 in.	to 92 in.
	58	63 - 72	77 - 86	93 - 96
	54	73 - 80	87 - 96	–
	50	81 - 88	–	–
	48	89 - 96	–	–
1.0 in. Dia.	74	to 92 in.	to 96 in.	to 96 in.
1 ¼ in. Dia.	96	to 96 in.		

Table 2–45 Internal Midpanel Tie Rod (MPT) Size (Dia.)

1500 Pa Negative Pressure			
EMT Size and Length for Duct Width (W)		Rod Spacing Between Qualified Joints		
		0.90 m RS	0.75 m RS	0.60 m RS
	Max. L, mm	Duct Width (W)		
12.7 mm Dia.	1194	to 1016 mm	to 1270 mm	to 1575 mm
	1118	1041 - 1194	1295 - 1422	1600 - 1778
	1067	1219 - 1321	1448 - 1575	1803 - 1981
	965	1346 - 1473	1600 - 1778	2007 - 2184
	914	1499 - 1676	1803 - 2032	2210 - 2438
19.1 mm Dia.	1575	to 1575 mm	to 1930	to 2337
	1473	1600 - 1829	1956 - 2184	2362 - 2438
	1372	1854 - 2032	2210 - 2438	–
	1270	2057 - 2235	–	–
	1219	2261 - 2438	–	–
25 mm Dia.	1880	to 2337 mm	to 2438 mm	to 2438 mm
31.8 mm Dia.	2400	to 2438 mm		

Table 2–45M Internal Midpanel Tie Rod (MPT) Size (Dia.)

W	RS	½"	1"	2"	3"	4"	6"	10"	W	RS	½"	1"	2"	3"	4"	6"	10"
37"	36	25	49	99	148	198	296	494	72"	36	47	94	187	281	374	562	936
	30	21	41	82	124	165	247	412		30	39	78	156	234	312	468	780
	28	19	38	77	115	154	231	384		28	36	73	146	218	291	437	728
	24	17	33	66	99	132	198	329		24	31	62	125	187	250	374	624
	22	15	30	60	91	121	181	302		22	29	57	114	172	229	343	572
	20	14	27	55	82	110	165	274		20	26	52	104	156	208	312	520
42"	36	27	55	109	164	218	328	546	78"	36	51	101	203	304	406	608	1014
	30	23	46	91	136	182	273	455		30	43	85	169	254	338	507	845
	28	21	43	85	127	170	255	425		28	39	79	158	237	315	473	789
	24	18	36	73	109	146	218	364		24	34	68	135	203	270	406	676
	22	17	33	67	100	134	200	334		22	31	62	124	186	248	372	620
	20	15	30	61	91	121	182	303		20	28	56	113	169	225	538	563
48"	36	31	62	125	187	250	374	624	84"	36	55	109	218	328	437	655	1092
	30	26	52	104	156	208	312	520		30	46	91	182	273	364	546	910
	28	24	49	97	146	194	291	485		28	42	85	170	255	340	510	849
	24	21	42	84	125	166	250	416		24	36	73	146	218	291	437	728
	22	19	38	76	114	153	229	381		22	33	67	133	200	267	400	667
	20	17	35	70	104	139	208	347		20	30	61	121	182	243	364	607
54"	36	35	70	140	211	281	421	702	90"	36	59	117	234	351	468	702	1170
	30	29	59	117	176	234	351	585		30	49	98	195	293	395	585	975
	28	27	55	109	164	218	328	546		28	46	91	182	273	364	546	910
	24	23	47	94	140	187	281	468		24	39	78	156	234	312	468	780
	22	22	43	86	129	172	257	429		22	36	72	143	215	286	429	715
	20	20	39	78	117	156	234	390		20	33	65	130	195	260	390	650
60"	36	39	78	156	234	312	468	780	96"	36	62	125	250	374	499	749	1248
	30	33	65	130	195	220	390	650		30	52	104	208	312	416	624	1040
	28	31	61	121	182	243	364	607		28	49	97	194	291	388	582	971
	24	26	52	108	156	216	312	520		24	42	83	166	250	333	494	832
	22	24	48	95	143	191	286	477		22	38	76	153	305	458	458	763
	20	22	43	87	130	173	260	433		20	35	69	139	208	277	416	693
66"	36	43	86	171	257	343	514	858									
	30	36	72	143	215	286	429	715									
	28	33	68	133	200	267	400	667									
	24	29	57	114	171	229	343	572									
	22	26	52	104	157	210	315	524									
	20	24	48	95	143	191	286	477									

Static Pressure Class, in. wg

Table 2–46 Midpanel Tie Rod (MPT) Design Load in Pounds

NOTES:

a. This table applies for tie rods at midpanel. It is based on 5.2 PSF/IN. WG on an area of duct width (W) times reinforcement spacing (RS). For sizes between W intervals use the load at the larger W or calculate it. Pressure is (+) or (-). 10 in. wg data is for independent custom design use only.

W	RS	\multicolumn{7}{c}{Static Pressure Class, Pa}	W	RS	\multicolumn{7}{c}{Static Pressure Class, Pa}
		125	250	500	750	1000	1500	2500			125	250	500	750	1000	1500	2500
1.0	900	11	23	46	69	91	137	229	1.8	900	21	41	82	123	165	247	411
	750	10	19	38	57	76	114	190		750	17	34	69	103	137	206	343
	700	9	18	36	53	71	107	178		700	16	32	64	96	128	192	320
	600	8	15	30	46	61	91	152		600	14	27	55	82	110	165	274
	550	7	14	28	56	75	112	140		550	13	25	50	75	101	151	251
	500	6	13	25	38	51	76	127		500	11	23	46	69	91	137	229
1.1	900	13	25	50	75	101	151	251	2.0	900	23	46	91	137	183	274	457
	750	11	21	42	63	84	126	210		750	19	38	76	114	152	229	381
	700	10	20	39	59	78	117	196		700	18	36	71	107	142	213	356
	600	8	17	34	50	67	101	168		600	15	30	61	91	122	183	305
	550	7	15	31	46	62	92	154		550	14	28	56	84	112	168	279
	500	7	14	28	42	56	84	140		500	13	25	51	76	102	152	254
1.2	900	14	27	55	82	110	165	274	2.1	900	24	48	96	144	192	288	480
	750	11	23	46	69	91	137	229		750	20	40	80	120	160	240	400
	700	11	21	43	64	85	128	213		700	19	37	75	112	149	224	373
	600	9	18	37	55	73	110	183		600	16	32	64	96	128	192	320
	550	8	17	34	50	67	101	168		550	15	29	59	88	117	176	293
	500	8	15	30	46	61	91	152		500	13	27	53	80	107	160	268
1.4	900	16	32	64	96	128	192	320	2.3	900	26	53	105	158	210	315	526
	750	13	27	53	80	107	160	267		750	22	44	88	131	175	263	438
	700	12	25	50	75	100	149	249		700	20	41	82	123	164	245	409
	600	11	21	43	64	85	128	213		600	18	35	70	105	140	210	350
	550	10	20	39	59	78	117	196		550	16	32	64	96	129	193	321
	500	9	18	36	53	71	107	178		500	15	29	58	88	117	175	292
1.5	900	17	34	69	103	137	206	343	2.4	900	27	55	110	165	219	329	549
	750	14	29	57	86	114	171	286		750	23	46	91	137	183	274	457
	700	13	27	53	80	107	160	267		700	21	43	85	128	171	256	427
	600	11	23	46	69	91	137	229		600	18	37	73	110	146	219	366
	550	11	21	42	63	84	126	210		550	17	34	67	101	134	201	335
	500	10	19	38	57	76	114	190		500	15	31	61	91	122	183	305
1.7	900	19	39	78	117	155	233	389									
	750	16	32	65	97	130	194	324									
	700	15	30	60	91	121	181	302									
	600	13	26	52	78	104	155	259									
	550	12	24	48	71	95	143	238									
	500	11	22	43	65	86	130	216									

Table 2–46M Midpanel Tie Rod (MPT) Design Load in Kilograms

NOTES:
a. This table applies for tie rods at midpanel. It is based on 0.101593 kg/m^2/Pa on an area of duct width (W) times reinforcement spacing (RS). For sizes between W intervals use the load at the larger W or calculate it. Pressure is (+) or (-). 1500 Pa data is for independent custom design use only.

Duct Dimension	Pressure Class, in. wg Positive or Negative							
	1/2 in.	1 in.	2 in.	3 in.	4 in.	6 in.	10 in.
8 in. and under	26	26	26	24	24	24	22
9 – 10 in.	26	26	26	24	22	22	20
11 – 12 in.	26	26	26	24	22	20	18
13 – 14 in.	26	26	24	22	20	20	18
15 – 16 in.	26	26	24	22	20	18	16
17 – 18 in.	26	24	22	20	18	18	16
19 – 20 in.	24	24	20	18	18	16	
21 – 22 in.	22	22	18	18	18	16	
23 – 24 in.	22	22	18	18	18	16	
25 – 26 in.	20	20	18	18	16		
27 – 28 in.	18	18	18	18	16		
29 – 30 in.	18	18	18	18	16		
31 – 36 in.	18	18	16	16			
37 – 42 in.	16	16					
43 – 48 in.	16	16					

Table 2–47 Unreinforced Duct (Wall Thickness)

This table gives minimum duct wall thickness (gage) for use of flat type joint systems. Plain S and hemmed S connectors are limited to 2 in. wg maximum. Slips and drives must not be less than two gages lighter than the duct wall nor below 24 ga. Double S slips must be 24 ga for ducts 30 in. wide or less and 22 ga for greater width.

Duct Gage	26 to 22	20	18	16
Minimum Flat Slip & Drive Gage	24	22	20	18

See Figure 2-9 for joint types.

Duct Dimension (mm)	Pressure Class, Pa Positive or Negative						
	125 Pa	250 Pa	500 Pa	750 Pa	1000 Pa	1500 Pa	2500 Pa
200 and under	0.55	0.55	0.55	0.70	0.70	0.70	0.85
230 – 250	0.55	0.55	0.55	0.70	0.85	0.85	1.00
251 – 300	0.55	0.55	0.55	0.70	0.85	1.00	1.31
301 – 350	0.55	0.55	0.70	0.85	1.00	1.00	1.31
351 – 400	0.55	0.55	0.70	0.85	1.00	1.31	1.61
401 – 450	0.55	0.70	0.85	1.00	1.31	1.31	1.61
451 – 500	0.70	0.70	1.00	1.31	1.31	1.61	
501 – 550	0.85	0.85	1.31	1.31	1.31	1.61	
551 – 600	0.85	0.85	1.31	1.31	1.31	1.61	
601 – 650	1.00	1.00	1.31	1.31	1.61		
651 – 700	1.31	1.31	1.31	1.31	1.61		
701 – 750	1.31	1.31	1.31	1.31	1.61		
751 – 900	1.61	1.31	1.61	1.61			
901 – 1000	1.61	1.61					
1001 – 1200	1.61	1.61					

Table 2–47M Unreinforced Duct (Wall Thickness)

This table gives minimum duct wall thickness (mm) for use of flat type joint systems. Plain S and hemmed S connectors are limited to 500 Pa maximum. Slips and drives must not be less than two gages lighter than the duct wall nor below 0.70 mm. Double S slips must be 0.70 mm for ducts 762 mm wide or less and 0.85 mm for greater width.

Duct Thickness (mm)	0.55 to 0.85	1.00	1.31	1.61
Minimum Flat Slip & Drive Thickness (mm)	0.70	0.85	1.00	1.31

See Figure 2-9 for joint types.

Duct Wall	26 ga		24 ga		22 ga		20 ga or Heavier	
Static Pressure	Maximum Duct Width (W) and Maximum Reinforcement Spacing (RS)							
	W	RS	W	RS	W	RS	W	RS
½ in. wg	20 in. 18 in.	10 ft N.R.	20 in.	N.R.	20 in.	N.R.	20 in.	N.R.
1 in. wg	20 in. 14 in. 12 in.	8 ft 10 ft N.R.	20 in. 14 in.	8 ft N.R.	20 in. 18 in.	10 ft N.R.	20 in.	N.R.
2 in. wg	18 in.	5 ft	18 in. 12 in.	8 ft N.R.	18 in. 14 in.	10 ft N.R.	18 in.	N.R
3 in. wg	12 in. 10 in.	5 ft 6 ft	18 in. 10 in.	5 ft N.R.	18 in. 12 in.	5 ft N.R.	18 in. 14 in.	6 ft N.R.
4 in. wg	Not Accepted		16 in. 8 in.	5 ft N.R.	12 in. 8 in.	6 ft N.R.	12 in.	N.R.

Table 2–48 T-1 Flat Drive Accepted as Reinforcement

Although the flat drive slip T-1 does not satisfy the EI calculation requirements for Classes A, B or C reinforcement, tests predict its suitability for use as reinforcement within the limits of the table.

N.R. – No reinforcement is required; however, the T-1 Joint may be used.

Duct Wall	0.55 mm		0.70 mm		0.80 mm		1.00 mm or Heavier	
Static Pressure (Pa)	Maximum Duct Width (W) and Maximum Reinforcement Spacing (RS)							
	W (mm)	RS (m)	W (mm)	RS (m)	W (mm)	RS (m)	W (mm)	RS (m)
125	508 457	3 N.R.	508	N.R.	508	N.R.	508	N.R.
250	508 356 305	2.4 3 N.R.	508 356	2.4 N.R.	508 457	3 N.R.	508	N.R.
500	457	1.5	457 305	2.4 N.R.	457 356	3 N.R.	457	N.R
750	305 254	1.5 1.8	457 254	1.5 N.R.	457 305	1.5 N.R.	457 356	1.8 N.R.
1000	Not Accepted		406 203	1.5 N.R.	305 254	1.8 N.R.	305	N.R.

Table 2–48M T-1 Flat Drive Accepted as Reinforcement

Although the flat drive slip T-1 does not satisfy the EI calculation requirements for Classes A, B or C reinforcement, tests predict its suitability for use as reinforcement within the limits of the table.

N.R. – No reinforcement is required; however, the T-1 Joint may be used.

NOTES:

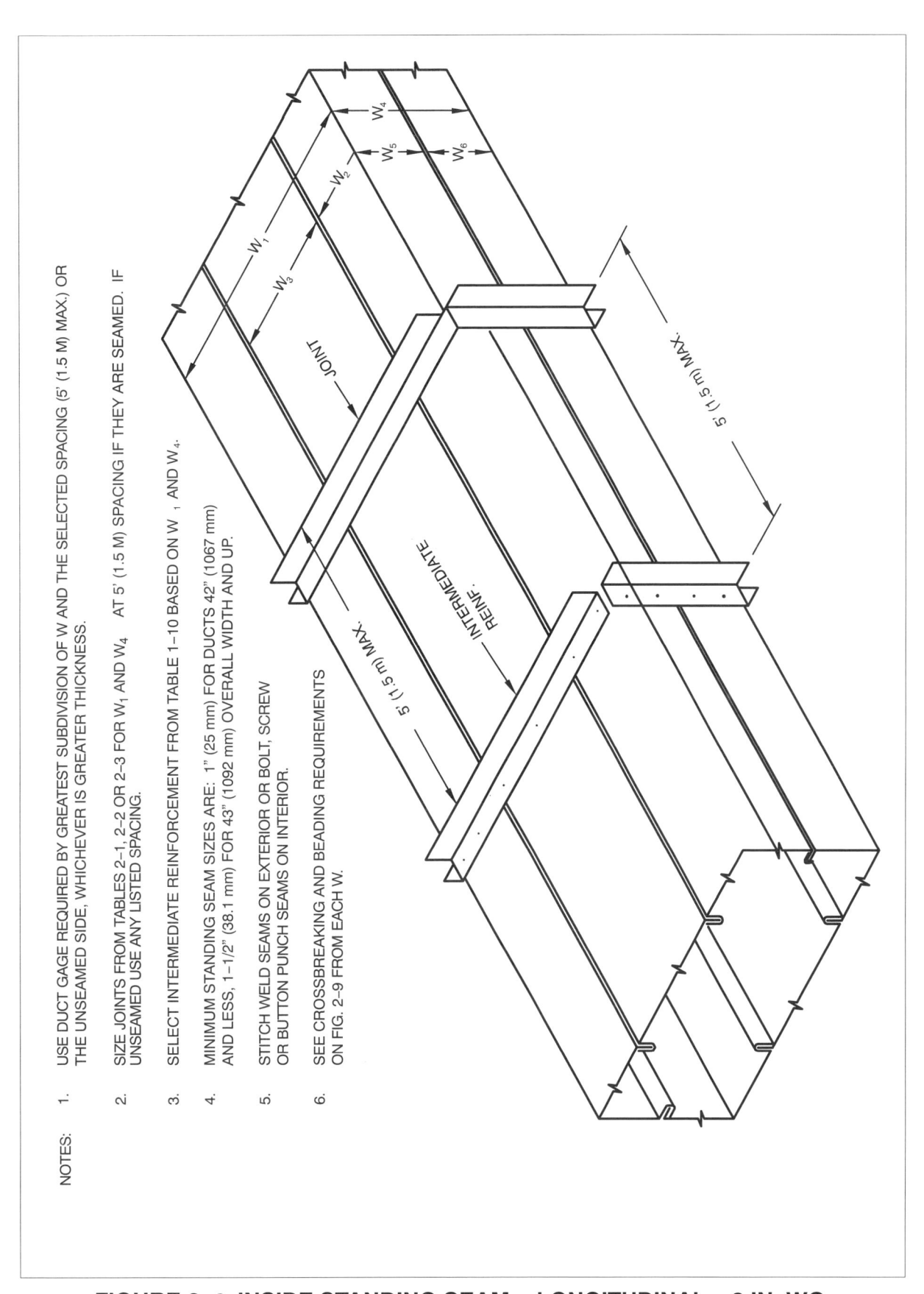

1. USE DUCT GAGE REQUIRED BY GREATEST SUBDIVISION OF W AND THE SELECTED SPACING (5' (1.5 M) MAX.) OR THE UNSEAMED SIDE, WHICHEVER IS GREATER THICKNESS.

2. SIZE JOINTS FROM TABLES 2-1, 2-2 OR 2-3 FOR W_1 AND W_4 AT 5' (1.5 M) SPACING IF THEY ARE SEAMED. IF UNSEAMED USE ANY LISTED SPACING.

3. SELECT INTERMEDIATE REINFORCEMENT FROM TABLE 1-10 BASED ON W_1 AND W_4.

4. MINIMUM STANDING SEAM SIZES ARE: 1" (25 mm) FOR DUCTS 42" (1067 mm) AND LESS, 1-1/2" (38.1 mm) FOR 43" (1092 mm) OVERALL WIDTH AND UP.

5. STITCH WELD SEAMS ON EXTERIOR OR BOLT, SCREW OR BUTTON PUNCH SEAMS ON INTERIOR.

6. SEE CROSSBREAKING AND BEADING REQUIREMENTS ON FIG. 2-9 FROM EACH W.

FIGURE 2-8 INSIDE STANDING SEAM – LONGITUDINAL – 2 IN. WG (500 Pa) MAXIMUM

JOINT OPTIONS

DRIVE SLIP
T-1

PLAIN "S" SLIP
T-5

HEMMED "S" SLIP
T-6

DOUBLE "S" SLIP
T-8

SEE TABLES 2-47 AND 2-48.
DUCTS WITH FLAT SLIP CONNECTORS
AND NO REINFORCEMENT
SEE OTHER FIGURES AND TEXT
FOR COMPLETE REQUIREMENTS
AND LIMITATIONS

TRANSVERSE JOINT

LONGITUDINAL SEAM
FIG. 2-2

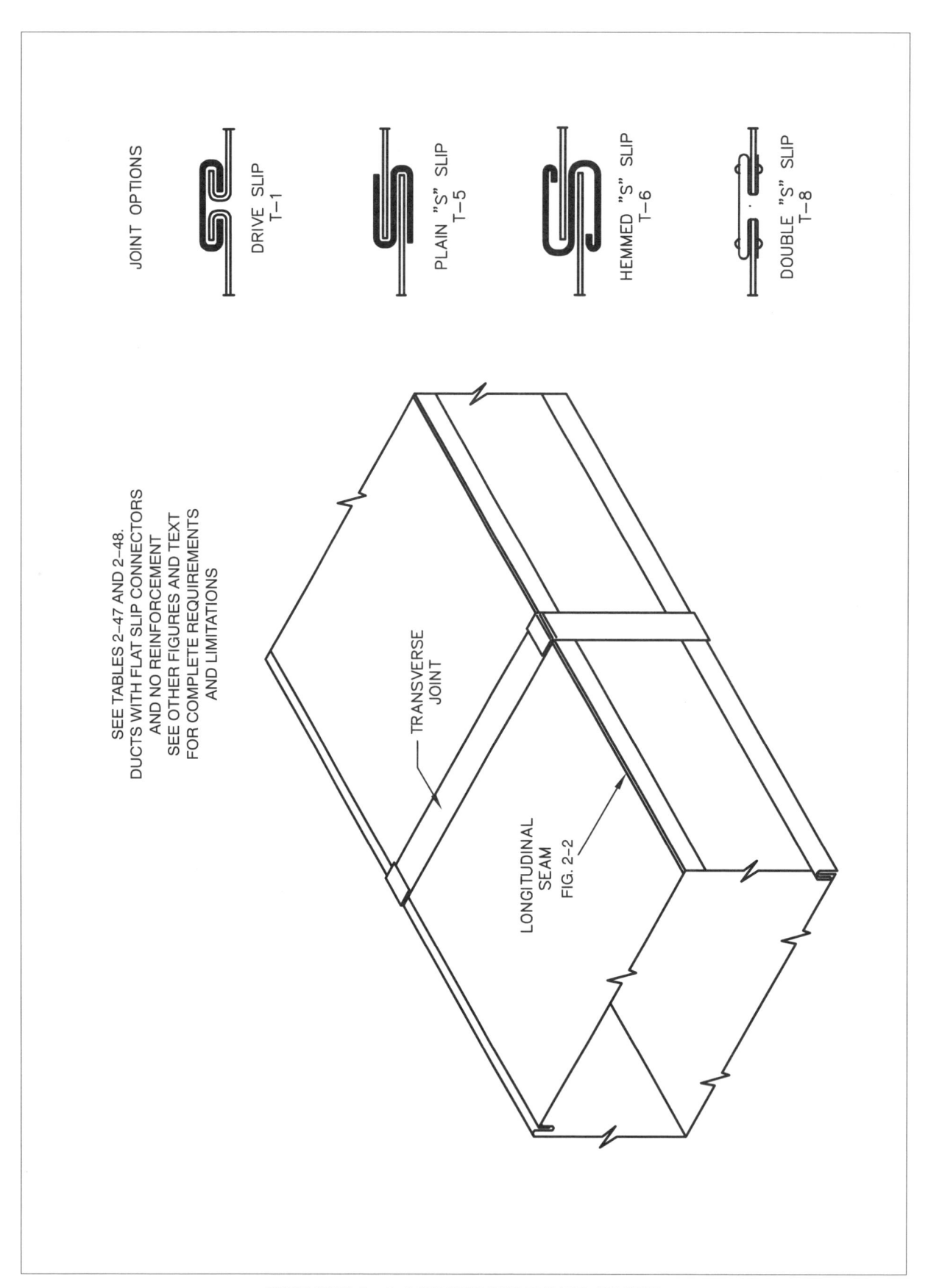

FIGURE 2-9 UNREINFORCED DUCT

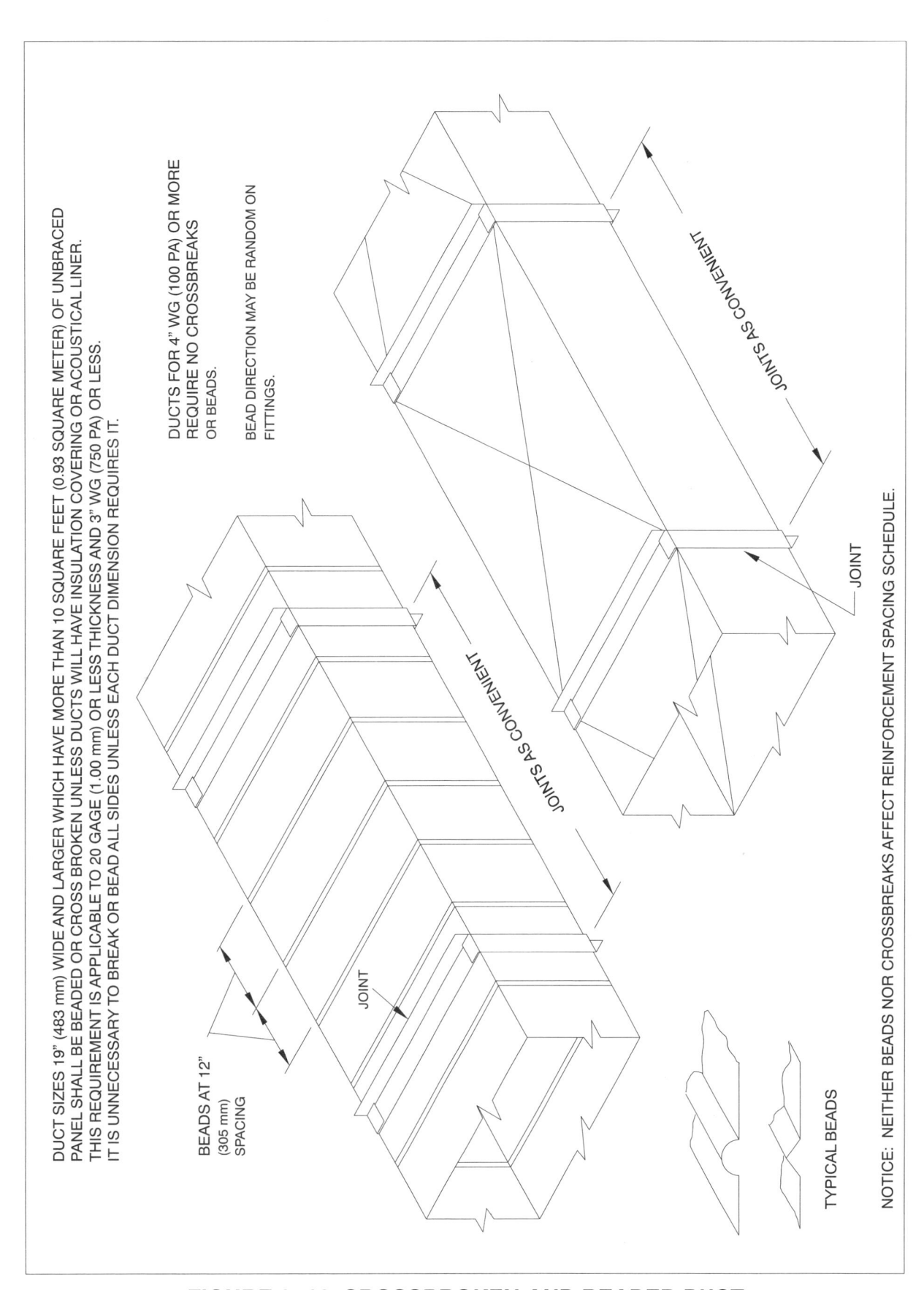

FIGURE 2–10 CROSSBROKEN AND BEADED DUCT

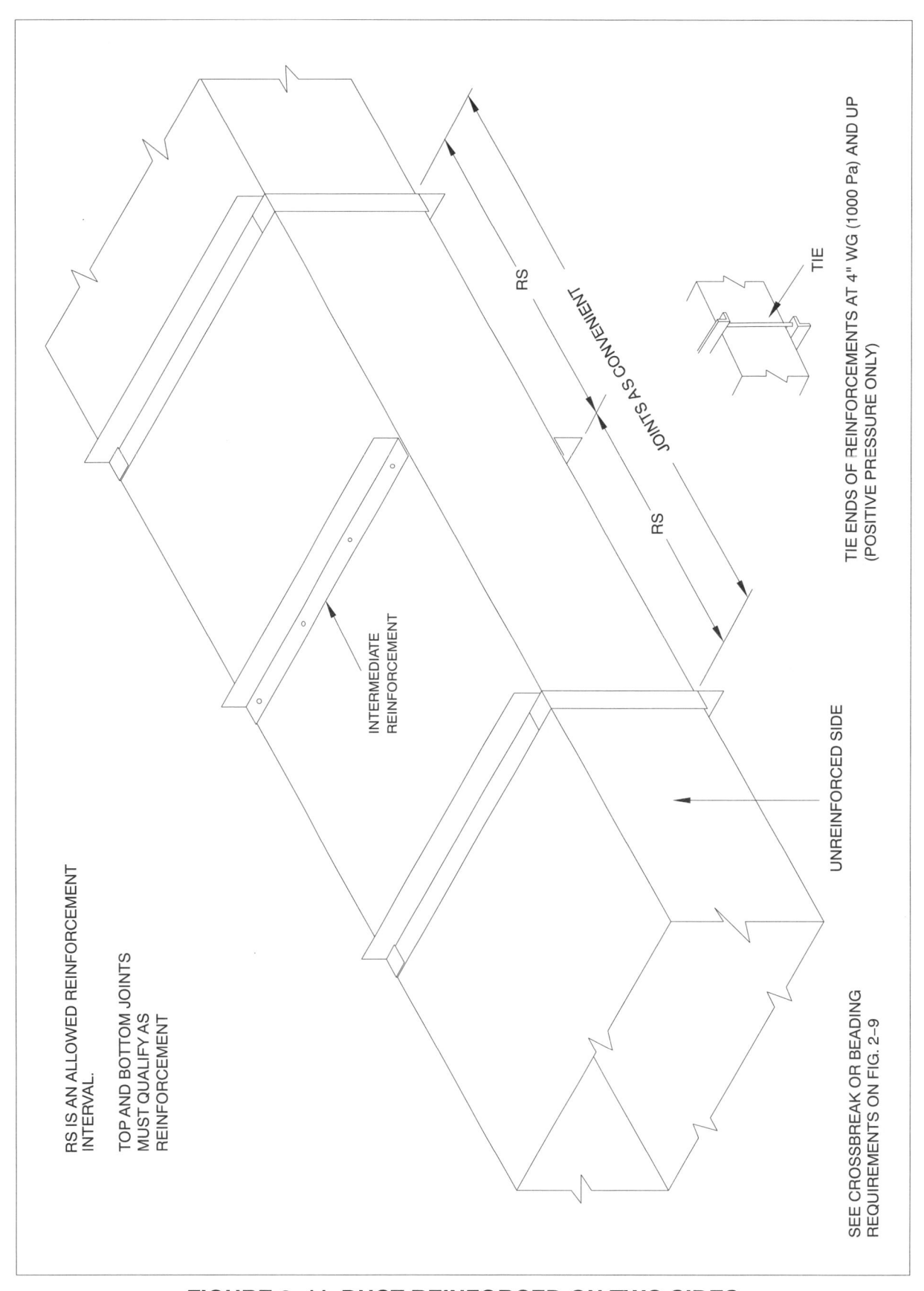

FIGURE 2-11 DUCT REINFORCED ON TWO SIDES

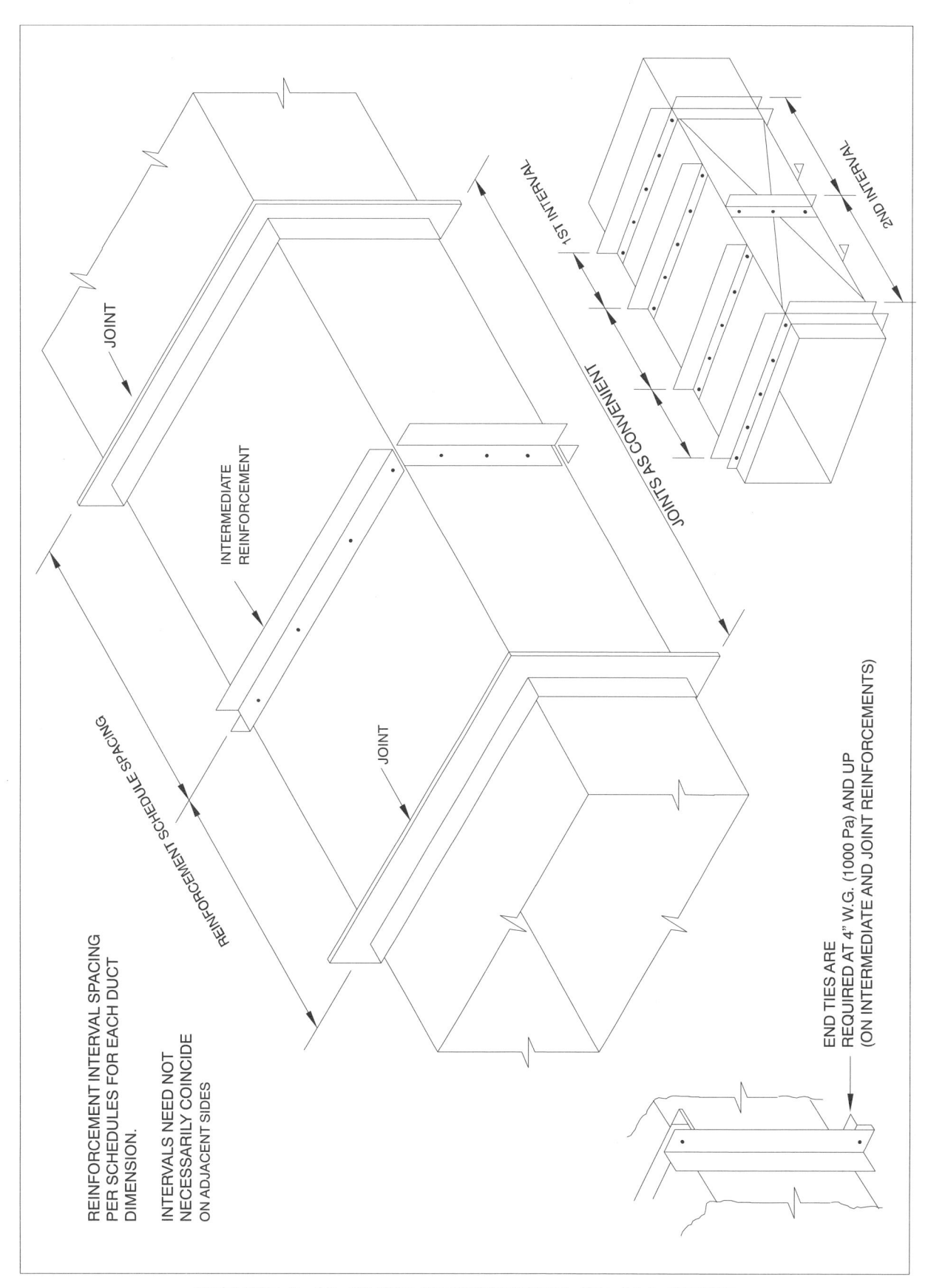

FIGURE 2-12 DUCT REINFORCED ON ALL SIDES

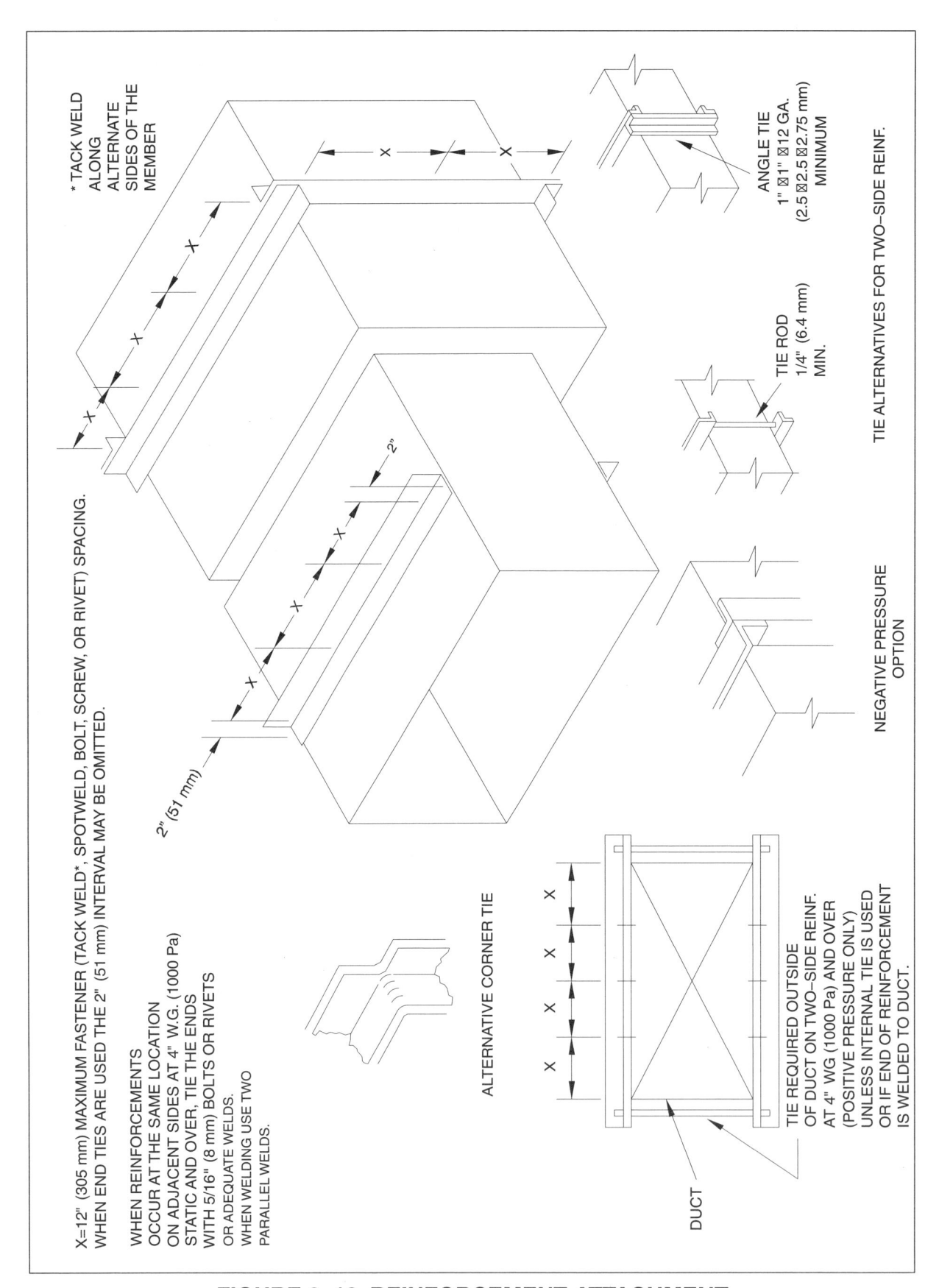

FIGURE 2-13 REINFORCEMENT ATTACHMENT

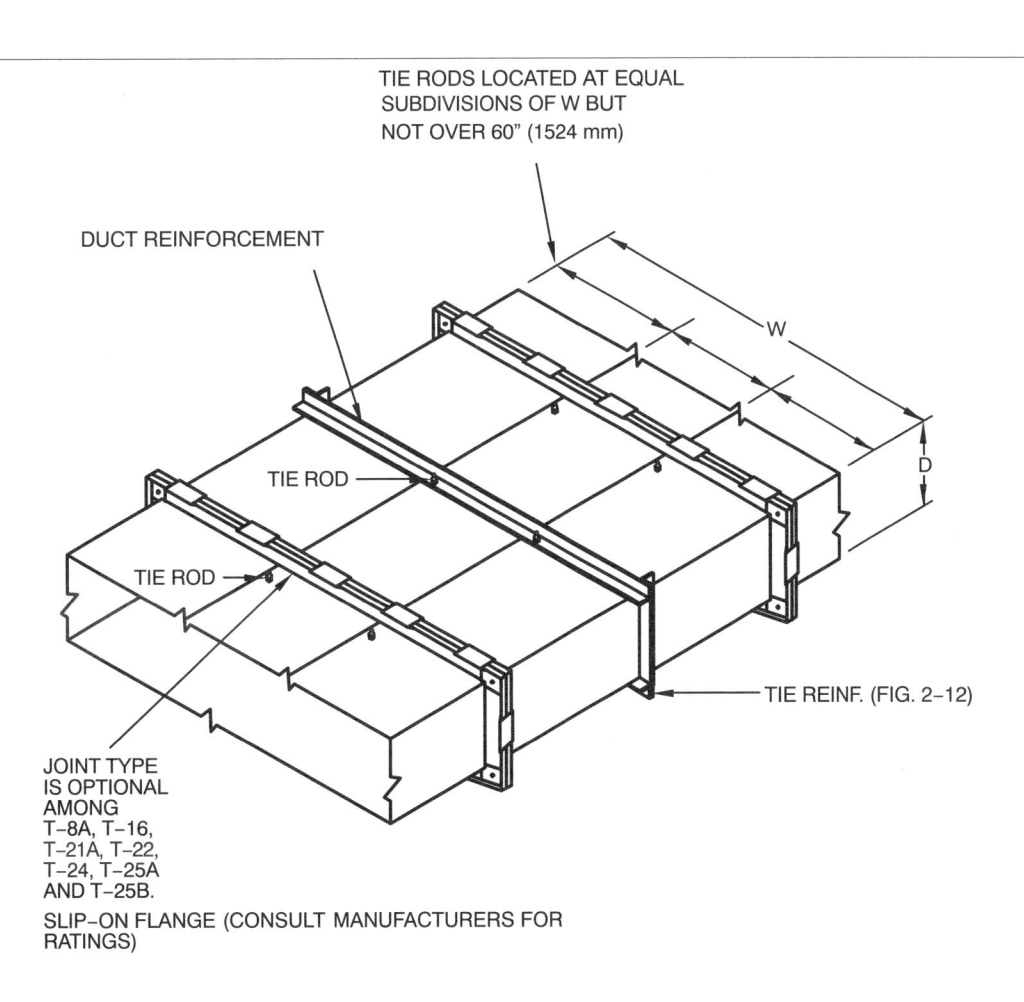

TIE RODS LOCATED AT EQUAL SUBDIVISIONS OF W BUT NOT OVER 60" (1524 mm)

DUCT REINFORCEMENT

TIE ROD

TIE ROD

TIE REINF. (FIG. 2-12)

JOINT TYPE IS OPTIONAL AMONG T-8A, T-16, T-21A, T-22, T-24, T-25A AND T-25B.

SLIP-ON FLANGE (CONSULT MANUFACTURERS FOR RATINGS)

Duct Pressure Class

wg (Pa)	½ in. (125 Pa)	1 in. (250 Pa)	2 in. (500 Pa)	3 in. (750 Pa)	4 in. (1000 Pa)	6 in. (1500 Pa)	10 in. (2500 Pa)
Panel Ga (mm)	18 (1.31 mm)	18 (1.31 mm)	18 (1.31 mm)	18 (1.31 mm)	18 (1.31 mm)	18 (1.31 mm)	16 (1.61 mm)
Reinf. Size	It	It	It	It	Jt	Kt	Lt
Reinf. Spacing ft (m)	2 ½ (0.75 m)	2 ½ (0.75 m)	2 ½ (0.75 m)	2 ½ (0.75 m)	2 ½ (0.75 m)	2 (0.60 m)	2 (0.60 m)
Max. Tie Rod Spacing ft (m)	5 (1.50 m)	5 (1.50 m)	5 (1.50 m)	5 (1.50 m)	5 (1.50 m)	5 (1.50 m)	4 (1.20 m)

Table 2-49 Duct Over 120 in. (3000 mm) Duct Construction

a. See tie rod text.

b. See Reinforcement Attachment in Figure 2-13.

c. See Figure 5-7 for large duct supports. Duct over 100 in. (2540 mm) width may require other internal supports for shape retention.

FIGURE 2-14 DUCT OVER 120 IN. (3000 MM) WIDE

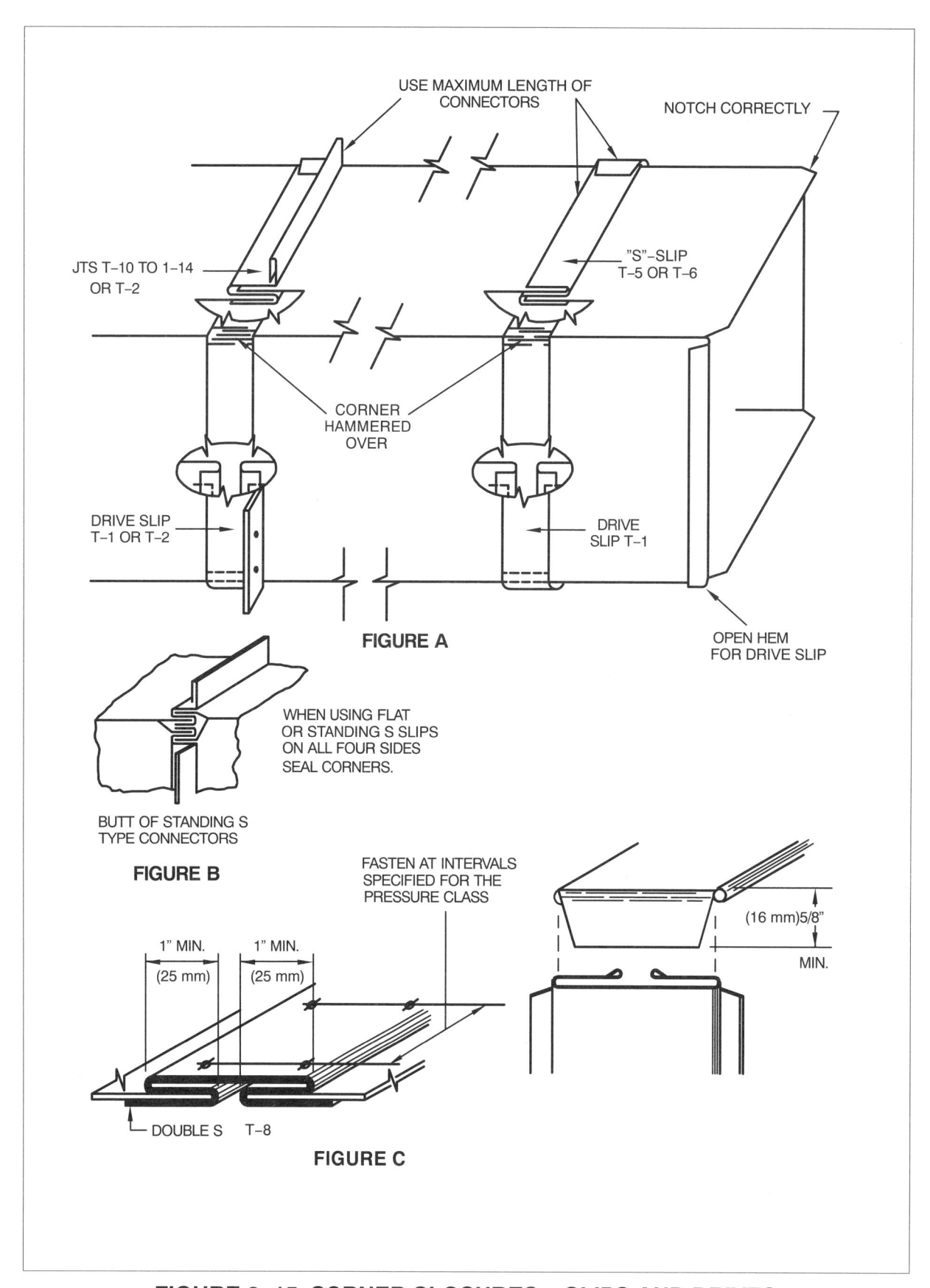

FIGURE 2-15 CORNER CLOSURES – SLIPS AND DRIVES

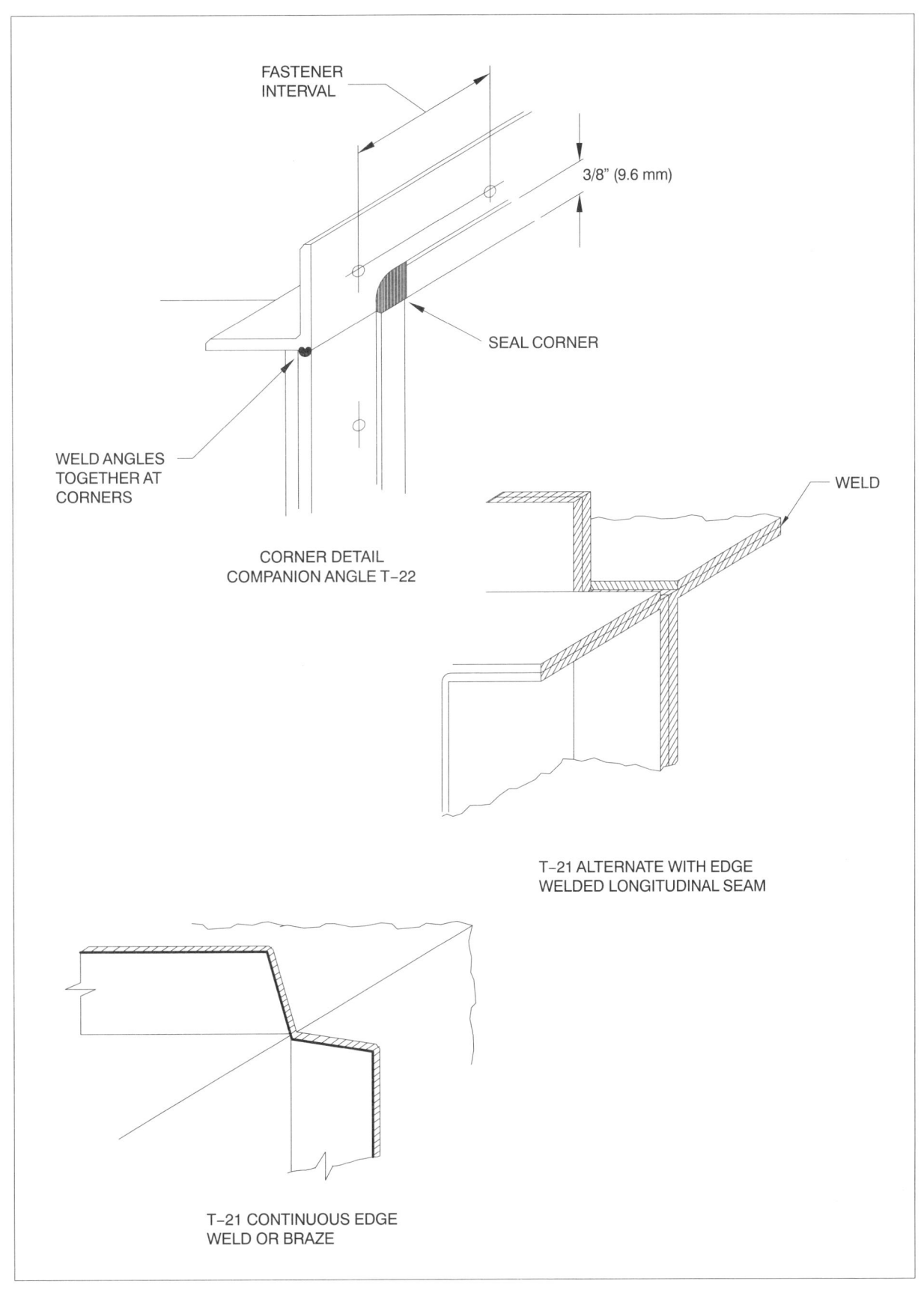

FIGURE 2-16 CORNER CLOSURES – FLANGES

BOLT OR RIVET FASTENING
1" (25 mm) MAX.
FROM THE END AND
AT 6" (150 mm)
MAX. INTERVALS

GASKET OR
SEALANT
USED IN THE JOINT

CONTINUOUS
CLEATS MAY
BE USED

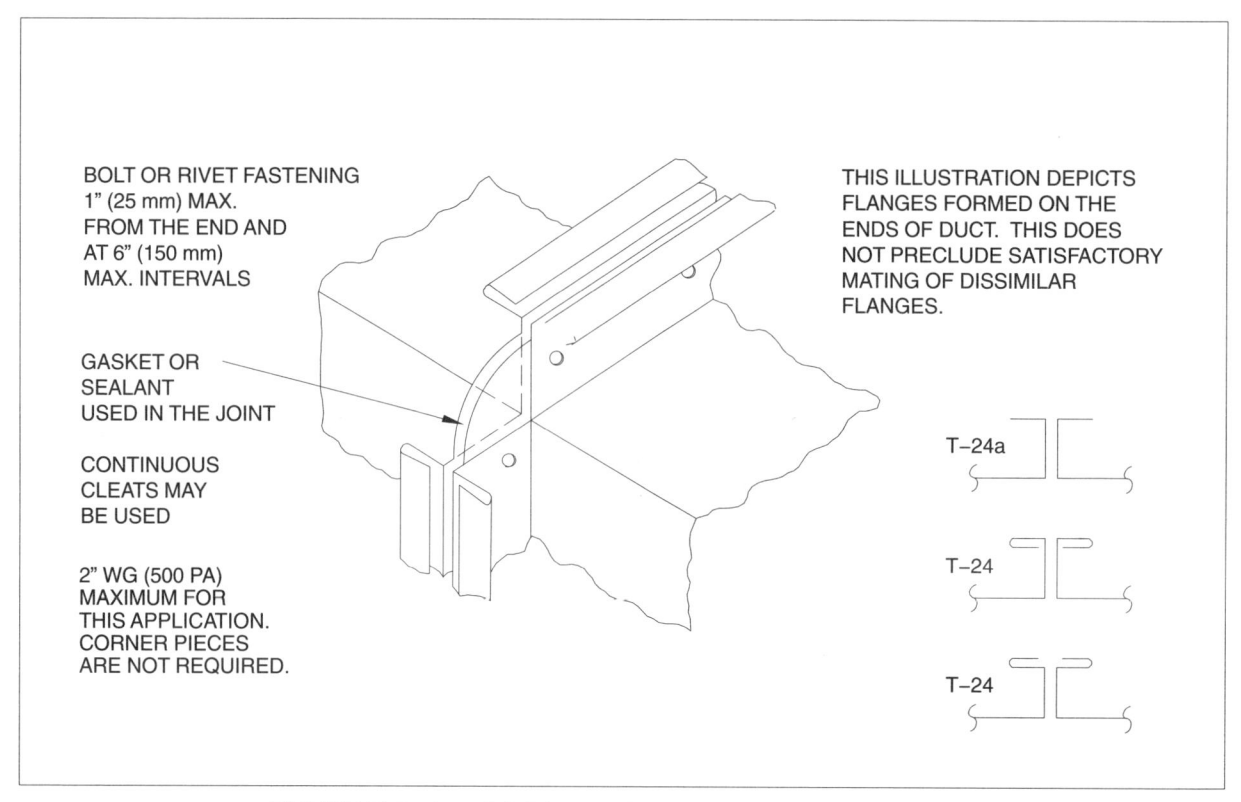

2" WG (500 PA)
MAXIMUM FOR
THIS APPLICATION.
CORNER PIECES
ARE NOT REQUIRED.

THIS ILLUSTRATION DEPICTS
FLANGES FORMED ON THE
ENDS OF DUCT. THIS DOES
NOT PRECLUDE SATISFACTORY
MATING OF DISSIMILAR
FLANGES.

T-24a

T-24

T-24

FIGURE 2-17 CORNER CLOSURES - FLANGES

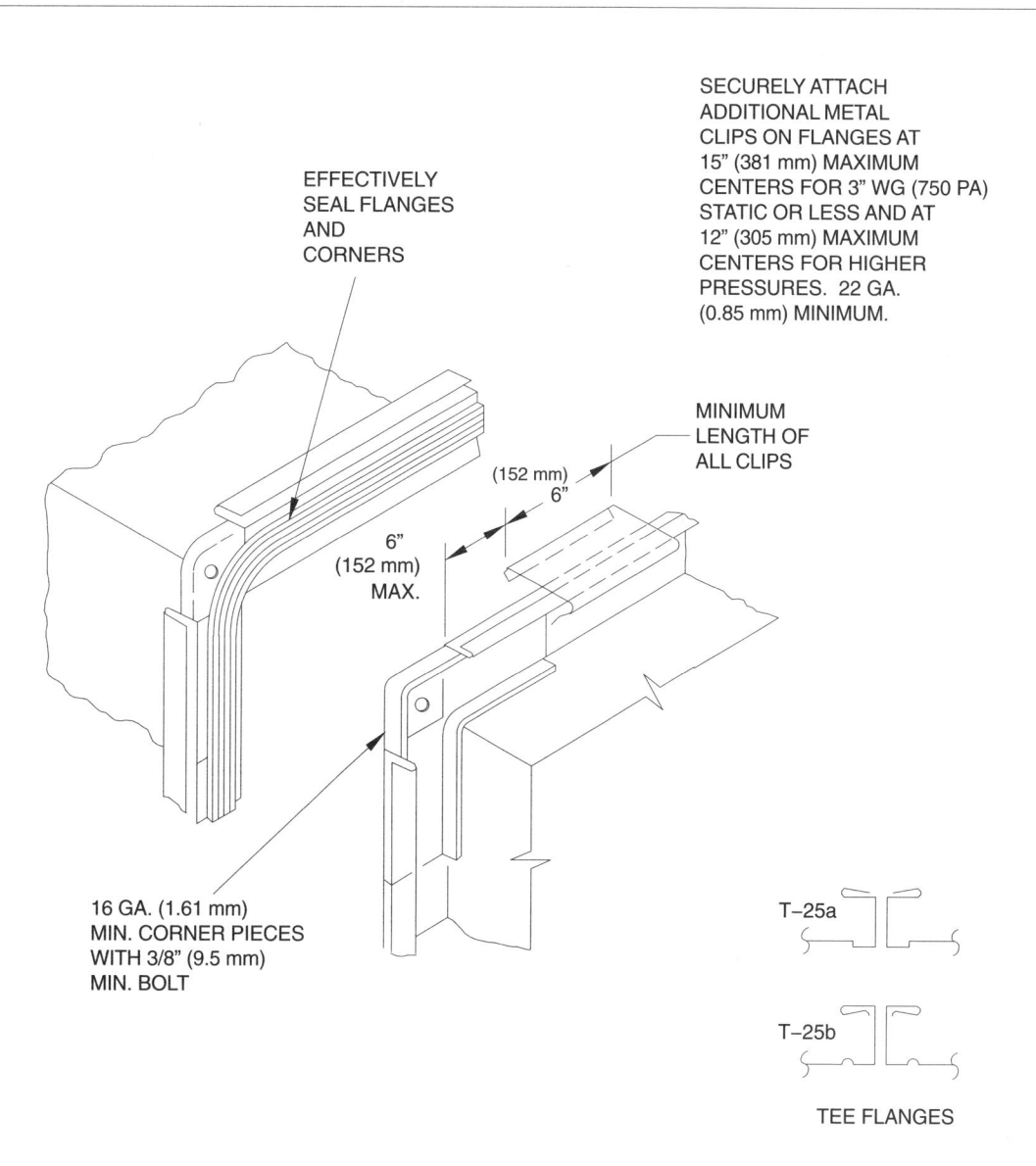

EFFECTIVELY SEAL FLANGES AND CORNERS

SECURELY ATTACH ADDITIONAL METAL CLIPS ON FLANGES AT 15" (381 mm) MAXIMUM CENTERS FOR 3" WG (750 PA) STATIC OR LESS AND AT 12" (305 mm) MAXIMUM CENTERS FOR HIGHER PRESSURES. 22 GA. (0.85 mm) MINIMUM.

MINIMUM LENGTH OF ALL CLIPS

(152 mm) 6"

6" (152 mm) MAX.

16 GA. (1.61 mm) MIN. CORNER PIECES WITH 3/8" (9.5 mm) MIN. BOLT

T-25a

T-25b

TEE FLANGES

SCREWS MAY BE USED IN LIEU OF METAL CLIPS. INSTALL 1" (25MM) MAX. FROM END OF CORNER PIECE AND AT 6" (152 MM) MAX. INTERVALS.

EQUIVALENT FIXATION OF JOINTS MAY BE USED. CONTINUOUS CLEATS MAY BE USED.

FIGURE 2–18 CORNER CLOSURES – FLANGES

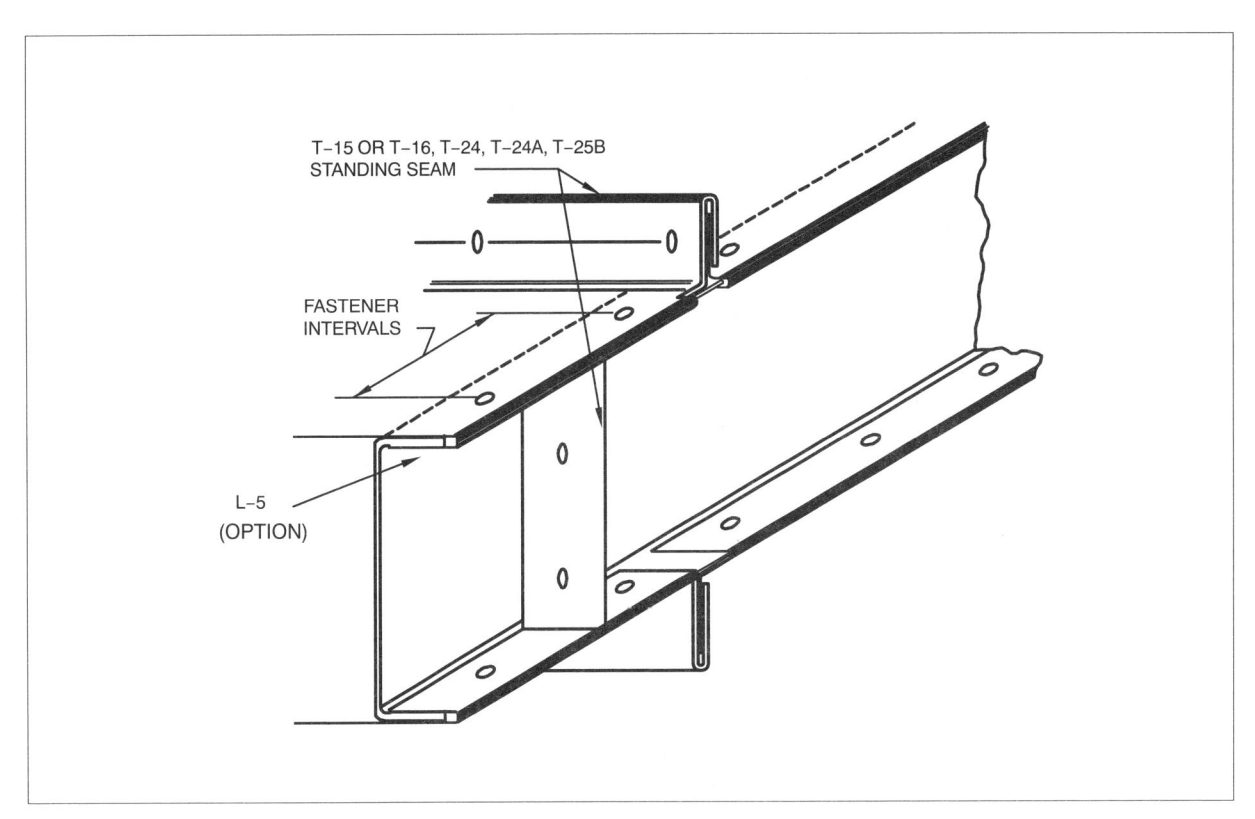

FIGURE 2-19 CORNER CLOSURES

2.10 COMMENTARY ON ALUMINUM DUCT

The traditional use of aluminum sheet two gages (Brown and Sharp schedule) heavier than standard galvanized sheet gage DOES NOT MEET THE REQUIREMENTS FOR EQUIVALENT STRENGTH AND RIGIDITY. The modulus of elasticity of aluminum is one-third that of steel and the yield strength is approximately one-half that of steel. Thus, aluminum has to be approximately 44 percent thicker. Table 2-50 gives the metal thickness conversion comparison. Tables 2-51 and 2-52 and notes explain how to adapt the steel duct reinforcement schedules to create comparable aluminum tables. However, tests have not been conducted on all of the indicated constructions to verify that deflections are the same as those of steel, to confirm that all construction will withstand a 50 percent overload, or to refine the fastener (screw, rivet, etc.) spacing, type, and size. Nevertheless, these provisions are more reliable than the tradition of simply increasing the duct gage by two size numbers. No failure at the rated pressure is anticipated, and none has been reported since this approach was introduced in 1976.

2.10.1 Conversion of Steel Tables to Aluminum

To convert the steel tables to aluminum:

1. Select a set of construction requirements for steel duct.

2. Substitute the aluminum thickness in Table 2-50 for the steel duct wall gage.

3. Change the thickness of the flat type of slips and drives (for unreinforced duct) per Table 2-50. If the aluminum thickness exceeds the capacity of the lock forming machine, use .032 in. (0.81 mm) minimum. The options in Table 2-48 using the flat drive as reinforcement have not been investigated for aluminum by SMACNA.

4. Find the thickness in dimensions (in steel) of the standing type of joint connector (Tables 2-31, 2-32, or 2-33). Change its thickness per Table 2-50 and change its dimension per the adjusted reinforcement code in Table 2-51. For example, a 1 in. × 22 ga (25 × 0.70 mm) (Code D) T-10 standing S in steel becomes 1⅛ in. × .050 in. (29 × 1.27 mm) in aluminum.

However, if the joint is one that enfolds an angle or bar (T-13, or T-14), equivalency is based on changing the thickness of the connector only and retaining a galvanized steel bar or angle. Otherwise, if the bar or angle must be aluminum, change the thickness and dimensions as necessary to accommodate the aluminum extrusions.

Alternative: Use a flat connector, change its thickness per Table 2-50, and back it up with a galvanized steel member from Table 2-29 (attaching it with aluminum fasteners), or back it up with an aluminum angle from Table 2-52 that is equivalent to the required steel angle code.

The alternative of using tie rods is also acceptable for aluminum. It is assumed that the reason for using aluminum duct would necessitate use of aluminum internal tie rods. However, since aluminum tie rods are not in this standard, the user will have to qualify his own selections. Round aluminum duct construction is given in Table 3-14.

RECTANGULAR ALUMINUM DUCT
ADAPTED FROM 3 IN. WG (750 PA) OR LOWER

Galv. Steel ga (mm) nominal	28 (0.48)	26 (0.55)	24 (0.70)	22 (0.78)	20 (1.00)	18 (1.31)	16 (1.61)
Min. Alum. equivalent* (mm)	0.023 (0.58)	0.027 (0.69)	0.034 (0.86)	0.043 (1.09)	0.052 (1.32)	0.067 (1.70)	0.083 (2.11)
Commercial size (mm)	0.025 (0.60)	0.032 (0.80)	0.04 (1.00)	0.05 (1.27)	0.063 (1.60)	0.071 (1.80)	0.09 (2.29)
Lbs wt/Sf. Alum.	Consult Appendix page A.5 for Weights						

Table 2-50 Thickness Adjustments

*Alloy 3003-H-14.

Galv. Rigidity Class	A	B	C	D	E	F	G	H	I	J	K	L
Alum. dim. per Galv. Class	C	E	E	F	H	I	I	K	**	**	**	**

Table 2-51 Dimension Adjustments

**Calculate an effective I_x = 3 x that used for steel.

Steel Angle Size In. (mm)	Cod	Equivalent Alum.*** Angle Size, In.	Steel Bar	Alum. Bar***
1 × 1 × 16 ga (25 × 25 × 1.61)	C	1¼ × 1¼ × ⅛ (31.8 × 31.8 × 3.2)	1 × ⅛ (25 × 3.2)	1½ × ⅛ or 1¼ × 3⁄16 (38. 1 × 38.1 or 31.8 × 4.8)
1 × 1 × ⅛ (25 × 25 × 3.2)	D	1½ × 1½ × ⅛ (38.1 × 38.1 × 3.2)	1½ × ⅛ (38.1 × 3.2)	1½ × ⅛ or 1¼ × 3⁄16 (38.1 × 38.1 or 31.8 × 4.8)
1¼ × 1¼ × ⅛ (31.8 × 31.8 × 3.2)	E	1¾ × 1¾ × ⅛ (44.5 × 44.5 × 3.2)		
1½ × 1½ × ⅛ (31.8 × 31.8 × 3.2)	F	2½ × 2½ × ⅛ (63.5 × 63.5 × 3.2)		
1½ × 1½ × 3⁄16 (31.8 × 31.8 × 4.8)	G	2 × 2 × ¼ (51 × 51 × 6.4)		
2 × 2 × ⅛ (51 × 51 × 3.2)	H	2½ × 2½ × 3⁄16 (63.5 × 63.5 × 4.8)		
2 × 2 × 3⁄16 (51 × 51 × 4.8)	I	2½ × 2½ × ⅜ or 3 × 3 × ¼ (63.5 × 63.5 × 7.9 or 76.2 × 76.2 × 6.4)		
2 × 2 × ¼ (51 × 51 × 6.4)	J	2½ × 2½ × ⅜ or 3 × 3 × ¼ (63.5 × 63.5 × 7.9 or 76.2 × 76.2 × 6.4)		
2½ × 2½ × 3⁄16 (63.5 ×. 63.5 × 4.8)	K	3 × 3 × ⅜ or 3½ × 3½ × ¼ (76.2 × 76.2 × 9.5 or 88.9 × 88.9 × 6.4)		

Table 2-52 Reinforcements

***Allow 6061-T Strength normally.

Any aluminum shape substitute must have a moment of inertia three times that of steel and have 30,000 psi minimum yield strength.

Sl.29 Rectangular aluminum duct construction using ASTM Standard B209 alloy sheet and the adaptations of the steel duct construction tables set forth in Tables 2-50 to 2-52 is acceptable for pressure classes not exceeding 3 in. wg (750 Pa).

Sl.30 For Tables 2-1, 2-2, 2-3, and 2-4, use equivalent sheet thickness from Table 2-50.

Sl.31 For Tables 2-31, 2-32, and 2-33, a connector not using angles or bar stock must have its thickness increased per Table 2-50 and its dimensions increased per Table 2-51.

Sl.32 For Tables 2-31, 2-32, and 2-33, a connector using angles or bar stock must have its aluminum thickness increased per Table 2-50 and must use either aluminum stock or galvanized stock from Table 2-51.

S1.33 For Table 2-29, use only galvanized steel members in Table 2-52 or the equivalent aluminum members. Use either galvanized steel members of dimensions given or aluminum members having both thickness and dimension conforming to Table 2-52. Other suitable aluminum shapes having a moment of inertia three times that of steel may be used.

Sl.34 Add fasteners as necessary to carry loadings.

Sl.35 Consider the need for dielectric isolation by zinc chromate paint, asphalt impregnated paper, bituminous paint, or other method.

Sl.36 Follow construction details for steel construction standards unless they are superseded by data on this page or by other considerations pertinent to aluminum. Use a lock-forming grade of sheet material.

THIS PAGE INTENTIONALLY LEFT BLANK

CHAPTER 3

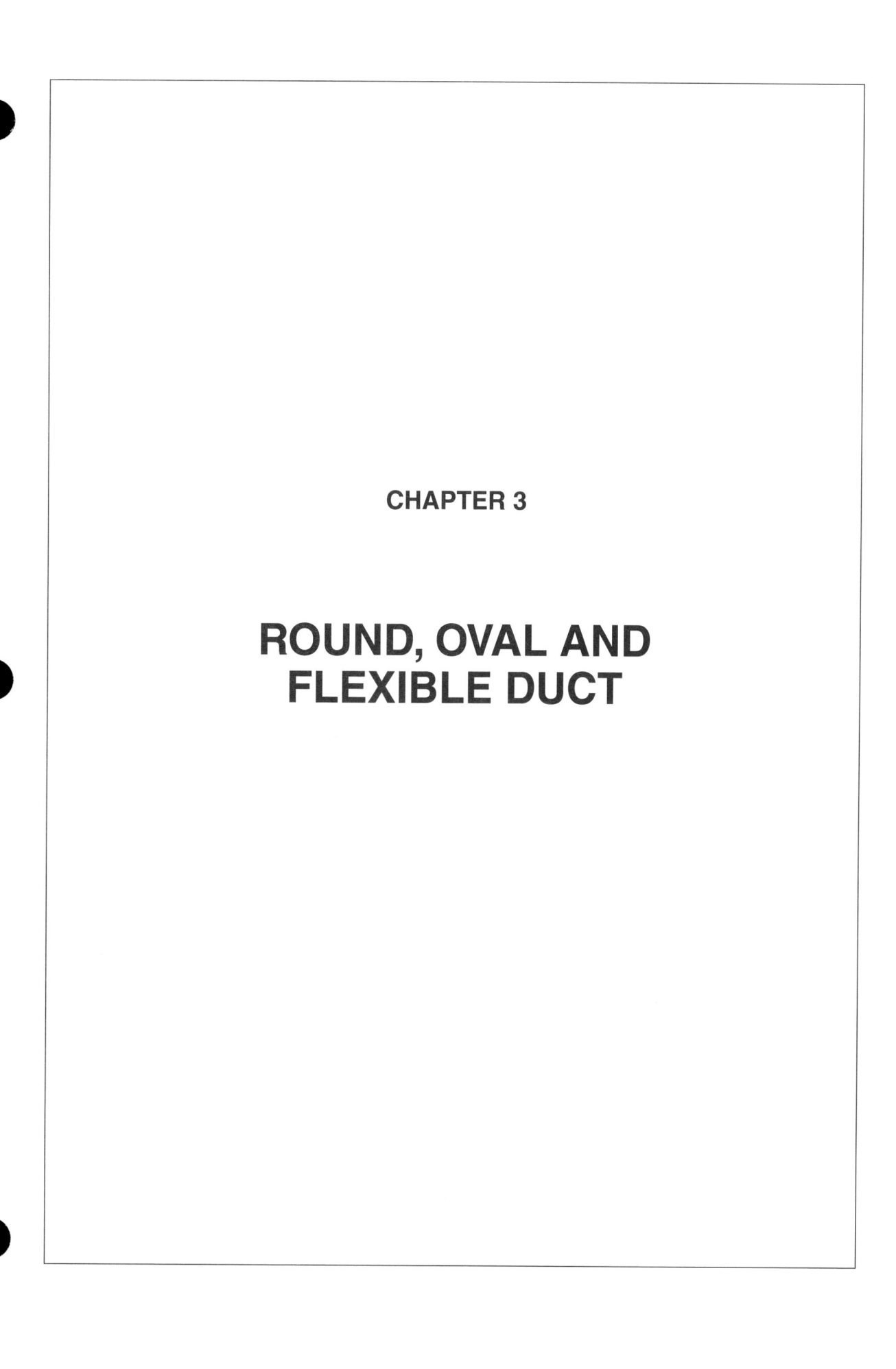

ROUND, OVAL AND FLEXIBLE DUCT

CHAPTER 3 — ROUND, OVAL AND FLEXIBLE DUCT

3.1 ROUND DUCT CONSTRUCTION STANDARDS

Classes available for designer use in project specifications or contractor selection as being fit for the project specifications that adopt these standards are as follows. Category listings are not intended to preclude different selections for fittings that function as area change, direction change, converging flow, diverging flow, or special purpose. Category listings also do not necessarily apply to their end connections to other fittings, straight duct sections or equipment.

1. All continuously welded or brazed.
2. Tack or spot welded (and sealed or unsealed).
3. Seam locked (and sealed or unsealed).
4. Rivet, screw, or punched-die-stamp locked (and sealed or unsealed).

The preceding categories may have additional forming prescriptions such as rolled, stamped, gored, spun, pleated, semi-pleated, or other methods. For purposes of distinction, openings in sections of straight ducts to receive taps of any connection method are not deemed to be fittings; but connection thereto may be specified by a prescribed method.

S3.0 Round ducts shall be constructed in accordance with Tables 3-5 and 3-14. Tables 3-5 through 3-12 are based on G-60 coated galvanized steel of ASTM Standards A653 and A924 grades. Uncoated, polyvinyl coated, aluminum alloy coated or aluminum-zinc alloy coated steel or stainless steel may be used if a minimum corresponding base metal thickness and material strength is provided. Lockforming quality is required. The use of an alternative material requires specification or approval by a designer.

S3.1 Fittings made with longitudinal seam bodies shall have a wall thickness not less than that specified for longitudinal-seam straight duct in Tables 3-5 through 3-14. Fittings with spiral bodies shall have a wall thickness not less than that specified for spiral-seam straight duct in Tables 3-5 through 3-14. The diameter of fittings shall be appropriate for mating with sections of the straight duct, equipment, and air terminals to which they connect.

S3.2 Sleeves, collars, and fittings to connect a round duct to a rectangular duct or to flexible ducts shall conform to S3.1 unless a different practice is supported by test data or affidavits confirming suitability for the service, *see* Figures 4-6 and 7-7.

S3.3 Nothing in this specification is meant to imply that the designer cannot by project specification designate acceptable construction methods.

S3.4 The use of a saddle or a direct connection of a branch into a larger duct is acceptable. Where they are used, the diameter of the branch shall not exceed two-thirds of the diameter of the main and protrusions into the interior of the main, are not allowed. Direct connection of a branch into a main shall include mechanical attachment sufficient to maintain the integrity of the assembly. All saddle fittings shall be sealed at all pressures.

S3.5 Where other limitations are not stated, mitered elbows shall be based on the velocity of flow and shall be constructed to comply with Table 3-1.

S3.6 The illustration of 90 degree elbows in Figure 3-4 does not preclude shapes of less than 90 degrees.

S3.7 Figure 4-7 is applicable for in-line offsets.

S3.8 Volume damper construction is provided in Figures 7-4 and 7-5.

Duct Velocity	R/D Ratio Centerline Radius to Duct Diameter	Number of Mitered Pieces 90 deg.	60 deg.	45 deg.
Up to 1000 fpm (5 mps)	0.6	3	2	2
1001 to 1500 fpm (5 to 7.5 mps)	1.0	4	3	2
Above 1500 fpm (7.5 mps)	1.5	5	4	3

Table 3-1 Mitered Elbows

S3.9　Ducts shall be suspended in accordance with Chapter 5. Additional supports shall be added if necessary to control deflection of ducts or to maintain their alignment at branch intersections. The support system shall not cause out-of-round shape.

S3.10　The requirements of Table 1-1 for sealing are applicable.

3.2　COMMENTARY

Round duct has a high strength to weight ratio, uses the least material to convey air at a given friction loss, and is comparatively easy to seal. The wall thickness suitable for positive pressure application is generally less than that for negative pressure. For positive pressure (and low negative pressure), girth ring reinforcement is not necessary. However, rings may be used to maintain the round shape to facilitate handling, shipment, or connection.

The tables indicate that a 10 in. wg (2500 Pa) negative pressure is the maximum classification. Some of the constructions in the tables will qualify at higher negative levels. For spiral ducts, higher negative pressure service information (and bursting pressure in positive mode) is available from industry sources.

Designers should consult SMACNA's *Round Industrial Duct Construction Standards* manual for:

a. Construction of any system carrying particulate or corrosive fumes (*i.e.*, systems for other than clean air),

b. Use of high negative pressure construction or (conservatively) for higher positive pressure than this document provides for,

c. Extended hanger spacing,

d. Engineering design of bolted flanged joints,

e. Negative pressure construction alternatives, and

f. Pressure service levels over 10 in. wg (2500 Pa).

This manual also does not indicate preference for any one type of longitudinal seam. The length of straight longitudinal seam duct will generally be determined by the size of the fabricator's rolling equipment. The length of spiral seam duct is limited by considerations such as in-line fitting frequency, potential for damage in shipment, maneuverability of the sections on the job, the number of support points needed to place the duct in its final location, and other factors.

The most popular transverse joints are the slip or lap types. The flanged joint is typically used in ducts over 60 in. (1524 mm) in diameter because of its advantage in retaining the circular shape.

Access to joints for makeup and orientation in vertical or horizontal positions will influence the choice of connection.

The SMACNA *HVAC Systems Duct Design* manual and the *ASHRAE* Duct Fitting Database contain far more configurations of round fittings than this manual. Friction loss data is provided in these design manuals. Where fittings of comparable or better performance are illustrated in duct design handbooks, designers are encouraged to consider allowing a substitution. Omissions from this document are not intended as prohibitions against using other constructions.

Double-wall rigid round duct is available from several industry sources. It is used for its acoustical value, and the perforated (typically metal) inner wall provides resistance to erosion of the duct liner. Single wall lined round duct is also available. Like double walled duct it primary function is sound attenuation but it does not have an inner liner.

Round spiral seam ducts with thinner than traditional wall thickness and with one or more corrugations (ribs) formed between the lock seams have been introduced in industry. Some of these forms have been tested for compliance with UL Standard 181 and have qualified for Class O listing. As the industry develops more experience with these in installation and service, and as more functional performance criteria are identified, it is anticipated that such forms will be added to SMACNA construction standards. Authorities and contractors are invited to evaluate them by information currently available.

Precaution:

Small differences occur in the diameter of ducts and fittings. Proper clearances are necessary. Verify suitability of fit, particularly when procurement is from outside sources.

BEADED SLEEVE JOINT RT-1

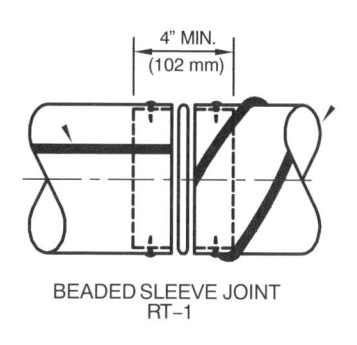

- Longitudinal or Spiral Seam
- Sleeve to be at least the same gage as duct
- Screws must be used at uniform intervals of at most 15 in. along the circumference
- Three screws minimum on 14 in. or less diameter

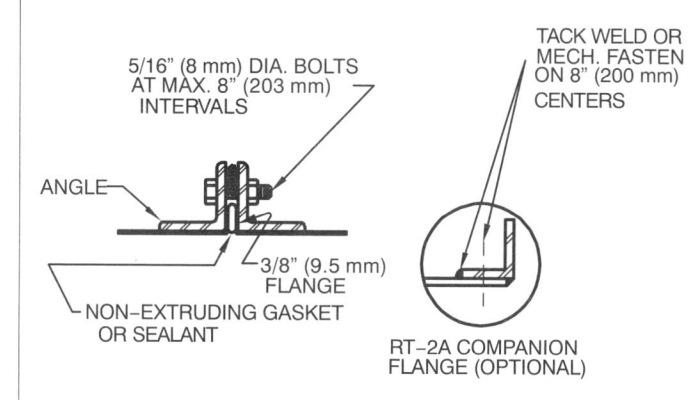

4" MIN. (102 mm)

5/16" (8 mm) DIA. BOLTS AT MAX. 8" (203 mm) INTERVALS
ANGLE
3/8" (9.5 mm) FLANGE
NON-EXTRUDING GASKET OR SEALANT
TACK WELD OR MECH. FASTEN ON 8" (200 mm) CENTERS
RT-2A COMPANION FLANGE (OPTIONAL)

- Longitudinal or spiral seam
- Minimum Flange Sizes:
- 1 in. × 1 in. × 10 ga up to 14 in. Dia.
- 1 ½ in. × 1 ½ in. × ⅛ in. over 14 in. Dia. If flanges are used as reinforcement *see* Table 3-4
- Male (internal) rings are permitted

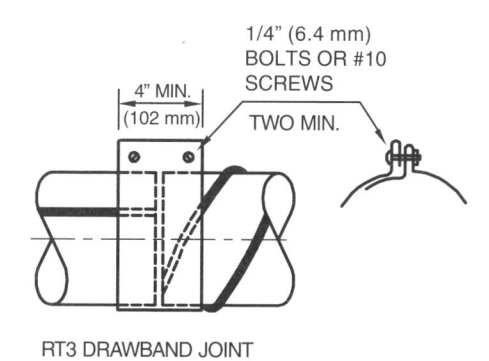

RT3 DRAWBAND JOINT

1/4" (6.4 mm) BOLTS OR #10 SCREWS TWO MIN.
4" MIN. (102 mm)

- Longitudinal or spiral seam
- Drawband to be at least same gage as duct

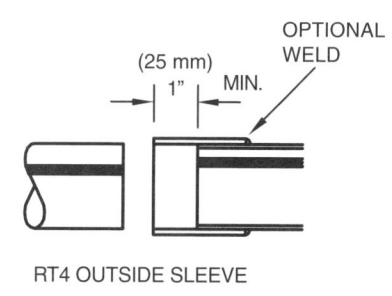

RT4 OUTSIDE SLEEVE

(25 mm) 1" MIN.
OPTIONAL WELD

- Longitudinal seam only
- See RT-1 for screw requirements

FIGURE 3-1 ROUND DUCT TRANSVERSE JOINTS

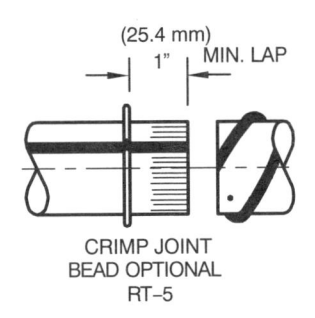

CRIMP JOINT
BEAD OPTIONAL
RT-5

(25.4 mm) 1" MIN. LAP

- Longitudinal or spiral seam
- See RT-1 for screw requirements

SWEDGE (BELL)
RT-6

(25 mm) 1" MIN.

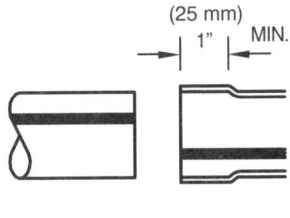

- Longitudinal seam only
- See RT-1 for screw requirements

GASKET
SLIP-ON
FLANGE
(CONSULT MFRS.)

- Consult manufacturers for ratings established by performance documented to functional criteria in Chapter 11.

FIGURE 3-1 ROUND DUCT TRANSVERSE JOINTS (CONTINUED)

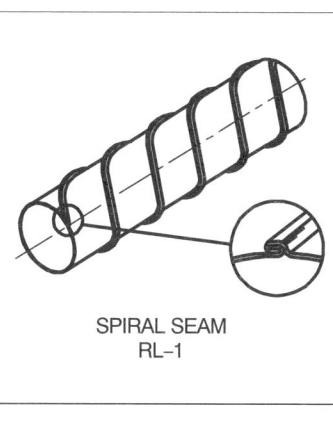

SPIRAL SEAM
RL-1

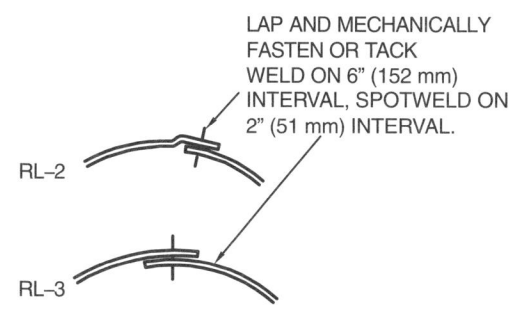

- To ± 10 in. wg

LAP AND MECHANICALLY FASTEN OR TACK WELD ON 6" (152 mm) INTERVAL, SPOTWELD ON 2" (51 mm) INTERVAL.

RL-2

RL-3

- To ± 4 in. wg
- Acceptable to 10 in. wg if spot welded on 1 in. intervals or tack welded on 3 in. intervals

RL-4
BUTT WELD
(OR LAP & SEAM WELDED)

- To ± 10 in. wg
- See RL 2 for weld options or continuously weld

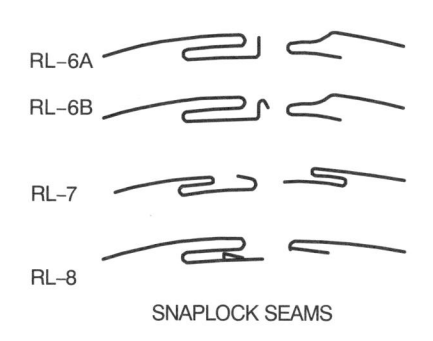

RL-5
GROOVED SEAM
PIPE LOCK
FLAT LOCK

- To ± 10 in. wg

RL-6A
RL-6B
RL-7
RL-8
SNAPLOCK SEAMS

- To + 2 in. wg
- To − 1 in. wg

FIGURE 3-2 ROUND DUCT LONGITUDINAL SEAMS

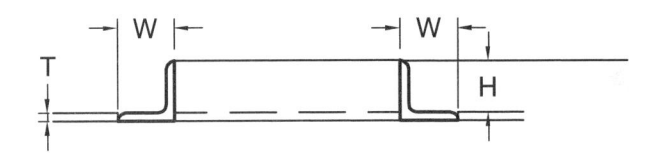

Angle Rings

FIGURE 3–3 ROUND DUCT REINFORCEMENT

Reinforcement Class	Size W × H × T
A	1 × 1 × ⅛
B	1 ¼ × 1 ¼ × 3/16
C	1 ½ × 1 ½ × 3/16
D	1 ½ × 1 ½ × ¼
E	2 × 2 × 3/16
F	2 × 2 × ¼
G	3 × 3 × ¼

Table 3–2 Angle Ring Size

Duct Dia, in.	Number of Attachments
6 and under	4
12 and under	6
18 and under	8
30 and under	12
54 and under	16
78 and under	20
96 and under	24

Table 3–3 Ring Attachment Schedule

NOTES:

a. Rings may be attached to the duct wall using screws, rivets, or tack welds.

b. Companion Flanges used for reinforcement shall be:

Duct Dia. in.	Flange Selection
up to 9	1 × 1 × ⅛*
10 – 12	1 ¼ × 1 ¼ × ⅛*
13 – 25	1 ½ × 1 ½ × 3/16
26 – 48	2 × 2 × 3/16
49 – 60	2 ½ × 2 ½ × 3/16
61 – 96	3 × 3 × ¼

Table 3–4 Companion Flange Joints Used As Reinforcement

*Standard rings in 10 ga are an acceptable slightly heavier alternative to the specified ⅛ in. thickness rings.

3.6 HVAC Duct Construction Standards Metal and Flexible • Fourth Edition

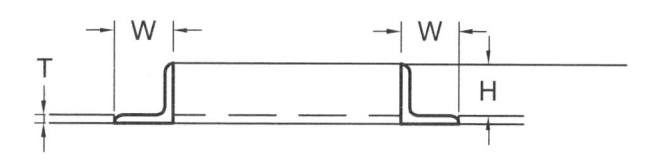

Angle Rings

FIGURE 3-3M ROUND DUCT REINFORCEMENT

Reinforcement Class	Size W × H × T (mm)
A	25 × 25 × 3.2
B	31.8 × 31.8 × 4.8
C	38.1 × 38.1 × 4.8
D	38.1 × 38.1 × 6.4
E	51 × 51 × 4.8
F	51 × 51 × 6.4
G	76 × 76 × 6.4

Table 3-2M Angle Ring Size

Duct Dia (mm)	Number of Attachments
150 and under	4
300 and under	6
450 and under	8
750 and under	12
1300 and under	16
1950 and under	20
2400 and under	24

Table 3-3M Ring Attachment Schedule

NOTES:

a. Rings may be attached to the duct wall using screws, rivets, or tack welds.

b. Companion Flanges used for reinforcement shall be:

Duct Dia. (mm)	Flange Selection
up to 225	25 × 25 × 3.2*
250 – 300	31.8 × 31.8 × 3.2*
301 – 601	38.1 × 38.1 × 4.8
650 – 1200	51 × 51 × 4.8
1201 – 1500	63.5 × 63.5 × 4.8
1501 – 2400	76 × 76 × 6.4

Table 3-4M Companion Flange Joints Used As Reinforcement

*Standard rings in 3.21 mm are an acceptable slightly heavier alternative to the specified 3.2 mm thickness rings.

MAX. Diameter, in.	Longitudinal Seam	Spiral Seam
4	28	28
6	28	28
8	28	28
10	28	28
12	28	28
14	28	28
16	26	26
18	26	26
20	24	26
22	24	26
24	24	26
30	22	24
36	22	24
42	22	24
48	20	22
54	20	22
60	20	22
66	18	22
72	18	20
78	18	20
84	18	20
90	18	20
96	18	20

Table 3–5 Round Duct Gage Unreinforced Positive Pressure To 10 in. wg

MAX. Diameter, mm	Longitudinal Seam	Spiral Seam
100	0.48	0.48
150	0.48	0.48
200	0.48	0.48
250	0.48	0.48
300	0.48	0.48
350	0.48	0.48
400	0.55	0.55
450	0.55	0.55
500	0.70	0.55
550	0.70	0.55
600	0.70	0.55
750	0.85	0.70
900	0.85	0.70
1000	0.85	0.70
1200	1.00	0.85
1300	1.00	0.85
1500	1.00	0.85
1650	1.31	0.85
1800	1.31	1.00
1950	1.31	1.00
2100	1.31	1.00
2250	1.31	1.00
2400	1.31	1.00

Table 3–5M Round Duct Gage Unreinforced Positive Pressure To 2500 Pa

Neg. Pressure 2 in. wg	Unstiff.		Stiffener Spacing								
			20 ft		12 ft		10 ft		6 ft		5 ft	
Max Diameter, in.	GA	R	GA	R	GA	R	GA	R	GA	R	GA	R
4	28	NR										
6	28	NR	Use Unstiffened Solution									
8	28	NR										
10	28	NR										
12	26	NR	28	A	28	A	28	A	28	A	28	A
14	24	NR	28	A	28	A	28	A	28	A	28	A
16	24	NR	26	A	28	A	28	A	28	A	28	A
18	22	NR	26	A	28	A	28	A	28	A	28	A
20	22	NR	24	A	28	A	28	A	28	A	28	A
22	22	NR	24	A	26	A	28	A	28	A	28	A
24	20	NR	24	A	26	A	26	A	28	A	28	A
30	18	NR	22	A	24	A	26	A	28	A	28	A
36	16	NR	22	A	24	A	24	A	26	A	28	A
42	16	NR	22	A	22	A	24	A	26	A	26	A
48			20	B	22	A	22	A	24	A	26	A
54			20	B	22	B	22	A	24	A	24	A
60			20	B	22	B	22	B	24	A	24	A
66			18	C	20	B	22	B	24	B	24	A
72			18	C	20	B	20	B	22	B	24	B
78			18	D	20	C	20	C	22	B	22	B
84			18	E	20	C	20	C	22	B	22	B
90			18	E	18	D	20	C	22	B	22	B
96			18	E	18	E	20	D	22	C	22	B

Table 3–6 Min. Required Gage for Longitudinal Seam Duct Under Neg. Pressure

NOTES:

a. N/A – Not Applicable

b. NR – Not Required

c. R – Reinforcement (stiffener) Class

d. For solutions in the shaded region consult SMACNA's Round Industrial Standard

Neg. Pressure 500 Pa	Unstiff.		6.00 m		3.6 m		3.00 m		1.80 m		1.50 m	
Max. Diameter (mm)	GA	R	GA	R	GA	R	GA	R	GA	R	GA	R
100	0.48	NR										
150	0.48	NR										
200	0.48	NR				Use Unstiffened Solution						
250	0.48	NR										
300	0.55	NR	0.48	A	0.48	A	0.48	A	0.48	A	0.48	A
350	0.70	NR	0.48	A	0.48	A	0.48	A	0.48	A	0.48	A
400	0.70	NR	0.55	A	0.48	A	0.48	A	0.48	A	0.48	A
450	0.85	NR	0.55	A	0.48	A	0.48	A	0.48	A	0.48	A
500	0.85	NR	0.70	A	0.48	A	0.48	A	0.48	A	0.48	A
550	0.85	NR	0.70	A	0.55	A	0.48	A	0.48	A	0.48	A
600	1.00	NR	0.70	A	0.55	A	0.55	A	0.48	A	0.48	A
750	1.31	NR	0.85	A	0.70	A	0.55	A	0.48	A	0.48	A
900	1.61	NR	0.85	A	0.70	A	0.70	A	0.55	A	0.48	A
1000	1.61	NR	0.85	A	0.85	A	0.70	A	0.55	A	0.55	A
1200			1.00	B	0.85	A	0.85	A	0.70	A	0.55	A
1300			1.00	B	0.85	B	0.85	A	0.70	A	0.70	A
1500			1.00	B	0.85	B	0.85	B	0.70	A	0.70	A
1650			1.31	C	1.00	B	0.85	B	0.70	B	0.70	A
1800			1.31	C	1.00	B	1.00	B	0.85	B	0.70	B
1950			1.31	D	1.00	C	1.00	C	0.85	B	0.85	B
2100			1.31	E	1.00	C	1.00	C	0.85	B	0.85	B
2250			1.31	E	1.31	D	1.00	C	0.85	B	0.85	B
2400			1.31	E	1.31	E	1.00	D	0.85	C	0.85	B

Table 3–6M Min. Required Gage for Longitudinal Seam Duct Under Neg. Pressure

NOTES:

a. N/A – Not Applicable

b. NR – Not Required

c. R – Reinforcement (stiffener) Class

d. For solutions in the shaded region consult SMACNA's Round Industrial Standard

Neg. Pressure 4 in. wg	Stiffener Spacing												
	Unstiff.		20 ft		12 ft		10 ft		6 ft		5 ft	
Max. Diameter, in.	GA	R	GA	R	GA	R	GA	R	GA	R	GA	R
4	28	NR										
6	28	NR		Use Unstiffened Solution									
8	28	NR										
10	26	NR	26	A	28	A	28	A	28	A	28	A
12	24	NR	26	A	28	A	28	A	28	A	28	A
14	22	NR	24	A	26	A	28	A	28	A	28	A
16	22	NR	24	A	26	A	26	A	28	A	28	A
18	20	NR	24	A	24	A	26	A	28	A	28	A
20	20	NR	22	A	24	A	24	A	28	A	28	A
22	18	NR	22	A	24	A	24	A	26	A	28	A
24	18	NR	22	A	24	A	24	A	26	A	26	A
30	16	NR	20	A	22	A	22	A	24	A	26	A
36			20	B	22	A	22	A	24	A	24	A
42			18	B	20	B	22	A	22	A	24	A
48			18	B	20	B	20	B	22	A	22	A
54			18	C	18	B	20	B	22	B	22	A
60			18	D	18	C	20	B	22	B	22	B
66			16	E	18	C	18	C	20	B	22	B
72			16	E	18	D	18	C	20	B	20	B
78			16	E	18	E	18	D	20	C	20	C
84			16	F	18	E	18	E	20	C	20	C
90					16	E	18	E	18	D	20	C
96					16	E	16	E	18	E	20	D

Table 3–7 Min. Required Gage for Longitudinal Seam Duct Under Neg. Pressure

NOTES:

a. N/A – Not Applicable

b. NR – Not Required

c. R – Reinforcement (stiffener) Class

d. For solutions in the shaded region consult SMACNA's Round Industrial Standard

Neg. Pressure 1000 Pa	Stiffener Spacing											
	Unstiff.		6.00 m		3.6 m		3.00 m		1.80 m		1.50 m	
MAX. Diameter (mm)	GA	R	GA	R	GA	R	GA	R	GA	R	GA	R
100	0.48	NR										
150	0.48	NR			Use Unstiffened Solution								
200	0.48	NR										
250	0.55	NR	0.55	A	0.48	A	0.48	A	0.48	A	0.48	A
300	0.70	NR	0.55	A	0.48	A	0.48	A	0.48	A	0.48	A
350	0.85	NR	0.70	A	0.55	A	0.48	A	0.48	A	0.48	A
400	0.85	NR	0.70	A	0.55	A	0.55	A	0.48	A	0.48	A
450	1.00	NR	0.70	A	0.70	A	0.55	A	0.48	A	0.48	A
500	1.00	NR	0.85	A	0.70	A	0.70	A	0.48	A	0.48	A
550	1.31	NR	0.85	A	0.70	A	0.70	A	0.55	A	0.48	A
600	1.31	NR	0.85	A	0.70	A	0.70	A	0.55	A	0.55	A
750	1.61	NR	1.00	A	0.85	A	0.85	A	0.70	A	0.55	A
900			1.00	B	0.85	A	0.85	A	0.70	A	0.70	A
1000			1.31	B	1.00	B	0.85	A	0.85	A	0.70	A
1200			1.31	B	1.00	B	1.00	B	0.85	A	0.85	A
1300			1.31	C	1.31	B	1.00	B	0.85	B	0.85	A
1500			1.31	D	1.31	C	1.00	B	0.85	B	0.85	B
1650			1.61	E	1.31	C	1.31	C	1.00	B	0.85	B
1800			1.61	E	1.31	D	1.31	C	1.00	B	1.00	B
1950			1.61	E	1.31	E	1.31	D	1.00	C	1.00	C
2100			1.61	F	1.31	E	1.31	E	1.00	C	1.00	C
2250					1.61	E	1.31	E	1.31	D	1.00	C
2400					1.61	E	1.61	E	1.31	E	1.00	D

Table 3–7M Min. Required Gage for Longitudinal Seam Duct Under Neg. Pressure

NOTES:

a. N/A – Not Applicable

b. NR – Not Required

c. R – Reinforcement (stiffener) Class

d. For solutions in the shaded region consult SMACNA's Round Industrial Standard

Neg. Pressure 6 in. wg	Unstiff.		Stiffener Spacing									
			20 ft		12 ft		10 ft		6 ft		5 ft	
MAX. Diameter, in.	GA	R	GA	R	GA	R	GA	R	GA	R	GA	R
4	28	NR	\multicolumn{10}{c	}{Use Unstiffened Solution}
6	28	NR										
8	26	NR	26	A	28	A	28	A	28	A	28	A
10	24	NR	24	A	26	A	28	A	28	A	28	A
12	24	NR	24	A	26	A	26	A	28	A	28	A
14	22	NR	24	A	24	A	26	A	28	A	28	A
16	20	NR	22	A	24	A	24	A	26	A	28	A
18	20	NR	22	A	24	A	24	A	26	A	26	A
20	18	NR	22	A	22	A	24	A	26	A	26	A
22	18	NR	20	A	22	A	24	A	24	A	26	A
24	18	NR	20	A	22	A	22	A	24	A	24	A
30	16	NR	18	A	20	A	22	A	24	A	24	A
36			18	B	20	B	20	A	22	A	22	A
42			18	B	18	B	20	B	22	A	22	A
48			16	C	18	B	18	B	20	B	22	B
54			16	D	18	C	18	C	20	B	20	B
60			16	E	18	C	18	C	20	B	20	B
66					16	E	18	D	18	C	20	B
72					16	E	18	E	18	C	20	C
78					16	E	16	E	18	D	18	C
84					16	F	16	E	18	E	18	D
90					16	G	16	F	18	E	18	E
96							16	G	18	E	18	E

Table 3–8 Min. Required Gage for Longitudinal Seam Duct Under Neg. Pressure

NOTES:

a. N/A – Not Applicable

b. NR – Not Required

c. R – Reinforcement (stiffener) Class

d. For solutions in the shaded region consult SMACNA's Round Industrial Standard

Neg. Pressure 1500 Pa	Unstiff.		Stiffener Spacing								
			6.00 m		3.6 m		3.00 m		1.80 m		1.50 m	
MAX. Diameter (mm)	GA	R	GA	R	GA	R	GA	R	GA	R	GA	R
100	0.48	NR	Use Unstiffened Solution									
150	0.48	NR										
200	0.55	NR	0.55	A	0.48	A	0.48	A	0.48	A	0.48	A
250	0.70	NR	0.70	A	0.55	A	0.48	A	0.48	A	0.48	A
300	0.70	NR	0.70	A	0.55	A	0.55	A	0.48	A	0.48	A
350	0.85	NR	0.70	A	0.70	A	0.55	A	0.48	A	0.48	A
400	1.00	NR	0.85	A	0.70	A	0.70	A	0.55	A	0.48	A
450	1.00	NR	0.85	A	0.70	A	0.70	A	0.55	A	0.55	A
500	1.31	NR	0.85	A	0.85	A	0.70	A	0.55	A	0.55	A
550	1.31	NR	1.00	A	0.85	A	0.70	A	0.70	A	0.55	A
600	1.31	NR	1.00	A	0.85	A	0.85	A	0.70	A	0.70	A
750	1.61	NR	1.31	A	1.00	A	0.85	A	0.70	A	0.70	A
900			1.31	B	1.00	B	1.00	A	0.85	A	0.85	A
1000			1.31	B	1.31	B	1.00	B	0.85	A	0.85	A
1200			1.61	C	1.31	B	1.31	B	1.00	B	0.85	B
1300			1.61	D	1.31	C	1.31	C	1.00	B	1.00	B
1500			1.61	E	1.31	C	1.31	C	1.00	B	1.00	B
1650					1.61	E	1.31	D	1.31	C	1.00	B
1800					1.61	E	1.31	E	1.31	C	1.00	C
1950					1.61	E	1.61	E	1.31	D	1.31	C
2100					1.61	F	1.61	E	1.31	E	1.31	D
2250					1.61	G	1.61	F	1.31	E	1.31	E
2400							1.61	G	1.31	E	1.31	E

Table 3–8M Min. Required Gage for Longitudinal Seam Duct Under Neg. Pressure

NOTES:

a. N/A – Not Applicable

b. NR – Not Required

c. R – Reinforcement (stiffener) Class

d. For solutions in the shaded region consult SMACNA's Round Industrial Standard

Neg. Pressure 10 in. wg	Unstiff.		20 ft		12 ft		10 ft		6 ft		5 ft	
MAX. Diameter, in.	GA	R	GA	R	GA	R	GA	R	GA	R	GA	R
4	28	NR	\multicolumn{10}{c	}{Use Unstiffened Solution}
6	28	NR										
8	24	NR	24	A	26	A	26	A	28	A	28	A
10	24	NR	24	A	24	A	26	A	28	A	28	A
12	22	NR	22	A	24	A	24	A	26	A	28	A
14	20	NR	22	A	24	A	24	A	26	A	26	A
16	18	NR	20	A	22	A	24	A	24	A	26	A
18	18	NR	20	A	22	A	22	A	24	A	24	A
20	18	NR	20	A	22	A	22	A	24	A	24	A
22	16	NR	18	A	20	A	22	A	24	A	24	A
24	16	NR	18	A	20	A	20	A	22	A	24	A
30			18	B	18	A	20	A	22	A	22	A
36			16	C	18	B	18	B	20	A	22	A
42			16	C	18	B	18	B	20	B	20	B
48					16	C	18	C	18	B	20	B
54					16	D	16	C	18	C	18	B
60					16	E	16	E	18	C	18	C
66							16	E	18	D	18	C
72							16	E	18	E	18	D
78									16	E	18	E
84									16	E	16	E
90									16	F	16	E
96									16	G	16	F

Table 3–9 Min. Required Gage for Longitudinal Seam Duct Under Neg. Pressure

NOTES:

a. N/A – Not Applicable

b. NR – Not Required

c. R – Reinforcement (stiffener) Class

d. For solutions in the shaded region consult SMACNA's Round Industrial Standard

| Neg. Pressure 2500 Pa | Stiffener Spacing ||||||||||||
| MAX. Diameter (mm) | Unstiff. || 6.00 m || 3.6 m || 3.00 m || 1.80 m || 1.50 m ||
	GA	R	GA	R	GA	R	GA	R	GA	R	GA	R
100	0.48	NR	Use Unstiffened Solution									
150	0.48	NR											
200	0.70	NR	0.70	A	0.55	A	0.55	A	0.48	A	0.48	A
250	0.70	NR	0.70	A	0.70	A	0.55	A	0.48	A	0.48	A
300	0.85	NR	0.85	A	0.70	A	0.70	A	0.55	A	0.48	A
350	1.00	NR	0.85	A	0.70	A	0.70	A	0.55	A	0.55	A
400	1.31	NR	1.00	A	0.85	A	0.70	A	0.70	A	0.55	A
450	1.31	NR	1.00	A	0.85	A	0.85	A	0.70	A	0.70	A
500	1.31	NR	1.00	A	0.85	A	0.85	A	0.70	A	0.70	A
550	1.61	NR	1.31	A	1.00	A	0.85	A	0.70	A	0.70	A
600	1.61	NR	1.31	A	1.00	A	1.00	A	0.85	A	0.70	A
750			1.31	B	1.31	A	1.00	A	0.85	A	0.85	A
900			1.61	C	1.31	B	1.31	B	1.00	A	0.85	A
1000			1.61	C	1.31	B	1.31	B	1.00	B	1.00	B
1200					1.61	C	1.31	C	1.31	B	1.00	B
1300					1.61	D	1.61	C	1.31	C	1.31	B
1500					1.61	E	1.61	E	1.31	C	1.31	C
1650							1.61	E	1.31	D	1.31	C
1800							1.61	E	1.31	E	1.31	D
1950									1.61	E	1.31	E
2100									1.61	E	1.61	E
2250									1.61	F	1.61	E
2400									1.61	G	1.61	F

Table 3–9M Min. Required Gage for Longitudinal Seam Duct Under Neg. Pressure

NOTES:

a. N/A – Not Applicable

b. NR – Not Required

c. R – Reinforcement (stiffener) Class

d. For solutions in the shaded region consult SMACNA's Round Industrial Standard

Neg. Pressure 2 in. wg	Stiffener Spacing											
	Unstiff.		20 ft		12 ft		10 ft		6 ft		5 ft	
Max Diameter, in.	GA	R	GA	R	GA	R	GA	R	GA	R	GA	R
4	28	NR										
6	28	NR										
8	28	NR			Use Unstiffened Solution							
10	28	NR										
12	28	NR										
14	28	NR										
16	26	NR	28	A	28	A	28	A	28	A	28	A
18	24	NR	28	A	28	A	28	A	28	A	28	A
20	24	NR	28	A	28	A	28	A	28	A	28	A
22	22	NR	28	A	28	A	28	A	28	A	28	A
24	22	NR	26	A	28	A	28	A	28	A	28	A
30	20	NR	26	A	28	A	28	A	28	A	28	A
36	18	NR	24	A	26	A	28	A	28	A	28	A
42	18	NR	24	A	26	A	26	A	28	A	28	A
48	16	NR	22	B	24	A	26	A	28	A	28	A
54	16	NR	22	B	24	B	24	A	26	A	28	A
60			22	B	24	B	24	B	26	A	26	A
66			22	C	24	B	24	B	26	B	26	A
72			20	C	22	B	24	B	24	B	26	B
78			20	D	22	C	22	C	24	B	26	B
84			20	E	22	C	22	C	24	B	24	B
90			20	E	22	D	22	C	24	B	24	B
96			20	E	22	E	22	D	24	C	24	B

Table 3–10 Min. Required Gage for Spiral Seam Duct Under Neg. Pressure

NOTES:

a. N/A – Not Applicable

b. NR – Not Required

c. R – Reinforcement (stiffener) Class

d. For solutions in the shaded region consult SMACNA's Round Industrial Standard

Neg. Pressure 500 Pa	Unstiff.		Stiffener Spacing									
			6.00 m		3.6 m		3.00 m		1.80 m		1.50 m	
Max Diameter (mm)	GA	R	GA	R	GA	R	GA	R	GA	R	GA	R
100	0.48	NR										
150	0.48	NR										
200	0.48	NR				Use Unstiffened Solution						
250	0.48	NR										
300	0.48	NR										
350	0.48	NR										
400	0.55	NR	0.48	A	0.48	A	0.48	A	0.48	A	0.48	A
450	0.70	NR	0.48	A	0.48	A	0.48	A	0.48	A	0.48	A
500	0.70	NR	0.48	A	0.48	A	0.48	A	0.48	A	0.48	A
550	0.85	NR	0.48	A	0.48	A	0.48	A	0.48	A	0.48	A
600	0.85	NR	0.55	A	0.48	A	0.48	A	0.48	A	0.48	A
750	1.00	NR	0.55	A	0.48	A	0.48	A	0.48	A	0.48	A
900	1.31	NR	0.70	A	0.55	A	0.48	A	0.48	A	0.48	A
1000	1.31	NR	0.70	A	0.55	A	0.55	A	0.48	A	0.48	A
1200	1.61	NR	0.85	B	0.70	A	0.55	A	0.48	A	0.48	A
1300	1.61	NR	0.85	B	0.70	B	0.70	A	0.55	A	0.48	A
1500			0.85	B	0.70	B	0.70	B	0.55	A	0.55	A
1650			0.85	C	0.70	B	0.70	B	0.55	B	0.55	A
1800			1.00	C	0.85	B	0.70	B	0.70	B	0.55	B
1950			1.00	D	0.85	C	0.85	C	0.70	B	0.55	B
2100			1.00	E	0.85	C	0.85	C	0.70	B	0.70	B
2250			1.00	E	0.85	D	0.85	C	0.70	B	0.70	B
2400			1.00	E	0.85	E	0.85	D	0.70	C	0.70	B

Table 3–10M Min. Required Gage for Spiral Seam Duct Under Neg. Pressure

NOTES:

a. N/A – Not Applicable

b. NR – Not Required

c. R – Reinforcement (stiffener) Class

d. For solutions in the shaded region consult SMACNA's Round Industrial Standard

Neg. Pressure 4 in. wg	Unstiff.		Stiffener Spacing									
			20 ft		12 ft		10 ft		6 ft		5 ft	
Max Diameter, in.	GA	R	GA	R	GA	R	GA	R	GA	R	GA	R
4	28	NR										A
6	28	NR				Use Unstiffened Solution						A
8	28	NR										A
10	28	NR										A
12	26	NR	28	A	28	A	28	A	28	A	28	A
14	24	NR	28	A	28	A	28	A	28	A	28	A
16	24	NR	26	A	28	A	28	A	28	A	28	A
18	22	NR	26	A	28	A	28	A	28	A	28	A
20	22	NR	24	A	28	A	28	A	28	A	28	A
22	20	NR	24	A	26	A	28	A	28	A	28	A
24	20	NR	24	A	26	A	26	A	28	A	28	A
30	18	NR	22	A	24	A	26	A	28	A	28	A
36	16	NR	22	B	24	A	24	A	26	A	28	A
42	16	NR	22	B	22	B	24	A	26	A	26	A
48			20	B	22	B	22	B	24	A	26	A
54			20	C	22	B	22	B	24	B	24	A
60			20	D	22	C	22	B	24	B	24	B
66			18	E	20	C	22	C	24	B	24	B
72			18	E	20	D	20	C	22	B	24	B
78			18	E	20	E	20	D	22	C	22	C
84			18	F	20	E	20	E	22	C	22	C
90			18	G	18	E	20	E	22	D	22	C
96			16	G	18	F	20	E	22	E	22	D

Table 3–11 Min. Required Gage for Spiral Seam Duct Under Neg. Pressure

NOTES:

a. N/A – Not Applicable

b. NR – Not Required

c. R – Reinforcement (stiffener) Class

d. For solutions in the shaded region consult SMACNA's Round Industrial Standard

| Neg. Pressure 1000 Pa | Stiffener Spacing ||||||||||||
| Max Diameter (mm) | Unstiff. || 6.00 m || 3.6 m || 3.00 m || 1.80 m || 1.50 m ||
	GA	R	GA	R	GA	R	GA	R	GA	R	GA	R
100	0.48	NR										
150	0.48	NR										
200	0.48	NR		Use Unstiffened Solution
250	0.48	NR										
300	0.55	NR	0.48	A	0.48	A	0.48	A	0.48	A	0.48	A
350	0.70	NR	0.48	A	0.48	A	0.48	A	0.48	A	0.48	A
400	0.70	NR	0.55	A	0.48	A	0.48	A	0.48	A	0.48	A
450	0.85	NR	0.55	A	0.48	A	0.48	A	0.48	A	0.48	A
500	0.85	NR	0.70	A	0.48	A	0.48	A	0.48	A	0.48	A
550	1.00	NR	0.70	A	0.55	A	0.48	A	0.48	A	0.48	A
600	1.00	NR	0.70	A	0.55	A	0.55	A	0.48	A	0.48	A
750	1.31	NR	0.85	A	0.70	A	0.55	A	0.48	A	0.48	A
900	1.61	NR	0.85	B	0.70	A	0.70	A	0.55	A	0.48	A
1000	1.61	NR	0.85	B	0.85	B	0.70	A	0.55	A	0.55	A
1200			1.00	B	0.85	B	0.85	B	0.70	A	0.55	A
1300			1.00	C	0.85	B	0.85	B	0.70	B	0.70	A
1500			1.00	D	0.85	C	0.85	B	0.70	B	0.70	B
1650			1.31	E	1.00	C	0.85	C	0.70	B	0.70	B
1800			1.31	E	1.00	D	1.00	C	0.85	B	0.70	B
1950			1.31	E	1.00	E	1.00	D	0.85	C	0.85	C
2100			1.31	F	1.00	E	1.00	E	0.85	C	0.85	C
2250			1.31	G	1.31	E	1.00	E	0.85	D	0.85	C
2400			1.61	G	1.31	F	1.00	E	0.85	E	0.85	D

Table 3–11M Min. Required Gage for Spiral Seam Duct Under Neg. Pressure

NOTES:

a. N/A – Not Applicable

b. NR – Not Required

c. R – Reinforcement (stiffener) Class

d. For solutions in the shaded region consult SMACNA's Round Industrial Standard

| Neg. Pressure 6 in. wg | Stiffener Spacing ||||||||||||
| Max Diameter, in. | Unstiff. || 20 ft || 12 ft || 10 ft || 6 ft || 5 ft ||
	GA	R	GA	R	GA	R	GA	R	GA	R	GA	R
4	28	NR										
6	28	NR	Use Unstiffened Solution									
8	28	NR										
10	26	NR	28	A	28	A	28	A	28	A	28	A
12	24	NR	26	A	28	A	28	A	28	A	28	A
14	24	NR	26	A	28	A	28	A	28	A	28	A
16	22	NR	24	A	26	A	28	A	28	A	28	A
18	22	NR	24	A	26	A	26	A	28	A	28	A
20	20	NR	24	A	26	A	26	A	28	A	28	A
22	20	NR	24	A	24	A	26	A	28	A	28	A
24	18	NR	22	A	24	A	24	A	28	A	28	A
30	18	NR	22	A	24	A	24	A	26	A	26	A
36	16	NR	20	B	22	B	22	A	24	A	26	A
42			20	B	22	B	22	B	24	A	24	A
48			18	C	20	B	22	B	24	B	24	B
54			18	D	20	C	20	C	22	B	24	B
60			18	E	20	C	20	C	22	B	22	B
66			18	E	18	E	20	D	22	C	22	B
72			18	F	18	E	20	E	22	C	22	C
78			16	G	18	E	18	E	20	D	22	C
84			16	G	18	F	18	E	20	E	22	D
90			16	G	18	G	18	F	20	E	20	E
96			16	G	18	G	18	G	20	E	20	E

Table 3–12 Min. Required Gage for Spiral Seam Duct Under Neg. Pressure

NOTES:

a. N/A – Not Applicable

b. NR – Not Required

c. R – Reinforcement (stiffener) Class

d. For solutions in the shaded region consult SMACNA's Round Industrial Standard

| Neg. Pressure 1500 Pa | \multicolumn{12}{c}{Stiffener Spacing} |
Max Diameter (mm)	Unstiff. GA	R	6.00 m GA	R	3.6 m GA	R	3.00 m GA	R	1.80 m GA	R	1.50 m GA	R
100	0.48	NR										
150	0.48	NR	\multicolumn{10}{c}{Use Unstiffened Solution}
200	0.48	NR										
250	0.55	NR	0.48	A	0.48	A	0.48	A	0.48	A	0.48	A
300	0.70	NR	0.55	A	0.48	A	0.48	A	0.48	A	0.48	A
350	0.70	NR	0.55	A	0.48	A	0.48	A	0.48	A	0.48	A
400	0.85	NR	0.70	A	0.55	A	0.48	A	0.48	A	0.48	A
450	0.85	NR	0.70	A	0.55	A	0.55	A	0.48	A	0.48	A
500	1.00	NR	0.70	A	0.55	A	0.55	A	0.48	A	0.48	A
550	1.00	NR	0.70	A	0.70	A	0.55	A	0.48	A	0.48	A
600	1.31	NR	0.85	A	0.70	A	0.70	A	0.48	A	0.48	A
750	1.31	NR	0.85	A	0.70	A	0.70	A	0.55	A	0.55	A
900	1.61	NR	1.00	B	0.85	B	0.85	A	0.70	A	0.55	A
1000			1.00	B	0.85	B	0.85	B	0.70	A	0.70	A
1200			1.31	C	1.00	B	0.85	B	0.70	B	0.70	B
1300			1.31	D	1.00	C	1.00	C	0.85	B	0.70	B
1500			1.31	E	1.00	C	1.00	C	0.85	B	0.85	B
1650			1.31	E	1.31	E	1.00	D	0.85	C	0.85	B
1800			1.31	F	1.31	E	1.00	E	0.85	C	0.85	C
1950			1.61	G	1.31	E	1.31	E	1.00	D	0.85	C
2100			1.61	G	1.31	F	1.31	E	1.00	E	0.85	D
2250			1.61	G	1.31	G	1.31	F	1.00	E	1.00	E
2400			1.61	G	1.31	G	1.31	G	1.00	E	1.00	E

Table 3–12M Min. Required Gage for Spiral Seam Duct Under Neg. Pressure

NOTES:

a. N/A – Not Applicable

b. NR – Not Required

c. R – Reinforcement (stiffener) Class

d. For solutions in the shaded region consult SMACNA's Round Industrial Standard

Neg. Pressure 10 in. wg	Stiffener Spacing												
	Unstiff.		20 ft		12 ft		10 ft		6 ft		5 ft	
Max Diameter, in.	GA	R	GA	R	GA	R	GA	R	GA	R	GA	R
4	28	NR	\multicolumn{10}{c}{Use Unstiffened Solution}									
6	28	NR										
8	26	NR	26	A	28	A	28	A	28	A	28	A
10	26	NR	26	A	28	A	28	A	28	A	28	A
12	24	NR	24	A	26	A	28	A	28	A	28	A
14	22	NR	24	A	26	A	26	A	28	A	28	A
16	22	NR	24	A	24	A	26	A	28	A	28	A
18	20	NR	22	A	24	A	24	A	26	A	28	A
20	18	NR	22	A	24	A	24	A	26	A	26	A
22	18	NR	22	A	24	A	24	A	26	A	26	A
24	18	NR	20	A	22	A	24	A	24	A	26	A
30	16	NR	20	B	22	A	22	A	24	A	24	A
36			18	C	20	B	22	B	22	A	24	A
42			18	C	20	B	20	B	22	B	22	B
48			18	E	18	C	20	C	22	B	22	B
54			18	E	18	D	18	C	20	C	22	B
60			16	F	18	E	18	E	20	C	20	C
66			16	G	18	E	18	E	20	D	20	C
72			16	G	18	F	18	E	20	E	20	D
78			16	G	16	G	18	F	18	E	20	E
84					16	G	16	G	18	E	18	E
90					16	G	16	G	18	F	18	E
96					16	G	16	G	18	G	18	F

Table 3–13 Min. Required Gage for Spiral Seam Duct Under Neg. Pressure

NOTES:

a. N/A – Not Applicable

b. NR – Not Required

c. R – Reinforcement (stiffener) Class

d. For solutions in the shaded region consult SMACNA's Round Industrial Standard

Neg. Pressure 2500 Pa	Unstiff.		6.00 m		3.6 m		3.00 m		1.80 m		1.50 m	
Max Diameter (mm)	GA	R	GA	R	GA	R	GA	R	GA	R	GA	R
100	0.48	NR										
150	0.48	NR			Use Unstiffened Solution							
200	0.55	NR	0.55	A	0.48	A	0.48	A	0.48	A	0.48	A
250	0.55	NR	0.55	A	0.48	A	0.48	A	0.48	A	0.48	A
300	0.70	NR	0.70	A	0.55	A	0.48	A	0.48	A	0.48	A
350	0.85	NR	0.70	A	0.55	A	0.55	A	0.48	A	0.48	A
400	0.85	NR	0.70	A	0.70	A	0.55	A	0.48	A	0.48	A
450	1.00	NR	0.85	A	0.70	A	0.70	A	0.55	A	0.48	A
500	1.31	NR	0.85	A	0.70	A	0.70	A	0.55	A	0.55	A
550	1.31	NR	0.85	A	0.70	A	0.70	A	0.55	A	0.55	A
600	1.31	NR	1.00	A	0.85	A	0.70	A	0.70	A	0.55	A
750	1.61	NR	1.00	B	0.85	A	0.85	A	0.70	A	0.70	A
900			1.31	C	1.00	B	0.85	B	0.85	A	0.70	A
1000			1.31	C	1.00	B	1.00	B	0.85	B	0.85	B
1200			1.31	E	1.31	C	1.00	C	0.85	B	0.85	B
1300			1.31	E	1.31	D	1.31	C	1.00	C	0.85	B
1500			1.61	F	1.31	E	1.31	E	1.00	C	1.00	C
1650			1.61	G	1.31	E	1.31	E	1.00	D	1.00	C
1800			1.61	G	1.31	F	1.31	E	1.00	E	1.00	D
1950			1.61	G	1.61	G	1.31	F	1.31	E	1.00	E
2100					1.61	G	1.61	G	1.31	E	1.31	E
2250					1.61	G	1.61	G	1.31	F	1.31	E
2400					1.61	G	1.61	G	1.31	G	1.31	F

Table 3–13M Min. Required Gage for Spiral Seam Duct Under Neg. Pressure

NOTES:

a. N/A – Not Applicable

b. NR – Not Required

c. R – Reinforcement (stiffener) Class

d. For solutions in the shaded region consult SMACNA's Round Industrial Standard

Duct Diameter in Inches	Maximum 2 in. wg Static Positive		Maximum 2 in. wg Static Negative	
	Spiral Seam Gage	Longitudinal Seam Gage	Spiral Seam Gage	Longitudinal Seam Gage
3 thru 8	.025 in.	.032 in.	.025 in.	.040 in.
9 thru 14	.025 in.	.032 in.	032 in.	.040 in.
15 thru 26	.032 in.	.040 in.	.040 in.	.050 in.
27 thru 36	.040 in.	.050 in.	.050 in.	.063 in.
37 thru 50	.050 in.	.063 in.	.063 in.	.071 in.
51 thru 60	.063 in.	.071 in.	N.A.	.090 in.
61 thru 84	N.A.	.090 in.	N.A.	N.A.

Table 3–14 Aluminum Round Duct Gage Schedule

NOTES:

Construction of aluminum duct and fittings shall otherwise correspond in the same relationship as for steel duct.

Sheet material shall be alloy 3003-H14 unless otherwise specified. Aluminum fasteners shall be used. Structural members (if used) shall be alloy 6061-T6 or galvanized steel as related in Table 2-52 (for rectangular duct). Hangers in contact with the duct shall be galvanized steel or aluminum.

N.A. means not readily available or not assigned.

Duct Diameter (mm)	Maximum 500 Pa Static Positive		Maximum 500 Pa Static Negative	
	Spiral Seam Gage (mm)	Longitudinal Seam Gage (mm)	Spiral Seam Gage (mm)	Longitudinal Seam Gage (mm)
75 thru 200	0.64	0.81	0.64	1.02
230 thru 350	0.64	0.81	0.81	1.02
351 thru 650	0.81	1.02	1.02	1.27
651 thru 900	1.02	1.27	1.27	1.60
901 thru 1250	1.27	1.60	1.60	1.80
1251 thru 1500	1.60	1.80	N.A.	2.29
1501 thru 2100	N.A.	2.29	N.A.	N.A.

Table 3–14M Aluminum Round Duct Gage Schedule

NOTES:

Construction of aluminum duct and fittings shall otherwise correspond in the same relationship as for steel duct.

Sheet material shall be alloy 3003-H14 unless otherwise specified. Aluminum fasteners shall be used. Structural members (if used) shall be alloy 6061-T6 or galvanized steel as related in Table 2-52 (for rectangular duct). Hangers in contact with the duct shall be galvanized steel or aluminum.

N.A. means not readily available or not assigned.

3.3 FLAT OVAL DUCT CONSTRUCTION STANDARDS

S3.11 Flat oval duct shall be provided where shown and as shown on the contract drawings.

S3.12 Minimum wall thickness for longitudinal seam flat oval duct shall be as indicated in Table 3–15.

S3.13 Reinforcement for flat sides of longitudinal seam flat oval duct shall be of the same size and spacing interval as specified for rectangular duct or shall be provided to limit wall deflection to ¾ in. (19 mm) and reinforcement deflection to ¼ in. (6.4 mm).

S3.14 Minimum duct wall thickness and reinforcement spacing, type, and size for flat sides of spiral flat oval duct shall be selected from tables 3-16 through 3-22M and are suitable for negative pressure applications.

S3.15 Unless otherwise specified, joints and seams shall be similar to those indicated for round duct.

S3.16 Fittings used in conjunction with longitudinal seam duct shall conform to the thickness schedules in Table 3–15, shall conform to the seam, joint, and connection arrangements permitted for round duct, and shall be reinforced to conform to S3.13.

S3.17 Fittings used in conjunction with spiral seam flat oval duct will be fabricated by a gage that is two gages thicker (one even gage) than the duct provided the reinforcement size, type and spacing are maintained.

S3.18 The duct construction shall be capable of withstanding a pressure 50 percent greater than that of the assigned pressure class without structural failure or permanent deformation.

S3.19 Duct wall deflection at atmospheric pressure, with reinforcements and connections in place, shall not exceed ¼ in. (6.4mm) on widths of 36 in. (914 mm) or less or ½ w in. (13 mm) on greater widths, *see* criteria in Chapter 11.

3.4 COMMENTARY

Flat oval duct combines the advantages of round duct and rectangular duct because it may fit in spaces where there is not enough room for round duct, and it can be joined using the techniques of round duct assembly.

Spiral flat oval duct is machine-made from round spiral lockseam duct and is available in varying sizes and aspect ratios. It can also be made with longitudinal seams.

Flat oval duct has considerably less flat surface that is susceptible to vibration and may require less reinforcement than a corresponding size of rectangular duct. The deflection of the flat oval duct under pressure is related to the flat span rather than the overall width of the duct.

Any round duct fitting can have an equivalent fitting made in flat oval. As in rectangular duct, a hard bend elbow denotes the bend in the plane of the duct width, whereas an easy bend elbow denotes the bend in the plane of the duct height. Any branch fitting can be made with the branch tap either round or flat oval. The tap of the flat oval fitting can be located anywhere on the circumference of the fitting body. If the diameter of a round tap is greater than the height of the flat oval body, a transition can be made from flat oval to round, providing an equivalent area at the base of the transition.

Major Dimension Duct Width (in)	Longitudinal Seam	Fitting Gage
To 24	20	20
30	20	20
36	20	20
42	18	18
48	18	18
54	18	18
60	18	18
66	16	16
71 and up	16	16

Table 3–15 Longitudinal Seam Flat Oval Duct Gage Positive Pressure To 10 in. wg

Major Dimension Duct Width (mm)	Longitudinal Seam (mm)	Fitting Gage (mm)
To 600	1.00	1.00
750	1.00	1.00
900	1.00	1.00
1000	1.31	1.31
1200	1.31	1.31
1300	1.31	1.31
1500	1.31	1.31
1650	1.61	1.61
1775 and up	1.61	1.61

Table 3–15M Longitudinal Seam Flat Oval Duct Gage Positive Pressure To 2500 Pa

Spiral Flat Oval Table Instructions:

1. Determine the flat span of your duct.

    a. Flat span = Major (larger) dimension – Minor (smaller) dimension

2. Find the appropriate table based on pressure class

    a. Tables 3.16 – 3.22

3. Using the flat span from step 1 find the appropriate row

4. For an unreinforced option use the gage listed in column 2. If no gage is listed then use a reinforced option.

5. For a reinforced option first find the appropriate columns under the reinforcement spacing being considered

6. Determine the minimum gage from columns 4, 6, or 9 depending on the reinforcement spacing being considered

7. For external reinforcement select a reinforcement class from columns 3, 5, or 8 depending on the reinforcement spacing being considered.

    a. For column 3 if no reinforcement is listed the gage is the same as the unreinforced gage so no reinforcement is required.

    b. These reinforcement classes correspond to Table 2-29 through Table 2-33

8. For optional internal supports, tie rods, determine the quantity required from column 7 or column 10 depending on the reinforcement spacing being considered.

    a. These supports replace the external support.

    b. Tie rod only support is not permitted for 10 in. w.g. construction.

External reinforcement is to be attached per Figure 2-12. Consult Figure 3-7 for options of tied external reinforcement (required at + 4, +6, and +10 in. w.g.).

Internal tie rod loads are to be calculated using the Major (larger) dimension as the width of the duct.

Fittings are to be fabricated from one even gage thicker material than the duct so long as the reinforcement spacing and class is equivalent to those used on the duct. Use the centerline for spacing purposes. Internal slip couplings can be fabricated from the same gage as the duct.

Tables are limited to minor dimensions up to 30 inches

If a cell is shaded this indicates that the option is lighter than the corresponding option with a larger reinforcement spacing.

Negative pressure applications are limited to the following options:

1. Use the unreinforced option

2. Use the internal (tie rod) option

3. Use a male flange or ring that meets the reinforcement class at the required spacing

4. Use external reinforcement meeting the reinforcement class in conjunction with an internal support (tie rod) type 1 per figure 3-7

5. A combination of the above options can be used. For example use a male flange on the ends of the duct with internal supports at locations not to exceed the spacing listed in the appropriate table.

1/2 in. w.g. +/−

Flat-Span (in.)	Unreinforced	12 ft. reinforcement spacing		6 ft. reinforcement spacing			3 ft. reinforcement spacing		
	Minimum Gage	External Reinforcement Class	Minimum Gage	External Reinforcement Class	Minimum Gage	Optional Tie rod(s)	External Reinforcement Class	Minimum Gage	Optional Tie rod(s)
1	2	3	4	5	6	7	8	9	10
1 – 10	26		26		26			26	
11 – 12	24		24	B	26	1	B	26	1
13 – 14	24		24	B	26	1	B	26	1
15 – 16	22		22	B	26	1	B	26	1
17 – 18	22		22	B	26	1	B	26	1
19 – 20	22		22	B	24	1	B	24	1
21 – 22	20		20	B	24	1	B	24	1
23 – 24	20		20	C	24	1	B	24	1
25 – 26	20		20	C	24	1	B	24	1
27 – 28	18		18	C	24	1	B	24	1
29 – 30	18		18	C	24	1	B	24	1
31 – 32	18		18	C	22	1	C	22	1
33 – 34	18		18	C	22	1	C	22	1
35 – 36	18		18	C	22	1	C	22	1
37 – 38	16	D	18	D	22	1	C	22	1
39 – 40	16	D	18	D	22	1	C	22	1
41 – 42	16	D	18	D	22	1	C	22	1
43 – 44	16	E	18	E	22	1	D	22	1
45 – 46	16	E	18	E	22	1	D	22	1
47 – 48	16	E	18	E	22	1	D	22	1
49 – 50		E	18	E	22	2	E	22	1
51 – 52		E	18	E	22	2	E	22	1
53 – 54		E	18	E	20	2	E	20	1
55 – 56		F	18	F	20	2	E	20	1
57 – 58		F	18	F	20	2	E	20	1
59 – 60		F	18	F	20	2	E	20	1
61 – 62		F	18	F	20	2	E	20	1
63 – 64		F	18	F	20	2	E	20	1
65 – 66		F	18	F	20	2	E	20	1
67 – 68		F	18	F	20	2	E	20	1
69 – 70		F	18	F	20	2	E	20	1
71 – 72		F	18	F	20	2	E	20	1

Tables are limited to minor dimensions up to 30 inches
If a cell is shaded this indicates that the option is lighter than the corresponding option with a larger reinforcement spacing.
NP = Not Permitted

◪ = No Solution Provided

Negative pressure applications are limited to the following options:
   Use the unreinforced option
   Use the internal (tie rod) option
   Use a male flange or ring that meets the reinforcement class at the required spacing
   Use external reinforcement meeting the reinforcement class in conjunction with an internal support (tie rod) type 1 per Figure 3-7
   A combination of the above options can be used.

Table 3–16 Spiral Flat Oval Reinforcement Table

125 Pa +/−

Flat-Span (mm)	Unreinforced Minimum Gage	3.6 m reinforcement spacing			1.8 m reinforcement spacing				0.9 m reinforcement spacing			
		External Reinforcement Class	Minimum Gage		External Reinforcement Class	Minimum Gage	Optional Tie rod(s)	External Reinforcement Class	Minimum Gage	Optional Tie rod(s)
1	2	3	4		5	6	7	8	9	10
1 – 250	0.55		0.55			0.55			0.55	
251 – 300	0.70		0.70		B	0.55	1	B	0.55	1
301 – 350	0.70		0.70		B	0.55	1	B	0.55	1
351 – 400	0.85		0.85		B	0.55	1	B	0.55	1
401 – 450	0.85		0.85		B	0.55	1	B	0.55	1
451 – 500	0.85		0.85		B	0.70	1	B	0.70	1
501 – 550	1.00		1.00		B	0.70	1	B	0.70	1
551 – 600	1.00		1.00		C	0.70	1	B	0.70	1
601 – 650	1.00		1.00		C	0.70	1	B	0.70	1
651 – 700	1.31		1.31		C	0.70	1	B	0.70	1
701 – 750	1.31		1.31		C	0.70	1	B	0.70	1
751 – 800	1.31		1.31		C	0.85	1	C	0.85	1
801 – 850	1.31		1.31		C	0.85	1	C	0.85	1
851 – 900	1.31		1.31		C	0.85	1	C	0.85	1
901 – 950	1.61	D	1.31		D	0.85	1	C	0.85	1
951 – 1000	1.61	D	1.31		D	0.85	1	C	0.85	1
1001 – 1050	1.61	D	1.31		D	0.85	1	C	0.85	1
1051 – 1100	1.61	E	1.31		E	0.85	1	D	0.85	1
1101 – 1150	1.61	E	1.31		E	0.85	1	D	0.85	1
1151 – 1200	1.61	E	1.31		E	0.85	1	D	0.85	1
1201 – 1250		E	1.31		E	0.85	2	E	0.85	1
1251 – 1300		E	1.31		E	0.85	2	E	0.85	1
1301 – 1350		E	1.31		E	1.00	2	E	1.00	1
1351 – 1400		F	1.31		F	1.00	2	E	1.00	1
1401 – 1450		F	1.31		F	1.00	2	E	1.00	1
1451 – 1500		F	1.31		F	1.00	2	E	1.00	1
1501 – 1550		F	1.31		F	1.00	2	E	1.00	1
1551 – 1600		F	1.31		F	1.00	2	E	1.00	1
1601 – 1650		F	1.31		F	1.00	2	E	1.00	1
1651 – 1700		F	1.31		F	1.00	2	E	1.00	1
1701 – 1750		F	1.31		F	1.00	2	E	1.00	1
1751 – 1800		F	1.31		F	1.00	2	E	1.00	1

Tables are limited to minor dimensions up to 750 mm
If a cell is shaded this indicates that the option is lighter than the corresponding option with a larger reinforcement spacing.
NP = Not Permitted
▱ = No Solution Provided

Negative pressure applications are limited to the following options:
  Use the unreinforced option
  Use the internal (tie rod) option
  Use a male flange or ring that meets the reinforcement class at the required spacing
  Use external reinforcement meeting the reinforcement class in conjunction with an internal support (tie rod) type 1 per Figure 3-7
  A combination of the above options can be used.

Table 3–16M Spiral Flat Oval Reinforcement Table

1 in. w.g. +/−

Flat-Span (in.)	Unreinforced Minimum Gage	12 ft. reinforcement spacing External Reinforcement Class	12 ft. reinforcement spacing Minimum Gage	6 ft. reinforcement spacing External Reinforcement Class	6 ft. reinforcement spacing Minimum Gage	6 ft. reinforcement spacing Optional Tie rod(s)	3 ft. reinforcement spacing External Reinforcement Class	3 ft. reinforcement spacing Minimum Gage	3 ft. reinforcement spacing Optional Tie rod(s)
1	2	3	4	5	6	7	8	9	10
1 – 10	24		24	B	26	1	B	26	1
11 – 12	22		22	B	26	1	B	26	1
13 – 14	22		22	B	26	1	B	26	1
15 – 16	22		22	B	24	1	B	24	1
17 – 18	20		20	B	24	1	B	24	1
19 – 20	20		20	C	24	1	B	24	1
21 – 22	20		20	C	24	1	B	24	1
23 – 24	18	E	20	C	22	1	C	22	1
25 – 26	18	E	20	C	22	1	C	22	1
27 – 28	18	E	20	D	22	1	C	22	1
29 – 30	18	E	20	D	22	1	C	22	1
31 – 32	18	E	20	E	22	1	C	22	1
33 – 34	18	E	20	E	22	1	C	22	1
35 – 36	18	E	20	E	22	1	C	22	1
37 – 38	16	E	18	E	22	1	D	22	1
39 – 40	16	E	18	E	22	1	D	22	1
41 – 42	16	E	18	E	20	1	D	20	1
43 – 44	16	F	18	F	20	1	E	20	1
45 – 46	16	F	18	F	20	1	E	20	1
47 – 48	16	F	18	F	20	1	E	20	1
49 – 50		G	18	G	20	2	E	20	1
51 – 52		G	18	G	20	2	E	20	1
53 – 54		G	18	G	20	2	E	20	1
55 – 56				G	20	2	F	20	1
57 – 58				G	20	2	F	20	1
59 – 60				G	20	2	F	20	1
61 – 62				H	18	2	F	20	1
63 – 64				H	18	2	F	20	1
65 – 66				H	18	2	F	18	1
67 – 68				H	18	2	F	18	1
69 – 70				H	18	2	F	18	1
71 – 72				H	18	2	F	18	1

Tables are limited to minor dimensions up to 30 inches
If a cell is shaded this indicates that the option is lighter than the corresponding option with a larger reinforcement spacing.
NP = Not Permitted
☐ = No Solution Provided
Negative pressure applications are limited to the following options:
  Use the unreinforced option
  Use the internal (tie rod) option
  Use a male flange or ring that meets the reinforcement class at the required spacing
  Use external reinforcement meeting the reinforcement class in conjunction with an internal support (tie rod) type 1 per Figure 3-7
  A combination of the above options can be used.

Table 3–17 Spiral Flat Oval Reinforcement Table

250 Pa +/−

Flat-Span (mm)	Unreinforced Minimum Gage	3.6 m reinforcement spacing			1.8 m reinforcement spacing			0.9 m reinforcement spacing		
		External Reinforcement Class	Minimum Gage	External Reinforcement Class	Minimum Gage	Optional Tie rod(s)	External Reinforcement Class	Minimum Gage	Optional Tie rod(s)
1	2	3	4	5	6	7	8	9	10
1 – 250	0.70		0.70	B	0.55	1	B	0.55	1
251 – 300	0.85		0.85	B	0.55	1	B	0.55	1
301 – 350	0.85		0.85	B	0.55	1	B	0.55	1
351 – 400	0.85		0.85	B	0.70	1	B	0.70	1
401 – 450	1.00		1.00	B	0.70	1	B	0.70	1
451 – 500	1.00		1.00	C	0.70	1	B	0.70	1
501 – 550	1.00		1.00	C	0.70	1	B	0.70	1
551 – 600	1.31	E	1.00	C	0.85	1	C	0.85	1
601 – 650	1.31	E	1.00	C	0.85	1	C	0.85	1
651 – 700	1.31	E	1.00	D	0.85	1	C	0.85	1
701 – 750	1.31	E	1.00	D	0.85	1	C	0.85	1
751 – 800	1.31	E	1.00	E	0.85	1	C	0.85	1
801 – 850	1.31	E	1.00	E	0.85	1	C	0.85	1
851 – 900	1.31	E	1.00	E	0.85	1	C	0.85	1
901 – 950	16.00	E	1.31	E	0.85	1	D	0.85	1
951 – 1000	16.00	E	1.31	E	0.85	1	D	0.85	1
1001 – 1050	16.00	E	1.31	E	1.00	1	D	1.00	1
1051 – 1100	16.00	F	1.31	F	1.00	1	E	1.00	1
1101 – 1150	16.00	F	1.31	F	1.00	1	E	1.00	1
1151 – 1200	16.00	F	1.31	F	1.00	1	E	1.00	1
1201 – 1250		G	1.31	G	1.00	2	E	1.00	1
1251 – 1300		G	1.31	G	1.00	2	E	1.00	1
1301 – 1350		G	1.31	G	1.00	2	E	1.00	1
1351 – 1400				G	1.00	2	F	1.00	1
1401 – 1450				G	1.00	2	F	1.00	1
1451 – 1500				G	1.00	2	F	1.00	1
1501 – 1550				H	1.31	2	F	1.00	1
1551 – 1600				H	1.31	2	F	1.00	1
1601 – 1650				H	1.31	2	F	1.31	1
1651 – 1700				H	1.31	2	F	1.31	1
1701 – 1750				H	1.31	2	F	1.31	1
1751 – 1800				H	1.31	2	F	1.31	1

Tables are limited to minor dimensions up to 750 mm
If a cell is shaded this indicates that the option is lighter than the corresponding option with a larger reinforcement spacing.
NP = Not Permitted
▭ = No Solution Provided
Negative pressure applications are limited to the following options:
  Use the unreinforced option
  Use the internal (tie rod) option
  Use a male flange or ring that meets the reinforcement class at the required spacing
  Use external reinforcement meeting the reinforcement class in conjunction with an internal support (tie rod) type 1 per Figure 3-7
  A combination of the above options can be used.

Table 3–17M Spiral Flat Oval Reinforcement Table

2 in. w.g. +/−

Flat-Span (in.)	Unreinforced Minimum Gage	12 ft. reinforcement spacing External Reinforcement Class	12 ft. reinforcement spacing Minimum Gage	6 ft. reinforcement spacing External Reinforcement Class	6 ft. reinforcement spacing Minimum Gage	6 ft. reinforcement spacing Optional Tie rod(s)	3 ft. reinforcement spacing External Reinforcement Class	3 ft. reinforcement spacing Minimum Gage	3 ft. reinforcement spacing Optional Tie rod(s)
1	2	3	4	5	6	7	8	9	10
1 – 10	22		22	B	26	1	B	26	1
11 – 12	22		22	B	24	1	B	24	1
13 – 14	20		20	B	24	1	B	24	1
15 – 16	20		20	C	24	1	C	24	1
17 – 18	18	D	20	C	24	1	C	24	1
19 – 20	18	D	20	C	22	1	C	22	1
21 – 22	18	D	20	D	22	1	C	22	1
23 – 24	18		18	D	22	1	D	22	1
25 – 26	18		18	E	22	1	D	22	1
27 – 28	18		18	E	22	1	D	22	1
29 – 30	18		18	E	22	1	D	22	1
31 – 32	16	F	18	F	22	1	E	22	1
33 – 34	16	F	18	F	20	1	E	20	1
35 – 36	16	F	18	F	20	1	E	20	1
37 – 38		G	18	G	20	1	E	20	1
39 – 40				G	20	1	E	20	1
41 – 42				G	20	1	E	20	1
43 – 44				H	20	1	F	20	1
45 – 46				H	20	1	F	20	1
47 – 48				H	20	1	F	20	1
49 – 50				I	18	2	G	20	1
51 – 52				I	18	2	G	20	1
53 – 54				I	18	2	G	20	1
55 – 56				I	18	2	G	20	1
57 – 58				I	18	2	G	18	1
59 – 60				I	18	2	G	18	1
61 – 62				J	16	2	H	18	1
63 – 64				J	16	2	H	18	1
65 – 66				J	16	2	H	18	1
67 – 68				J	16	2	H	18	1
69 – 70				J	16	2	H	18	1
71 – 72				J	16	2	H	18	1

Tables are limited to minor dimensions up to 30 inches
If a cell is shaded this indicates that the option is lighter than the corresponding option with a larger reinforcement spacing.
NP = Not Permitted
☐ = No Solution Provided
Negative pressure applications are limited to the following options:
　Use the unreinforced option
　Use the internal (tie rod) option
　Use a male flange or ring that meets the reinforcement class at the required spacing
　Use external reinforcement meeting the reinforcement class in conjunction with an internal support (tie rod) type 1 per Figure 3-7
　A combination of the above options can be used.

Table 3–18 Spiral Flat Oval Reinforcement Table

500 Pa +/−

Flat-Span (mm)	Unreinforced	3.6 m reinforcement spacing		1.8 m reinforcement spacing			0.9 m reinforcement spacing		
	Minimum Gage	External Reinforcement Class	Minimum Gage	External Reinforcement Class	Minimum Gage	Optional Tie rod(s)	External Reinforcement Class	Minimum Gage	Optional Tie rod(s)
1	2	3	4	5	6	7	8	9	10
1 – 250	0.85		0.85	B	0.55	1	B	0.55	1
251 – 300	0.85		0.85	B	0.70	1	B	0.70	1
301 – 350	1.00		1.00	B	0.70	1	B	0.70	1
351 – 400	1.00		1.00	C	0.70	1	C	0.70	1
401 – 450	1.31	D	1.00	C	0.70	1	C	0.70	1
451 – 500	1.31	D	1.00	C	0.85	1	C	0.85	1
501 – 550	1.31	D	1.00	D	0.85	1	C	0.85	1
551 – 600	1.31		1.31	D	0.85	1	D	0.85	1
601 – 650	1.31		1.31	E	0.85	1	D	0.85	1
651 – 700	1.31		1.31	E	0.85	1	D	0.85	1
701 – 750	1.31		1.31	E	0.85	1	D	0.85	1
751 – 800	1.61	F	1.31	F	0.85	1	E	0.85	1
801 – 850	1.61	F	1.31	F	1.00	1	E	1.00	1
851 – 900	1.61	F	1.31	F	1.00	1	E	1.00	1
901 – 950		G	1.31	G	1.00	1	E	1.00	1
951 – 1000				G	1.00	1	E	1.00	1
1001 – 1050				G	1.00	1	E	1.00	1
1051 – 1100				H	1.00	1	F	1.00	1
1101 – 1150				H	1.00	1	F	1.00	1
1151 – 1200				H	1.00	1	F	1.00	1
1201 – 1250				I	1.31	2	G	1.00	1
1251 – 1300				I	1.31	2	G	1.00	1
1301 – 1350				I	1.31	2	G	1.00	1
1351 – 1400				I	1.31	2	G	1.00	1
1401 – 1450				I	1.31	2	G	1.31	1
1451 – 1500				I	1.31	2	G	1.31	1
1501 – 1550				J	1.61	2	H	1.31	1
1551 – 1600				J	1.61	2	H	1.31	1
1601 – 1650				J	1.61	2	H	1.31	1
1651 – 1700				J	1.61	2	H	1.31	1
1701 – 1750				J	1.61	2	H	1.31	1
1751 – 1800				J	1.61	2	H	1.31	1

Tables are limited to minor dimensions up to 750 mm
If a cell is shaded this indicates that the option is lighter than the corresponding option with a larger reinforcement spacing.
NP = Not Permitted
☐ = No Solution Provided
Negative pressure applications are limited to the following options:
  Use the unreinforced option
  Use the internal (tie rod) option
  Use a male flange or ring that meets the reinforcement class at the required spacing
  Use external reinforcement meeting the reinforcement class in conjunction with an internal support (tie rod) type 1 per Figure 3-7
  A combination of the above options can be used.

Table 3–18M Spiral Flat Oval Reinforcement Table

3 in. w.g. +/−

Flat-Span (in.)	Unreinforced Minimum Gage	12 ft. reinforcement spacing External Reinforcement Class	12 ft. reinforcement spacing Minimum Gage	6 ft. reinforcement spacing External Reinforcement Class	6 ft. reinforcement spacing Minimum Gage	6 ft. reinforcement spacing Optional Tie rod(s)	3 ft. reinforcement spacing External Reinforcement Class	3 ft. reinforcement spacing Minimum Gage	3 ft. reinforcement spacing Optional Tie rod(s)
1	2	3	4	5	6	7	8	9	10
1 – 10	22		22	B	24	1	B	24	1
11 – 12	20		20	B	24	1	B	24	1
13 – 14	20		20	C	24	1	C	24	1
15 – 16	18		18	C	24	1	C	24	1
17 – 18	18		18	D	22	1	C	22	1
19 – 20	18		18	D	22	1	C	22	1
21 – 22	18		18	E	22	1	D	22	1
23 – 24	18		18	E	22	1	D	22	1
25 – 26	18		18	E	22	1	D	22	1
27 – 28	18		18	F	20	1	E	22	1
29 – 30	18		18	F	20	1	E	20	1
31 – 32	16	H	18	H	18	1	F	20	1
33 – 34	16		16	H	18	1	F	20	1
35 – 36	16		16	H	18	1	F	20	1
37 – 38				H	18	1	F	20	1
39 – 40				H	18	1	F	20	1
41 – 42				H	18	1	F	20	1
43 – 44				I	18	1	G	20	1
45 – 46				I	18	1	G	20	1
47 – 48				I	18	1	G	20	1
49 – 50				J	16	2	H	20	1
51 – 52				J	16	2	H	20	1
53 – 54				J	16	2	H	18	1
55 – 56				J	16	2	H	18	1
57 – 58				J	16	2	H	18	1
59 – 60				J	16	2	H	18	1
61 – 62							I	18	1
63 – 64							I	18	1
65 – 66							I	18	1
67 – 68							I	18	1
69 – 70							I	18	1
71 – 72							I	18	1

Tables are limited to minor dimensions up to 30 inches
If a cell is shaded this indicates that the option is lighter than the corresponding option with a larger reinforcement spacing.
NP = Not Permitted
☐ = No Solution Provided
Negative pressure applications are limited to the following options:
  Use the unreinforced option
  Use the internal (tie rod) option
  Use a male flange or ring that meets the reinforcement class at the required spacing
  Use external reinforcement meeting the reinforcement class in conjunction with an internal support (tie rod) type 1 per Figure 3-7
  A combination of the above options can be used.

Table 3–19 Spiral Flat Oval Reinforcement Table

750 Pa. +/−

Flat-Span (mm)	Unreinforced Minimum Gage	3.6 m reinforcement spacing External Reinforcement Class	3.6 m reinforcement spacing Minimum Gage	1.8 m reinforcement spacing External Reinforcement Class	1.8 m reinforcement spacing Minimum Gage	1.8 m reinforcement spacing Optional Tie rod(s)	0.9 m reinforcement spacing External Reinforcement Class	0.9 m reinforcement spacing Minimum Gage	0.9 m reinforcement spacing Optional Tie rod(s)
1	2	3	4	5	6	7	8	9	10
1 – 250	0.85		0.85	B	0.70	1	B	0.70	1
251 – 300	1.00		1.00	B	0.70	1	B	0.70	1
301 – 350	1.00		1.00	C	0.70	1	C	0.70	1
351 – 400	1.31		1.31	C	0.70	1	C	0.70	1
401 – 450	1.31		1.31	D	0.85	1	C	0.85	1
451 – 500	1.31		1.31	D	0.85	1	C	0.85	1
501 – 550	1.31		1.31	E	0.85	1	D	0.85	1
551 – 600	1.31		1.31	E	0.85	1	D	0.85	1
601 – 650	1.31		1.31	E	0.85	1	D	0.85	1
651 – 700	1.31		1.31	F	1.00	1	E	0.85	1
701 – 750	1.31		1.31	F	1.00	1	E	1.00	1
751 – 800	1.61	H	1.31	H	1.31	1	F	1.00	1
801 – 850	1.61		1.61	H	1.31	1	F	1.00	1
851 – 900	1.61		1.61	H	1.31	1	F	1.00	1
901 – 950				H	1.31	1	F	1.00	1
951 – 1000				H	1.31	1	F	1.00	1
1001 – 1050				H	1.31	1	F	1.00	1
1051 – 1100				I	1.31	1	G	1.00	1
1101 – 1150				I	1.31	1	G	1.00	1
1151 – 1200				I	1.31	1	G	1.00	1
1201 – 1250				J	1.61	2	H	1.00	1
1251 – 1300				J	1.61	2	H	1.00	1
1301 – 1350				J	1.61	2	H	1.31	1
1351 – 1400				J	1.61	2	H	1.31	1
1401 – 1450				J	1.61	2	H	1.31	1
1451 – 1500				J	1.61	2	H	1.31	1
1501 – 1550							I	1.31	1
1551 – 1600							I	1.31	1
1601 – 1650							I	1.31	1
1651 – 1700							I	1.31	1
1701 – 1750							I	1.31	1
1751 – 1800							I	1.31	1

Tables are limited to minor dimensions up to 750 mm
If a cell is shaded this indicates that the option is lighter than the corresponding option with a larger reinforcement spacing.
NP = Not Permitted
▱ = No Solution Provided
Negative pressure applications are limited to the following options:
  Use the unreinforced option
  Use the internal (tie rod) option
  Use a male flange or ring that meets the reinforcement class at the required spacing
  Use external reinforcement meeting the reinforcement class in conjunction with an internal support (tie rod) type 1 per Figure 3-7
  A combination of the above options can be used.

Table 3–19M Spiral Flat Oval Reinforcement Table

4 in. w.g. +/−

Flat-Span (in.)	Unreinforced	12 ft. reinforcement spacing		6 ft. reinforcement spacing			3 ft. reinforcement spacing		
	Minimum Gage	External Reinforcement Class	Minimum Gage	External Reinforcement Class	Minimum Gage	Optional Tie rod(s)	External Reinforcement Class	Minimum Gage	Optional Tie rod(s)
1	2	3	4	5	6	7	8	9	10
1 – 10	20		20	B	24	1	B	24	1
11 – 12	20		20	C	24	1	C	24	1
13 – 14	18		18	C	22	1	C	24	1
15 – 16	18	D	20	D	22	1	C	22	1
17 – 18	18		18	D	22	1	C	22	1
19 – 20	18		18	E	22	1	D	22	1
21 – 22	18		18	E	20	1	D	22	1
23 – 24	18		18	F	20	1	E	22	1
25 – 26	16	F	18	F	20	1	E	22	1
27 – 28	16	G	18	G	20	1	E	20	1
29 – 30	16		16	G	18	1	E	20	1
31 – 32				H	18	1	F	20	1
33 – 34				H	16	1	F	20	1
35 – 36				H	16	1	F	20	1
37 – 38				I	16	1	G	20	1
39 – 40				I	16	1	G	20	1
41 – 42				I	16	1	G	20	1
43 – 44				J	16	1	H	20	1
45 – 46				J	16	1	H	20	1
47 – 48				J	16	1	I	20	1
49 – 50				J	16	2	I	20	1
51 – 52				J	16	2	I	18	1
53 – 54				J	16	2	I	18	1
55 – 56							I	18	1
57 – 58							I	18	1
59 – 60							I	18	1
61 – 62							J	18	2
63 – 64							J	18	2
65 – 66							J	18	2
67 – 68							J	18	2
69 – 70							J	18	2
71 – 72							J	18	2

Tables are limited to minor dimensions up to 30 inches
If a cell is shaded this indicates that the option is lighter than the corresponding option with a larger reinforcement spacing.
NP = Not Permitted
☐ = No Solution Provided
Negative pressure applications are limited to the following options:
  Use the unreinforced option
  Use the internal (tie rod) option
  Use a male flange or ring that meets the reinforcement class at the required spacing
  Use external reinforcement meeting the reinforcement class in conjunction with an internal support (tie rod) type 1 per Figure 3-7
  A combination of the above options can be used.

Table 3–20 Spiral Flat Oval Reinforcement Table

1000 Pa +/−

Flat-Span (mm)	Unreinforced	3.6 m reinforcement spacing		1.8 m reinforcement spacing			0.9 m reinforcement spacing		
	Minimum Gage	External Reinforcement Class	Minimum Gage	External Reinforcement Class	Minimum Gage	Optional Tie rod(s)	External Reinforcement Class	Minimum Gage	Optional Tie rod(s)
1	2	3	4	5	6	7	8	9	10
1 – 250	1		1	B	0.7	1	B	0.7	1
251 – 300	1		1	C	0.7	1	C	0.7	1
301 – 350	1.31		1.31	C	0.85	1	C	0.7	1
351 – 400	1.31	D	1	D	0.85	1	C	0.85	1
401 – 450	1.31		1.31	D	0.85	1	C	0.85	1
451 – 500	1.31		1.31	E	0.85	1	D	0.85	1
501 – 550	1.31		1.31	E	1	1	D	0.85	1
551 – 600	1.31		1.31	F	1	1	E	0.85	1
601 – 650	1.61	F	1.31	F	1	1	E	0.85	1
651 – 700	1.61	G	1.31	G	1	1	E	1	1
701 – 750	1.61		1.61	G	1.31	1	E	1	1
751 – 800				H	1.31	1	F	1	1
801 – 850				H	1.61	1	F	1	1
851 – 900				H	1.61	1	F	1	1
901 – 950				I	1.61	1	G	1	1
951 – 1000				I	1.61	1	G	1	1
1001 – 1050				I	1.61	1	G	1	1
1051 – 1100				J	1.61	1	H	1	1
1101 – 1150				J	1.61	1	H	1	1
1151 – 1200				J	1.61	1	I	1	1
1201 – 1250				J	1.61	2	I	1	1
1251 – 1300				J	1.61	2	I	1.31	1
1301 – 1350				J	1.61	2	I	1.31	1
1351 – 1400							I	1.31	1
1401 – 1450							I	1.31	1
1451 – 1500							I	1.31	1
1501 – 1550							J	1.31	2
1551 – 1600							J	1.31	2
1601 – 1650							J	1.31	2
1651 – 1700							J	1.31	2
1701 – 1750							J	1.31	2
1751 – 1800							J	1.31	2

Tables are limited to minor dimensions up to 750 mm
If a cell is shaded this indicates that the option is lighter than the corresponding option with a larger reinforcement spacing.
NP = Not Permitted
☐ = No Solution Provided
Negative pressure applications are limited to the following options:
  Use the unreinforced option
  Use the internal (tie rod) option
  Use a male flange or ring that meets the reinforcement class at the required spacing
  Use external reinforcement meeting the reinforcement class in conjunction with an internal support (tie rod) type 1 per Figure 3-7
  A combination of the above options can be used.

Table 3–20M Spiral Flat Oval Reinforcement Table

6 in. w.g. +/−

Flat-Span (in.)	Unreinforced	12 ft. reinforcement spacing		6 ft. reinforcement spacing			3 ft. reinforcement spacing		
	Minimum Gage	External Reinforcement Class	Minimum Gage	External Reinforcement Class	Minimum Gage	Optional Tie rod(s)	External Reinforcement Class	Minimum Gage	Optional Tie rod(s)
1	2	3	4	5	6	7	8	9	10
1 – 10	20		20	B	24	1	B	24	1
11 – 12	18		18	C	22	1	C	24	1
13 – 14	18		18	D	20	1	C	24	1
15 – 16	18		18	D	20	1	D	22	1
17 – 18	18		18	E	20	1	D	22	1
19 – 20	16	F	18	F	20	1	D	22	1
21 – 22	16	F	18	F	20	1	E	22	1
23 – 24	16		16	G	20	1	E	22	1
25 – 26				G	18	1	F	20	1
27 – 28				H	18	1	F	20	1
29 – 30				H	18	1	F	20	1
31 – 32				I	18	1	H	20	1
33 – 34				I	18	1	H	20	1
35 – 36				I	18	1	H	20	1
37 – 38				J	16	2	H	20	1
39 – 40				J	16	2	H	20	1
41 – 42				J	16	2	H	20	1
43 – 44							I	20	2
45 – 46							I	20	2
47 – 48							I	18	1
49 – 50							I	18	1
51 – 52							I	18	1
53 – 54							I	18	1
55 – 56							J	18	2
57 – 58							J	18	2
59 – 60							J	18	2
61 – 62							K	16	2
63 – 64							K	16	2
65 – 66							K	16	2
67 – 68							K	16	2
69 – 70							K	16	2
71 – 72							K	16	2

Tables are limited to minor dimensions up to 30 inches
If a cell is shaded this indicates that the option is lighter than the corresponding option with a larger reinforcement spacing.
NP = Not Permitted
☐ = No Solution Provided
Negative pressure applications are limited to the following options:
  Use the unreinforced option
  Use the internal (tie rod) option
  Use a male flange or ring that meets the reinforcement class at the required spacing
  Use external reinforcement meeting the reinforcement class in conjunction with an internal support (tie rod) type 1 per Figure 3-7
  A combination of the above options can be used.

Table 3–21 Spiral Flat Oval Reinforcement Table

1500 Pa +/−

Flat-Span (mm)	Unreinforced	3.6 m reinforcement spacing		1.8 m reinforcement spacing			0.9 m reinforcement spacing		
	Minimum Gage	External Reinforcement Class	Minimum Gage	External Reinforcement Class	Minimum Gage	Optional Tie rod(s)	External Reinforcement Class	Minimum Gage	Optional Tie rod(s)
1	2	3	4	5	6	7	8	9	10
1 – 250	1.00		1.00	B	0.70	1	B	0.70	1
251 – 300	1.31		1.31	C	0.85	1	C	0.70	1
301 – 350	1.31		1.31	D	1.00	1	C	0.70	1
351 – 400	1.31		1.31	D	1.00	1	D	0.85	1
401 – 450	1.31		1.31	E	1.00	1	D	0.85	1
451 – 500	1.61	F	1.31	F	1.00	1	D	0.85	1
501 – 550	1.61	F	1.31	F	1.00	1	E	0.85	1
551 – 600	1.61		1.61	G	1.00	1	E	0.85	1
601 – 650				G	1.31	1	F	1.00	1
651 – 700				H	1.31	1	F	1.00	1
701 – 750				H	1.31	1	F	1.00	1
751 – 800				I	1.31	1	H	1.00	1
801 – 850				I	1.31	1	H	1.00	1
851 – 900				I	1.31	1	H	1.00	1
901 – 950				J	1.61	2	H	1.00	1
951 – 1000				J	1.61	2	H	1.00	1
1001 – 1050				J	1.61	2	H	1.00	1
1051 – 1100							I	1.00	2
1101 – 1150							I	1.00	2
1151 – 1200							I	1.31	1
1201 – 1250							I	1.31	1
1251 – 1300							I	1.31	1
1301 – 1350							I	1.31	1
1351 – 1400							J	1.31	2
1401 – 1450							J	1.31	2
1451 – 1500							J	1.31	2
1501 – 1550							K	1.61	2
1551 – 1600							K	1.61	2
1601 – 1650							K	1.61	2
1651 – 1700							K	1.61	2
1701 – 1750							K	1.61	2
1751 – 1800							K	1.61	2

Tables are limited to minor dimensions up to 750 mm
If a cell is shaded this indicates that the option is lighter than the corresponding option with a larger reinforcement spacing.
NP = Not Permitted
⬜ = No Solution Provided
Negative pressure applications are limited to the following options:
  Use the unreinforced option
  Use the internal (tie rod) option
  Use a male flange or ring that meets the reinforcement class at the required spacing
  Use external reinforcement meeting the reinforcement class in conjunction with an internal support (tie rod) type 1 per Figure 3-7
  A combination of the above options can be used.

Table 3–21M Spiral Flat Oval Reinforcement Table

10 in. w.g. +/−

Flat-Span (in.)	Unreinforced Minimum Gage	12 ft. reinforcement spacing External Reinforcement Class	Minimum Gage	6 ft. reinforcement spacing External Reinforcement Class	Minimum Gage	Optional Tie rod(s)	3 ft. reinforcement spacing External Reinforcement Class	Minimum Gage	Optional Tie rod(s)
1	2	3	4	5	6	7	8	9	10
1 – 10	18		18	C	20	NP	C	24	NP
11 – 12	18		18	D	20	NP	C	24	NP
13 – 14	18		18	E	20	NP	D	22	NP
15 – 16	16	E	18	E	18	NP	E	22	NP
17 – 18	16		16	F	18	NP	E	22	NP
19 – 20				G	18	NP	F	22	NP
21 – 22				H	18	NP	F	22	NP
23 – 24				H	18	NP	G	20	NP
25 – 26				I	16	NP	G	20	NP
27 – 28				I	16	NP	H	20	NP
29 – 30				J	16	NP	H	20	NP
31 – 32							I	20	NP
33 – 34							I	20	NP
35 – 36							I	20	NP
37 – 38							I	18	NP
39 – 40							I	18	NP
41 – 42							I	18	NP
43 – 44							J	18	NP
45 – 46							J	18	NP
47 – 48							J	18	NP
49 – 50							K	18	NP
51 – 52							K	18	NP
53 – 54							K	18	NP
55 – 56							L	16	NP
57 – 58							L	16	NP
59 – 60							L	16	NP
61 – 62							L	16	NP
63 – 64							L	16	NP
65 – 66							L	16	NP
67 – 68							L	16	NP
69 – 70							L	16	NP
71 – 72							L	16	NP

Tables are limited to minor dimensions up to 30 inches
If a cell is shaded this indicates that the option is lighter than the corresponding option with a larger reinforcement spacing.
NP = Not Permitted
☐ = No Solution Provided
Negative pressure applications are limited to the following options:
  Use the unreinforced option
  Use the internal (tie rod) option
  Use a male flange or ring that meets the reinforcement class at the required spacing
  Use external reinforcement meeting the reinforcement class in conjunction with an internal support (tie rod) type 1 per Figure 3-7
  A combination of the above options can be used.

Table 3–22 Spiral Flat Oval Reinforcement Table

2500 Pa +/−

Flat-Span (mm)	Unreinforced Minimum Gage	3.6 m reinforcement spacing External Reinforcement Class	3.6 m Minimum Gage	1.8 m reinforcement spacing External Reinforcement Class	1.8 m Minimum Gage	Optional Tie rod(s)	0.9 m reinforcement spacing External Reinforcement Class	0.9 m Minimum Gage	Optional Tie rod(s)
1	2	3	4	5	6	7	8	9	10
1 – 250	1.31		1.31	C	1.00	NP	C	0.70	NP
251 – 300	1.31		1.31	D	1.00	NP	C	0.70	NP
301 – 350	1.31		1.31	E	1.00	NP	D	0.85	NP
351 – 400	1.61	E	1.31	E	1.31	NP	E	0.85	NP
401 – 450	1.61		1.61	F	1.31	NP	E	0.85	NP
451 – 500				G	1.31	NP	F	0.85	NP
501 – 550				H	1.31	NP	F	0.85	NP
551 – 600				H	1.31	NP	G	1.00	NP
601 – 650				I	1.61	NP	G	1.00	NP
651 – 700				I	1.61	NP	H	1.00	NP
701 – 750				J	1.61	NP	H	1.00	NP
751 – 800							I	1.00	NP
801 – 850							I	1.00	NP
851 – 900							I	1.00	NP
901 – 950							I	1.31	NP
951 – 1000							I	1.31	NP
1001 – 1050							I	1.31	NP
1051 – 1100							J	1.31	NP
1101 – 1150							J	1.31	NP
1151 – 1200							J	1.31	NP
1201 – 1250							K	1.31	NP
1251 – 1300							K	1.31	NP
1301 – 1350							K	1.31	NP
1351 – 1400							L	1.61	NP
1401 – 1450							L	1.61	NP
1451 – 1500							L	1.61	NP
1501 – 1550							L	1.61	NP
1551 – 1600							L	1.61	NP
1601 – 1650							L	1.61	NP
1651 – 1700							L	1.61	NP
1701 – 1750							L	1.61	NP
1751 – 1800							L	1.61	NP

Tables are limited to minor dimensions up to 750 mm
If a cell is shaded this indicates that the option is lighter than the corresponding option with a larger reinforcement spacing.
NP = Not Permitted
☐ = No Solution Provided
Negative pressure applications are limited to the following options:
  Use the unreinforced option
  Use the internal (tie rod) option
  Use a male flange or ring that meets the reinforcement class at the required spacing
  Use external reinforcement meeting the reinforcement class in conjunction with an internal support (tie rod) type 1 per Figure 3-7
  A combination of the above options can be used.

Table 3–22M Spiral Flat Oval Reinforcement Table

PLEATED

STAMPED

ADJUSTABLE

SPIRAL

SEGMENTED

SEGMENTED STANDING SEAM

FIGURE 3–4 ROUND DUCT ELBOWS

(51 mm) (51 mm)
2" C + 4 2"

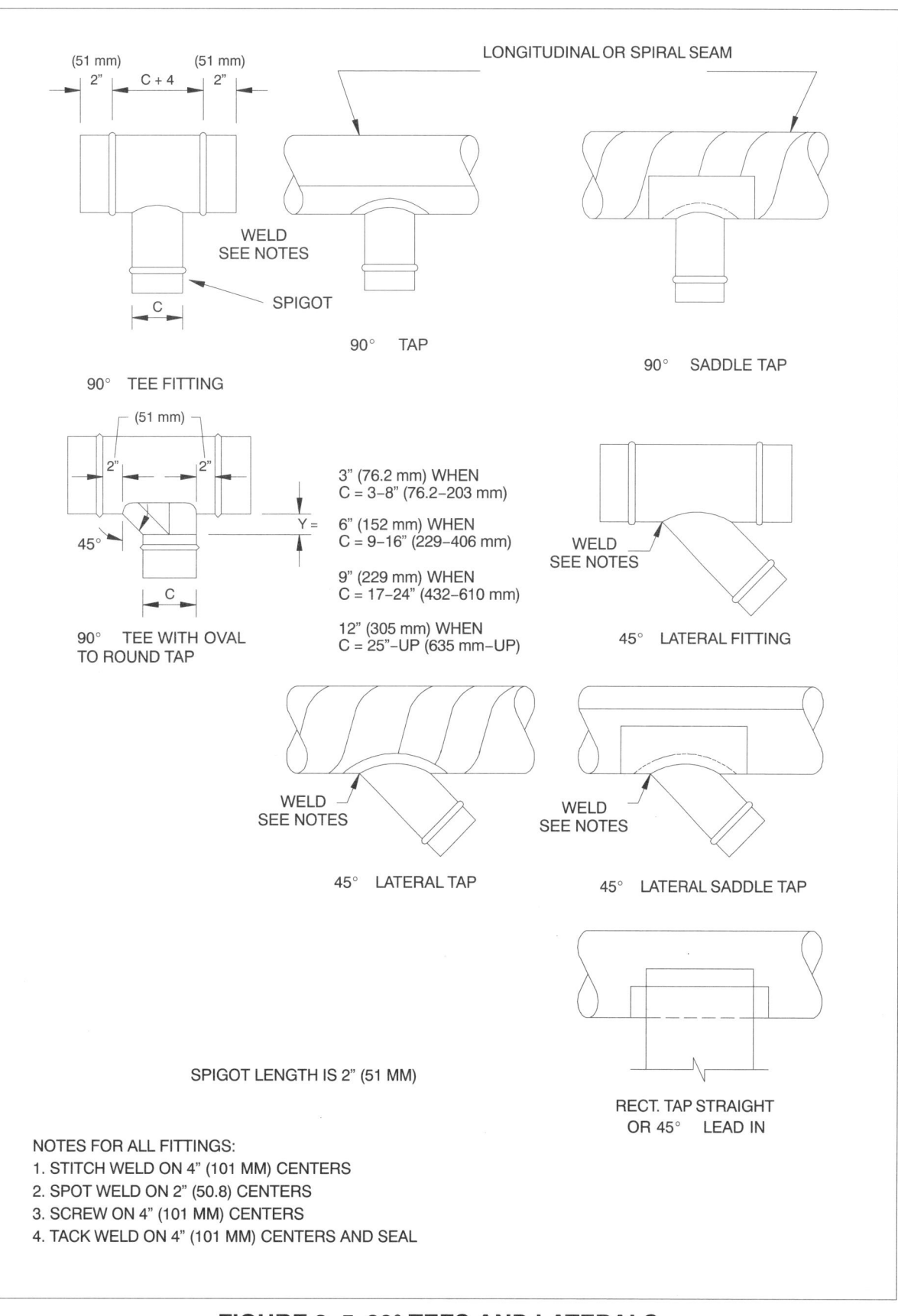

LONGITUDINAL OR SPIRAL SEAM

WELD SEE NOTES
SPIGOT
C

90° TEE FITTING

90° TAP

90° SADDLE TAP

(51 mm)
2" 2"
45°
C

Y = 3" (76.2 mm) WHEN C = 3–8" (76.2–203 mm)
6" (152 mm) WHEN C = 9–16" (229–406 mm)
9" (229 mm) WHEN C = 17–24" (432–610 mm)
12" (305 mm) WHEN C = 25"–UP (635 mm–UP)

90° TEE WITH OVAL TO ROUND TAP

WELD SEE NOTES

45° LATERAL FITTING

WELD SEE NOTES

45° LATERAL TAP

WELD SEE NOTES

45° LATERAL SADDLE TAP

RECT. TAP STRAIGHT OR 45° LEAD IN

SPIGOT LENGTH IS 2" (51 MM)

NOTES FOR ALL FITTINGS:
1. STITCH WELD ON 4" (101 MM) CENTERS
2. SPOT WELD ON 2" (50.8) CENTERS
3. SCREW ON 4" (101 MM) CENTERS
4. TACK WELD ON 4" (101 MM) CENTERS AND SEAL

FIGURE 3–5 90° TEES AND LATERALS

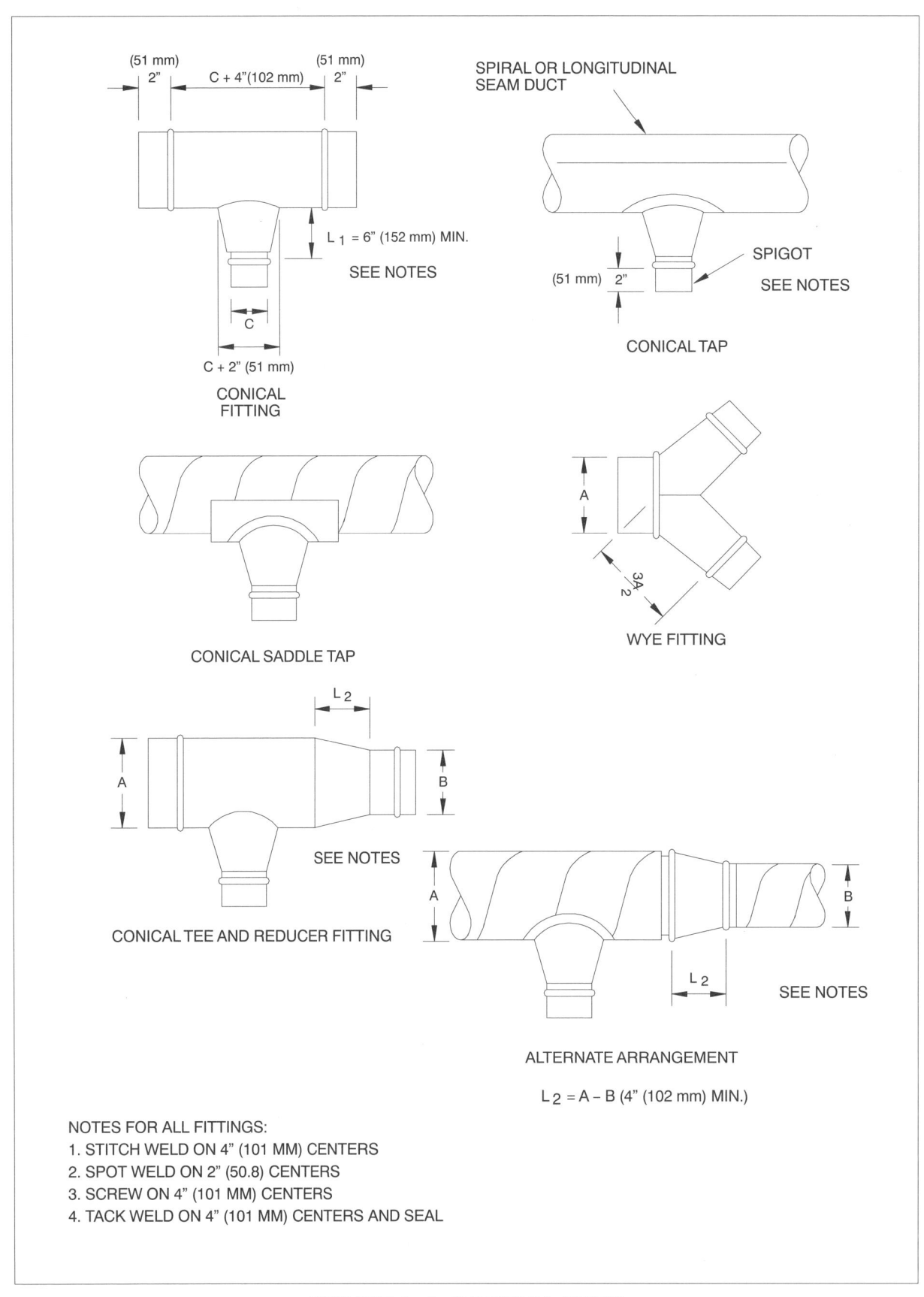

CONICAL FITTING
- (51 mm) 2"
- C + 4" (102 mm)
- (51 mm) 2"
- $L_1 = 6"$ (152 mm) MIN.
- SEE NOTES
- C
- C + 2" (51 mm)

CONICAL TAP
- SPIRAL OR LONGITUDINAL SEAM DUCT
- SPIGOT
- (51 mm) 2"
- SEE NOTES

CONICAL SADDLE TAP

WYE FITTING
- A
- 3A/2

CONICAL TEE AND REDUCER FITTING
- L_2
- A
- B
- SEE NOTES

ALTERNATE ARRANGEMENT
- A
- B
- L_2
- SEE NOTES

$L_2 = A - B$ (4" (102 mm) MIN.)

NOTES FOR ALL FITTINGS:
1. STITCH WELD ON 4" (101 MM) CENTERS
2. SPOT WELD ON 2" (50.8) CENTERS
3. SCREW ON 4" (101 MM) CENTERS
4. TACK WELD ON 4" (101 MM) CENTERS AND SEAL

FIGURE 3–6 CONICAL TEES

GROOVED OR WELDED SEAM

TYPE 1
TYPE 2
F

TYPE 1 HAS AN INTERNAL TIE ROD

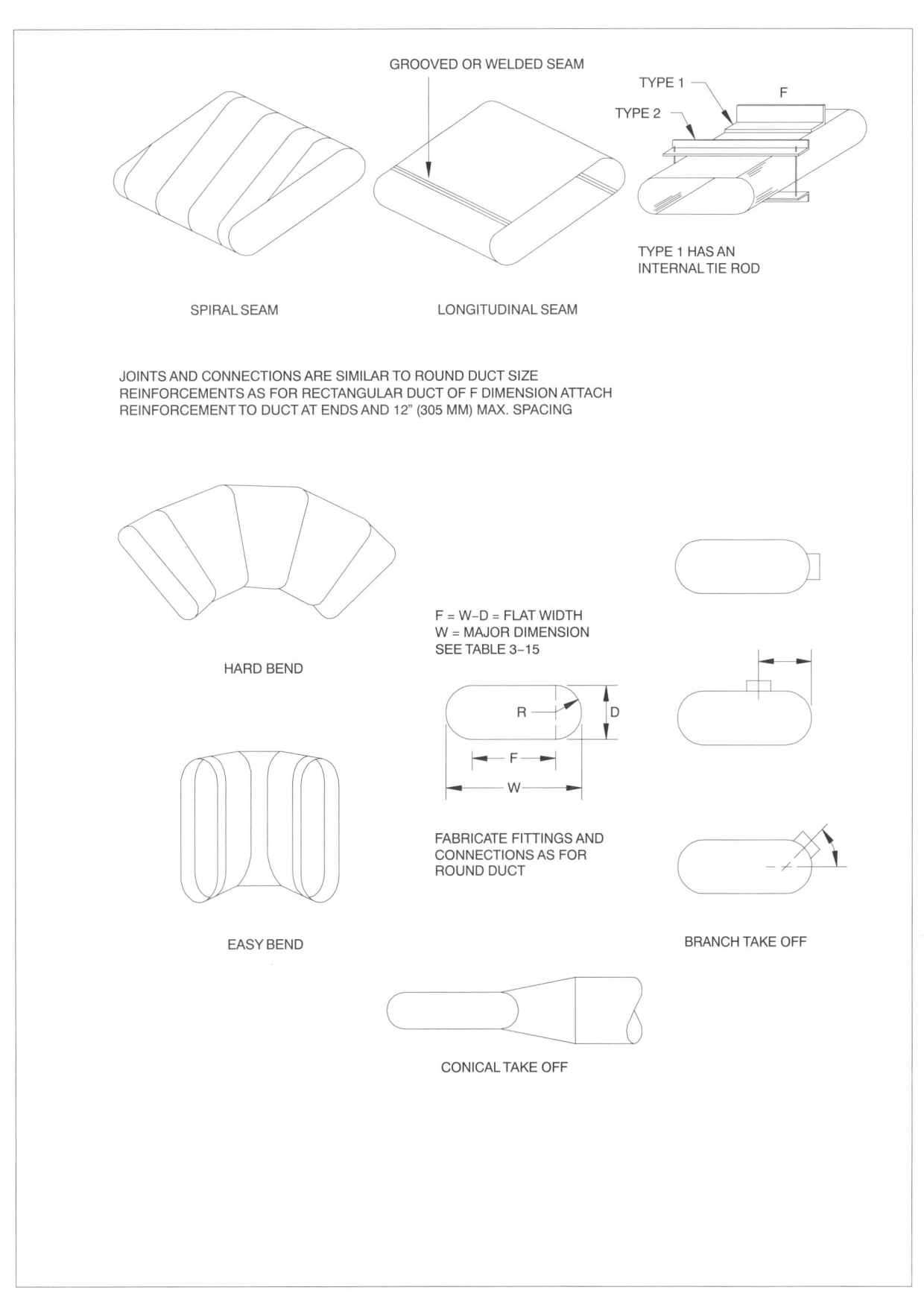

SPIRAL SEAM

LONGITUDINAL SEAM

JOINTS AND CONNECTIONS ARE SIMILAR TO ROUND DUCT SIZE REINFORCEMENTS AS FOR RECTANGULAR DUCT OF F DIMENSION ATTACH REINFORCEMENT TO DUCT AT ENDS AND 12" (305 MM) MAX. SPACING

HARD BEND

$F = W-D =$ FLAT WIDTH
$W =$ MAJOR DIMENSION
SEE TABLE 3–15

FABRICATE FITTINGS AND CONNECTIONS AS FOR ROUND DUCT

EASY BEND

BRANCH TAKE OFF

CONICAL TAKE OFF

FIGURE 3–7 FLAT OVAL DUCTS

HVAC Duct Construction Standards Metal and Flexible • Fourth Edition

3.5 FLEXIBLE AIR DUCT INSTALLATION STANDARDS

S3.19 Unless otherwise designated, the term "flexible air duct" is used for all ducts classified by UL as either flexible air ducts or air connectors.

S3.20 These provisions apply to ducts used for indoor comfort heating, ventilating, and air conditioning service. They do not apply to service for conveying particulates, corrosive fumes and vapors, high temperature air, corrosive or contaminated atmosphere, etc.

S3.21 It is presumed that project specifications define the specific materials, pressure limits, velocity limits, friction rate, thermal conductivity, acoustical ratings, and other attributes.

S3.22 When ducts must conform to NFPA Standard 90A or 90B, flexible ducts must be tested in accordance with Underwriters Laboratories *UL Standard for Safety, Factory-Made Air Ducts and Air Connectors*, UL-181, and must be installed in accordance with the conditions of their UL listing. Separate installation limitations for air connectors and flexible air ducts are identified in NFPA Standard 90A or 90B.

Refer to UL Standard 181 for details.

S3.23 The minimum length of flexible duct should be used.

S3.24 Bends shall be made with not less than 1 duct diameter centerline radius. Ducts should extend a few inches beyond the end of a sheet metal connection before bending. Ducts should not be compressed.

S3.25 Ducts shall be located away from hot equipment such as furnaces and steam pipes to avoid excess temperature exposure.

S3.26 Illustrations of accessories, sleeves, and collars are representative of classes of items. The use of components not precisely identical to these is acceptable.

S3.27 If the application guidelines dictated by the flexible duct manufacturer are more stringent than the specifications in this manual, those of the manufacturer shall govern.

3.6 SPECIFICATION FOR JOINING AND ATTACHING FLEXIBLE DUCT

S3.28 The provisions for sealing ducts specified on Section 1.4 apply. Adhesives shall be chemically compatible with materials they contact. Flexible air ducts and air connectors shall be sealed using tape or mastic that is listed and labeled to the UL 181B Standard and marked UL 181B-FX (tape) or UL 181B-M (mastic). Non-metallic mechanical fasteners (plastic straps) shall be listed and labeled to the UL 181B Standard and marked UL 181B-C

S3.29 The ends of ducts shall be trimmed square before installation.

S3.30 Collars to which flexible duct is attached shall be a minimum of 2 in. (51 mm) in length. Sleeves used for joining two sections of flexible duct shall be a minimum of 4 in. (102 mm) in length. When non-metallic mechanical fasteners are used, collars and sleeves shall be beaded and pressure is limited to 6" W.G. maximum.

S3.31 Collars and sleeves shall be inserted into flexible duct a minimum of 1 in. (25 mm) before fastening.

S3.32 Metallic flexible duct shall be attached with at least three #8 sheet metal screws equally spaced around the duct's circumference. Ducts larger than 12 in. (305 mm) in diameter shall have at least five #8 sheet metal screws. Screws shall be located at least 1/2 in. (13 mm) from the duct end.

S3.33 Insulation and vapor barriers on flexible ducts shall be fitted over the core connection and shall be secured using approved tape. A draw band may be used in combination with, or in place of, the tape

3.7 SPECIFICATION FOR SUPPORTING FLEXIBLE DUCT

S3.34 Flexible duct shall be supported at the manufacturer's recommended intervals but at least every 4 ft (1.5 m). Maximum permissible sag is a ½ in. per foot (41.7 mm/m) of spacing between supports. A connection to another duct or to equipment is considered a support point.

S3.35　Hanger or saddle material in contact with the flexible duct shall be wide enough so that it does not reduce the internal diameter of the duct when the supported section rests on the hanger or saddle material. In no case will the material contacting the flexible duct be less than 1 ½ in. (25 mm) wide. Narrower hanger material may be used in conjunction with a sheet metal saddle that meets this specification. This saddle must cover one-half the circumference of the outside diameter of the flexible duct and fit neatly around the lower half of the duct's outer circumference.

S3.36　Pre-installed suspension systems that are integral to the flexible duct are acceptable for hanging when the manufacturer's recommended procedures are followed.

S3.37　Hangers shall be adequately attached to the building structure.

S3.38　To avoid tearing the vapor barrier, do not support the entire weight of the flexible duct on any one hanger during installation. Avoid contacting the flexible duct with sharp edges of the hanger material. Damage to the vapor barrier may be repaired with approved tape. If the internal core is penetrated, replace the flexible duct or treat the tear as a connection.

S3.39　Terminal devices connected to a flexible duct shall be supported independently of the flexible duct.

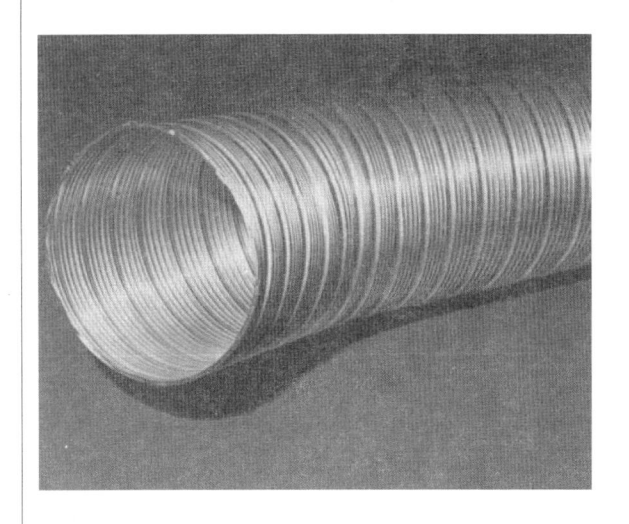

Form "M – UN" — Metallic, uninsulated
(Figure A)

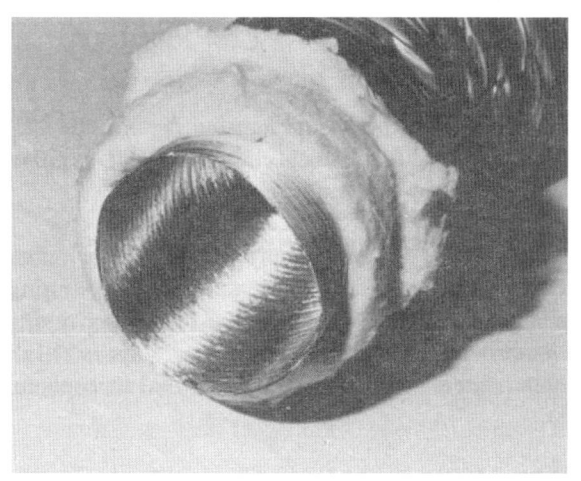

Form "M – I" — Metallic, insulated
(Figure B)

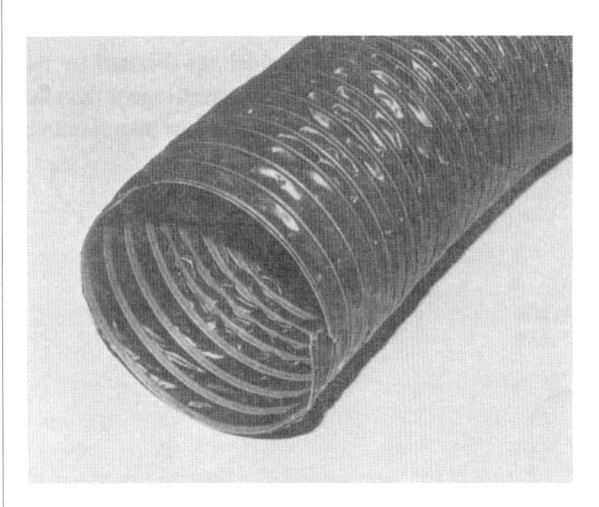

Form "NM – UN" — Nonmetallic, uninsulated
(Figure C)

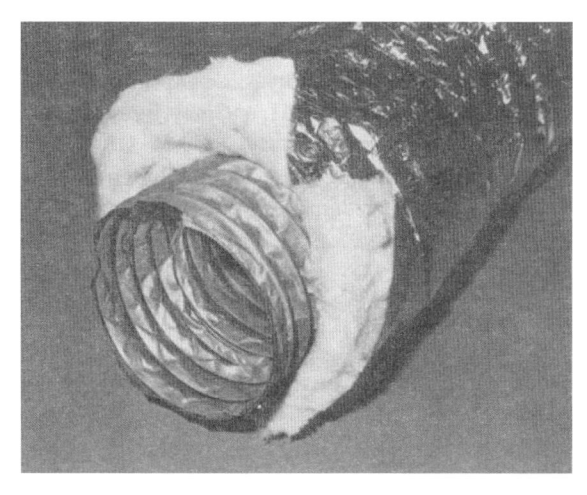

Form "NM – IL" — Nonmetallic, insulated (lined)
(Figure D)

FIGURE 3-8 TYPES OF FLEXIBLE DUCT

These photographs depict typical accessories but do not represent all available accessories. Coincidence with proprietary features is unintentional. The standard is not intended to limit the selection or the development of accessories for use with flexible duct.

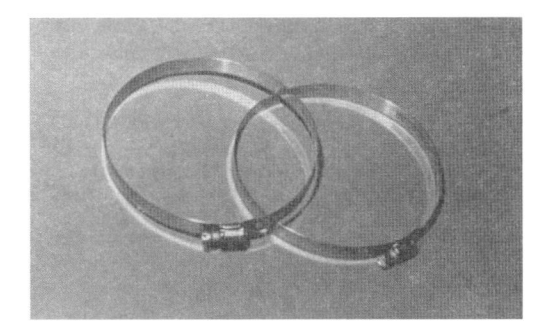

Figure A — Metal Clamp

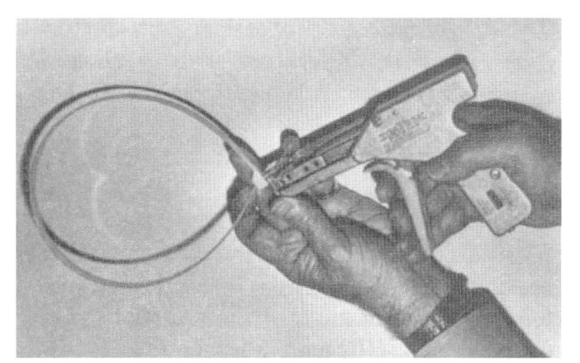

Figure B — Nonmetallic Duct Clamp

Figure C — Collar (Dovetail)

Figure D — Collar (Spin-in, Flared)

Figure E — Collar (Spin-in Straight)

Figure F — Collar (Spin-in Conical)

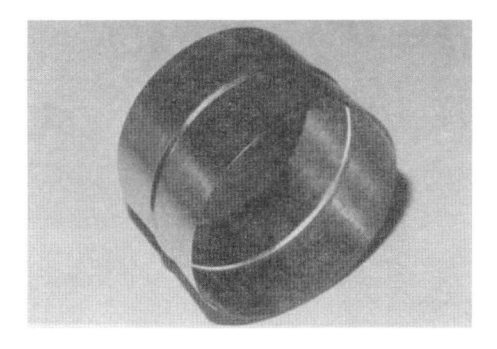

Figure G — 4" sleeve

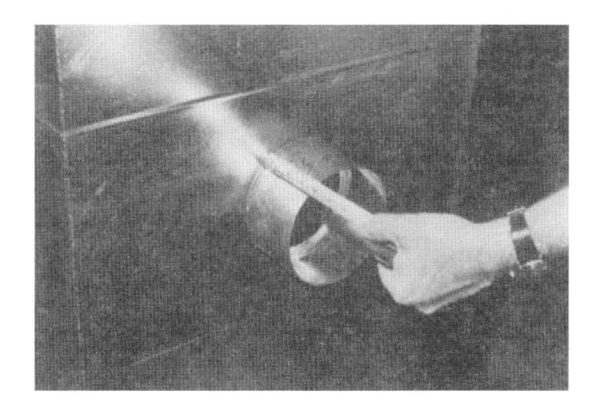

Figure H — Collar in duct min. 2"

FIGURE 3-9 TYPICAL ACCESSORIES

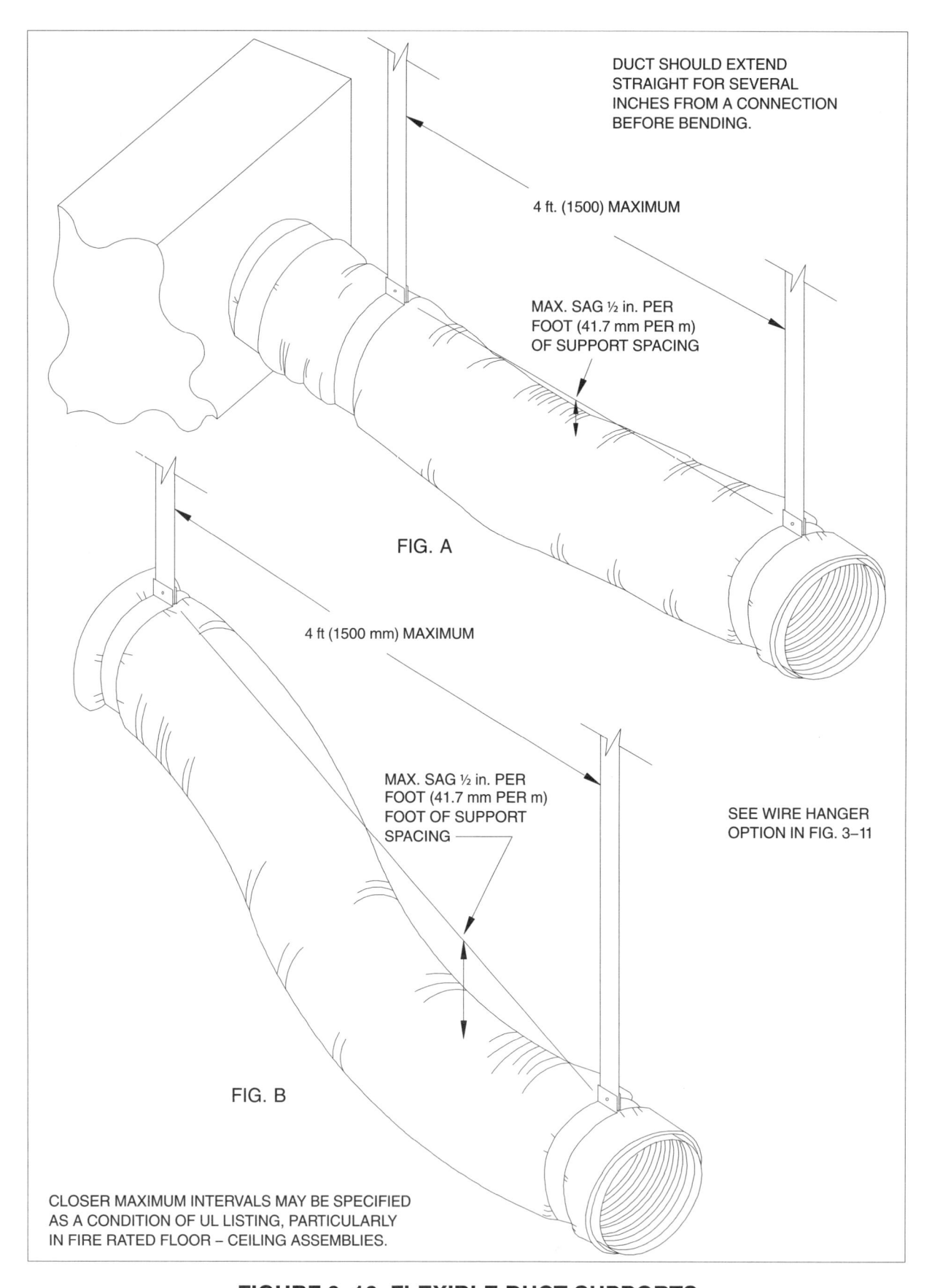

FIGURE 3–10 FLEXIBLE DUCT SUPPORTS

1½ in. (38 mm) MINIMUM

1½ in. (38 mm) BAND CLAMP WITH WIRE IS OPTIONAL.

WIRE

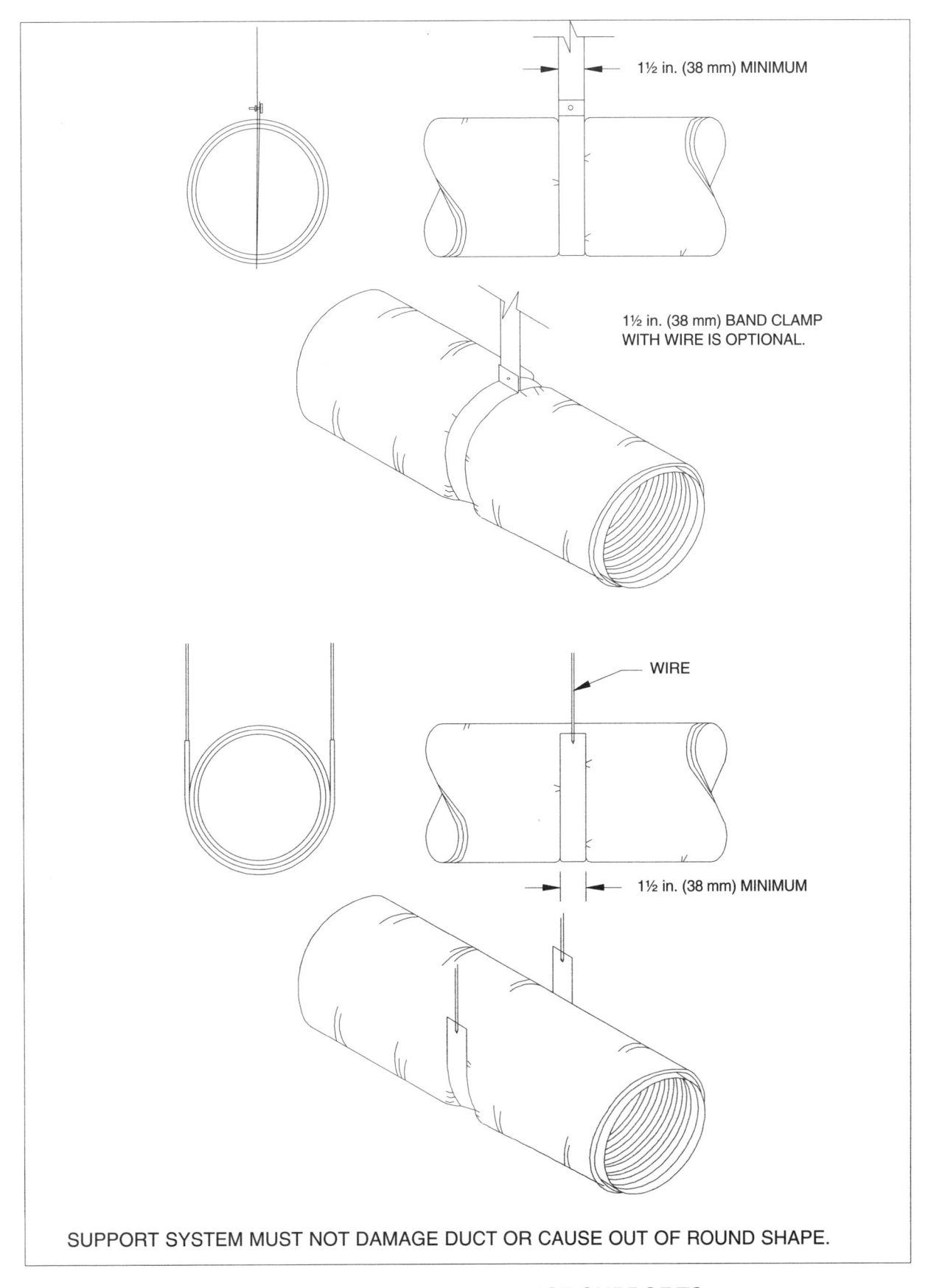

1½ in. (38 mm) MINIMUM

SUPPORT SYSTEM MUST NOT DAMAGE DUCT OR CAUSE OUT OF ROUND SHAPE.

FIGURE 3–11 FLEXIBLE DUCT SUPPORTS

3.8 COMMENTARY

Flexible air ducts have rectangular UL labels attached or printed at a maximum of 10 ft (3.05 m); flexible air connectors have round labels at least every 10 ft (3.05 m). UL, NFPA, and most codes make distinctions between these two products in their limits of application. Connectors are more restricted and are currently limited to 14 ft (4.27 m) of installed length. Regulations governing these forms of duct should be checked especially for floor penetrations, ceiling air plenums, and fire rated floor-ceiling or roof-ceiling assemblies.

These installation provisions were prepared for round ducts; however, they may also be usable for flexible flat oval ducts.

Some types of flexible duct have received listings as components of fan unit or air terminal unit systems, and they may be governed independently by the conditions of those listings.

The designer should consult the following references when considering the use of flexible ducts:

- UL Standard 181 and 181B (closure systems)

- NFPA Standards 90A and 90B

- UL Gas and Oil Equipment Directory

- UL Fire Resistance Directory

- ASTM Standard E96, *Water Vapor Transmission of Materials in Sheet Form*, American Society of Testing Materials

- ASTM Standard E477, *Duct Liner Materials and Prefabricated Silencer for Acoustical Performance*, American Society of Testing Materials

- ADC Flexible Duct Performance and Installation Standards, and ADC Flexible Duct Test Code FD-72, R1, Air Duct Council (covering thermal, acoustical and friction ratings)

The most common metallic duct is aluminum; however, galvanized steel and stainless steel varieties are available. Nonmetal ducts are available in a wide variety of materials and nominal shape-retaining reinforcements. Machines for producing the ducts are available from several suppliers.

Flexible ducts may come to the installer in compressed form in a variety of lengths. Their length can be determined by a measurement taken with a 25 lb. (11.3 Kg) axial load used to extend the duct. Repeated flexure of metallic ducts will probably result in fatigue stress cracking. Sections S3.23 and S3.24 contain statements that ducts "should" have minimum length and "should not" be compressed. "Should" is used instead of "must" in these instances because some discretionary judgement is necessary. Compressing duct increases first cost and friction loss. The minimum length refers to the practical route between connection points but not to the degree that the material is overstressed or to the degree that all available stretch is removed. SMACNA discourages the practice of providing excess length in case of future building modifications.

CHAPTER 4

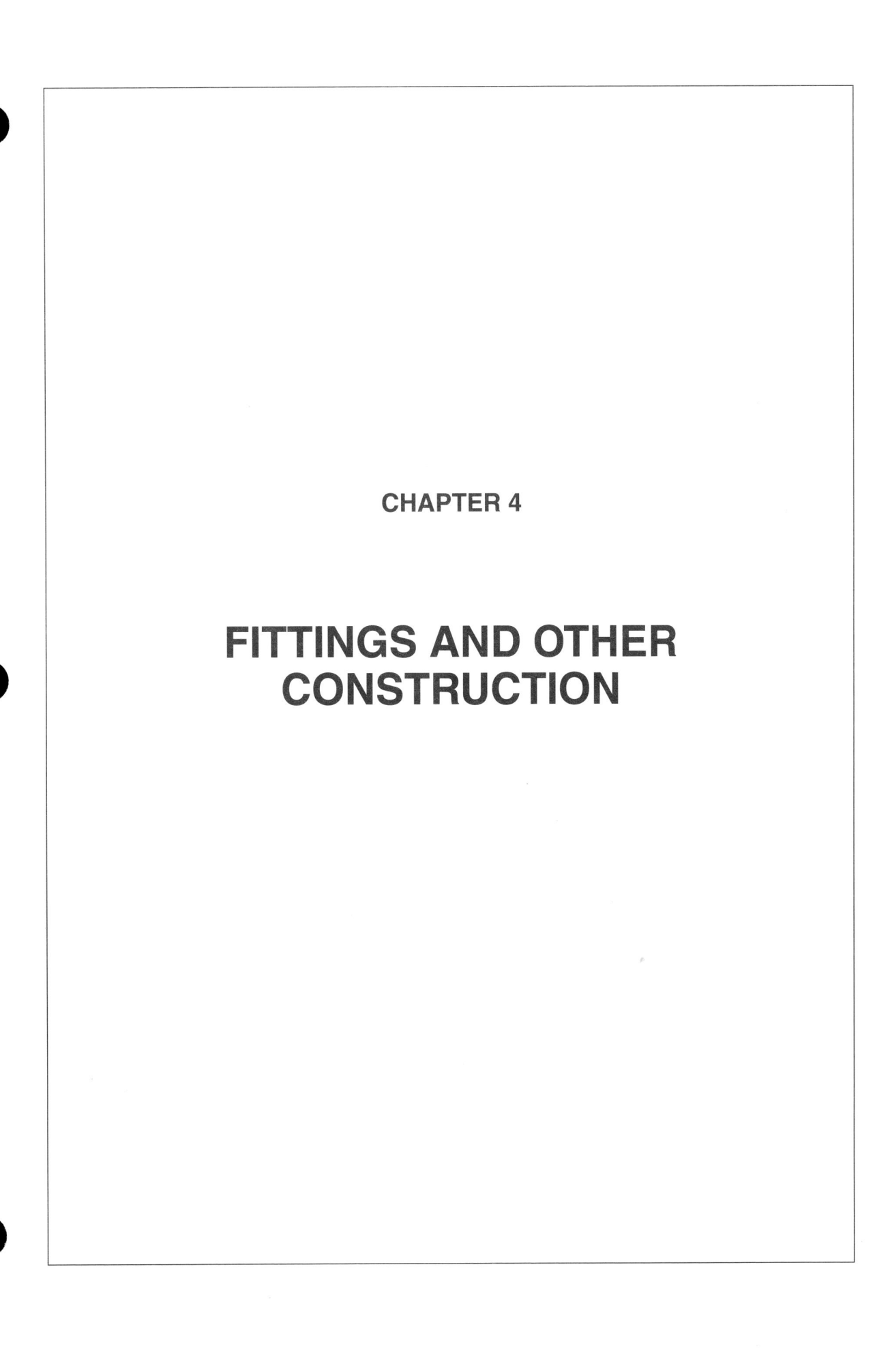

FITTINGS AND OTHER CONSTRUCTION

CHAPTER 4   FITTINGS AND OTHER CONSTRUCTION

4.1 REQUIREMENTS

The illustrations of fittings, equipment connections, and duct liners in this section presuppose that the designer is familiar with performance data published by organizations such as ASHRAE, AMCA, SMACNA, NAIMA, ACGIH, and coil, damper, air terminal, and fan manufacturers. They assume that system designers understand friction and dynamic losses in HVAC systems and have accounted for these in the design of systems for particular projects.

The purpose of this section is to provide geometries, configurations, and construction detail alternatives that relate to and enhance the performance of fittings that the designer may incorporate in his systems. More construction detail is provided than is given in design handbooks. The many alternatives included in this document would not have the same pressure loss factors. Also, equipment manufacturer installation requirements may differ from the illustrations herein.

To the extent that the designer is inconsistent with the requirements stated in S1.3 on page 1.1, installers may assume that construction alternatives herein are left for their choice.

Within this section as in other sections specifications considered to be obligatory are designated by "S" paragraph numbers. When not preempted, Section S1 will control the construction of fittings. To a significant extent S1.16 on page 1.3 addresses reinforcement of fittings that appear in this section.

S paragraphs for Chapter 2 begin on page 2.4. Compliance with Figures in Chapter 2 that are not specifically referenced in the S specification text is presumed when not preempted by specifications external to this document. However, the inclusion of performance requirements in this section, as in other sections, is intended to acknowledge the provisions of Section S1.2 on page 1.1 when alternatives to the prescriptive requirements are proposed.

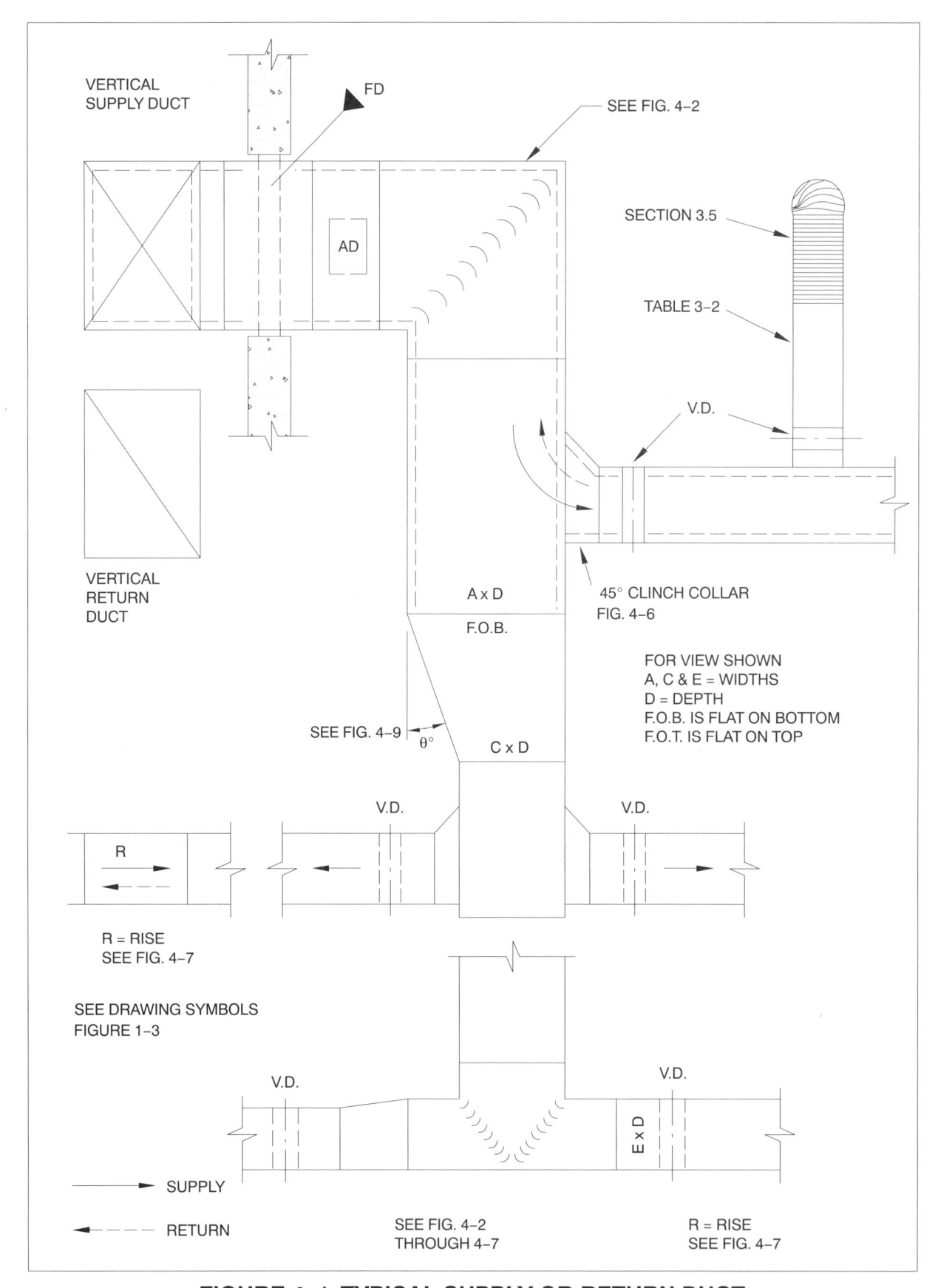

FIGURE 4-1 TYPICAL SUPPLY OR RETURN DUCT

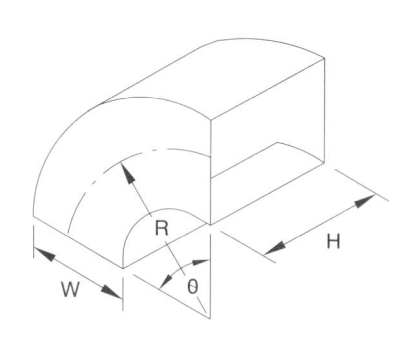

TYPE RE 1
RADIUS ELBOW

CENTERLINE $R = \dfrac{3W}{2}$ UNLESS OTHERWISE SPECIFIED – IS NOT RESTRICTED TO 90° SQUARE THROAT, $\dfrac{R}{W} = 0.5$, MAY BE USED, UP TO 1000 FPM (5 mps).

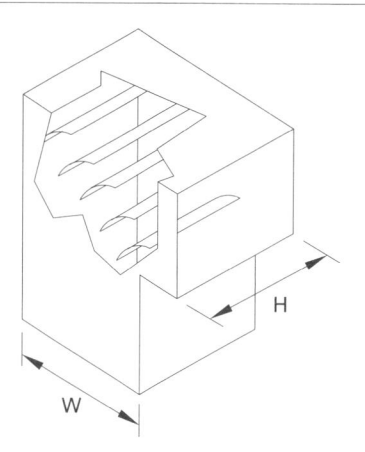

TYPE RE 2
SQUARE THROAT ELBOW
WITH VANES

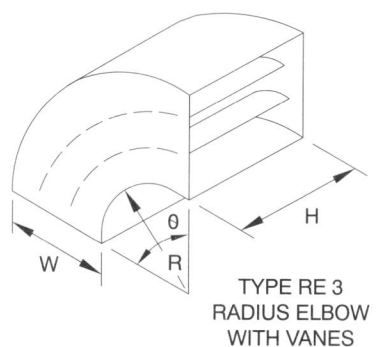

TYPE RE 3
RADIUS ELBOW
WITH VANES

NOTE:
FOR RE 3 *SEE* SPLITTER VANES IN SMACNA *HVAC SYSTEMS DUCT DESIGN*

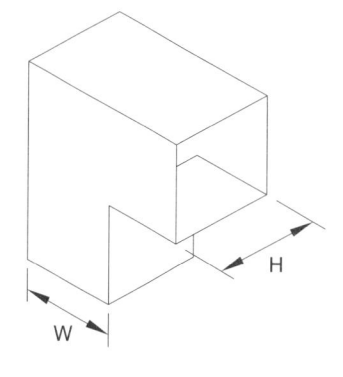

TYPE RE 4
SQUARE THROAT ELBOW
WITHOUT VANES
(1000 FPM (5 mps) MAXIMUM VELOCITY)

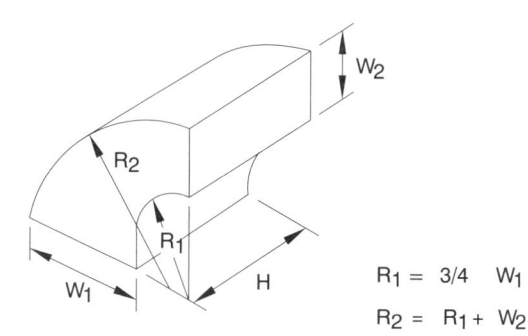

$R_1 = 3/4 \ W_1$
$R_2 = R_1 + W_2$

TYPE RE 5
DUAL RADIUS ELBOW

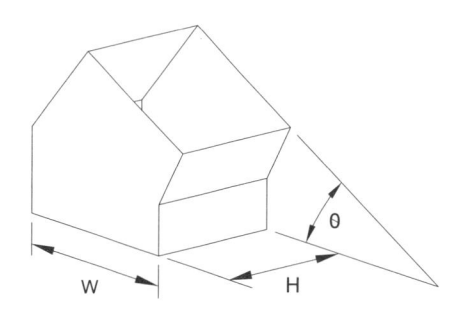

TYPE RE 6
MITERED ELBOW

BEAD, CROSSBREAK AND REINFORCE FLAT SURFACES AS IN STRAIGHT DUCT

FIGURE 4–2 RECTANGULAR ELBOWS

TYPE RE 7
45° THROAT
45° HEEL

TYPE RE 8
45° THROAT
RADIUS HEEL

ALL 45° THROATS ARE 4" (100 MM) MINIMUM

TYPE RE 9
45° THROAT
90° HEEL

TYPE RE 10
RADIUS THROAT
90° HEEL

BEAD, CROSSBREAK AND REINFORCE FLAT SURFACES AS IN STRAIGHT DUCT

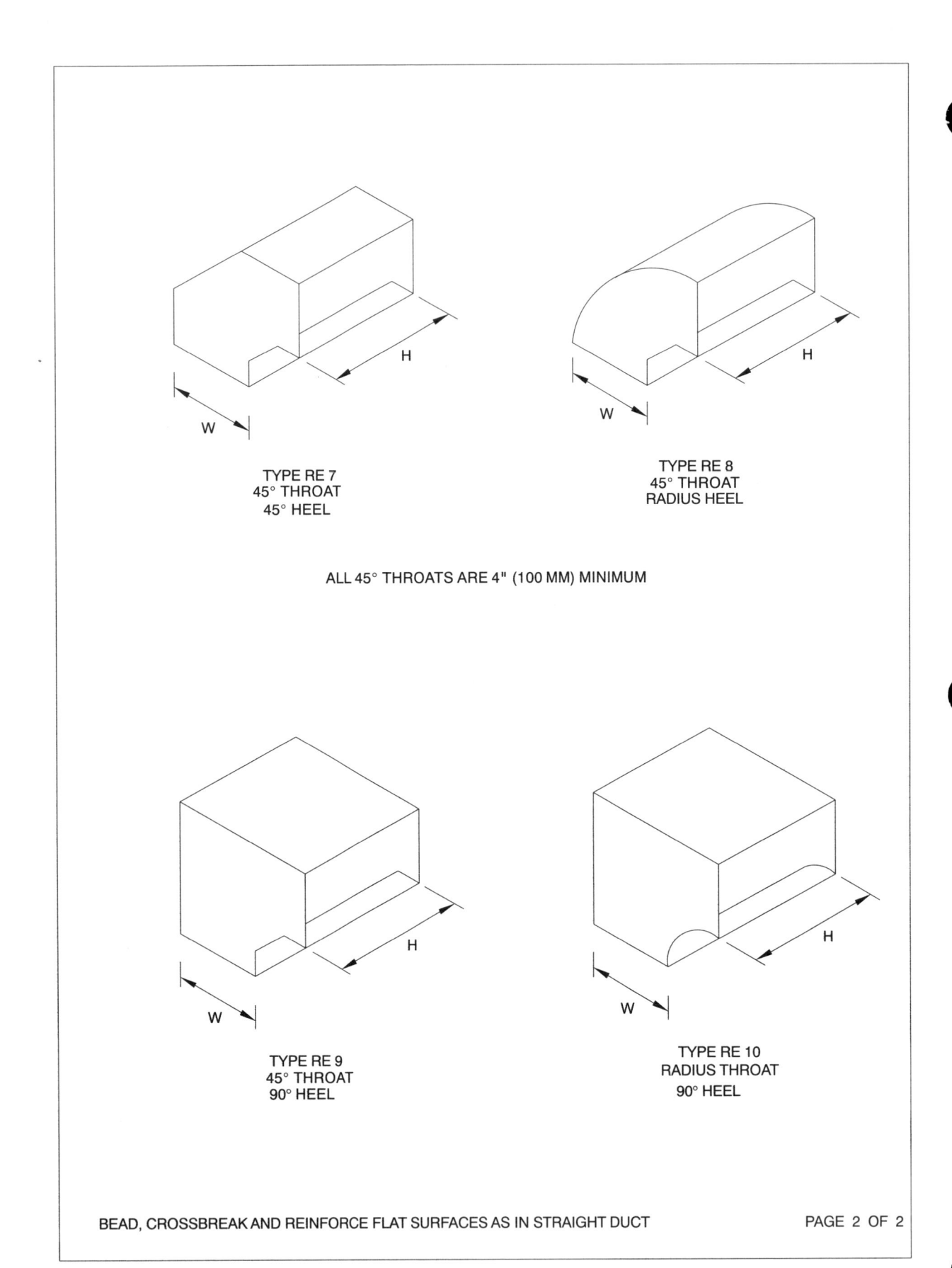

FIGURE 4–2 RECTANGULAR ELBOWS (CONTINUED)

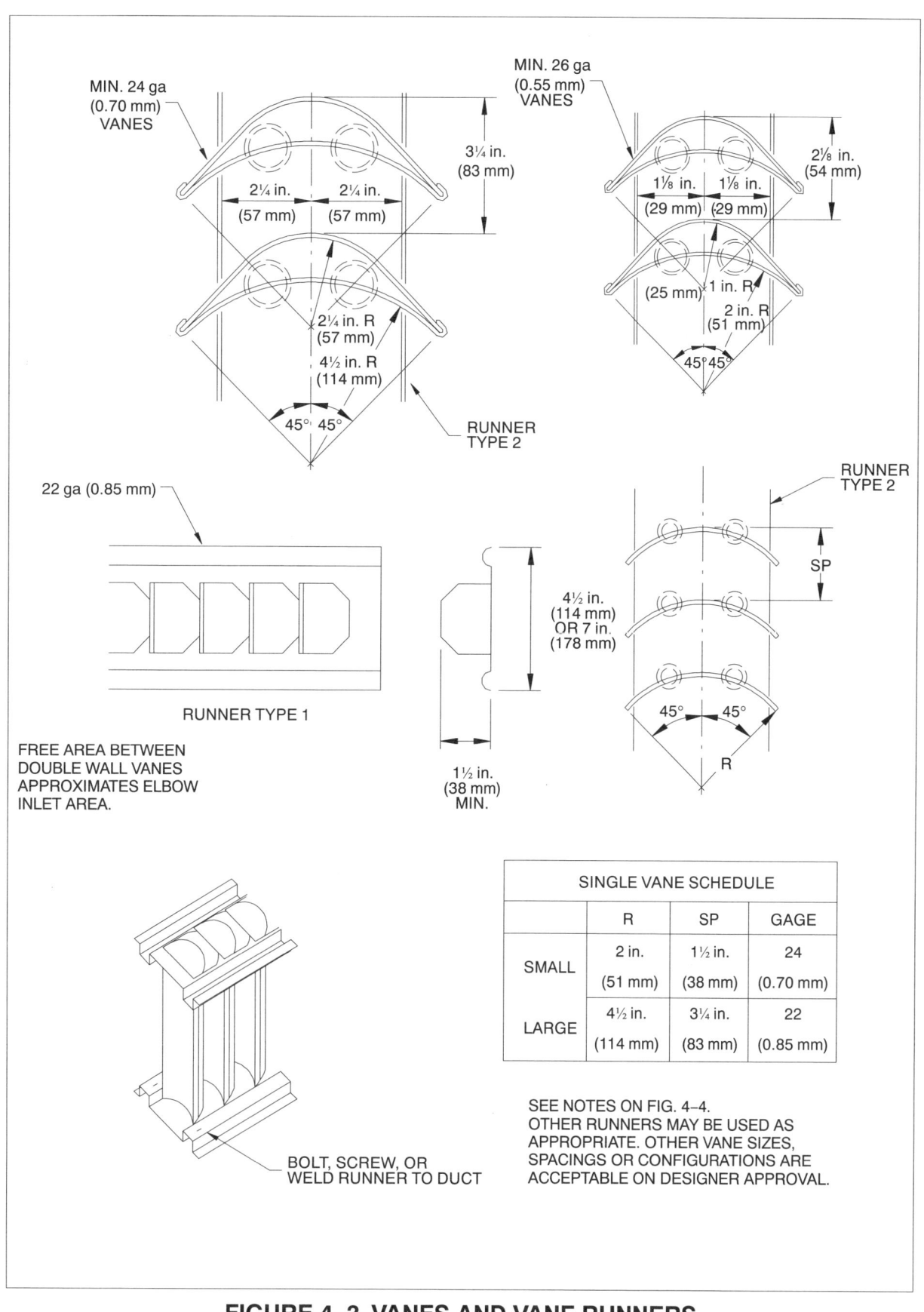

FIGURE 4–3 VANES AND VANE RUNNERS

SINGLE VANE SCHEDULE			
	R	SP	GAGE
SMALL	2 in. (51 mm)	1½ in. (38 mm)	24 (0.70 mm)
LARGE	4½ in. (114 mm)	3¼ in. (83 mm)	22 (0.85 mm)

SEE NOTES ON FIG. 4–4.
OTHER RUNNERS MAY BE USED AS APPROPRIATE. OTHER VANE SIZES, SPACINGS OR CONFIGURATIONS ARE ACCEPTABLE ON DESIGNER APPROVAL.

FREE AREA BETWEEN DOUBLE WALL VANES APPROXIMATES ELBOW INLET AREA.

* MAXIMUM UNSUPPORTED VANE LENGTH

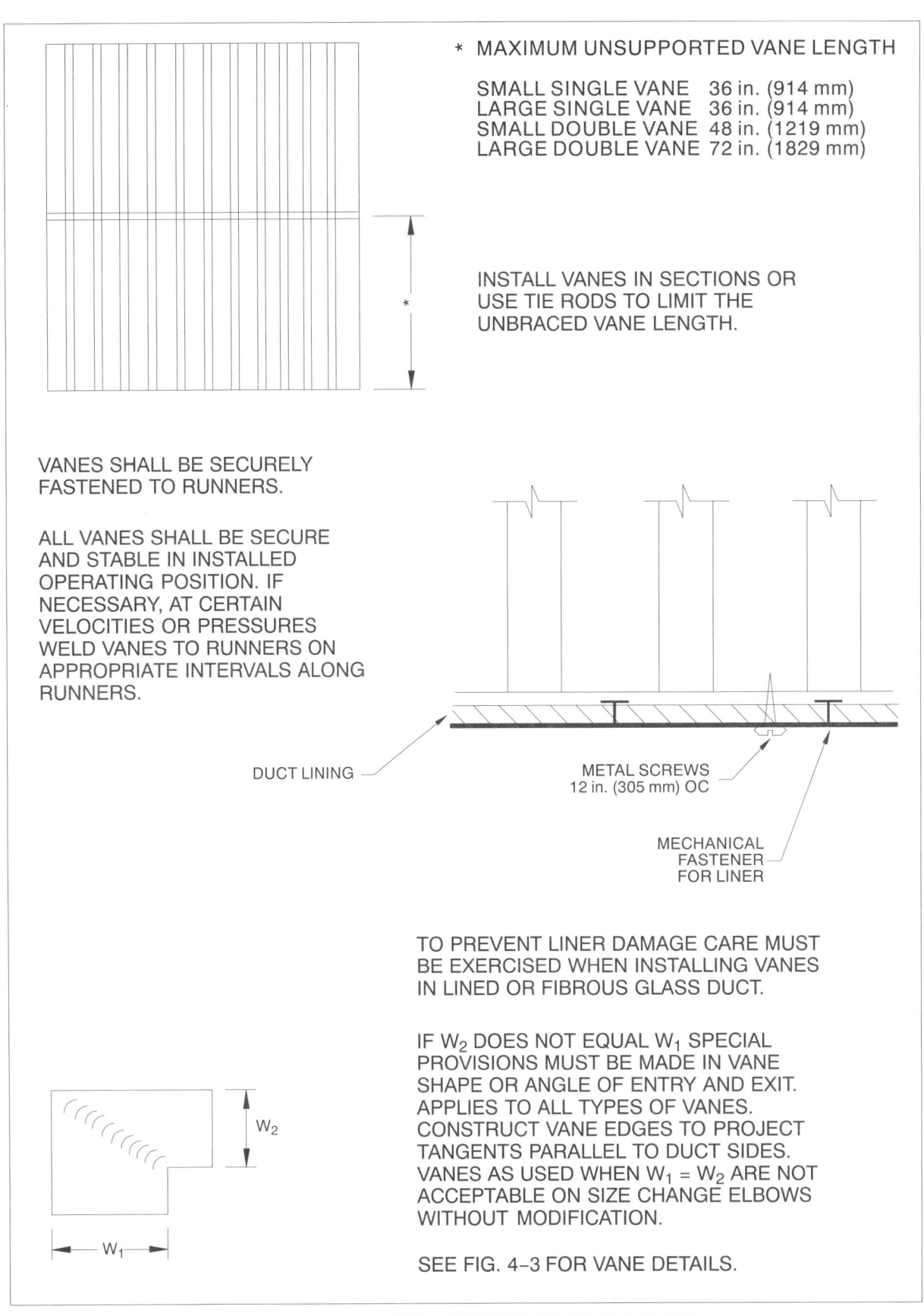

SMALL SINGLE VANE   36 in. (914 mm)
LARGE SINGLE VANE   36 in. (914 mm)
SMALL DOUBLE VANE   48 in. (1219 mm)
LARGE DOUBLE VANE   72 in. (1829 mm)

INSTALL VANES IN SECTIONS OR USE TIE RODS TO LIMIT THE UNBRACED VANE LENGTH.

VANES SHALL BE SECURELY FASTENED TO RUNNERS.

ALL VANES SHALL BE SECURE AND STABLE IN INSTALLED OPERATING POSITION. IF NECESSARY, AT CERTAIN VELOCITIES OR PRESSURES WELD VANES TO RUNNERS ON APPROPRIATE INTERVALS ALONG RUNNERS.

DUCT LINING

METAL SCREWS 12 in. (305 mm) OC

MECHANICAL FASTENER FOR LINER

TO PREVENT LINER DAMAGE CARE MUST BE EXERCISED WHEN INSTALLING VANES IN LINED OR FIBROUS GLASS DUCT.

IF W_2 DOES NOT EQUAL W_1 SPECIAL PROVISIONS MUST BE MADE IN VANE SHAPE OR ANGLE OF ENTRY AND EXIT. APPLIES TO ALL TYPES OF VANES. CONSTRUCT VANE EDGES TO PROJECT TANGENTS PARALLEL TO DUCT SIDES. VANES AS USED WHEN $W_1 = W_2$ ARE NOT ACCEPTABLE ON SIZE CHANGE ELBOWS WITHOUT MODIFICATION.

SEE FIG. 4-3 FOR VANE DETAILS.

FIGURE 4-4 VANE SUPPORT IN ELBOWS

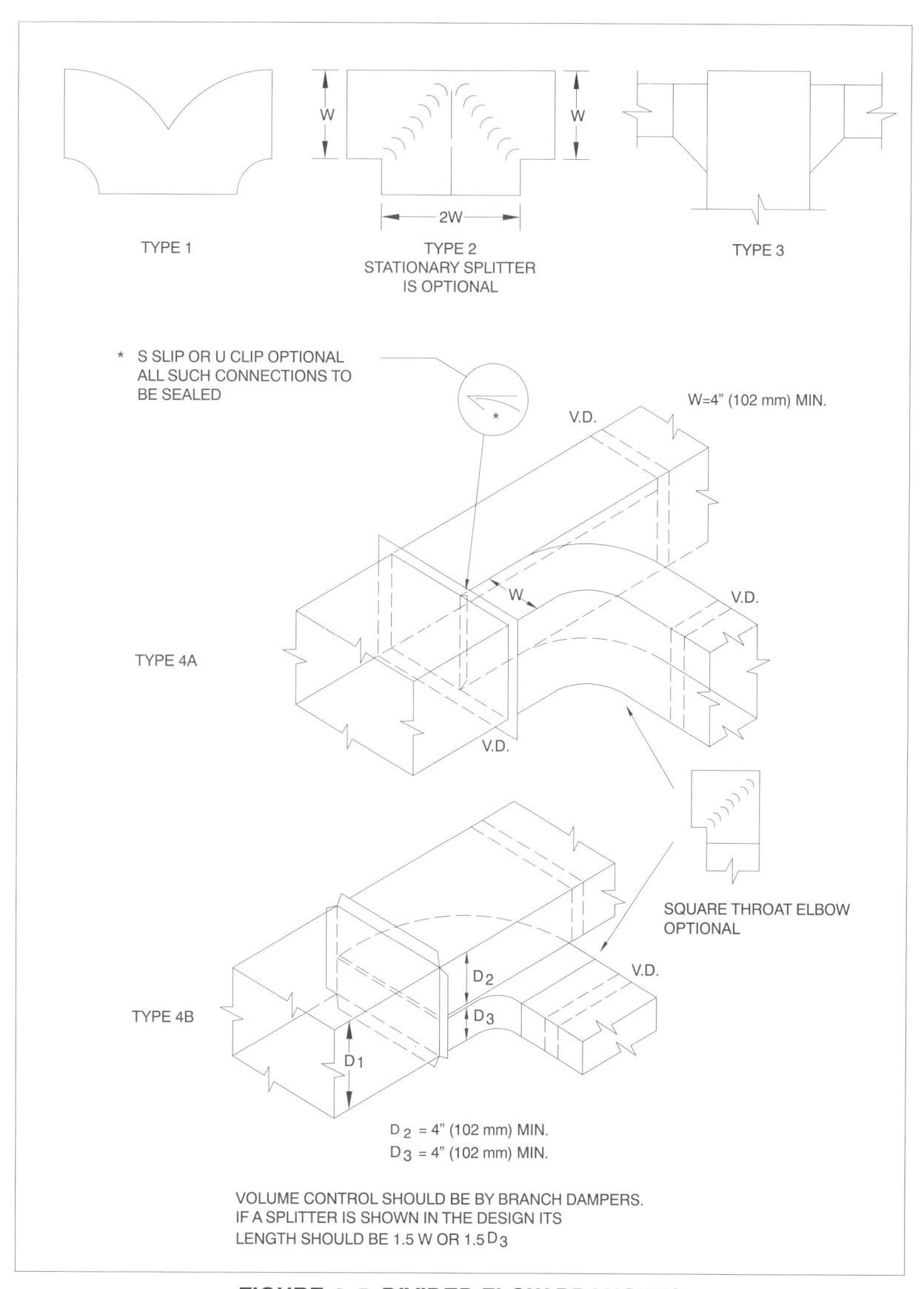

FIGURE 4–5 DIVIDED FLOW BRANCHES

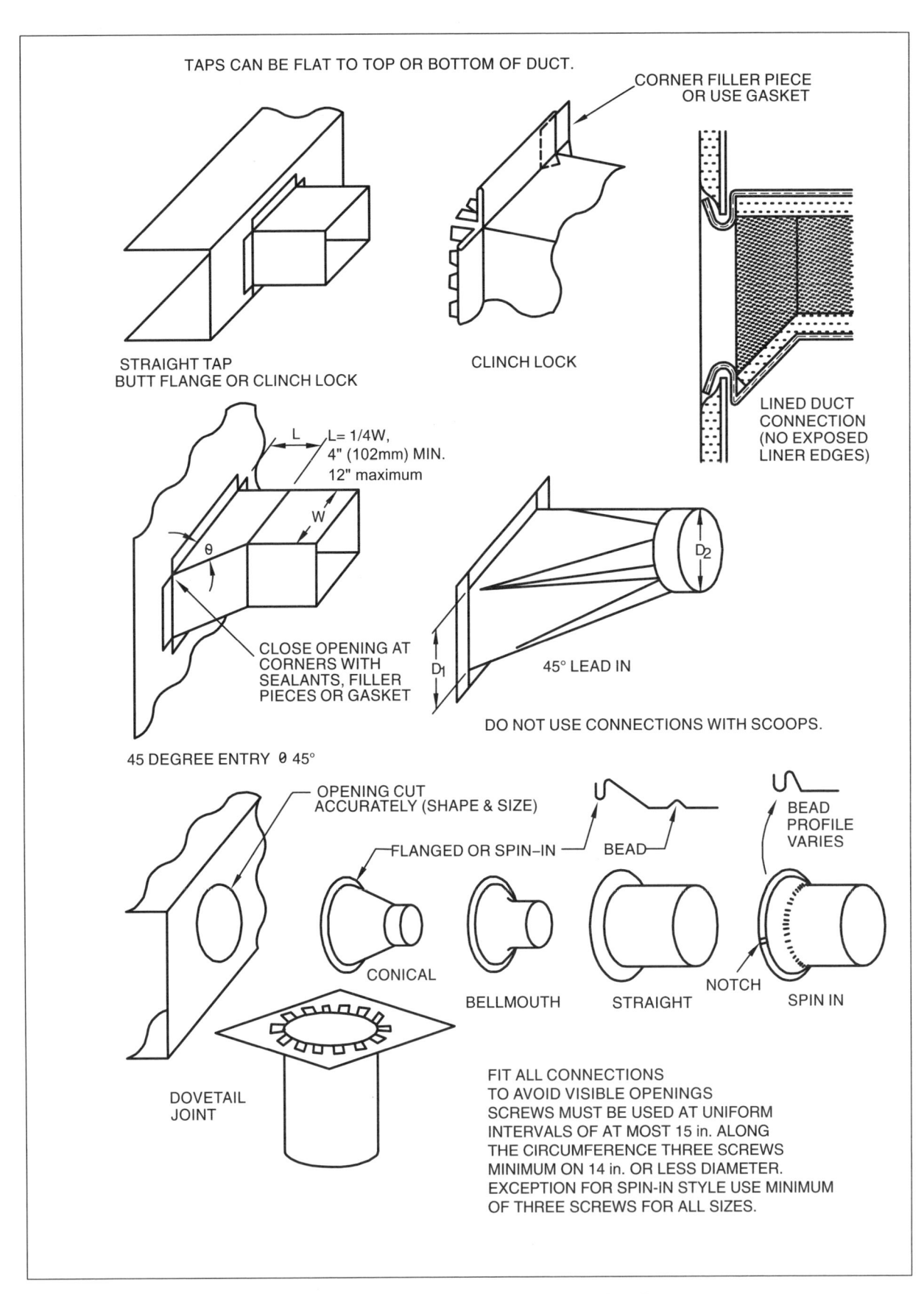

FIGURE 4–6 BRANCH CONNECTION

OFFSETS 2 AND 3 AND TRANSITIONS MAY HAVE EQUAL OR UNEQUAL INLET AND OUTLET AREAS. TRANSITIONS MAY CONVERT DUCT PROFILES TO ANY COMBINATION FOR RECTANGULAR, ROUND OR FLAT OVAL SHAPES.

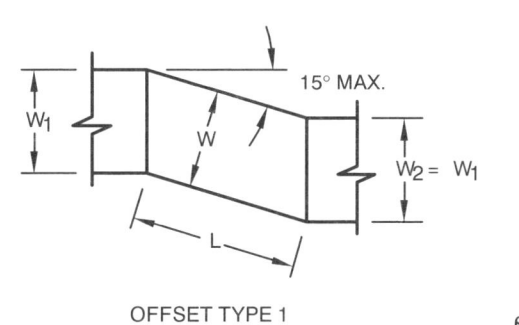

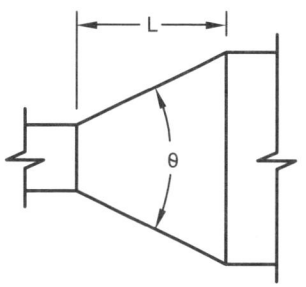

OFFSET TYPE 1
(ANGLED)

CONCENTRIC TRANSITION
θ MAX. 45° DIVERGING, 60° CONVERGING

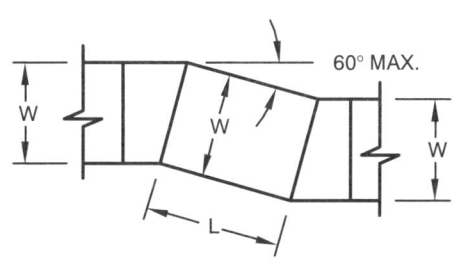

OFFSET TYPE 2
(MITERED)

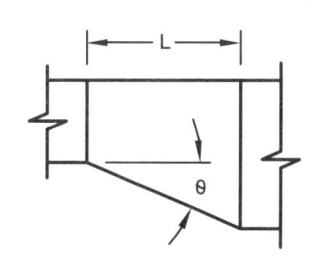

ECCENTRIC TRANSITION
θ MAX. 30°
(EXCEPT 45° IS PERMITTED AT ROUND TO FLAT OVAL)

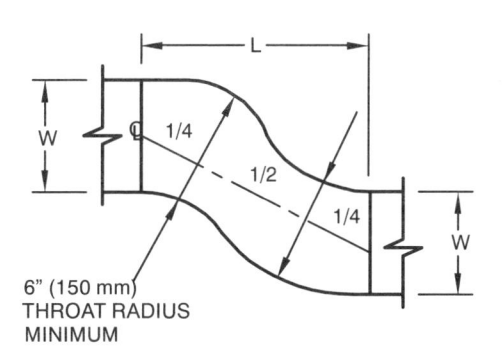

OFFSET TYPE 3
(RADIUSSED OR OGEE)

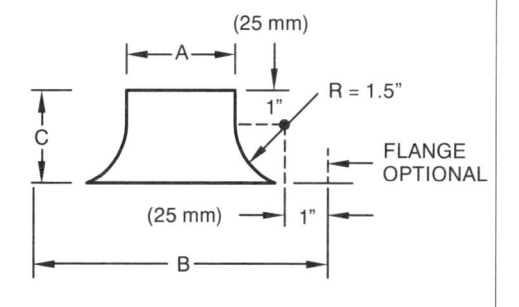

6" (150 mm) THROAT RADIUS MINIMUM

STANDARD BELLMOUTH
(ON SHORT PATTERN BELL
C = 3" (76 mm)
B = A + 4" (102 mm))

FIGURE 4-7 OFFSETS AND TRANSITIONS

HVAC Duct Construction Standards Metal and Flexible • Fourth Edition

FIG. A IS APPLICABLE FOR UP TO 20% AREA OBSTRUCTION WITH ROUND SHAPED MEMBER AND 10% WITH FLAT PROFILE. Y IS THE DISTANCE FROM DUCT CENTER.

FIG. A

R = H (MIN.)

FIG. B

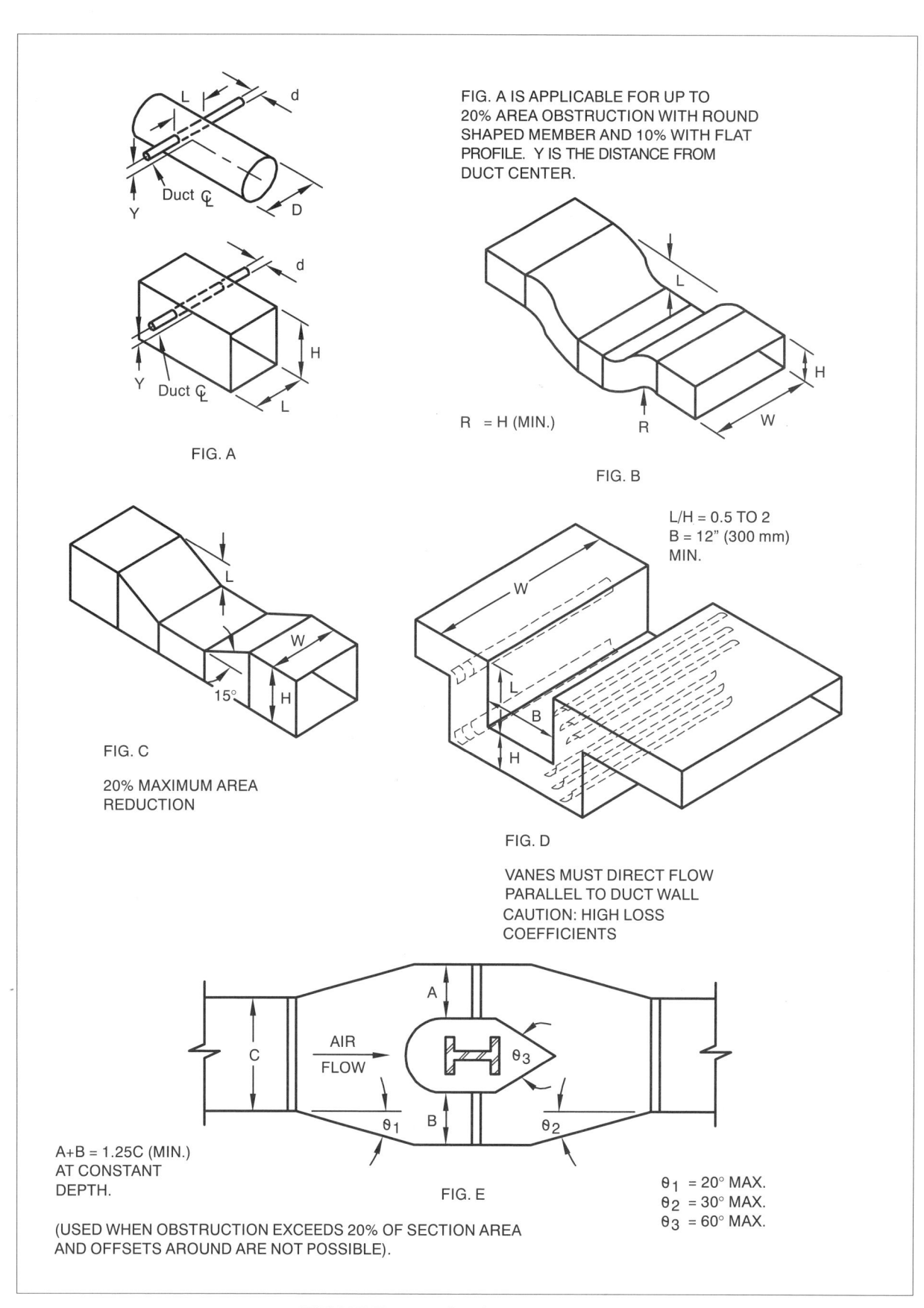

FIG. C

20% MAXIMUM AREA REDUCTION

L/H = 0.5 TO 2
B = 12" (300 mm) MIN.

FIG. D

VANES MUST DIRECT FLOW PARALLEL TO DUCT WALL
CAUTION: HIGH LOSS COEFFICIENTS

A+B = 1.25C (MIN.) AT CONSTANT DEPTH.

FIG. E

θ_1 = 20° MAX.
θ_2 = 30° MAX.
θ_3 = 60° MAX.

(USED WHEN OBSTRUCTION EXCEEDS 20% OF SECTION AREA AND OFFSETS AROUND ARE NOT POSSIBLE).

FIGURE 4-8 OBSTRUCTIONS

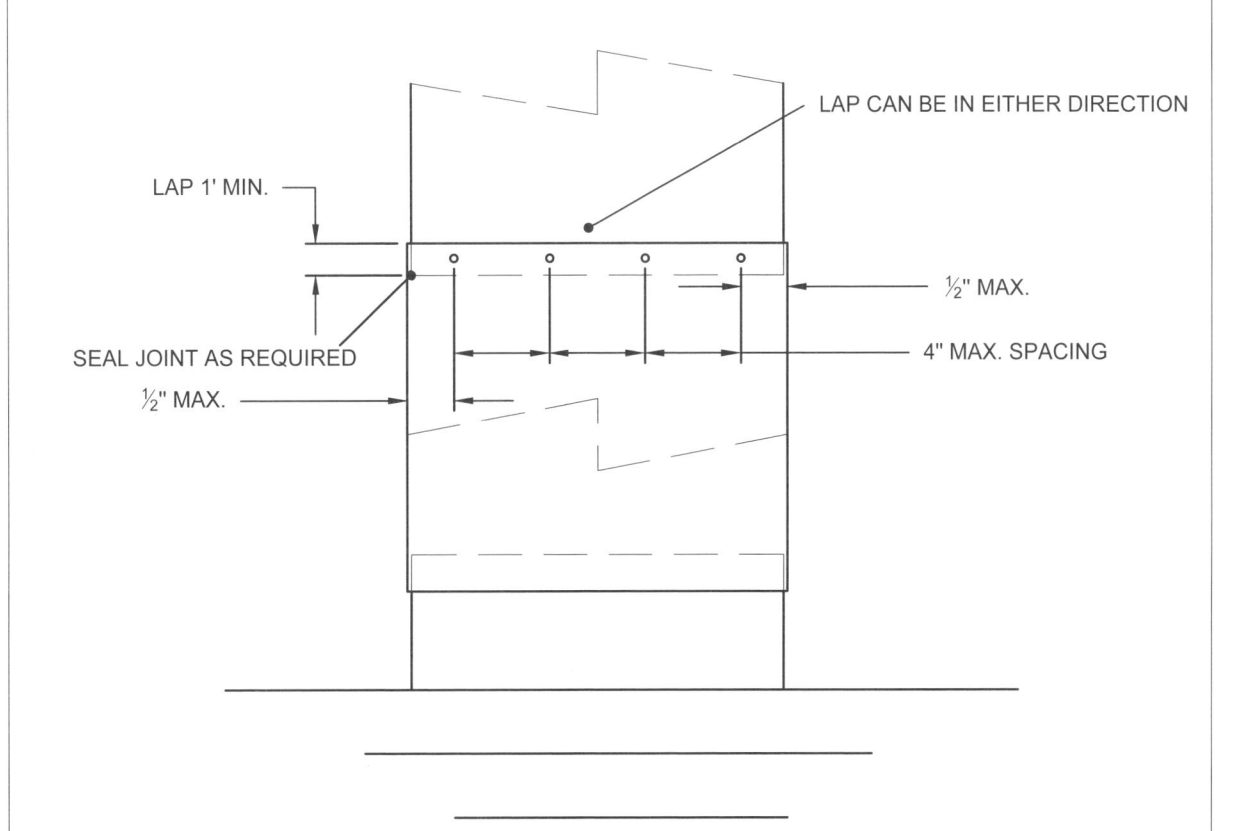

FIGURE 4–9 TELESCOPE CONNECTION

HVAC Duct Construction Standards Metal and Flexible • Fourth Edition

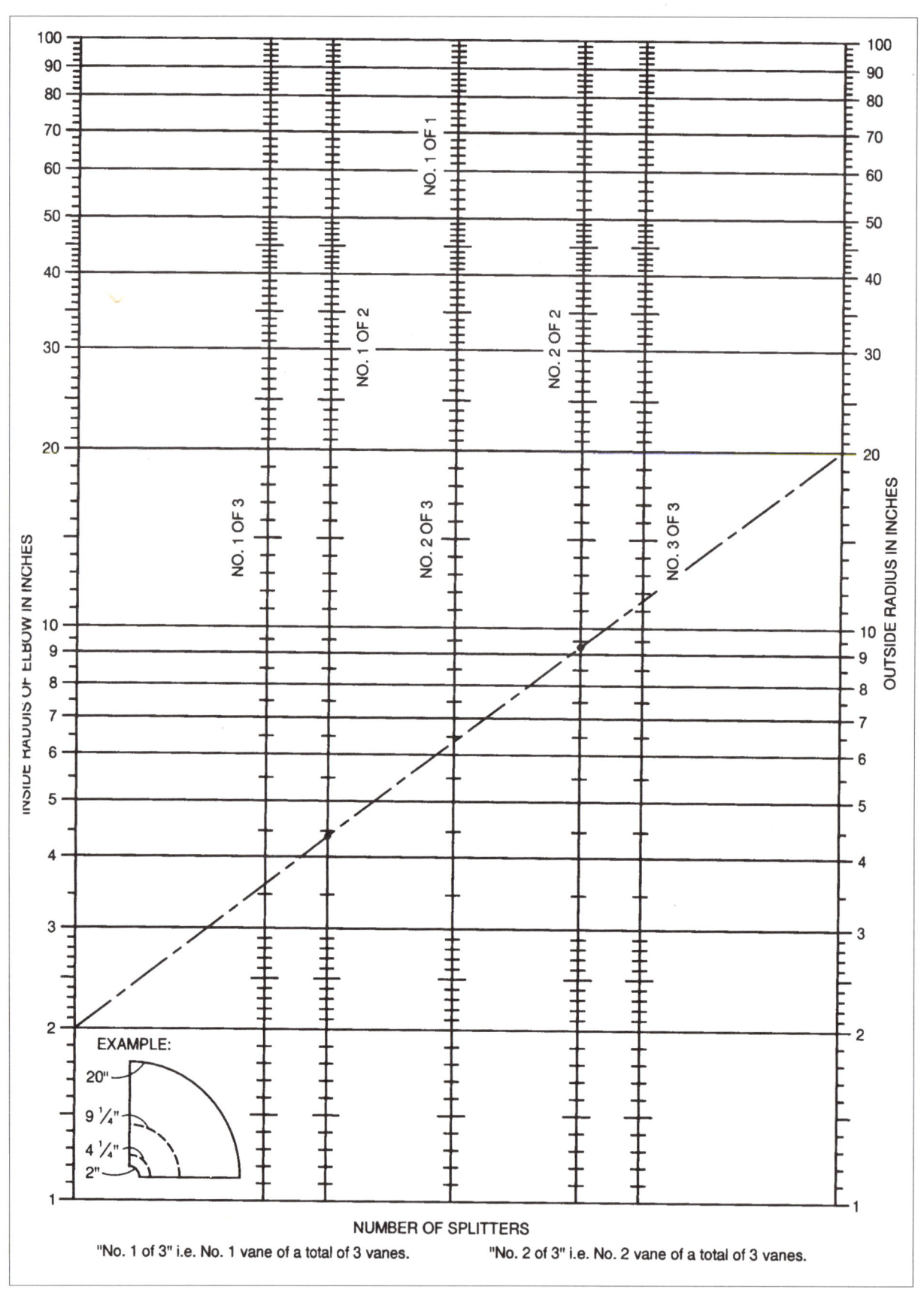

CHART 4-1 NUMBER OF SHORT RADIUS VANES

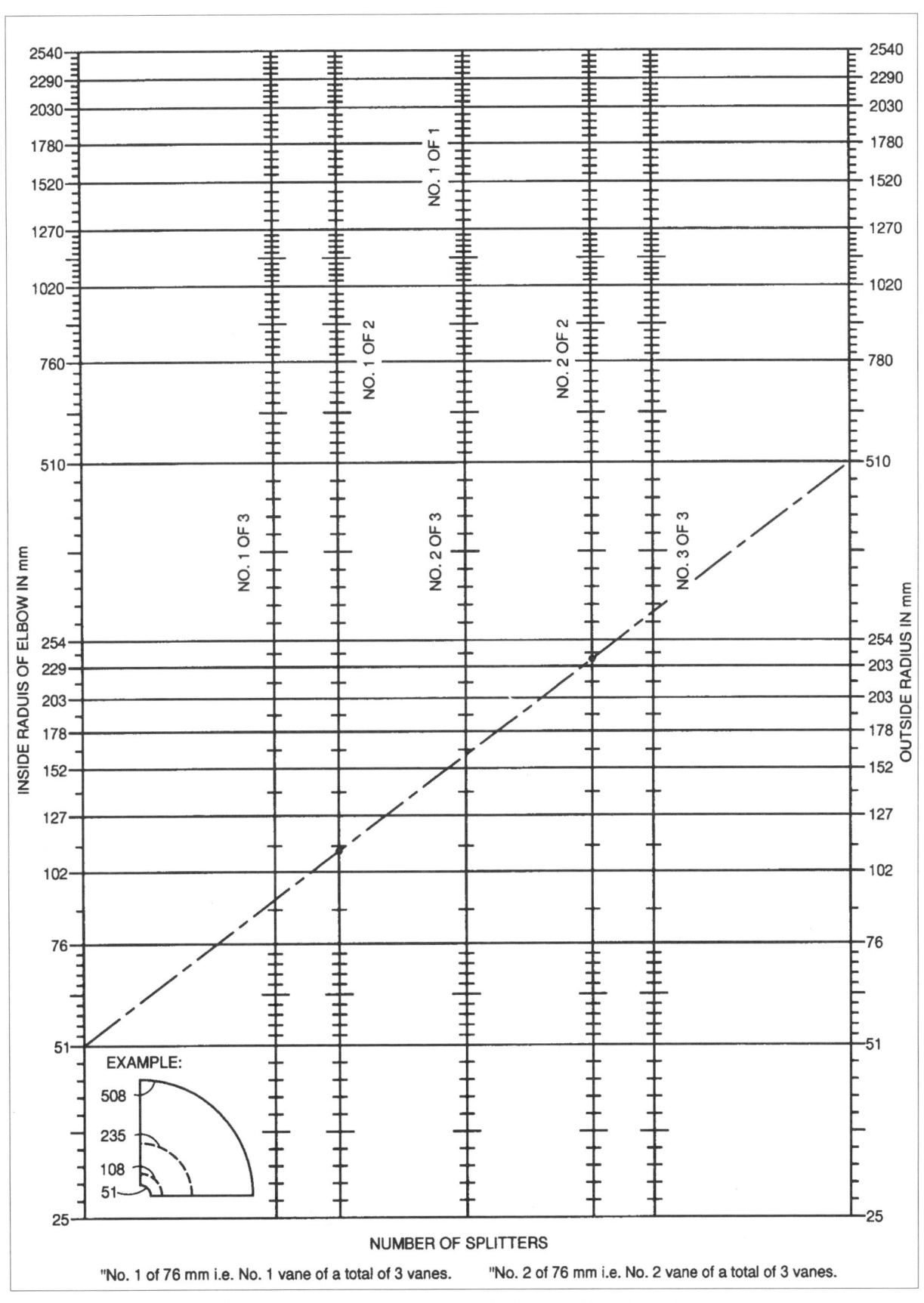

CHART 4–1M NUMBER OF SHORT RADIUS VANES

"No. 1 of 76 mm i.e. No. 1 vane of a total of 3 vanes. "No. 2 of 76 mm i.e. No. 2 vane of a total of 3 vanes.

HVAC Duct Construction Standards Metal and Flexible • Fourth Edition

LOSS COEFFICIENTS FOR USE OF 1,2, OR 3 VANES DEPENDS ON ASPECT RATION (H/W) AND A CURVE RATIO (CR) WHICH DEFINES VANNE LOCATION IN TERMS OF THROAT RADIUS. THIS DATA IS IN SMACNA'S HVAC SYSTEMS DUCT DESIGN 1990 SMACNA DUCT DESIGN.

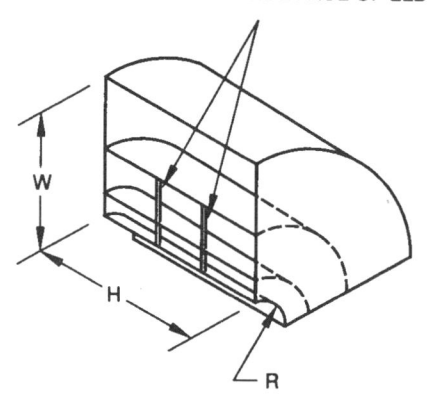

1/4" (6.4 mm) TIE RODS ON INLET & OUTLET WELDED TO VANES AND INSIDE FACE OF ELBOW

ELBOW DEPTH H REQUIRED (mm)	NUMBER OF TIE RODS
0 - 12" (305)	NONE
13 - 20" (330 - 508)	1
21 - 48" (533 - 1219)	2
49 - 64" (1243 - 1626)	3
65 - 80" (1651 - 2032)	4

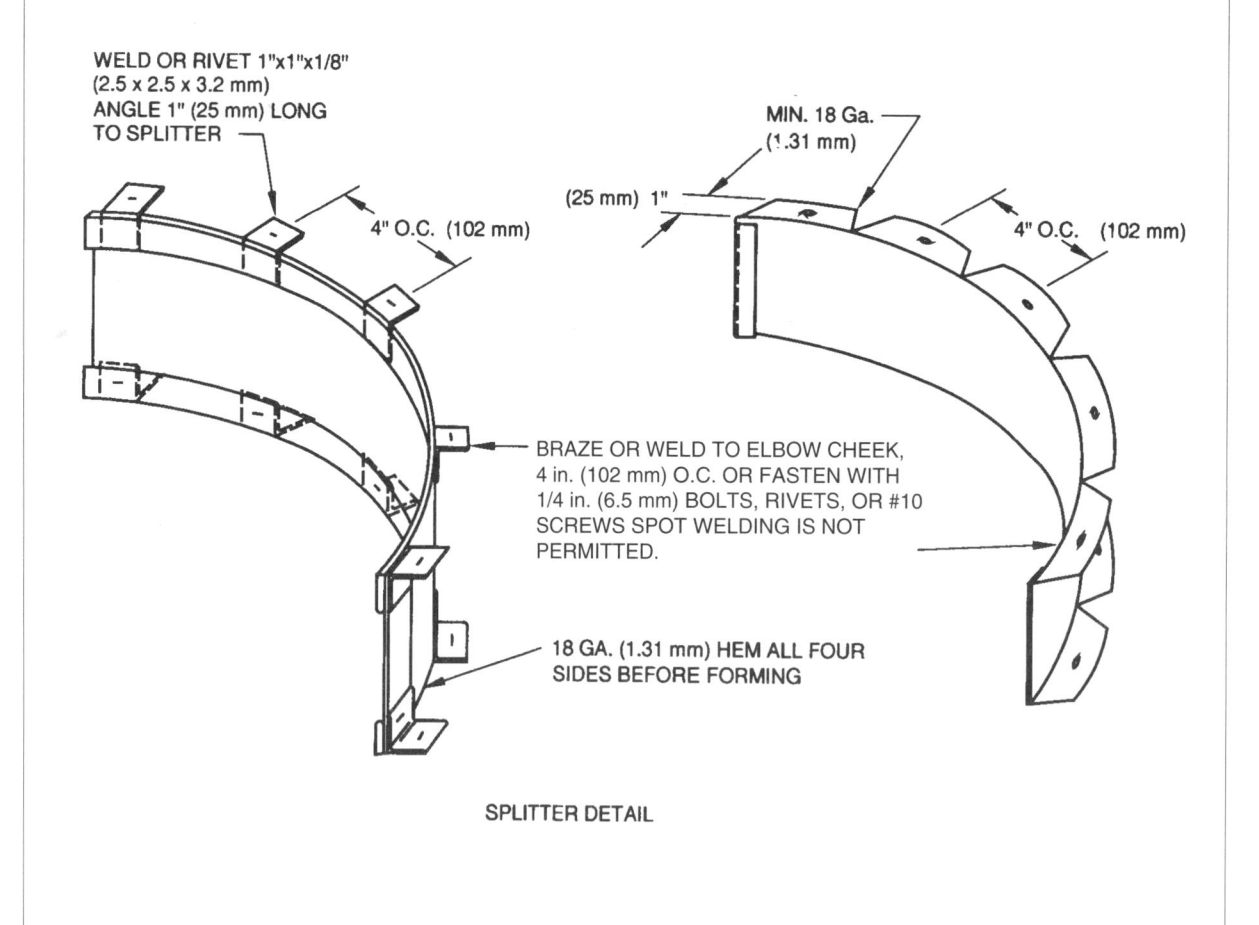

WELD OR RIVET 1"x1"x1/8" (2.5 x 2.5 x 3.2 mm) ANGLE 1" (25 mm) LONG TO SPLITTER

4" O.C. (102 mm)

MIN. 18 Ga. (1.31 mm)

(25 mm) 1"

4" O.C. (102 mm)

BRAZE OR WELD TO ELBOW CHEEK, 4 in. (102 mm) O.C. OR FASTEN WITH 1/4 in. (6.5 mm) BOLTS, RIVETS, OR #10 SCREWS SPOT WELDING IS NOT PERMITTED.

18 GA. (1.31 mm) HEM ALL FOUR SIDES BEFORE FORMING

SPLITTER DETAIL

FIGURE 4–10 CONSTRUCTION OF SHORT RADIUS VANES

CHAPTER 5

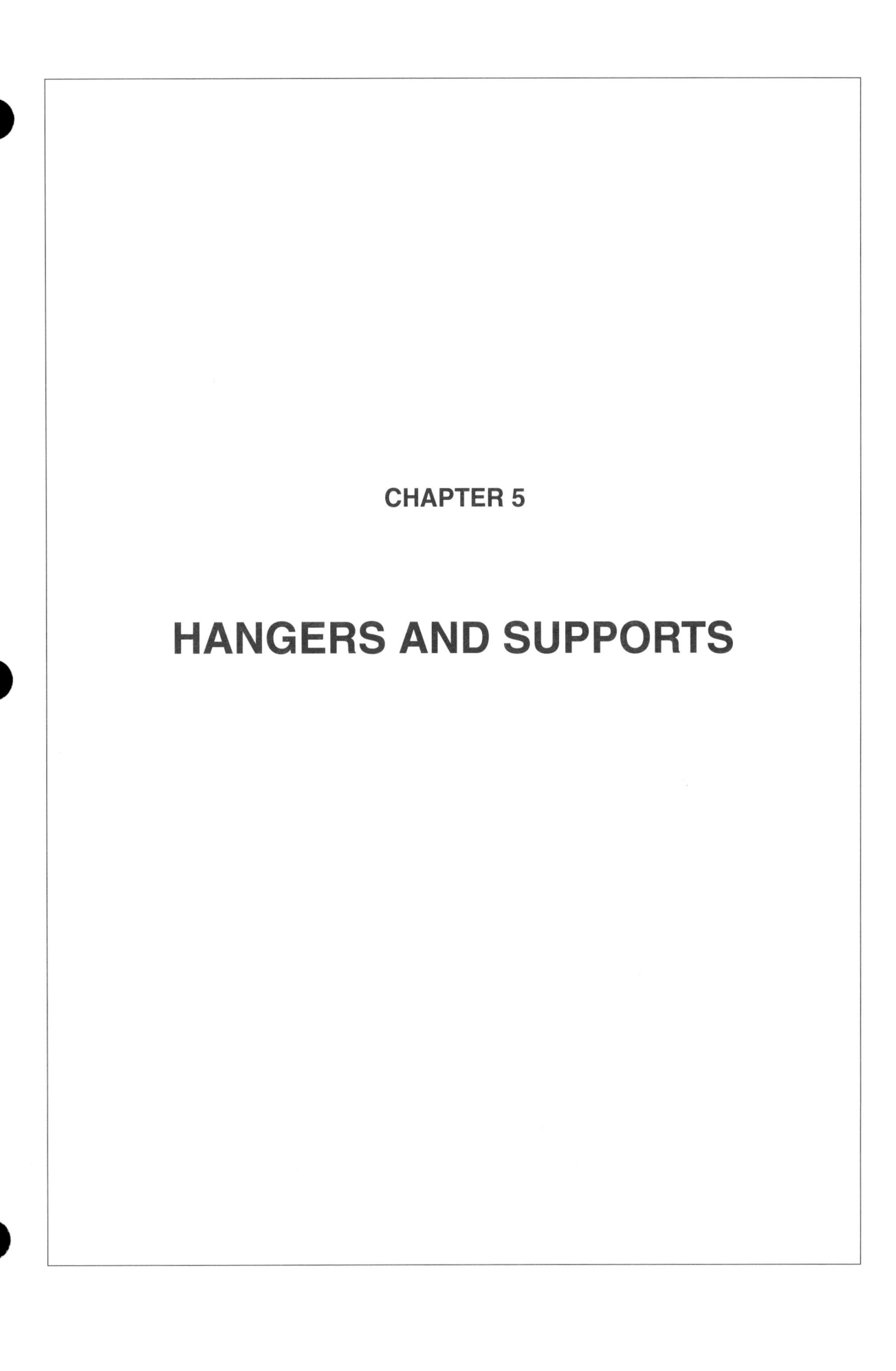

HANGERS AND SUPPORTS

CHAPTER 5   HANGERS AND SUPPORTS

5.1 HANGING AND SUPPORTING SYSTEMS

5.1.1 Requirements

S4.0   Rigid round, rectangular, and flat oval metal ducts shall be installed with support systems indicated in Tables 5-1 to 5-3 and Figures 5-1 to 5-10. They shall be installed as required to maintain alignment. Horizontal ducts shall have a support within 2 ft (0.61 m) of each elbow and within 4 ft (1.2 m) of each branch intersection. Upper attachments to structures shall have an allowable load not more than one-fourth of the failure (proof test) load but are not limited to the specific methods shown here.

5.2 COMMENTARY

The duct hanging system is composed of three elements, the upper attachment to the building, the hanger itself, and the lower attachment to the duct. The manufacturer's load ratings and application data should be followed for all devices and materials.

5.2.1 Concrete Inserts

Concrete inserts must be installed before the concrete is poured. They are used primarily where the duct layout is simple and there is enough lead time to determine accurate placement. The simplest insert is a piece of bent flat bar. Manufactured inserts are available individually or in long lengths; the latter are generally used where many hangers will be installed in a small area, or where individual inserts cannot be precisely spotted at the time of placing the concrete.

5.2.2 Concrete Fasteners

Concrete fasteners are installed after the concrete has been poured and the forms have been removed. Their application allows greater flexibility than concrete inserts because their exact location can be determined after all interferences between the various trades' work have been coordinated.

There are several variations of powder-actuated fasteners, which are installed with powder-actuated tools and booster cartridges. Gas driven fasteners are also used for upper attachments. Powder-actuated or gas driven fasteners should be used within the manufacturer's published application limits. Load capacities are based on tests in representative base materials in accordance with ASTM E1190.

5.2.3 Structural Steel Fasteners

Several types of beam clamps are available. Some should be used with a retaining clip. Powder-actuated and gas driven fasteners or threaded studs may also be used on steel. Welded studs may be installed using special welding equipment. Certain manufactured devices that are driven onto the flange will support either a rod or a band type hanger.

5.2.4 Cellular Metal Deck

Many office buildings are now built with a cellular steel deck that carries the electrical and communication systems and is covered with concrete fill. The wiring in the cells and the concrete above the deck preclude the use of fasteners, such as sheet metal screws, that must pierce the deck. Some manufacturers of this type of deck now offer an integral hanging system. In cases where there are no integral hangers at the required hanging points, install the rod or strap hangers before concrete placement, or install welded studs after concrete placement. In all cases, the upper attachments to the decking should be in place before the application of fireproofing materials.

5.2.5 Upper Attachment

Upper attachment methods should be selected with care. A safety factor of 4 or 5 (based on ultimate failure) is practical unless it can be shown that few unpredictable variables exist and that quality control is disciplined.

5.2.6 Hangers

Hangers are usually strips of galvanized steel or round steel rod. For hangers made of round steel rod, use uncoated hot-rolled steel except where the installation is in a corrosive atmosphere. Where corrosion is a problem, hanger rods should be electro-galvanized, all-thread rods or hot-dipped galvanized rods with their threads painted after installation.

5.2.7 Lower Attachment

The lower attachment is the connection between the hanger and the duct section. Fasteners that penetrate the duct may be sheet metal screws, blind rivets, or self-tapping metal screws.

5.2.8 Hanger Spacing

A straight duct section is actually a box section beam of considerable strength. As in many structures, the joint is the weakest point, so that is where the support is. Duct joints, however, are normally strong enough to permit maximum hanger spacing at 8 ft (2.44 m) or 10 ft (3.05 m) intervals, even with one or two intermediate joints. Very wide ducts require closer hanger spacing in order to limit individual hanger loads to safe values. They also require intermediate hangers to prevent the upper portion of the duct from sagging.

5.2.9 Trapeze Selection

Trapeze members must be selected with careful attention to the position of the loads on the horizontal bar. Load analysis is discussed in the notes of Figure 5–6.

5.2.10 Riser Supports

Rectangular risers should be supported by angles or channels secured to the sides of the duct with welds, bolts, sheet metal screws, or blind rivets. Here again, for ducts over 30 in. (762 mm) wide, caution must be used in fastening the support to the sheet because the expansion of the sheet due to internal pressures will tend to tear the fasteners out. Riser support intervals must not exceed 24 feet unless specifically designed to do so. Another method is to support the riser by its reinforcing. The load can be transferred to the riser support by angles or by rods.

5.2.11 Hanging System Selection

The selection of a hanging system should not be taken lightly not only because it involves a significant portion of the erection labor, but also because an inadequate hanging system can be disastrous. In any multiple hanger system, the failure of one hanger transfers its load to adjacent hangers. If one of these fails, an even greater load is transferred to the next. The result is a cascading failure in which an entire run of duct might fall.

There are many hanger alternatives, especially in the upper attachments. Besides structural adequacy, the contractor's choice of hanging system must also take into account the particulars of the building structure, the skills of the workmen, the availability of tooling, and the recommendations of the fastener manufacturer. Because of these variables, it is suggested that the hanging system be the contractor's choice, subject to the approval of the mechanical engineer.

Figures in this manual show typical hanger constructions. When special conditions require high safety factors or the ability to withstand vibrations, individual concrete or steel attachments can be specified to be capable of supporting test loads equal to the minimum rating listed when they are tested in accordance with methods described by Underwriters' Laboratories, Inc., for Pipe Hanger Equipment, Bulletin UL 203, latest edition, *see* Figures 3–10 and 3–11 for support of flexible duct.

The supports discussed here are not seismically qualified. Refer to SMACNA's Seismic Restraint Manual for additional reinforcement required by earthquake hazards.

ALPHABET LETTER ONLY INDICATES AN ALTERNATIVE LOCATION OR SITUATION
THAT MAY BE PERMITTED OR RESTRICTED BY DESIGN DOCUMENTS. ILLUSTRATIONS
OF CONCRETE AND STEEL DO NOT PRECLUDE ATTACHMENTS TO WOOD.

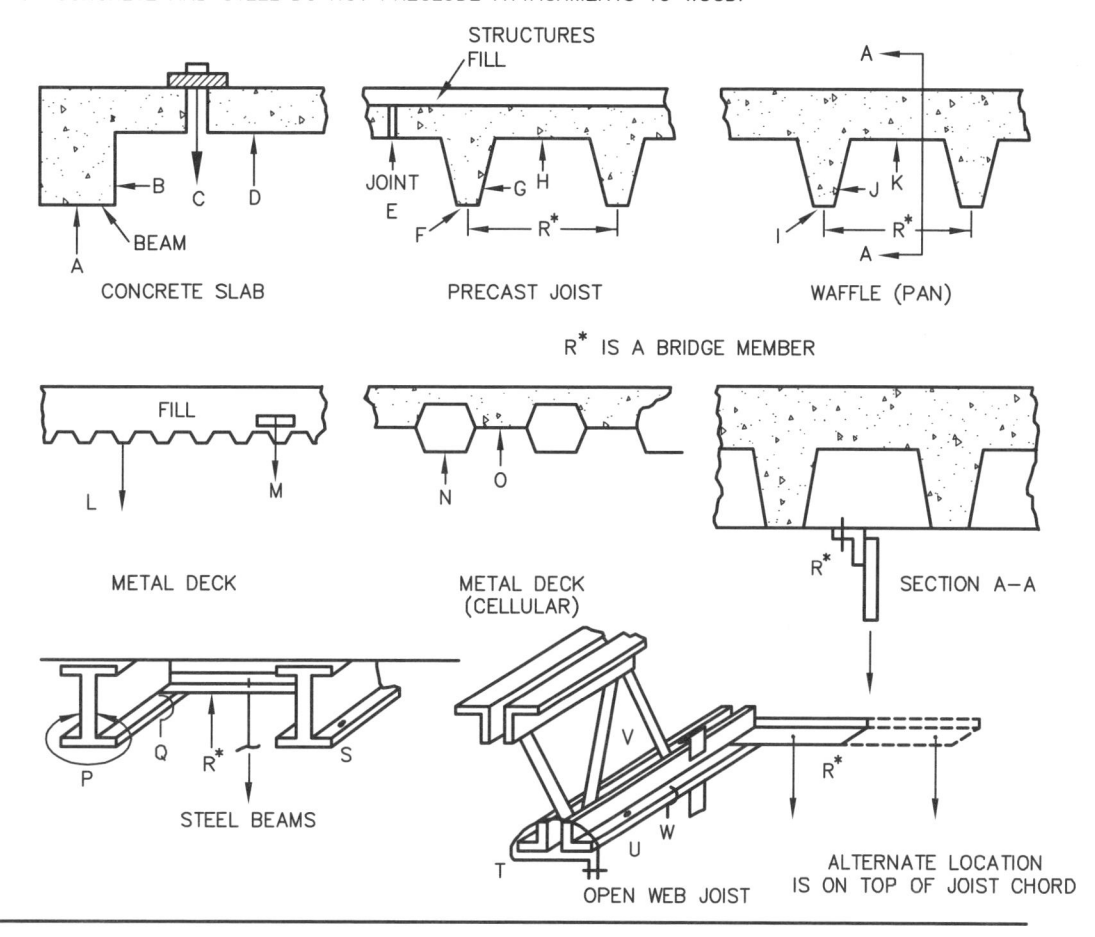

CONCRETE SLAB

PRECAST JOIST

WAFFLE (PAN)

R* IS A BRIDGE MEMBER

METAL DECK

METAL DECK (CELLULAR)

SECTION A-A

STEEL BEAMS

OPEN WEB JOIST

ALTERNATE LOCATION IS ON TOP OF JOIST CHORD

CONVENTIONAL HANGER METHODS AND DEVICES

CONCRETE SCREW ANCHORS
CONCRETE INSERTS, SINGLE
CONCRETE INSERTS, SLOTTED
POWDER ACTUATED FASTENERS
GAS DRIVEN FASTENERS
"C" CLAMPS
WELDED STUDS
FRICTION CLAMPS
STRAP
ROD, THREADED, UNTHREADED
BRIDGE
BEAM CLAMP, HALF FLANGE
BEAM CLAMP, FULL FLANGE
EYE BOLT (OR ROD)
TOGGLE BOLTS

DRILLED HOLE AND BOLT
STANCHION
SELF TAPPING SCREWS PLUS STRAPS
DROP IN EXPANSION ANCHORS
KNEE BRACKET FROM WALL
LAG SCREW EXPANSION ANCHOR
NAILED PIN FASTENERS
RIVETS
SWAY BRACING
"FISH" PLATE OR WASHER AND ROD
HOOK OR LOOP
VIBRATION ISOLATOR
WIRE

NOTE: CABLE HANGING SYSTEMS WITH ADJUSTABLE MECHANICAL DEVICE
SELECT HANGERS FOR TYPE OF STRUCTURE AND SUSPENSION.
DO NOT EXCEED ALLOWABLE OR SPECIFIED LOAD LIMITS.

ALLOWABLE LOAD ON UPPER ATTACHMENT IS 1/4 OF FAILURE LOAD

FIGURE 5-1 HANGER ATTACHMENTS TO STRUCTURES

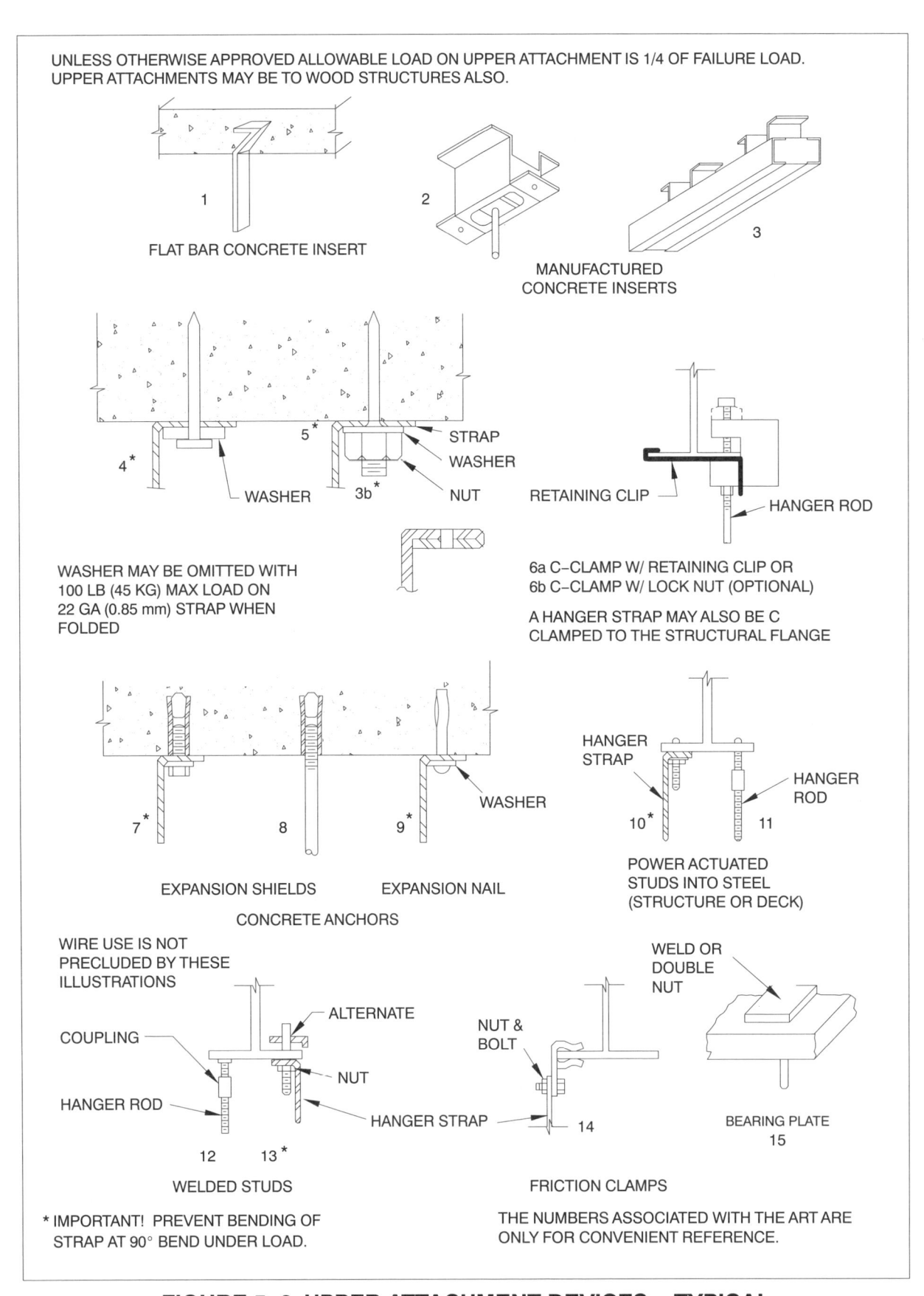

FIGURE 5-2 UPPER ATTACHMENT DEVICES – TYPICAL

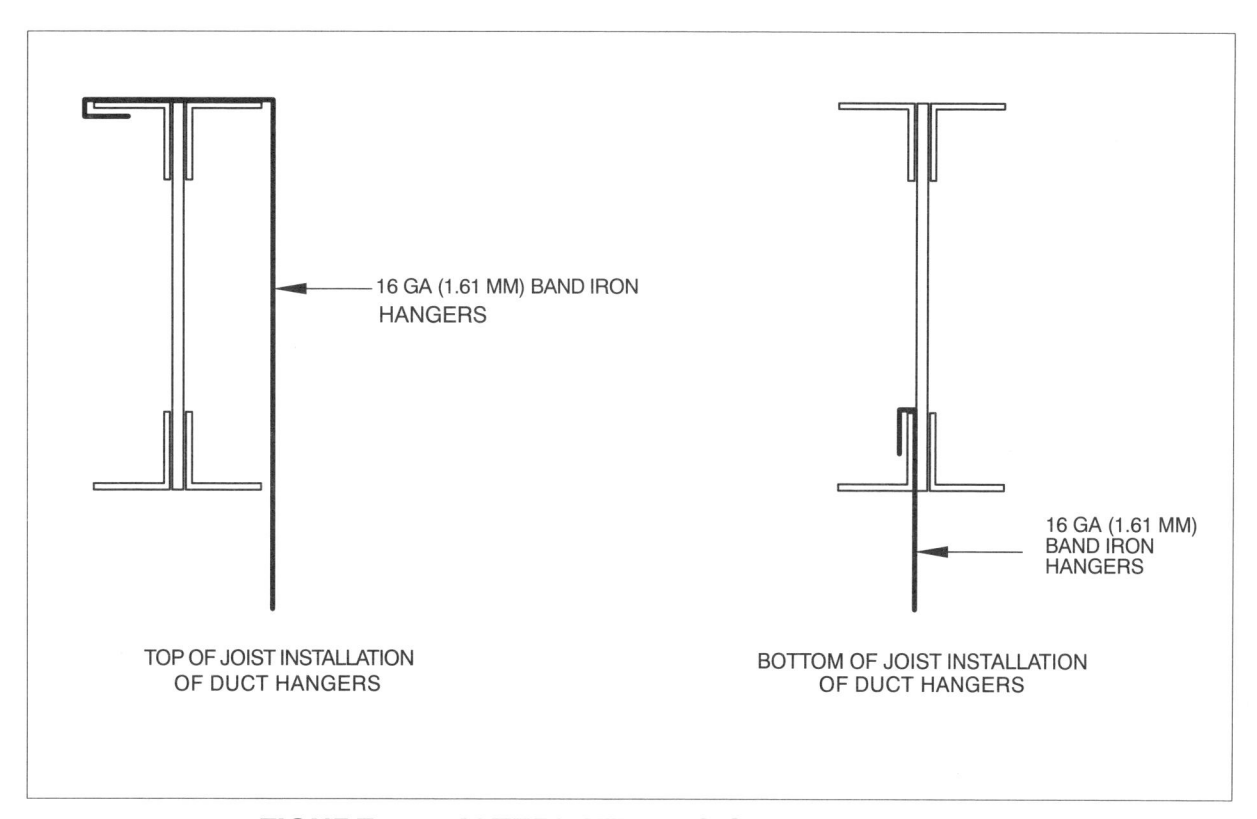

FIGURE 5-3 ALTERNATIVE JOIST ATTACHMENTS

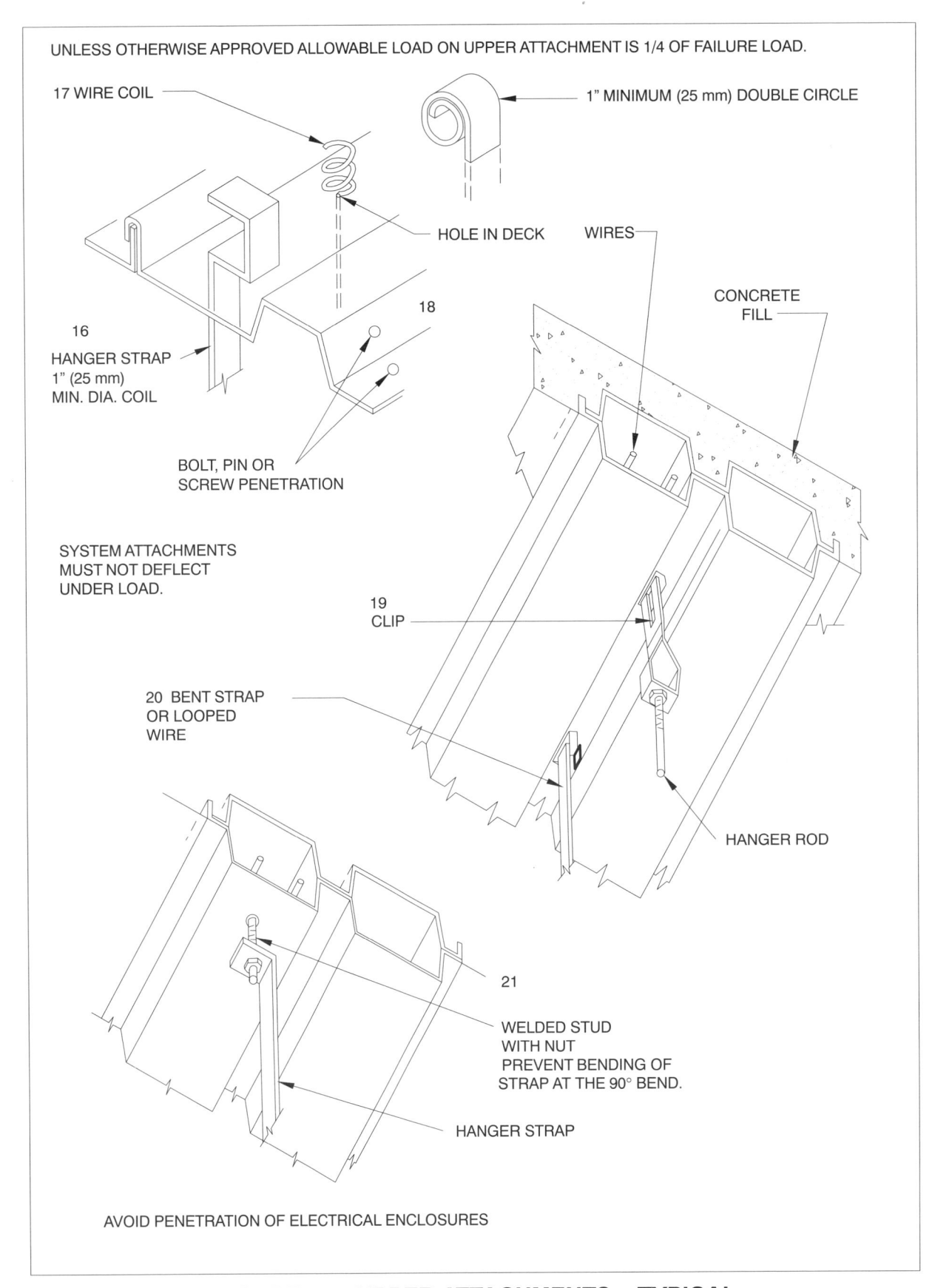

FIGURE 5–4 UPPER ATTACHMENTS – TYPICAL

Maximum Half of Duct Perimeter	Pair at 10 ft Spacing Strap	Pair at 10 ft Spacing Wire/Rod	Pair at 8 ft Spacing Strap	Pair at 8 ft Spacing Wire/Rod	Pair at 5 ft Spacing Strap	Pair at 5 ft Spacing Wire/Rod	Pair at 4 ft Spacing Strap	Pair at 4 ft Spacing Wire/Rod
P/2 = 30"	1" × 22 ga	10 ga (.135")	1" × 22 ga	10 ga (.135")	1" × 22 ga	12 ga (.106")	1" × 22 ga	12 ga (.106")
P/2 = 72"	1" × 18 ga	⅜"	1" × 20 ga	¼"	1" × 22 ga	¼"	1" × 22 ga	¼"
P/2 = 96"	1" × 16 ga	⅜"	1" × 18 ga	⅜"	1" × 20 ga	⅜"	1" × 22 ga	¼"
P/2 = 120"	1½" × 16 ga	½"	1" × 16 ga	⅜"	1" × 18 ga	⅜"	1" × 20 ga	¼"
P/2 = 168"	1½" × 16 ga	½"	1½" × 16 ga	½"	1" × 16 ga	⅜"	1" × 18 ga	⅜"
P/2 = 192"	Not Given	½"	1½" × 16 ga	½"	1" × 16 ga	⅜"	1" × 16 ga	⅜"
P/2 = 193" up	Special Analysis Required							

When Straps are Lap Joined Use These Minimum Fasteners:	Single Hanger Maximum Allowable Load	
	Strap	Wire or Rod (Dia.)
1" × 18, 20, 22 ga -two #10 or one ¼" bolt 1" × 16 ga -two ¼" dia. 1½" × 16 ga -two ⅜" dia Place fasteners in series, not side by side.	1" × 22 ga - 260 lbs. 1" × 20 ga - 320 lbs. 1" × 18 ga - 420 lbs. 1" × 16 ga - 700 lbs. 1½" × 16 ga - 1100 lbs.	0.106" - 80 lbs. 0.135" - 120 lbs. 0.162" - 160 lbs. ¼" - 270 lbs. ⅜" - 680 lbs. ½" - 1250 lbs. ⅝" - 2000 lbs. ¾" - 3000 lbs.

Table 5–1 Rectangular Duct Hangers Minimum Size

NOTES:

a. Dimensions other than gage are in inches.

b. Tables allow for duct weight, 1 lb./sf insulation weight and normal reinforcement and trapeze weight, but no external loads!

c. For custom design of hangers, designers may consult SMACNA's *Rectangular Industrial Duct Construction Standards,* the AISI *Cold Formed Steel Design Manual* and the AISC Steel *Construction Manual.*

d. Straps are galvanized steel; other materials are uncoated steel.

e. Allowable loads for P/2 assume that ducts are 16 ga maximum, except that when maximum duct dimension (w) is over 60 in. then P/2 maximum is 1.25 w.

f. For upper attachments *see* Figs. 5-2, 5-3 and 5-4.

g. For lower attachments *see* Fig. 5-5.

h. For trapeze sizes *see* Table 5-3 and Fig. 5-6.

i. 12, 10, or 8 ga wire is steel of black annealed, bright basic, or galvanized type.

j. Cable hanging systems with adjustable mechanical device.

k. Edge distance for holes in strap minimum of one hole diameter.

Maximum Half of Duct Perimeter	Pair at 3 m Spacing Strap	Pair at 3 m Spacing Wire/Rod	Pair at 2.2 m Spacing Strap	Pair at 2.2 m Spacing Wire/Rod	Pair at 1.5 m Spacing Strap	Pair at 1.5 m Spacing Wire/Rod	Pair at 1.2 m Spacing Strap	Pair at 1.2 m Spacing Wire/Rod
P/2 = 760	25.4 × 0.85	3.4	25.4 × 0.85	3.4	25.4 × 0.85	2.7	25.4 × 0.85	2.7
P/2 = 1830	25.4 × 1.31	9.5	25.4 × 1.00	6.4	25.4 × 0.85	6.4	25.4 × 0.85	6.4
P/2 = 2440	25.4 × 1.61	9.5	25.4 × 1.31	9.5	25.4 × 1.00	9.5	25.4 × 0.85	6.4
P/2 = 3050	38.1 × 1.61	12.7	25.4 × 1.61	9.5	25.4 × 1.31	9.5	25.4 × 1.00	6.4
P/2 = 4270	38.1 × 1.61	12.7	38.1 × 1.61	12.7	25.4 × 1.61	9.5	25.4 × 1.31	9.5
P/2 = 4880	Not Given	12.7	38.1 × 1.61	12.7	25.4 × 1.61	9.5	25.4 × 1.61	9.5
P/2 = More	Special Analysis Required							

When Straps are Lap Joined Use These Minimum Fasteners:	Single Hanger Maximum Allowable Load	
	Strap	Wire or Rod (Dia.)
25.4 × 1.31, 1.00, 0.85 mm – one 6.4 bolt 25.4 × 1.61 mm – two 6.4 bolts 38.1 × 1.61 mm – two 9.5 bolts Two bolts must be in series, not side by side	25.4 × 0.85 – 118 Kg. 25.4 × 1.00 – 145 Kg. 25.4 × 1.31 – 191 Kg. 25.4 × 1.61 – 318 Kg. 38.1 × 1.61 – 500 Kg.	2.7 – 36 Kg. 3.4 – 54 Kg. 4.1 – 73 Kg. 6.4 – 122 Kg. 9.5 – 308 Kg. 12.7 – 567 Kg. 15.9 – 9.7 Kg. 19.1 – 1360 Kg.

Table 5–1M Rectangular Duct Hangers Minimum Size

NOTES:

a. Dimensions other than hanger spacing are in millimeters.

b. Tables allow for duct weight, 4.89 kg./m² insulation weight and normal reinforcement and trapeze weight, but no external loads!

c. For custom design of hangers, designers may consult SMACNA's *Rectangular Industrial Duct Standards*, the AISI *Cold Formed Steel Design Manual* and the AISC Steel *Construction Manual*.

d. Straps are galvanized steel; other materials are uncoated steel.

e. Allowable loads for P/2 assume that ducts are 1.61 mm maximum, except that when maximum duct dimension (w) is over 1520 mm then p/2 maximum is 1.25 w.

f. For upper attachments *see* Figs. 5-2, 5-3 and 5-4.

g. For lower attachments *see* Fig. 5-5.

h. For trapeze sizes *see* Table 5-3 and Fig. 5-6.

i. 2.7, 3.4, and 4.1 mm wire is steel of black annealed, bright basic, or galvanized type.

j. Cable hanging systems with adjustable mechanical device.

k. Edge distance for holes in strap minimum of one hole diameter.

Dia.	Maximum Spacing	Wire Dia.	Rod	Strap
10 in. dn 250 mm dn	12 ft 3.7 m	One 12 ga One 2.75 mm	¼ in. 6.4 mm	1 in. × 22 ga 25.4 × 0.85 mm
11-18 in. 460 mm	12 ft 3.7 m	Two 12 ga or One 8 ga One 4.27 mm	¼ in. 6.4 mm	1 in. × 22 ga 25.4 × 0.85 mm
19-24 in. 610 mm	12 ft 3.7 m	Two 10 ga Two 3.51 mm	¼ in. 6.4 mm	1 in. × 22 ga 25.4 × 0.85 mm
25-36 in. 900 mm	12 ft 3.7 m	Two 8 ga Two 2.7 mm	⅜ in. 9.5 mm	1 in. × 20 ga 25.4 × 1.00 mm
37-50 in. 1270 mm	12 ft 3.7 m	⟶	Two ⅜ in. Two 9.5 mm	Two 1 in. × 20 ga (2) 25.4 × 1.00 mm
51-60 in. 1520 mm	12 ft 3.7 m	⟶	Two ⅜ in. Two 9.5 mm	Two 1 in. × 18 ga (2) 25.4 × 1.31 mm
61-84 in. 2130 mm	12 ft 3.7 m	⟶	Two ⅜ in. Two 9.5 mm	Two 1 in. × 16 ga (2) 25.4 × 1.61 mm
85-96 in. 2400 mm	12 ft 3.7 m	⟶	Two ½ in. Two 12 mm	Two 1½ in. × 16 ga (2) 38 × 1.61 mm

Table 5–2 Minimum Hanger Sizes for Round Duct

NOTES:

a. Straps are galvanized steel; rods are uncoated or galvanized steel; wire is black annealed, bright basic or galvanized steel. All are alternatives.

b. *See* Figure 5-5 for lower supports.

c. *See* Figs. 5-2, 5-3 and 5-4 for upper attachments.

d. Table allows for conventional wall thickness, and joint systems plus one lb./sf (4.89 Kg/m^2) insulation weight. If heavier ducts are to be installed, adjust hanger sizes to be within their load limits; see allowable loads with Table 5-1. Hanger spacing may be adjusted by special analysis.

e. Designers: For industrial grade supports, including saddles, single point trapeze loads, longer spans and flanged joint loads, *see* SMACNA's *Round Industrial Duct Construction Standards*.

f. *See* Figs. 3-9 and 3-10 for flexible duct supports.

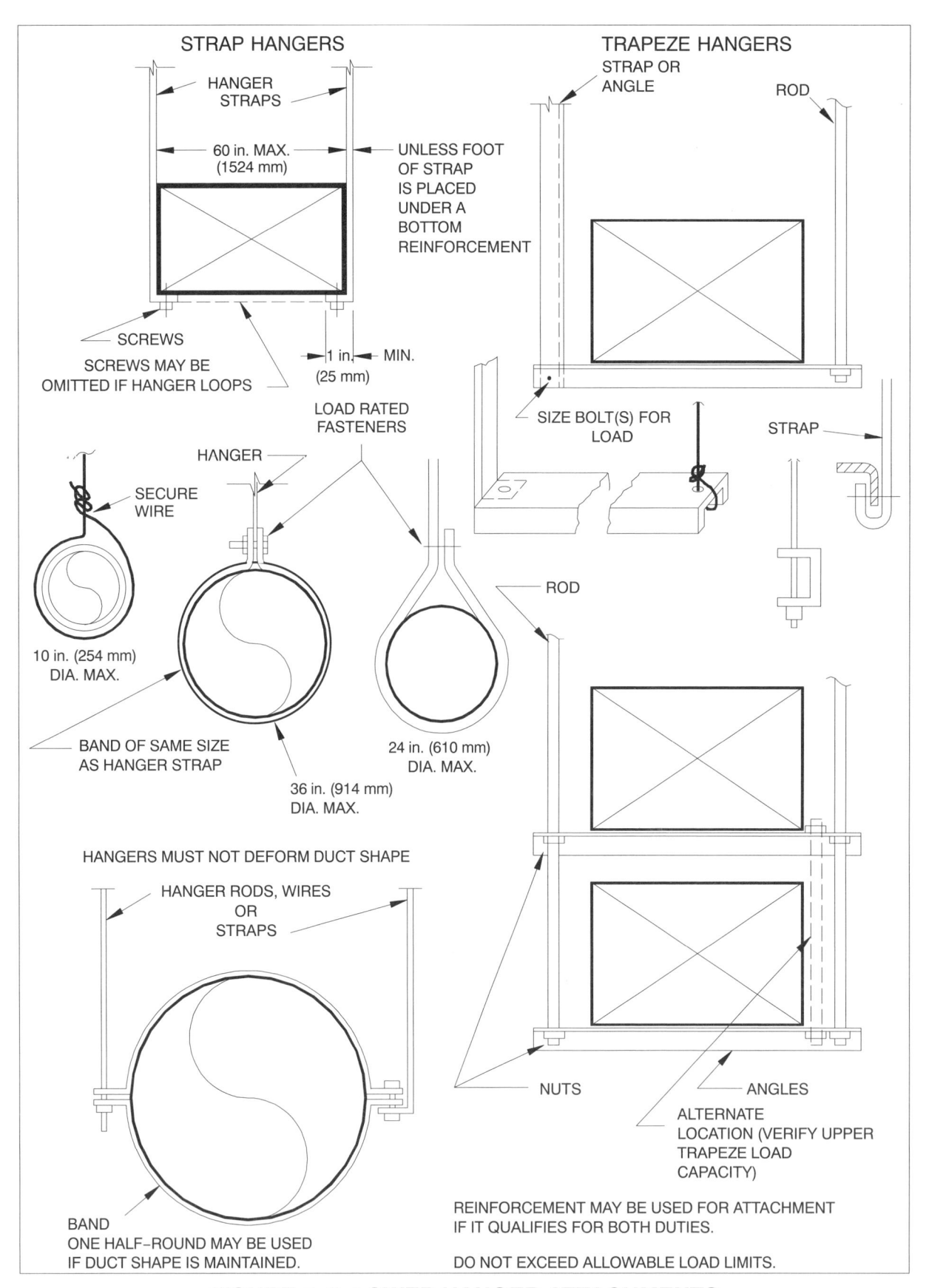

FIGURE 5–5 LOWER HANGER ATTACHMENTS

Table 5-3 Allowable Loads in Pounds for Trapeze Bars

Trapeze		A	B	C	D	E	F	G	H	I	J	K	L	M	N	O	P
		_	Angles												Channels		
		1" × 1" × 16 ga	1" × 1" × 1/8"	1-1/2" × 1-1/2" × 16ga	1-1/2" × 1-1/2" × 1/8"	1-1/2" × 1-1/2" × 3/16"	1-1/2" × 1-1/2" × 1/4"	2" × 2" × 1/8"	2" × 2" × 3/16"	2" × 2" × 1/4"	2-1/2" × 2-1/2" × 3/16"	2-1/2" × 2-1/2" × 1/4"	3" × 3" × 1/4"	4" × 4" × 1/4"	3" × 4.1 lb/ft	3" × 6.0 lb/ft	4" × 5.4 lb/ft
Length, in.	18	80	150	180	350	510	650	650	940	1230	1500	1960	-	-	-	-	-
	24	75	150	180	350	510	650	650	940	1230	1500	1960	-	-	-	-	-
	30	70	150	180	350	510	650	650	940	1230	1500	1960	-	-	-	-	-
	36	60	130	160	340	500	620	620	920	1200	1480	1940	-	-	-	-	-
	42	40	110	140	320	480	610	610	900	1190	1470	1930	-	-	-	-	-
	48	-	80	110	290	450	580	580	870	1160	1440	1900	-	-	-	-	-
	54	-	-	-	250	400	540	540	840	1120	1400	1860	-	-	-	-	-
	60	-	-	-	190	350	490	490	780	1060	1340	1800	-	-	-	-	-
	66	-	-	-	100	270	400	400	700	980	1260	1720	-	-	-	-	-
	72	-	-	-	-	190	320	320	620	900	1180	1640	-	-	-	-	-
	78	-	-	-	-	-	210	210	500	790	1070	1530	-	-	-	-	-
	84	-	-	-	-	-	-	-	380	660	940	1400	2310	4680	4650	5980	9080
	96	-	-	-	-	-	-	-	-	320	600	1060	1970	4340	3870	4950	8740
	108	-	-	-	-	-	-	-	-	-	-	-	2510	7240	5760	7780	15650
	120	-	-	-	-	-	-	-	-	-	-	-	1220	5950	4120	5930	13200
	132	-	-	-	-	-	-	-	-	-	-	-	-	4350	2540	3920	10820
	144	-	-	-	-	-	-	-	-	-	-	-	-	2420	-	2000	8330
Section Properties	I_x	0.012	0.022	0.041	0.078	0.110	0.139	0.190	0.272	0.348	0.547	0.703	1.240	3.040	1.660	2.070	3.850
	Z	0.016	0.031	0.037	0.072	0.104	0.13	0.130	0.190	0.247	0.303	0.394	0.577	1.050	1.100	1.380	1.930
	A	0.120	0.234	0.180	0.359	0.527	0.688	0.484	0.715	0.938	0.902	1.190	1.440	1.940	1.210	1.760	1.590
	lb/ft	0.440	0.800	0.660	1.230	1.800	2.340	1.650	2.440	3.190	3.070	4.100	4.900	6.600	4.100	6.000	5.400

NOTES:

a. It is assumed that steel with a yield strength of 30,000 psi or greater is used.
b. Loads above assume that a hanger rod is 6 in. max distance from the duct side for lengths of 96 in. or less, and 3 in. for greater lengths.
c. Framing Struts, see Table 5-4 and other steel shapes having equal or greater (Ix and Z) properties may be used in place of listed shapes. Ix is in in.^{4}, Z is in in.^{3}, and A is in in.^{2}
d. See Fig. 5-6 for load calculation method and Table 5-1 for rod and strap load limits.

Table 5-3M Allowable Loads in Kilograms for Trapeze Bars

Trapeze Length (mm)	Angles 25 × 25 × 1.61 (A)	Angles 25 × 3.2 (B)	Angles 38.1 × 1.61 (C)	Angles 38.1 × 3.2 (D)	Angles 38.1 × 4.8 (E)	Angles 38.1 × 6.4 (F)	Angles 51 × 3.2 (G)	Angles 51 × 3.8 (H)	Angles 51 × 6.4 (I)	Angles 63.5 × 4.8 (J)	Angles 63.5 × 6.4 (K)	Angles 76 × 6.4 (L)	Angles 102 × 6.4 (M)	Channels 76 × 1.9 (N)	Channels 76 × 2.7 (O)	Channels 102 × 2.5 (P)
450	36	68	81	159	231	295	295	426	558	680	889	-	-	-	-	-
600	34	68	81	159	231	295	295	426	558	680	889	-	-	-	-	-
760	32	68	81	159	231	295	295	426	558	680	889	-	-	-	-	-
900	27	59	72	154	227	281	281	417	549	671	880	-	-	-	-	-
1060	18	50	63	145	218	277	277	408	540	667	875	-	-	-	-	-
1220	-	36	50	132	204	263	263	395	526	653	862	-	-	-	-	-
1370	-	-	-	113	181	245	245	381	508	635	844	-	-	-	-	-
1520	-	-	-	86	159	222	222	354	480	608	816	-	-	-	-	-
1670	-	-	-	45	86	181	181	318	444	571	780	-	-	-	-	-
1830	-	-	-	-	-	145	145	281	408	535	744	-	-	-	-	-
2010	-	-	-	-	-	95	95	227	358	485	694	-	-	-	-	-
2130	-	-	-	-	-	-	-	454	299	426	635	1048	2123	2109	2713	4119
2440	-	-	-	-	-	-	-	-	145	272	480	894	1969	1755	2245	3964
2740	-	-	-	-	-	-	-	-	-	-	-	1139	3284	2613	3529	7010
3050	-	-	-	-	-	-	-	-	-	-	-	553	2699	1869	2690	5987
3350	-	-	-	-	-	-	-	-	-	-	-	-	1973	1152	1778	4908
3660	-	-	-	-	-	-	-	-	-	-	-	-	1098	-	907	3778
Section Properties I_x	0.494	0.906	1.69	3.21	4.53	3.72	7.82	11.2	14.3	22.5	28.9	51.0	125	68.3	85.2	158
Z	0.262	0.508	0.606	1.18	1.70	2.13	2.13	3.11	4.05	4.97	6.46	9.46	17.2	18.0	22.6	31.6
A	77.4	151	116	232	340	444	312	461	605	582	768	929	1252	781	1136	1026
kg/m	0.65	1.20	0.98	1.83	2.66	3.48	2.46	3.63	4.75	4.57	6.10	7.29	9.82	6.10	8.93	8.04

NOTES:
a. It is assumed that steel with a yield strength of 172.4 MPa or greater is used.
b. Loads above assume that a hanger rod is 152 mm max distance from the duct side for lengths of 2440 mm or less, and 76 mm for greater lengths.
c. Framing Struts, see Table 5-4M and other steel shapes having equal or greater (I_x and Z) properties may be used in place of listed shapes. I_x is in mm^4, Z is in mm^3, and A is in mm^2.
d. See Fig. 5-6 for load calculation method and Table 5-1M for rod and strap load limits.

FRAMING CHANNEL (STRUT) MAY BE USED AS AN ALTERNATIVE TO THE TRAPEZE ANGLES SHOWN IN TABLE 5-3 AS FOLLOWS:

Channel (Strut)			Section Modulus (Z)	Moment of Inertia (I)	Trapeze
H	W	GA	in.³	in.⁴	Table 5-3
1 in.	1 ⅝ in.	12	0.0923	0.0533	A, B, C
1 ⅜ in.	1 ⅝ in.	12	0.1559	0.1209	D, E
1 ⅝ in.	1 ⅝ in.	12	0.2042	0.1850	F, G
2 ⁷⁄₁₆ in.	1 ⅝ in.	12	0.3927	0.5203	H, I
3 ¼ in.	1 ⅝ in.	12	0.5772	0.9379	J, K

Channel (Strut)			Section Modulus (Z)	Moment of Inertia (I)	Trapeze
H (mm)	W (mm)	MM	mm³	mm⁴	Table 5-3M
25.4	41.3	2.45	1500	22,200	A, B, C
34.9	41.3	2.45	2600	50,300	D, E
41.3	41.3	2.45	3300	77,000	F, G
61.9	41.3	2.45	6400	216,000	H, I
82.6	41.3	2.45	10,300	454,000	J, K

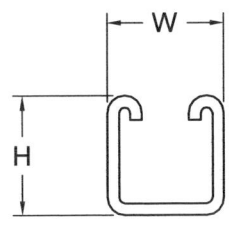

Table 5-4 Channel (Strut) Used as Trapeze

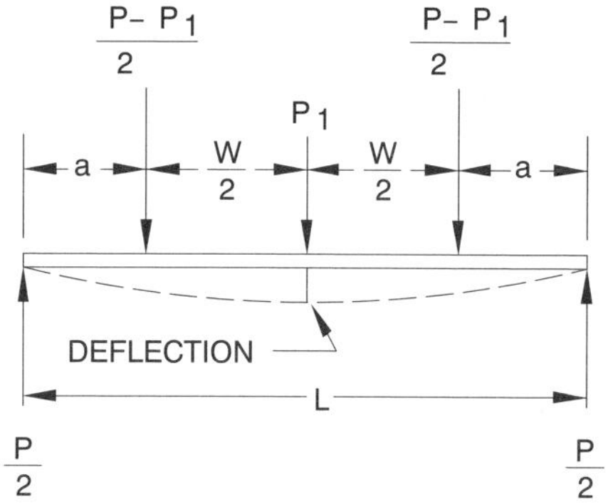

LOAD DIAGRAM

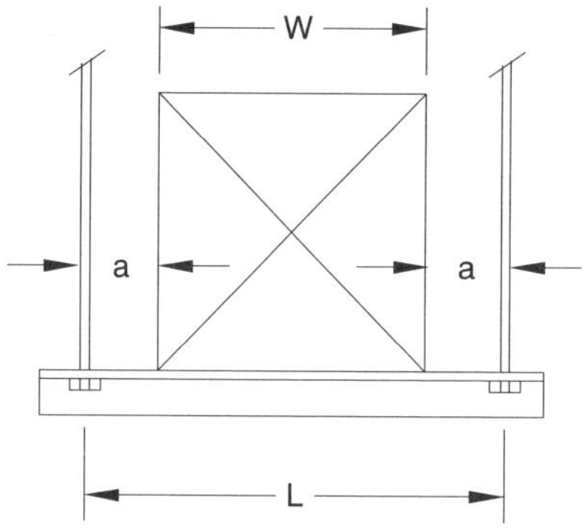

TRAPEZE SUPPORT

Weight of duct material of an areaW x W in ft (m) times 2.656 lb/ft (127 newtons/m)

W = Duct Width, inches
L = Distance between supports on the trapeze, inches (mm)
a = Distance between support and duct side, inches (mm)
D = Deflection, inches, suggested maximum 3/8" (9.5 mm)
E = Modulus of elasticity (29,000,000 psi for steel) (200 x 10^6 KPa)
I = Moment of Inertia, in.^{4} (mm^4)
Z = Section Modulus, in.^{3} (mm^3)
P = Weight of duct, reinforcements, insulation, etc.–not to exceed allowable load for stress or deflection limits
P_1 = Weight of duct material of an area W x W in ft^2 (m^2) times 2.656 lb/ft^2 (127 newtons/m^2)
M = Moment, in.–lb. (mN x m)
S = Allowable stress, steel = 15,000 psi (103,425 KPa) for bending stress. Shear stress alone should not exceed 7,500 psi. (51,713 KPa)
F = Shear load, lbs. (Kg.)
A = Cross sectional area, in.^{2} (mm^2)

BENDING STRESS

$$S_A = 15{,}000 \text{ psi} = \frac{M}{Z} \qquad P = 2\frac{SZ}{a} - P_1\left(\frac{L}{2a} - 1\right) = 30{,}000\frac{Z}{a} - P_1\left(\frac{L}{2a} - 1\right)$$

DEFLECTION

$$D = \frac{(P - P_1)\, a\, (3L^2 - 4a^2)}{2\,(24EI)} + \frac{P_1 L^3}{48\, EI}$$

Consult reference texts for other conditions of loading. For round duct loads on trapeze angles see the Round Industrial Duct Construction Standards

SHEAR STRESS

$$S_S = 7{,}500 \text{ Psi} = \frac{F}{A} = \frac{P}{2A} \qquad P = 15000\, A \text{ (maximum)}$$

Notice: Formula constants here are not in metric units.

FIGURE 5–6 TRAPEZE LOAD DIAGRAM

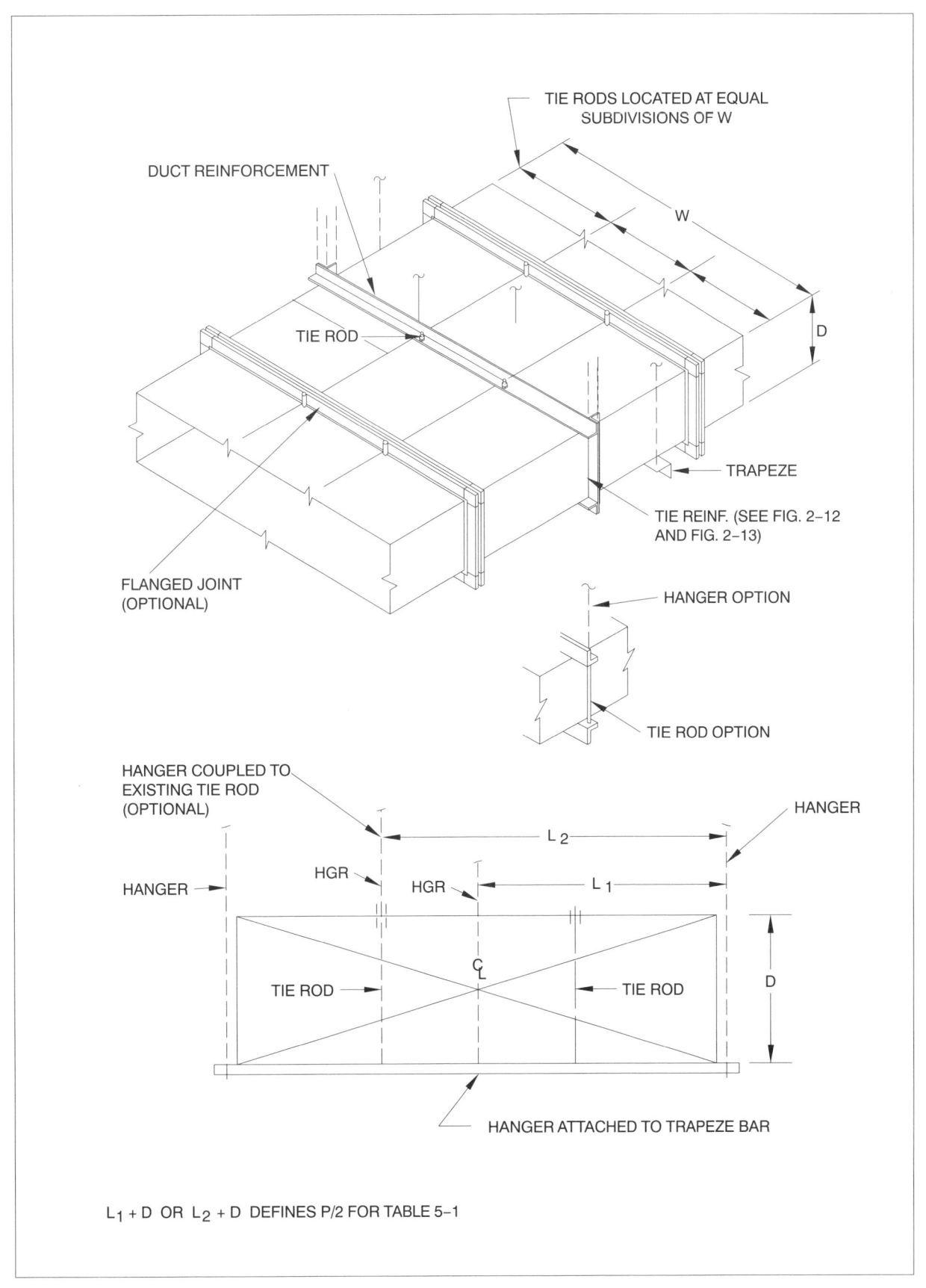

FIGURE 5-7 LARGE DUCT SUPPORT

$L_1 + D$ OR $L_2 + D$ DEFINES P/2 FOR TABLE 5-1

ALTERNATIVE SUPPORT TO RISER REINFORCEMENT ABOVE FLOOR

S = MAX DISTANCE FROM DUCT WALL TO SHAFT OPENING

HANGER ROD BETWEEN RISER SUPPORT & RISER REINFORCING

RISER REINFORCING (FOR DUAL DUTY)

FASTENERS *

FIG. B

* MINIMUM NUMBERS OF FASTENERS ON EACH OF TWO SUPPORT BARS

LARGEST DUCT DIM.	MINIMUM NUMBERS OF FASTENERS
16" AND DOWN	2
17" - 24"	3
OVER 24"	LARGEST DUCT DIM. DIVIDED BY 8

LOCATE A FASTENER WITHIN 2" OF THE DUCT EDGES. LOCATE OTHER AT EVENLY SPACED INTERVALS, SEE TABLE 5-5 IN FIG 5-9

DUCT JOINT

ANGLE

FIG. A

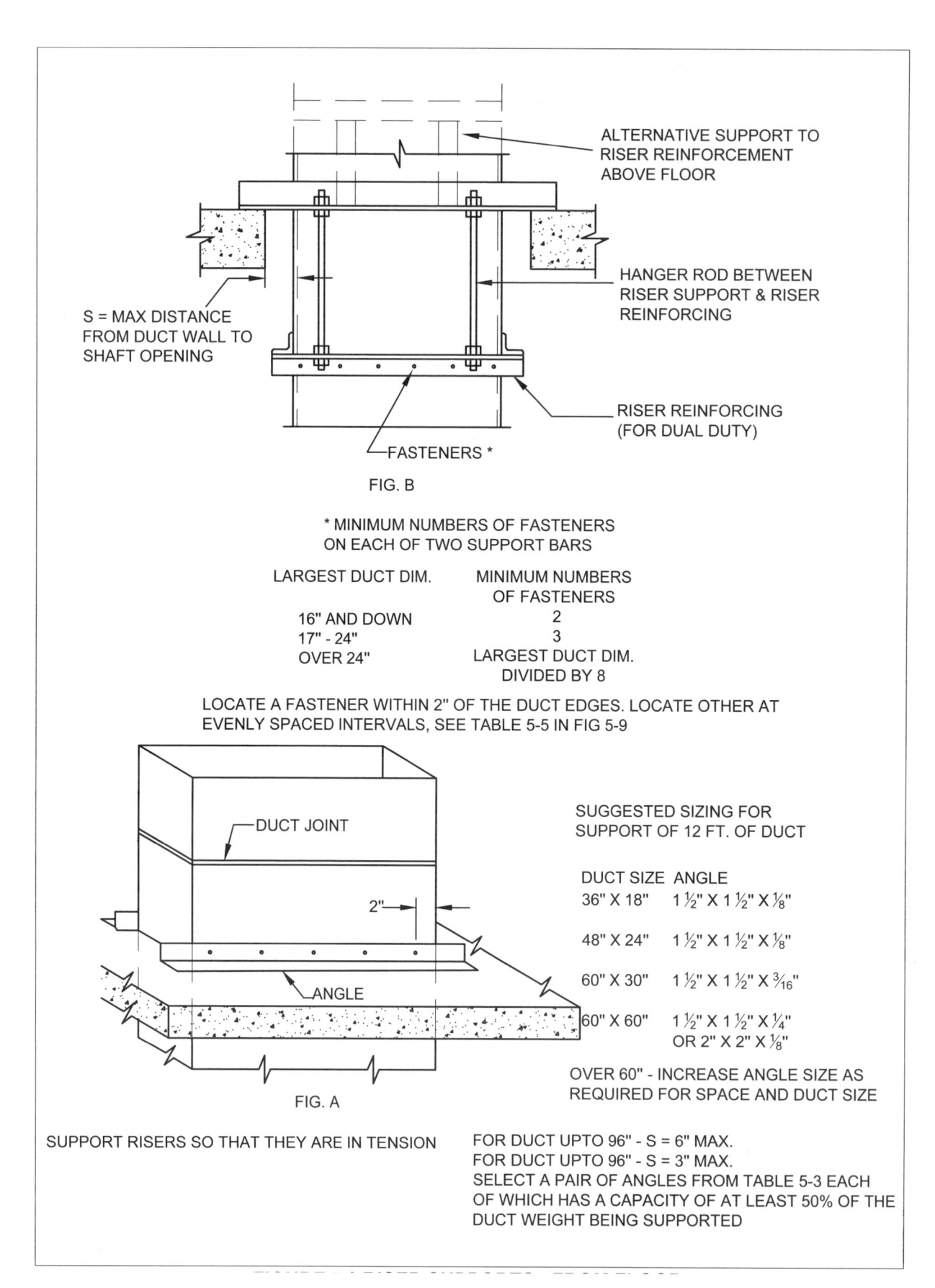

SUPPORT RISERS SO THAT THEY ARE IN TENSION

SUGGESTED SIZING FOR SUPPORT OF 12 FT. OF DUCT

DUCT SIZE	ANGLE
36" X 18"	1½" X 1½" X ⅛"
48" X 24"	1½" X 1½" X ⅛"
60" X 30"	1½" X 1½" X 3⁄16"
60" X 60"	1½" X 1½" X ¼" OR 2" X 2" X ⅛"

OVER 60" - INCREASE ANGLE SIZE AS REQUIRED FOR SPACE AND DUCT SIZE

FOR DUCT UPTO 96" - S = 6" MAX.
FOR DUCT UPTO 96" - S = 3" MAX.
SELECT A PAIR OF ANGLES FROM TABLE 5-3 EACH OF WHICH HAS A CAPACITY OF AT LEAST 50% OF THE DUCT WEIGHT BEING SUPPORTED

FIGURE 5–8 RISER SUPPORTS – FROM FLOOR

ALTERNATIVE SUPPORT TO RISER REINFORCEMENT ABOVE FLOOR

HANGER ROD BETWEEN RISER SUPPORT & RISER REINFORCING

RISER REINFORCING (FOR DUAL DUTY)

FASTENERS *

FIG. B

* MINIMUM NUMBER OF FASTENERS ON EACH OF TWO SUPPORT BARS

LARGEST DUCT DIM.	MINIMUM NUMBER OF FASTENERS
406 mm and down	2
432 mm – 610 mm	3
over 610 mm	Largest duct dim. Divided by 8

Locate a fastener within 51 mm of the duct edges. Locate others at evenly spaced intervals. See Table 5–5M in Figure 5–9M.

DUCT JOINT

51 mm

ANGLE

7.62 mm MAX. DISTANCE TO SUPPORT

FIG. A

SUGGESTED SIZING FOR SUPPORT OF 3.7 M OF DUCT

DUCT SIZE	ANGLE
914 x 457 mm	38.1 x 38.1 x 3.2 mm
1219 x 610 mm	38.1 x 38.1 x 3.2 mm
1524 x 762 mm	38.1 x 38.1 x 4.8 mm
1524 x 1524 mm	38.1 x 38.1 x 6.4 mm or 51 x 51 x 3.2 mm

OVER 1524 mm – INCREASE ANGLE SIZE AS REQUIRED FOR SPACE & DUCT SIZE

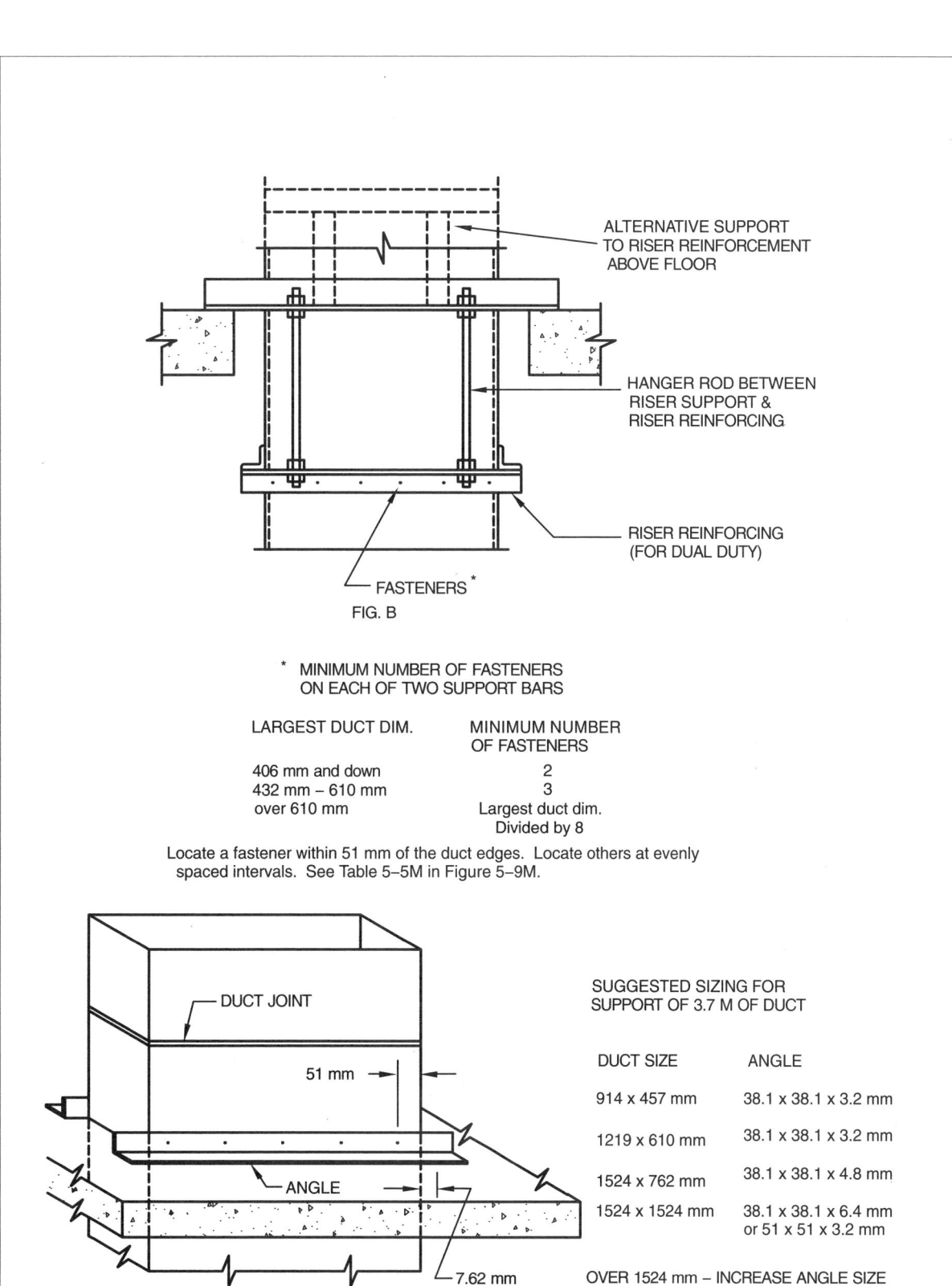

FIGURE 5–8M RISER SUPPORT – FROM FLOOR

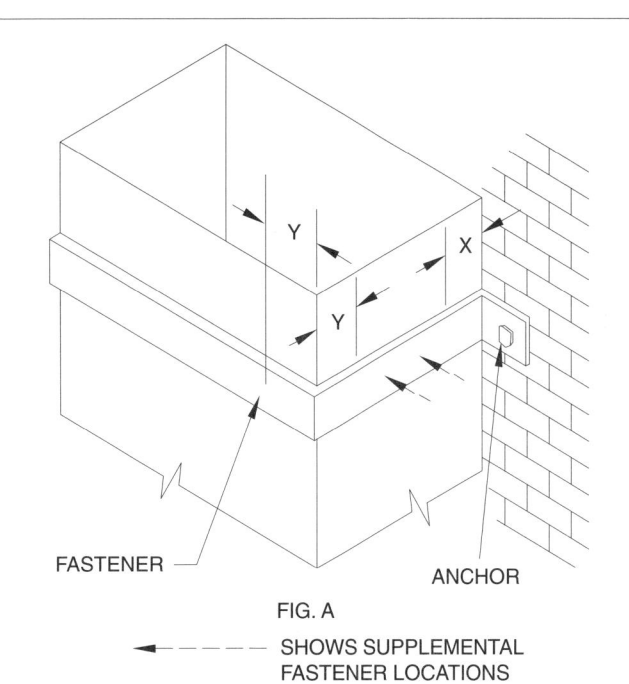

FIG. A – SUGGESTED SIZING

DUCT SIZE	BAND
18"x12"	1 1/2"x16 GA.
24"x20"	1"x1/8"

Table 5-5

DUCT GAGE	ALLOWABLE LOAD PER FASTENER*
28, 26	25 lb
24, 22, 20	35 lb
18, 16	50 lb

* WELD, BOLT OR NO. 8 SCREW (MIN.) DEVIATION PERMITTED BY OTHER ANALYSIS. X=1", Y=2"; ADD OTHERS TO ACCOMODATE LOAD. MINIMUM OF 3 ON 24" WIDTH AND UP. ADD ALONG SIDES NEAREST ANCHORS.

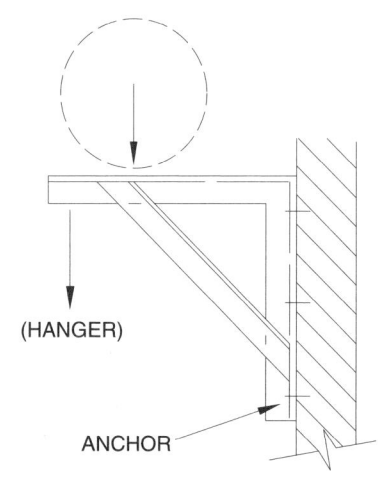

FASTENER
ANCHOR
FIG. A
◄ – – – – SHOWS SUPPLEMENTAL FASTENER LOCATIONS

(HANGER)
ANCHOR

SEE KNEE BRACKET TABLES IN THE ROUND INDUSTRIAL STDS.

FIG. B – SUGGESTED SIZING

DUCT SIZE	ANGLE
30" x 12"	1" x 1" x 1/8"
36" x 18"	1" x 1" x 1/8"
42" x 24"	1 1/4" x 1 1/4" x 1/8"
48" x 30"	1 1/4" x 1 1/4" x 1/8"

ANCHOR
FIG. B

NOTES:
1. BRACKETS ARE SIZED FOR 12 FEET OF DUCT, MAXIMUM.
2. LOCATE DUCTS AGAINST WALL OR MAXIMUM OF 2" AWAY FROM WALL.
3. EACH WALL ANCHOR SHALL SATISFY THE FOLLOWING CRITERIA UNLESS OTHER ANALYSIS IS MADE:
    A. TENSILE LOAD = 3/8 x DUCT WEIGHT; SAFETY FACTOR 4.
    B. SHEAR LOAD x 1/2 x DUCT WEIGHT; SAFETY FACTOR 4.

FIGURE 5–9 SUPPORTS FROM WALL

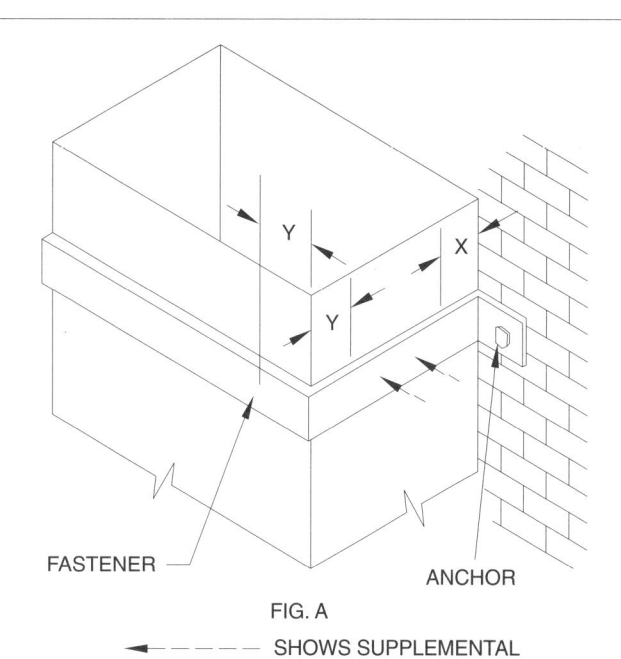

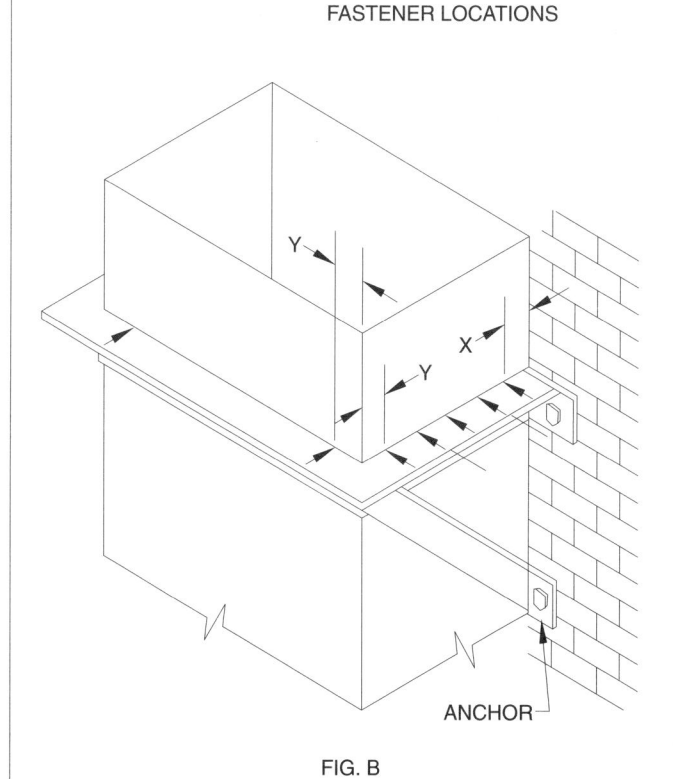

FIG. A – SUGGESTED SIZING

DUCT SIZE	BAND
457 x 300 mm	38.1 x 1.61 mm
610 x 508 mm	25 x 3.2 mm

Table 5-5M

DUCT THICKNESS	ALLOWABLE LOAD PER FASTENER*
0.48, 0.58 mm	11.3 KG
0.70, 1.00 mm	16 KG
1.31, 1.61 mm	23 KG

* WELD, BOLT OR NO. 8 SCREW (MIN.) DEVIATION PERMITTED BY OTHER ANALYSIS. X = 25 mm, Y = 51 mm; ADD OTHERS TO ACCOMODATE LOAD. MINIMUM OF 3 ON 610 mm WIDTH AND UP. ADD ALONG SIDES NEAREST ANCHORS.

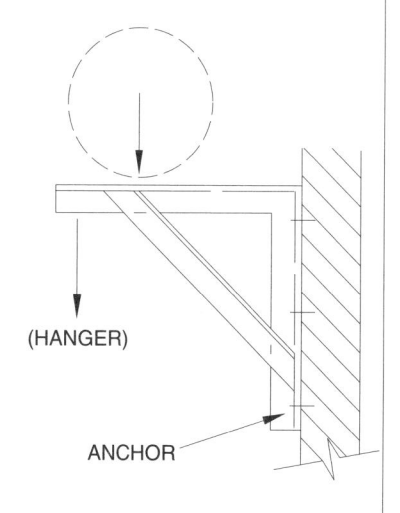

FASTENER
ANCHOR
FIG. A
SHOWS SUPPLEMENTAL FASTENER LOCATIONS

(HANGER)
ANCHOR

SEE KNEE BRACKET TABLES IN THE ROUND INDUSTRIAL STDS.

FIG. B – SUGGESTED SIZING

DUCT SIZE	ANGLE
762 x 305 mm	25 x 25 x 3.2 mm
914 x 457 mm	25 x 25 x 3.2 mm
1067 x 610 mm	31.8 x 31.8 x 3.2 mm
1219 x 914 mm	31.8 x 31.8 x 3.2 mm

ANCHOR
FIG. B

NOTES:
1. BRACKETS ARE SIZED FOR 3.7 M OF DUCT, MAXIMUM.
2. LOCATE DUCTS AGAINST WALL OR MAXIMUM OF 51 mm AWAY FROM WALL.
3. EACH WALL ANCHOR SHALL SATISFY THE FOLLOWING CRITERIA UNLESS OTHER ANALYSIS IS MADE:
   A. TENSILE LOAD = 3/8 x DUCT WEIGHT; SAFETY FACTOR 4.
   B. SHEAR LOAD x 1/2 x DUCT WEIGHT; SAFETY FACTOR 4.

FIGURE 5–9M SUPPORT FROM WALL

HVAC Duct Construction Standards Metal and Flexible • Fourth Edition

SPLIT BAND SUPPORT DIRECTLY ON FLOOR SLAB

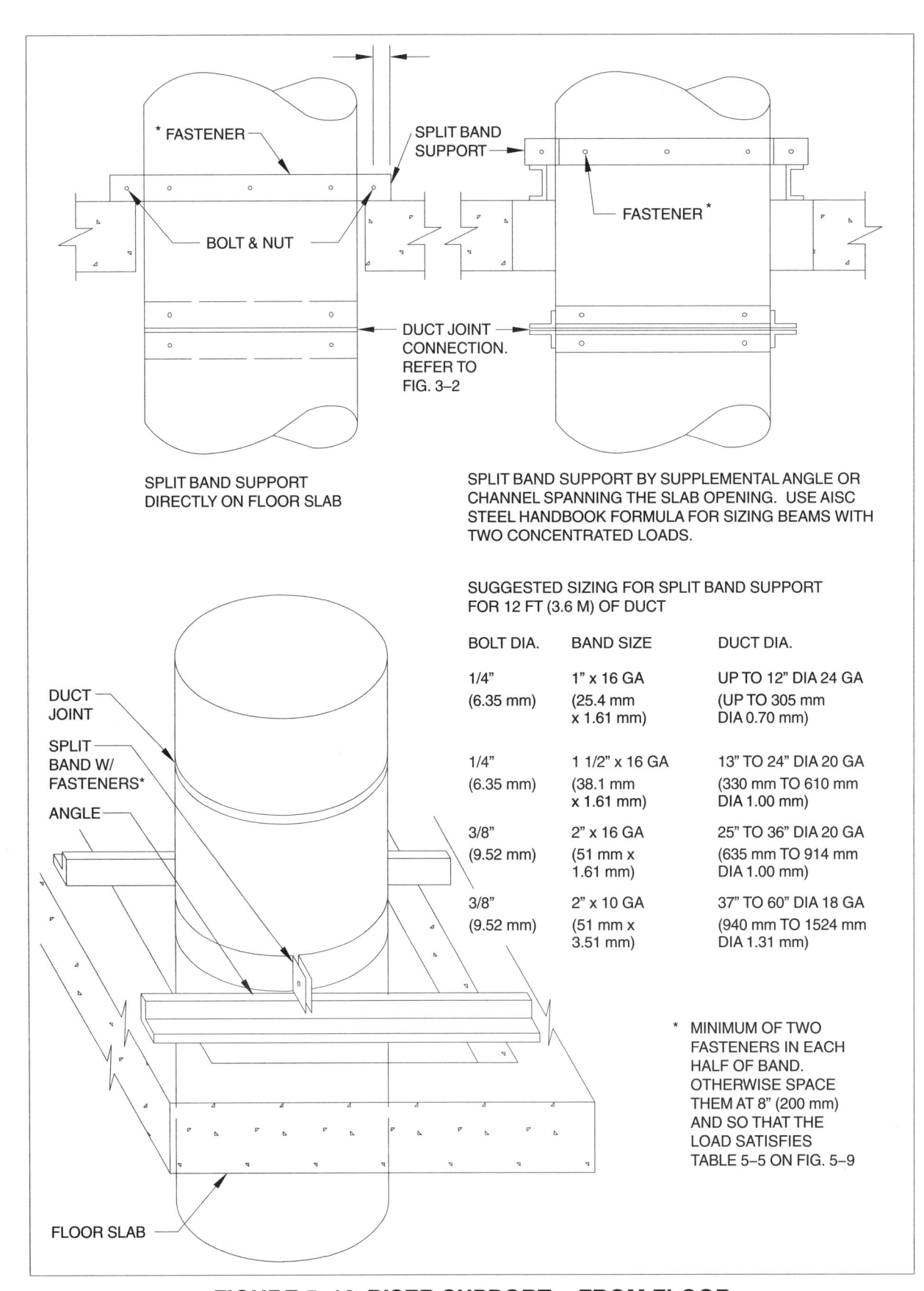

SPLIT BAND SUPPORT BY SUPPLEMENTAL ANGLE OR CHANNEL SPANNING THE SLAB OPENING. USE AISC STEEL HANDBOOK FORMULA FOR SIZING BEAMS WITH TWO CONCENTRATED LOADS.

SUGGESTED SIZING FOR SPLIT BAND SUPPORT FOR 12 FT (3.6 M) OF DUCT

BOLT DIA.	BAND SIZE	DUCT DIA.
1/4" (6.35 mm)	1" x 16 GA (25.4 mm x 1.61 mm)	UP TO 12" DIA 24 GA (UP TO 305 mm DIA 0.70 mm)
1/4" (6.35 mm)	1 1/2" x 16 GA (38.1 mm x 1.61 mm)	13" TO 24" DIA 20 GA (330 mm TO 610 mm DIA 1.00 mm)
3/8" (9.52 mm)	2" x 16 GA (51 mm x 1.61 mm)	25" TO 36" DIA 20 GA (635 mm TO 914 mm DIA 1.00 mm)
3/8" (9.52 mm)	2" x 10 GA (51 mm x 3.51 mm)	37" TO 60" DIA 18 GA (940 mm TO 1524 mm DIA 1.31 mm)

* MINIMUM OF TWO FASTENERS IN EACH HALF OF BAND. OTHERWISE SPACE THEM AT 8" (200 mm) AND SO THAT THE LOAD SATISFIES TABLE 5-5 ON FIG. 5-9

FIGURE 5-10 RISER SUPPORT - FROM FLOOR

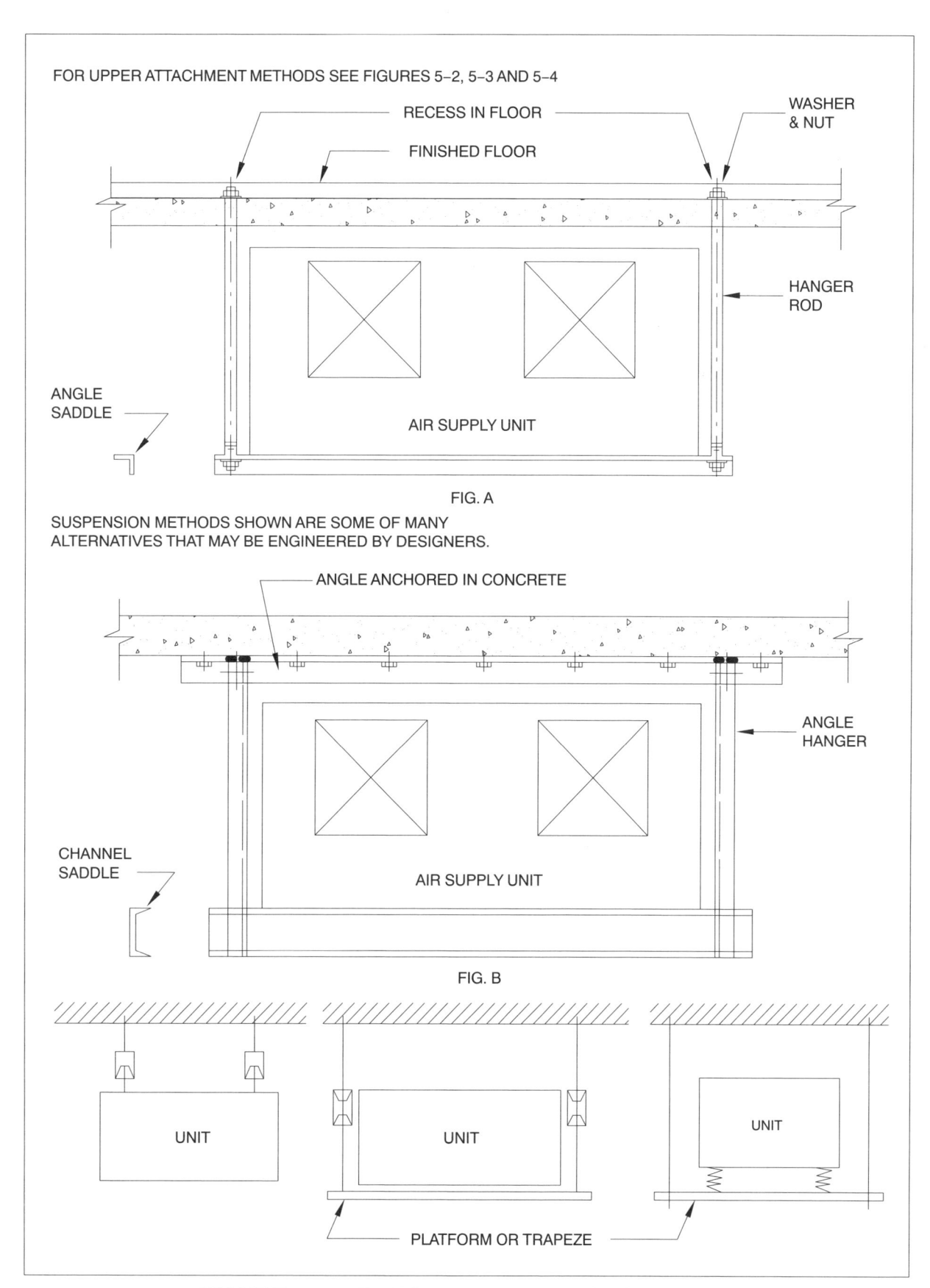

FIGURE 5-11 TYPICAL HVAC UNIT SUSPENSION

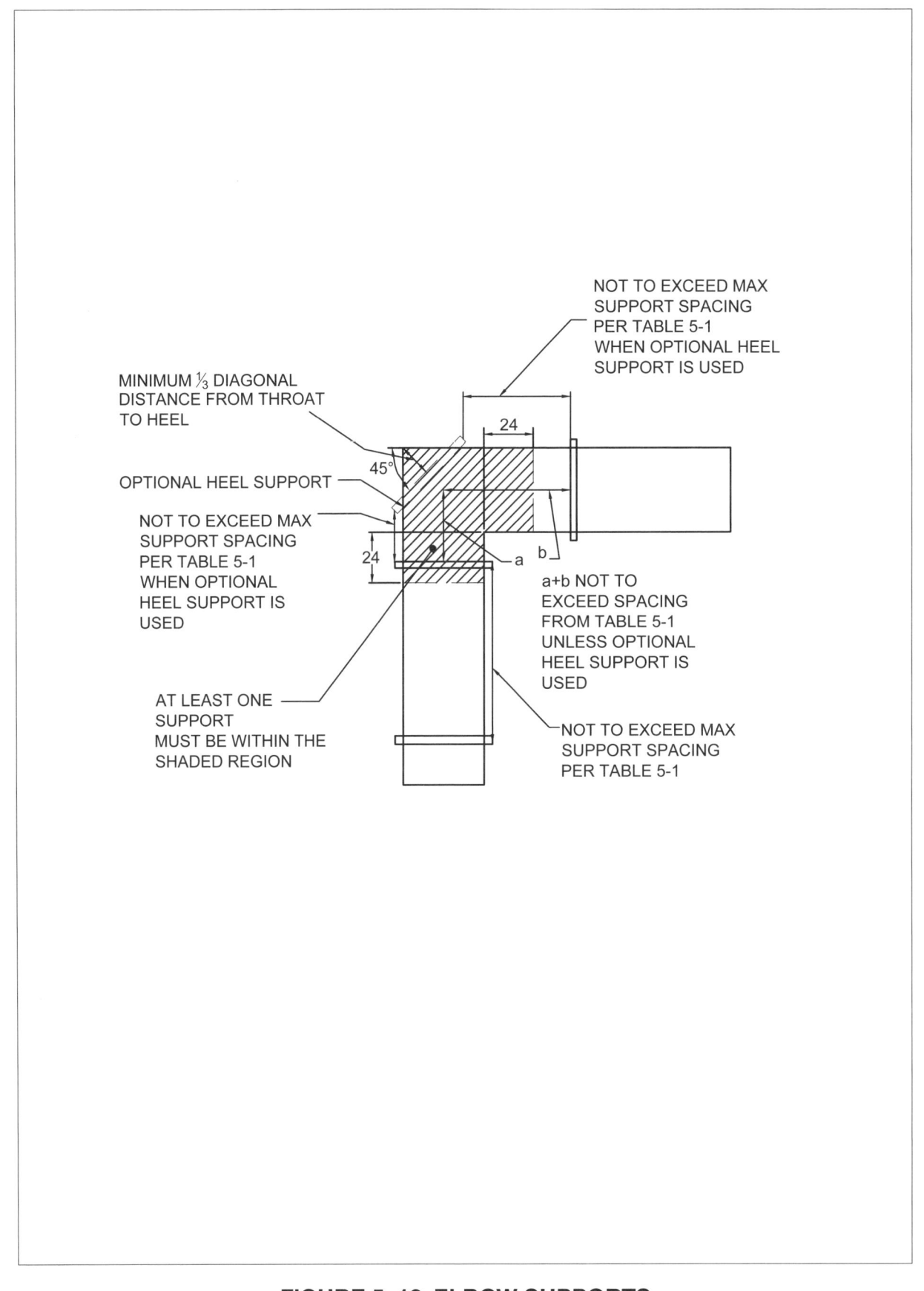

FIGURE 5–12 ELBOW SUPPORTS

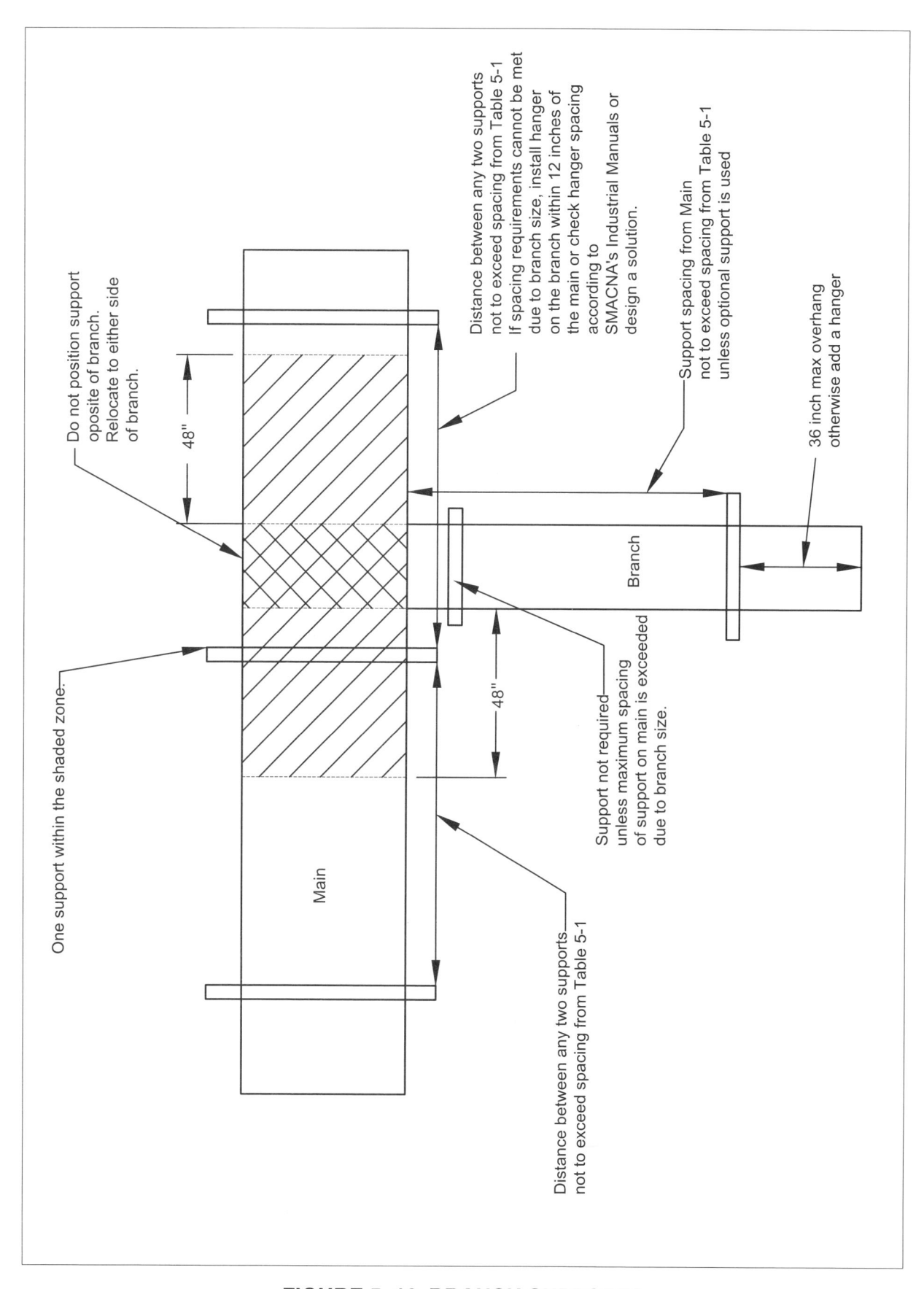

FIGURE 5–13 BRANCH SUPPORTS

THIS PAGE INTENTIONALLY LEFT BLANK

CHAPTER 6

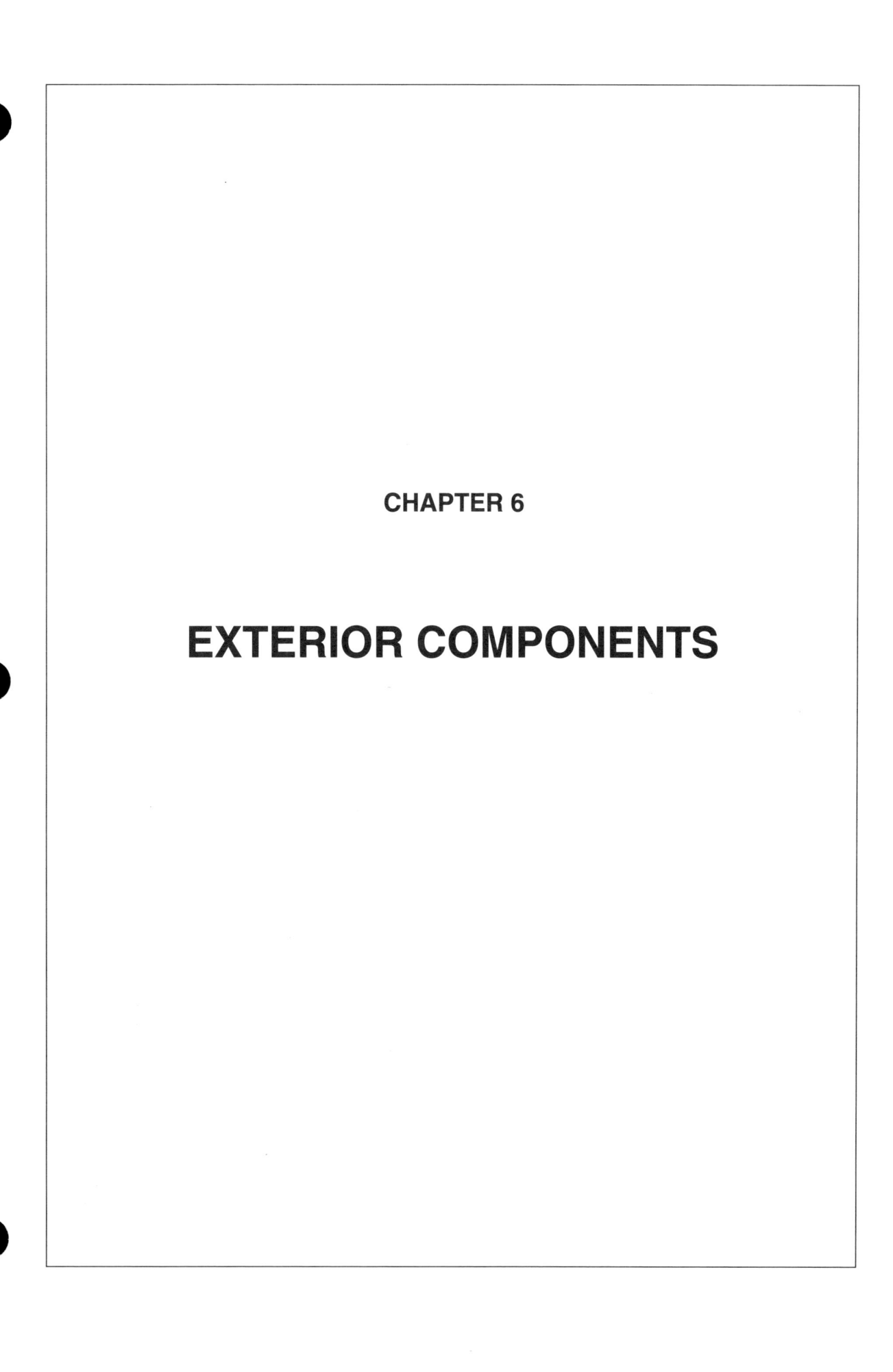

EXTERIOR COMPONENTS

CHAPTER 6 EXTERIOR COMPONENTS

6.1 INTRODUCTION

Among the deliberations that designers should consider in the selection of louvers, rooftop ducts, curbs, ventilators, supports, and other components are the following.

1. Waterproofing details

2. Durability/service life

3. Wind, snow and hail resistance

4. Corrosion rate - chemical, electrolytic and atmospheric

5. Maintenance/repair frequency

6. Orientation of air intakes and discharges to prevent hazards

7. Vibration control

8. How the presence and proximity of screen enclosures used for aesthetic purposes affect the performance of the HVAC systems

9. Infiltration, exfiltration and prevailing wind direction

10. The details and resource references dealing with the preceding in the SMACNA duct standards, *HVAC Systems Duct Design* and the *Architectural Sheet Metal Manual*.

Information on air flow pressure loss standard stock sizes, strength, corrosion, comparative cost and much other data on perforated metals is available from the Industrial Perforators Association. Some perforated metals have the appearance of wire mesh screens.

Similar data for bird screen, insect screen and other meshes for wire cloth is available from the American Wire Cloth Institute and its members.

SCHEDULE BLADES & FRAMES

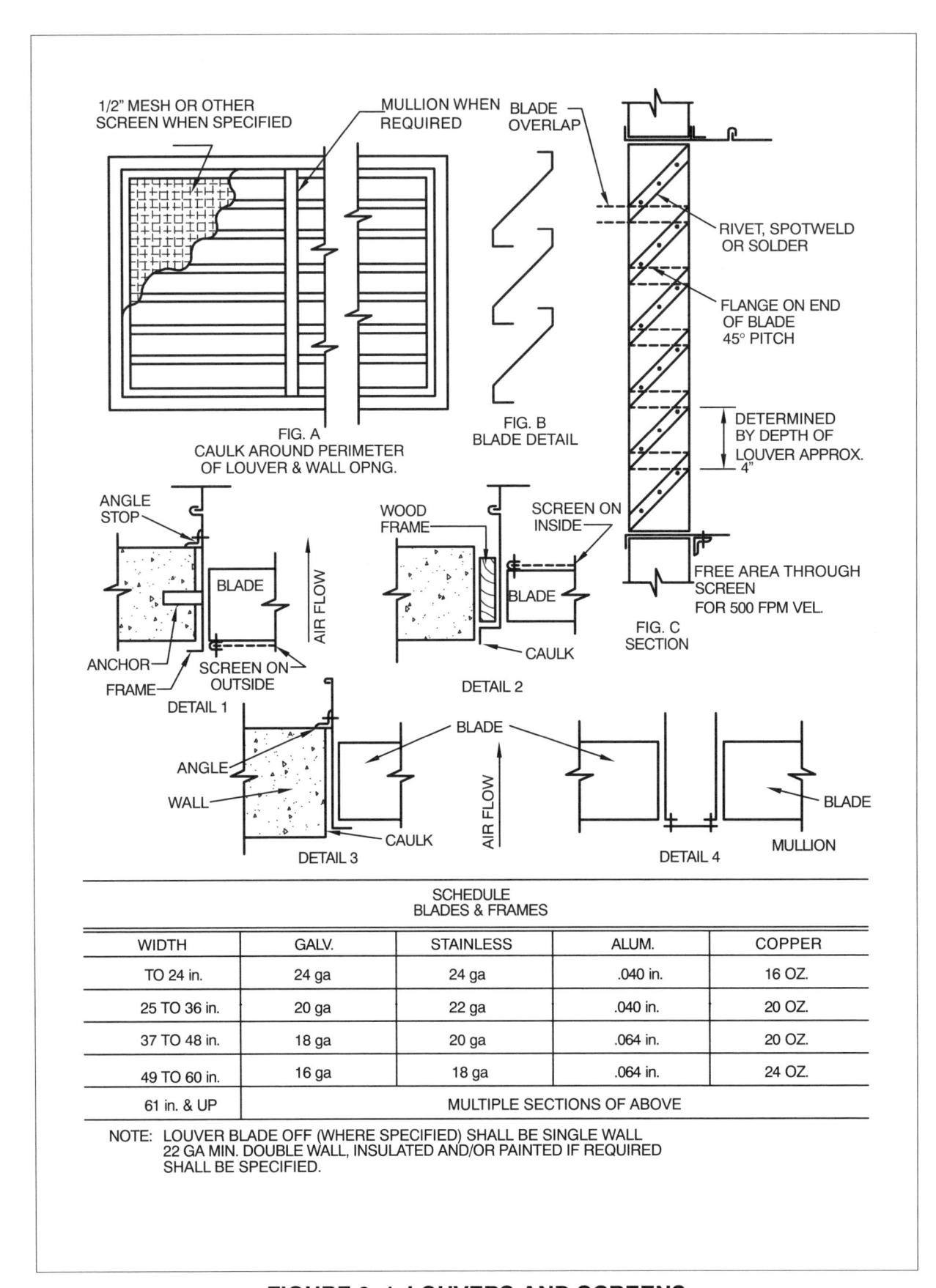

WIDTH	GALV.	STAINLESS	ALUM.	COPPER
TO 24 in.	24 ga	24 ga	.040 in.	16 OZ.
25 TO 36 in.	20 ga	22 ga	.040 in.	20 OZ.
37 TO 48 in.	18 ga	20 ga	.064 in.	20 OZ.
49 TO 60 in.	16 ga	18 ga	.064 in.	24 OZ.
61 in. & UP	MULTIPLE SECTIONS OF ABOVE			

NOTE: LOUVER BLADE OFF (WHERE SPECIFIED) SHALL BE SINGLE WALL 22 GA MIN. DOUBLE WALL, INSULATED AND/OR PAINTED IF REQUIRED SHALL BE SPECIFIED.

FIGURE 6-1 LOUVERS AND SCREENS

SCHEDULE
BLADES & FRAMES

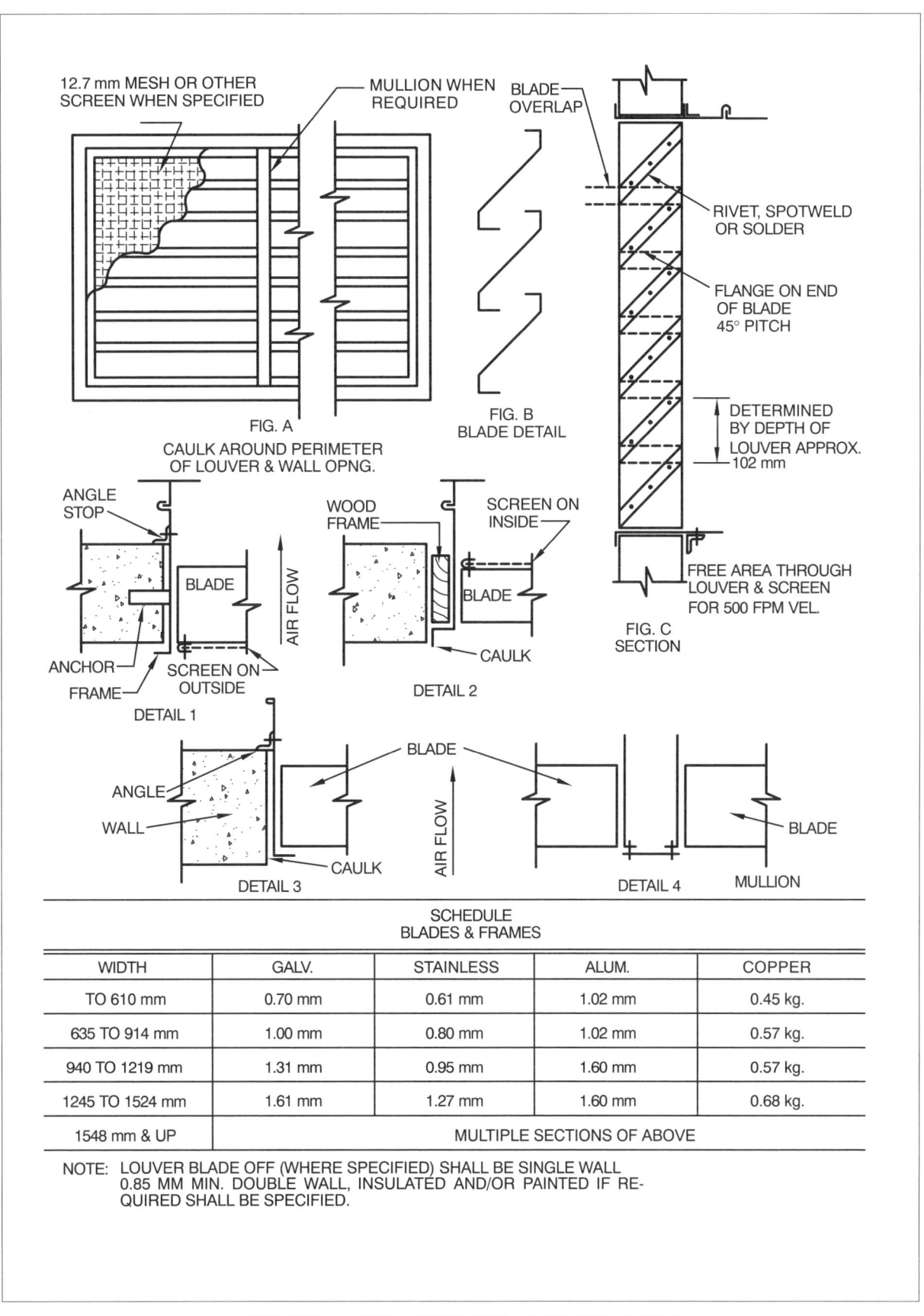

WIDTH	GALV.	STAINLESS	ALUM.	COPPER
TO 610 mm	0.70 mm	0.61 mm	1.02 mm	0.45 kg.
635 TO 914 mm	1.00 mm	0.80 mm	1.02 mm	0.57 kg.
940 TO 1219 mm	1.31 mm	0.95 mm	1.60 mm	0.57 kg.
1245 TO 1524 mm	1.61 mm	1.27 mm	1.60 mm	0.68 kg.
1548 mm & UP	MULTIPLE SECTIONS OF ABOVE			

NOTE: LOUVER BLADE OFF (WHERE SPECIFIED) SHALL BE SINGLE WALL 0.85 MM MIN. DOUBLE WALL, INSULATED AND/OR PAINTED IF REQUIRED SHALL BE SPECIFIED.

FIGURE 6-1M LOUVERS AND SCREENS

Consult AMCA Standard 500-L for complete information on free area, static pressure loss, water penetration and cfm ratings.

Free area is the minimum area through which air can pass and is determined by multiplying the sum of the minimum distances between intermediate blades, top blade and head and bottom blade and sill, by the minimum distance between jambs. The percent free area is the free area thus calculated, divided by the face area of the louver x 100. See cross sections of louvers and frames.

$$\text{Free Area (sq. ft. or mm)} = L[A+B+(N \times C)]$$

$$\text{Percent Free Area} = \frac{L[A+B+(N \times C)]\,100}{W \times H}$$

Where:

- A = Minimum distance, in inches (mm), between the head and top blade.
- B = Minimum distance, in inches (mm), between the sill and bottom blade.
- C = Minimum distance, in inches (mm), between adjacent blades.
  Note that in louver Type 2, C_1, may not be equal to C, and the minimum C should be used.
- N = Number of "C" openings in the louver.
- L = Minimum distance, in inches (mm), between louver jambs.
- W = Actual louver width, in inches (mm).
- H = Actual louver height, in inches (mm).

Size listing: conventional practice is to list width by height.

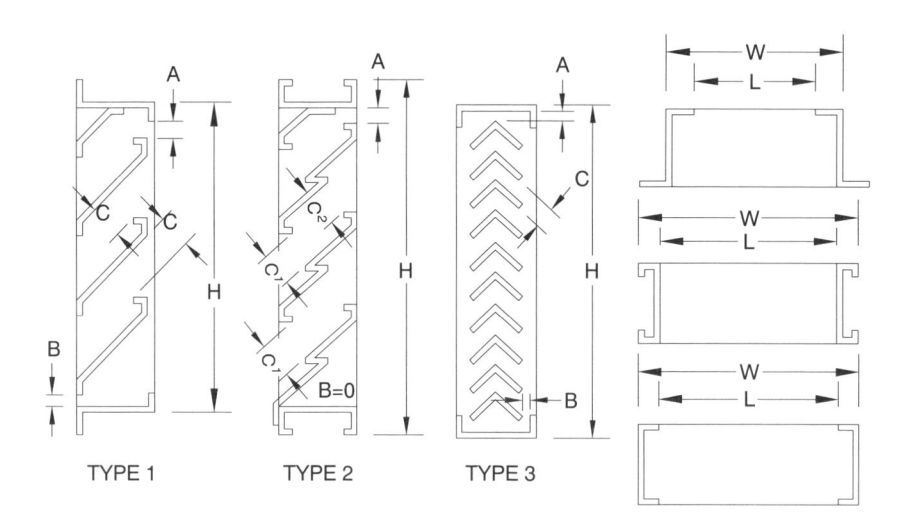

TYPICAL LOUVER AND FRAME CROSS SECTIONS
SHOWING MINIMUM DISTANCES IN FORMULA

FIGURE 6–2 LOUVER FREE AREA CALCULATION

6.2 ROOFTOP EQUIPMENT INSTALLATION

6.3 COMMENTARY

Each installation of a roof-mounted HVAC unit or roof-supported duct involves customized design requirements. The construction details and recommendations here are therefore advisory and depend on contract documents for clarification. Openings in roofs require coordination of the architectural, structural, mechanical, and electrical contract drawings. The height of equipment and ducts above the roof level may be influenced by snow loading, snow drifting, and wind loading as well as aesthetic considerations. Designers must specify constructions appropriate for the specific locality and circumstances.

All ducts that are not watertight through the use of welded constructions or protective shields and are exposed directly to weather and solar radiation should have secure, watertight mechanical connections and receive exterior duct sealant treatment as defined in S1.9g.

Exterior duct sealant treatment should consist of applying products marketed specifically as forming a positive airtight and watertight seal, bonding well to the metal involved, remaining watertight with metal movement, and having a service temperature range of -30°F (-34°C) to 175°F (79°C). If exposed to direct sunlight it should also be ultraviolet ray- and ozone-resistant or should, after curing, be painted with a compatible coating that provides these plus weather resistance. The term sealant is not limited to materials of adhesive or mastic nature, but is inclusive of tapes and combinations of woven fabric strips and mastics. Asphalt-based compounds should not be used for sealing ducts.

Duct systems should not be pressurized until the sealant has had time to cure. Follow the sealant manufacturer's recommendations on curing.

Unless otherwise prescribed by the HVAC equipment manufacturer, ducts should be flanged for attachment to equipment with mechanical fastening plus exterior duct sealant. Typical connections are shown in Figure 6-3. The attachment method should accommodate disconnection if this is required for routine maintenance of the equipment.

Where vibration isolation material is required at the connection of ducts to equipment, such material should be impervious to water. Ducts should be supported to avoid the transfer of duct weight across flexible connections.

Roof penetrations by ducts should have curbs. Ducts that are interrupted at the curb should overhang the top of the curb or be flashed to divert water over the curb. Ducts that are continuous through the curb should have flashing that slopes over the curb and is sealed to the duct with caulking or a suitable tape. Adequate clearances between ducts and roof penetration openings should be provided, *see* Figure 6-4.

Curbs may be supplied with rooftop units or provided independently. The equipment manufacturer may outline flashing methods, structural opening requirements, sealing techniques, etc., which must be coordinated with project construction. With considerable pitch in the roof, a subbase may be required to adapt to a pre-engineered curb. Furthermore, curb mountings may incorporate vibration isolation features.

All penetrations into ducts should be watertight. Duct reinforcements and supports attached to the duct should have external sealant at points of penetrations. Attach supports with a minimum number of duct penetrations.

Horizontal ducts should be pitched and provided with drainage outlets as illustrated by the system designer.

If airtight, waterproof flexible insulation jackets are applied on positive pressure ducts, the installation should accommodate some duct leakage; ducts are not completely airtight.

When moving rooftop units across the roof, handle them in a manner to prevent roof damage.

Supports for ducts should be as indicated in Figure 6-4. If the support does not rest on a cap-flashed curb, the penetration of the roof membrane should have base flashing and umbrella flashing.

Pitch pockets require periodic maintenance and are not permanently watertight. They are not recommended.

Designers should carefully consider the proximity of intakes to exhausts and the possibility of drawing in contaminated air. The direction and elevation of discharges may be controlled by codes or standards such as NFPA-89M, 90A, 91, 96, 204 or 211.

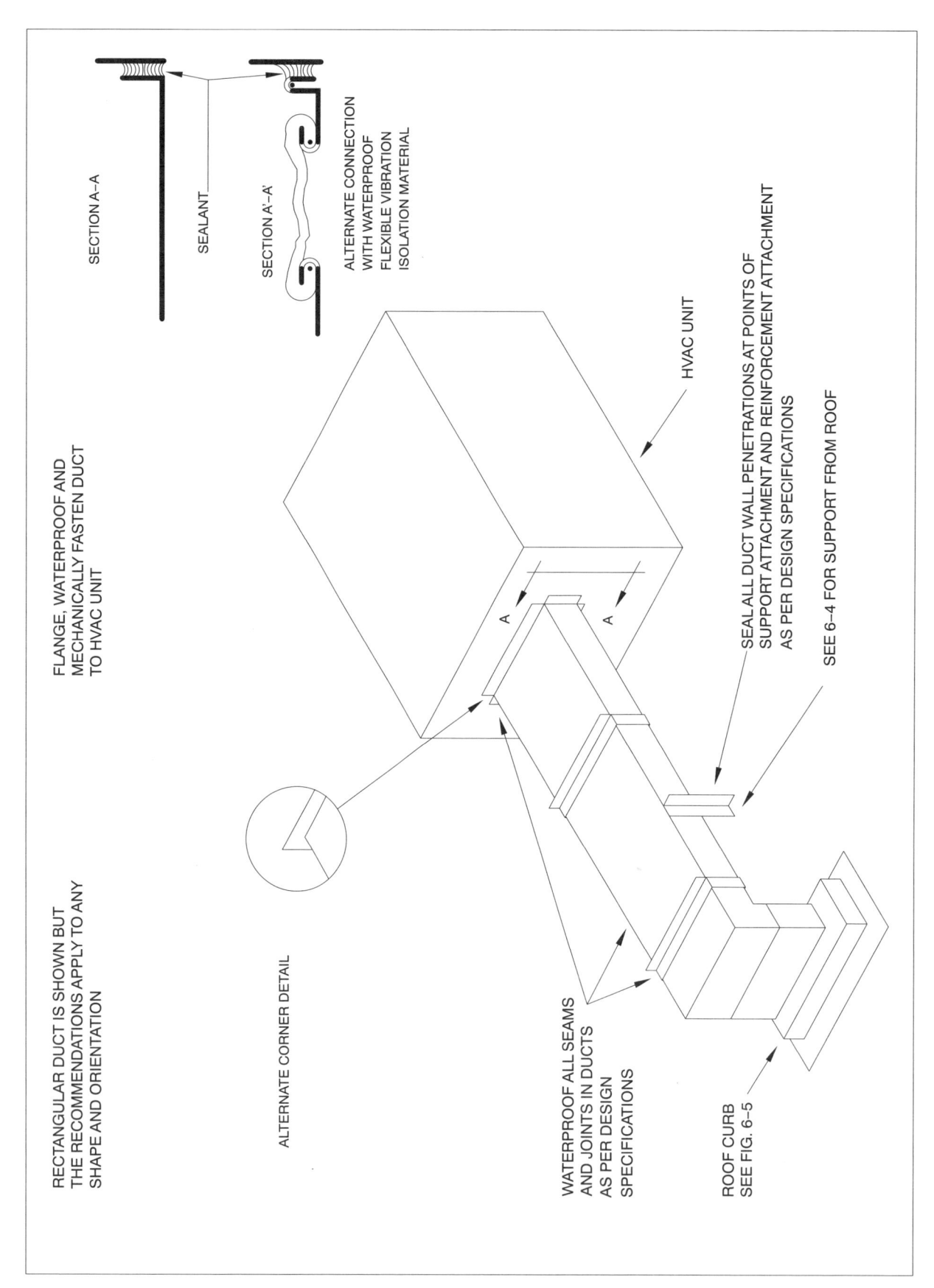

FIGURE 6–3 ROOFTOP DUCT INSTALLATION

HVAC Duct Construction Standards Metal and Flexible • Fourth Edition

PIPE OR ANGLE SUPPORT

CAP FLASHING

COMPOSITION FLASHING

PIER OR CURB BASE

ELASTOMERIC SEAL

DRAWBAND

WATERTIGHT UMBRELLA

FLASHING FLANGE

MASTIC BEAD

ROOF MEMBRANES

CONCRETE DECK

NAILER (ALL SIDES)

EQUIPMENT SUPPORT FRAME

BEARING PLATE

INSULATED STEEL DECK

ROOF JACK
FLASHING REQUIREMENTS

HEIGHT: 8" (203 mm) MIN. ABOVE ROOF
FLANGE: 3" TO 4" (76 mm TO 102 mm) WIDTH
CLEARANCE TO PIPE: 1/4" (6.4 mm) MIN.
CLEARANCE TO UMBRELLA: 1/4" (6.4 mm) MIN.
ALL ARE SET IN MASTIC AND STRIPPED IN.
FLANGE IS FASTENED TO WOOD NAILER ON
  INSULATED DECKS.
BOTTOM OF UMBRELLA TO BE 4" (102 mm) BELOW
  TOP OF FLASHING.

WIDTH OF EQUIPMENT	HEIGHT H
UP TO 24" (610 mm)	14" (356 mm)
25" TO 36" (635 mm TO 914 mm)	18" (457 mm)
37" TO 48" (940 mm TO 1219 mm)	24" (610 mm)
49" TO 60" (1245 mm TO 1524 mm)	30" (762 mm)
61" (1549 mm) AND WIDER	48" (1219 mm)

H CLEARANCE FOR ROOF MAINTENANCE IS RECOMMENDED FOR EQUIPMENT AND DUCTS.

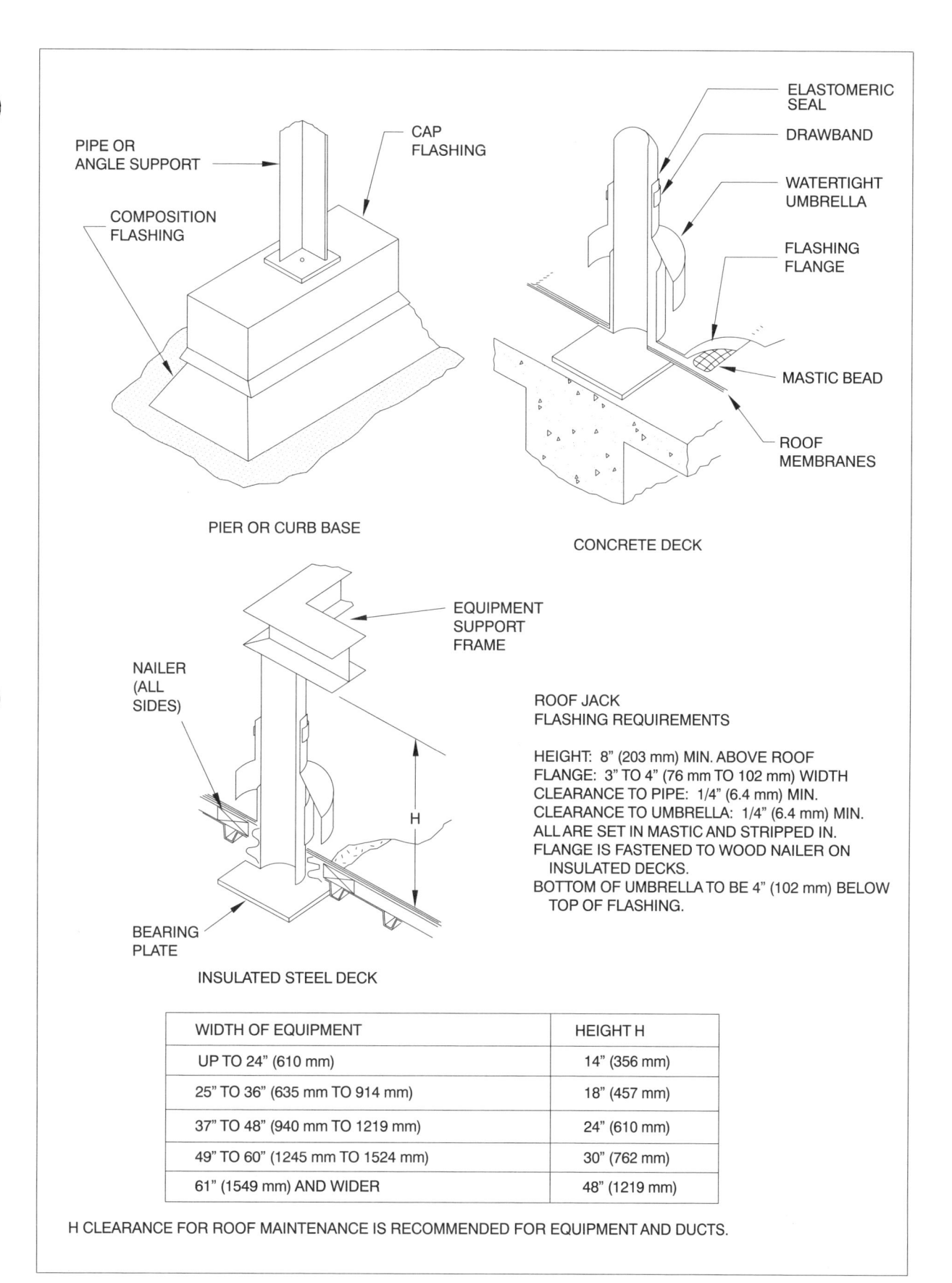

FIGURE 6-4 EQUIPMENT AND DUCT SUPPORT FLASHING

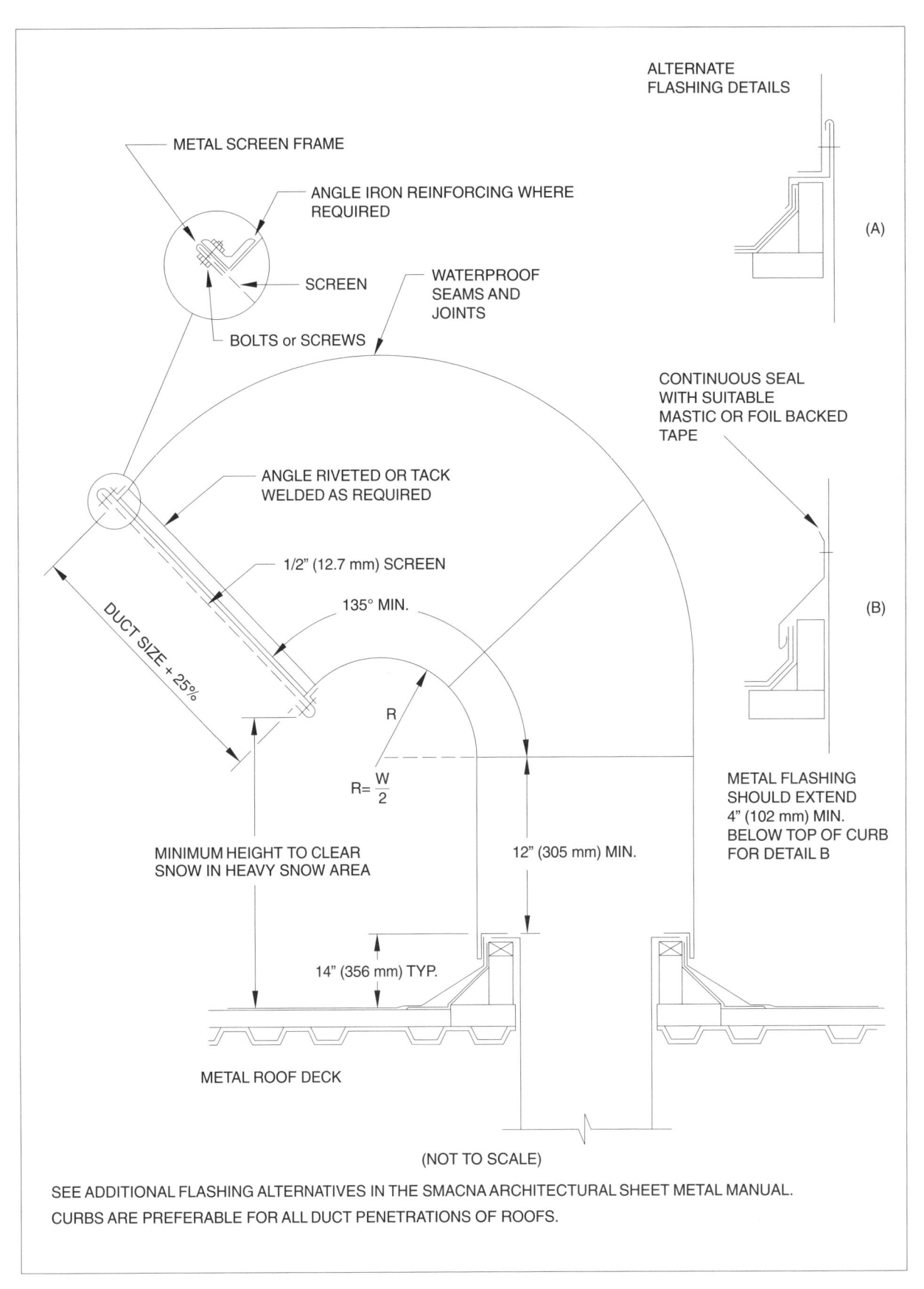

FIGURE 6–5 RECTANGULAR GOOSENECK

1/2" (12.7 mm) MESH SCREEN* 4 SIDES

* RAD. A

SAME AS A
HALF OF A
3" (76 mm)

CURBS MAY BE FLASHED AS SHOWN IN FIG. 6–5

*SEE ADDITIONAL NOTES ON FIG. 6–5 FOR SCREEN AREA COMPENSATION, DEFLECTORS, CURB HEIGHTS, AND RIM ELEVATION.

IF USED FOR DAMPER ACCESS, USE HINGES AND LATCHES

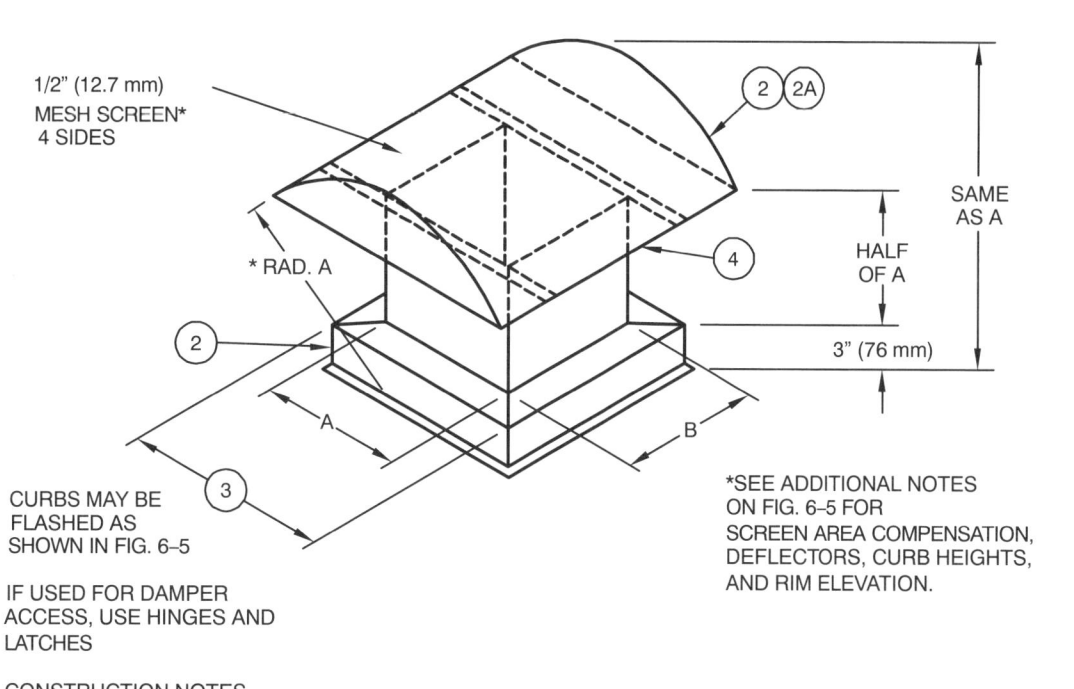

CONSTRUCTION NOTES

1. WHEN A x B = 12 SQ. FT. (1.11 SQ. M) USE 22 GA. (0.85 mm)
   WHEN A x B = 12 TO 18 SQ. FT. (1.11 TO 1.67 SQ. M) USE 20 GA. (1.00 mm)
   WHEN A x B = OVER 18 SQ. FT. (1.67 SQ. M) USE 18 GA. (1.31 mm)
   WHEN CONSTRUCTION IS GALVANIZED USE GA SCHEDULE SHOWN. WHEN CONSTRUCTION IS ALUMINUM USE FOUR GAUGES HEAVIER.

RADIUS = 1/2A + 3/4" (19 mm)
SUPPORT ANGLE

BIRD SCREEN*

18" (457 mm) MIN. TO ROOF*

1/2 A OR 6" (152 mm) MIN.

3" (76 mm)

CONSTRUCTION NOTES

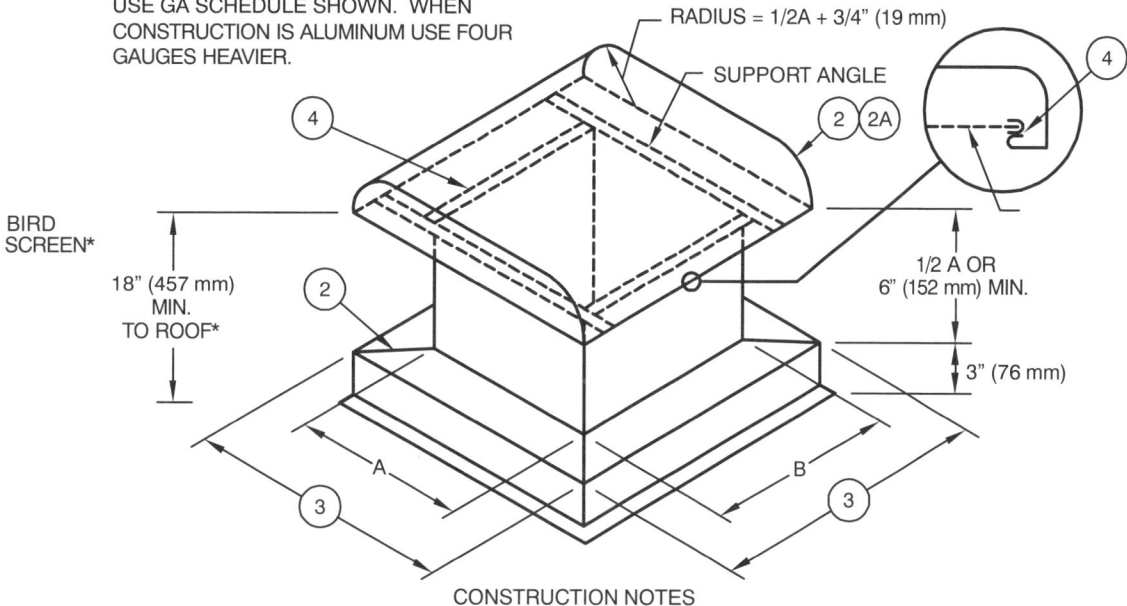

2. WELDED OR RIVETED AND SOLDERED.
2A. COVER END SEAMS ON UNITS MAY BE SEALED PITTSBURGH.
3. DIMENSIONS AS REQ'D. TO FLASH OVER CURB.
4. SUPPORT SCREEN ON 3/4" (19 mm) HEMMED FLANGE.

FIGURE 6–6 INTAKE OR EXHAUST VENTILATORS

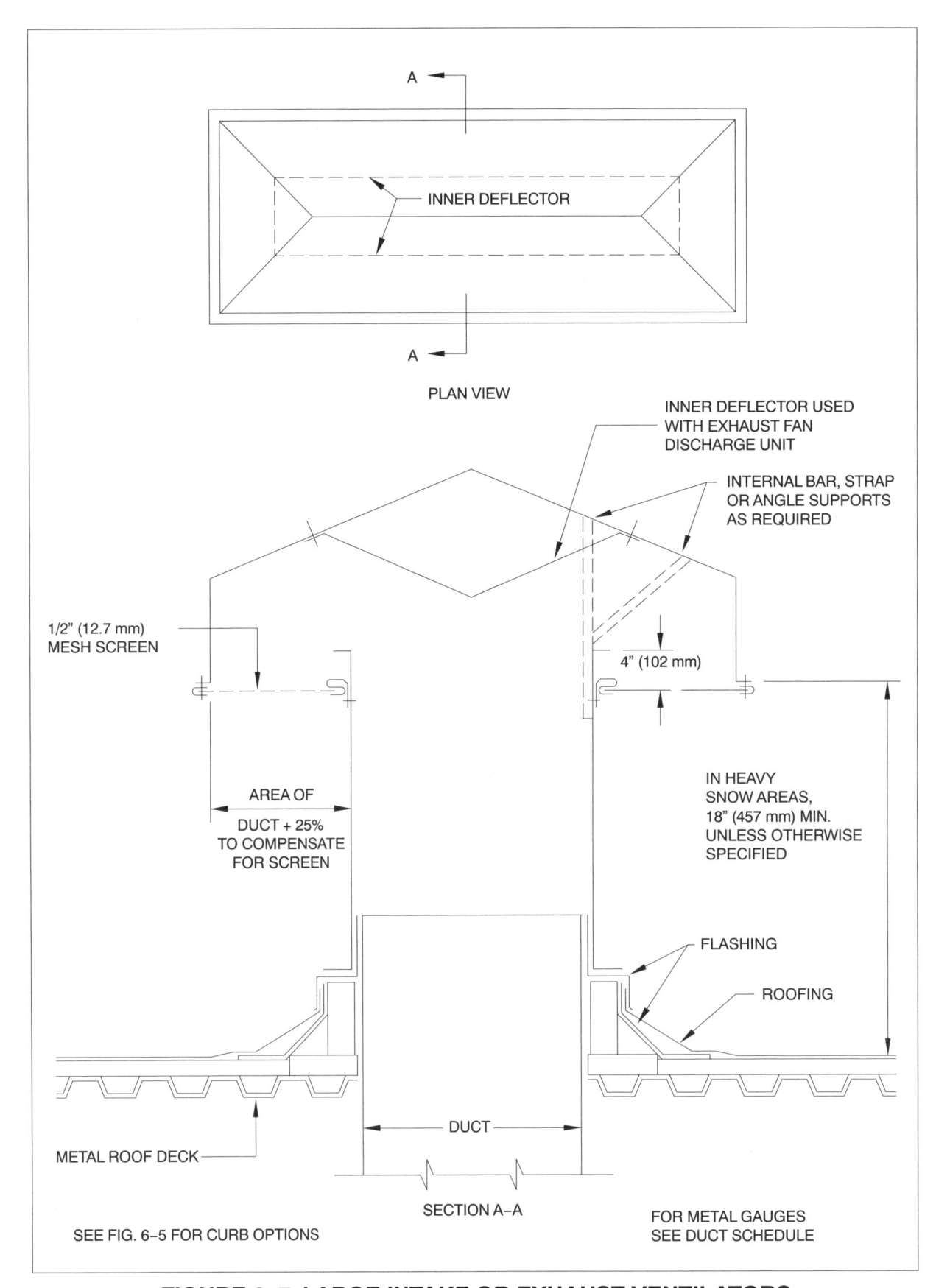

FIGURE 6-7 LARGE INTAKE OR EXHAUST VENTILATORS

CHAPTER 7

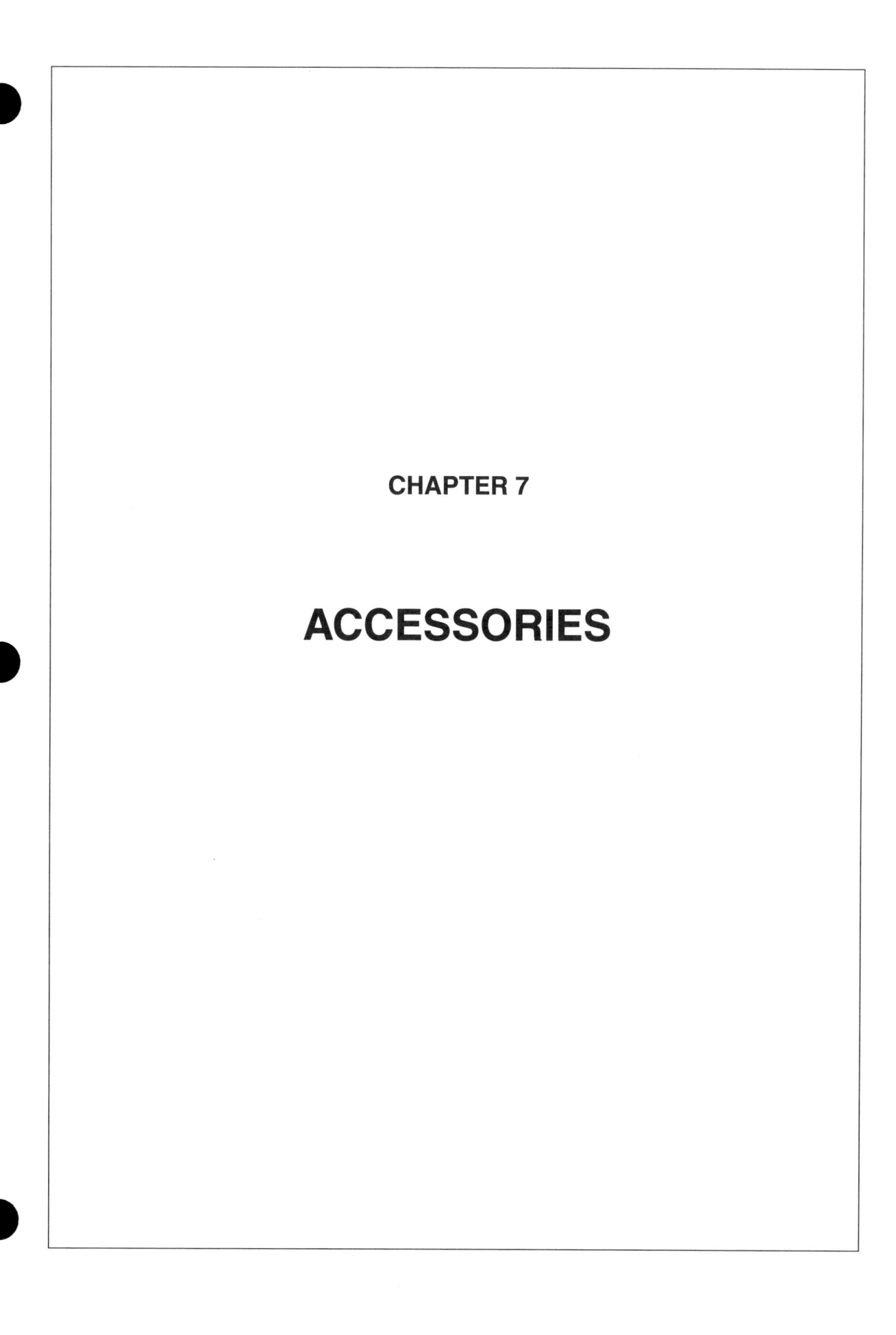

ACCESSORIES

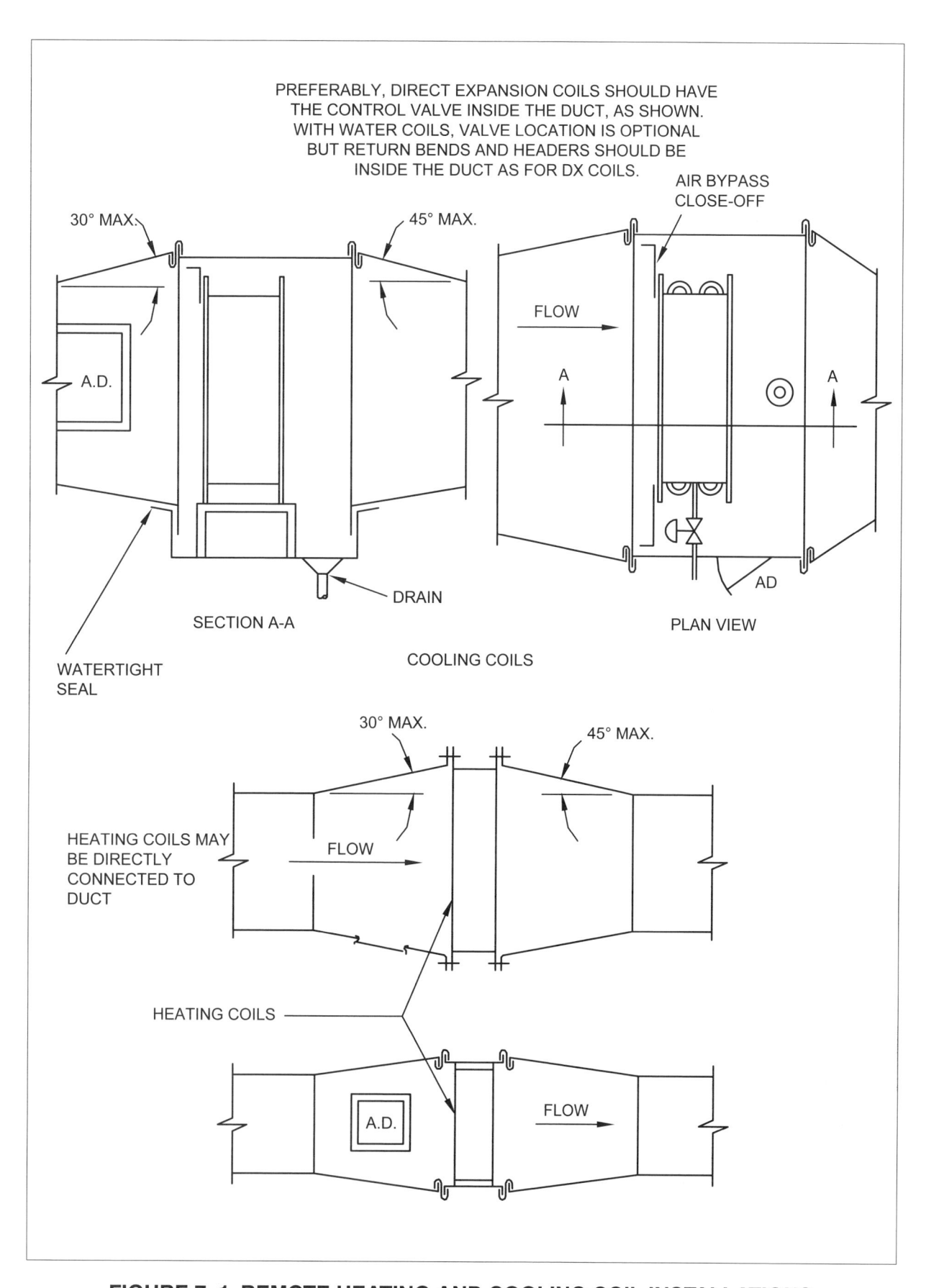

FIGURE 7–1 REMOTE HEATING AND COOLING COIL INSTALLATIONS

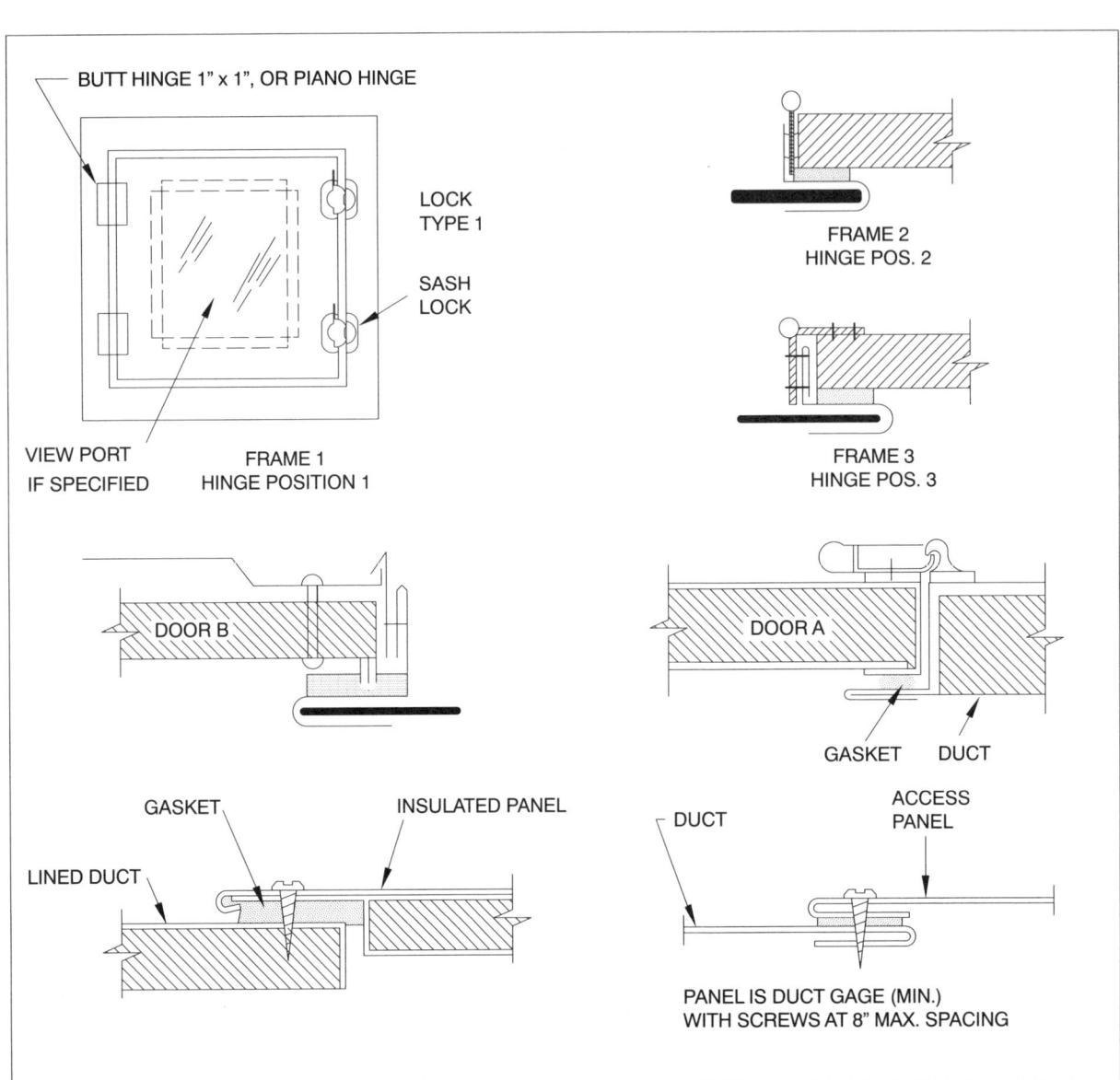

	Door Size	No. Hinges	No. Locks	Metal Gage - Frame	Metal Gage - Door	Metal Gage - Back
2" w.g. Static and Less	12" x 12"	2	1–S	24	26	26
	16" x 20"	2	2–S	22	24	26
	24" x 24"	3	2–S	22	22	26
3" w.g. Static	12" x 12"	2	1–S	22	22	26
	16" x 20"	2	1–S,1–T,1–B	20	20	26
	24" x 24"	3	2–S,1–T,1–B	20	20	24
4" w.g. to 10" w.g.	12" x 12"	2	1–S,1–T,1–B	20	20	26
	16" x 20"	3	2–S,1–T,1–B	20	18	24
	24" x 24"	3	2–S,2–T,2–B	18	18	24

S = Side opposite hinges, T = Top, B = Bottom

CONSTRUCTION AND AIRTIGHTNESS MUST BE SUITABLE FOR THE DUCT PRESSURE CLASS USED. THESE ILLUSTRATIONS DO NOT PRECLUDE THE USE OF OTHER METHODS AND HARDWARE.

FIGURE 7-2 DUCT ACCESS DOORS AND PANELS

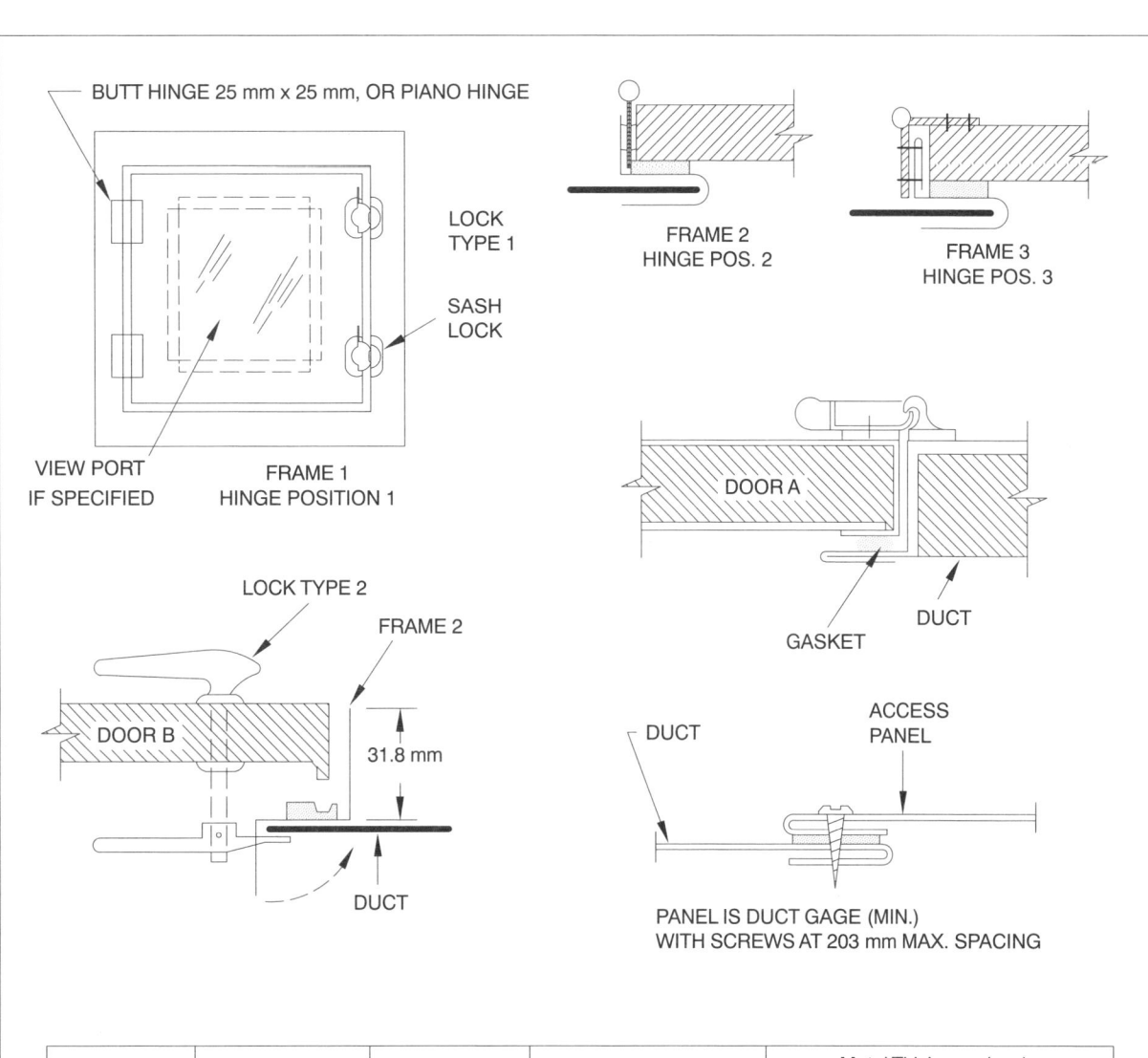

	Door Size (mm)	No. Hinges	No. Locks	Metal Thickness (mm)		
				Frame	Door	Back
500 Pa Static and Less	305 x 305	2	1-S	0.70	0.55	0.55
	406 x 508	2	2-S	0.85	0.70	0.55
	610 x 610	3	2-S	0.85	0.85	0.55
750 Pa Static	305 x 305	2	1-S	0.85	0.85	0.55
	406 x 508	2	1-S,1-T,1-B	1.00	1.00	0.55
	610 x 610	3	2-S,1-T,1-B	1.00	1.00	0.70
1000 Pa to 2500 Pa	305 x 305	2	1-S,1-T,1-B	1.00	1.00	0.55
	406 x 508	3	2-S,1-T,1-B	1.00	1.31	0.70
	610 x 610	3	2-S,2-T,2-B	1.31	1.31	0.70

S = Side opposite hinges, T = Top, B = Bottom

CONSTRUCTION AND AIRTIGHTNESS MUST BE SUITABLE FOR THE DUCT PRESSURE CLASS USED.

FIGURE 7-2M DUCT ACCESS DOORS AND PANELS

SPLIT SLEEVE

COMBINATION ACCESS
AND PRESSURE RELIEF
(MANUALLY OPERABLE
AND PRESSURE SENSITIVE
RELEASE LATCHES)

ROLLED HINGED
PLATE WITH
COMMERCIAL
CATCHES

A CONTOURED PANEL
WITH SCREW FASTENING
AND GASKET IS
ALSO ACCEPTABLE

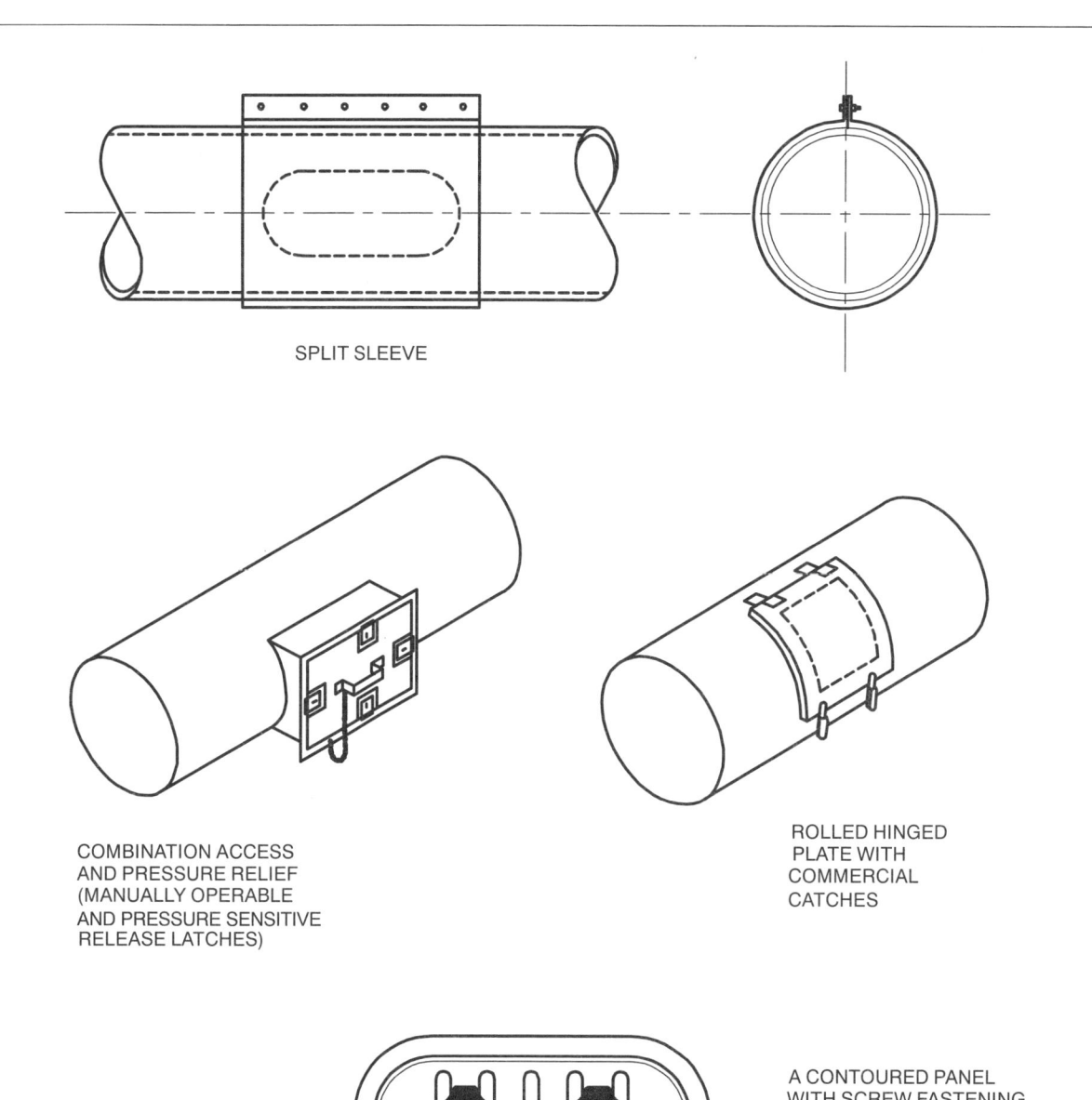

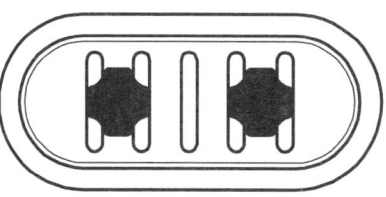

CLAMPING TYPE ACCESS DOOR

CONSTRUCTION AND AIRTIGHTNESS SHALL BE SUITABLE
FOR THE DUCT PRESSURE CLASS USED.

FIGURE 7-3 ACCESS DOORS – ROUND DUCT

7.1 VOLUME DAMPERS

7.2 NOTES FOR FIGURES 7–4 AND 7–5

1. Unless otherwise permitted, dampers shall be provided with the general configuration, materials, and application limits indicated in Figures 7–4 and 7–5 and in related notes.

2. Damper hardware must be durable and installed properly.

3. Dampers must be stable under operating conditions. Round and rectangular damper blades must be stiffened by forming or other method if required for the duty.

4. All single blade dampers must have a locking device to hold the dampers in a fixed position without vibration.

5. Damper component penetration of ducts must be closed, in keeping with the sealing classification applicable for the pressure class. End bearings or other seals are required on 3 in. wg (750 Pa) static pressure class.

6. The installation of a damper in a lined duct must not damage the liner or cause liner erosion.

7.3 COMMENTARY

Designers must show all required air volume control devices on the contract drawings. Nothing in this document implies an obligation to provide volume control devices that are not on the contract drawings.

The ASHRAE *Terminology Handbook* chapter on testing, adjusting, and balancing defines ducts as follows: a main duct serves the system's major or entire fluid flow; a sub-main serves two or more branch mains; a branch main serves two or more terminals; a branch serves a single terminal. Illustrating dampers on contract drawings relieves contractors from interpreting damper requirements.

The damper designs illustrated in Figures 7-4 and 7-5 are for reduced volume control, not for positive shut off. Modified versions can be constructed for tight shut off.

OBD (opposed blade damper) devices installed with grilles and diffusers should not be relied on to take more than ¼ to ½ closure without noise.

Splitters, extractors and scoops are not recommended.

Orifice plates or perforated metal with required pressure-drop characteristics may be used in lieu of dampers to set up permanent loss in duct runs.

Multiblade damper styles are normally parallel blade for two position operation; opposed blade for modulating position.

Dampers with blade lengths over 48 in. (1219 mm) are normally sectioned horizontally.

Motor operators for dampers should develop sufficient torque to operate properly. The motor supplier should select operators carefully. In certain cases, a fire damper may be used for flow rate control. If it serves a dual function, its operation as a fire damper must not be impaired. The installation must not develop noise or vibration.

Volume control devices that are capable of throttling flow over wide pressure diferentials without generating noise are normally special procurement items. Low-pressure drop dampers should not be used for wide-pressure differentials.

Consult duct design texts and manufacturer's data for loss coefficients.

The designer must carefully evaluate pressure change in ducts and provide pressure relief measures where necessary. System status changes, as in smoke control mode or energy conservation use, impose different requirements for normally open, normally closed, and modulating dampers.

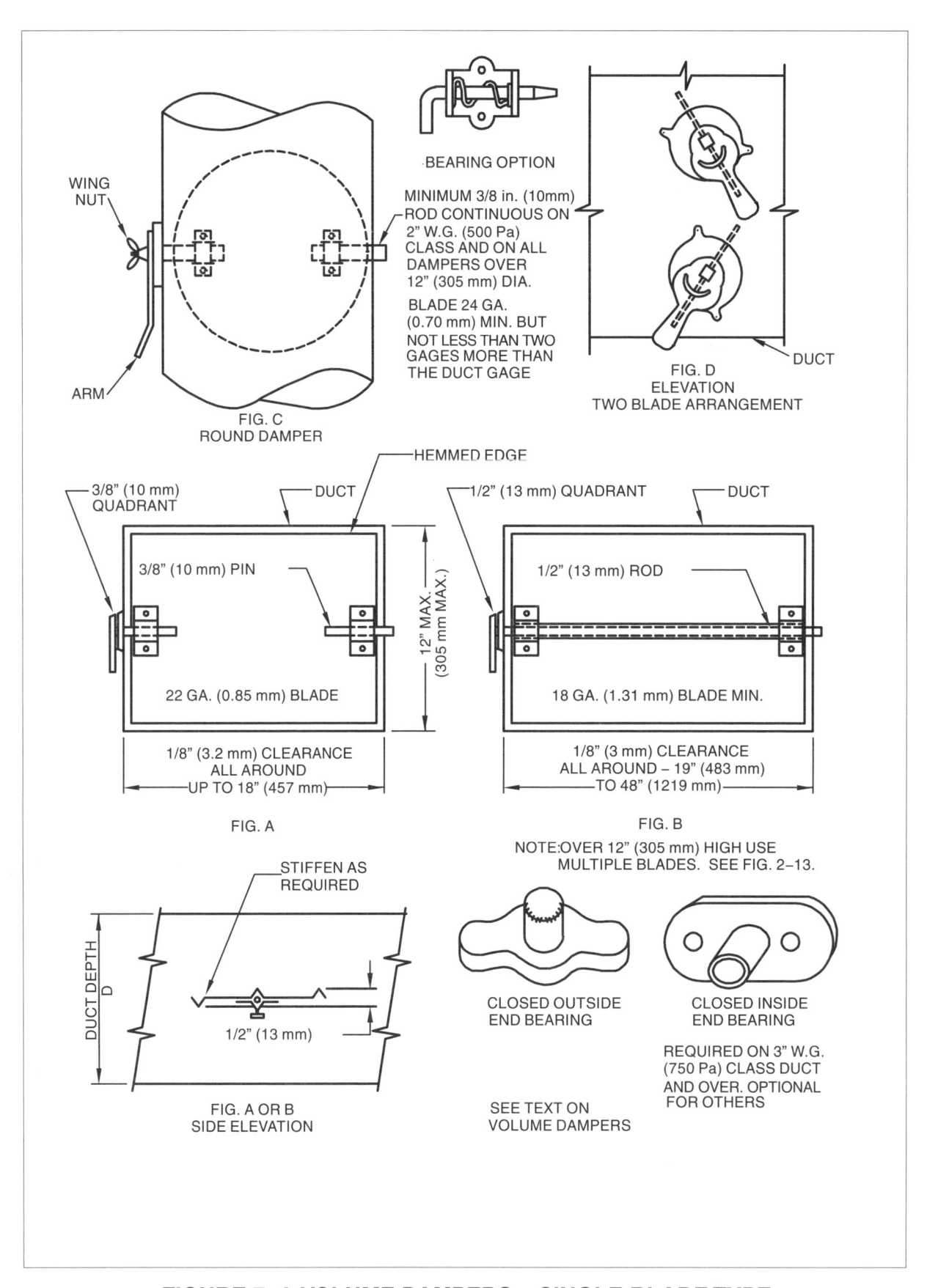

FIGURE 7–4 VOLUME DAMPERS – SINGLE BLADE TYPE

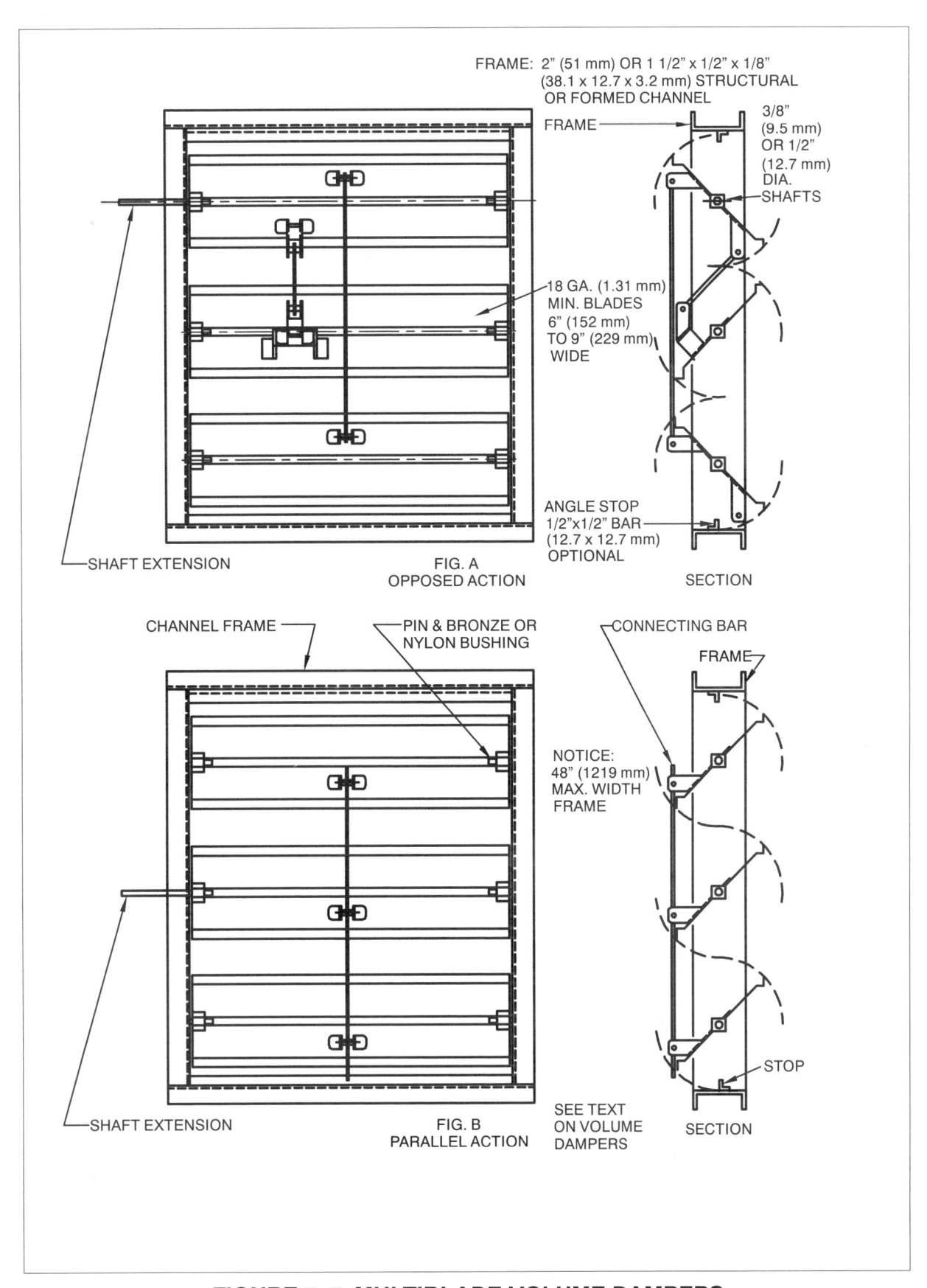

FIGURE 7-5 MULTIBLADE VOLUME DAMPERS

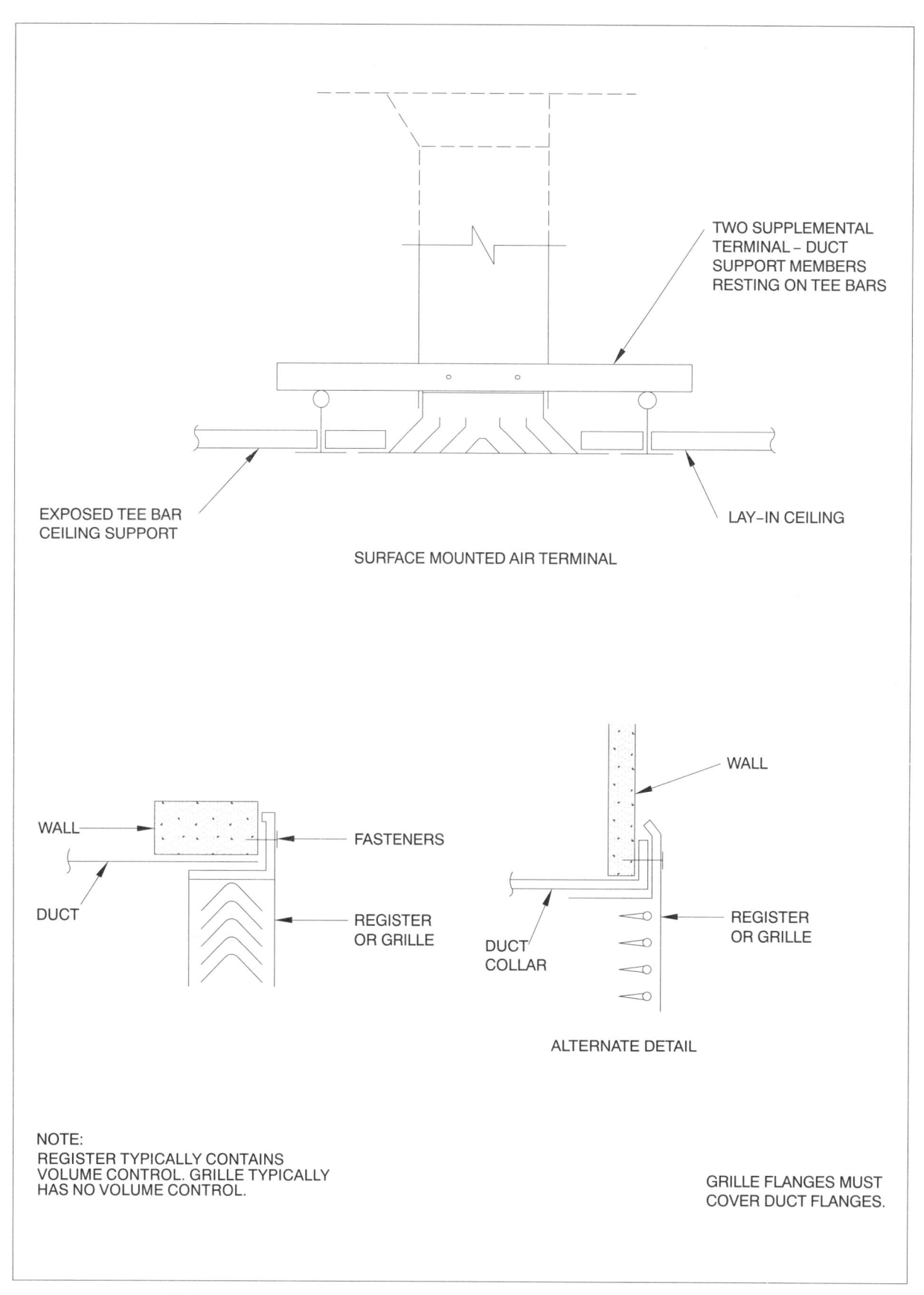

FIGURE 7-6 GRILLE AND REGISTER CONNECTIONS

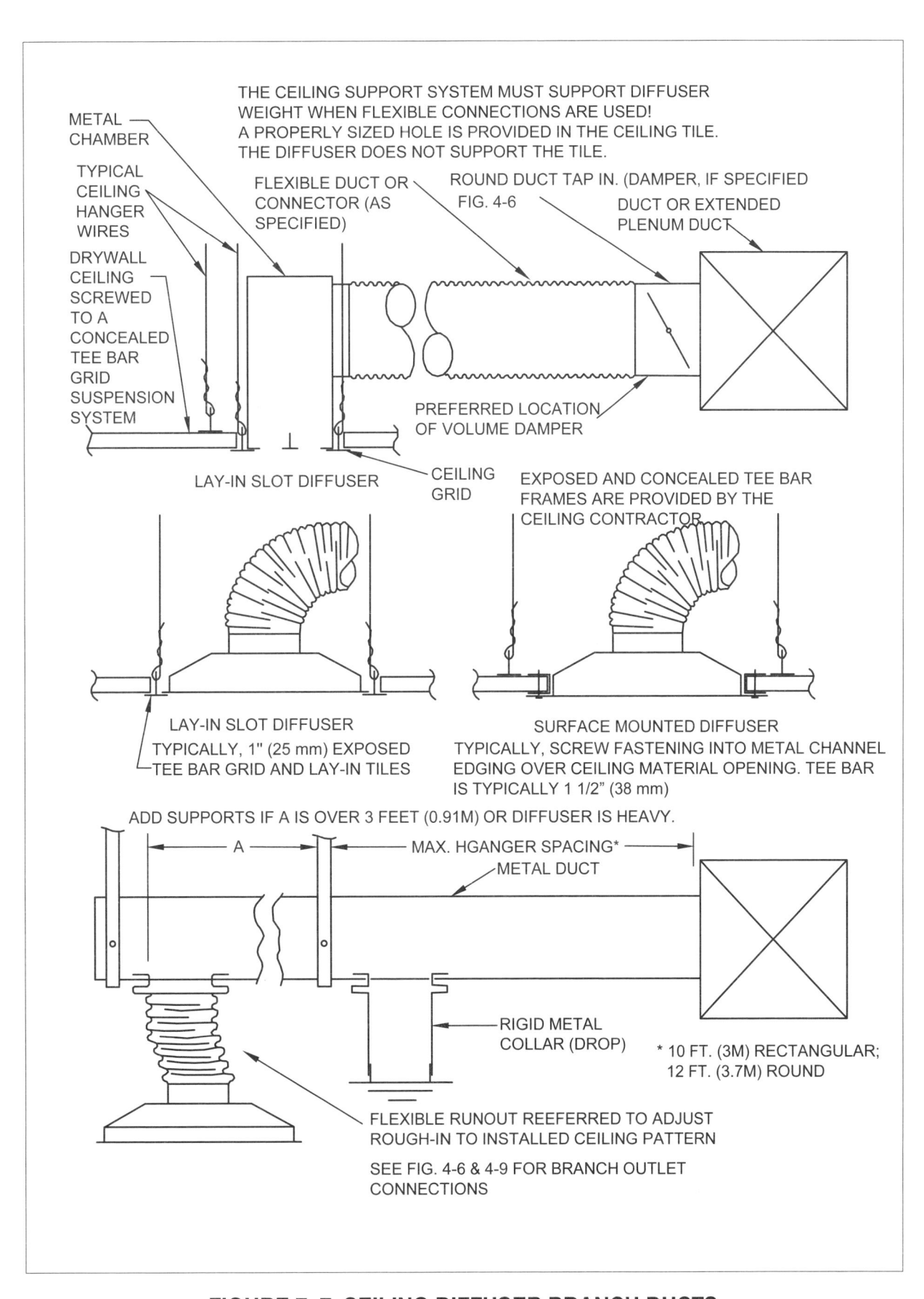

FIGURE 7–7 CEILING DIFFUSER BRANCH DUCTS

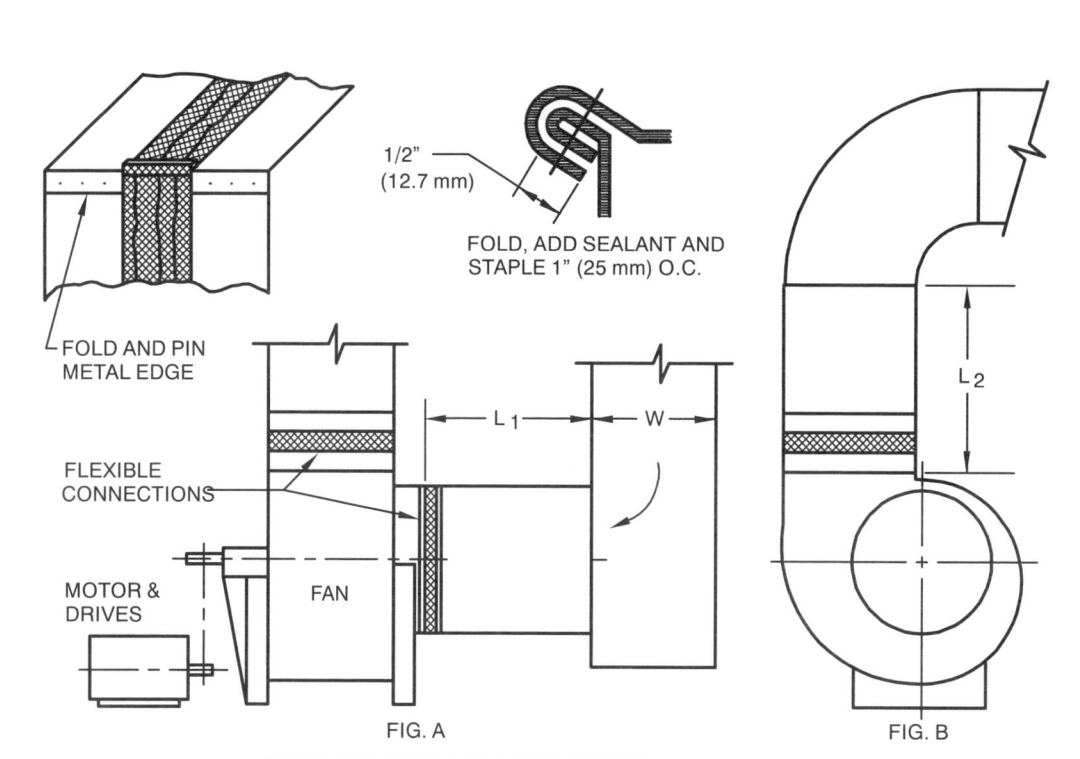

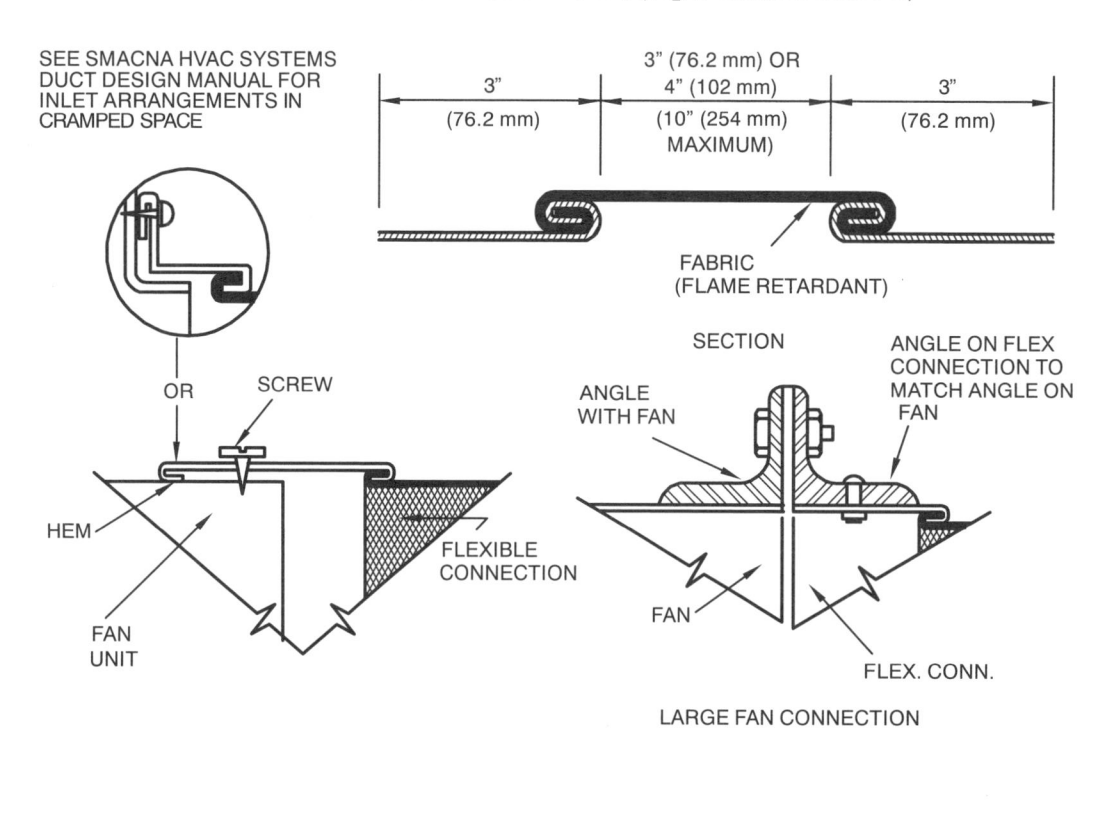

FIGURE 7-8 FLEXIBLE CONNECTIONS AT FAN

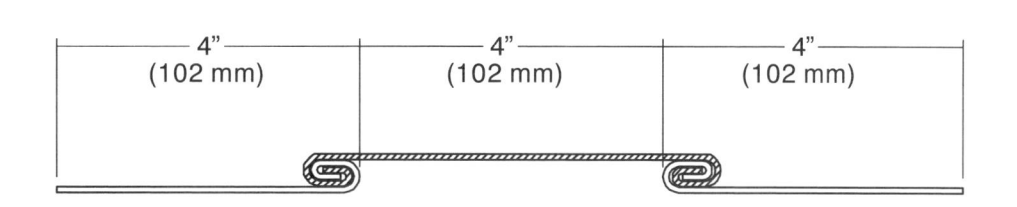

4/4/4 FLEX CONNECTION

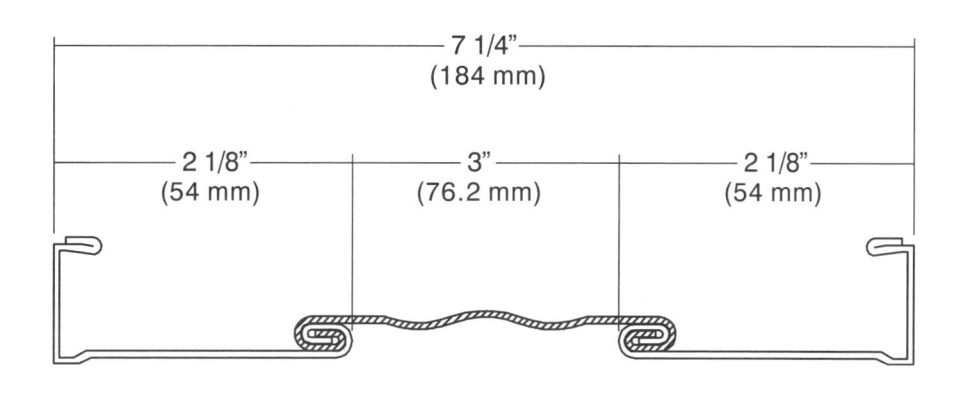

T-25 a FLANGES
ON A 4/4/4 FLEX CONNECTION

FIGURE 7-9 ALTERNATIVE FLEX CONNECTOR DETAILS

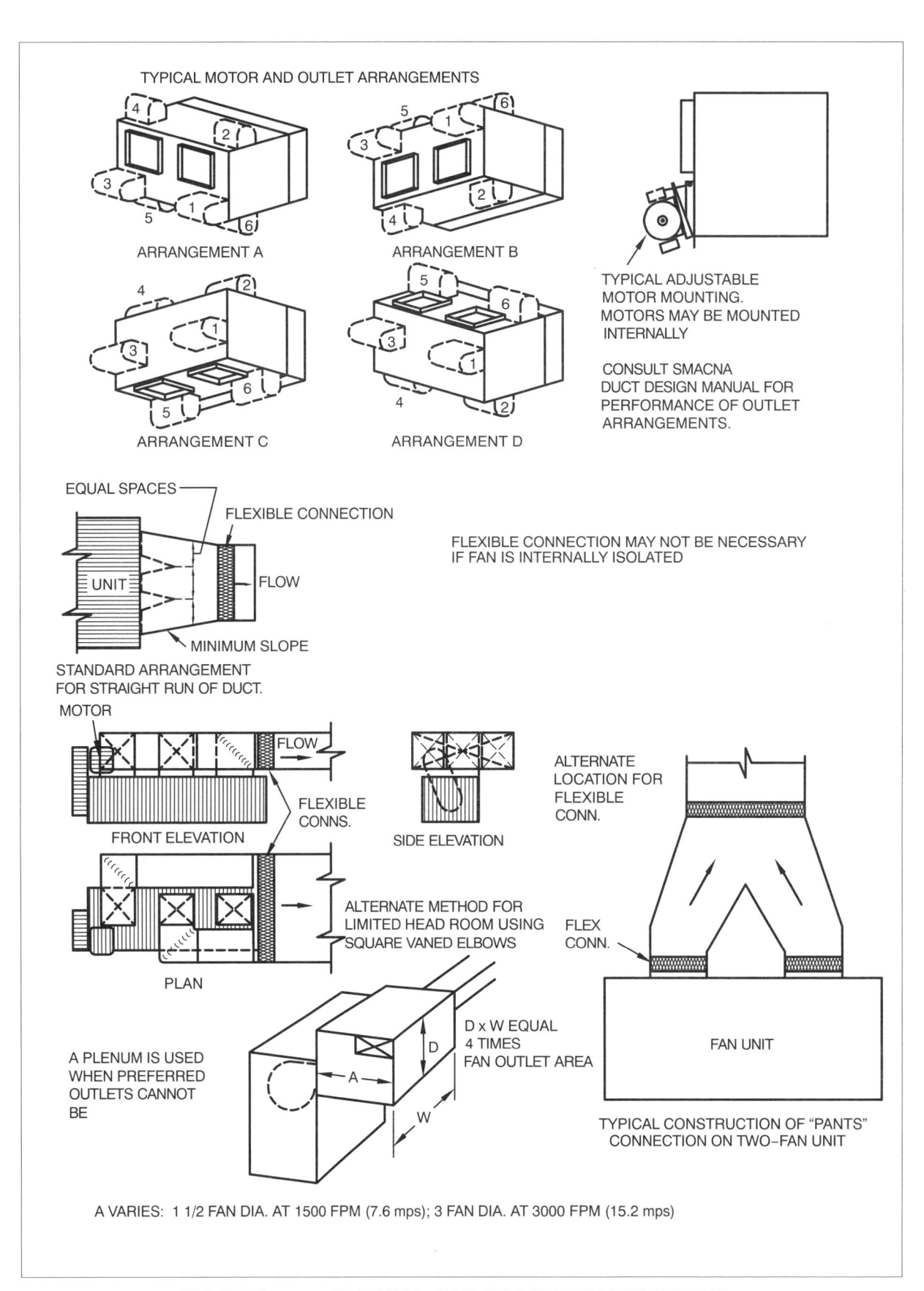

FIGURE 7-10 TYPICAL HVAC UNIT CONNECTIONS

NOTE:

SEE TYPICAL DUCT BRANCH ENTRY CONDITION IN FIG. 4-6.

METAL NOSING MUST BE USED WHEREVER LINER IS PRECEDED BY UNLINED METAL; OTHERWISE WHEN VELOCITY EXCEEDS 4000 FPM (20.3 MPS) USE METAL NOSING ON EVERY LEADING EDGE. NOSING MAY BE FORMED ON DUCT OR BE CHANNEL OR ZEE ATTACHED BY SCREWS, RIVETS OR WELDS.

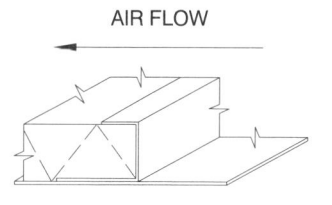

INTERIOR WIDTH OF 8" (200 mm) AND LESS DOES NOT REQUIRE PINS.

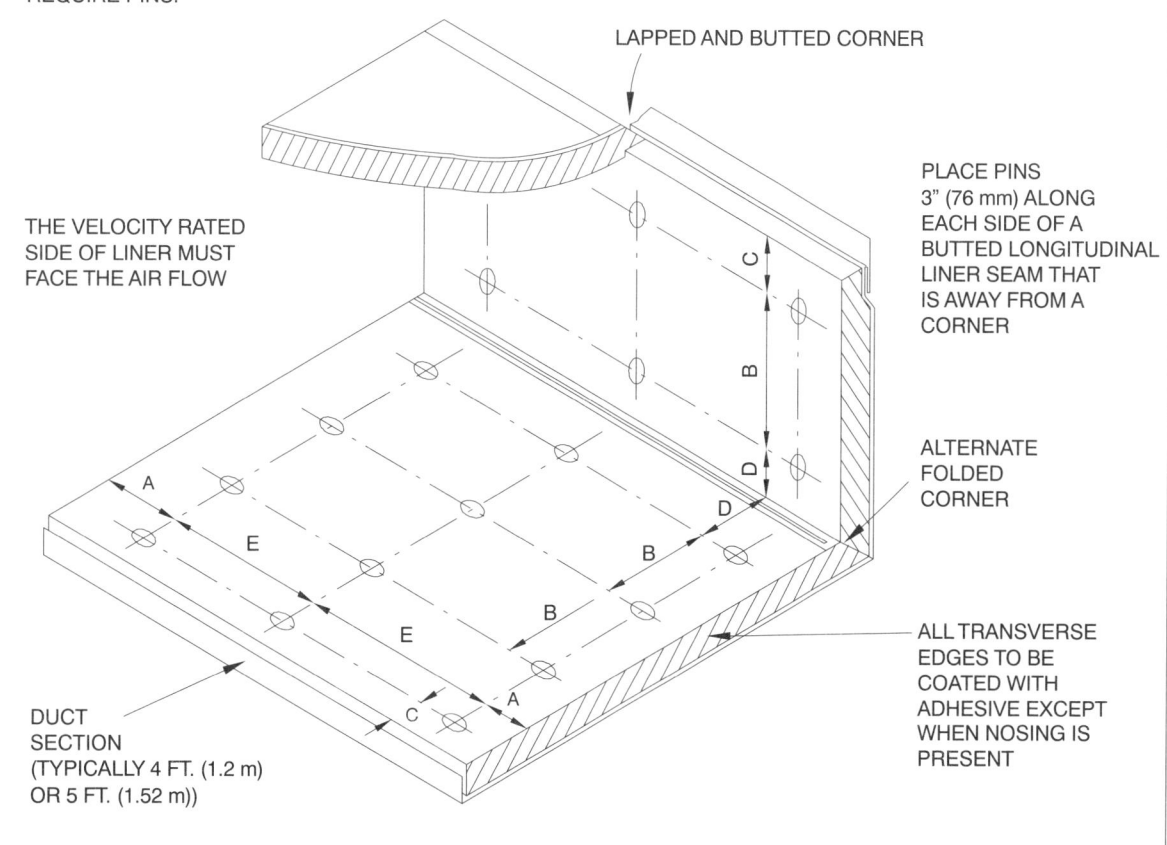

AIR FLOW

DETAIL – A
METAL NOSING
CHANNEL OR ZEE

LAPPED AND BUTTED CORNER

THE VELOCITY RATED SIDE OF LINER MUST FACE THE AIR FLOW

PLACE PINS 3" (76 mm) ALONG EACH SIDE OF A BUTTED LONGITUDINAL LINER SEAM THAT IS AWAY FROM A CORNER

ALTERNATE FOLDED CORNER

ALL TRANSVERSE EDGES TO BE COATED WITH ADHESIVE EXCEPT WHEN NOSING IS PRESENT

DUCT SECTION (TYPICALLY 4 FT. (1.2 m) OR 5 FT. (1.52 m))

MAXIMUM SPACING FOR FASTENERS. ACTUAL INTERVALS ARE APPROXIMATE.

"A" PIN ROW MAY BE OMITTED WHEN METAL NOSING IS USED. "E" THEN STARTS FROM THE NOSING.

LINER ADHERED TO THE DUCT WITH 90% MIN. AREA COVERAGE OF ADHESIVE

Velocity *	Dimensions				
	A	B	C	D	E
0 – 2500 FPM (0 – 12.7 MPS)	3" (76.2)	12" (305)	4" (102)	6" (152)	18" (457)
2501 – 6000 FPM (12.7 – 30.5 MPS)	3" (76.2)	6" (152)	4" (102)	6" (152)	16" (406)

* UNLESS A LOWER LEVEL IS SET BY MANUFACTURER OR LISTING AGENCY

FIGURE 7-11 FLEXIBLE DUCT LINER INSTALLATION

7.4 INSTALLATION STANDARDS FOR RECTANGULAR DUCTS USING FLEXIBLE LINER

S2.0 Flexible duct liner of the specified material, thickness, and density shall be furnished and installed where shown on the contract drawings.

S2.1 Unless otherwise indicated, the net free area of the duct dimensions given on the contract drawings shall be maintained. The duct dimensions shall be increased as necessary to compensate for liner thickness.

S2.2 The liner surface designated to be exposed shall face the airstream.

S2.3 Each layer of duct liner shall be attached with adequate coverage of adhesive at the liner contact surface area.

S2.4 All transversely oriented edges of fibrous liner not receiving metal nosing shall be coated with adhesive. Liner shall be neatly butted without gaps at transverse joints and fibrous liner shall be coated with adhesive at such joints before butting. Non-fibrous liner is not required to have the edges coated with adhesive.

S2.5 Liner shall be folded and compressed in the corners of rectangular duct sections or shall be cut and fit to ensure butted edge overlapping. Longitudinal joints in the duct liner shall not occur except at the corners of ducts, unless the size of the duct and standard liner product dimensions make them necessary.

S2.6 Ducts with interior widths of 8 in. (203 mm) or less do not require mechanical fasteners in addition to adhesive. Non-fibrous liners using a "peel and stick" adhesive, or that utilize a quick drying adhesive do not require mechanical fasteners.

S2.7 Except as noted in S2.6, mechanical fasteners shall be located with respect to interior dimensions and regardless of airflow direction as in the accompanying table and in Figure 7–11.

S2.8 Longitudinal joints in liners shall be coated with adhesive when velocities over 2500 fpm (12.7 mps) are anticipated.

S2.9 Metal nosings that are either channel or zee profile or are integrally formed from the duct wall shall be securely installed over transversely oriented liner edges facing the airstream, at fan discharge and at any interval of lined duct preceded by unlined duct. In addition, where velocities exceed 4000 fpm (20.3 mps), metal nosing shall be used on upstream edges of liner at every transverse joint.

S2.10 Where dampers, turning vane assemblies, or other devices are placed inside lined ducts or fittings, the installation must not damage the liner or cause erosion of the liner. The use of metal hat sections or other buildout means is optional; when used, buildouts shall be secured to the duct wall with bolts, screws, rivets, or welds.

S2.11 Liners shall also be installed with mechanical fastening devices that:

   a. Are spaced in accordance with Figure 7-11,

   b. When installed, are as corrosion resistant as G60 coated galvanized steel,

   c. Will not adversely affect the fire resistance classification of liner and adhesives,

   d. Do not damage the liner when applied as recommended by the manufacturer,

   e. Do not cause leakage in the duct,

Velocity	Transversely Around Perimeter	Longitudinally
2500 fpm (12.7 mps) and less	At 4 in. (102 mm) from longitudinal liner edges, at 6 in. (152 mm) from folded corners and at intervals not exceeding 12 in. (305 mm)	At 3 in. (76 mm) from transverse joints and at intervals not exceeding 18 in. (457 mm)
2501 fpm (12.7 mps) to 6000 fpm (30.5 mps)	At 4 in. (102 mm) from longitudinal liner edges, at 6 in. (152 mm) from folded corners and at intervals not exceeding 6 in. (152 mm)	At 3 in. (76 mm) from transverse joints and at intervals not exceeding 16 in. (406 mm)

f. Do not project more than nominally into the airstream,

g. Will indefinitely sustain a 50 lb. (22.7 Kg) tensile dead load test perpendicular to the duct wall,

h. Are the correct length specified for the liner thickness used, and

i. Are installed with pins perpendicular to the duct wall.

7.5 COMMENTARY

These standards assume that the designer of a duct system has:

a. Examined the liner reference texts listed in the front of this document;

b. Clearly designated on the contract drawings the amount of ductwork to receive lining;

c. Specified the type of liner, the thickness and density of liner and the type of liner, adhesive to be used;

d. Determined that the specified liner materials have the acoustical, friction loss, and other performance characteristics required for the application; and

e. Provided for condensation control where the interruption of the liner would cause a problem.

Typically, duct liner is of flexible material of 1 in. (25 mm) thickness and 1½ lbs. per cubic foot (24 Kg/m3) density. It is primarily used for its sound absorption characteristics, although it may have some thermal resistance value. Metal wall inner lining is available for all conventional duct shapes; typically it is of 22 gage (0.85 mm) galvanized steel with 3/32 in. (2.4 mm) diameter holes on 3/16 in. (4.8 mm) or ¼ in. (6.4 mm) centers. The double-wall style of lined duct is used where increased resistance to damage is desired or where erosion of the inner surface might occur.

Standard flexible liner is normally shop-installed. Minor damage to the liner surface may occur in transportation and handling. Small cuts, tears, or abrasions may be repaired with fire retardant adhesive. Material that has significant damage cannot be considered to be in new condition.

Liner is normally prequalified for a certain resistance to moisture absorption, mold growth, and degradation from high humidity. Occasional exposure to wet weather during transportation or to prebuilding enclosure conditions in new construction does not necessarily impair the liner's performance. In such cases, drying or other corrective measures recommended by the material manufacturer should be followed.

Installing two layers of material to meet a minimum liner thickness is not recommended. For special circumstances, when it must be done, 90 percent minimum adhesive coverage of each layer should make the two layers act as one. In addition, pay special attention to the leading edge conditions.

Normally, duct linings must be interrupted at fire dampers (to avoid adverse effects on damper operation) and at heat sources (to meet minimum clearances specified in an equipment listing).

Note: Some appliances are rated for a zero clearance to combustible material.

Liner adhesives are usually water-based or solvent-based, and they may be flammable in wet or dry states. Designers should select adhesives that meet construction and code requirements. So-called safety standards may involve tests that report various characteristics but do not meet up to a hazard classification under installed conditions. Contractors are invited to follow ventilation, storage, and other precautions published by the adhesive manufacturers.

7.5.1 Liner Fastener Commentary

Three types of fasteners are commonly used with duct liners. For each type of fastener, a specific pin length is appropriate for each type and thickness of liners. It is important that the proper pin length be used; otherwise a faulty installation will result.

Fasteners designed to be secured with adhesives have a large base on which to apply the adhesive. After waiting enough time to achieve adequate bond strength which will vary, depending on the air temperature, impale the duct liner on the pin and add the spring clip or washer.

Mechanically secured fasteners form a positive attachment to the sheet metal. Typically, they are impact-applied, hardened steel fasteners which bite into the sheet metal.

Weld-secured fasteners are attached by two techniques: resistance welding and capacitance discharge welding. Correct adjustment of the timing devices is necessary to obtain a solid weld without burn-through.

The type of pin that is applied before duct liner installation takes a spring-clip or washer. Pins with pre-at-Attached caps are pressed through the insulation and attached to the duct in a single operation.

Depending on the type of fastener, discoloration or dimpling may be evident when fasteners are properly attached to the sheet metal. This does not affect the serviceability of the fastener or of the sheet metal.

7.6 INSTALLATION STANDARDS FOR SINGLE WALL, ROUND DUCT INSULATION DUCT LINERS

a. Determine Circumference of the round duct. Obtain the actual circumference of the round duct to be lined. Duct diameters vary due to differences in metal gauge and fabrication equipment, it is important to determine internal circumference using a flat flexible tape.

b. Unless otherwise indicated, the net free area of the duct diameter given on the contract drawings shall be maintained. The duct diameter shall be increased as necessary to compensate for liner thickness.

c. Single Wall, Round duct liner of the specified material, thickness, R value and NRC rating shall be furnished and installed where shown on the contract drawings.

d. The liner surface designated to be exposed shall face the airstream.

e. Calculate stretch-out dimension of single wall, Round Duct Insulation material. The Initial stretch-out dimension should be cut approximately ½" less than the actual measured duct circumference. Always cut a trial liner strip to verify correct stretch out for tight, snug fit within the round pipe.

f. Any excess product remaining after stretch out is determined, exceeding the length of the single wall round insulation, shall be spliced together utilizing a UL 181 approved pressure sensitive tape, UL approved closure method, or manufacturers recommended closure method before the final product is measured and trimmed.

g. All Longitudinal joints in liner must apply closure tabs perpendicular to the butt-edge seam, approximately 6" (minimum)-12" (maximum) on centers, three to six per side. The installer must reference the manufacturer's closure method for all longitudinal seams for the product being applied for the installation.

7.6.1 Single Wall Round Applications Requiring Additional Support or Mechanical Fastening:

a. Round Ducts Using single wall, kerfed, rigid board insulation liners do not normally require pins, adhesive or other types of mechanical securement in straight duct sections. However, there are several applications where fastening may be necessary:

- Applications where the insulation slides easily in the duct (loose fit), as with smaller, slip fit diameters.

- In systems where high-velocity fans will be operated before the duct system installation is completed.

- In very large (> 60" ID) duct sections prior to the installation of connection flanges or reinforcement rings.

- In any duct where the round shape will not be retained after installation, such as in special clearance fittings or architectural design applications.

- Vertical runs or other risers greater than 45° from horizontal.

- Where the vertical drop exceeds 16 feet, clips must be installed on every other liner section and finished with a row on the end section. Clips must be applied around the duct circumference, maximum 12" on center, with a minimum of three clips per liner section.

- In addition to the clips described above, vertical duct runs of 60" ID or greater must have mechanical fasteners (weld pins or metal screws with washers) on 24" centers (max.) at the upstream and downstream edges of each liner section. The fasteners should be approximately 3" in from the ends of the liner section.

- Partial liner applications, where single wall round duct lining ends and unlined metal continues. The downstream (last) section of liner must be mechanically secured.

- Mechanical fasteners shall be located with respect to interior dimensions of the round pipe section and regardless of airflow direction

- Negative Pressure Applications

- Some Round Duct Applications do not require mechanical fasteners or adhesives as the insulation is considered self-supporting. Please reference the manufacturer's guidelines for specific application recommendations and mechanical fastening schedules for the product being installed.

7.6.2 Single Wall Round Applications Requiring Nosings:

A. All transversely oriented edges of the liner shall receive a metal nosing at fan discharge and at any interval of lined duct preceded by unlined duct. The first exposed, transverse edge of the liner on the edge facing the air stream (first section of liner following unlined duct) must receive a metal nosing.

B. All transversely oriented edges of liner, not receiving metal nosing, shall be neatly butted without gaps at the transverse joint. Any transverse joint with greater than 1/8" gap shall be coated with adhesive or duct sealant at such joints as per manufacturer's instructions.

C. Any leading edge of the insulation exposed to airflow by normal or emergency system operation must have a metal nosing.

Fastening Requirements for Negative Pressure Systems

Where negative pressure greater than 0.5" w.g. (125 Pa) exist, or in any supply air duct that may be used for emergency smoke exhaust, the use of mechanical fasteners to secure Single Wall Round Insulation Liners into the air duct is required. The minimum requirements for fastening are described below:

- Care should be taken during installation to cut the insulation sections to the tight end of the recommended size range.

- Any insulation that will be exposed to negative pressure must be secured with mechanical fasteners, 3" (75mm) in from the ends of each insulation section and as needed to maintain a spacing not to exceed 6 ft. (1.8m). The fasteners should be spaced evenly around the circumference of the duct, with the spacing not to exceed 16 in. (400 mm).

Additional Considerations:

S2.10 Where dampers, turning vane assemblies, or other devices are placed inside lined ducts or fittings, the installation must not damage the liner or cause erosion of the liner. The use of metal hat sections or other build out means is optional; when used, build outs shall be secured to the duct wall with bolts, screws, rivets, or welds.

S2.11 Liners shall also be installed with mechanical fastening devices that:

a. When installed, are as corrosion resistant as G60 coated galvanized steel,

b. Will not adversely affect the fire resistance classification of liner and adhesives,

c. Do not damage the liner when applied as recommended by the manufacturer,

d. Do not cause leakage in the duct

e. Will indefinitely sustain a 50 lb. (22.7 Kg) tensile dead load test perpendicular to the duct wall,

f. Are the correct length specified for the liner thickness used, and

g. Are installed with pins perpendicular to the duct wall.

h. Do not project more than nominally into the airstream

7.7 COMMENTARY

These standards assume that the designer of a duct system has:

a. Examined the liner reference texts listed in the front of this document;

b. Clearly designated on the contract drawings the amount of ductwork to receive lining;

c. Specified the type of liner, the thickness, the R value and the NRC rating of the liner as well as the needed fasteners and adhesive to be used;

d. Determined that the specified liner materials have the acoustical, friction loss, and other performance characteristics required for the application; and

e. Provided for condensation control where the interruption of the liner would cause a problem.

Typically, duct liner is primarily used for its sound absorption characteristics, although it does have thermal resistance value as well. Molded round liner is available. Single wall lined applications, can be used where weight restrictions, acoustical and thermal needs may be required.

Standard Single Wall Round Duct liner is normally shop-installed. Minor damage to the liner surface may occur in transportation and handling. Small cuts, tears, or abrasions may be repaired with fire retardant adhesive.

Material that has significant damage cannot be considered to be in new condition.

Liner is normally prequalified for a certain resistance to moisture absorption, mold growth, and degradation from high humidity. Occasional exposure to wet weather during transportation or to prebuilding enclosure conditions in new construction does not necessarily impair the liner's performance. In such cases, drying or other corrective measures recommended by the material manufacturer should be followed.

Normally, duct linings must be interrupted at fire dampers (to avoid adverse effects on damper operation) and at heat sources (to meet minimum clearances specified in an equipment listing).

Note: Some appliances are rated for a zero clearance to combustible material.

Liner adhesives are usually water-based or solvent-based, and they may be flammable in wet or dry states. Designers should select adhesives that meet construction and code requirements. So-called safety standards may involve tests that report various characteristics but do not meet up to a hazard classification under installed conditions. Contractors are invited to follow ventilation, storage, and other precautions published by the adhesive manufacturers.

Contractors installing single wall round duct insulation should reference the manufacturers guidelines for the product for any detailed or specific information relevant to the application or installation of the specific product being used to avoid any installation or warranty violations of the product.

7.7.1 Liner Fastener Commentary

Three types of fasteners are commonly used with duct liners. For each type of fastener, a specific pin length is appropriate for each type and thickness of liners. It is important that the proper pin length be used; otherwise a faulty installation will result.

Fasteners designed to be secured with adhesives have a large base on which to apply the adhesive. After waiting enough time to achieve adequate bond strength which will vary, depending on the air temperature, impale the duct liner on the pin and add the spring clip or washer.

Mechanically secured fasteners form a positive attachment to the sheet metal. Typically, they are impact-applied, hardened steel fasteners which bite into the sheet metal.

Weld-secured fasteners are attached by two techniques: resistance welding and capacitance discharge welding. Correct adjustment of the timing devices is necessary to obtain a solid weld without burn-through.

The type of pin that is applied before duct liner installation takes a spring-clip or washer. Pins with pre-at-Attached caps are pressed through the insulation and attached to the duct in a single operation.

Depending on the type of fastener, discoloration or dimpling may be evident when fasteners are properly attached to the sheet metal. This does not affect the serviceability of the fastener or of the sheet metal.

FIGURE 7-12 LINER FASTENERS

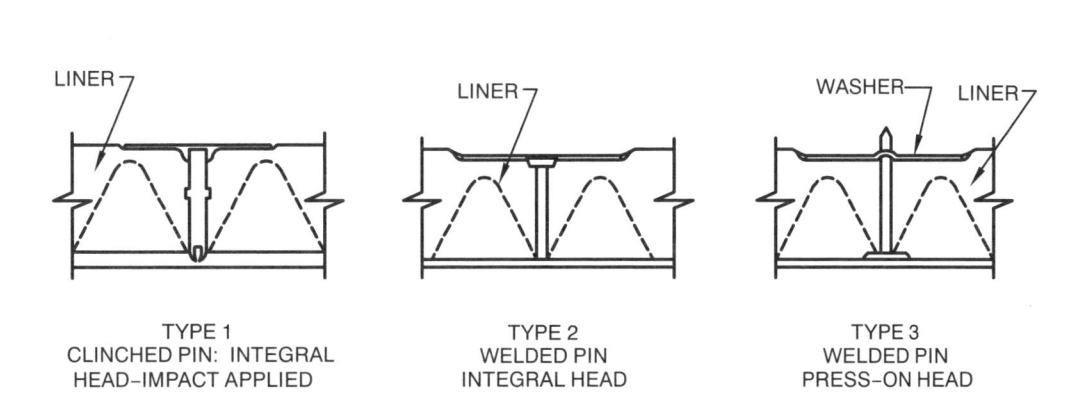

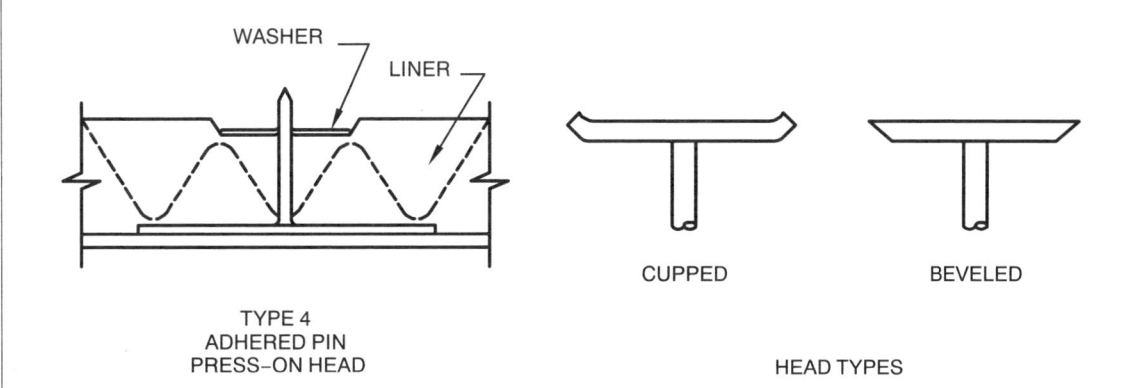

INSTALLED PINS AND WASHERS SHALL NOT COMPRESS LINER MORE THAN THE CORRECT LENGTH SPECIFIED FOR THE LINEAR THICKNESS USED.

STANDARD SYMBOLS NOW REFLECT THE PROPER DESIGNATION FOR SHOWING DUCT LINER ON DRAWINGS. DUCT DIMENSIONS DESIGNATE NET FREE AREA.

ACOUSTICAL LINING DUCT DIMENSIONS FOR NET FREE AREA	

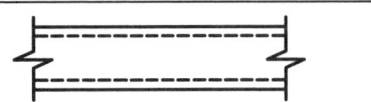

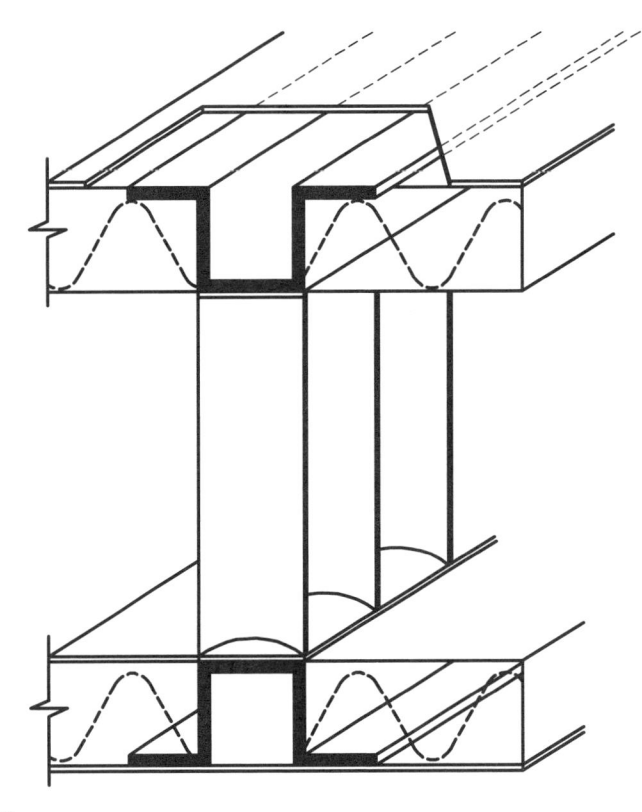

* HAT SECTION USED AS INSULATED "BUILD OUT". BUILD OUT IS ATTACHED TO DUCT WITH SHEET
* METAL SCREWS, BOLTS OR WELDS.
  usage range 4001 FPM (20.3 mps) – 6000 FPM (30.5 mps)

VANES AND DAMPERS MUST BE INSULATED IN A MANNER THAT WILL NOT DISRUPT LINER, RESTRICT DAMPER OPERATION OR INCREASE FRICTION LOSS.

FIGURE 7-13 OPTIONAL HAT SECTION

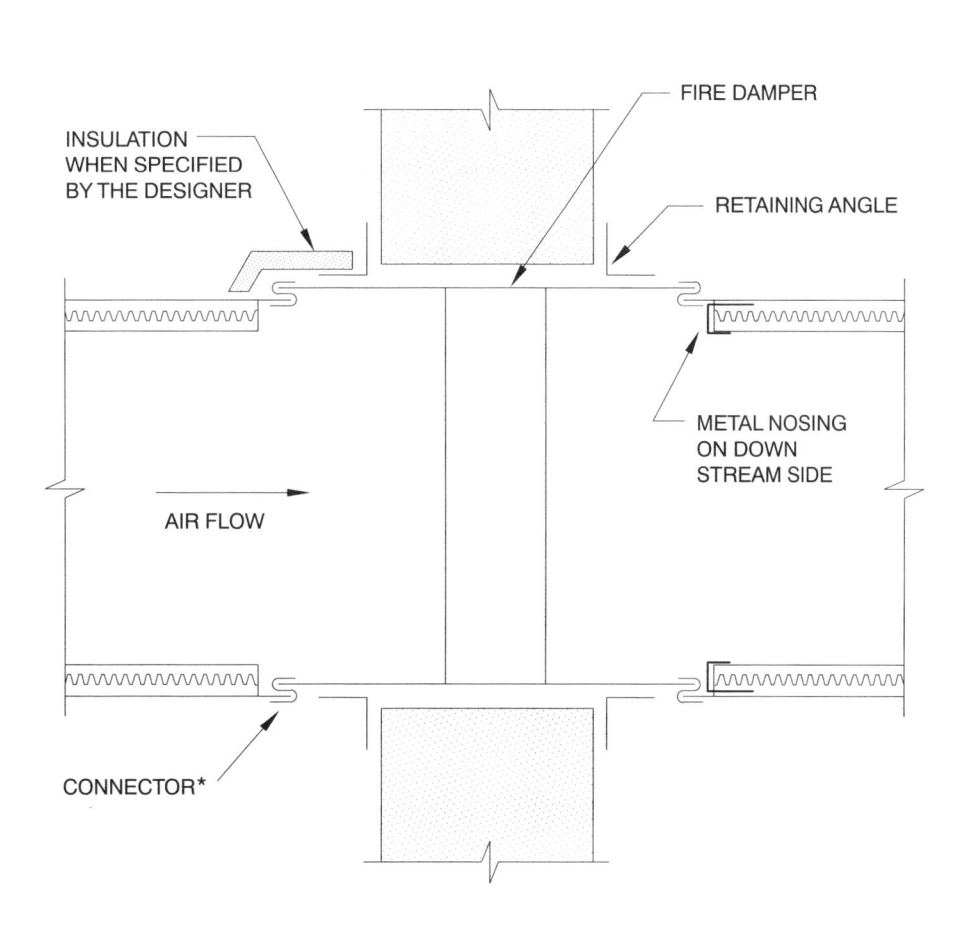

Interruption of duct liner at fire damper (to avoid impairing damper operation) is required by NFPA Standard 90A. Where 90A is applicable, installation may be made as shown and should otherwise conform to the Duct Liner Installation Standards.

The designer should consider the possibility and consequences of condensation occuring on unlined or uninsulated metal at penetrations and should specify control measures.

This illustration and text does not address features of fire damper installations unrelated to duct liner.

* S Slip illustrated; see type of connections permitted as a condition of damper listing.

FIGURE 7-14 DUCT LINER INTERRUPTION

THIS PAGE INTENTIONALLY LEFT BLANK

CHAPTER 8

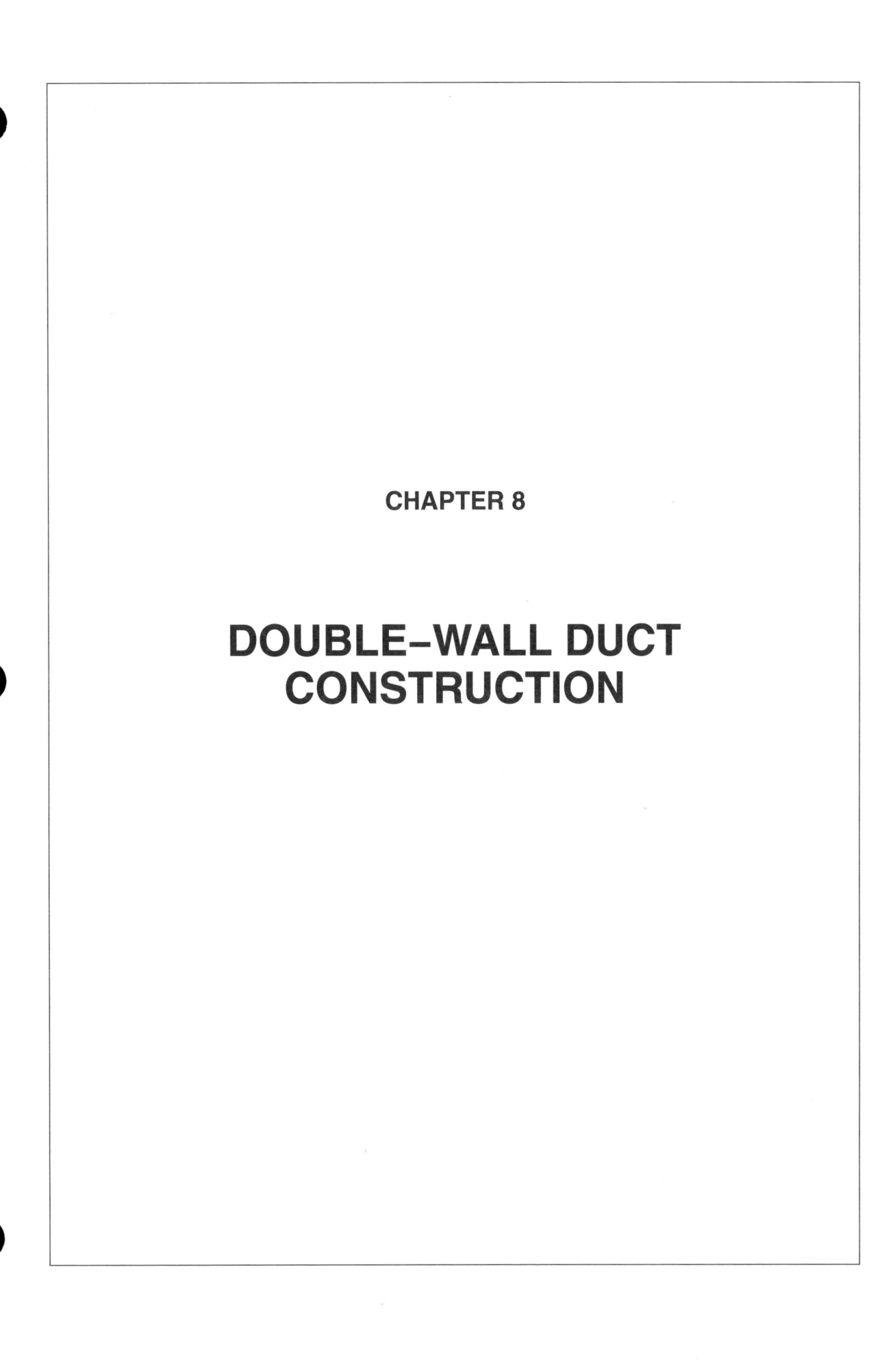

DOUBLE-WALL DUCT CONSTRUCTION

CHAPTER 8 — DOUBLE–WALL DUCT CONSTRUCTION

8.1 INSTALLATION STANDARDS COMMENTARY

Double-wall rigid duct is used for its acoustical value, and the perforated (metal typically) inner wall provides resistance to erosion of the duct liner.

The outer shell is the structural (pressure) shell and is the basis of construction. Unless otherwise indicated, the net free area of the duct dimensions given on the contract drawings shall be maintained. The duct dimensions shall be increased as necessary to compensate for liner thickness.

Metal wall inner lining is available for all conventional duct shapes; typically it is of 22 ga (0.85 mm) galvanized steel with 3/32 in. (2.4 mm) diameter holes on 3/16 in. (4.8 mm) or ¼ in. (6.4 mm) centers. The double-wall style of lined duct is used where increased resistance to damage is desired or where erosion of the inner surface might occur.

Where dampers, turning vane assemblies, or other devices are placed inside lined ducts or fittings, the installation must not damage the liner or cause erosion of the liner. The use of metal hat sections or other buildout means is optional; when used, buildouts shall be secured to the duct wall with bolts, screws, rivets, or welds.

Hanger and support requirements shall be calculated to be in conformance with Chapter 5 based on the size and weight of the double-wall duct system.

Equipment and casings requirements shall be in conformance with Chapter 9. Casing for negative pressure greater than 3 in. wg (750 Pa) may be constructed in accordance with the SMACNA *Rectangular Industrial Duct Construction Standards*.

Unless otherwise specified all duct and fittings shall be G-60 coated galvanized steel of lockforming grade conforming to ASTM A653 and A924 standards.

Double-wall to single-wall transitions shall be provided where insulated duct connects to non-insulated, single-wall duct.

All double-wall duct and fittings shall be furnished with both an inner and an outer pressure shell coupling.

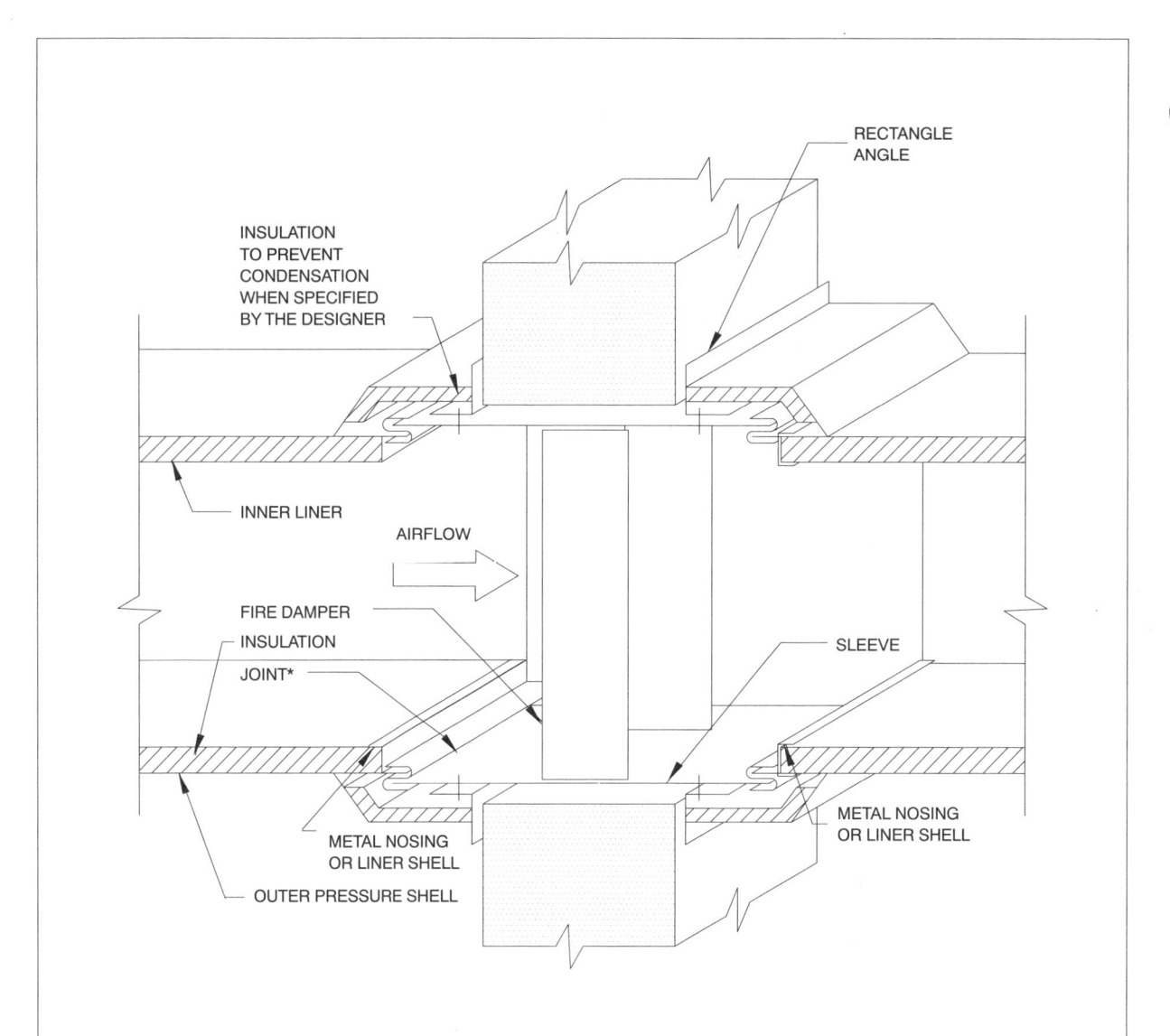

INTERRUPTION OF INTERNAL INSULATION AT THE FIRE DAMPER IS REQUIRED BY NFPA STANDARD 90A. WHERE 90A IS APPLICABLE INSTALLATION SHOULD BE MADE AS SHOWN AND SHOULD OTHERWISE CONFORM TO THE SMACNA HVAC DUCT CONSTRUCTION STANDARDS–METAL AND FLEXIBLE.

THE DESIGNER SHOULD SPECIFY EXTERNAL INSULATION AS SHOWN TO PREVENT CONDENSATION OCCURRING ON UNLINED METAL AT PENETRATIONS. WHERE THE PROVISIONS OF NFPA 90A AS APPLICABLE, NEITHER INSULATION NOR LINER CAN EXTEND THROUGH THE WALLS OF FLOORS.

* S SLIP IS ILLUSTRATED; SEE SMACNA FIRE, SMOKE AND RADIATION DAMPER MANUAL FOR RANGE OF APPROVED TYPES OF CONNECTOR.

FIGURE 8-1 FIRE DAMPER INSTALLATION IN DOUBLE-WALL DUCT

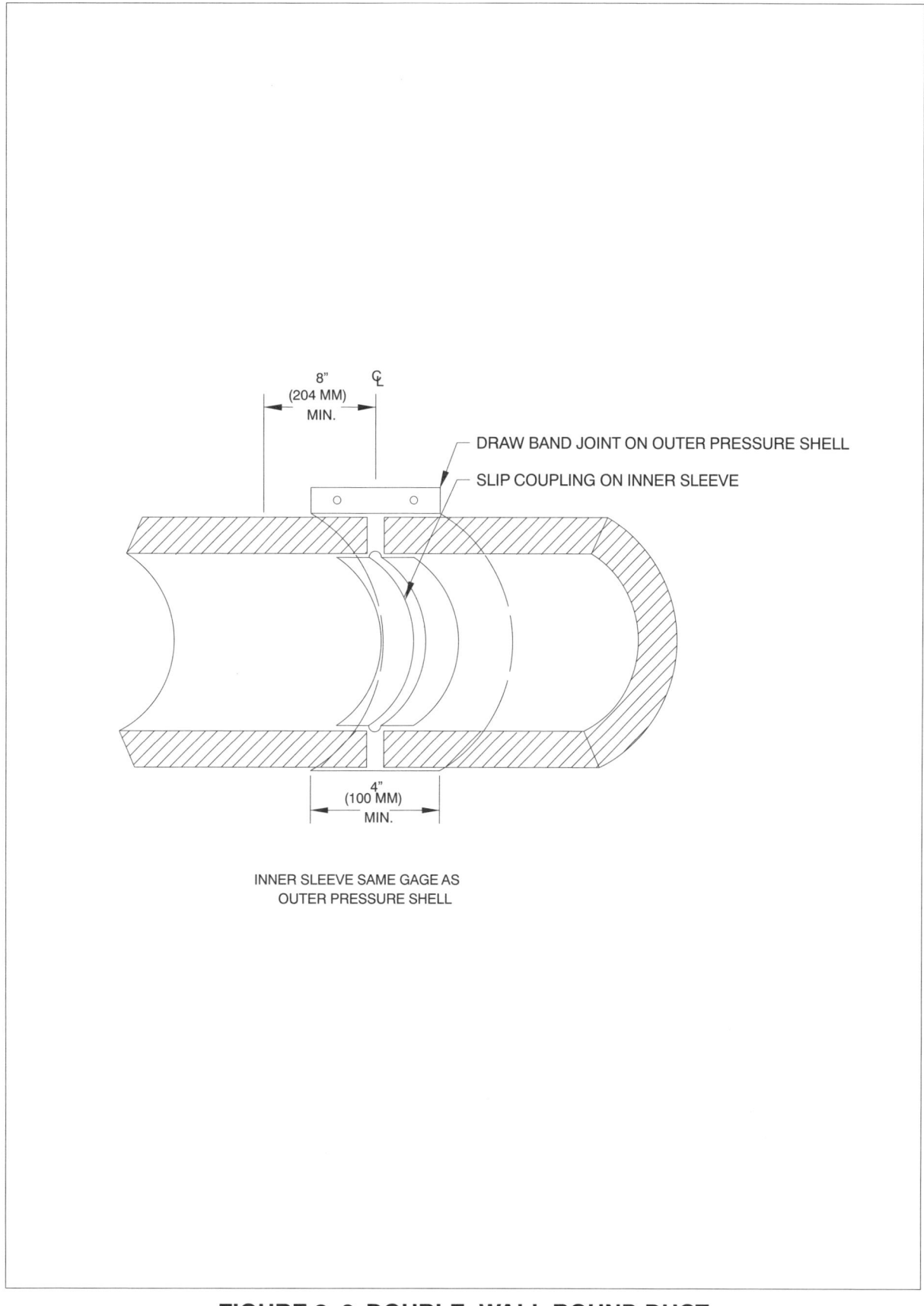

FIGURE 8-2 DOUBLE-WALL ROUND DUCT

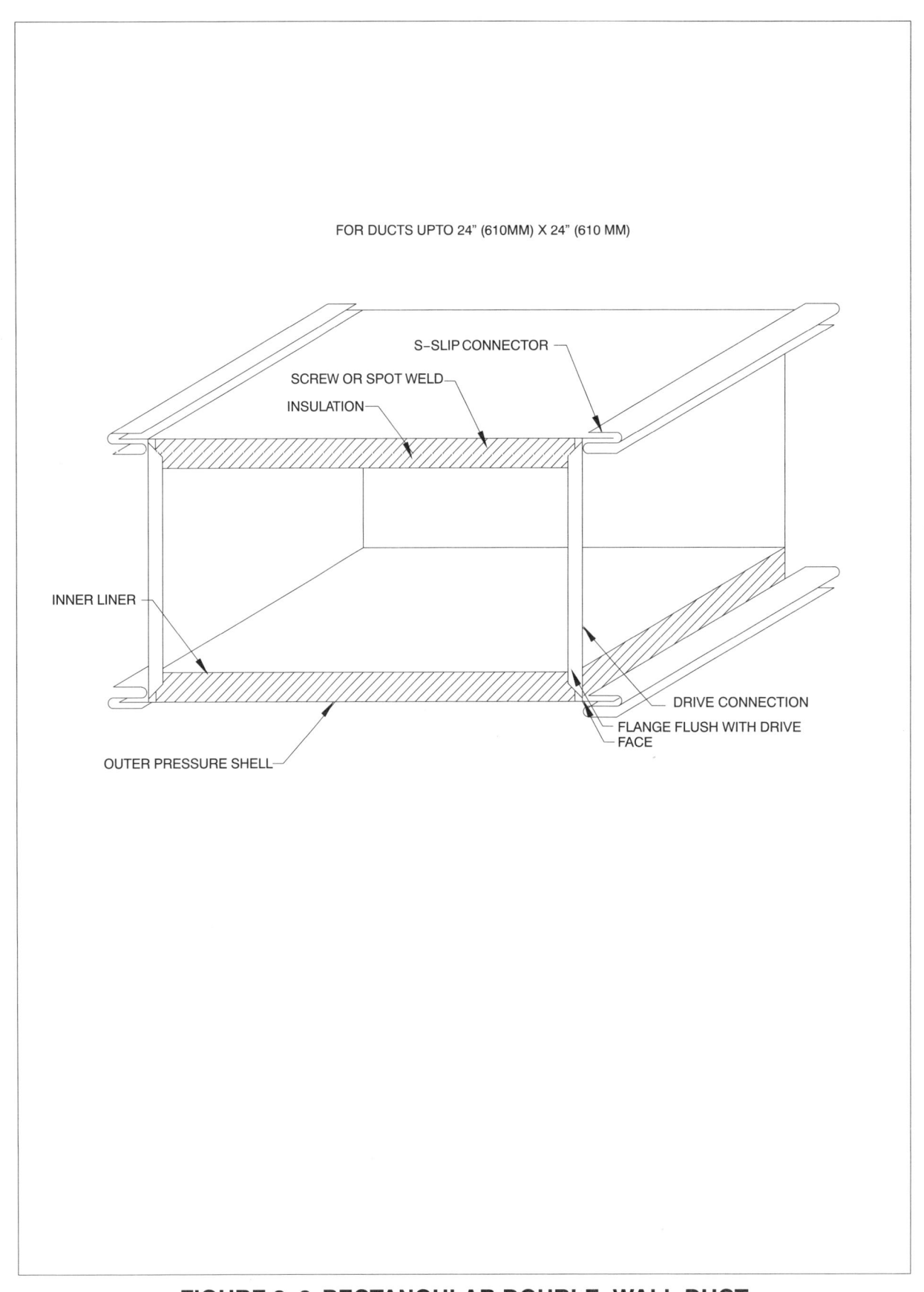

FIGURE 8-3 RECTANGULAR DOUBLE-WALL DUCT

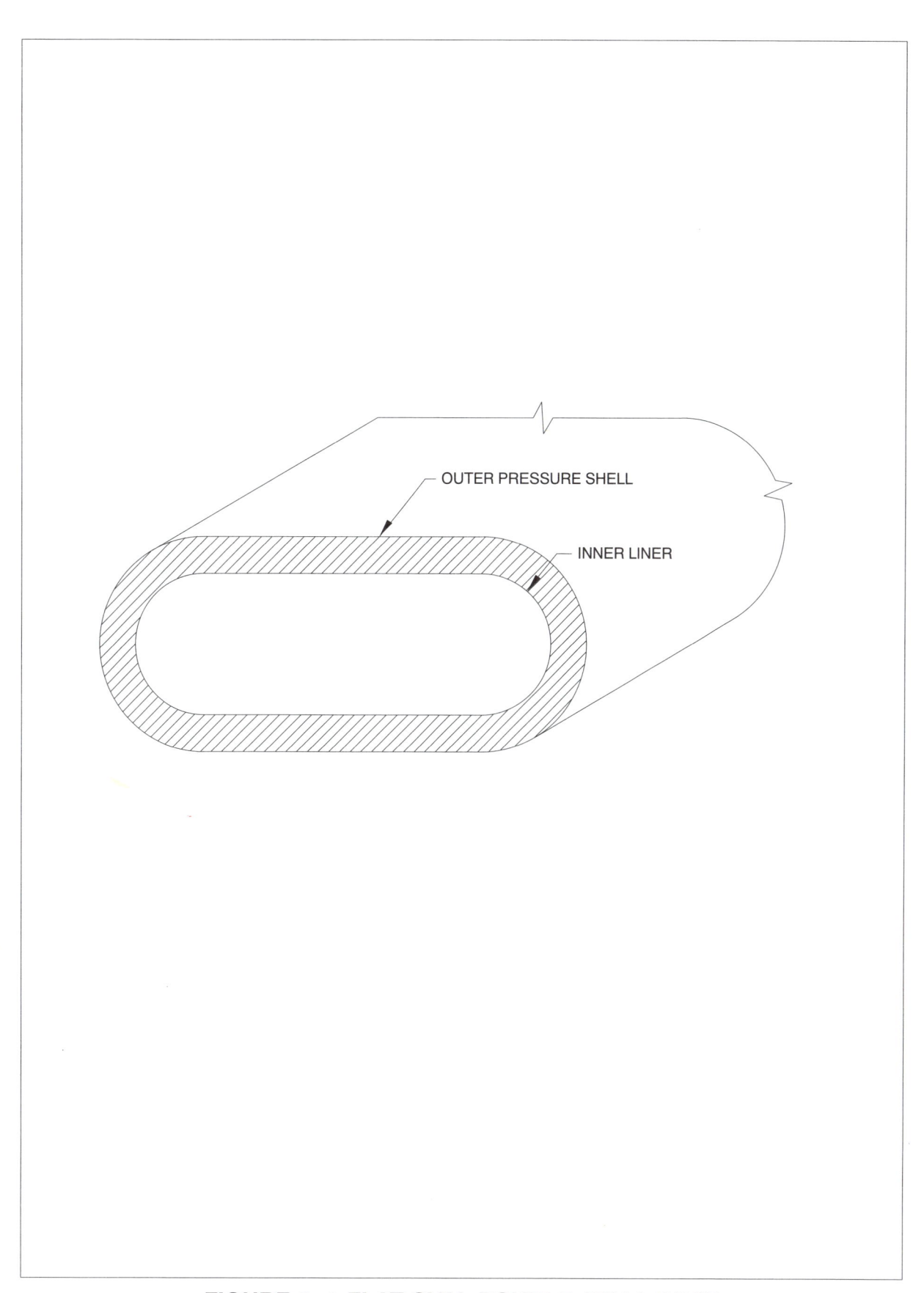

FIGURE 8-4 FLAT OVAL DOUBLE-WALL DUCT

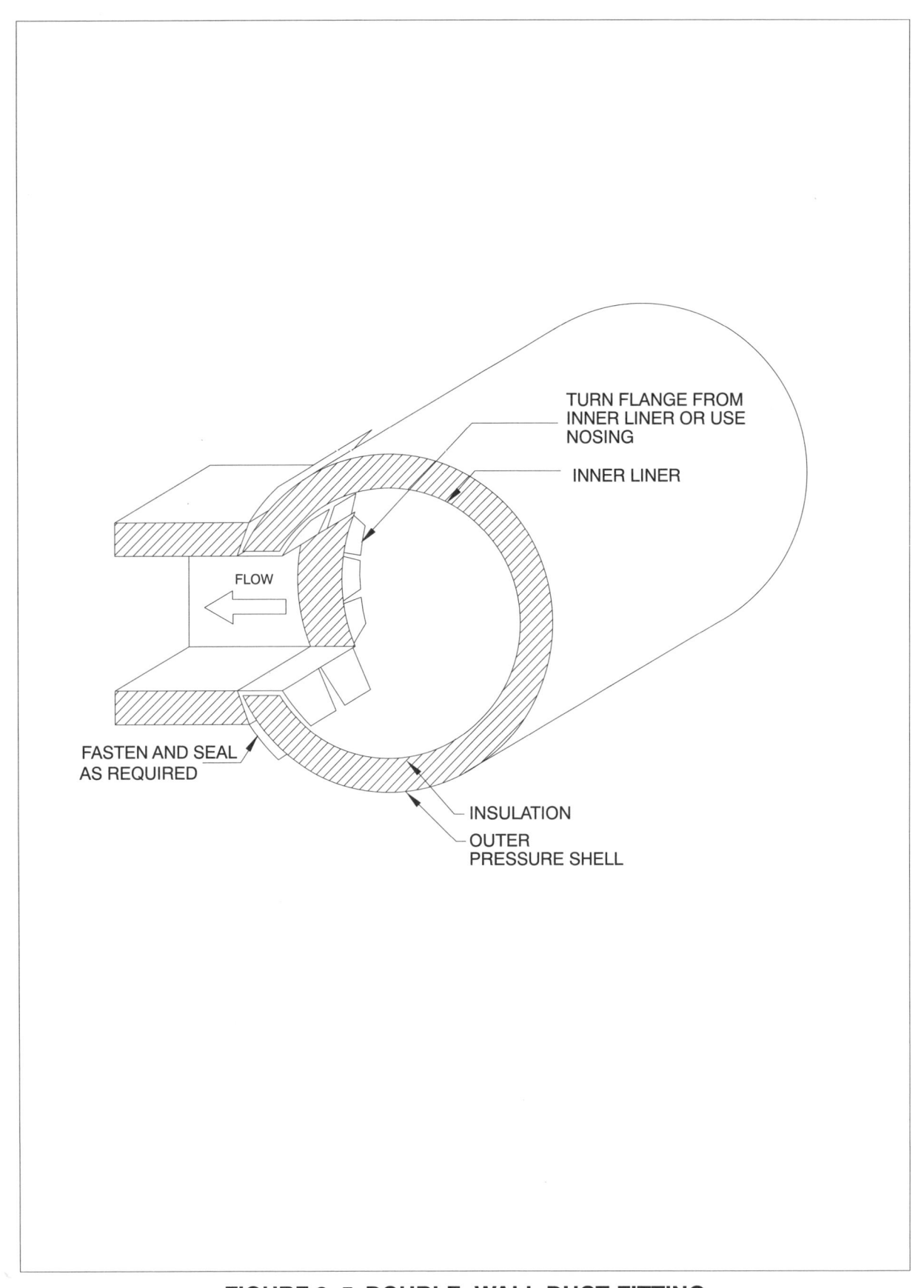

FIGURE 8-5 DOUBLE-WALL DUCT FITTING

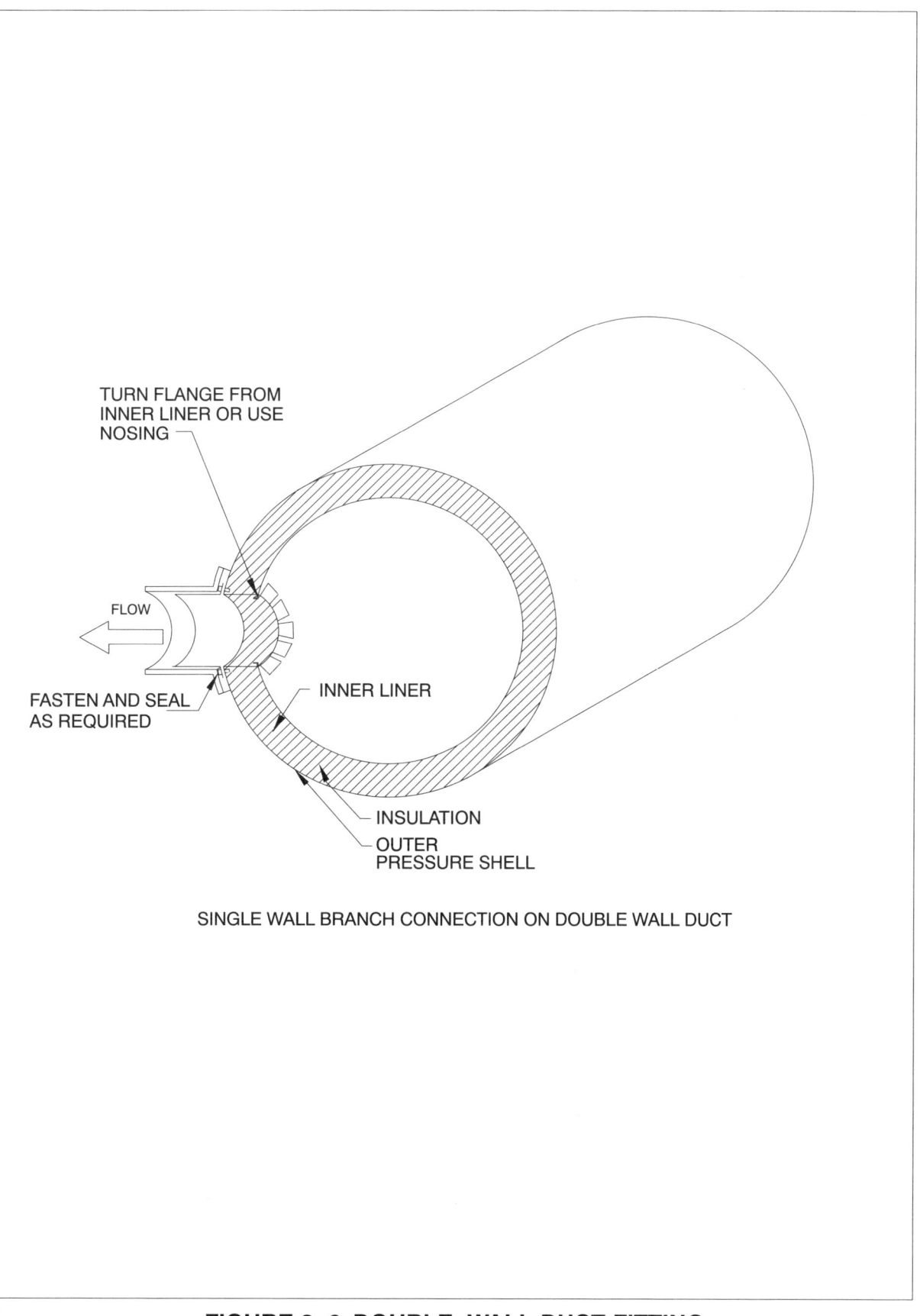

FIGURE 8-6 DOUBLE-WALL DUCT FITTING

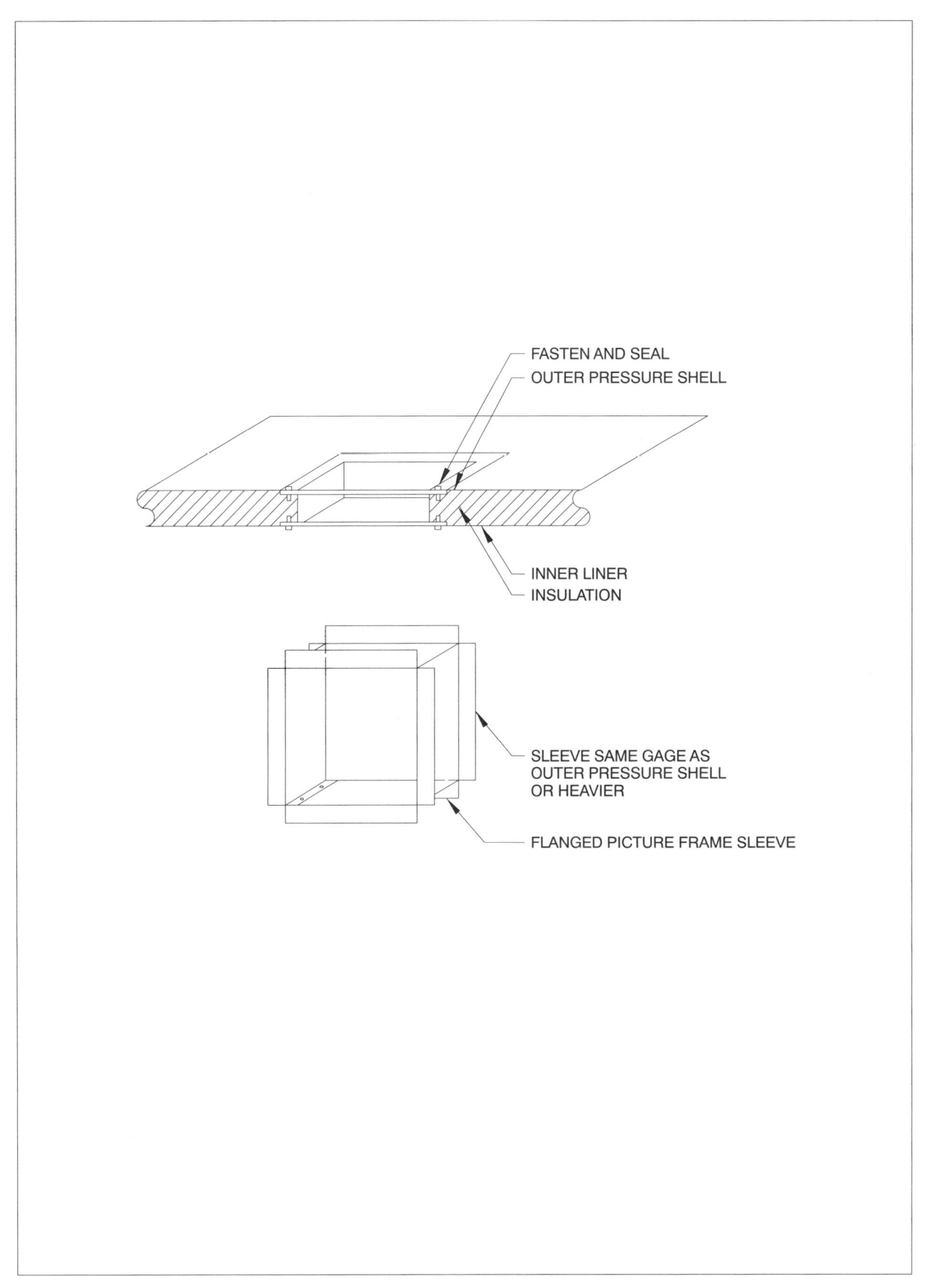

FIGURE 8-7 DOUBLE-WALL DUCT SLEEVE

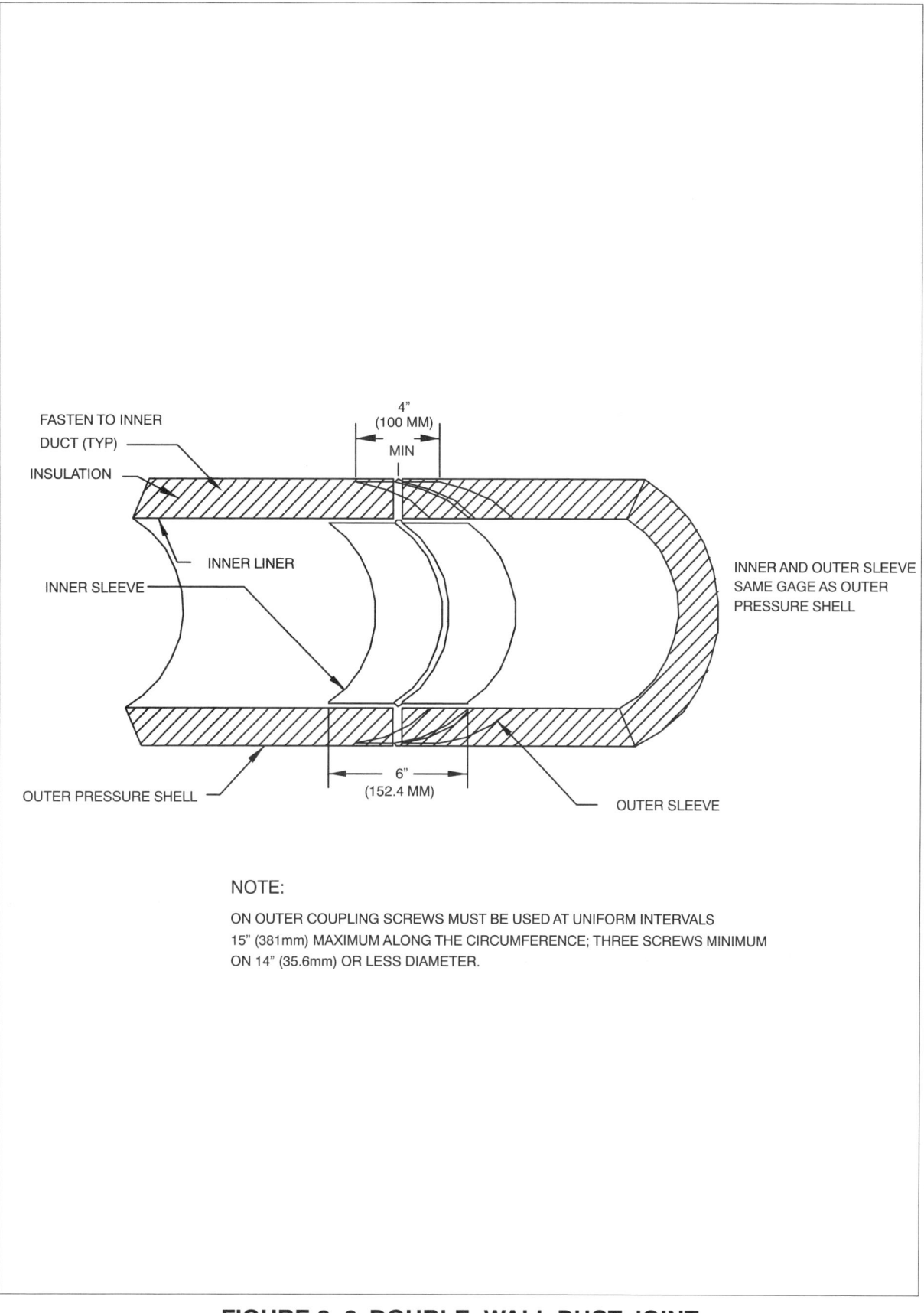

FIGURE 8-8 DOUBLE-WALL DUCT JOINT

CONDUIT

INNER LINER

OUTER PRESSURE SHELL

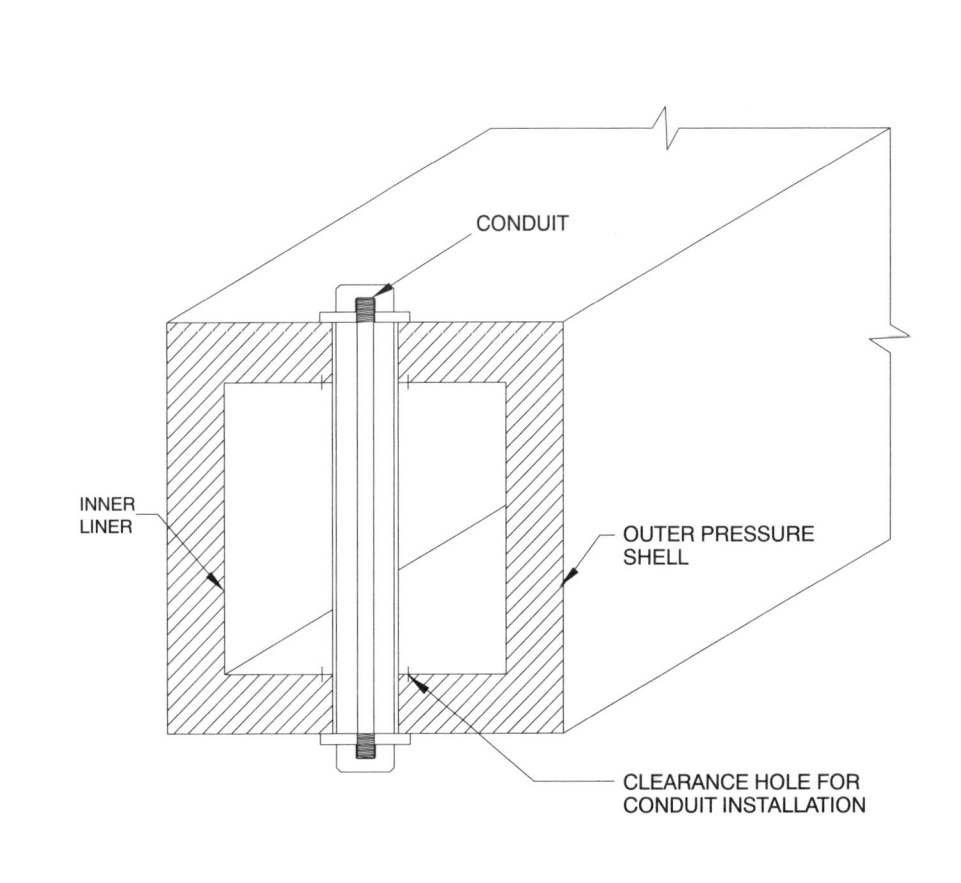

CLEARANCE HOLE FOR CONDUIT INSTALLATION

NOTE:

OUTER PRESSURE SHELL IS POSITIVE OR NEGATIVE.
INNER LINER IS NEUTRAL.
SEE CHAPTER 2 FOR USE OF
MID-PANEL TIE RODS.

FIGURE 8-9 DOUBLE-WALL DUCT TIE ROD INSTALLATION

FIGURE 8-10 DOUBLE-WALL DUCT – VAN STONE JOINT

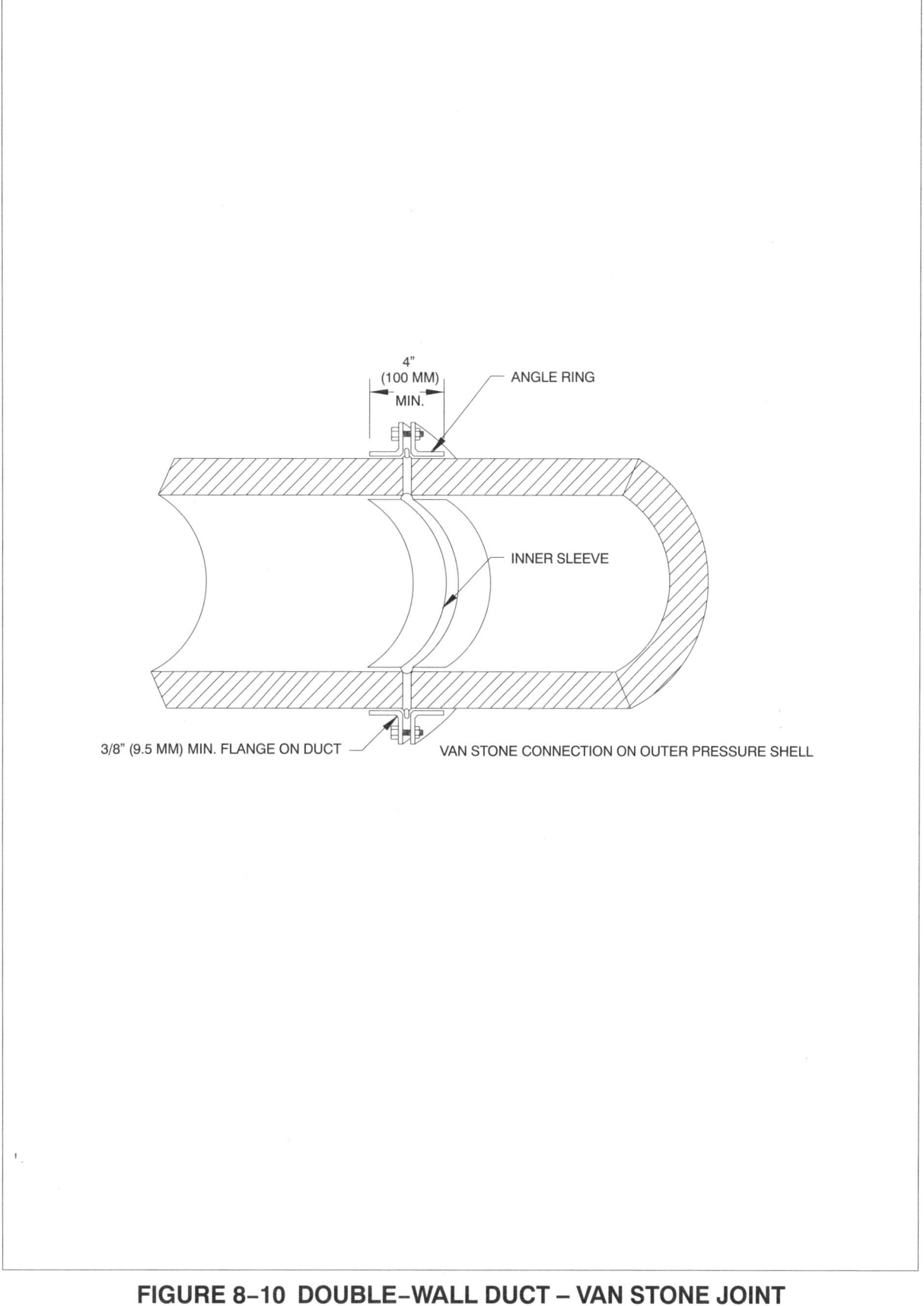

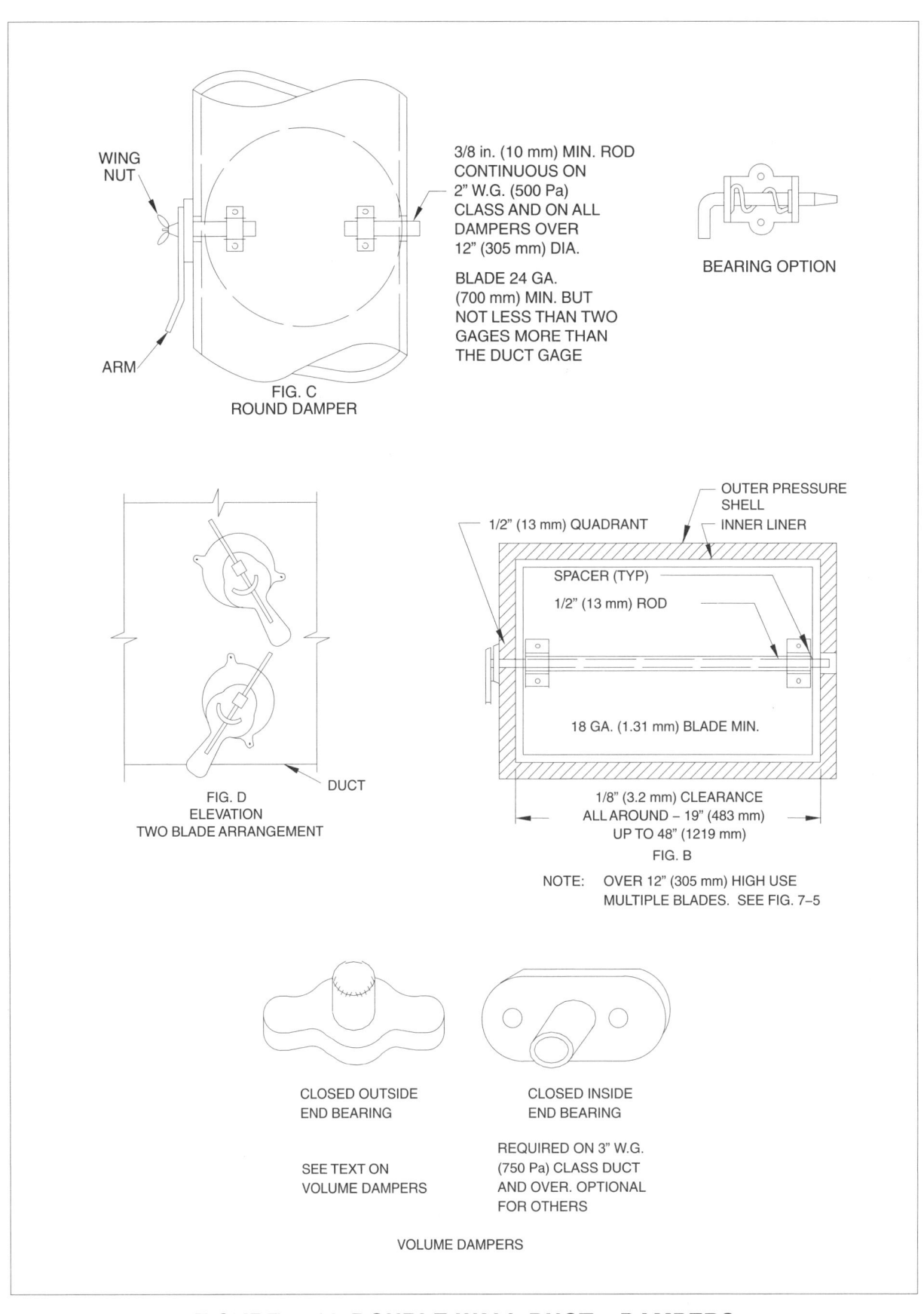

FIGURE 8–11 DOUBLE-WALL DUCT – DAMPERS

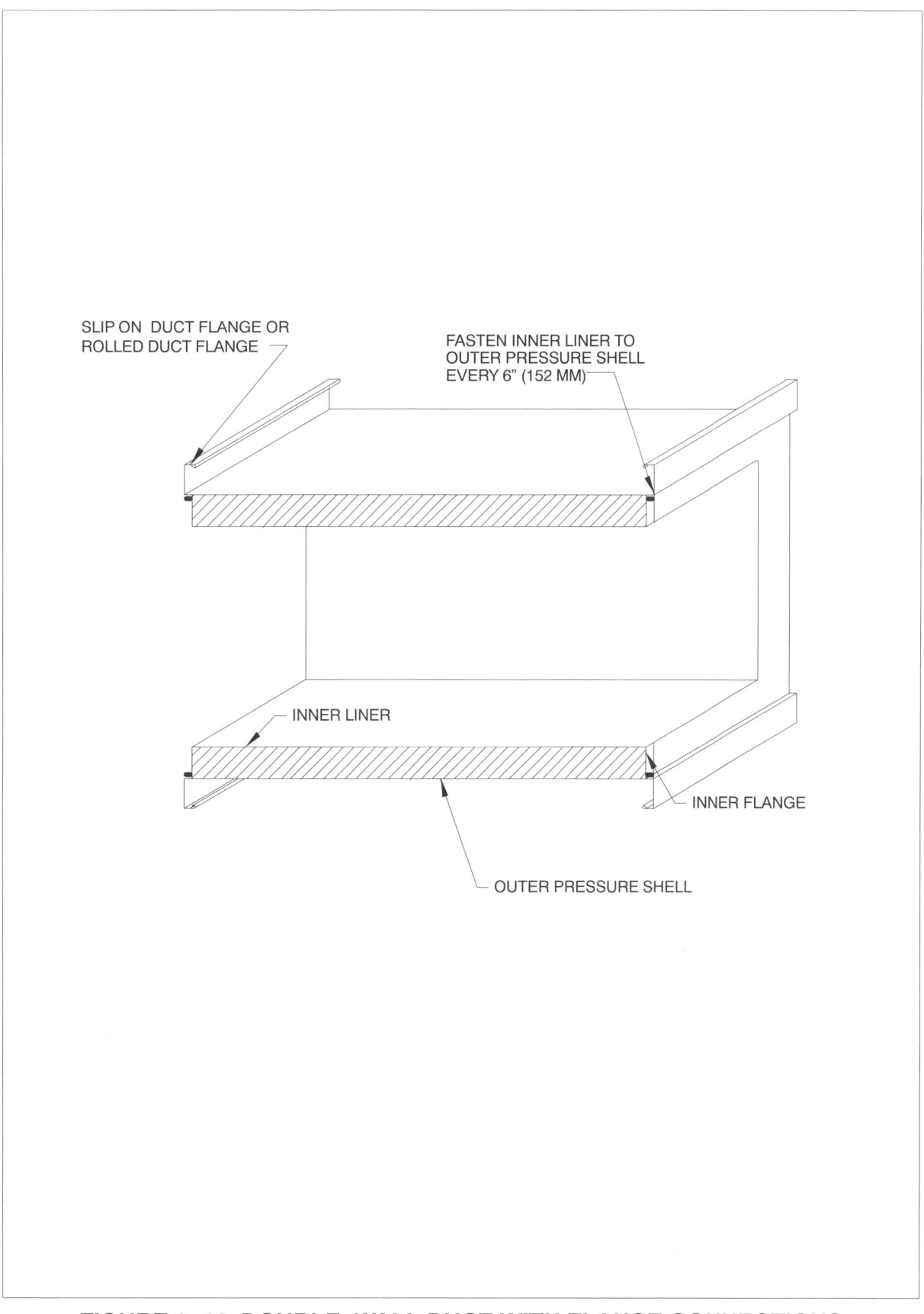

FIGURE 8–12 DOUBLE-WALL DUCT WITH FLANGE CONNECTIONS

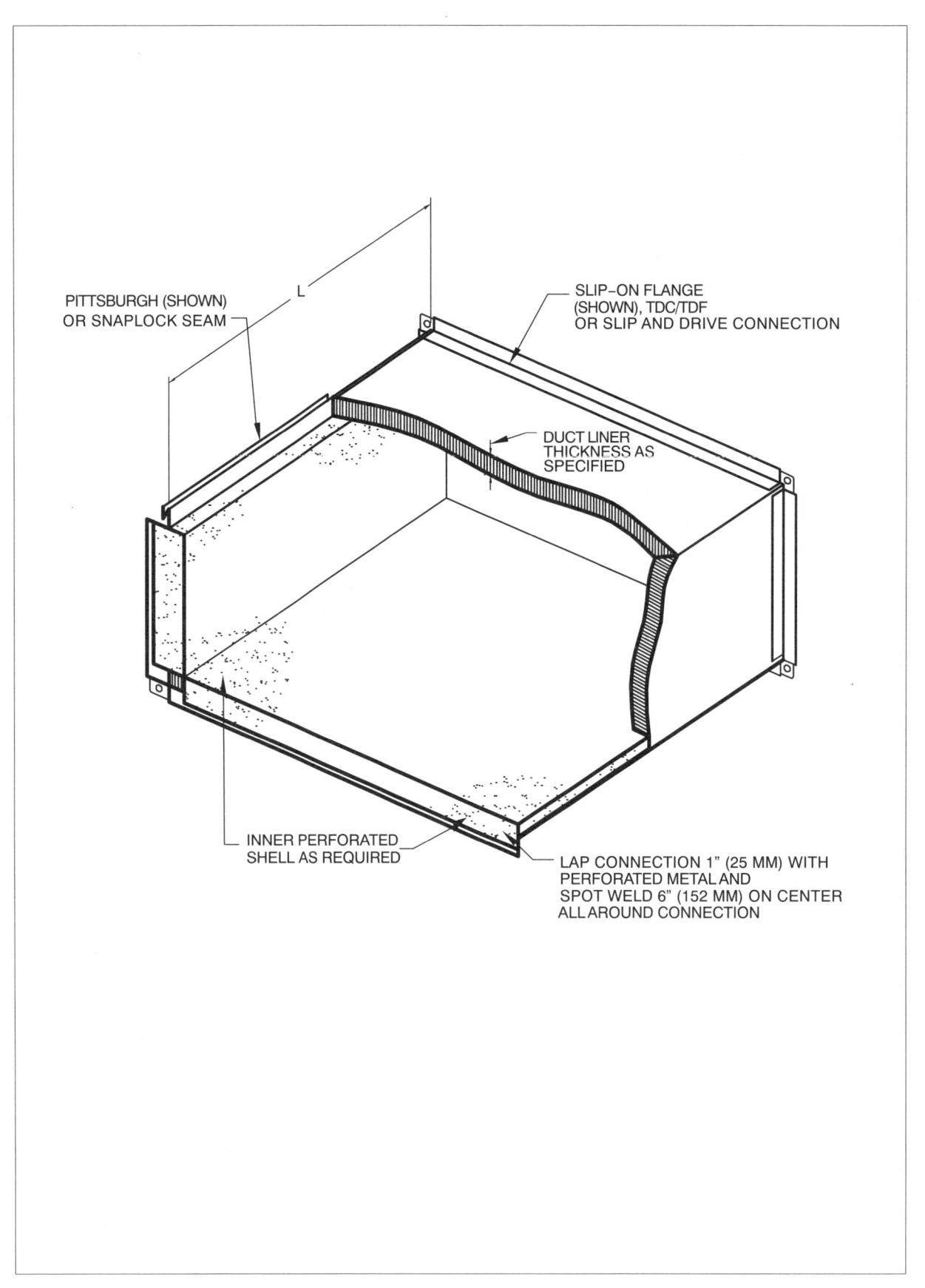

FIGURE 8–13 DOUBLE-WALL DUCT – FLANGE CONNECTION

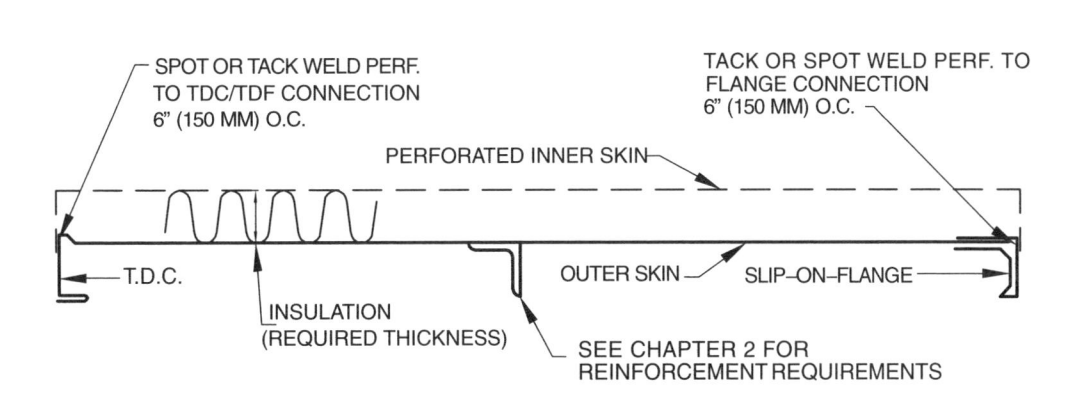

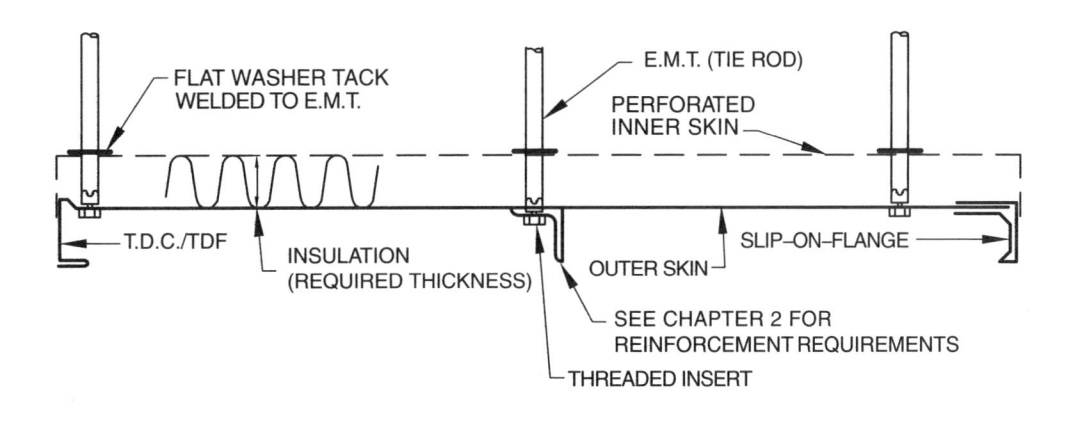

FIGURE 8–14 DOUBLE-WALL DUCT DETAILS

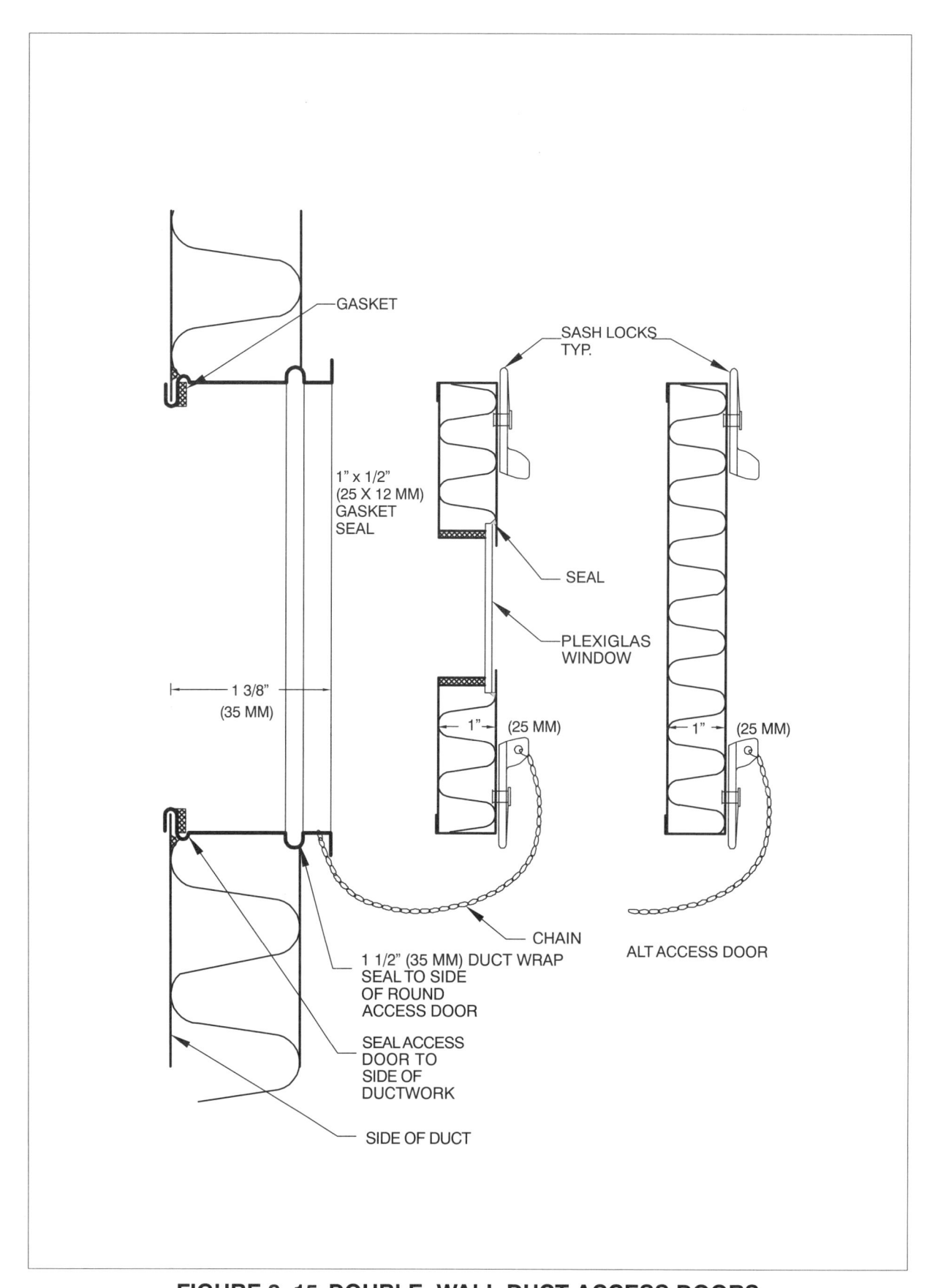

FIGURE 8–15 DOUBLE-WALL DUCT ACCESS DOORS

CHAPTER 9

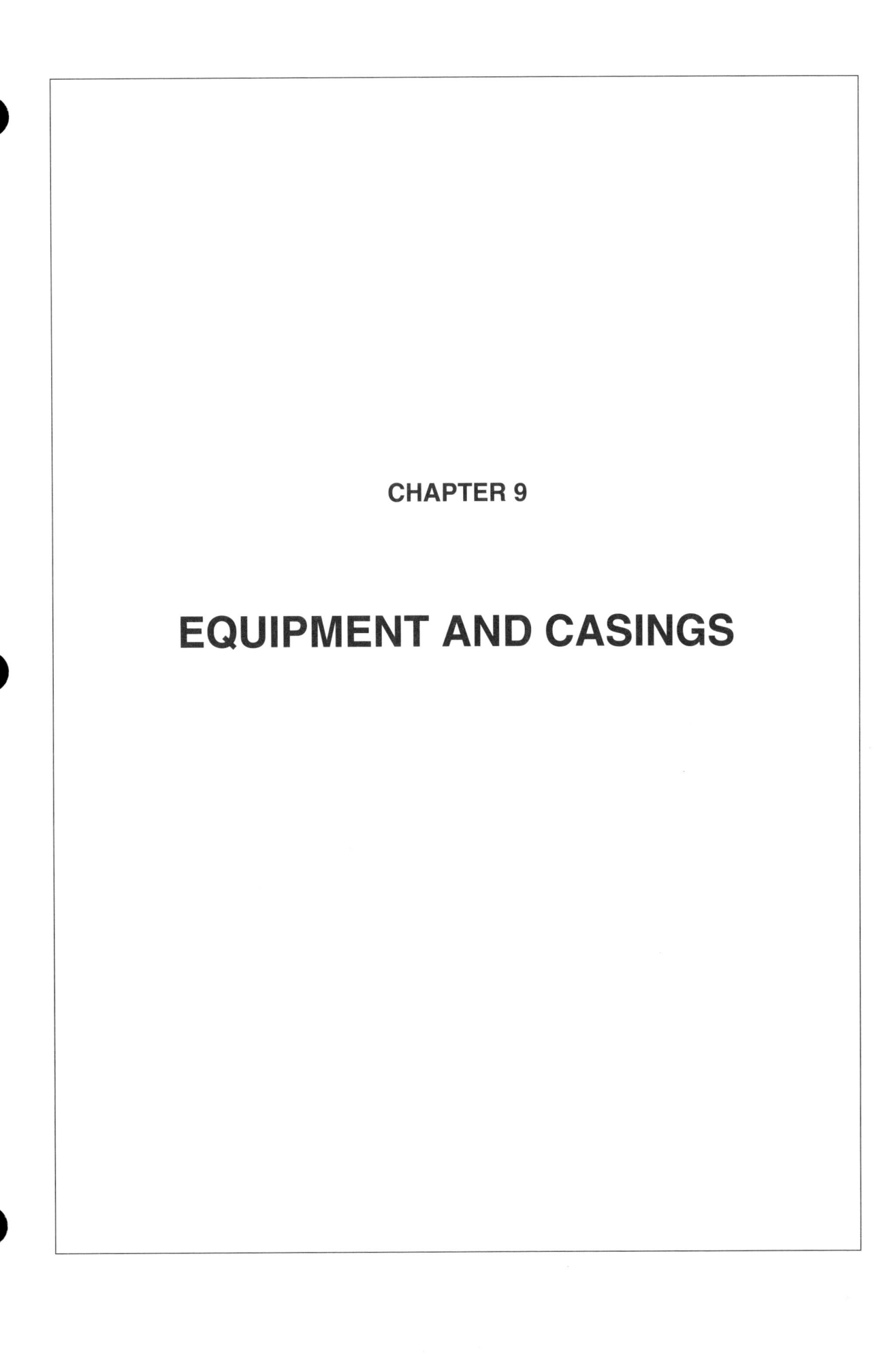

EQUIPMENT AND CASINGS

CHAPTER 9

EQUIPMENT AND CASINGS

9.1 CASING AND PLENUM CONSTRUCTION STANDARDS

S6.0 Unless details are shown otherwise on contract drawings, provide casings and plenums of the designated pressure classification as required by this standard.

S6.1 Submit details selected from the illustrated alternatives for approval of the contracting authority. When equivalent construction is proposed as substitution, clearly identify the substitution. Use construction appropriate for the pressure classification.

S6.2 All casing on the suction side of the fan shall be of 2 in. wg (500 Pa) pressure classification. Casing on fan discharge shall be of the designated pressure class.

S6.3 All joints, seams, connections, and abutments to the building structure shall be sealed with suitable compounds or gaskets.

S6.4 Drains shall have water seals not less than 2 in. wg (500 Pa) greater than the maximum operating pressure in the chamber.

S6.5 Pipe penetrations shall be sealed to prevent air leakage and condensation movement through the seal.

S6.6 Casing material shall be of the same commercial grades as for ducts except that G90 coated galvanized steel shall be used in all chambers with moisture present.

S6.7 Metal drain pans shall be of G90 coated galvanized steel.

S6.8 All welds on casing interiors shall be painted.

S6.9 Close-off or safing sheets and strips shall be of G90 galvanized steel of thickness not less than that of the duct widths and shall be securely attached. They shall not be used for structural support of equipment.

S6.10 Casings and plenums shall be constructed to withstand 133 percent of the rated pressure without structural failure. Wall and roof deflections at the rated pressure shall not exceed 1/8 in. per foot (0.97 mm/m) of width.

S6.11 Casings for negative pressures greater than 3 in. wg (750 Pa) may be constructed in accordance with the SMACNA *Rectangular Industrial Duct Construction Standards*.

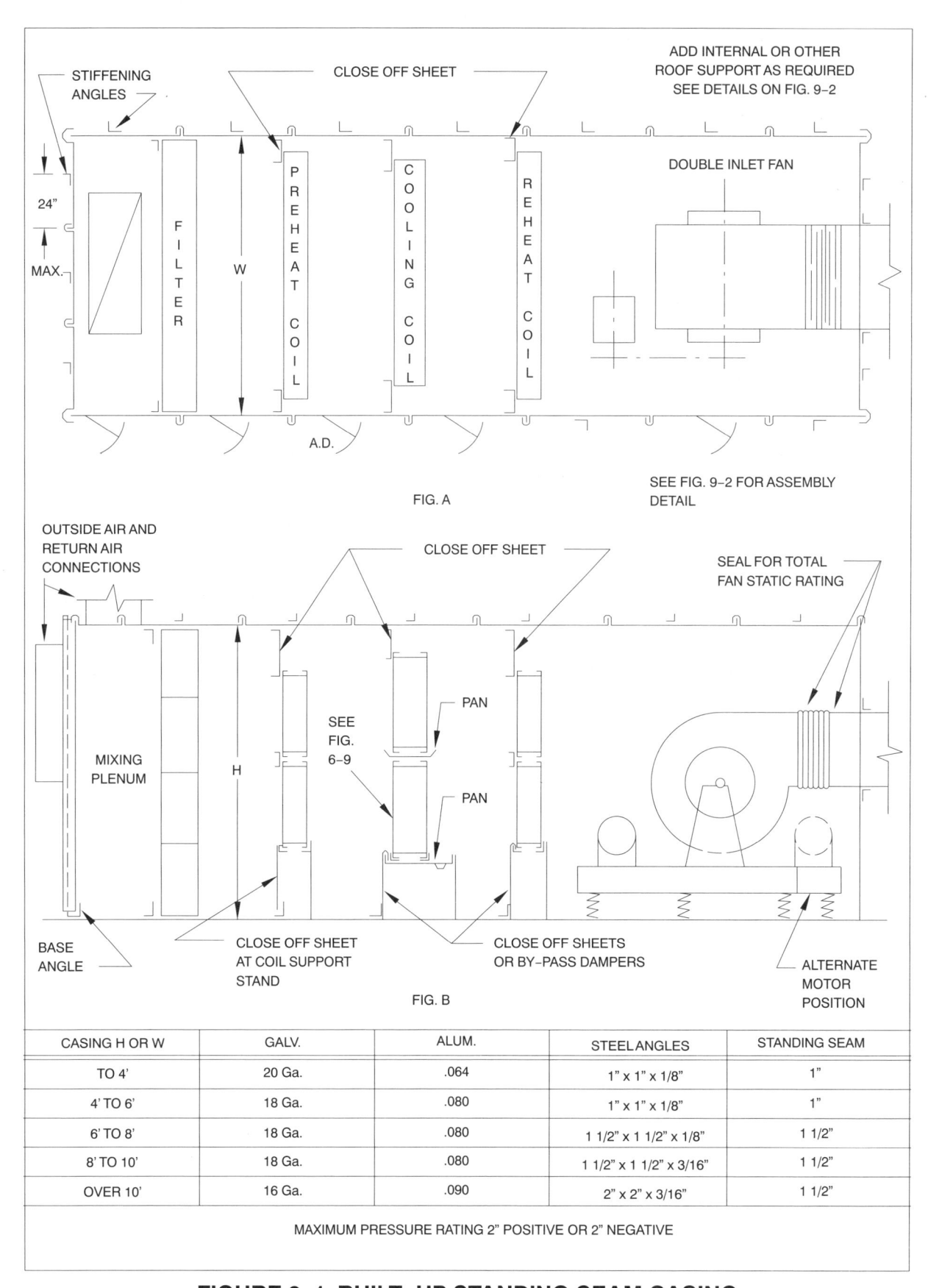

CASING H OR W	GALV.	ALUM.	STEEL ANGLES	STANDING SEAM
TO 4'	20 Ga.	.064	1" x 1" x 1/8"	1"
4' TO 6'	18 Ga.	.080	1" x 1" x 1/8"	1"
6' TO 8'	18 Ga.	.080	1 1/2" x 1 1/2" x 1/8"	1 1/2"
8' TO 10'	18 Ga.	.080	1 1/2" x 1 1/2" x 3/16"	1 1/2"
OVER 10'	16 Ga.	.090	2" x 2" x 3/16"	1 1/2"

MAXIMUM PRESSURE RATING 2" POSITIVE OR 2" NEGATIVE

FIGURE 9-1 BUILT-UP STANDING SEAM CASING

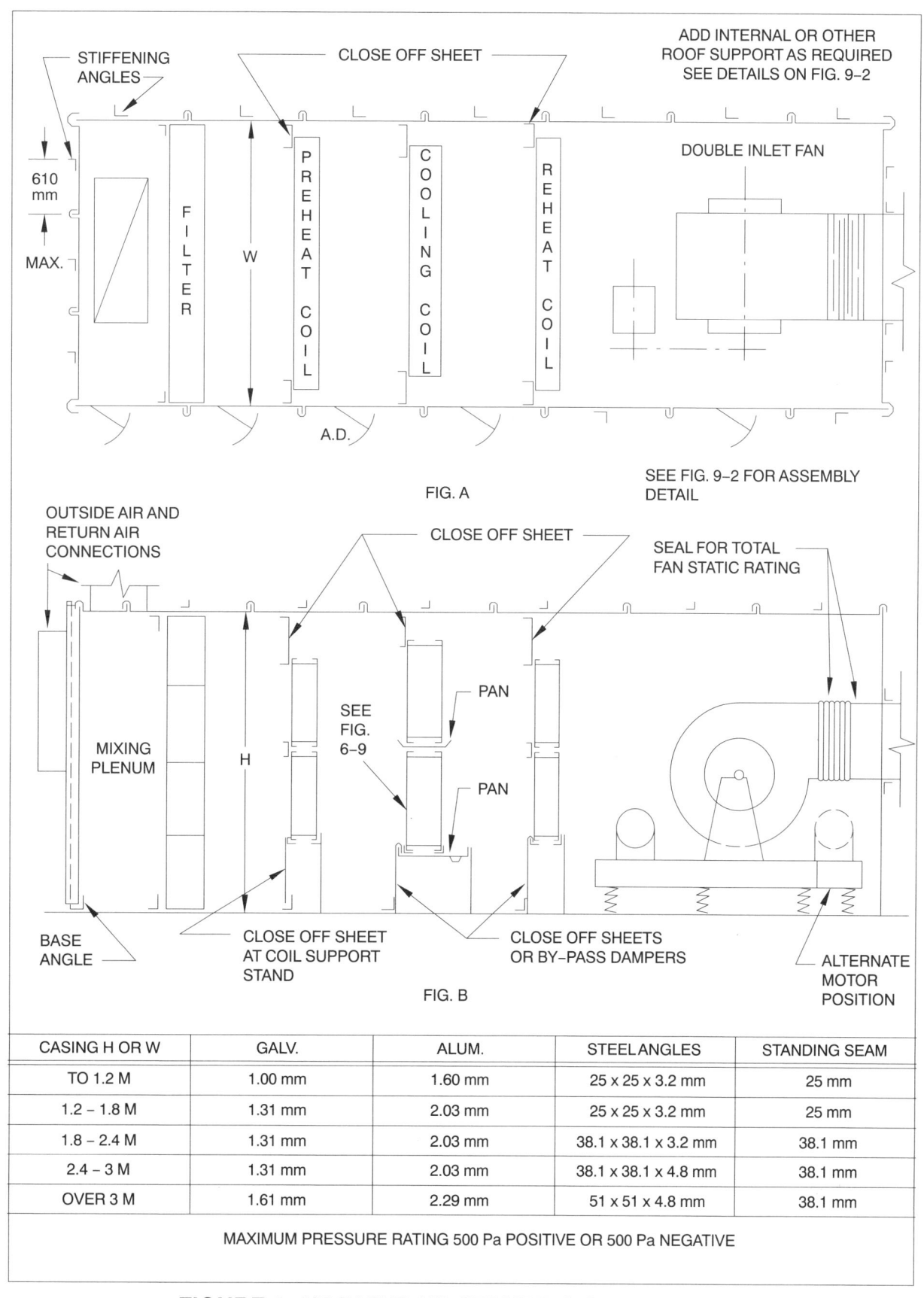

CASING H OR W	GALV.	ALUM.	STEEL ANGLES	STANDING SEAM
TO 1.2 M	1.00 mm	1.60 mm	25 x 25 x 3.2 mm	25 mm
1.2 – 1.8 M	1.31 mm	2.03 mm	25 x 25 x 3.2 mm	25 mm
1.8 – 2.4 M	1.31 mm	2.03 mm	38.1 x 38.1 x 3.2 mm	38.1 mm
2.4 – 3 M	1.31 mm	2.03 mm	38.1 x 38.1 x 4.8 mm	38.1 mm
OVER 3 M	1.61 mm	2.29 mm	51 x 51 x 4.8 mm	38.1 mm

MAXIMUM PRESSURE RATING 500 Pa POSITIVE OR 500 Pa NEGATIVE

FIGURE 9-1M BUILT-UP STANDING SEAM CASING

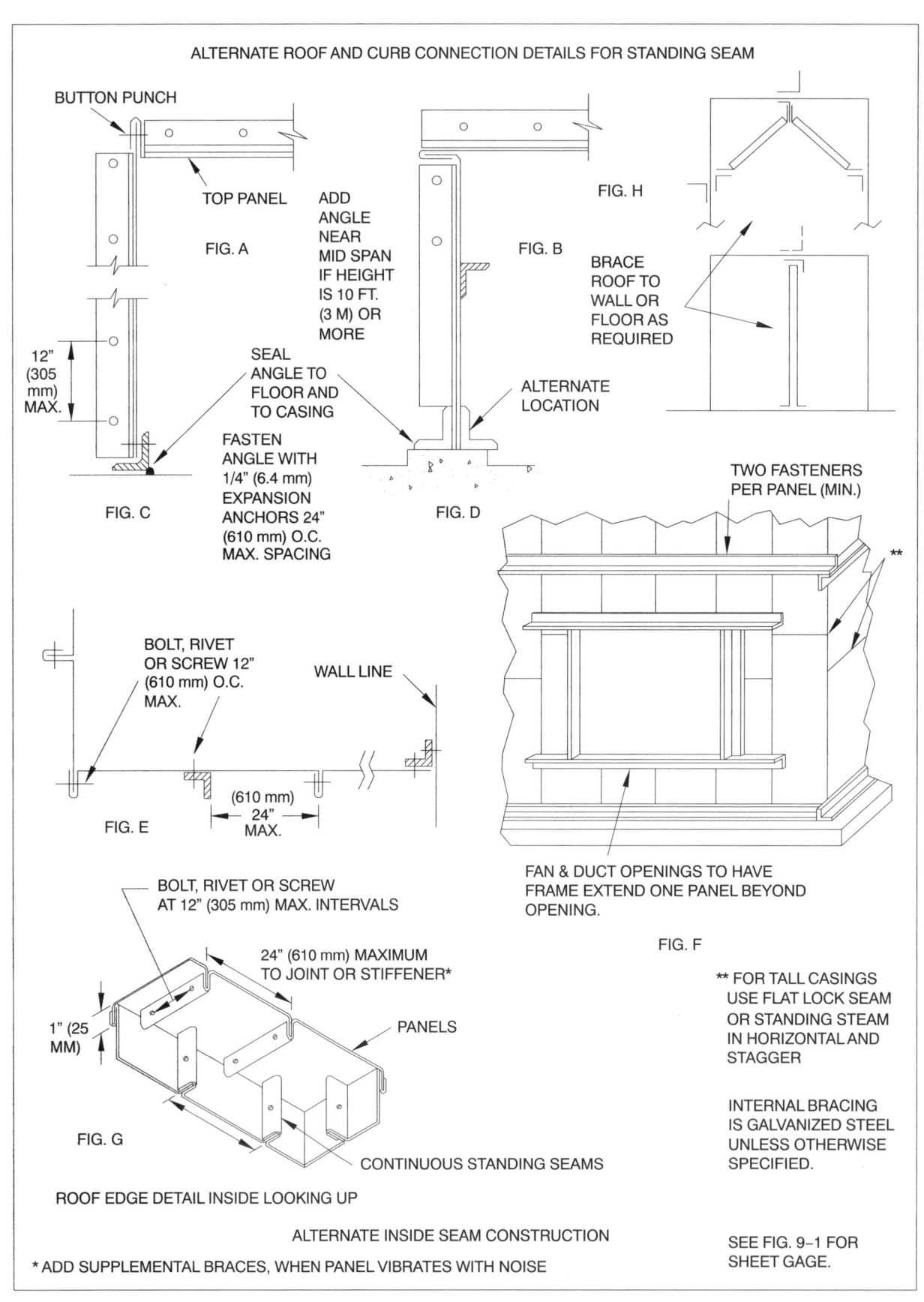

FIGURE 9-2 STANDING SEAM CASINGS

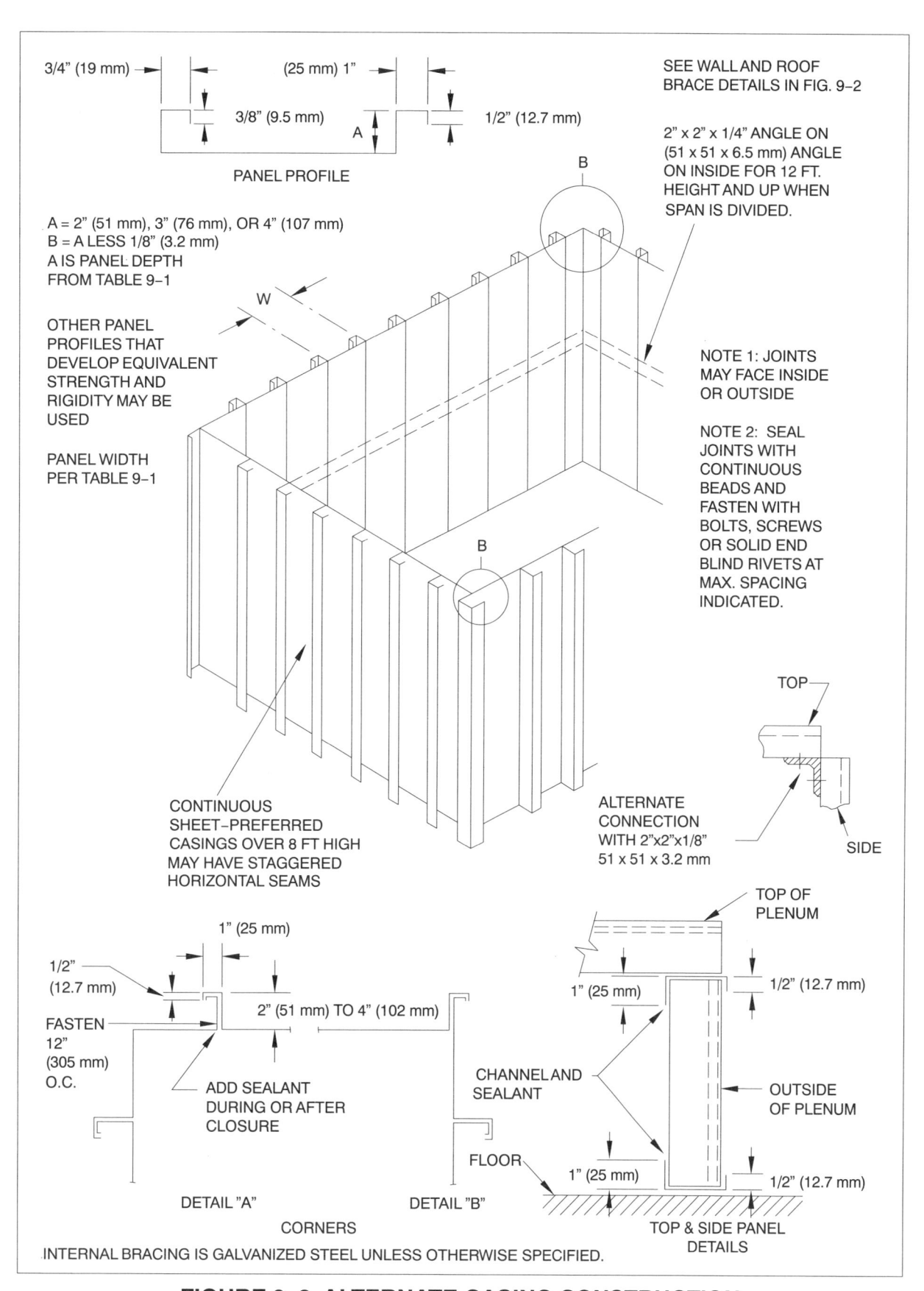

FIGURE 9-3 ALTERNATE CASING CONSTRUCTION

Maximum Allowable Panel Width For a Panel Gage, Span and Load Class

Span (ft)	Panel Gage	Depth	Load Class (in. wg Static) 2" (500 Pa)	3" (750 Pa)	4" (1000 Pa)	6" (1500 Pa)	10" (2500 Pa)
6 ft (1.8 m)	#22 (0.85 mm) #22 #22	2" (51 mm) 3" (76 mm) 4" (102 mm)	20" (508 mm) 20" (508 mm) 22" (559 mm)	14" (356 mm) 16" (406 mm) 16" (406 mm)	12" (305 mm) 14" (356 mm) 14" (356 mm)	– – 12" (305 mm)	– – –
	#20 (1.00 mm) #20 #20	2" (51 mm) 3" (76 mm) 4" (102 mm)	24" (610 mm) 24" (610 mm) 24" (610 mm)	18" (457 mm) 20" (508 mm) 20" (508 mm)	16" (406 mm) 18" (457 mm) 18" (457 mm)	12" (305 mm) 14" (356 mm) 14" (356 mm)	– – –
	#18 (1.31 mm) #18 #18	2" (51 mm) 3" (76 mm) 4" (102 mm)	24" (610 mm) 24" (610 mm) 24" (610 mm)	24" (610 mm) 24" (610 mm) 24" (610 mm)	22" (559 mm) 24" (610 mm) 24" (610 mm)	16" (406 mm) 18" (457 mm) 20" (508 mm)	12" (305 mm) 14" (356 mm) 14"
	#16 (1.61 mm) #16 #16	2" (51 mm) 3" (76 mm) 4" (102 mm)	24" (610 mm) 24" (610 mm) 24" (610 mm)	24" (610 mm) 24" (610 mm) 24" (610 mm)	24" (610 mm) 24" (610 mm) 24" (610 mm)	22" (559 mm) 24" (610 mm) 24" (610 mm)	16" (406 mm) 18" (457 mm) 18" (457 mm)
8 ft (2.4 m)	#22 (0.85 mm) #22 #22	2" (51 mm) 3" (76 mm) 4" (102 mm)	16" (406 mm) 18" (457 mm) 20" (508 mm)	12" (305 mm) 14" (358 mm) 16" (406 mm)	– 12" (305 mm) 14" (356 mm)	– – –	– – –
	#20 (1.00 mm) #20 #20	2" (51 mm) 3" (76 mm) 4" (102 mm)	20" (508 mm) 24" (610 mm) 24" (610 mm)	16" (406 mm) 18" (457 mm) 20" (508 mm)	12" (305 mm) 16" (406 mm) 16" (406 mm)	– 12" (305 mm) 12" (305 mm)	– – –
	#18 (1.31 mm) #18 #18	2" (51 mm) 3" (76 mm) 4" (102 mm)	24" (610 mm) 24" (610 mm) 24" (610 mm)	22" (559 mm) 24" (610 mm) 24" (610 mm)	18" (457 mm) 22" (559 mm) 22" (559 mm)	14" (356 mm) 16" (406 mm) 18" (457 mm)	– 12" (305 mm) 12" (305 mm)
	#16 (1.61 mm) #16 #16	2" (51 mm) 3" (76 mm) 4" (102 mm)	24" (610 mm) 24" (610 mm) 24" (610 mm)	24" (610 mm) 24" (610 mm) 24" (610 mm)	24" (610 mm) 24" (610 mm) 24" (610 mm)	18" (457 mm) 22" (559 mm) 22" (559 mm)	12" (305 mm) 14" (356 mm) 16" (406 mm)
10 ft (3 m)	#22 (0.85 mm) #22 #22	2" (51 mm) 3" (76 mm) 4" (102 mm)	12" (305 mm) 16" (406 mm) 18" (457 mm)	– 12" (305 mm) 14" (358 mm)	– – 12" (305 mm)	– – –	– – –
	#20 (1.00 mm) #20 #20	2" (51 mm) 3" (76 mm) 4" (102 mm)	16" (406 mm) 22" (559 mm) 24" (610 mm)	12" (305 mm) 16" (406 mm) 18" (457 mm)	– 12" (305 mm) 14" (356 mm)	– – –	– – –
	#18 (1.31 mm) #18 #18	2" (51 mm) 3" (76 mm) 4" (102 mm)	24" (610 mm) 24" (610 mm) 24" (610 mm)	18" (457 mm) 22" (559 mm) 24" (610 mm)	14" (356 mm) 18" (457 mm) 20" (508 mm)	– 14" (356 mm) 16" (406 mm)	– – –
	#16 (1.61 mm) #16 #16	2" (51 mm) 3" (76 mm) 4" (102 mm)	24" (610 mm) 24" (610 mm) 24" (610 mm)	24" (610 mm) 24" (610 mm) 24" (610 mm)	20" (508 mm) 24" (610 mm) 24" (610 mm)	12" (305 mm) 18" (457 mm) 20" (508 mm)	– 12" (305 mm) 14" (356 mm)

Table 9–1 Alternate Casing Panels

NOTES:

a. Use table to determine maximum panel width for load class, panel span and gage.

b. – Indicates panel gage not suitable for this load class and span condition.

c. For casings with interior support angle, use larger of spans either side of angle to select panel gage and width.

d. *See* Fig. 9-3 for assembly.

Maximum Allowable Panel Width For a Panel Gage, Span and Load Class

Span (m)	Panel Gage	Depth	2" (500 Pa)	3" (750 Pa)	4" (1000 Pa)	6" (1500 Pa)	10" (2500 Pa)
12 ft (3.7 m)	#22 (0.85 mm)	3" (76 mm)	14" (356 mm)	–	–	–	–
	#22	4" (102 mm)	16" (406 mm)	12" (305 mm)	–	–	–
	#20 (1.0 mm)	2" (51 mm)	14" (356 mm)	–	–	–	–
	#20	3" (76 mm)	18" (457 mm)	14" (356 mm)	–	–	–
	#20	4" (102 mm)	22" (559 mm)	16" (406 mm)	12" (305 mm)	–	–
	#18 (1.31 mm)	2" (51 mm)	20" (508 mm)	14" (356 mm)	–	–	–
	#18	3" (76 mm)	24" (610 mm)	20" (508 mm)	16" (406 mm)	–	–
	#18	4" (102 mm)	24" (610 mm)	22" (559 mm)	18" (457 mm)	14" (356 mm)	–
	#16 (1.61 mm)	2" (51 mm)	24" (610 mm)	18" (457 mm)	14" (356 mm)	–	–
	#16	3" (76 mm)	24" (610 mm)	24" (610 mm)	22" (559 mm)	16" (406 mm)	–
	#16	4" (102 mm)	24" (610 mm)	24" (610 mm)	24" (610 mm)	18" (457 mm)	12" (305 mm)
14 ft (4.3 m)	#22 (0.85 mm)	3" (76 mm)	12" (305 mm)	–	–	–	–
	#22	4" (102 mm)	14" (356 mm)	–	–	–	–
	#20 (1.0 mm)	3" (76 mm)	16" (406 mm)	–	–	–	–
	#20	4" (102 mm)	18" (457 mm)	14" (356 mm)	–	–	–
	#18 (1.31 mm)	2" (51 mm)	12" (305 mm)	–	–	–	–
	#18	3" (76 mm)	22" (559 mm)	16" (406 mm)	12" (305 mm)	–	–
	#18	4" (102 mm)	24" (610 mm)	20" (508 mm)	16" (406 mm)	12" (305 mm)	–
	#16 (1.61 mm)	2" (51 mm)	16" (406 mm)	–	–	–	–
	#16	3" (76 mm)	24" (610 mm)	22" (559 mm)	18" (457 mm)	12" (305 mm)	–
	#16	4" (102 mm)	24" (610 mm)	24" (610 mm)	22" (559 mm)	16" (406 mm)	–
16 ft (4.9 m)	#22 (0.85 mm)	4" (102 mm)	12" (305 mm)	–	–	–	–
	#20 (1.00 mm)	3" (76 mm)	12" (305 mm)	–	–	–	–
	#20	4" (102 mm)	16" (406 mm)	12" (305 mm)	–	–	–
	#18 (1.31 mm)	3" (76 mm)	18" (457 mm)	12" (305 mm)	–	–	–
	#18	4" (102 mm)	24" (610 mm)	18" (457 mm)	14" (356 mm)	–	–
	#16 (1.61 mm)	3" (76 mm)	24" (610 mm)	16" (406 mm)	12" (305 mm)	–	–
	#16	4" (102 mm)	24" (610 mm)	24" (610 mm)	18" (457 mm)	14" (356 mm)	–
18 ft (5.5 m)	#20 (1.0 mm)	4" (102 mm)	14" (356 mm)	–	–	–	–
	#18 (1.31 mm)	3" (76 mm)	12" (305 mm)	–	–	–	–
	#18	4" (102 mm)	22" (559 mm)	14" (356 mm)	–	–	–
	#16 (1.61 mm)	3" (76 mm)	16" (406 mm)	–	–	–	–
	#16	4" (102 mm)	24" (610 mm)	20" (508 mm)	14" (356 mm)	–	–

Table 9-1 Alternate Casing Panels (Continued)

NOTES:

a. Use table to determine maximum panel width for load class, panel span and gage.

b. – Indicates panel gage not suitable for this load class and span condition.

c. For casings with interior support angle, use larger of spans either side of angle to select panel gage and width.

d. *See* Fig. 9-3 for assembly.

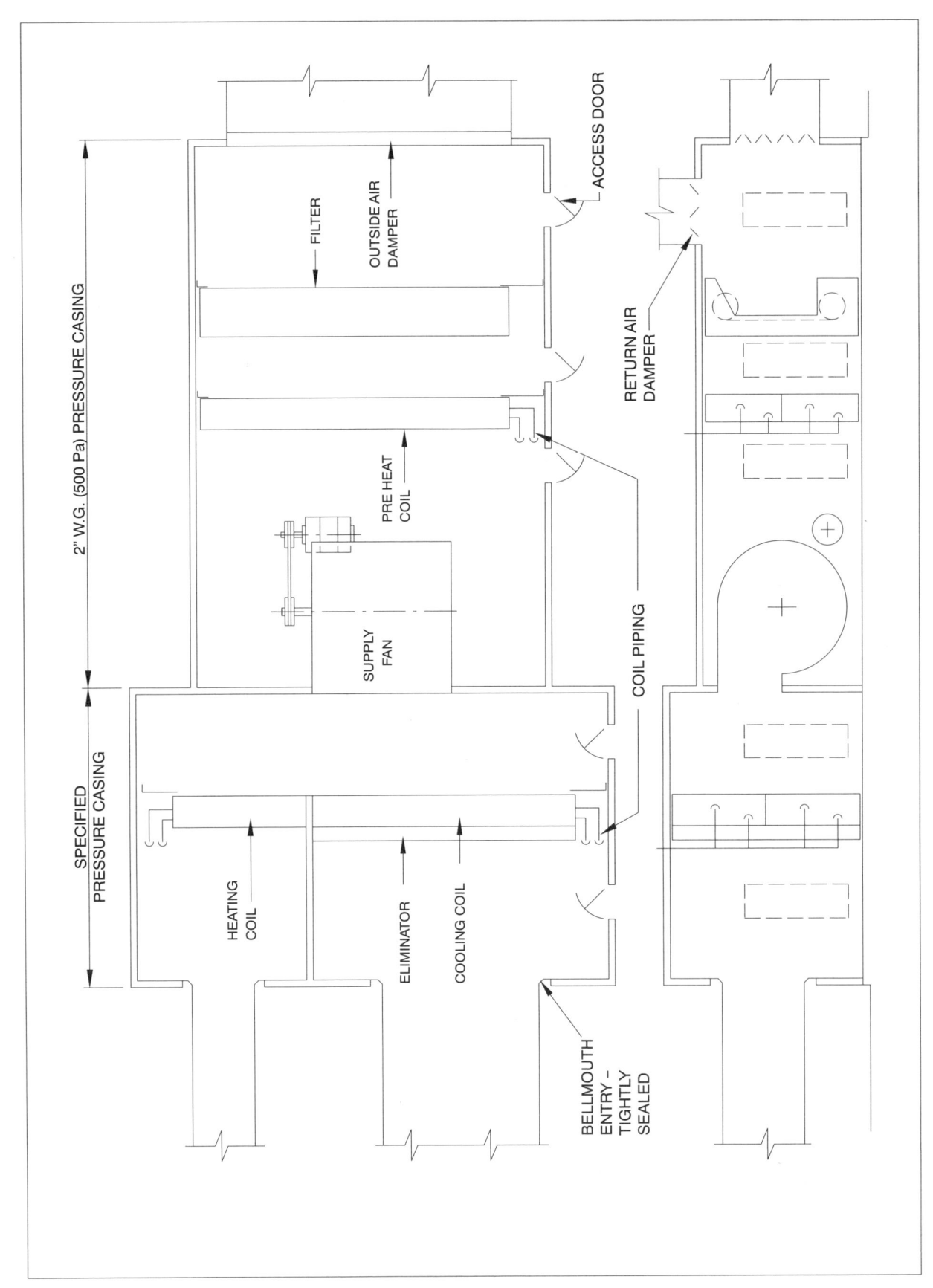

FIGURE 9-4 OVER 2 IN. WG (500 PA) CASING ARRANGEMENT

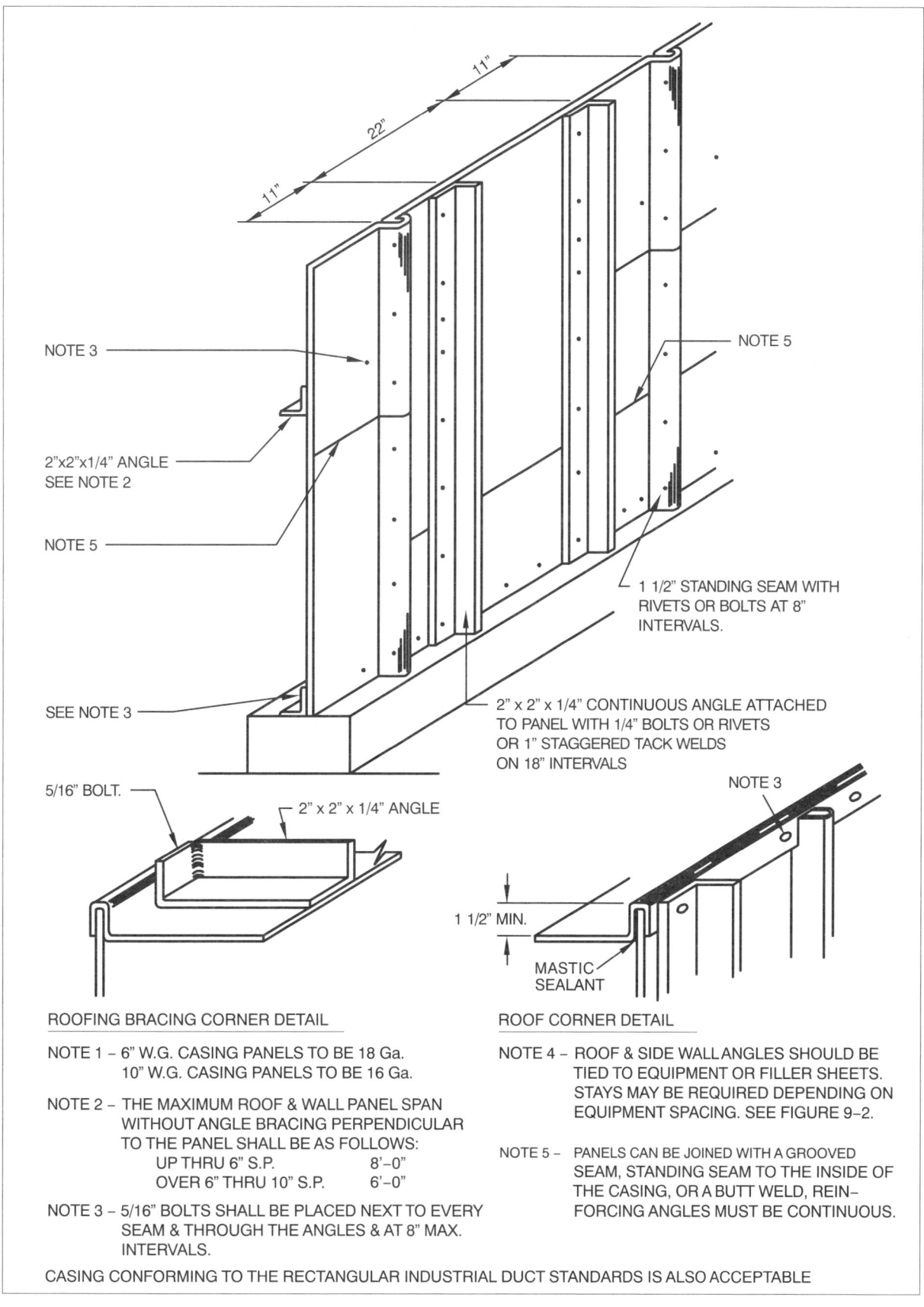

FIGURE 9–5 OVER 2 IN. WG PRESSURE APPARATUS CASING

ROOFING BRACING CORNER DETAIL

ROOF CORNER DETAIL

NOTE 1 – 6" W.G. CASING PANELS TO BE 18 Ga.
10" W.G. CASING PANELS TO BE 16 Ga.

NOTE 2 – THE MAXIMUM ROOF & WALL PANEL SPAN WITHOUT ANGLE BRACING PERPENDICULAR TO THE PANEL SHALL BE AS FOLLOWS:
UP THRU 6" S.P.   8'-0"
OVER 6" THRU 10" S.P. 6'-0"

NOTE 3 – 5/16" BOLTS SHALL BE PLACED NEXT TO EVERY SEAM & THROUGH THE ANGLES & AT 8" MAX. INTERVALS.

NOTE 4 – ROOF & SIDE WALL ANGLES SHOULD BE TIED TO EQUIPMENT OR FILLER SHEETS. STAYS MAY BE REQUIRED DEPENDING ON EQUIPMENT SPACING. SEE FIGURE 9-2.

NOTE 5 – PANELS CAN BE JOINED WITH A GROOVED SEAM, STANDING SEAM TO THE INSIDE OF THE CASING, OR A BUTT WELD, REINFORCING ANGLES MUST BE CONTINUOUS.

CASING CONFORMING TO THE RECTANGULAR INDUSTRIAL DUCT STANDARDS IS ALSO ACCEPTABLE

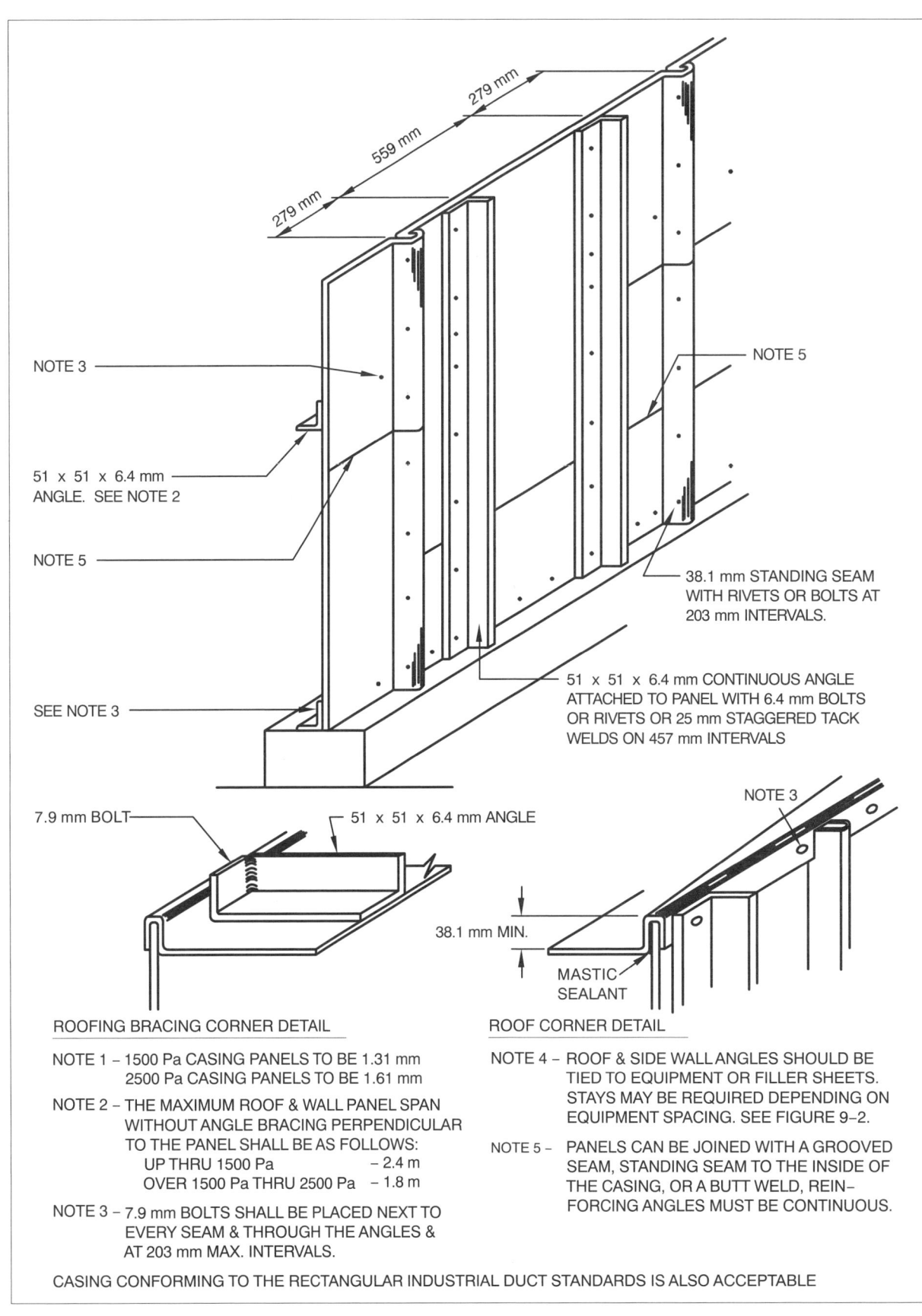

FIGURE 9–5M OVER 500 PA PRESSURE APPARATUS CASING

Labels on main illustration:
- 279 mm, 559 mm, 279 mm
- NOTE 3
- NOTE 5
- 51 x 51 x 6.4 mm ANGLE. SEE NOTE 2
- NOTE 5
- SEE NOTE 3
- 38.1 mm STANDING SEAM WITH RIVETS OR BOLTS AT 203 mm INTERVALS.
- 51 x 51 x 6.4 mm CONTINUOUS ANGLE ATTACHED TO PANEL WITH 6.4 mm BOLTS OR RIVETS OR 25 mm STAGGERED TACK WELDS ON 457 mm INTERVALS

Roofing Bracing Corner Detail:
- 7.9 mm BOLT
- 51 x 51 x 6.4 mm ANGLE

Roof Corner Detail:
- NOTE 3
- 38.1 mm MIN.
- MASTIC SEALANT

ROOFING BRACING CORNER DETAIL

ROOF CORNER DETAIL

NOTE 1 – 1500 Pa CASING PANELS TO BE 1.31 mm
2500 Pa CASING PANELS TO BE 1.61 mm

NOTE 2 – THE MAXIMUM ROOF & WALL PANEL SPAN WITHOUT ANGLE BRACING PERPENDICULAR TO THE PANEL SHALL BE AS FOLLOWS:
UP THRU 1500 Pa – 2.4 m
OVER 1500 Pa THRU 2500 Pa – 1.8 m

NOTE 3 – 7.9 mm BOLTS SHALL BE PLACED NEXT TO EVERY SEAM & THROUGH THE ANGLES & AT 203 mm MAX. INTERVALS.

NOTE 4 – ROOF & SIDE WALL ANGLES SHOULD BE TIED TO EQUIPMENT OR FILLER SHEETS. STAYS MAY BE REQUIRED DEPENDING ON EQUIPMENT SPACING. SEE FIGURE 9–2.

NOTE 5 – PANELS CAN BE JOINED WITH A GROOVED SEAM, STANDING SEAM TO THE INSIDE OF THE CASING, OR A BUTT WELD, REINFORCING ANGLES MUST BE CONTINUOUS.

CASING CONFORMING TO THE RECTANGULAR INDUSTRIAL DUCT STANDARDS IS ALSO ACCEPTABLE

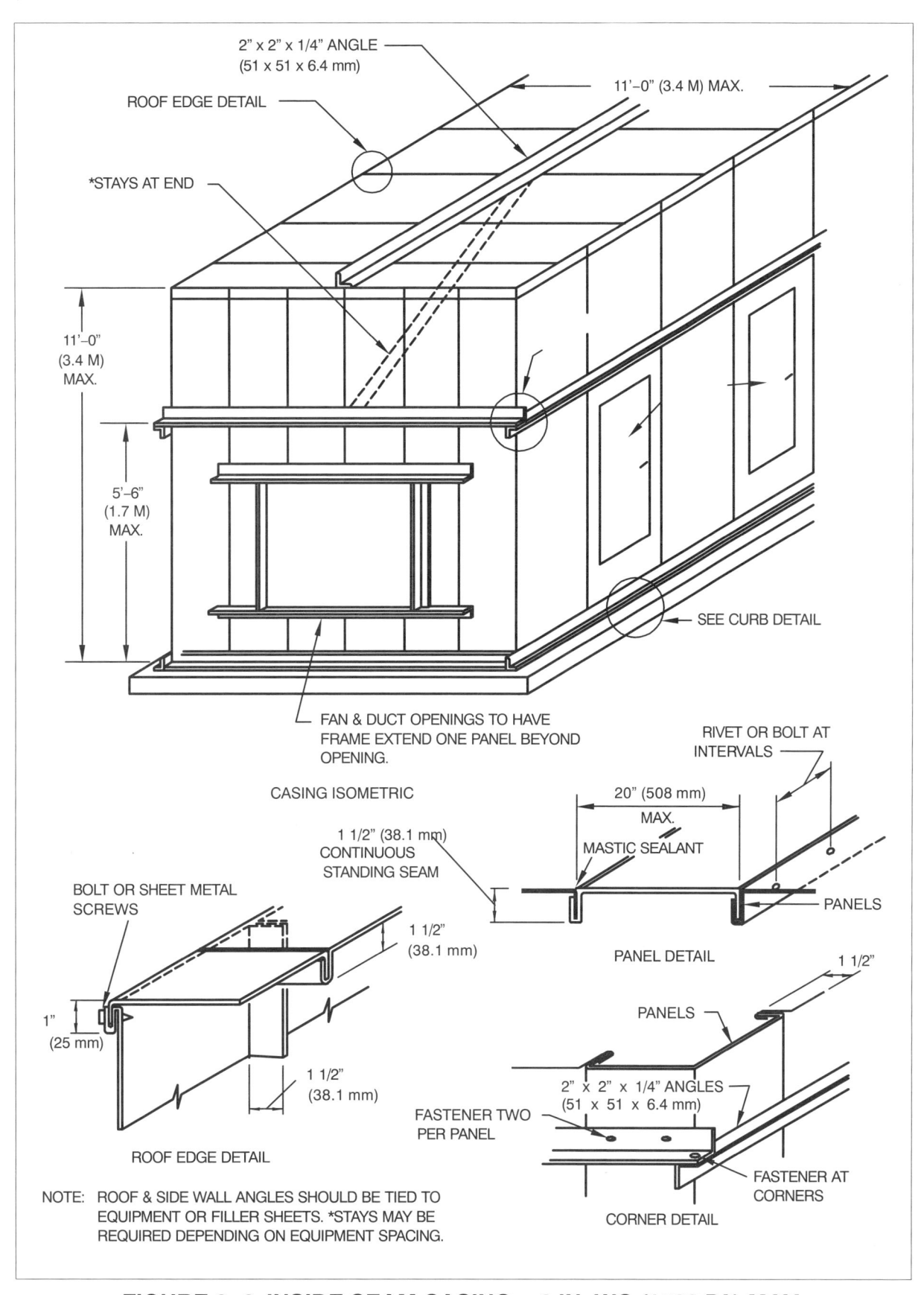

FIGURE 9-6 INSIDE SEAM CASING – 6 IN. WG (1500 PA) MAX.

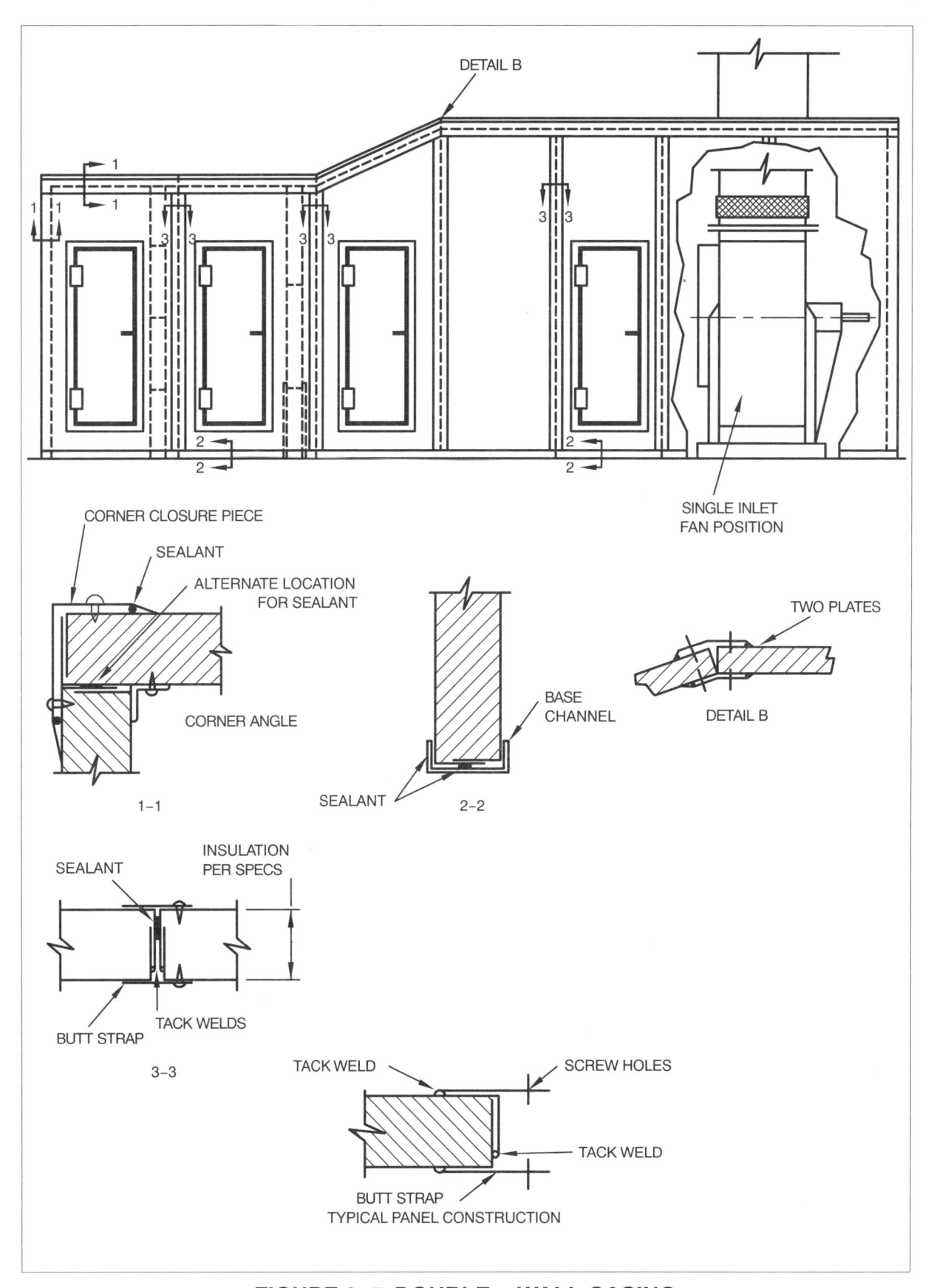

FIGURE 9-7 DOUBLE – WALL CASING

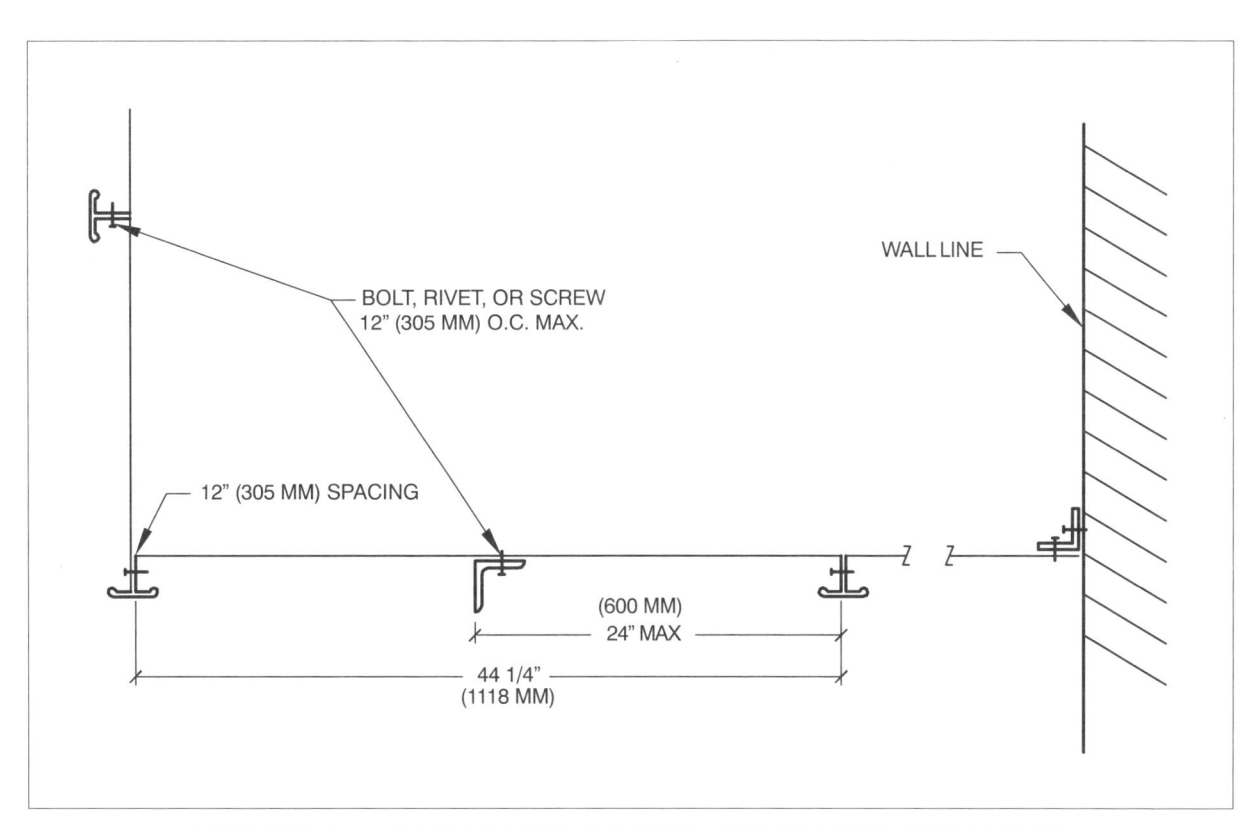

FIGURE 9-8 ALTERNATE CASING CONSTRUCTION USING TDC OR TDF FLANGES

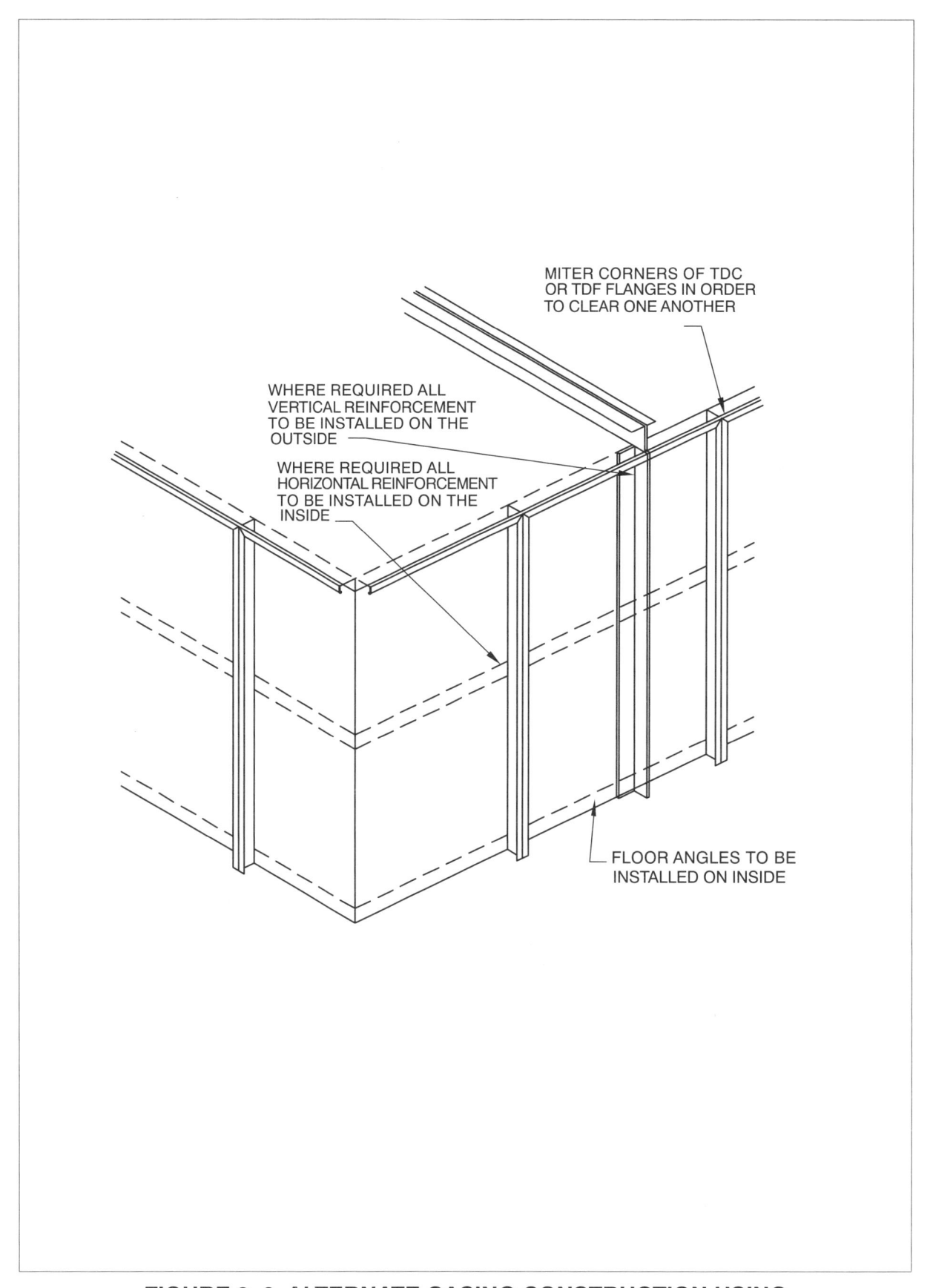

FIGURE 9-9 ALTERNATE CASING CONSTRUCTION USING TDC OR TDF FLANGES

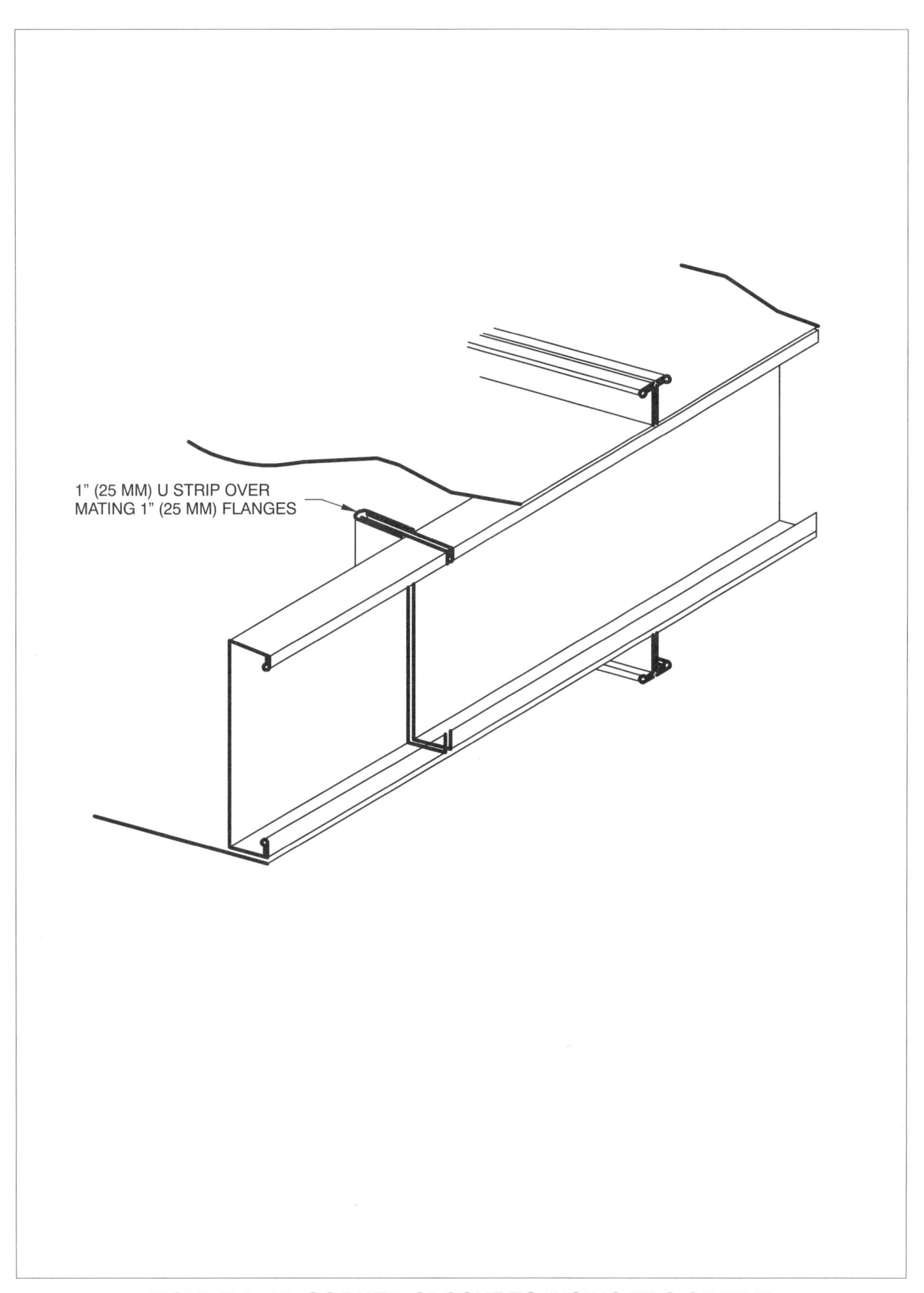

FIGURE 9-10 CORNER CLOSURES (USING TDC OR TDF)

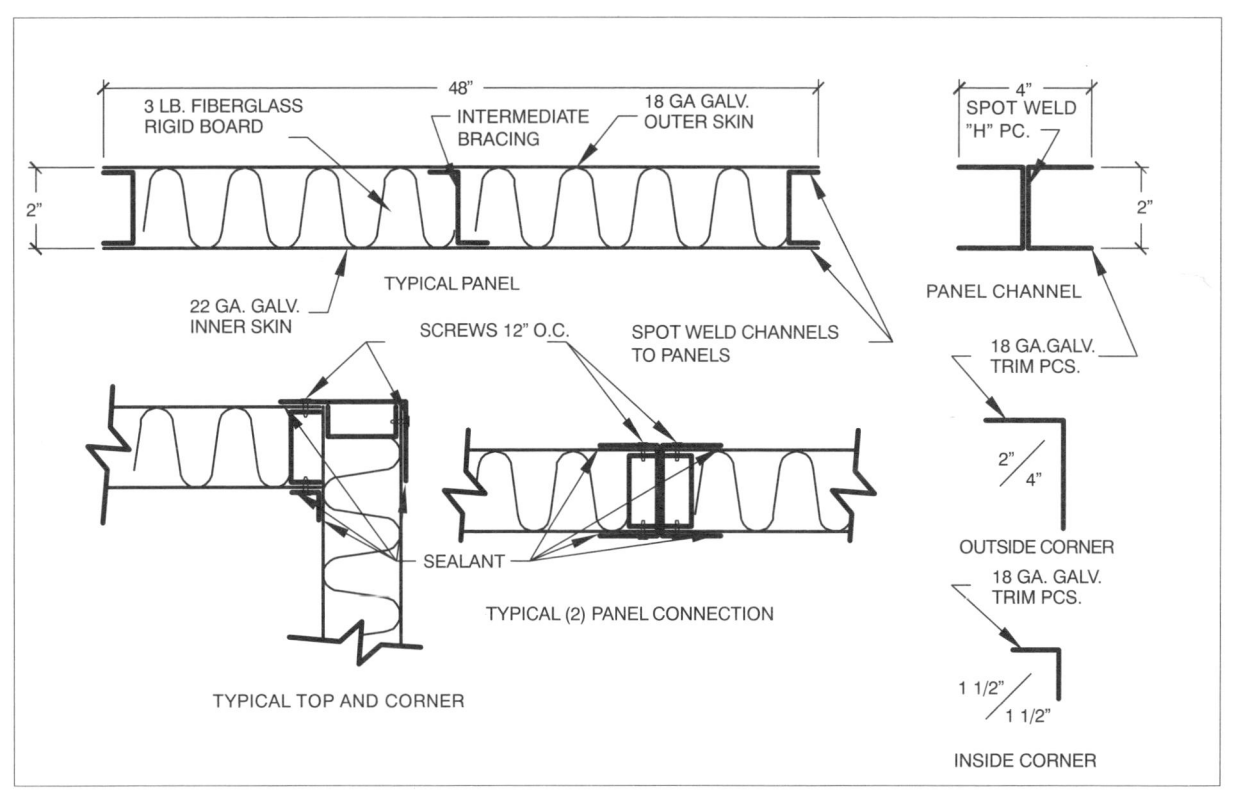

FIGURE 9-11 DOUBLE-WALL CASING DETAILS

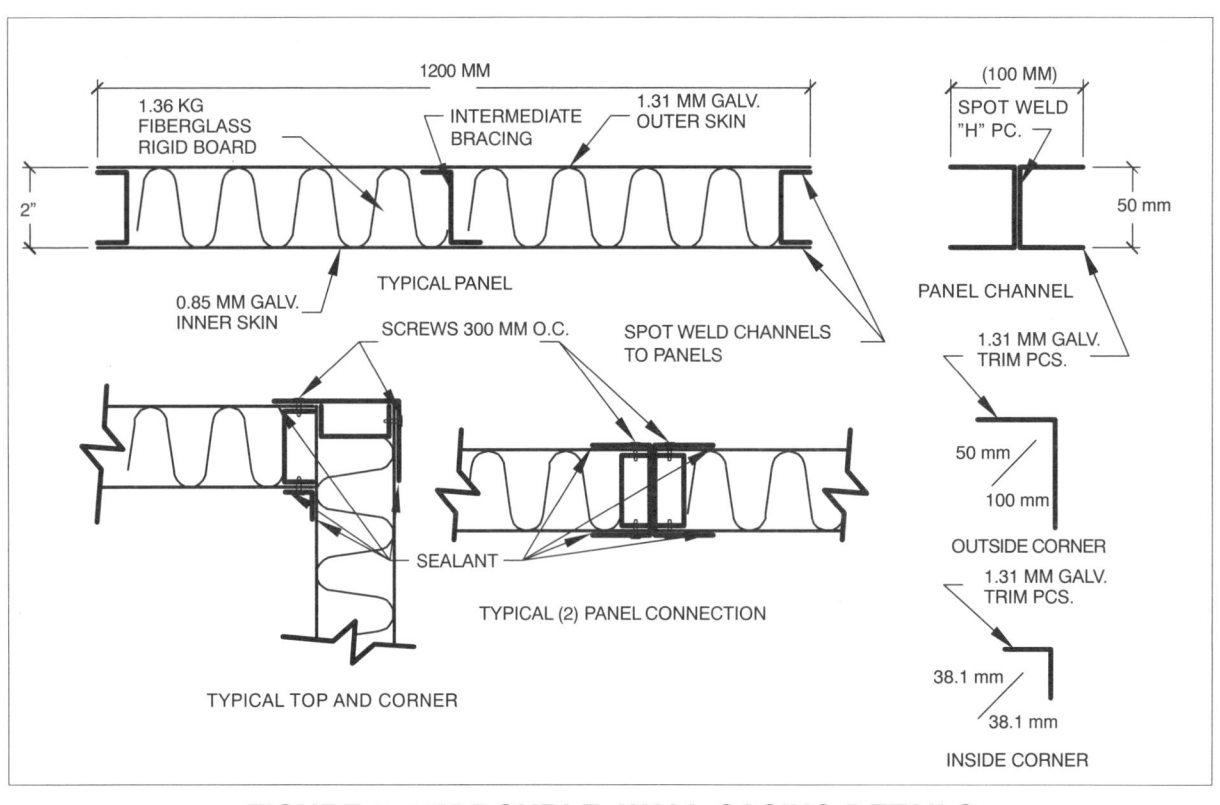

FIGURE 9-11M DOUBLE-WALL CASING DETAILS

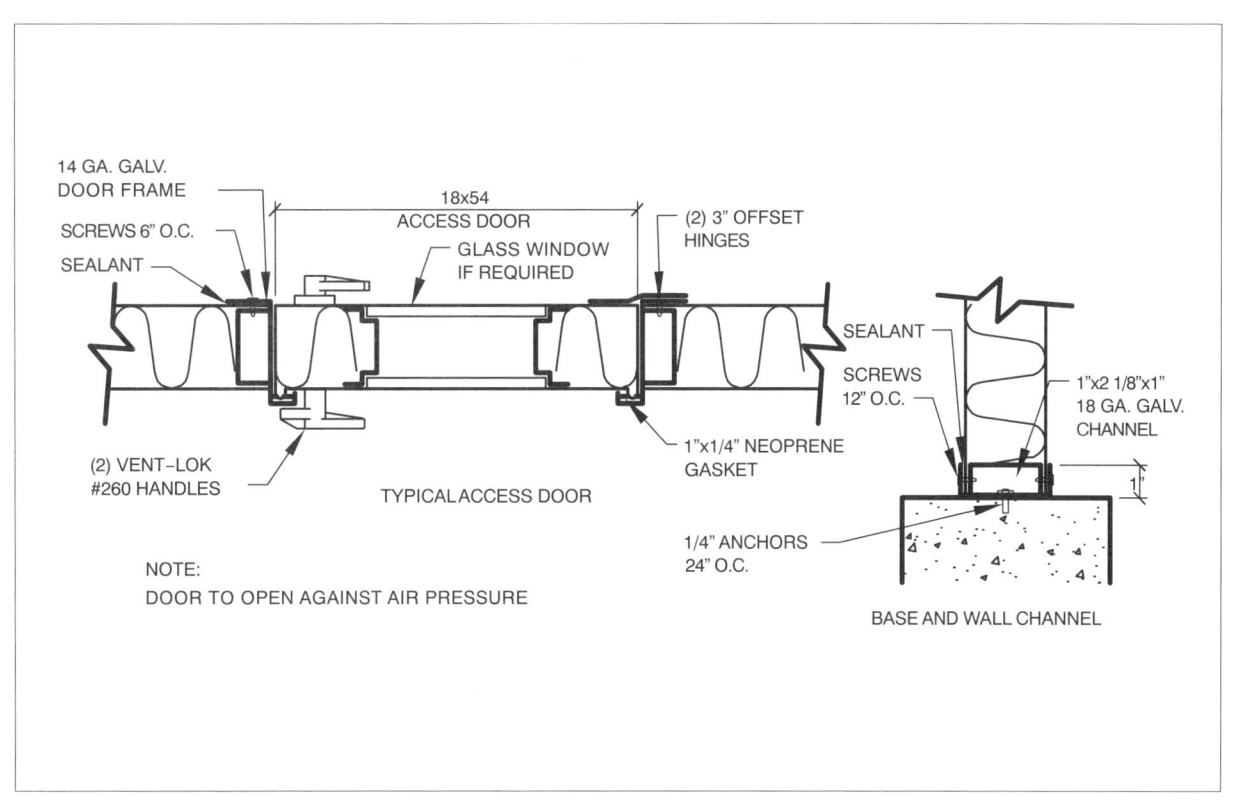

FIGURE 9-11 DOUBLE-WALL CASING DETAILS (CONTINUED)
TYPICAL ACCESS DOOR

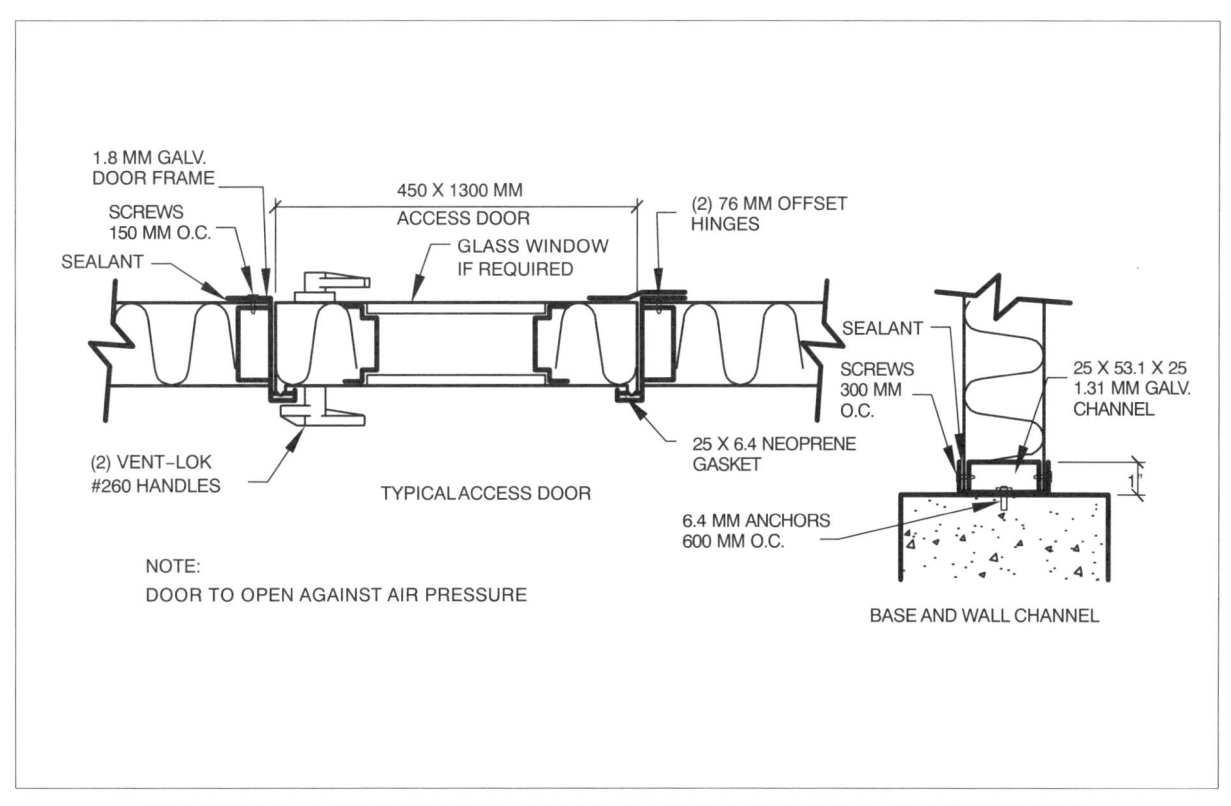

FIGURE 9-11M DOUBLE-WALL CASING DETAILS (CONTINUED)
TYPICAL ACCESS DOOR

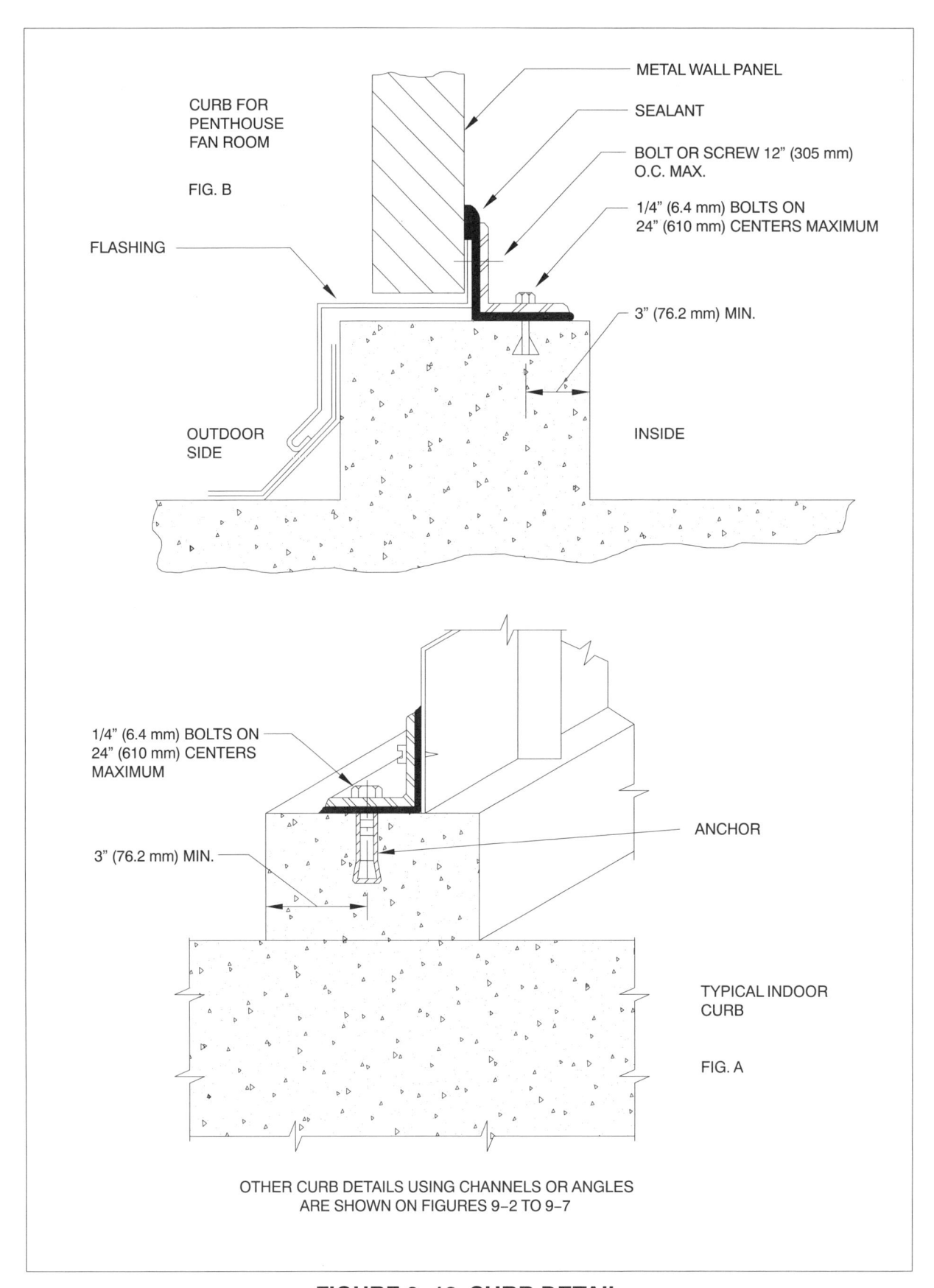

FIGURE 9–12 CURB DETAIL

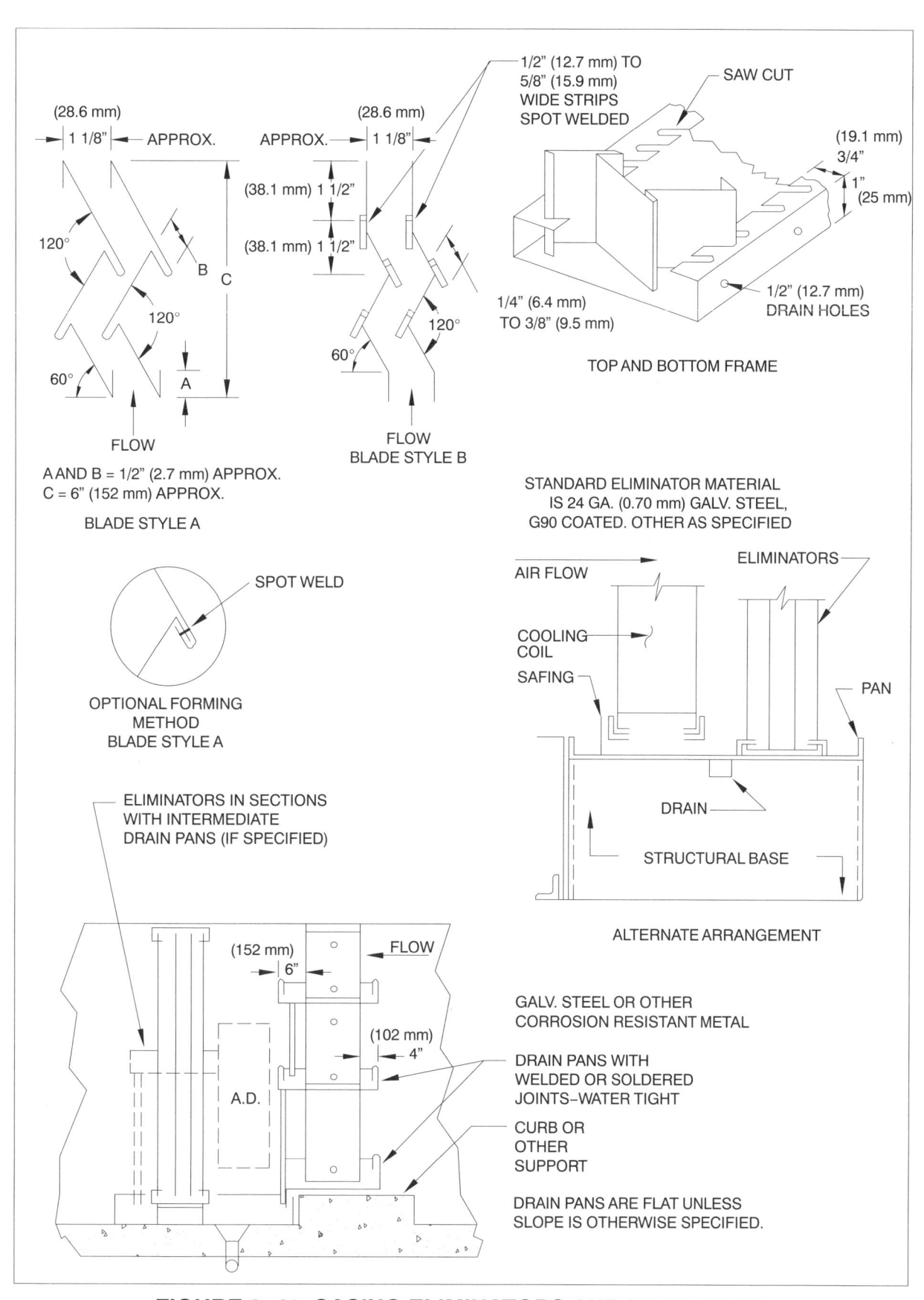

FIGURE 9-13 CASING ELIMINATORS AND DRAIN PANS

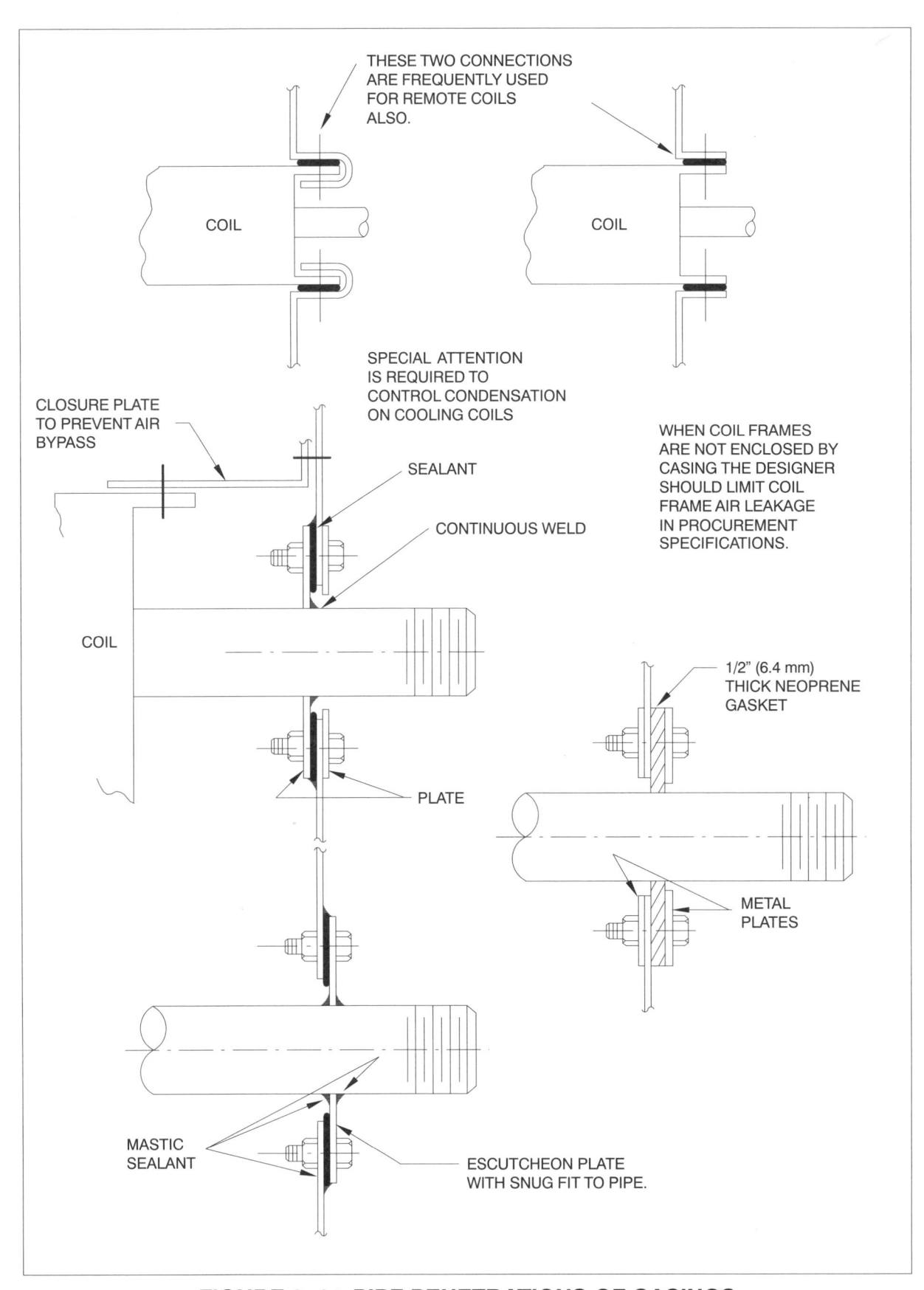

FIGURE 9–14 PIPE PENETRATIONS OF CASINGS

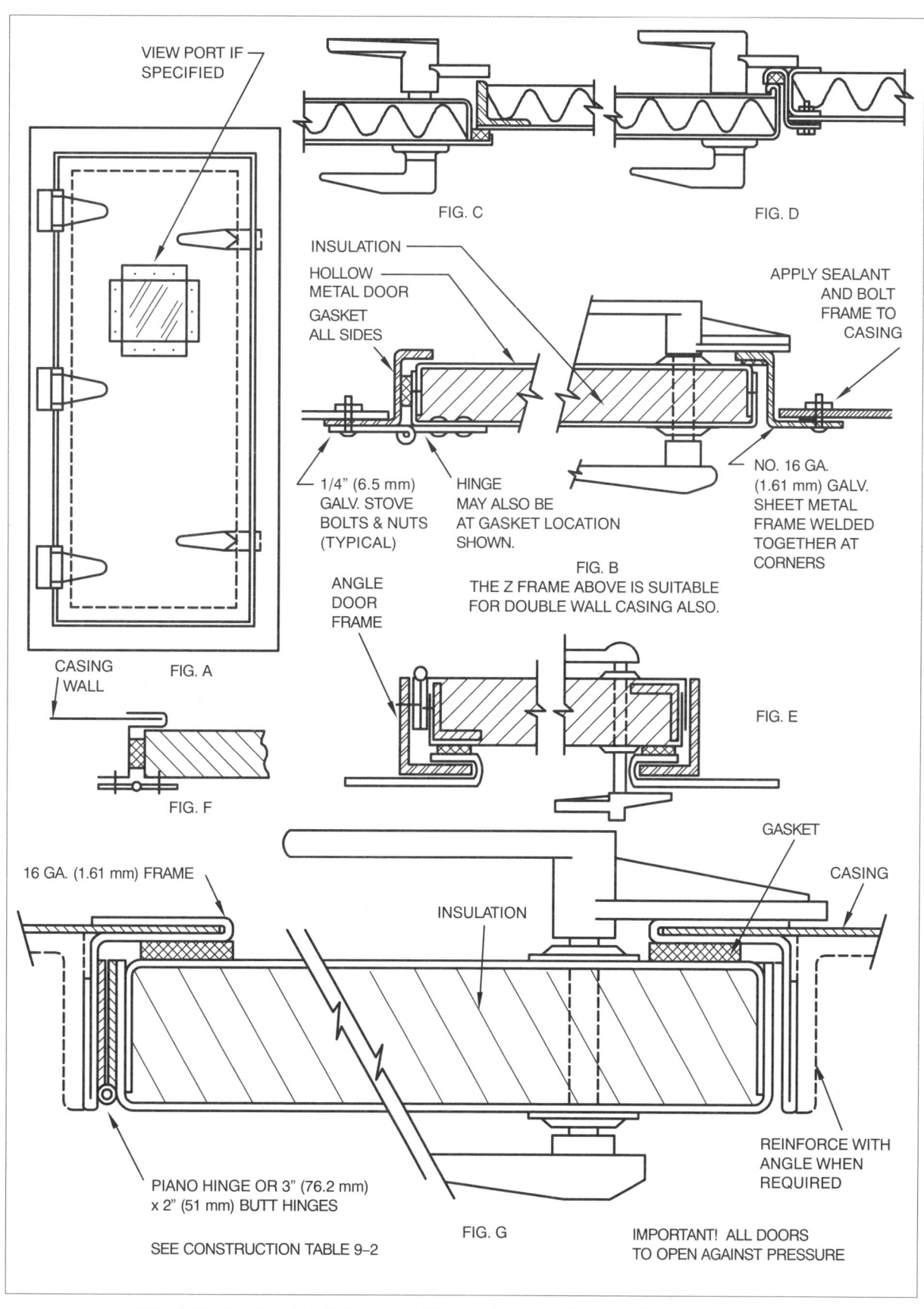

FIGURE 9–15 CASING ACCESS DOORS – 2 IN. WG (500 Pa)

Door Size	No. Hinges *	No. Handles	Gage Door	Gage Back	Gage Frame	Insulation (if req'd) (in.)
72 in. × 18 in. up	4	3	20	22	1½ in. × 1½ in. × ⅛ in.	1
57 in. × 18 in. up	3	2	22	24	16 ga	1
45 in. × 18 in. up	3	2	22	24	18 ga	1
36 in. × 18 in. up	3	2	22	24	18 ga	1

Table 9–2 Plenum and Casing Access Doors – 2 in. wg

See Figure 7-2 for other construction details that may be suitable for small doors.

*Continuous piano hinge is optional.

Door Size	No. Hinges *	No. Handles	Gage Door	Gage Back	Gage Frame	Insulation (if req'd) (in.)
1800 × 450	4	3	1.00	0.85	38.1 × 38.1 × 3.2	25.4
1450 × 450	3	2	0.85	0.70	1.61	25.4
1150 × 450	3	2	0.85	0.70	1.61	25.4
900 × 450	3	2	0.85	0.70	1.61	25.4

Table 9–2M Plenum and Casing Access Doors – 500 Pa

See Figure 7-2 for other construction details that may be suitable for small doors.

*Continuous piano hinge is optional.

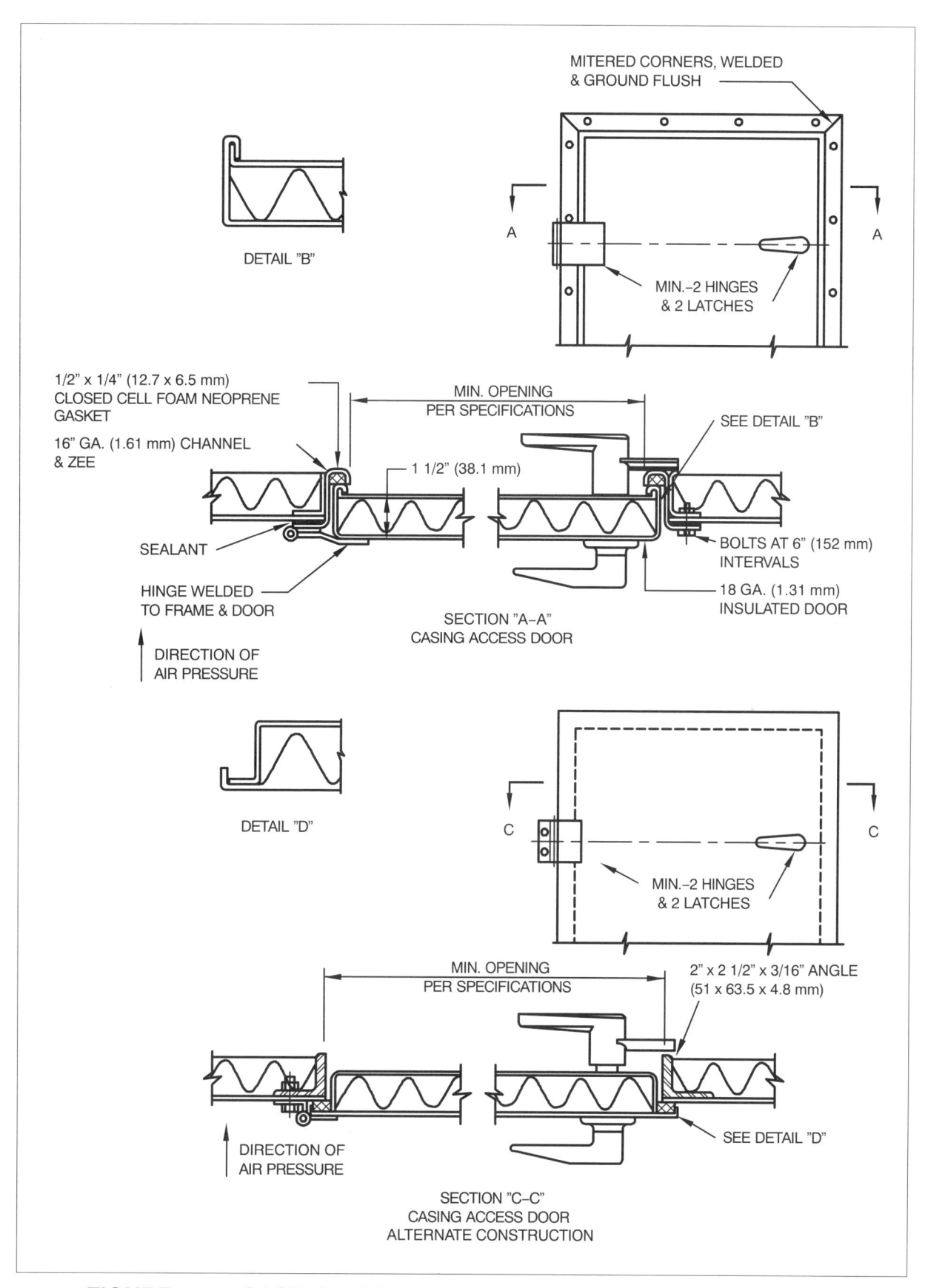

FIGURE 9–16 CASING ACCESS DOORS – 3–10 IN. WG (750–2500 Pa)

9.2 COMMENTARY

9.3 CASING ARRANGEMENT

Casings should be built in a rectangular box shape. Tapered sides and roofs should be avoided primarily because of the difficulty in developing adequate strength and air tightness at the joints. In theory, the tapered casings conserve energy and facilitate uniform air distribution. However, as a practical matter, the tapers required for ideal expansion or contraction are such that there is seldom enough space to accommodate them in typical equipment rooms.

Several alternative constructions are illustrated. The contractor is obligated to select and use these construction details or their equivalent to satisfy the pressure level designated by the designer.

Therefore, all details such as bracing, curb connections, roof and side wall connections, access doors, etc., must be carefully constructed to carry their share of the load.

CASING ASSEMBLY DETAILS SHOWN ARE NOT THE ONLY SATISFACTORY METHODS. OTHER TECHNIQUES ARE EQUIVALENT OR SUPERIOR. AUTHORITIES SHOULD JUDGE ALTERNATIVES ON THE BASIS OF ACCEPTABLE EVIDENCE.

9.3.1 Single-Thickness Wall Construction

Single-wall casings may be constructed from continuous standing seam reinforced panels or one of the alternative constructions. The same gage of metal is used on all sides. Galvanized steel is standard sheet material. Black iron stiffeners are standard.

9.3.2 Double-Thickness Wall Construction

Double-wall, casings are fabricated in a variety of types and thicknesses by specialized producers. Some offer acoustical control through a perforated inner liner.

There are so many possible variations of the double-wall casing construction that it is impractical to detail them in this manual. If a contractor wants to fabricate this type of casing, it is suggested that strength of the panels be determined by structural calculations or pressure tests on mock-ups. Particular attention should be given to the design of airtight joints for panels with perforated liners.

A cubic foot (28.32 L) of water weighs approximately 62.4 lbs. (28.3 kg). A one-inch (25 mm)-high column of water exerts a pressure of $\frac{1}{1726}$ of 62.4 (28.3 kg.) or 361 lbs. (1.64 kg.) on one square inch (645 mm^2). On one square foot (0.0929 m^2) the load is $\frac{1}{12}$ of 62.4 (28.3 kg.) or 5.2 lbs. (2.36 kg.). The following table relates static pressure to pounds per square foot:

Static Pressure		
(in.)	(Pa)	psf
1 in. water gage	(250)	5.2
2 in. water gage	(500)	10.4
3 in. water gage	(750)	15.6
4 in. water gage	(1000)	20.8
6 in. water gage	(1500)	31.2
8 in. water gage	(2000)	41.6
10 in. water gage	(2500)	52.0
1 in. water gage is 0.036 psi (0.25 kPa).		
1 psi is 27.36 in. wg (6897 Pa)		

9.3.3 Anchorage

Casings are normally set on a 4 to 6 in. high (102 to 152 mm) concrete curb to facilitate housekeeping and also to contain any water which may leak from the coils or eliminators. The concrete curbs are normally poured on top of the finished floor. In order to prevent the forces on the casing walls from shearing off the curb, the curb should be securely doweled to the floor. If the floor is waterproofed, the curb should be doweled through the waterproof membrane into the structural slab.

9.3.4 Casing Access Doors

Unless required to permit replacement of larger equipment such as a fan motor, duct access door size should be limited to approximately 20 in. (508 mm) wide by 54 in. (1372 mm) high. This is an adequate size for personnel and most equipment. Larger doors should be avoided since they break the continuity of the wall reinforcing. DOORS SHOULD OPEN AGAINST THE AIR PRESSURE. This arrangement utilizes the air pressure rather than the door latches to force the door against the sealing gasket.

9.3.5 Joint Sealing

All joints, seams, and connections should be sealed. Sealing is equally important on suction and discharge sides of the fan. Gasketing may suffice for some assemblies.

Leakage testing of casing is not routinely practical. Attention to workmanship and inspection of the pressurized installation will normally suffice for airtightness.

9.3.6 Drainage

Drainage facilities must be provided in the coil and eliminator sections of the casing to handle condensation on the cooling coil.

Conventional drains without deep seal traps will not give satisfactory performance. Drainage may be directly into the sewer system through a floor drain in the casing, or indirectly through the casing curb to an exterior floor drain. In either case, THE DRAIN LINE MUST BE PROVIDED WITH A WATER SEAL AT LEAST 2 IN. (51 mm) GREATER THAN THE MAXIMUM NEGATIVE STATIC PRESSURE ON THE CASING.

9.3.7 Piping Penetrations

If space is available, water and steam coil connections should be manifolded inside the casing to minimize the number of penetrations through the casing walls. Piping penetrations must be carefully sealed, especially on chilled water piping because any leakage will force condensation along the pipe insulation.

9.3.8 Low Pressure Casing Protection

The casing up to the suction side of the fan is normally constructed as a conventional low-pressure casing.

If the fan and the return and fresh air damper controls are not properly synchronized, it is possible that the supply fans will exert an extreme negative static pressure on the low pressure casings. It is not necessary to build these casings to withstand these unusual pressures. However, the fan and damper controls must be carefully coordinated so that it is impossible for such a negative pressure condition to occur. Safety relief panels or dampers may be designed into the system to prevent damage.

CONTRACTORS SHOULD BE PARTICULARLY AWARE OF THE POTENTIAL DAMAGE WHICH CAN BE CAUSED BY IMPROPER MANIPULATION OF THE DAMPER CONTROLS DURING CONSTRUCTION AND INITIAL START-UP.

THE OUTSIDE AIR OR RETURN AIR DAMPER SHOULD BE BLOCKED OPEN UNTIL THE AUTOMATIC CONTROL SYSTEM IS PUT INTO OPERATION AND PROPERLY ADJUSTED.

THIS PAGE INTENTIONALLY LEFT BLANK

CHAPTER 10

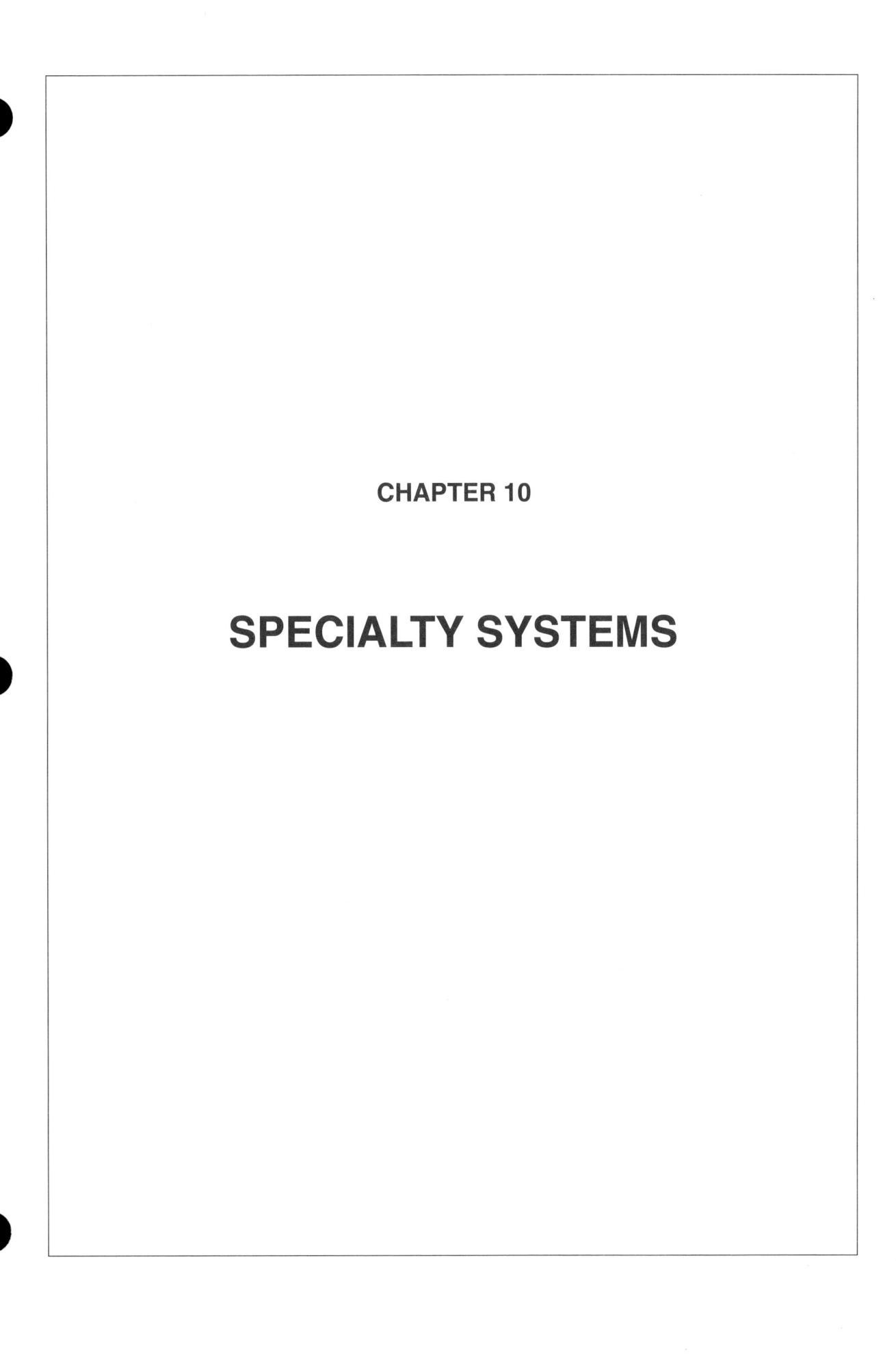

SPECIALTY SYSTEMS

CHAPTER 10

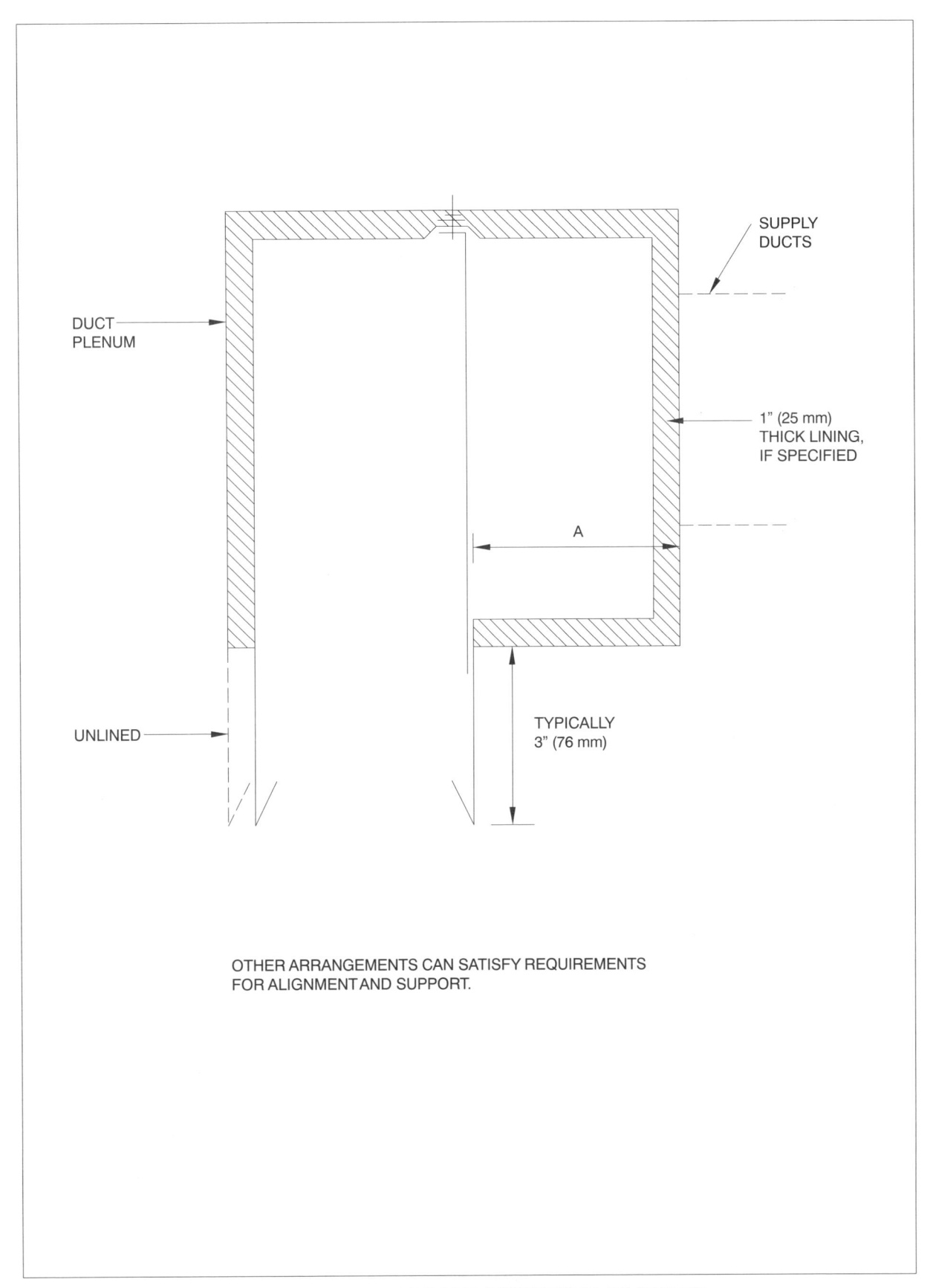

SPECIALTY SYSTEMS

FIGURE 10-1 LINEAR DIFFUSER PLENUM

10.1 HOODS

In recent years, there has been a great increase in the extent of construction detail for dust, fume, and grease removal systems that appears in codes and code-invoked standards such as NFPA-91, "Standard for Exhaust Systems for Air Conveying of Vapors, Gases, Mists, and Noncombustible Particulate Solids" and NFPA-96, "Standard for Ventilation Control and Fire Protection of Commercial Cooking Operations." Such detail now sets forth material, wall thickness, and joint construction, among other features. Furthermore, much data on the shape, size, and location of kitchen range and other hoods is published in the book *Industrial Ventilation,* by the American Conference of Governmental Industrial Hygienists. Examples are Kitchen Range Hood Plates VS-30-10 and VS-30-11, Paint Spray Booth Plates VS-75-01 and VS-75-02, and Charcoal Broiler Hood Plate VS-30-12.

Chapter 3 is devoted to hood design data and Chapter 10 to specific operations involving hoods and ducts. Moreover, new emphasis on energy conservation has prompted the increased use of localized exhaust and makeup air.

These and similar industry changes have resulted in reliance on customized designs rather than standard designs such as those formerly published by SMACNA.

Designers should consult these references, illustrate the complete design on contract drawings, and make limited reference to the duct construction detail in this manual, if necessary.

"Hooded" air intakes and exhausts for the exterior of buildings are detailed in the Appendix.

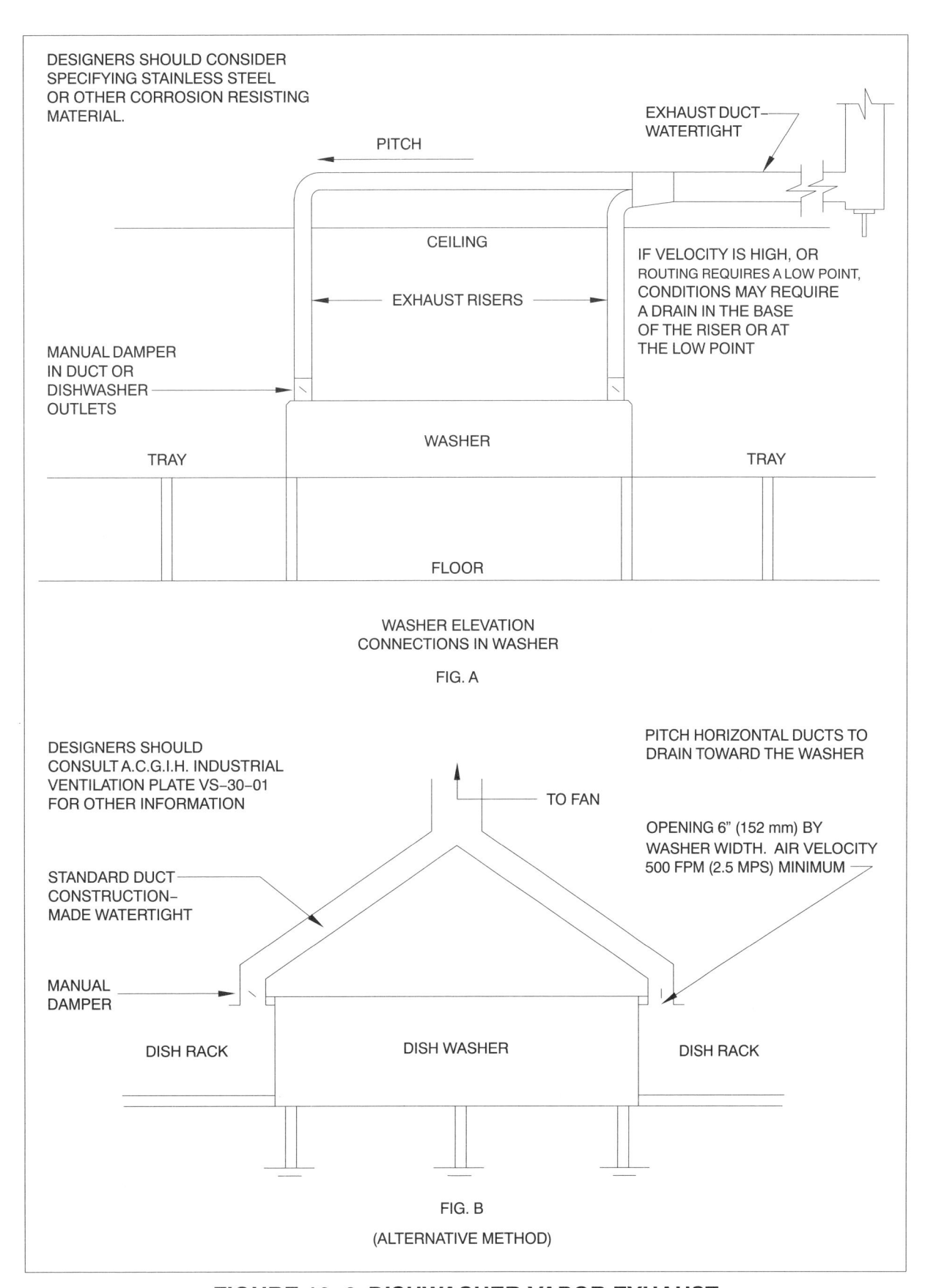

FIGURE 10-2 DISHWASHER VAPOR EXHAUST

10.2 UNDERGROUND DUCT CONSTRUCTION STANDARDS

S3.41 This installation standard is applicable to ducts placed in or beneath concrete floors or in areas free from vehicle traffic.

S3.42 Materials shall conform to the project specifications.

S3.43 Ducts shall be located as shown on the contract drawings.

S3.44 The duct contractor shall provide:

a. Proper assembly of the duct, including connections and sealing as prescribed;

b. Verification of the undamaged condition of the duct before enclosure with fill or encasement;

c. Anchorage for the duct, if any;

d. Notices of requirements for successive placements of fill, if any;

e. Precautions against use of powered vibrators in placing concrete on or around ducts;

f. Witnessing of backfill or encasement; and

g. Temporary protection of openings in ducts.

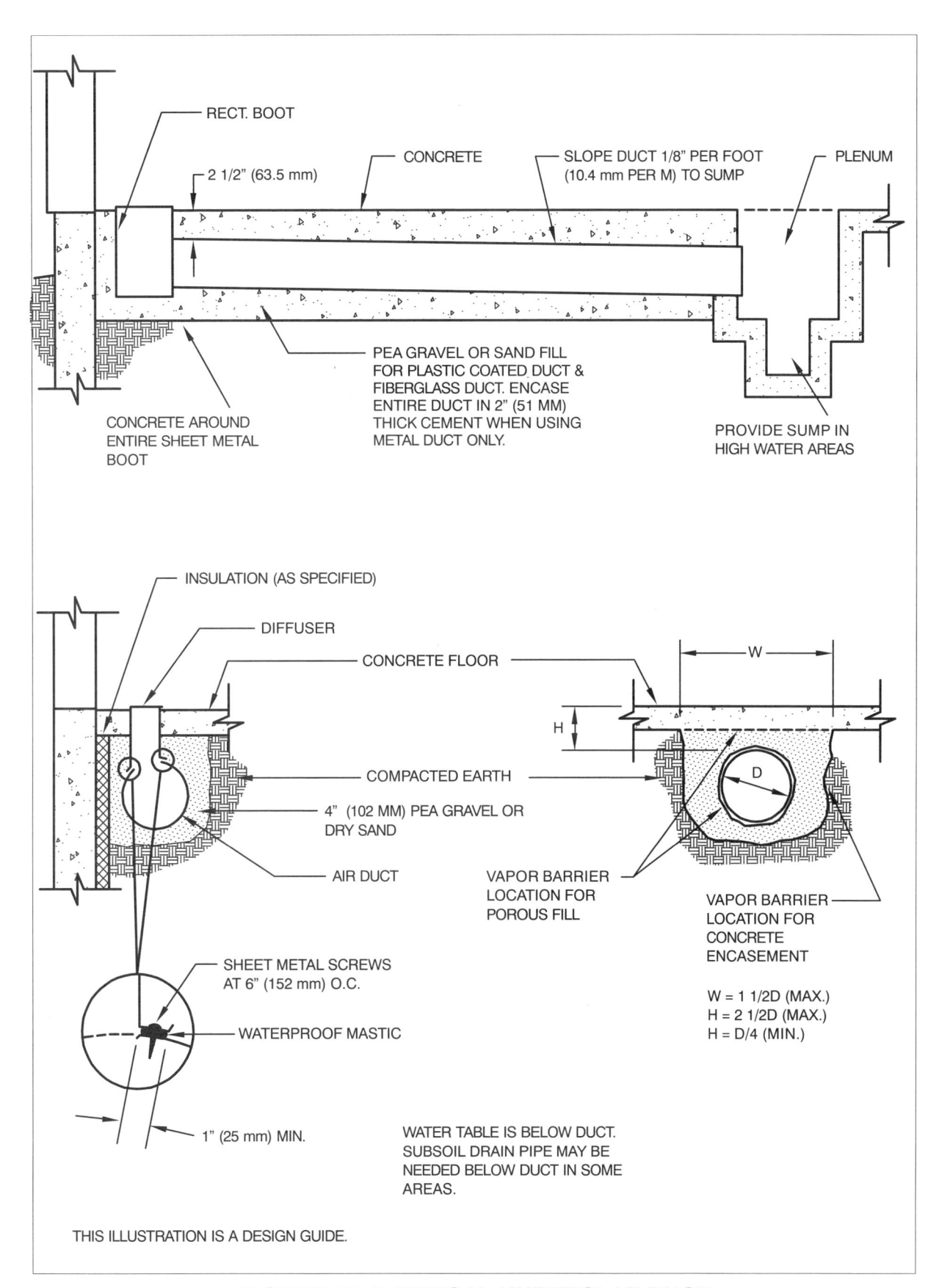

FIGURE 10-3 TYPICAL UNDERSLAB DUCT

HVAC Duct Construction Standards Metal and Flexible • Fourth Edition

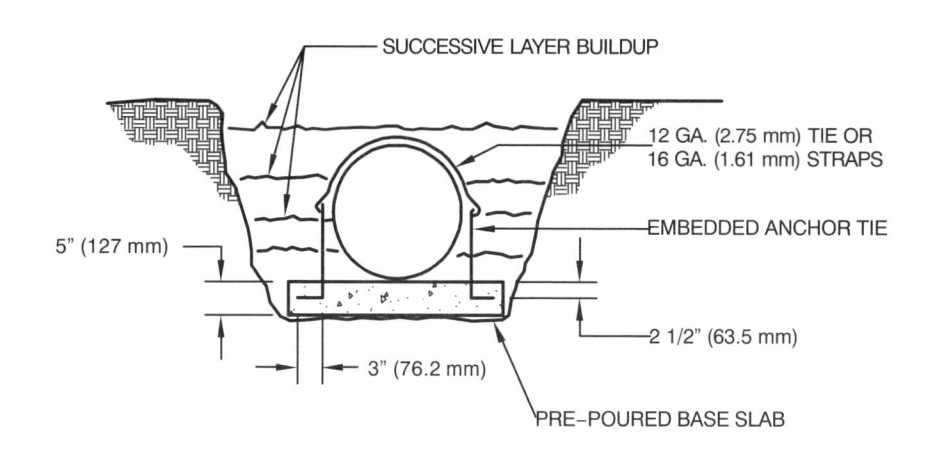

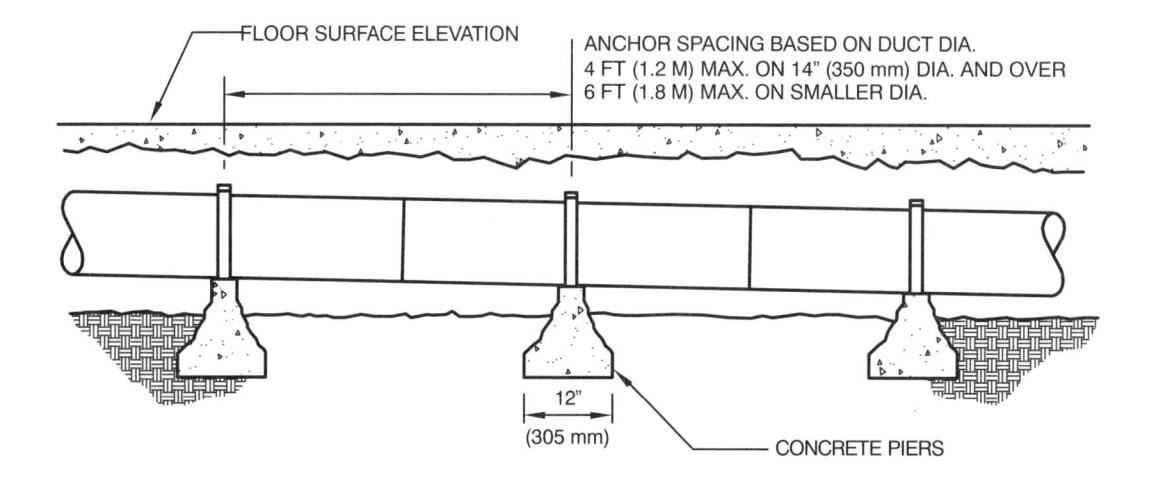

FIGURE 10-4 ANCHORS FOR DUCT ENCASEMENT

10.3 COMMENTARY

Materials commonly used for this application include galvanized steel, vinyl chloride-coated steel, and stainless steel. Glass fiber-reinforced resin, asbestos, cement, tile, and other nonmetal ducts are also used. Ducts are not generally deemed to be or required to be waterproof. Ducts should always be above the water table. The designer should carefully evaluate the exposure to moisture or ground water and require vapor barriers, sumps, porous fill, and subsoil drainage pipe as necessary Master Format Specification 023000 provides useful references for subsoil drainage. The top of drain tile should be below the bottom of the duct.

Corrosion resistance is an important characteristic of both in-slab and under-slab ducts. The Portland Cement Association has guidelines for protection of metals in contact with concrete. *ASHRAE Handbook - Systems* addresses the corrosion of materials in soil environments.

The strength of round ducts makes them the preferred shape for underground application. Round duct wall thicknesses in these standards are generally acceptable for below-grade installation. Ribbed or corrugated styles have additional crushing strength. Temporary internal supports can be appropriate at times. Ducts should have continuous bedding.

Ducts to be embedded in concrete are subject to floating and they must be restrained. The first pour should be the base support for the duct and anchors should be included. Twelve gage (2.68 mm) wire, 16 ga (2.75 mm) straps, or other appropriate ties should be specified for hold-down.

Ducts buried in sand or pea gravel are not known to float. Porous fill and earth fill should not be dumped directly on ducts in trenches. Fill should be firmly but not heavily tamped under and around the duct. The first foot of fill should be shoveled on top of the duct. Fill should not contain stones larger than 2 in. (51 mm).

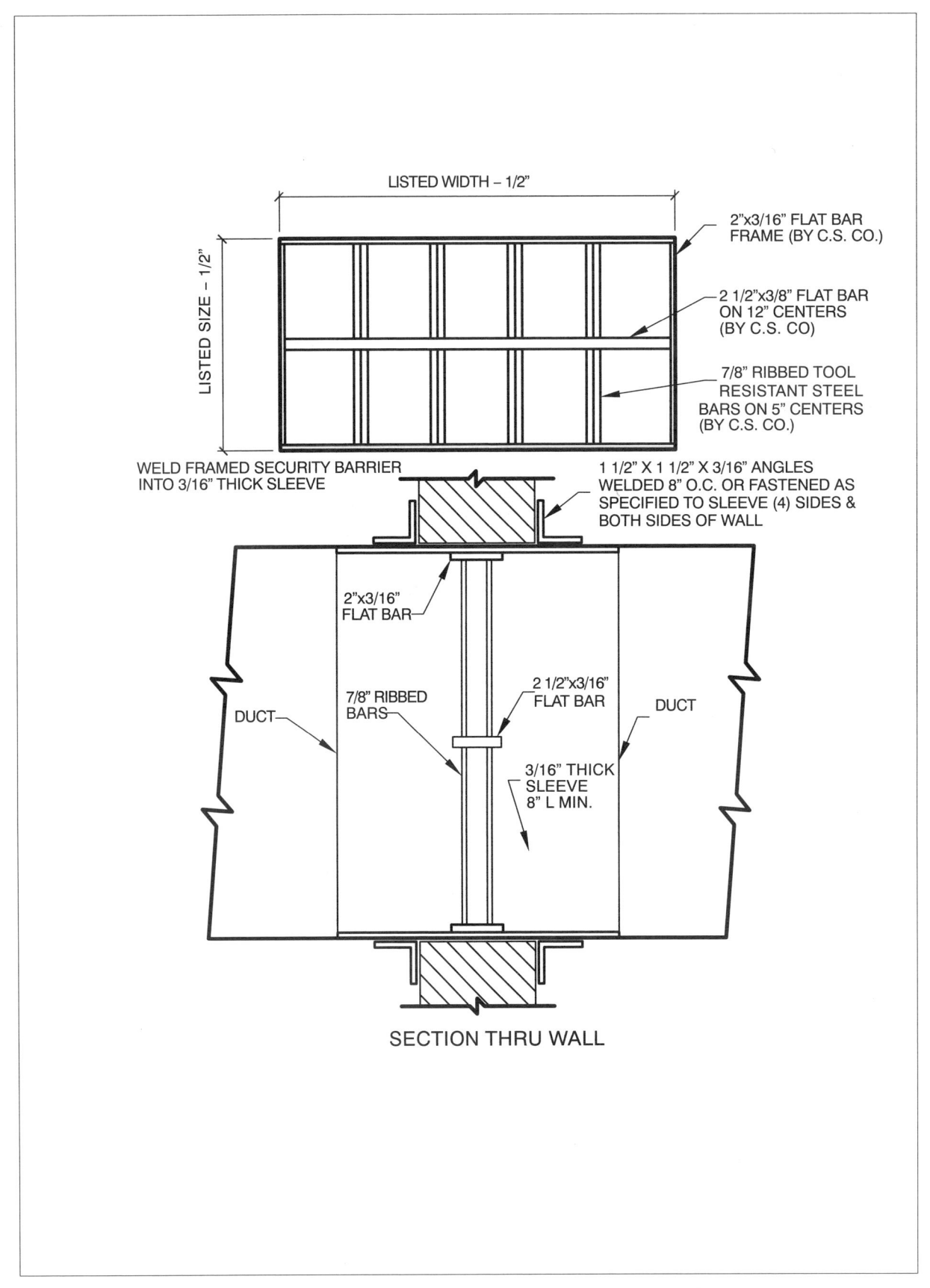

FIGURE 10-5 SECURITY DUCT BARRIER DETAIL

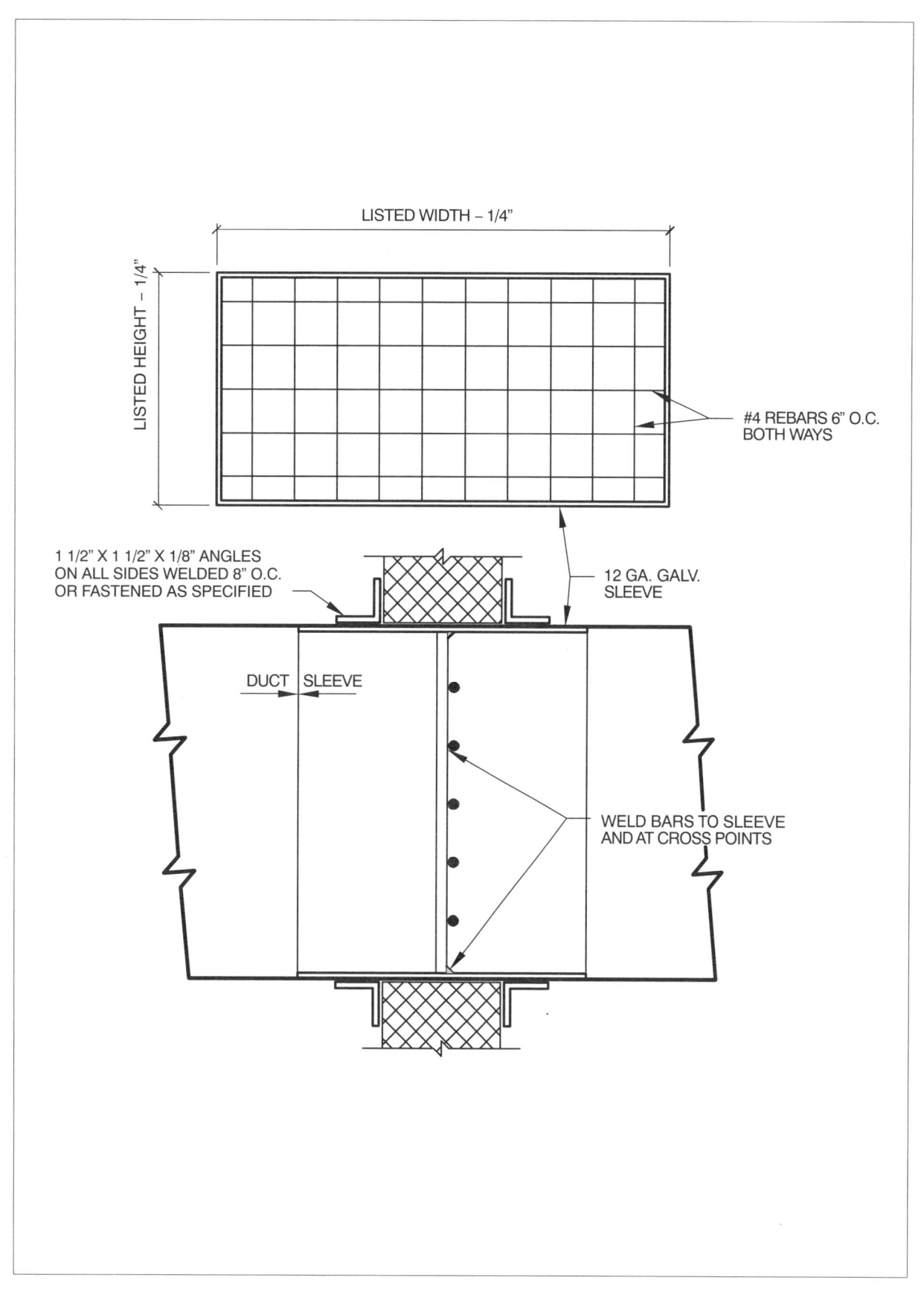

FIGURE 10-6 ALTERNATIVE SECURITY BARRIER DETAIL

CHAPTER 11

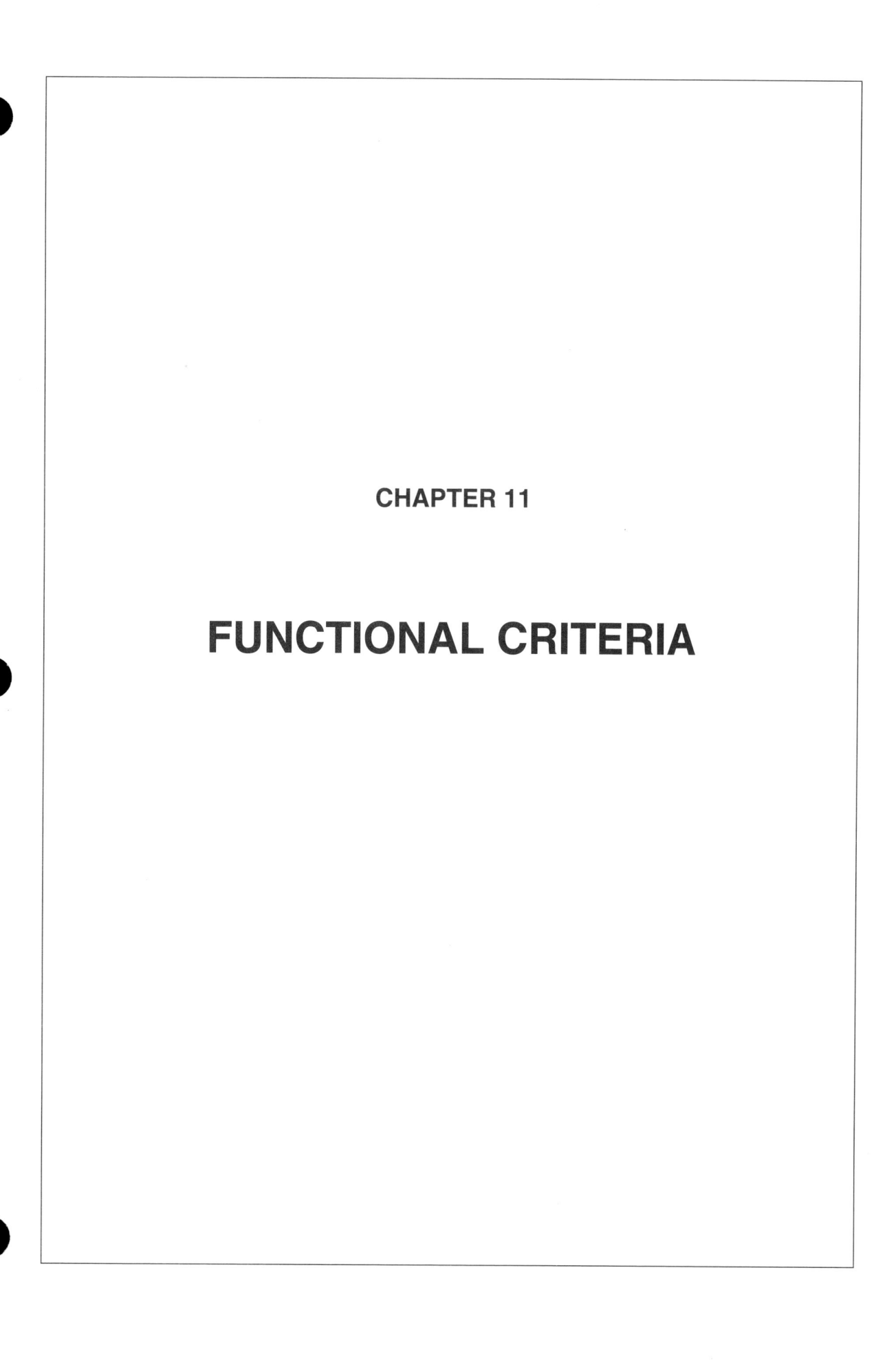

FUNCTIONAL CRITERIA

CHAPTER 11

11.1 FUNCTIONAL CRITERIA FOR DUCTS

11.2 RECTANGULAR DUCTS

SMACNA has conducted testing and analysis of galvanized steel ducts up to 96 in. in size, of gages between 28 (0.48 mm) and 16 (1.61 mm), inclusive, at static pressure levels ranging from 0.1 in. wg (25 Pa) to 10 in. wg (2500 Pa). Tests were conducted in both positive and negative pressure modes. The study recorded pressure, deflection, and other duct element behavior. It concluded that the structural behavior of duct is reasonably predictable in terms of pressure, deflection, metal thickness, and stiffener spacing. Committees conclude that the functional criteria previously used are valid with some new provisions for tolerances. The general performance criteria for ducts is reviewed in Section 1.5.5 and outlined in 11.3.1.

The criteria used by SMACNA in its test program and in development of new duct tables is as follows.

1. Sheet

   The sheet must resist both deflection caused by internal pressure and vibration due to turbulent air flow. Because space is a limiting factor, and there is a need to maintain an approximately rectangular cross section, sheet deflections for ducts were limited as listed in Figure 11-1.

   The current test program did not include vibration analysis. A discussion of vibration parameters follows in this chapter. Commentary also appears with Table 1-1 and in the notes for Tables 2-1 to 2-7. It was concluded that the limited risk of an occasional problem is preferable to postponing use of multiple sheet gages until the boundaries of stability can be completely defined.

   Cross breaking or beading of unbraced duct sides larger than certain dimensions is effective in dealing with commercial tolerances on out-of-flatness, natural sag from dead weight, and with the flexure reversals that may result when duct pressure is inadequate to stretch the sheet taut. If pressure does not produce a taut sheet, vibration may result. Beading is considered as effective as cross breaking, but formation of a suitable bead requires adjustment for each sheet thickness. Criteria for cross breaking or beading is given in Figure 2–10. NEITHER IS A SUBSTITUTE FOR REINFORCEMENT.

   The provisions for flexure control do not eliminate rumble during start-up and shutdown. Lagging or other measures must be designed if rumble is to be eliminated.

2. Reinforcing

   The reinforcing members must restrain the deflection of the sheet and must resist their own deflection. They must also handle bending moments so that allowable stresses are not exceeded.

3. Seams

   Longitudinal seams must be able to withstand 1.5 times the maximum operating pressure without deformation or failure.

4. Joints

   Transverse joints must be able to withstand 1.5 times the maximum operating pressure without failure. Where a transverse joint acts as a reinforcing member, it must not deflect excessively nor incur excessive stress.

5. Beam Strength of Duct Section

   A duct section between adjacent hangers must be able to carry its own weight and to resist external loads for which it is constructed. The joints and sheets listed in the current construction tables are not specifically designed to support the weight of a person. The support systems are not qualified for supplemental loads either.

6. Leakage

   See Table 1-1 and the discussion of leakage in relation to pressure level. Ducts are not absolutely airtight and designers should not impose unreasonably low limits of leakage. Careful selection of closure methods can ensure adequate performance. However, designers must consider that even slight leakage may cause bulges in an airtight, flexible skin that encloses a positive pressure duct.

   Leakage is primarily a function of the static pressure differential. It is independent of joint orientation and of velocity levels of

2000 fpm (11.6 mps) and less. Rectangular longitudinal seam leakage for Pittsburgh and snaplock seams is low compared to that in transverse joints.

11.3 COMMENTARY

Because the tables are derived from test data averages, construction conforming to Tables 2-1 to 2-28 will not always limit deflections of sheets and stiffeners to the stated levels. Also, cross breaks establish an initial deflection which, when added to that generated by pressure, may result in sheet deflections slightly more than the limits discussed.

Furthermore, the ability of a reinforcing member to perform its function is critically affected by the location and adequacy of its attachment to the duct. These variables change with the negative pressure and positive pressure modes.

A further advancement to establish a methodology for future duct construction has been the development of modeling through Finite Element Analysis (FEA). FEA modeling was developed through a combination of theoretical analysis and experimental testing of rectangular steel duct. More than 800 finite-element models were generated, including both non-linear stress analysis and non-linear buckling analyses, along with experiments tests of over 20 full-scale ducts in various sizes. Additionally translational/rotational restraint; internal/external pressure (+/-); total displacement; surface and membrane stress (panel, joints, seams) were analyzed.

This development of FEA has enabled expanding the efficient use of stiffened and unstiffened sheet metal panels. Additionally, the tables in previous editions precluded the use of certain thickness for larger sheet metal panels, which through FEA it was possible to expand the tables for sheet metal panels previously not rated.

11.3.1 General Requirements for All Ducts

A duct system is an assembly whose primary function is to convey air between specified points. In fulfilling this function, the duct assembly must perform satisfactorily with regard to certain fundamental performance characteristics. Elements of the assembly are sheets (duct envelope), reinforcement, seams, and joints. With regard to the duct assembly and its elements, theoretical and practical limits must be established for:

1. Dimensional stability deformation and deflection.

2. Leakage.

3. Vibration.

4. Noise generation and transmission.

5. Exposure to damage from the rigors of handling and transportation, weather, temperature extremes, flexure cycles, chemical corrosion, or other in-service conditions.

6. Support (including supplemental loads, if any).

7. Impact loading such as conditions of fire, earthquake, or sudden stoppage of the moving air stream.

In establishing limitations for these factors, consideration must be given to the effects of the pressure differential across the duct wall, airflow friction losses, air velocities, infiltration or exfiltration, as well as the inherent strength characteristics of the duct components. Construction methods that economically achieve the predicted and desired performance must be determined.

Selected specific performance requirements for rectangular, round and flat-oval ducts are codified in SMACNA Duct Performance Test Standard No. DPTS-2005.

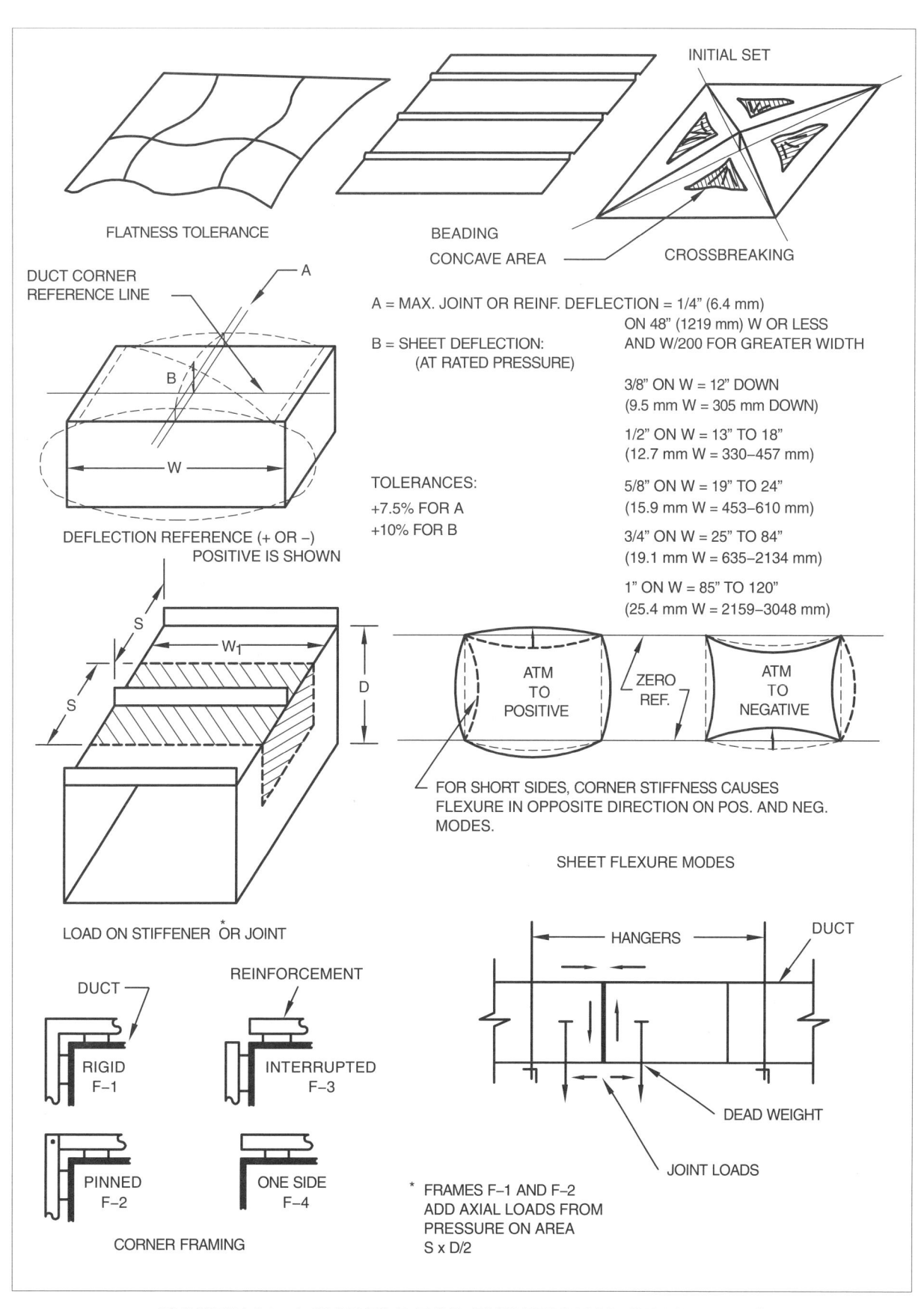

FIGURE 11–1 MODELS FOR FUNCTIONAL STANDARDS

THE NUMBER OF POINTS OF DEFLECTION MEASUREMENT DEPENDS ON THE ITEM TO BE QUALIFIED. POINTS P_1 TO P_4 ARE PANEL CENTERS. J_1 AND J_2 ARE JOINT CENTERS. R_1 AND R_2 ARE JOINT INTERMEDIATE REINFORCEMENT CENTERS. WHEN TIE RODS ARE AT R_1, R_2, J_1, J_2, ETC., DEFLECTIONS SHALL BE MEASURED AT THESE POINTS AND BETWEEN THEM AND THE DUCT CORNERS.

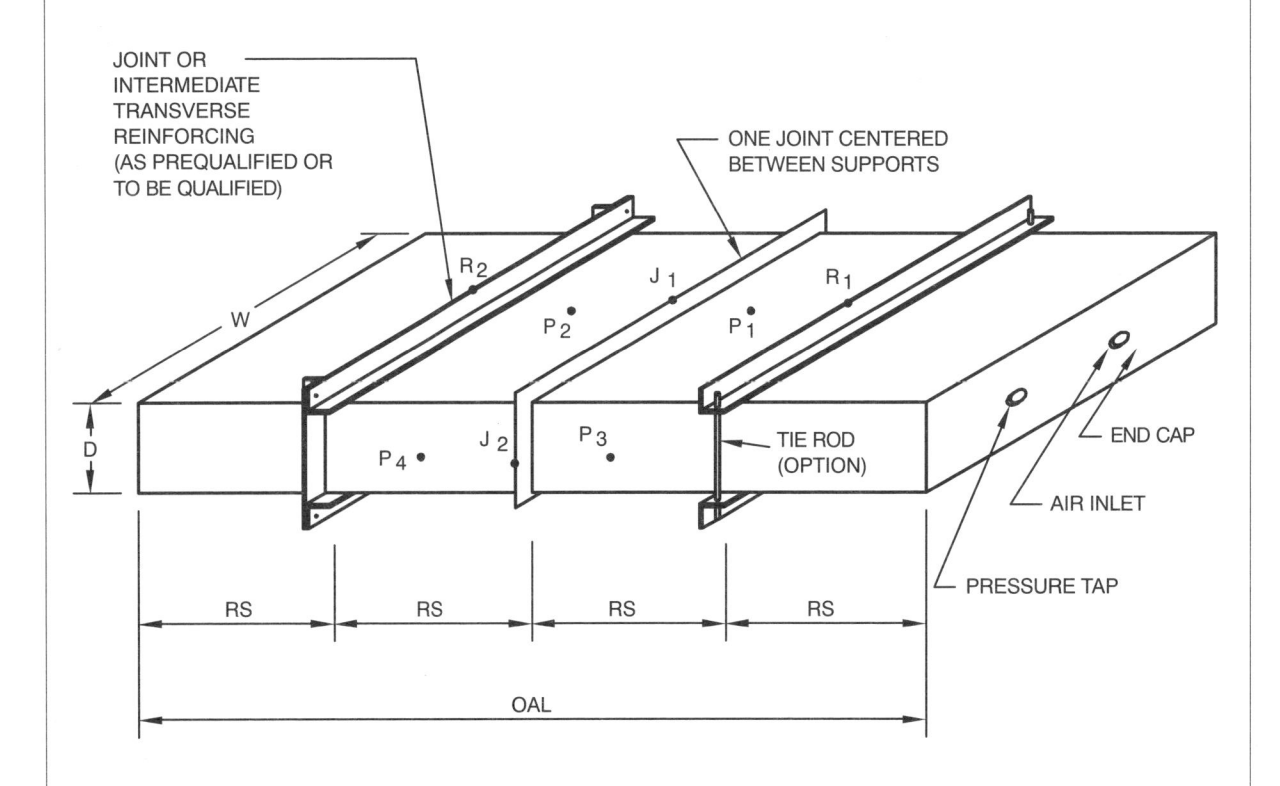

END CAPS SHALL NOT INFLUENCE POINTS OF MEASUREMENT FOR WHICH QUALIFICATION IS BEING INVESTIGATED.

| RECTANGULAR DUCT |||
JOINT SPACING	REINFORCEMENT BETWEEN JOINTS	OVERALL LENGTH
ANY	NONE	4 x Jt SPACING
ANY	YES	4 x RS SPACING
NONE*	NONE	10 W

* END CAPS ONLY

IT IS SUGGESTED THAT $D = W$, $\frac{W}{2}$ OR $\frac{W}{4}$ AND THAT PANEL WIDTH TO SPACING RATIOS OF 0.5:1, 1:1 AND 2:1 BE INVESTIGATED.

FIGURE 11-2 TEST DUCT CONFIGURATION

LOCATE DIAL GAGE IN CENTER OF SPAN FOR ELEMENTS WITHOUT TIE RODS. IF TIE RODS ARE USED, DETERMINE THE POINT OF MAXIMUM DEFLECTION BY TRIAL & ERROR MEASUREMENT. CENTER POINT OF DIAL GAGE OVER POINT OF MAXIMUM DEFLECTION.

FIG. A   DEFLECTION MEASUREMENTS

FIG. B   LEAKAGE MEASUREMENTS

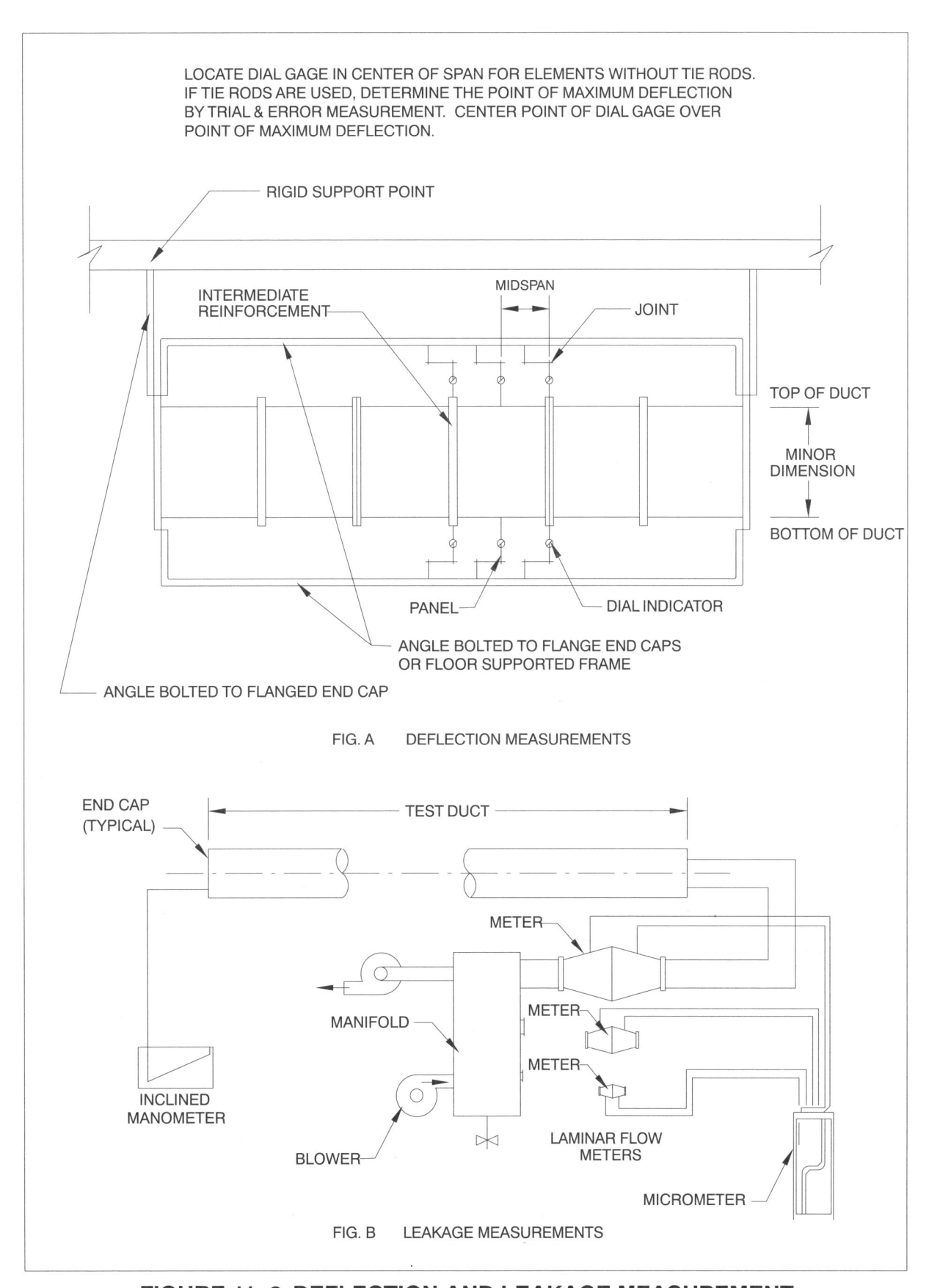

FIGURE 11-3 DEFLECTION AND LEAKAGE MEASUREMENT

SMACNA DUCT PERFORMANCE TEST STANDARD NO. DPTS–2005

1.0 PURPOSE

1.1 The purpose of this standard is to provide a uniform reliable laboratory test procedure for evaluating various performance attributes of HVAC air ducts.

2.0 SCOPE

2.1 The scope of this standard covers test methods and evaluation criteria for the following:

    a. Burst pressure capacity or resistance;

    b. Collapse pressure capacity or resistance;

    c. Wall deflection measurement;

    d. Leakage;

    e. Suspension (an optional test)

3.0 PERFORMANCE REQUIREMENTS

3.1 Burst and Collapse Tests

These shall determine that a minimum safety factor of 2 on round and oval duct and 1.5 on rectangular duct exists for the desired duct construction pressure classifications.

3.2 Rectangular Duct Deflection Limits

Duct Wall	Limit
W= 12 in. (305 mm) or less	3/8 in. (9.5 mm)
W= 13 in. (330 mm) to 18 in. (457 mm)	1/2 in. (12.7 mm)
W= 19 in. (483 mm) to 24 in. (610 mm)	5/8 in. (15.9 mm)
W= 25 in. (635 mm) to 84 in. (2134 mm)	3/4 in. (19.1 mm)
W= 85 in. (2159 mm) to 120 in. (3048 mm)	1 in. (25.4 mm)
Tolerance of +10%	

Joints and Reinforcements	Limit
W=48 in. (1219 mm) or less	1/4 in. (6.35 mm)
W=49 in. (1245 mm) to 120 in. (3048 mm)	W/200
Tolerance of +7.5%	

3.3 Oval Duct Deflection Limits

At Rated Pressure			
	(in.)	(mm)	Tolerance
Duct Wall	3/4	19.1	10%
Reinforcements	1/4	6.35	7.5%
At Atmospheric Pressure			
Duct wall when W <= 36 in. (914 mm)	1/4	6.35	10%
Duct wall when W > 36 in. (914 mm)	1/2	12.7	10%

3.4 Round Duct Deflection Limits

Duct Wall	Limit
Positive Pressure	Not applicable if shape is round at rated pressure
Negative Pressure	D/200

3.5 Leakage Evaluation

Only applicable for the determination of a leakage class within the *SMACNA HVAC Air Duct Leakage Test Manual* for experimental purposes.

3.6 Suspension Effects (Optional)

Suspension

Using supports at the maximum specified interval a weight equal to the dead weight of the duct is suspended at midpoint between hangers (over a joint if a joint could occur in the span and also on an unjointed span if the joint spacing could equal or exceed the hanger span). Leakage and sag (referenced to support points) are measured before and at the end of one hour. Report Leakage Classes as in Leakage Evaluation.

4.0 TEST SETUP

4.1 *See* Figures 11-1, 11-2, and 11-3, the instrumentation requirements and the data to be recorded and reported. Ducts shall be assembled in accordance with the test sponsor's instructions.

4.2 The support frame for dial indicators may not rest on ducts except at end caps.

4.3 On rectangular and oval ducts, the test sponsor may have only top measurements for (+)

pressure qualification and only bottom measurements for (-) pressure service. The greater duct dimension must be on the top, not on the side. The setup must provide for recording for both the top and bottom sides of rectangular and oval duct concave or convex sag for the theoretical flat spans. A rigid straight cross-member or other appropriate means of determining zero pressure deflections for the flat spans must be provided.

4.4 Test setups for round and oval duct are not required to evaluate circular or semi-circular portions of flanges or angle reinforcements.

4.5 Test setups for round duct wall deflections require placement of displacement indicators at 12, 3, 6, and 9 o'clock around the perimeter.

5.0 INSTRUMENTATION

5.1 **Accuracy and Precision.** For the purposes of this standard, requirements for accuracy and precision, or for maximum error, are specified. The systematic error in an instrument can be minimized by suitable calibration procedures. Random error in an instrument can to some extent be reduced by careful technique in reading and by choosing scale divisions so as to assist in estimating values.

5.2 **Temperature Measurement.** Wet- and dry-bulb thermometers, transducers, or sensors shall have an accuracy of ±1°C and a precision of ±0.5°C or better. Calibration thermometers, transducers, and sensors shall be calibrated over the range of temperatures expected to be encountered during a test, using a reference thermometer having a calibration that can be traceable to the National Institute of Standards and Technology (NIST), or another national laboratory recognized by NIST.

5.3 **Pressure Measurement.** Duct pressure shall be measured with a manometer or other instrument with an accuracy of ±t percent or less and the precision shall be ±0.5 percent or less. Manometer readings must be corrected for variation of specific weight of gage fluid with temperature, any difference in gas column balancing effect from standard, change in length of the graduated scale due to temperature, or capillary effects.

5.4 **Dial Indicators.** Displacement indicators shall have a suitable range, 0.001 in. or 0.01 mm maximum graduations and an accuracy of 1 percent.

5.5 **Laminar Flow Meter.** Laminar flow elements shall have a 1 percent precision, and be calibrated to within ±0.5 percent of flow standards traceable to NIST. A micro-manometer shall be used to measure the pressure drop across the laminar flow element.

5.6 **Piping.** The Figure 11-3B manifold shall be 6 in. (150 mm) diameter pipe minimum. Piping between the manifold and a test duct end cap shall be 2 in. (50 mm) diameter minimum.

5.7 **Prime Movers.** The number and capacity of blowers shall maintain positive and negative test pressures. Blowers may be operated individually or in parallel at full or reduced speed using variable frequency or voltage control. A bleed valve may be installed in the fan discharge manifold to provide fine flow adjustment.

6.0 TEST SEQUENCE

Step 1. Set up the dial indicator(s) over the test point(s). Record the dial indicator reading (D1) at zero gage pressure. Determine the sag for top and bottom flat surfaces as required for Section 4.3 even though the DAVE calculation might apply for only one surface. Record sag or bow at P1, P2, J1, R1 and R2 (for both top and bottom panels).

Step 2. Pressurize the duct to the target classification. After pressure is stable for one minute, record the dial indicator reading (D2). Examine the duct.

Step 3. Relieve pressure and record the dial indicator reading (D3).

Step 4. Pressurize rectangular duct 50 percent above the step 2 level for a minimum of five minutes. Pressurize round and oval ducts 100 percent above the step 2 level for five minutes minimum. Examine the duct. A dial indicator record is optional.

Step 5. Relieve the pressure. Examine the duct. Record the dial indicator reading (D4).

Calculate the average deflection DAVE.

$$DAVE = \frac{(D2 - D1) + (D2 - D3)}{2}$$

Where:

D1 = Dial indicator reading per Step 1.

D2 = Dial indicator reading per Step 2.

D3 = Dial indicator reading per Step 3.

This relates to the performance requirements in Section 3 of this test standard. The DAVE calculation does not require that the performance limits for Section 3.2 and 3.3 apply to theoretical flat zero reference data.

7.0 DATA TO BE INCLUDED IN REPORTS OF TESTS

1. Diagram of the test specimen.

2. Complete description of the specimen: sheet thickness; galvanized coating weight; if any; longitudinal seam locations; seam size; model of machines on which seams, joint members, and intermediate members are roll-formed, (or if brake-formed, so state); approximate inside radius of bends in formed stiffener and joint members; type, size, and spacing for fastener, (*e.g.*, bolt, weld, or self-tapping screw); type of sealants; gasket dimensions, etc. Include any observed imperfection or irregularity which might influence the results; if sealants are used, state whether they were applied before, during, or after assembly of parts.

3. The test setup including apparatus, least scale division and estimated accuracy of measurement instruments, support points and support method for specimen, measurement points on specimen, etc.

4. The sequence of observing and recording of data, the increments of pressure, the zero pressure level deflections, etc.

5. Any corrective adjustments made in the condition of the specimen after the start of testing. The location and nature of any failure points or conditions.

6. (Optional). Pressurize the duct in 1 in. wg (250 Pa) increments above the qualifying pressure until failure occurs. Record the observations and the failure pressure. Use precautions to avoid injury from parts dislocated at failure pressure.

The laboratory may just report its findings or may certify that compliance with a particular standard or requirement has been met.

11.4 PROCEDURE FOR RATING DUCT CONSTRUCTION METHODS RELATIVE TO THE SMACNA CONSTRUCTION TABLES

Method 1

Show by written analysis and commentary that any features that are different from the reinforcement and assembly scheme will result in:

a. Construction that satisfies the general requirements described in Section 1 for all ducts to the same extent that the published standards do;

b. Compliance with the stated performance requirements of Test Standard No. DPTS-2005.

Method 2

Present substantial evidence of historical acceptability for the use intended, and show that the previous use has been subjected to the pressures, velocity levels, and other conditions for which rating is desired.

Method 3

Construct, test, and rate specimens of the contemplated design.

Method 3A

Test only the component being substituted or test the component plus any connected components in a manner that will simulate the actual loading and will correlate with actual performance. Show that this approach will not impair or reduce the performance of the entire assembly.

Method 3B

Test a full specimen. Construct a specimen using the desired scheme of sheet thickness, joint type, intermediate stiffener, sealant, fasteners, etc. Conduct tests in the positive or negative mode of pressurization, as desired. Use instrumentation and follow procedures that will produce laboratory accuracy. Record the proceedings and observations. Write conclusions showing equivalence to the construction tables published by SMACNA. Include a diagram of the specimen tested.

NOTICE: Test procedures 3A and 3B may result in showing compliance with the performance criteria published by SMACNA, and not result in structural failure in the specimen. It is also desirable (but not required) to know the conditions under which failure occurs. If feasible, increase the pressure on the specimen until buckling, permanent deformation, or separation of parts occurs. This will indicate the safety factor of the construction and show the nature of the failure.

11.5 NOTES ON SPECIMEN TESTING

1. Observe that the SMACNA pressure classifications are positive and negative at several pressure levels. Tests for negative pressure qualification are similar to those described for positive pressure except that suction apparatus is used.

2. Tests in the negative pressure mode are more critical for sheet deflection and joint and stiffener buckling than those in the positive pressure mode. *See* the diagrams of models for functional standards. A test in one mode will not substitute for one in the other mode. Where the same specimen is tested in both positive and negative modes, the positive test should be conducted first. The approach of failure is usually more evident in the positive pressure mode on rectangular shapes. The pressure capacity of ducts is usually higher in the positive mode than in the negative.

3. For corner attachments and end restraints on rectangular joints and intermediate stiffeners, ties are required on 4 in. (1000 Pa), 6 in. (1500 Pa), and 10 in. wg (2500 Pa) pressure classes.

4. The deflection limits are at the rated pressure class. The freedom-from-structural-failure limit is at a safety factor level.

5. Make sure that end caps and their attachment are secure enough and leak-free enough for the test pressure range. End cap failure at lower than target pressure makes more testing necessary.

6. Returning to zero pressure and checking joints or reinforcements between pressure level increments enables testers to identify set, the residual deflection in excess of that originally present at atmospheric pressure. Some set may occur from slippage or cold working of the metal. Considerable set may indicate that failure is imminent or that excess deflection may occur at the next pressure level. Periodic release and restoration of pressure may help identify metal separation or loss of seal adhesion that will contribute to more leakage even though structural failure or excess deflection do not occur. This is not true for some connection and reinforcement systems.

7. Typical failures under positive pressure are joint separation from the duct, opening of joints, tearing of joint corners, screw or rivet pullout from duct near corners, and longitudinal seam separation. Reinforcements break at corners or, if they are not corner-tied, move away from the duct near the corner, thereby pulling fasteners out of the duct wall. Typical failures under negative pressure are buckling of duct wall at the corners, buckling of joints and reinforcements near the center, openings anywhere in the duct surface that change in size or orientation to adversely affect seal effectiveness, fastener release, and excessive deflection.

Structural Inadequacies

- Joint separation

- Seam separation

- Permanent warp, buckling, or collapse

- Excessive sag or misalignment at zero pressure

- Excessive deflection in duct wall, reinforcements, or joints under pressure

- Component or fastener breaking, pullout, or slip

- Changing alignment or fit-up of components causing loss of seal effectiveness

- Stress cracking

- Susceptibility to damage from routine handling and from impact at assembly and installation

Inadequate Integration with Support Systems

- Insufficient support causing misalignment of duct sections

- Support detaching from duct assembly (if attached)

- Support deflecting under load, adversely affecting duct integrity or shape retention

- Support contact with duct being periodic and causing noise

NOTE: Where riser or horizontal duct supports transmit loads to joints or reinforcements, these loads can affect the integrity of the duct system.

8. Consult the SMACNA *HVAC Air Duct Leakage Test Manual* for evaluation of leakage. Allow sealants to cure before conducting tests.

9. The investigation of a single specimen will not provide enough data to confirm adequacy for all duct sizes, gages, and reinforcement arrangements. Also, marginal failure of one specimen will not necessarily mean that the construction is necessarily unsuitable.

10. Inserting flow meters in the air line between the blower or vacuum unit and the specimen and recording air leaks at stabilized pressure levels, while evaluating the structure can confirm joint separation or seal degradation and provide other useful information.

11. Joints and intermediate reinforcements influence the deflection of the duct wall at midpoints between such members. Checking the amount of wall midpoint deflection can lead to the development of new reinforcement schedules. The corners of the duct may deform more between joints than at joints, and the duct ends at the joint may more longitudinally as well as laterally. Both of these conditions can contribute to span midpoint deflection. This suggests that the wall deflection measurement might better be referenced diagonally to the duct wall edges at joints and reinforcements than referenced transversely from corner to corner at midspan.

Sponsors of new or proprietary transverse joining systems are encouraged to have their tests witnessed and certified by a disinterested responsible party such as a commercial testing laboratory Recommended construction tables and details should follow a format similar to that used in this manual if an indication of equivalency is intended. Evidence of equivalency should include information on the EI rigidity classification calculation. SMACNA does not endorse or approve proprietary constructions and does not validate their analysis or tests as being equivalent to SMACNA classifications. Authorities are invited to evaluate such constructions based on evidence presented by their sponsors.

11.6 SOUND AND VIBRATION

The following discussion reviews vibration research conducted by SMACNA and reported in the May 1984 issue of the ASHRAE Journal. It is extracted and used by permission of the American Society of Heating, Refrigerating & Air Conditioning Engineers, Inc. No inference that ASHRAE agrees with these opinions is intended. For a more recent discussion of acoustical analysis of ducts see the "Sound and Vibration" Chapter in the *ASHRAE Handbook - Systems.*

IMPORTANT NOTICE! The rectangular duct reinforcement tables in these standards and in former editions do not eliminate rumble on system start-up and shutdown. Lagging, diagonal bracing, or other acoustical treatment will be necessary to reduce or eliminate rumble.

11.6.1 Test Objectives

The object of the test was to determine the behavior of a variety of rectangular duct constructions for various air velocities and static pressures. Behavior was measured in terms of deflection and vibration amplitude.

11.6.2 Equipment

The test apparatus is illustrated in Figure 11-4. Air from the fan passed through a calibrated orifice and a square-throat elbow into the test specimen. Then it discharged into a plenum with an outlet damper. Air pressure and flow were controlled by the fan inlet damper and the outlet damper at the end of the system. A manually operated bypass damper was used whenever the desired airflow through the specimen was below the normal operating range of the fan. Four sizes of orifices were used for different flow ranges. The square-throat elbow with turning vanes was installed upstream of the test specimen in order to create a turbulent airflow like that found in actual installations. The pressure in the test specimen was sensed by a static pressure probe installed in each of the test specimens. The displacement of the sheet was measured by a calibrated linear potentiometer. The movable arm of the potentiometer was secured to the sheet by a permanent magnet, and the housing of the potentiometer was secured to an aluminum channel superstructure, which was in turn supported by the corners of the duct. Thus the sheet displacement was measured relative to the duct itself. This arrangement prevented false readings caused by movement of the testing system relative to the building structure.

The static pressure and differential orifice pressure were measured by electronic pressure transducers, which in turn were calibrated and monitored by liquid manometers. The static pressure, differential orifice pressure, and sheet displacement were simultaneously recorded on an oscillograph chart. The deflection of the reinforcing angles was measured with a dial indicator using as a reference the same superstructure used for the potentiometers, and these measurements were recorded manually.

11.6.3 Ducts Tested

Most of the tested ducts had a uniform depth of 8 in. (203 mm). Because the top, bottom, and sides of a rectangular duct act as independent load bearing panels, there was no reason to make a separate study of each of these panels, or to study the effects of combining various sizes of top and side panels.

Duct widths tested were 10 in. (254 mm), 12 in. (305 mm), 18 in. (457 mm), 24 in. (610 mm), 36 in. (914 mm), 48 in. (1219 mm), 54 in. (1372 mm), 60 in. (1524 mm), 72 in. (1829 mm), and 84 in. (2134 mm). Ducts wider than 84 in. (2134 mm) could not be tested due to limited capacity of the supply fan to provide sufficient velocities at the higher test pressures.

Duct specimens were 8 (2.44) to 12 ft (3.66 m) long, usually with 2 (0.61) to 4 ft (1.22 m) connecting pieces on each end. Longitudinal seams were button punch snap lock for 24 (0.70) through 20 ga (1.00 mm) sheets. Lock seams were used for 18 ga (1.31) ducts. 16 (1.61) and 14 ga (1.99 mm) ducts had welded seams. Reinforcing angles were secured with sheet metal screws and tie rods on each end. Transverse joints were flanged and edge-welded. Each specimen normally included two transverse joints.

For each width of duct, the sheet gage, reinforcing size, and reinforcing spacing were varied in order to determine the lowest cost construction that would perform within the standards.

Constant-pressure test runs were made on each duct specimen, varying the velocity continuously from about 6500 (33) down to about 2000 fpm (10 mps). The constant pressure runs were made at 10.0 (2500), 6.0 (1500), 2.0 (500), 1.5, (375) and 1.0 in. wg (250 Pa) static pressure as measured in the specimen.

Static Pressure in wg (Pa)	Average Velocity fpm	(mps)
1.5 (375)	2500	(12.7)
2.0 (500)	2750	(14)
4.0 (1000)	3500	(17.8)
8.0 (2000)	5500	(27.9)
10.0 (2500)	6500	(33)

Table 'A' Minimum Threshold Velocities at Various Internal Static Pressures

11.6.4 Threshold Velocity

The oscillograph traces were examined to determine, for each pressure, the maximum sheet deflection and the maximum air velocity at which the amplitude of sheet vibration was equal to the arbitrary maximum value established as standard. With amplification available from the recording instruments, this value was the width of one line on the trace, which was equal to a movement of the sheet of .01785 in. (0.4534 mm) (slightly over 1/64 in.). This velocity is termed the "threshold velocity."

It was not feasible to conduct the tests to establish the exact relationship between the threshold velocity and each of the variable of duct size, sheet gage, and reinforcing spacing. Instead it was decided to arbitrarily establish minimum threshold velocities for various static pressures. The intent was that the resulting criteria would cover all of the operating conditions in normal- to high-velocity air conditioning systems.

Because operating conditions are the designer's choice, these criteria were established through a poll of consulting mechanical engineers. Based on their responses, Table A lists the minimum threshold velocities used in evaluating the test results.

11.6.5 Test Results

In all cases the performance of the duct specimen followed the same pattern.

1. Deflection of the sheet

    a. Increasing velocity does not affect deflection.

b. Increasing reinforcing spacing increases deflection.

c. Increasing duct width increases deflection.

d. Increasing internal static pressure increases deflection.

e. Increasing sheet gage decreases deflection.

2. Amplitude of vibration

a. Increasing velocity increases vibration.

b. Increasing reinforcing spacing increases vibration.

c. Increasing duct width increases vibration.

d. Increasing internal static pressure decreases vibration.

e. Increasing sheet gage increases vibration.

All of the above phenomena would seem to be readily predictable with the exception of the last two. Why would a light gage sheet resist vibration more than a heavy gage sheet, and why would a sheet vibrate more at lower pressures?

Careful observation of all specimens showed that the sheet acts more as a membrane than as a beam. A sheet acting as a beam would require a much greater section modulus, calling for thicknesses beyond those of operating pressures, some concave areas might be on the verge of "popping out" or snapping over center to conform to the overall convex shape of the sheet. If an area is near this equilibrium condition, then relatively small but rapid variations in static pressure caused by turbulence will make that area vibrate violently.

In addition to the random waves in commercial sheets, the sheet forming the top of the duct will sag and form a concave area between the reinforcing members. This is due to the dead weight of the sheet and occurs at zero or low internal static pressures. The top sheet will not be stretched taut until the internal static pressure is adequate to overcome both the dead weight of the sheet and the internal forces which cause the waves. Here again, the equilibrium static pressure for heavy gage sheets, can occur well within operating pressure ranges, while for light gage sheets, equilibrium will occur below operating pressure.

From the foregoing, it might appear that it would always be best to use a light gage sheet. However, as the duct width increases, it is also necessary to increase sheet gage in order to meet the deflection criteria.

11.6.6 Cross Breaking

A natural approach for maintaining a sheet in a convex shape is to cross break it. Unfortunately, cross breaking results in concave areas between the break lines. The technique of cross breaking is successful in reducing vibration when applied to low velocity ducts because internal static pressures are seldom high enough to cause the concave areas to "pop out." Also, low velocity ducts are not normally subjected to the turbulence found in high velocity ducts. Therefore, the forces causing vibration are much smaller.

The test results showed that the effect of cross breaking high velocity ducts is dependent on the sheet gage. Because they were stretched taut at low pressures, cross breaking had a minimum effect on light gage ducts. On the other hand, higher pressures were required to stretch taut the heavy gage sheets which had been cross broken than those not cross broken. It was observed that in general, cross breaking was not beneficial to high velocity duct performances.

11.6.7 Vibration and Noise

Vibration of the sheet is undesirable:

1. If it can cause fatigue failure in the sheet;

2. If it causes other objects to vibrate by contact, *e.g.*, ceilings, light fixtures, etc.; or

3. If it makes excessive noise.

Complete and definitive testing in these three problem areas was not practical under the financial and time limitations of this program. It was instead decided to rely on the judgment of experienced parties to determine the criteria for acceptability. Thirty ventilation contractors and design engineers witnessed various test runs and expressed their opinions on the effects of vibration when the sheets were made to vibrate at 1, 1½ and 2 times the maximum standard (0.01785 in.) (0.4534 mm).

11.6.8 Fatigue

Fatigue failure in steel ducts is uncommon. The consultants had seen fatigue failure only in cases of

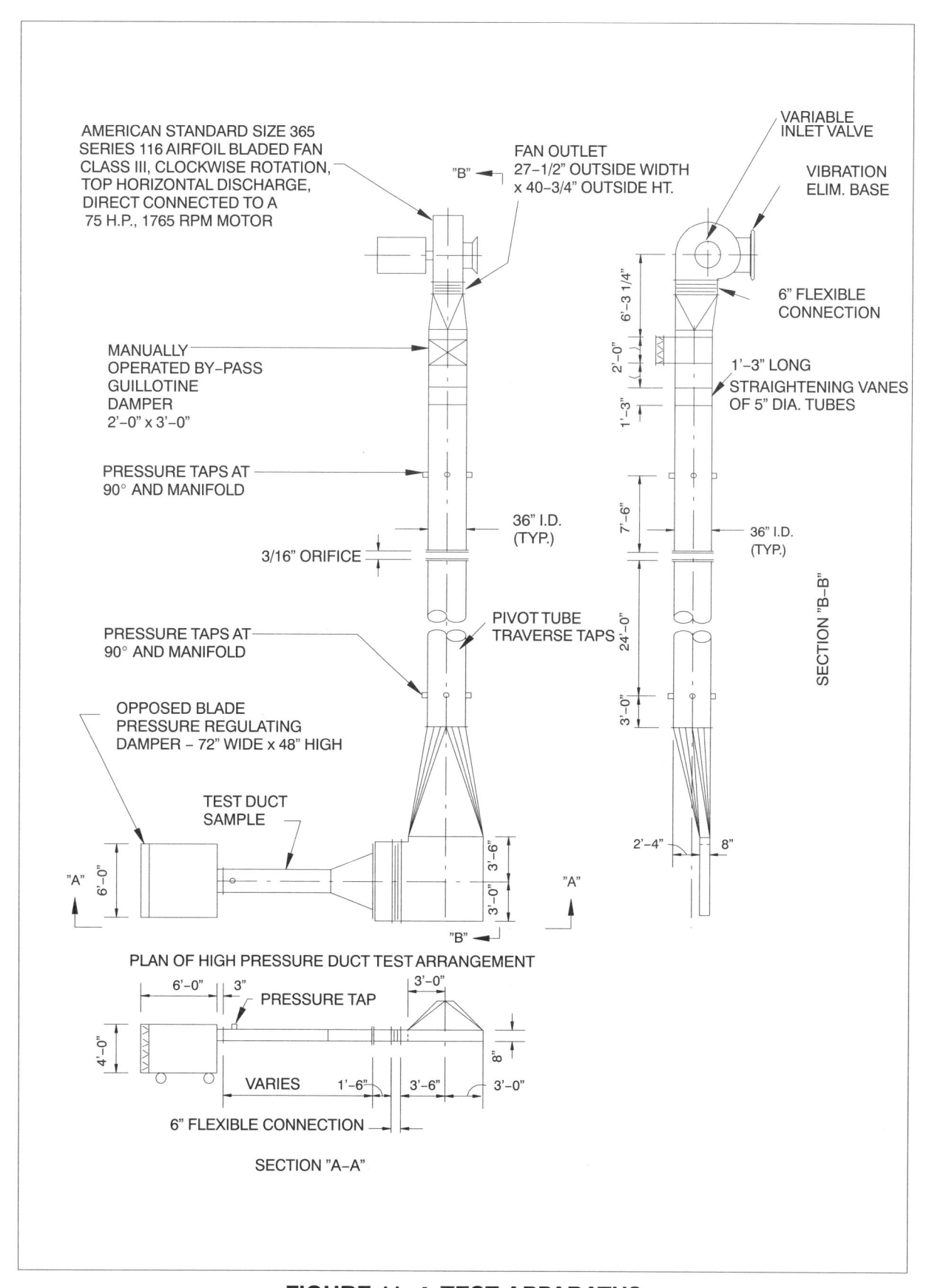

FIGURE 11-4 TEST APPARATUS

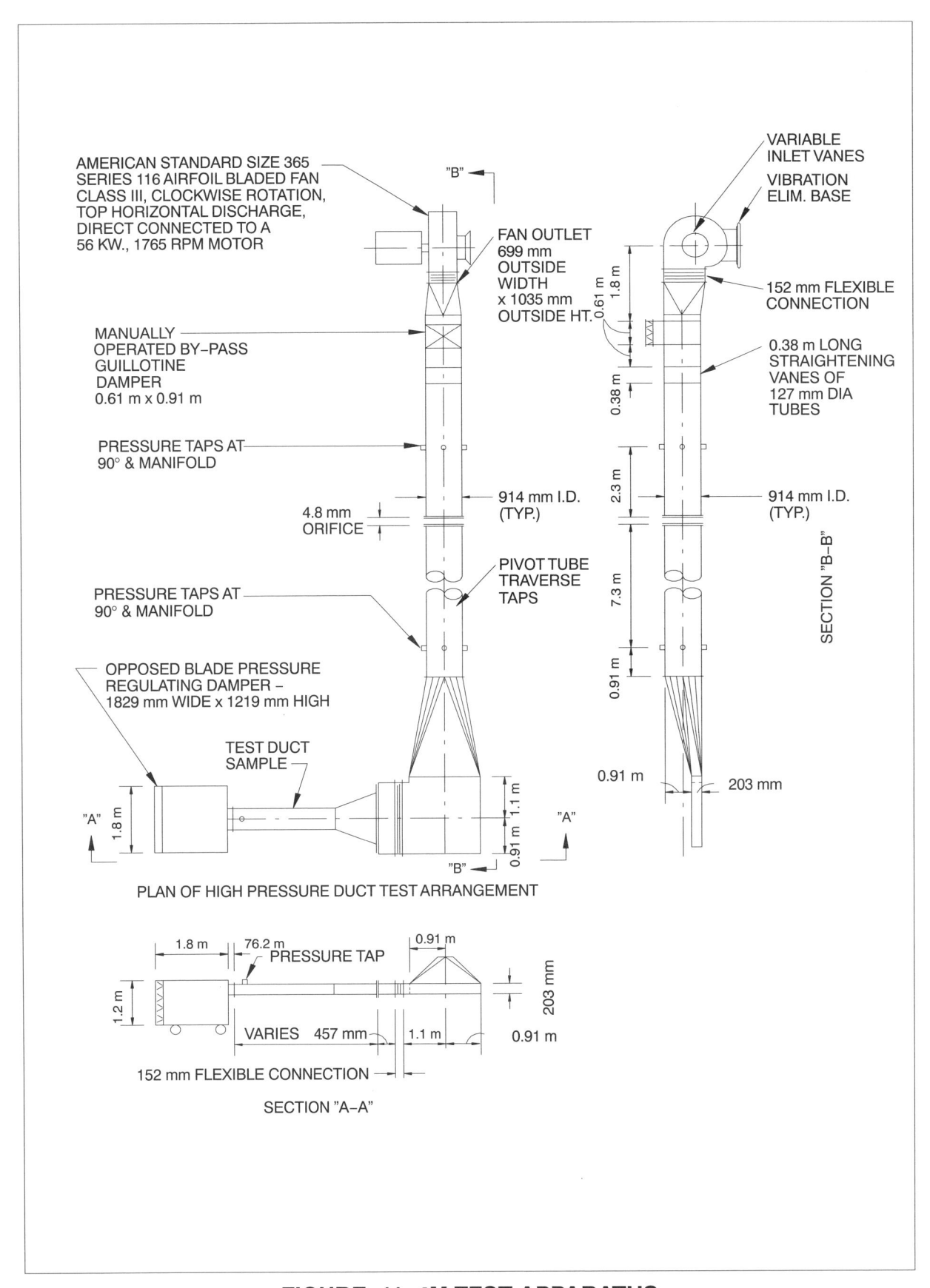

FIGURE 11-4M TEST APPARATUS

11.14 HVAC Duct Construction Standards Metal and Flexible • Fourth Edition

much more severe vibration, usually where there were stress reversals such as that created by a poorly secured turning vane flapping in the airstream.

11.6.9 Vibration Transmission by Contact

It is not good practice for the duct sheet to come in contact with other parts of a building. It was agreed that the maximum deflection and amplitude values set as standard were reasonable enough to prevent such contact. Where ducts are covered with insulation, vibration transmission by contact is further minimized.

11.6.10 Noise

As a practical matter, the foregoing two problems were not as great a concern as the possibility of excessive noise. Due to the high ambient noise caused by having the complete air handling system in one room, it was impossible to measure the amount of noise radiated by the duct specimen. Our consultants evaluated the test runs by visual observation, by touch, and by ear. On this basis, they unanimously agreed that the maximum amplitude of vibration established as a standard was well within the limits of vibration considered acceptable.

It was possible to take vibration readings of the various specimens and system components. Magnetic tape recordings were made of the vibration of duct walls as detected by an accelerometer pickup. A preamplifier was used that had uniform characteristics throughout the audio frequency range. After the test runs, the consultants listened to the recordings in a quiet room and judged them. Certain qualitative judgments were made concerning these listening tests. Additional measurements were made concerning the relative noise intensity as a function of sheet gage and static pressure.

The levels in Table B indicate the relative vibration under the various conditions of test on a logarithmic scale as used for sounds. The absolute values are of no importance, but the relative values are similar to those obtained if it had been possible to measure noise directly on a decibel scale; that is, for an increase of 3, the ratio of vibration is doubled.

For an increase in 10, the vibration intensity is increased tenfold. The basis of interpretation of the readings of relative vibration is the assumption that the intensity of radiated sound will vary with the intensity of vibration. In actuality, the relationship between surface vibration and sound radiation is also a function of frequency. In our tests, the differences in relative vibration however are significant enough to assume that an increase in radiated sound will result from an increase in vibration of the sheet. The significance of the tests was the determination of trends rather than the measurement of levels.

In assessing the differences between the various conditions, it should be realized that the isolation between the various portions of the duct are minimal, especially for the case where a heavy gage and a light gage duct are connected in series in the test rig. Furthermore, with the existing test setup, vibration is easily conducted along the entire system with little reduction in amplitude. The differences that are noted therefore are minimal and it can be expected that considerably more differences would have occurred under ideal test conditions.

Vibration readings on a 42 × 8 in. (1067 × 203 mm) duct specimen, constructed of a 10 ft (3.05 m) long, 22 ga (0.85 mm) section, joined directly to a 10 ft (3.05 m) long, 16 ga (1.61 mm) section, are tabulated in Table B, Run No. 5.

| Run No. 5 - 42 in. Wide Ducts ||||
Static Pressure in wg (Pa)	Velocity fpm (mps)	Relative Vibration 22 ga (0.85 mm) Duct	Vibration 16 ga (1.61 mm) Duct
10.1 (2500)	5,680 (28.9)	30	32
8.1 (2000)	6.560 (33.3)	31	33
6.1 (1500)	6.560 (33.3)	30	32
4.1 (1000)	6.660 (33.8)	30	33
2.5 (6.25)	6.440 (32.7)	32	42

Table 'B' Relative Vibration of Various Ducts

Under these test conditions, the vibration intensity of the thinner duct was consistently lower in level than the heavier duct and showed a maximum difference at the lower pressures, for which visible motion of the duct walls was apparent in the heavier gages.

RUN NO. 6 (Continued) 42 in. (1067 mm) Wide Duct 6270 fpm (31.6 mps) Velocity, 6.0 in. (1500 Pa) static pressure

Position	Relative Vibration
Outlet plenum box	32
16 ga (1.61 mm) duct section	32
22 ga (0.85 mm) duct sections	29
Floor next to duct specimens	11
Inlet plenum upstream of duct specimens	37
Top of elbow	39
Top of round to rectangular transition	38
Round duct on outlet side of orifice	35
Round duct on inlet side of orifice	39
Round duct on outlet of fan under bleed-off	38

A most interesting set of measurements was obtained in Run No. 6 during which recordings were made at 10 different locations throughout the entire system. The lowest vibration in the system was obtained in the section of duct having the thinnest gage. The readings are not indicative of noise reduction because the frequency characteristic of the noise also changes. The thinner duct appears to sound significantly less loud than the heavier duct. This is in part due to less intensity, but also to the lower pitch or frequency of the sounds.

Our study of noise radiation was conducted under less than ideal conditions. However, its results appear to substantiate the assumption that light gages in high velocity duct will not result in greater noise radiation than heavy gages.

1" W.G.

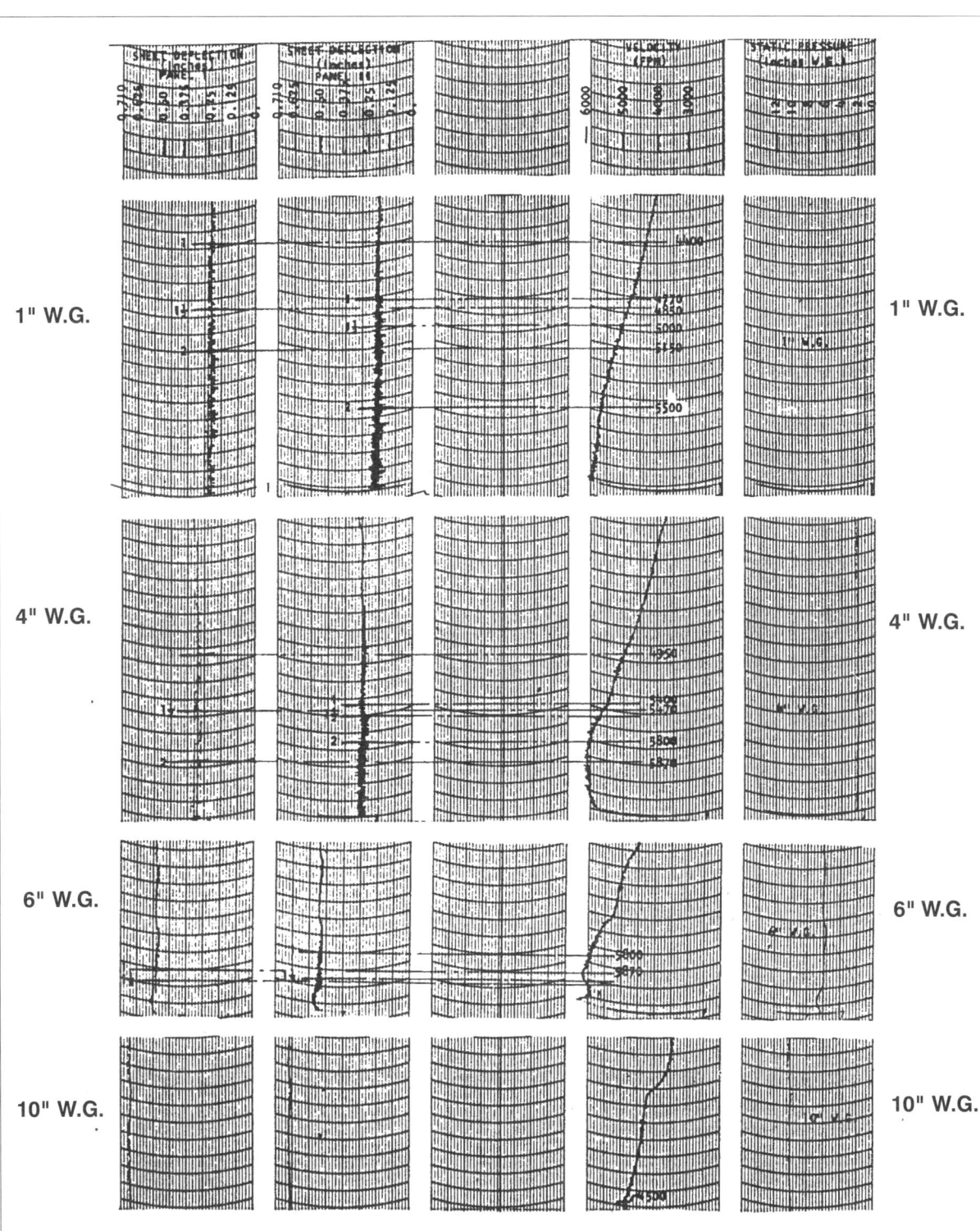

1" W.G.

4" W.G.

4" W.G.

6" W.G.

6" W.G.

10" W.G.

10" W.G.

Typical oscillograph traces for test runs at 1, 2, 6, and 10 in. wg. static pressure. Lines marked 1, 1-½, and 2 indicate where the sheet vibration was approximately 1, 1-½ and 2 chart lines amplitude. It can be seen that as the velocity decreased, the amplitude of vibration also decreased. It can also be seen that as the pressure was increased, a higher velocity was required before a given amplitude of vibration was reached. Total sheet deflection also increased with increases in pressure.

FIGURE 11–5 OSCILLOGRAPH TRACES

THIS PAGE INTENTIONALLY LEFT BLANK

APPENDIX

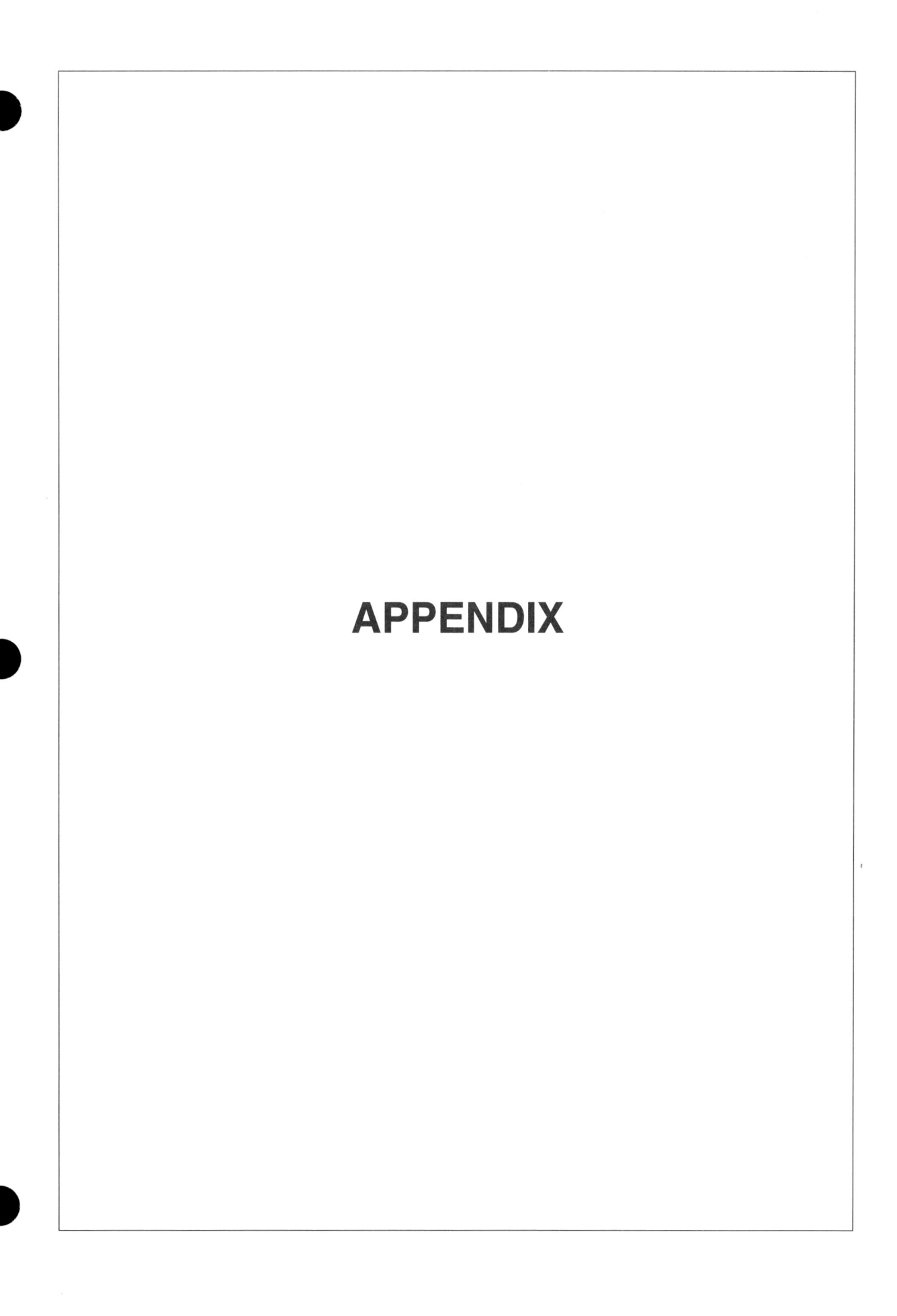

APPENDIX A

SECTIONS

		Page
A.1	CONTRACTOR'S ANALYSIS OF SHOP STANDARDS	A.12
A.2	NOTES	A.12
A.3	RADIATION PROTECTION AT WALL OPENINGS FOR DUCT OR PIPE	A.21

TABLES

	Page
Galvanized Sheet Thickness Tolerances	A.1
Manufacturers Standard Gage-Thickness—Uncoated Steel	A.2
Stainless Steel Sheet Thickness	A.3
Aluminum Sheet Thickness—Alloy 3003-H14	A.4
Metric Conversion Chart	A.5
Duct Surface Area In Square Feet Per Linear Foot	A.6
Galvanized Sheet Weight	A.7
Galvanized Sheet Weight (Continued)	A.8
Approximate Weight - Round Duct in Pounds Per Linear Foot	A.9
Area And Circumferences of Circles	A.10
Angle, Bar & Channel Properties	A.11
Sample Worksheet	A.13

FIGURES

	Page
Single Path Air Ssystems	A.14
Dual Path Air Systems	A.15
Terminology For Central Station Apparatus	A.16
Motor Arrangements	A.17
Fan Rotation And Discharge Positions	A.18
Typical Belt Guards	A.19
Typical Isolation Devices	A.20
Radiation Protection At Wall Openings	A.23
Radiation Protection At Wall Openings	A.24

APPENDIX A

Gage	Thickness in Inches Min.	Thickness in Inches Max.	Thickness in Inches Nom.	Weight Min lb/sf	Weight Nom. lb/sf	Weight Max. lb/sf	Nom. kg/m²	Thickness in Millimeters Min.	Thickness in Millimeters Max.	Thickness in Millimeters Nom.
33	.0060	.0120	.0090	.2409	.376	.486		.1524	.3048	.2286
32	.0104	.0164	.0134	.4204	.563	.665		.2642	.4166	.3404
31	.0112	.0172	.0142	.4531	.594	.698		.2845	.4369	.3607
30	.0127	.0187	.0157	.5143	.656	.759	3.20	.3188	.4783	.3988
29	.0142	.020	.0172	.5755	.719	.820		.3569	.5169	.4369
28	.0157	.0217	.0187	.6367	.781	.881	3.81	.3950	.5550	.4750
27	.0172	.0232	.0202	.6979	.844	.943		.4331	.5931	.5131
26	.0187	.0247	.0217	.7591	.906	1.004	4.42	.4712	.6312	.5512
25	.0217	.0287	.0247	.8407		1.167		.5274	.7274	.6274
24	.0236	.0316	.0276	.9590	1.156	1.285	5.64	.6010	.8010	.7010
23	.0266	.0346	.0306	1.0814		1.408		6772	.8772	.7772
22	.0296	.0376	.0336	1.2038	1.406	1.530	6.86	.7534	.9534	.8534
21	.0326	.0406	.0336	1.3263		1.653		.8296	1.0296	.9296
20	.0356	.0436	.0396	1.4486	1.656	1.775	8.08	.906	1.106	1.006
19	.0406	.0506	.0456	1.6526		2.061		1.028	1.288	1.158
18	.0466	.0566	.0516	1.8974	2.156	2.305	10.52	1.181	1.441	1.311
17	.0525	.0625	.0575	2.1381		2.546		1.331	1.591	1.461
16	.0575	.0695	.0635	2.342	2.656	2.832	12.96	1.463	1.763	1.613
15	.0650	.0770	.0710	2.6481		3.138		1.653	1.953	1.803
14	.0705	.0865	.0785	2.8725	3.281	3.525	16.01	1.784	2.204	1.994
13	.0854	.1014	.0934	3.4804		4.133		2.162	2.5823	2.372
12	.0994	.1174	.1084	4.0516	4.531	4.786	22.11	2.523	2.983	2.753
11	.1143	.1323	.1233	4.6505		5.394		2.902	3.362	3.132
10	.1292	.1472	.1382	5.2675	5.781	6.002	28.21	3.280	3.740	3.510
9	.1442	.1622	.1532	5.8795		6.614		3.661	4.121	3.891
8	.1591	.1771	.1681	6.4874	6.875	7.222		4.040	4.500	4.270

Galvanized Sheet Thickness Tolerances

NOTES:

a. Based on ASTM A924/924M-94, Standard Specification for General Requirements for Sheet Steel, Metallic Coated by the Hot-Dip Process (formerly ASTMA525); and ASTMA653/A653M-94, Standard Specification for Sheet Steel, Zinc-Coat (Galvanized) or Zinc-Iron Alloy Coated (Galvanized) by the Hot-Dip Process.

b. Tolerances are valid for 48 in. and 60 in. wide coil and cut length stock - other dimensions apply to other sheet widths and to strip.

c. The lock forming grade of steel will conform to ASTM A653 (formerly ASTM A527).

d. The steel producing industry recommends that steel be ordered by decimal thickness only. Thickness and zinc coating class can be stenciled on the sheet. The gage designation is retained for residual familiarity reference only.

e. Minimum weight in this table is based on the following computation:
Minimum sheet thickness minus 0.001 in. of G60 coating times 40.8 lb. per sf. per in. plus 0.0369 lb./sf of zinc.
G90 stock would be comparably calculated from:
(t - .00153 in.) 40.8 ÷ 0.05564 = minimum weight.
However, scale weight may run 2% (or more) greater than theoretical weight. Actual weight may be near 40.82 lb. per sf per in.

f. G60 coating, per ASTM A653 and ASTM A90, has 0.60 oz/sf (triple spot test) total for two sides. 0.59 oz/sf of zinc equals 0.001 in. 1 oz is 0.0017 in. and is 305.15 g/m².
G90 coating is 0.90 oz/sf (triple spot test), or 0.00153 in. Magnetic gage measurement of zinc coating may have 15% error.

g. ASTM D2092, Practice for Preparation of Zinc-Coated Galvanized Steel Surfaces for Paint, includes mill phosphatizing.

h. ASTM A755 is the Specification for Sheet Steel, Metallic Coated by the Hot-Dip Process and Prepainted by the Coating Process for Exterior Building Products. Other information is available from the National Coal Coaters Association, Philadelphia, PA.

i. Much chemical and atmospheric corrosion information is available from ASM International in Metals Park, Ohio and from NACE International in Houston, TX.

j. A principle international standard is ISO 3575, Continuous Hot-Dip Process, Zinc-Coated Carbon Steel Sheet of Commercial, Lock Forming and Drawing Qualities.

M.S. Gage	Weight lb/sf (kg/m²)	Thickness Nominal	Hot Rolled Min.	Hot Rolled Max.	Cold Rolled Min.	Cold Rolled Max.	ANSI STANDARD B32.3 Preferred in Thickness Millimeters First	Second
28	.625 (3.051)	.0149 in .378 mm			.0129 in .328 mm	.0169 in .429 mm	.30	.35
26	.750 (3.661)	.0179 in .455 mm			.0159 in .404 mm	.0199 in .505 mm	.40	.45
24	1.000 (4.882)	.0239 in .607 mm			.0209 in .531 mm	.0269 in .683 mm	.50	
22	1.250 (6.102)	.0299 in .759 mm			.0269 in .683 mm	.0329 in .826 mm	.60	.65 .70
20	1.500 (7.232)	.0359 in .912 mm			.0329 in .836 mm	.0389 in .988 mm	.80 1.00	.90
18	2.000 (9.764)	.0478 in 1.214 mm	.0428 in 1.087 mm	.0528 in 1.341 mm	.0438 in 1.113 mm	.0518 in 1.316 mm	1.2	1.10 1.40
16	2.500 (12.205)	.0598 in 1.519 mm	.0538 in 1.367 mm	.0658 in 1.341 mm	.0548 in 1.392 mm	.0548 in 1.649 mm	1.6	1.8
14	3.125 (15.256)	.0747 in 1.897 mm	.0677 in 1.720 mm	.0817 in 2.075 mm	.0697 in 1.770 mm	.0797 in 2.024 mm	2.0 2.5	2.2
12	4.125 (21.359)	.1046 in 1.657 mm	.0966 in 2.454 mm	.112 in 2.860 mm	.0986 in 2.504 mm	.1106 in 2.809 mm	3.0	2.8
10	5.625 (27.461)	.1345 in 3.416 mm	.1265 in 3.213 mm	.1425 in 3.619 mm	.1285 in 3.264 mm	.1405 in 3.569 mm	3.5 4.0	3.2 3.8
8	6.875 (33.564)	.1644 in 4.176 mm	.1564 in 3.973 mm	.1724 in 4.379 mm				

Manufacturers Standard Gage-Thickness—Uncoated Steel

NOTES:

Manufacturers Standard Gage is based on a theoretical steel density of 489.6 lb./cf, or 40.80 lb/sf per in. of thickness plus 2.5% normally experienced increase in delivery weight. Thus, the weight basis associated with thickness specifications as 41.82 lb./sf per in.

U.S. Standard Gage, the legal gage since 1893, although based on the density of wrought iron 480#/cf, used 40.00 lb/sf/in for both iron and steel. Thus, U.S. gage thickness are derived from weights 2% lighter than steel.

The table is based on 48 in. width coil and sheet stock. 60 in. stock has the same tolerance for gages listed except for 16 ga which has ± 0.007 in. in hot rolled sheet.

See ASTM Standards A 366 (cold rolled order form), A 568 (properties of hot rolled and cold rolled sheet of commercial quality), and A 569 (hot rolled order form).

Thickness and weight in customary units are based on data in the AISI *Carbon Sheet Steel Products* Manual. Metric conversions listed here are straight multiplications for comparison purposes. Individual manufacturers may quote other tolerances.

ANSI is the American National Standards Institute. Standards B-32.3 actually covers a wider range of thickness than listed here.

	Thickness in Inches				Weight				Thickness in Millimeters		
					lb./sf		kg./m²				
Gage	Min.	Max.	Tolerance	Nom.	300	400	300	400	Nom.	Min.	Max.
31	.0089	.0129	.002	.0109	.459	.451	2.239	2.200	.2769	.2269	.3269
30	.0105	0.145	.002	.0125	.525	.515	2.562	2.512	.3175	.2675	.3675
29	.0121	.0161	.002	.0141	.591	.579	2.883	2.825	.3581	.3081	.4081
28	.0136	.0176	.002	.0456	.656	.644	3.200	3.142	.3962	.3462	.4462
27	.0142	.0202	.003	.0172	.722	.708	3.522	3.454	.4369	.3569	.5169
26	.0158	.0218	.003	.0188	.788	.773	3.844	3.771	.4775	.3975	.5575
25	.0189	.0249	.003	.0219	.919	.901	4.483	4.395	.5562	.4762	.6362
24	.0220	.0280	.003	.0250	1.050	1.030	5.122	5.025	.6350	.5550	.7150
23	.0241	.0321	.004	.0281	1.181	1.159	5.761	5.654	.7137	.6137	.8137
22	.0273	.0353	.004	.0313	1.313	1.288	6.405	6.283	.7950	.6950	.8950
21	.0304	.0384	.004	.0344	1.444	1.416	7.044	6.908	.8738	.7738	.9738
20	.0335	.0415	.004	.0375	1.575	1.545	7.683	7.537	.9525	.8525	1.0525
19	.0388	.0488	.005	.0438	1.838	1.803	8.966	8.796	1.1125	.9835	1.2425
18	.0450	.0550	.005	.0500	2.100	2.060	10.245	10.050	1.2700	1.1400	1.4000
17	.0513	.0613	.005	.0563	2.363	2.318	11.528	11.308	1.4300	1.300	1.5600
16	.0565	.0685	.006	.0625	2.625	2.575	12.806	12.562	1.5875	1.4375	1.7375
15	.0643	.0763	.006	.0703	2.953	2.897	14.406	14.133	1.7856	1.6356	1.9356
14	.0711	.0851	.007	.0781	3.281	3.219	16.006	15.704	1.9837	1.8037	2.1637
13	.0858	.1018	.008	.0938	3.938	3.863	19.211	18.845	2.3825	2.1825	2.5825
12	.1000	.1184	.009	.1094	4.594	4.506	22.411	21.982	2.7788	2.5488	2.9788
11	.1150	.1350	.010	.1250	5.250	5.150	25.612	25.124	3.1750	2.9250	3.4250
10	.1286	.1526	.012	.1406	5.906	5.794	28.812	28.265	3.5712	3.2712	3.8712
9	.1423	.1703	.014	.1563	6.563	6.438	32.017	31.407	3.9700	3.6100	4.3300
8	.1579	.1859	.014	.1719	7.219	7.081	35.217	34.544	4.3663	4.0063	4.7263

Stainless Steel Sheet Thickness

ASTM-A167 — "Stainless and Heat-Resisting Chromium-Nickel Steel Plate, Sheet, and Strip" (Properties of the 300 series)

ASTM-A480 — "Standard Specification for General Requirements for Flat-Rolled Stainless and Heat-Resisting Steel Plate, Sheet, and Strip"

Finishes:
No. 1 Finish — Hot-rolled, annealed, and descaled.
No. 2 D Finish — Cold-rolled, dull finish.
No. 3 B Finish — Cold-rolled, bright finish.
Bright Annealed Finish — A bright cold-rolled finish retained by annealing in a controlled atmosphere furnace.
No. 3 Finish — Intermediate polished finish, one or both sides.
No. 4 Finish — General purpose polished finish, one or both sides.
No. 6 Finish — Dull satin finish, Tampico brushed, one or both sides.
No. 7 Finish — High luster finish.
No. 8 Finish — Mirror finish.

The 300 series weight is based on 41.99 lb. per square foot per inch of thickness (or 504 lb./cf).

The 400 series weight is based on 41.20 lb. per square foot per inch of thickness (or 494 lb./cf).

ASTM A666 covers the structural grade of stainless steel (not used for ducts.). For design criteria, generally, consult the AISI *Stainless Steel Cold-Formed Structural Design Manual*. For general application and corrosion data consult the AISI *Design Guidelines for the Selection and Use of Stainless Steels* and the Speciality Steel industry of the United States in Washington, D.C.

Thickness in Inches				Weight		Thickness in Millimeters		
Nom.	Tolerance 48" & (60) Width	Min.	Max.	lb./ft²	kg./m²	Nom.	Min.	Max.
.016	.0015	.0145	.0175	.228	1.114	.4068	.3683	.4445
.020	.002 (.003)	.018	.022	.285	1.393	.508	.4572	.5588
.024	.002 (.003)	.022	.026	.342	1.671	.6096	.5588	.6604
.025	.002 (.003)	.023	.027	.356	1.7398	.635	.5842	.6858
.032	.0025 (.0035)	.0295	.0345	.456	2.228	.8128	.7493	.8763
.040	.0035 (.0045)	.0365	.0435	.570	2.786	1.016	.9271	1.1049
.050	.0035 (.0045)	.465	.0535	.713	3.484	1.27	1.1811	1.3589
.063	.0035 (.005)	.0595	.665	.898	4.389	1.600	1.5113	1.6891
.080	.0045 (.006)	.0755	.0845	1.140	5.571	2.032	1.9117	2.1463
.090	.0045 (.006)	.0855	.0945	1.283	6.270	2.286	2.1717	2.4003
.100	.0055 (.007)	.0945	.1055	1.426	6.969	2.54	2.4003	2.6797
.125	.0055 (.007)	.1195	.1305	1.782	8.709	3.175	3.0353	3.3147

Aluminum Sheet Thickness—Alloy 3003-H14

Weight is based on 14.256 lb. per square foot per inch of thickness (or 171.1 lb./cf). Alloy 1100 is of slightly lower density.

Specification references: ASTM B209 Standard Specification of Aluminum Alloy Sheet and Plate which references ANSI *Standard H-35.2 Dimensional Tolerance for Aluminum Mill Products.*

Other useful references are published by the Aluminum Association: *Specification for Aluminum Structures; Engineering Data for Aluminum Structures; Aluminum Standards and Data.*

INCHES INTO MILLIMETERS

INCHES	0 in.	1 in.	2 in.	3 in.	4 in.	5 in.	6 in.	7 in.	8 in.	9 in.	10 in.	11 in.
		25.4	50.8	76.2	101.6	127.0	152.4	177.8	203.2	228.6	254.0	279.4
1/16 in.	1.6	27.0	52.4	77.8	103.2	128.6	154.0	179.4	204.8	230.2	255.6	281.0
1/8 in.	3.2	28.6	54.0	79.4	104.8	130.2	155.6	181.0	206.4	231.8	257.2	282.6
3/16 in.	4.8	30.2	55.6	81.0	106.4	131.8	157.2	182.6	208.0	233.4	258.8	284.2
1/4 in.	6.4	31.8	57.2	82.6	108.0	133.4	158.8	184.2	209.6	235.0	260.4	285.8
5/16 in.	7.9	33.3	58.7	84.1	109.5	134.9	160.3	185.7	211.1	236.5	261.9	287.3
3/8 in.	9.5	34.9	60.3	85.7	111.1	136.5	161.9	187.3	212.7	238.1	263.5	288.9
7/16 in.	11.1	36.5	61.9	87.3	112.7	138.1	163.5	188.9	214.3	239.7	265.1	290.5
1/2 in.	12.7	38.1	63.5	88.9	114.3	139.7	165.1	190.5	215.9	241.3	266.7	292.1
9/16 in.	14.3	39.7	65.1	90.5	115.9	141.3	166.7	192.1	217.5	242.9	268.3	293.7
5/8 in.	15.9	41.3	66.7	92.1	117.5	142.9	168.3	193.7	219.1	244.5	269.9	295.3
11/16 in.	17.5	42.9	68.3	93.7	119.1	144.5	169.9	195.3	220.7	246.1	271.5	296.9
3/4 in.	19.1	44.5	69.9	95.3	120.7	146.1	171.5	196.9	222.3	247.7	273.1	298.5
13/16 in.	20.6	46.0	71.4	96.8	122.2	147.6	173.0	198.4	223.8	249.2	274.6	300.0
7/8 in.	22.2	47.6	73.0	98.4	123.8	149.2	174.6	200.0	225.4	250.8	276.2	301.6
15/16 in.	23.8	49.2	74.6	100.0	125.4	150.8	176.2	201.6	227.0	252.4	277.8	303.2

FEET TO METERS (1 METER = 1000 MILLIMETERS)

1 ft 0 in.	2 ft 0 in.	3 ft 0 in.	4 ft 0 in.	5 ft 0 in.	6 ft 0 in.	7 ft 0 in.	8 ft 0 in.	9 ft 0 in.	10 ft 0 in.	11 ft 0 in.	12 ft 0 in.	13 ft 0 in.
0.3048	0.6096	0.9144	1.2192	1.5240	1.8288	2.1336	2.4384	2.7432	3.0480	3.3528	3.6576	3.9624
14 ft 0 in.	15 ft 0 in.	16 ft 0 in.	17 ft 0 in.	18 ft 0 in.	19 ft 0 in.	20 ft 0 in.	21 ft 0 in.	22 ft 0 in.	23 ft 0 in.	24 ft 0 in.	25 ft 0 in.	26 ft 0 in.
4.2672	4.5720	4.8768	5.1816	5.4864	5.7912	6.0960	6.4008	6.7056	7.0104	7.3152	7.6200	7.9248
27 ft 0 in.	28 ft 0 in.	29 ft 0 in.	30 ft 0 in.	31 ft 0 in.	32 ft 0 in.	33 ft 0 in.	34 ft 0 in.	35 ft 0 in.	36 ft 0 in.	37 ft 0 in.	38 ft 0 in.	39 ft 0 in.
8.2296	8.5344	8.8392	9.1440	9.4488	9.7536	10.0584	10.3632	10.6680	10.9728	11.2776	11.5824	11.8872

Metric Conversion Chart

Duct Dimension (Width)

Duct Dimension (Depth)	6 in.	8 in.	10 in.	12 in.	14 in.	16 in.	18 in.	20 in.	22 in.	24 in.	26 in.	28 in.	30 in.	36 in.	42 in.	48 in.	54 in.	60 in.	66 in.	72 in.	84 in.	96 in.	108 in.
6 in.	2.00	2.33	2.67	3.00	3.33	3.67	4.00	4.33	4.67	5.00	5.33	5.67	6.00	7.00	8.00	9.00	10.00	11.00	12.00	13.00	15.00	17.00	19.00
8 in.		2.67	3.00	3.33	3.67	4.00	4.33	4.67	5.00	5.33	5.67	6.00	6.33	7.33	8.33	9.33	10.33	11.33	12.33	13.33	15.33	17.33	19.33
10 in.			3.33	3.67	4.00	4.33	4.67	5.00	5.33	5.67	6.00	6.33	6.67	7.67	8.67	9.67	10.67	11.67	12.67	13.67	15.67	17.67	19.67
12 in.				4.00	4.33	4.67	5.00	5.33	5.67	6.00	6.33	6.67	7.00	8.00	9.00	10.00	11.00	12.00	13.00	14.00	16.00	18.00	20.00
14 in.					4.67	5.00	5.33	5.67	6.00	6.33	6.67	7.00	7.33	8.33	9.33	10.33	11.33	12.33	13.33	14.33	16.33	18.33	20.33
16 in.						5.33	5.67	6.00	6.33	6.67	7.00	7.33	7.67	8.67	9.67	10.67	11.67	12.67	13.67	14.67	16.67	18.67	20.67
18 in.							6.00	6.33	6.67	7.00	7.33	7.67	8.00	9.00	10.00	11.00	12.00	13.00	14.00	15.00	17.00	19.00	21.00
20 in.								6.67	7.00	7.33	7.67	8.00	8.33	9.33	10.33	11.33	12.33	13.33	14.33	15.33	17.33	19.33	21.33
22 in.									7.33	7.67	8.00	8.33	8.67	9.67	10.67	11.67	12.67	13.67	14.67	15.67	17.67	19.67	21.67
24 in.										8.00	8.33	8.67	9.00	10.00	11.00	12.00	13.00	14.00	15.00	16.00	18.00	20.00	22.00
26 in.											8.67	9.00	9.33	10.33	11.33	12.33	13.33	14.33	15.33	16.33	18.33	20.33	22.33
28 in.												9.33	9.67	10.67	11.67	12.67	13.67	14.67	15.67	16.67	18.67	20.67	22.67
30 in.													10.00	11.00	12.00	13.00	14.00	15.00	16.00	17.00	19.00	21.00	23.00
36 in.														12.00	13.00	14.00	15.00	16.00	17.00	18.00	20.00	22.00	24.00
42 in.															14.00	15.00	16.00	17.00	18.00	19.00	21.00	23.00	25.00
48 in.																16.00	17.00	18.00	19.00	20.00	22.00	24.00	26.00
54 in.																	18.00	19.00	20.00	21.00	23.00	25.00	27.00
60 in.																		20.00	21.00	22.00	24.00	26.00	28.00
66 in.																			22.00	23.00	25.00	27.00	29.00
72 in.																				24.00	26.00	28.00	30.00
84 in.																					28.00	30.00	32.00
96 in.																						32.00	34.00
108 in.																							36.00

Duct Surface Area In Square Feet Per Linear Foot

LB./S.F. S.F.	23.2% 2.656 16 ga	30.2% 2.156 18 ga	17.8% 1.656 20 ga	21.8% 1.406 22 ga	27.6% 1.156 24 ga	16% .906 26 ga	.781 28 ga
2.33	6.19	5.02	3.86	3.28	2.69	2.11	1.82
2.67	7.09	5.56	4.42	3.75	3.09	2.42	2.09
3.00	7.96	6.47	4.97	4.22	3.47	2.72	2.34
3.33	8.84	7.18	5.51	4.68	3.85	3.02	2.60
3.67	9.75	7.91	6.08	5.16	4.24	3.33	2.87
4.00	10.62	8.62	6.62	5.62	4.62	3.62	3.12
4.33	11.50	9.34	7.17	6.09	5.01	3.92	3.38
4.67	12.40	10.07	7.73	6.57	5.40	4.23	3.65
5.00	13.28	10.78	8.28	7.03	5.78	4.53	3.91
5.33	14.16	11.49	8.83	7.49	6.16	4.83	4.16
5.67	15.06	12.22	9.39	7.97	6.55	5.14	4.43
6.00	15.94	12.94	9.94	8.44	6.94	5.44	4.69
6.33	16.81	13.65	10.48	8.90	7.32	5.73	4.94
6.67	17.72	14.38	11.05	9.38	7.71	6.04	5.21
7.00	18.59	15.09	11.59	9.84	8.09	6.34	5.47
7.33	19.47	15.80	12.14	10.31	8.47	6.64	5.72
7.67	20.37	16.54	12.70	10.78	8.87	6.95	5.99
8.00	21.25	17.28	13.20	11.25	9.25	7.25	6.25
8.33	22.12	17.96	13.79	11.71	9.63	7.55	6.51
8.67	23.03	18.69	14.36	12.91	10.02	7.86	6.77
9.00	23.90	19.40	14.90	12.65	10.40	8.15	7.03
9.33	24.78	20.12	15.45	13.12	10.79	8.45	7.29
9.67	25.68	20.85	16.01	13.60	11.18	8.76	7.55
10.00	26.56	21.56	16.56	14.06	11.56	9.06	7.81
10.33	27.44	22.27	17.11	14.52	11.94	9.36	8.07
10.67	28.34	23.00	17.67	15.00	12.33	9.67	8.33
11.00	29.22	23.72	18.22	15.47	12.72	9.97	8.50
11.33	30.09	24.43	18.76	15.93	13.10	10.26	8.85
11.63	30.96	25.16	19.33	16.41	13.49	10.57	9.11
12.00	31.87	25.87	19.87	16.87	13.87	10.87	9.37
12.33	32.75	26.58	20.42	17.34	14.25	11.17	9.63
12.67	33.65	27.32	20.96	17.81	14.65	11.48	9.90
13.00	34.53	28.03	21.53	18.28	15.03	11.78	10.15
13.33	35.40	28.74	22.07	18.74	15.41	12.08	10.41
13.67	36.31	29.47	22.64	19.22	15.08	12.39	10.68
14.00	37.18	30.18	23.18	19.68	16.18	12.68	10.93
14.33	38.06	30.90	23.73	20.15	16.57	12.98	11.19
14.67	38.96	31.63	24.29	20.63	16.96	13.29	11.46
15.00	39.84	32.34	24.84	21.09	17.34	13.59	11.72
15.33	40.72	33.05	25.39	21.55	17.72	13.89	11.97
15.67	41.62	33.78	25.95	22.03	18.11	14.20	12.24
16.00	42.50	34.50	26.50	22.50	18.50	14.50	12.50
16.33	43.37	35.21	27.04	22.96	18.88	14.79	12.75
16.67	44.28	35.94	27.61	23.44	19.27	15.10	13.02
17.00	45.15	36.65	28.15	23.90	19.65	15.40	13.28
17.33	46.03	37.36	28.70	24.37	20.03	15.70	13.53
17.67	46.93	38.10	29.26	24.84	20.43	16.01	13.80
18.00	47.81	38.81	29.81	25.31	20.81	16.31	14.06
18.33	48.68	39.52	30.35	25.77	21.19	16.61	14.32
18.67	49.59	40.25	30.92	26.25	21.58	16.92	14.58
19.00	50.46	40.96	31.46	26.71	21.96	17.21	14.84

Galvanized Sheet Weight

LB./S.F. / S.F.	23.2% / 2.656 / 16 ga	30.2% / 2.156 / 18 ga	17.8% / 1.656 / 20 ga	21.8% / 1.406 / 22 ga	27.6% / 1.156 / 24 ga	16% / .906 / 26 ga	.781 / 28 ga
19.33	51.34	41.68	32.01	27.18	22.35	17.51	15.10
19.67	52.24	42.41	32.57	27.66	22.74	17.82	15.36
20.00	53.12	43.12	33.12	28.12	23.12	18.12	15.62
20.33	54.00	43.83	33.67	28.58	23.50	18.42	15.88
20.67	54.90	44.56	34.23	29.06	23.89	18.73	16.14
21.00	55.78	45.28	34.78	29.53	24.28	19.03	16.40
21.33	56.65	45.99	35.32	29.99	24.66	19.32	16.66
21.67	57.56	46.72	35.89	30.47	25.05	19.63	16.92
22.00	58.43	47.43	36.43	30.93	25.43	19.93	17.18
22.33	59.31	48.14	36.98	31.40	25.81	20.23	17.44
22.67	60.21	48.88	37.54	31.87	26.21	20.54	17.71
23.00	61.09	49.59	38.09	32.34	26.59	20.84	17.96
23.33	61.96	50.30	38.63	32.80	26.97	21.14	18.22
23.67	62.87	51.03	39.20	33.28	27.36	21.45	18.49
24.00	63.74	51.74	39.74	33.74	27.74	21.74	18.74
24.33	64.62	52.46	40.29	34.20	28.13	22.04	19.00
24.67	65.52	53.19	40.85	34.69	28.52	22.35	19.27
25.00	66.40	53.90	41.20	35.15	28.90	22.65	19.53
26.33	67.28	54.61	41.95	35.61	29.28	22.95	19.78
25.67	68.18	55.34	42.51	36.09	29.67	23.26	20.05
26.00	69.06	56.06	43.01	36.56	30.06	23.56	20.31
26.33	69.93	56.77	43.60	37.02	30.44	23.85	20.56
26.67	70.84	57.50	44.17	37.50	30.83	24.16	20.83
27.00	71.71	58.21	44.71	37.96	31.21	24.46	21.09
27.33	72.59	58.92	45.26	38.43	31.59	24.76	21.34
27.67	73.49	59.66	45.82	38.90	31.99	25.07	21.61
28.00	74.37	60.37	46.36	39.37	32.37	25.37	21.87
28.33	75.24	61.08	46.91	39.83	32.75	25.67	22.13
28.67	76.15	61.81	47.48	40.31	33.14	25.98	22.39
29.00	77.02	62.52	48.02	40.77	33.52	26.27	22.65
29.33	77.90	63.24	48.57	41.24	33.91	26.57	22.91
29.67	78.80	63.97	49.13	41.72	34.30	26.88	23.17
30.00	79.80	64.68	49.68	42.18	34.68	27.18	23.43
30.33	80.56	65.39	50.23	42.64	35.06	27.48	23.69
30.67	81.46	56.12	50.79	43.12	35.45	27.79	23.95
31.00	82.34	66.84	51.34	43.59	35.84	28.09	24.21
31.33	83.21	67.55	51.88	44.05	36.22	28.38	24.47
31.67	84.12	68.28	52.45	44.53	36.61	28.69	24.73
32.00	84.79	68.99	52.99	44.99	36.99	28.99	24.99
32.33	85.87	69.70	53.54	45.46	37.37	29.29	25.25
32.67	86.77	70.44	54.10	45.93	37.77	29.60	25.52
33.00	87.65	71.15	54.65	46.40	38.15	29.90	25.77
33.33	88.52	71.86	55.19	46.86	38.53	30.20	26.03
33.67	89.43	72.59	55.76	47.34	38.97	30.51	26.30
34.00	90.30	73.30	56.30	47.80	39.30	30.80	26.55
34.33	91.18	74.02	56.85	48.27	39.69	31.10	26.81
34.67	92.08	74.75	57.41	48.75	40.08	31.41	27.08
35.00	92.96	75.46	57.96	49.21	40.46	31.71	27.34
35.33	93.84	76.17	58.51	49.67	40.84	32.01	27.59
35.67	94.74	76.90	59.07	50.15	41.23	32.32	27.86
36.00	95.62	77.62	59.62	50.62	41.62	32.62	28.12

Galvanized Sheet Weight (Continued)

DIA. \ GA.	30S	30L	28S	28L	26S	26L	24S	24L	22S	22L	20S	20L	18S	18L	16S	16L
3"	0.6	0.60	0.7	0.71	0.9	0.82	1.0	1.05	1.2	1.28	1.3	1.51	2.0	1.97		2.42
4"	0.8	0.77	0.9	0.92	1.2	1.06	1.3	1.36	1.5	1.65	1.8	1.94	2.6	2.53		3.12
5"	0.9	0.94	1.1	1.12	1.4	1.3	1.6	1.66	2.0	2.02	2.3	2.38	3.2	3.10		3.81
6"	1.1	1.11	1.4	1.32	1.7	1.54	2.0	1.96	2.4	2.39	2.6	2.81	3.7	3.66	5.0	4.51
7"	1.3	1.28	1.6	1.53	1.9	1.77	2.4	2.26	2.8	2.75	3.3	3.24	4.3	4.23	5.8	5.20
8"	1.5	1.46	1.9	1.73	2.1	2.01	2.6	2.57	3.2	3.12	3.7	3.68	4.8	4.79	6.7	5.90
9"	1.6	1.63	2.0	1.94	2.3	2.25	3.0	2.87	3.5	3.49	4.0	4.11	5.3	5.36	7.5	6.60
10"	1.9	1.80	2.2	2.14	2.5	2.48	3.3	3.17	4.0	3.86	4.7	4.54	6.0	5.92	8.3	7.29
11"	2.0	1.97	2.4	2.35	2.8	2.72	3.6	3.48	4.4	4.23	5.1	4.98	6.7	6.49		7.99
12"	2.2	2.14	2.6	2.55	30	2.96	3.8	3.78	4.7	4.60	5.2	5.41	7.2	7.05	10.0	8.68
14"		2.49	3.0	2.96	3.5	3.43	4.4	4.38	5.4	5.33	6.4	6.28	8.3	8.19	11.7	10.08
16"		2.83	3.4	3.37	4.0	3.91	5.1	4.99	6.2	6.07	7.3	7.15	9.4	9.32	13.4	11.47
18"		3.18	3.8	3.78	4.4	4.38	5.7	5.59	6.9	6.80	8.1	8.01	10.5	10.45	15.0	12.86
20"			4.2	4.19	5.0	4.85	6.4	6.20	7.8	7.54	9.0	8.88	11.7	11.58	16.7	14.25
22"			4.7	4.60	5.4	5.33	7.0	6.80	8.4	8.28	9.9	9.75	12.9	12.71	18.4	15.64
24"			5.2	5.01	6.0	5.80	7.8	7.41	9.5	9.01	11.0	10.62	14.4	13.64	20.0	17.04
26"					6.6	6.28	8.5	8.02	10.3	9.75	12.2	11.48	15.8	14.97	21.7	18.43
28"					7.0	6.75	8.9	8.62	11.0	10.49	12.9	12.35	16.5	16.10	23.4	19.82
30"					7.1	7.23	9.3	9.23	11.8	11.22	13.6	13.22	17.2	17.23	25.0	21.21
32"						7.70	10.1	9.83	12.6	11.96	14.6	14.09	18.9	18.36	26.7	22.60
34"						8.18		10.44		12.70		14.95		19.49		24.00
36"						8.65	11.5	11.05	14.2	13.43	16.6	15.82	21.5	20.62	30.0	25.39
40"						9.60	12.8	12.26	15.5	14.91	16.5	17.56	23.8	23.88	33.4	28.17
44"						10.55	14.4	13.47	17.4	16.38	20.5	19.29	26.7	25.15	36.7	30.96
48"						11.50	15.4	14.68	18.7	17.85	22.2	21.03	29.2	27.41	40.1	33.74
50"							16.0	15.28	19.5	18.59	23.3	21.89	30.0	28.54	41.7	35.13
54"								16.50		20.06		23.63		30.80	45.1	37.91
56"								17.10		20.79		24.50		31.93	46.7	39.31
60"								18.31		22.27		26.23		34.19	50.1	42.09
72"								21.95		26.69		31.44		40.98		50.44
84"								25.58		31.11		36.64		47.76		58.79

Approximate Weight - Round Duct in Pounds Per Linear Foot

S = Spiral duct - from manufacturers published tables
L = Longitudinal seam with 1½" seam allowance

NOTE: 1. Liner and/or exterior insulation weight excluded.
2. Based on galvanized steel. Investigate tolerance for closer estimates

Diameter Inches	Area Sq. In.	Area Sq. Ft.	Circumference In.	Circumference Ft.	Diameter Inches	Area Sq. In.	Area Sq. Ft.	Circumference In.	Circumference Ft.
1	0.7854	0.00545	3.142	0.2618	51	2042.82	14.19	160.22	13.35
2	3.1416	0.0218	6.283	0.5236	52	2123.72	14.75	163.36	13.61
3	7.0686	0.0491	9.425	0.7854	53	2206.18	15.32	166.50	13.88
4	12.5664	0.0873	12.566	1.047	54	2290.22	15.90	169.65	14.14
5	19.6350	0.1364	15.708	1.309	55	2375.83	16.50	172.79	14.40
6	28.2743	0.1964	18.850	1.571	56	2463.01	17.10	175.93	14.66
7	38.4845	0.2673	21.991	1.833	57	2551.76	17.72	179.07	14.92
8	50.2655	0.3491	25.133	2.094	58	2642.08	18.35	182.21	15.18
9	63.6173	0.4418	28.274	2.356	59	2733.97	18.99	185.35	15.45
10	78.5398	0.5454	31.416	2.618	60	2827.43	19.63	188.50	15.71
11	95.0332	0.6600	34.558	2.880	61	2922.47	20.29	191.64	15.97
12	113.097	0.7854	37.699	3.142	62	3019.07	20.97	194.78	16.23
13	132.732	0.9218	40.841	3.403	63	3117.25	21.65	197.92	16.49
14	153.938	1.069	43.982	3.665	64	3216.99	22.34	201.06	16.76
15	176.715	1.227	47.124	3.927	65	3318.31	23.04	204.20	17.02
16	201.062	1.396	50.265	4.189	66	3421.19	23.76	207.35	17.28
17	226.980	1.576	53.407	4.451	67	3525.65	24.48	210.49	17.54
18	254.469	1.767	56.549	4.712	68	3631.68	25.22	213.63	17.80
19	283.529	1.969	59.690	4.974	69	3739.28	25.97	216.67	18.06
20	314.159	2.182	62.832	5.236	70	3848.45	26.73	219.91	18.33
21	346.361	2.405	65.973	5.498	71	3959.19	27.49	233.05	18.69
22	380.133	2.640	69.115	5.760	72	4071.50	28.27	226.19	18.85
23	415.476	2.885	72.257	6.021	73	4185.39	29.07	229.34	19.11
24	452.389	3.142	75.398	6.283	74	4300.84	29.87	232.48	19.37
25	490.874	3.409	78.540	6.545	75	4417.86	30.68	235.62	19.63
26	530.929	3.687	81.681	6.807	76	4536.46	31.50	238.76	19.90
27	572.555	3.976	84.823	7.069	77	4656.63	32.34	241.90	20.16
28	615.752	4.276	87.965	7.330	78	4778.36	33.18	245.04	20.42
29	660.520	4.587	91.106	7.592	79	4901.67	34.04	248.19	20.68
30	706.859	4.909	94.248	7.854	80	5026.55	34.91	251.33	20.94
31	754.768	5.241	97.389	8.116	81	5153.00	35.78	254.47	21.21
32	804.248	5.585	100.531	8.378	82	5281.02	36.67	257.61	21.47
33	855.299	5.940	103.673	8.639	83	5410.61	37.57	260.75	21.73
34	907.920	6.305	106.814	8.901	84	5541.77	38.48	263.89	21.99
35	942.113	6.681	109.956	9.163	85	5674.50	39.41	267.04	22.25
36	1017.88	7.069	113.097	9.425	86	5808.80	40.34	270.18	22.51
37	1075.21	7.467	116.239	9.686	87	5944.68	41.28	273.32	22.78
38	1134.11	7.876	119.381	9.948	88	6082.12	42.24	276.46	23.04
39	1194.59	8.296	122.522	10.21	89	6221.14	43.20	279.60	23.30
40	1256.54	8.727	125.66	10.47	90	6361.73	44.18	282.74	23.56
41	1320.25	9.168	128.81	10.73	91	6503.88	45.17	285.88	23.82
42	1385.44	9.621	131.95	10.99	92	6647.61	46.16	289.03	24.09
43	1452.20	10.08	135.09	11.26	93	6792.91	47.17	292.17	24.35
44	1520.53	10.56	138.23	11.52	94	6939.78	48.19	295.31	24.61
45	1590.43	11.04	141.37	11.78	95	7088.78	49.22	298.45	24.87
46	1661.90	11.54	144.51	12.04	96	7238.23	50.27	301.59	25.13
47	1734.94	12.05	147.65	12.30	97	7389.81	51.32	304.73	25.39
48	1809.56	12.51	150.80	12.57	98	7542.96	52.38	307.88	25.66
49	1885.74	13.09	153.94	12.83	99	7699.69	53.46	311.02	25.92
50	1963.50	13.64	157.08	13.09	100	7853.98	54.54	314.16	26.18

Area And Circumferences of Circles

Size in.	Description	Weight lbs/ft	Rated Z	Rated I_x
1 × 1 × ⅛	Angle	.80	.031	.022
1 ¼ × 1 ¼ × ⅛	Angle	1.02	.049	.044
1 ½ × ⅛	Bar	.64	.035	.035
1 × ¼	Bar	.85	.042	.021
1 ½ × 1 ½ × ⅛	Angle	1.23	.072	.078
1 ½ × 1 ½ × 3/16	Angle	1.80	.104	.110
1 ½ × 1 ½ × ¼	Angle	2.34	.134	.139
2 × 2 × ⅛	Angle	1.65	.131	.190
2 × ¼	Bar	1.70	.167	.167
2 × 2 × 3/16	Angle	2.44	.190	.272
2 × 2 × 5/16	Angle	3.92	.30	.416
3 × ¼	Bar	2.55	.375	.563
2 ½ × 2 ½ × ¼	Angle	4.1	.394	.703
3 × 3/16	Bar	3.19	.469	.703
2 ½ × 2 ½ × ⅜	Angle	5.9	.566	.984
3 × 3 × ¼	Angle	4.9	.577	1.24
3 × 2 × ⅜	Angle	5.9	.781	1.53
4 × 4 ¼	Angle	6.6	1.05	3.04
4 × 4 × 5/16	Angle	8.2	1.29	3.71
4 × ½	Bar	6.8	1.334	2.667
C4	Channel	5.4	1.93	3.85
4 × 3 ½ × ½	Angle	11.9	1.94	5.32
C5	Channel	6.7	3.00	7.49
C5	Channel	9	3.56	8.90

Angle, Bar and Channel Properties

Z is section modulus in in^3.

Stress is M/Z where M is bending moment.
I_x is moment of inertia in in^4.

For steel, the nominal rigidity index EI is $290 \times 10^5 \times I_x$

A.1 CONTRACTOR'S ANALYSIS OF SHOP STANDARDS

What is the Preference in Primary Variables?

1. Metal Stock Size: 4 × 8 ft; 4 × 10 ft; 5 × 10 ft; 48 in. coil, 60 in. coil, other?

2. Joint spacing: 4 ft, 5 ft, 8 ft, or 10 ft?

3. Joint type?

4. Intermediate Reinforcement: type (and amount; i.e., reduce interval by using it on lighter duct wall or avoid it by selecting wall thickness not requiring it?)

Other Variables that Affect Production Costs and that may prompt Change in First Choice of Primary Variables

1. Sealing requirements

2. Leak Test requirements, if any

3. Access Space available for joint make up/closure/repair

4. Amount of Prefabrication off-site

5. Transportation storage and hoisting (damage risk and logistics control)

6. Job Schedule/manpower

7. Quality level of Workmanship anticipated on the specific project

8. Ratio of fittings to straight duct

9. Size changes, i.e., potential to make rectangular shape more square with contracting authority's approval; potential to convert to extended plenum; potential to convert rectangular to round.

10. Crossbreaking or beading obligations

11. Standardized Pressure Classification (Supply construction conforming to a higher pressure class than required in order to use fewer variations).

A.2 NOTES

1. Joints and intermediate reinforcements are labor intensive units and they may be more costly than the savings in a reduction in metal in duct wall thickness.

2. Use of a thicker duct wall or a stronger joint over a wider range of duct sizes than those required can be cost effective. Examples include using a 22 ga duct wall where 22 ga and 24 ga are minimums and using a D grade of joint over a range of sizes that would permit A, B, C, and D selections. However, substituting a larger-than-minimum element in one primary variable does not justify reducing another primary variable.

3. Some joint classifications have flanges or portions of the duct incorporated in their ratings; others do not. A thorough study is advised.

4. Flat joint systems can qualify when backed up with reinforcements. Sealing expense and effectiveness may make this alternative more attractive than other joint options.

wg Static Pos. or Neg. Duct Dimension	No Reinforcement Required	Shop Standards Rectangular Duct Reinforcement Reinforcement Code for Duct Gage No. Reinforcement Spacing Options							
		10 ft	8 ft	6 ft	5 ft	4 ft	3 ft	2½ ft	2 ft
①	②	③	④	⑤	⑥	⑦	⑧	⑨	⑩
10 in. dn									
11, 12 in.									
13, 14 in.									
15, 16 in.									
17, 18 in.									
19, 20 in.									
21, 22 in.									
23, 24 in.									
25, 26 in.									
27, 28 in.									
29, 30 in.									
31–36 in.									
37–42 in.									
43–48 in.									
49–54 in.									
55–60 in.									
61–72 in.									
73–84 in.									
85–96 in.									
97–108 in.									
109–120 in.									

Sample Worksheet

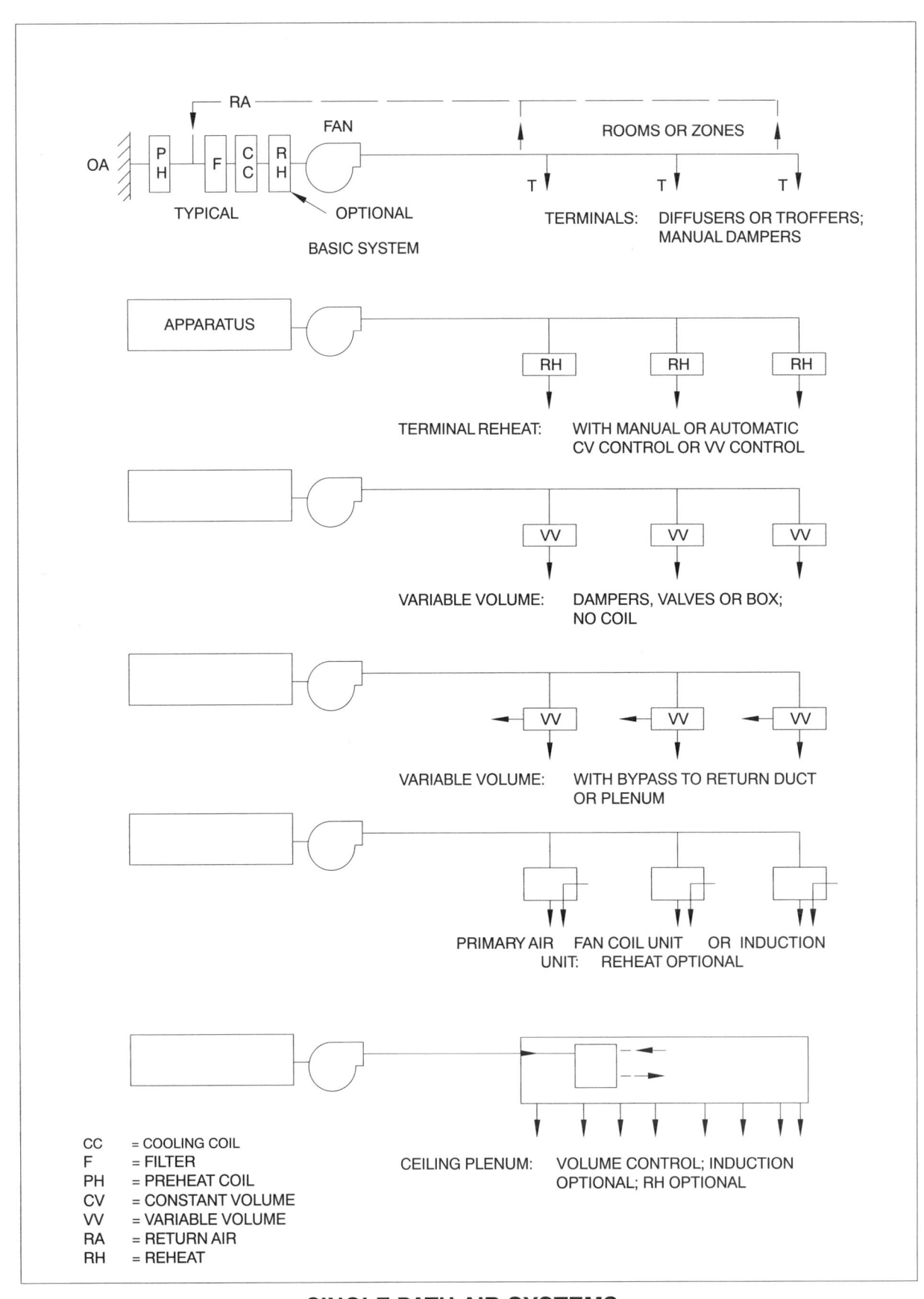

SINGLE PATH AIR SYSTEMS

BASIC SYSTEM
OA → PH → F → CC → RH (OPTIONAL) → FAN → RA → ROOMS OR ZONES
PH, F, CC = TYPICAL
TERMINALS: DIFFUSERS OR TROFFERS; MANUAL DAMPERS

APPARATUS → FAN → RH → RH → RH
TERMINAL REHEAT: WITH MANUAL OR AUTOMATIC CV CONTROL OR VV CONTROL

VV → VV → VV
VARIABLE VOLUME: DAMPERS, VALVES OR BOX; NO COIL

VV ← VV ← VV
VARIABLE VOLUME: WITH BYPASS TO RETURN DUCT OR PLENUM

PRIMARY AIR FAN COIL UNIT OR INDUCTION UNIT: REHEAT OPTIONAL

CEILING PLENUM: VOLUME CONTROL; INDUCTION OPTIONAL; RH OPTIONAL

CC = COOLING COIL
F = FILTER
PH = PREHEAT COIL
CV = CONSTANT VOLUME
VV = VARIABLE VOLUME
RA = RETURN AIR
RH = REHEAT

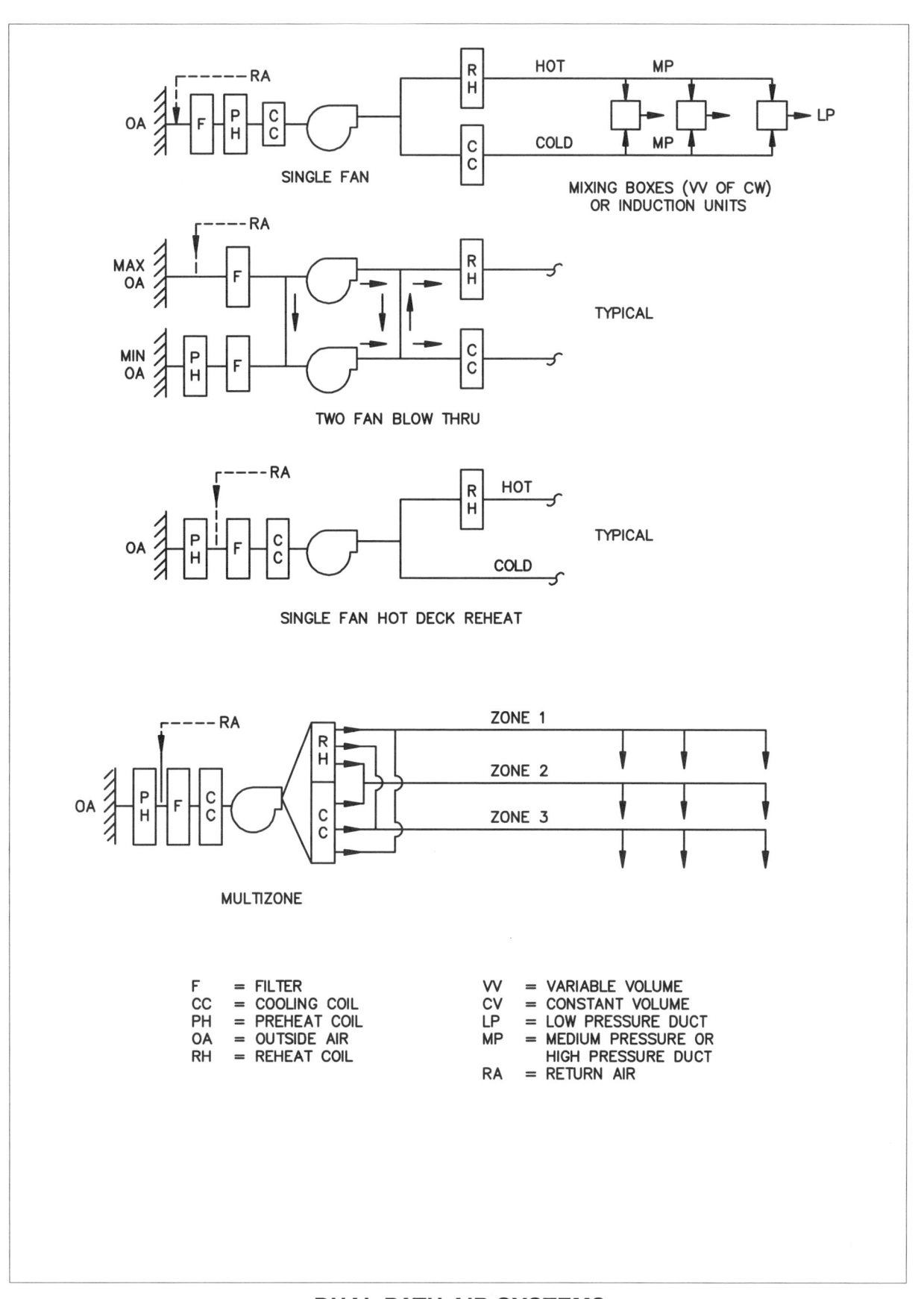

DUAL PATH AIR SYSTEMS

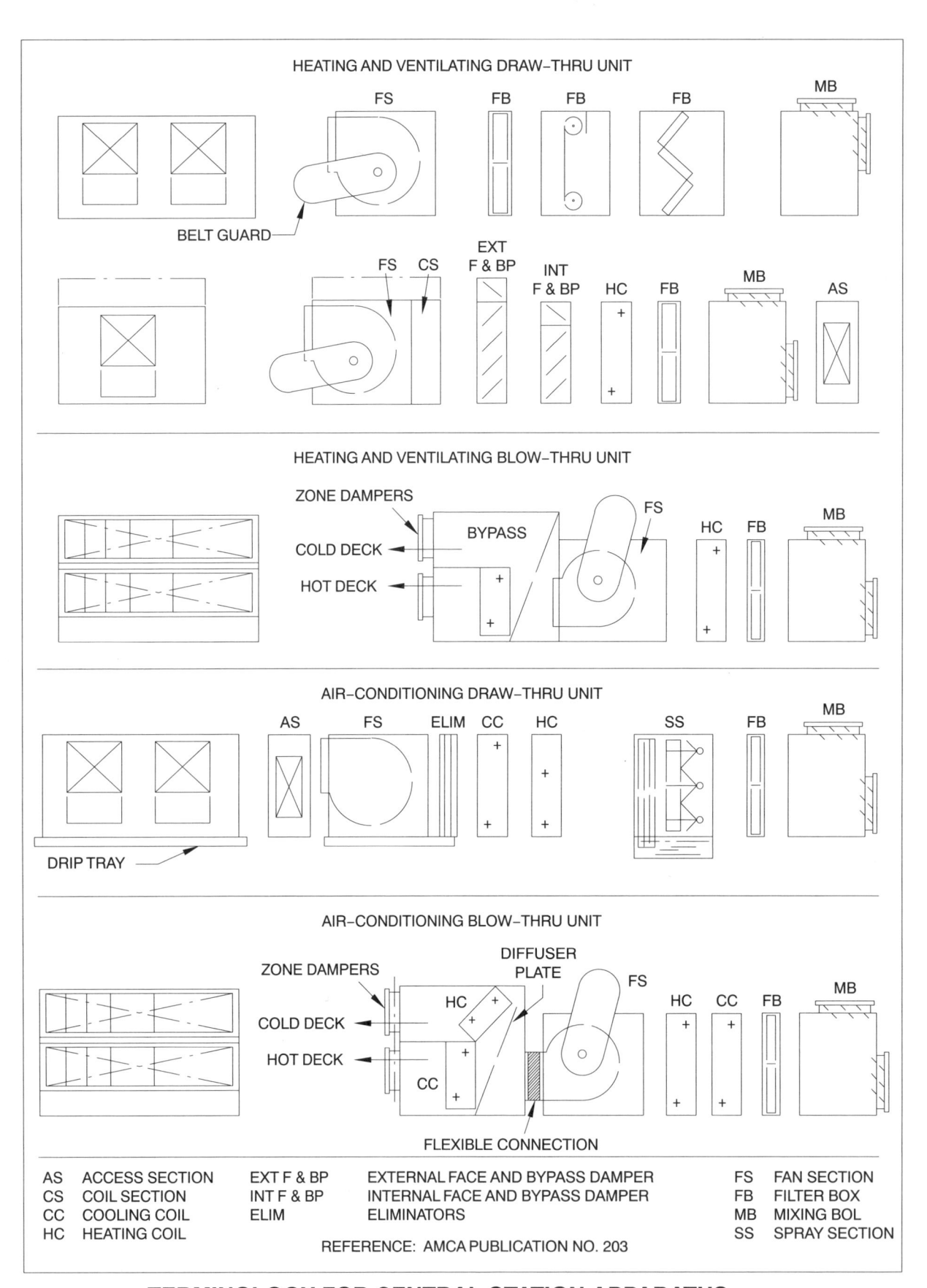

AS	ACCESS SECTION	EXT F & BP	EXTERNAL FACE AND BYPASS DAMPER	FS	FAN SECTION
CS	COIL SECTION	INT F & BP	INTERNAL FACE AND BYPASS DAMPER	FB	FILTER BOX
CC	COOLING COIL	ELIM	ELIMINATORS	MB	MIXING BOL
HC	HEATING COIL			SS	SPRAY SECTION

REFERENCE: AMCA PUBLICATION NO. 203

TERMINOLOGY FOR CENTRAL STATION APPARATUS

HVAC Duct Construction Standards Metal and Flexible • Fourth Edition

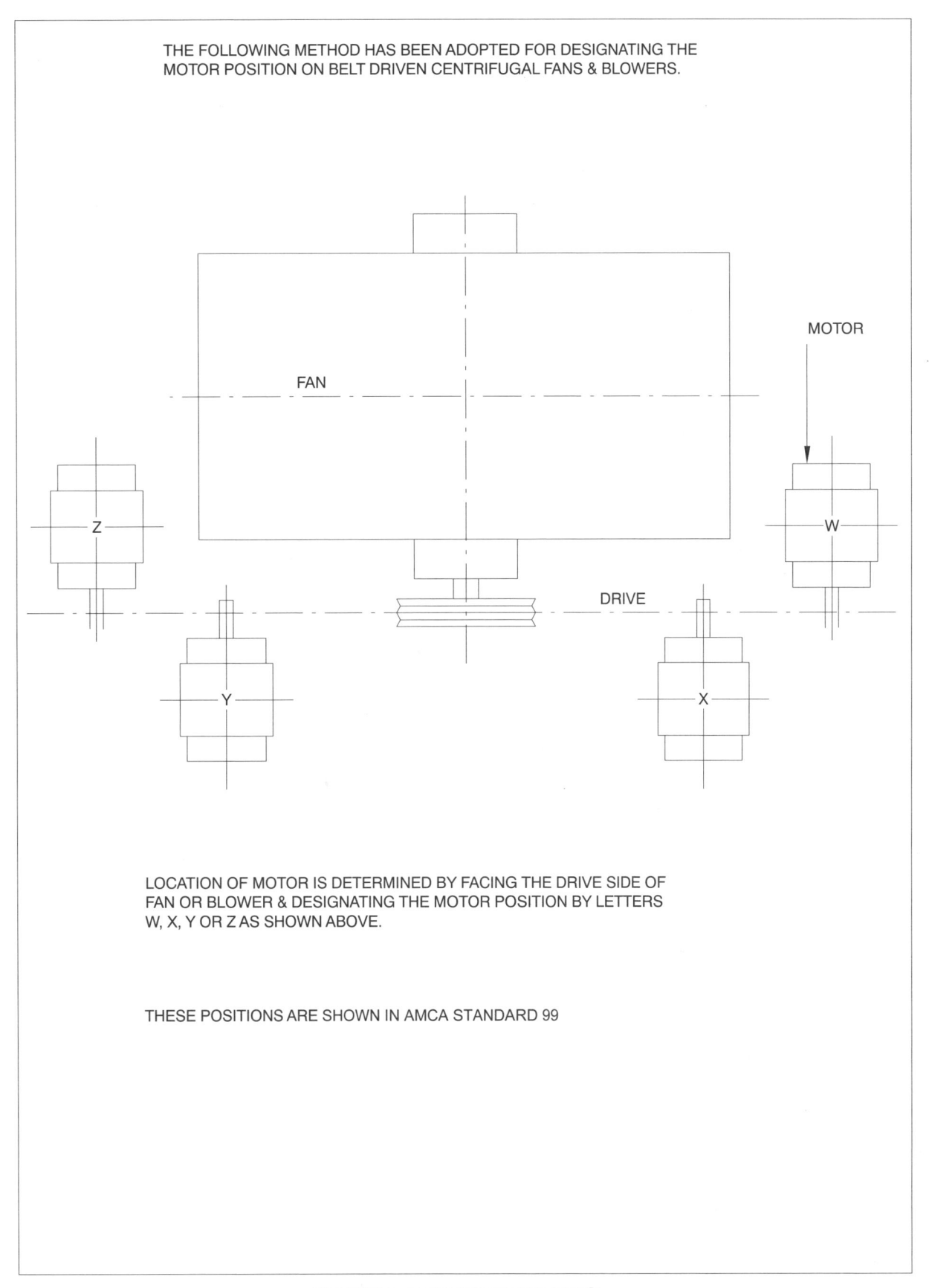

THE FOLLOWING METHOD HAS BEEN ADOPTED FOR DESIGNATING THE MOTOR POSITION ON BELT DRIVEN CENTRIFUGAL FANS & BLOWERS.

LOCATION OF MOTOR IS DETERMINED BY FACING THE DRIVE SIDE OF FAN OR BLOWER & DESIGNATING THE MOTOR POSITION BY LETTERS W, X, Y OR Z AS SHOWN ABOVE.

THESE POSITIONS ARE SHOWN IN AMCA STANDARD 99

MOTOR ARRANGEMENTS

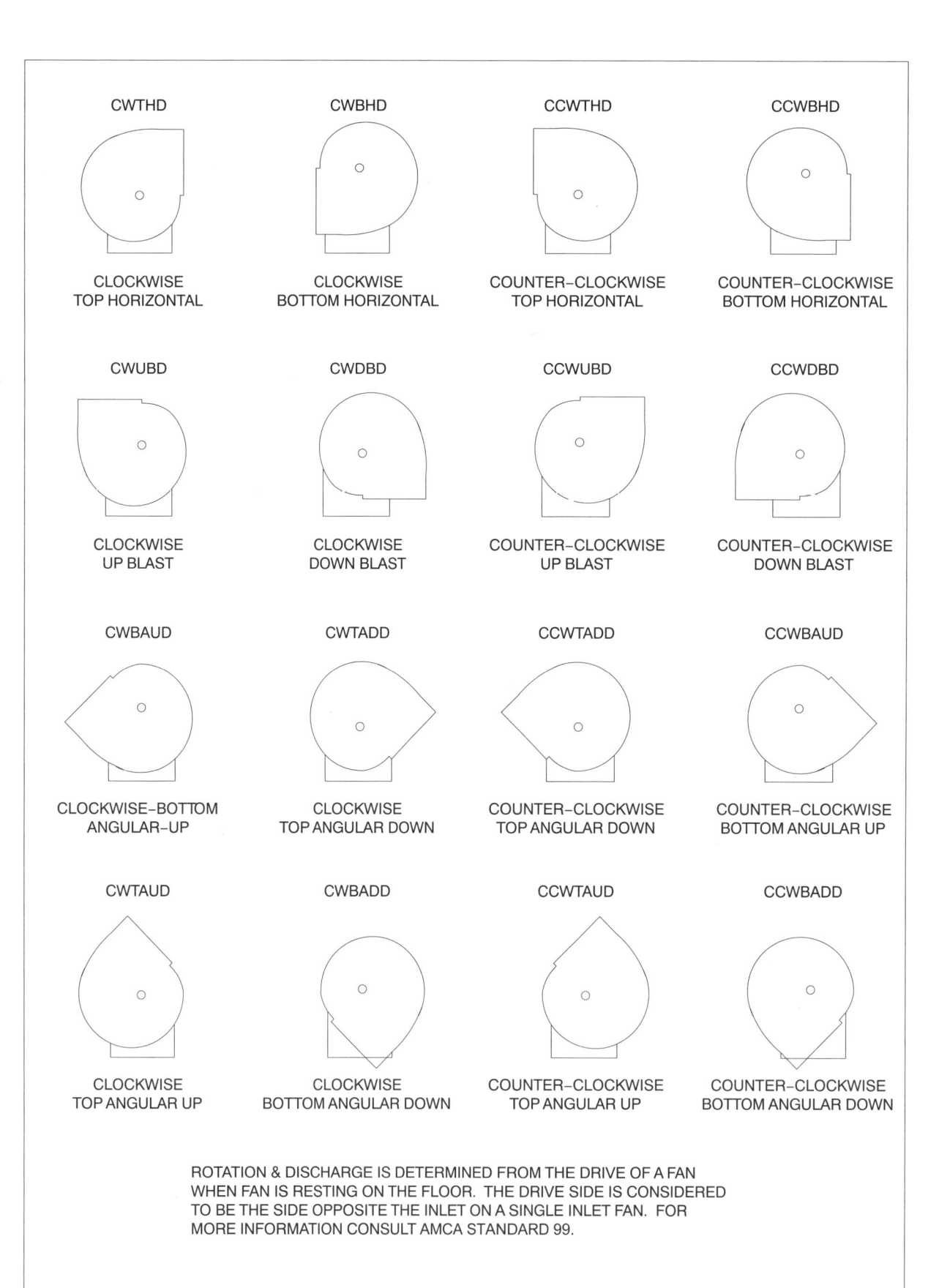

CWTHD	CWBHD	CCWTHD	CCWBHD
CLOCKWISE TOP HORIZONTAL	CLOCKWISE BOTTOM HORIZONTAL	COUNTER-CLOCKWISE TOP HORIZONTAL	COUNTER-CLOCKWISE BOTTOM HORIZONTAL
CWUBD	CWDBD	CCWUBD	CCWDBD
CLOCKWISE UP BLAST	CLOCKWISE DOWN BLAST	COUNTER-CLOCKWISE UP BLAST	COUNTER-CLOCKWISE DOWN BLAST
CWBAUD	CWTADD	CCWTADD	CCWBAUD
CLOCKWISE-BOTTOM ANGULAR-UP	CLOCKWISE TOP ANGULAR DOWN	COUNTER-CLOCKWISE TOP ANGULAR DOWN	COUNTER-CLOCKWISE BOTTOM ANGULAR UP
CWTAUD	CWBADD	CCWTAUD	CCWBADD
CLOCKWISE TOP ANGULAR UP	CLOCKWISE BOTTOM ANGULAR DOWN	COUNTER-CLOCKWISE TOP ANGULAR UP	COUNTER-CLOCKWISE BOTTOM ANGULAR DOWN

ROTATION & DISCHARGE IS DETERMINED FROM THE DRIVE OF A FAN WHEN FAN IS RESTING ON THE FLOOR. THE DRIVE SIDE IS CONSIDERED TO BE THE SIDE OPPOSITE THE INLET ON A SINGLE INLET FAN. FOR MORE INFORMATION CONSULT AMCA STANDARD 99.

FAN ROTATION & DISCHARGE POSITIONS

SOUND METAL GAGE VARIES WITH GUARD SIZE

ANGLE

PREFORATED OR EXPANDED METAL

TYPICAL SECTION

1" x 1" x 18 GA. (25 x 25 x 1.31 mm) ANGLES MIN. ON SPLIT GUARDS

ANGLE FRAME

EXPANDED METAL

TYPE D

SUPPORT FROM EQUIPMENT

SPLIT GUARD

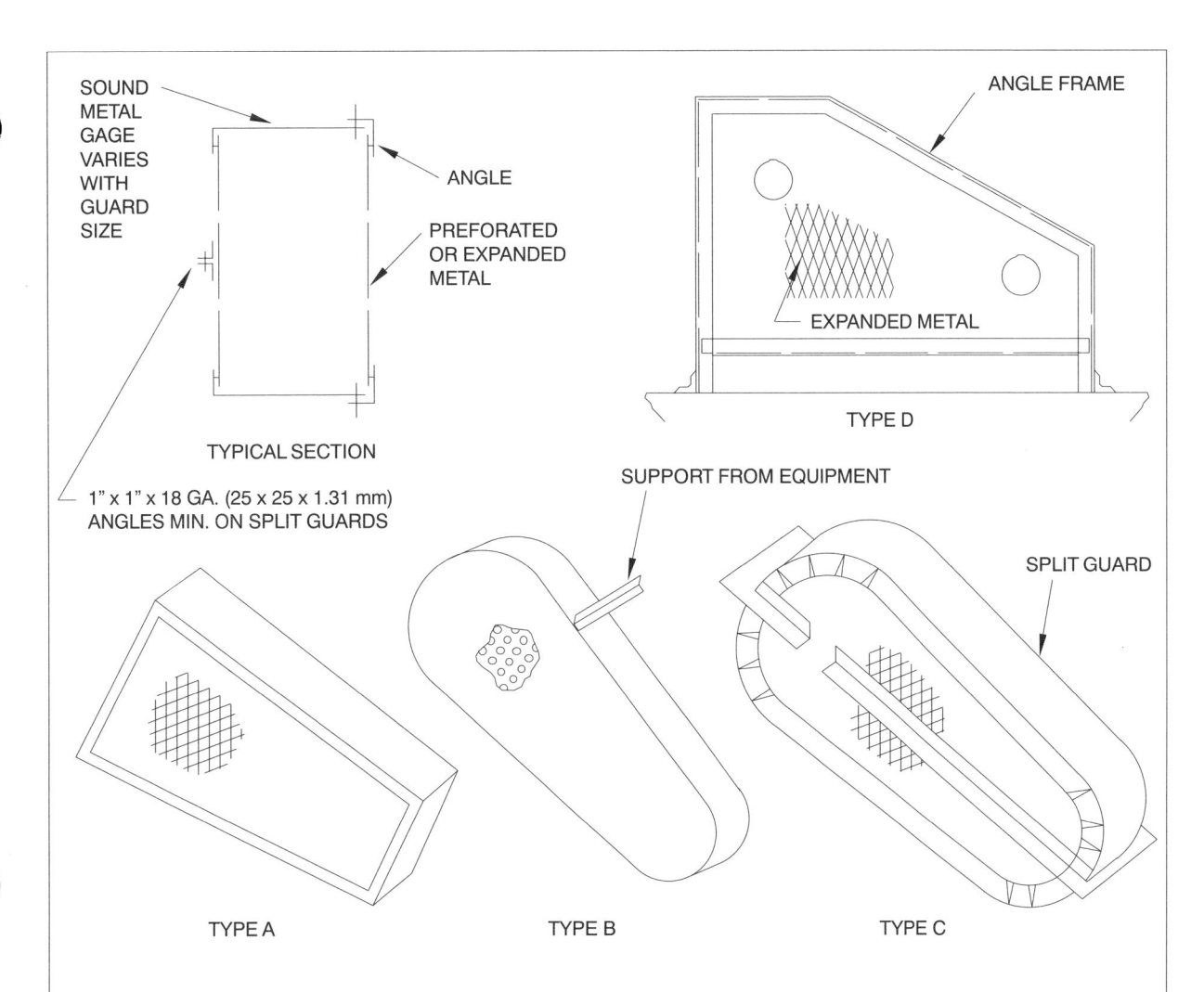

TYPE A   TYPE B   TYPE C

1. BELT GUARDS MUST CONFORM TO THE OCCUPATIONAL SAFETY & HEALTH ADMINISTRATION (OSHA) REGULATIONS.
2. TOTALLY ENCLOSED BELT GUARDS MAY BE REQUIRED. THE ENCLOSURE SHOULD BE PERFORATED OR EXPANDED METAL, IN PART, TO PROVIDE ADEQUATE VENTILATION.
3. BELT GUARDS MUST BE DESIGNED TO ACCOMMODATE MOTOR TRAVEL AND NORMAL ROTATING EQUIPMENT VIBRATION WITHOUT CONTACT WITH ADJACENT STRUCTURES. ADEQUATE CLEARANCE BETWEEN PULLEYS AND THE BELT GUARD, AND BELTS AND THE GUARD, MUST BE PROVIDED. ON LARGE DRIVES, BELT SAG SHOULD BE CONSIDERED.
4. ACCESS TO BELT, BEARINGS OR SHAFT MAY BE BY ONE OF SEVERAL METHODS: SMALL MOVABLE COVER PLATES, HINGED FRONT, SPLIT GUARD OR COMPLETE COVER REMOVAL. FACTORS TO BE CONSIDERED ARE SIZE AND WEIGHT OF THE GUARD, FREQUENCY OF ACCESS, METHOD OF SUPPORT, DISASSEMBLY TIME, INSPECTION ACCESS, ETC.
5. IN CONSIDERATION OF VIBRATION ISOLATION OR RIGID MOUNTING OF ROTATING EQUIPMENT, BELT GUARDS SHOULD BE SUPPORTED FROM THE VIBRATING MASS UNLESS CONTACT WITH MOVING PARTS IN IMPOSSIBLE.
6. THE THICKNESS OF THE BELT GUARD COMPONENTS VARIES WITH THE SIZE OF THE GUARD. SELECT ADEQUATELY FOR DUTY.
7. BELT GUARDS ARE FURNISHED IN UNCOATED METAL OR GALVANIZED STEEL UNLESS OTHERWISE SPECIFIED.

TYPICAL BELT GUARDS

HVAC Duct Construction Standards Metal and Flexible • Fourth Edition

A. OPEN SPRING MOUNT

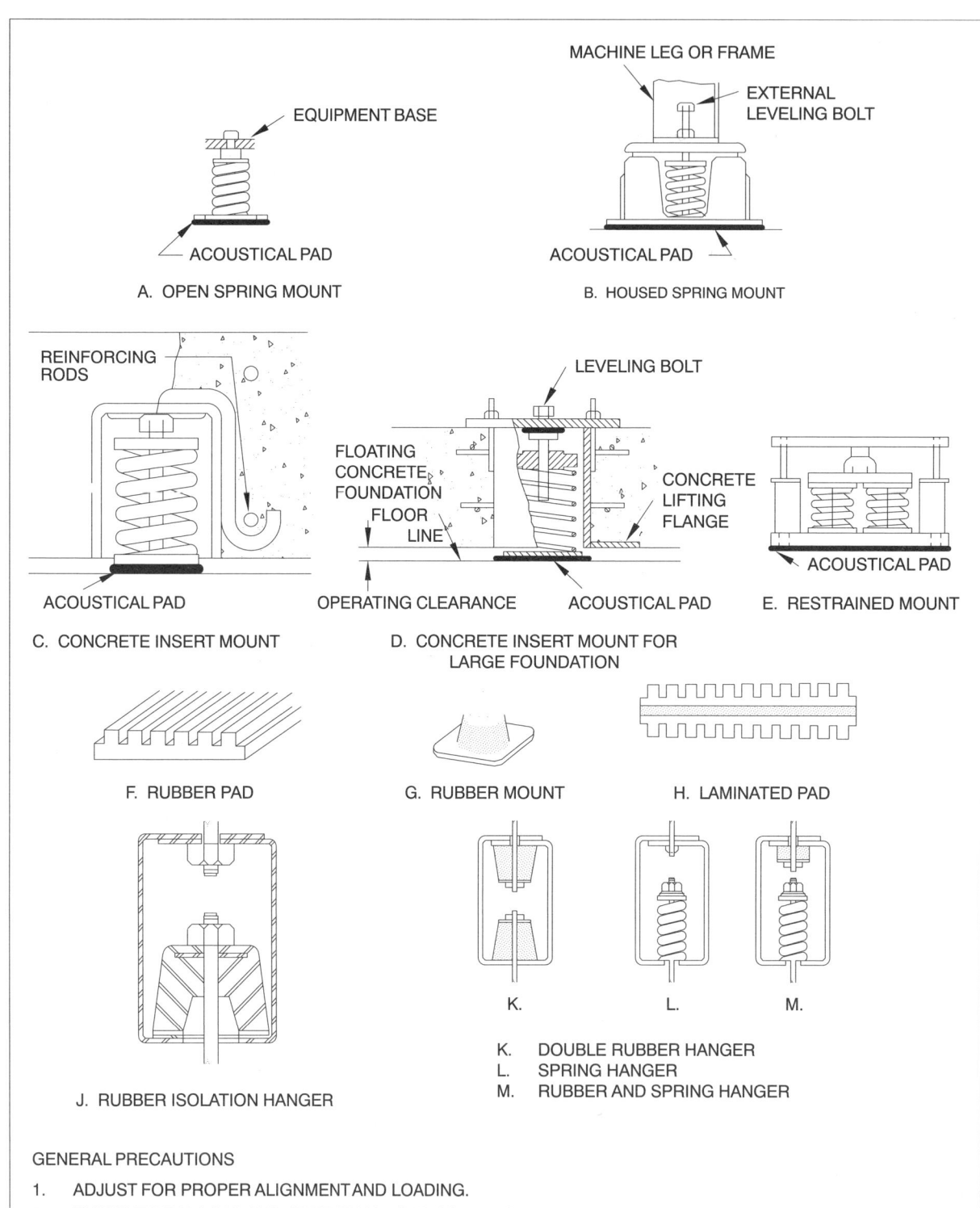

B. HOUSED SPRING MOUNT

C. CONCRETE INSERT MOUNT

D. CONCRETE INSERT MOUNT FOR LARGE FOUNDATION

E. RESTRAINED MOUNT

F. RUBBER PAD

G. RUBBER MOUNT

H. LAMINATED PAD

J. RUBBER ISOLATION HANGER

K. DOUBLE RUBBER HANGER
L. SPRING HANGER
M. RUBBER AND SPRING HANGER

GENERAL PRECAUTIONS

1. ADJUST FOR PROPER ALIGNMENT AND LOADING.
2. EXAMINE DEAL LOAD AND OPERATING LOAD CONDITION.
3. AVOID "GROUNDING" THE ISOLATOR.
4. MAINTAIN ALIGNMENT OF THE SYSTEM COMPONENTS BEING ISOLATED WITHOUT IMPOSING EXCESS STRESS.
5. CHECK HANGER ROD SIZE FOR ALLOWABLE LOADS AT THE ISOLATED DEVICE AND AT THE UPPER AND LOWER ATTACHMENTS TO STRUCTURES, DUCT, EQUIPMENT, ETC.
6. CONSULT MANUFACTURER FOR APPLICATION DATA.

TYPICAL ISOLATION DEVICES

A.3 RADIATION PROTECTION AT WALL OPENINGS FOR DUCT OR PIPE

Harrison D. Goodman* and George Hollands*

The purpose of these data sheets is to acquaint the air conditioning engineer with means for shielding ductwork and other openings that penetrate protective barriers around radiation facilities, particularly X-ray rooms.

Protection against radiation from X-ray tube, cyclotron, radium, or other radioactive material is primarily a question of shielding to reduce the level of radiation to a safe or specified amount, of maintaining safe distances from the rays, and/or of limiting the time of exposure.

The prime consideration in preventing penetration of rays is density of the shielding material. Lead is the densest of any commonly available. Where space is at a premium, particularly in modern buildings, and where utmost radiation protection is demanded, lead isinvariably used. Lead is useful, especially where neutron and gamma rays are concerned, in that it does not itself become contaminated and emit harmful rays.

Lead, usually in sheet form, is used to line the walls, floor, and often the ceiling of rooms containing radiation facilities. Openings through the barrier for air ductwork, piping, service boxes, conduit, etc., require shielding, usually obtained by a lead barrier around or behind these building utilities of sufficient coverage and thickness to prevent penetration of these rays.

Shielding of duct and other openings in the protective barriers of radiation facilities depends on energy of radiation, orientation of the beam, dimensions, and location of opening in the protective barrier, geometrical relationship between the radiation source and opening, and geometrical relationship between opening and perons, materials, or instruments to be protected. The complexity of these factors requires the services of a radiological physicist, who determines extent of shielding, materials for shielding (usually lead or concrete) and the thickness of the shielding material.

After the radiological physicist has done the basic design for this shielding, the protective barrier contractor provides the required shielding for the opening.

Role of Engineer

Design of ductwork, piping, etc., should *anticipate* some of the problems encountered both in the design and installation of shielding. Also, coordination between air conditioning contractor and shielding fabricator can best be achieved by understanding and forethought on the part of the air conditioning designer.

Figures 1 to 4 give some idea of the *area of shielding* required around ductwork. They show various duct installations which penetrate the protective barrier for walls or partitions of X-ray rooms. Lead shielding is used to cover these openings, *the approximate* extent of which is indicated in terms of simple equations in involving the opening dimensions and wall thickness. These are *conservative estimates,* which will aid the air conditioning designer to understand what what to expect as to the area of shielding ductwork. The radiological physicist actually determines for *each* case the *lead* thickness and the exact amount of shielding required.

Note in Figure 4 that the protective shielding deals with primary radiation, while Figures 1 to 3 show protection against *scattered* or *secondary* radiation. Primary radiation comes directly from the source; scattered radiation has been deviated in direction; and secondary radiation is emitted by an irradiated material. Primary radiation requires more protection because its energy level is higher.

Fabrication and Installation

Sheet lead is not structurally self-supporting, so must be mounted to prevent sagging by its own weight. For lead thickness up to 3.5 mm, sheet lead can be readily shaped around round and small rectangular ducts, say

---

* Mr. Goodman, formerly with Meyer, Strong, and Jones now has his own consulting practice in New York City. He has a masters degree in mechanical engineering from the University of Wisconsin, where he specialized in heat transfer, and is a licensed professional engineer.

** Mr. Hollands is chief engineer, in charge of design of radiation shielding materials and equipment, for Bar-Ray Products, Inc., Brooklyn, N.Y. He is a member of ASTM, Society for Nondestructive Testing, Acoustical Society of America, and American Institute of Physics.

24 in. maximum diameter or width, with all joints overlapping at least ½ in. To hold these lead sheets in place, 1 in. wide iron bands should be placed around the periphery of the duct on approximately 12 in. centers, care being taken not to cut into the lead when the bands are bolted up.

When lead thickness is greater than 3.5 mm or duct or duct width exceeds 24 in., lead shielding should be laminated on a plywood or similar structural core, which is made in sections or panels to conform to the sides of the duct. The laminated sections are mechanically fastened at the seams and corners. These joints are lapped with sheet lead angles or lead strips, the width of which is twice the thickness of the lead, but not less than ½ inch in any case. Nails, bolts, screws, or other fasteners used to secure the lead sheet or panel must be covered with lead of thickness equal to the lead sheet. Lead headed nails may be used as shown in Figure 5.

For lead shielding of 1.0 mm or less, flexible leaded vinyl sheets can be used for easy forming to complex shapes and contours. The flexible leader vinyl sheets can be applied in layers where heavier than 1.0 mm lead shielding is required. If the duct has a flexible vinyl sheets could be applied over it more readily than other forms of shielding.

Duct hangers are best installed on the outside of the lead shielding so that the hanger rods or straps do not have to pierce the shielding. The lead shielding adds considerably to the weight of the duct and the hangers should be substantial, with such adequate anchoring in the slab above as fish plates. For rectangular ducts, trapeze hangers would be the most practical. For design purposes, estimate each $\frac{1}{16}$ in. of lead at 4 lb. per sq. ft.

Tests for radiation leakage are usually made after the room is finished and the equipment is installed. It is very important to install shielding properly during the course of construction because of the expense in making corrections to the finished protective barrier. Moreover, equipment such as dampers should never be put in the shielded section of the ductwork, as repairs to this equipment would be very costly if the shielding must be dismantled.

A simple way to avoid penetration of the protective barrier's lead lining by pipes or wires is to offset them as close behind the lead lining as possible so that they can be backed with a lead sheet of sufficient size to prevent passage of the rays at any angle. This lead patch method is also used for electric switch boxes located in the wall.

Medical Installation

The extent of the protective barrier for medical installations is summarized below so that the air conditioning designer can tell whether ducts or pipes running through such spaces are likely to be a problem. For medical radiographic and fluoroscopic rooms the lead shielding generally does not extend above a line 7 ft 0 in. from the finished floor; and if the service lines and ducts can be located above this line, shielding around them is obviously unnecessary. For X-ray therapy rooms, lead shielding may extend to the ceiling or structural slab. The ceiling or slab above and the floor may also be lead lined, depending upon output of the machine and other conditions. For industrial X-ray work, wall shielding may extend to the ceiling. Both ceiling and floor in some cases will require lead lining.

For shielding in super voltage rooms, special conditions may apply. In any event, the radiological physicist should be consulted to design the proper protection. Where concrete is considered for the shielding material, it is often more practical to use lead of equivalent value for the shielding of openings. Where recesses occur in concrete barriers for equipment, lead backing, equivalent to the thickness of the concrete removed, should be provided.

Bibliography

Of the many publication available on the subject of radiation protection, these two are the most useful:

1. *Medical X-ray Protection Up to Three Million Volts*, Handbook No. 76, National Bureau of Standards, 1961;

2. *Radiation Protection,* Lead Industries Association, 292 Madison Avenue, New York, N.Y.

In addition, the New York City Health Department publishes the New York City Health Code requirements dealing with radiological hazards (Article 175).

Notice: This article and associated drawings are reproduced from a 1984 printing *of A Guide to The Use* of *Lead For Radiation Shielding* with permission of the Lead Industries Association.

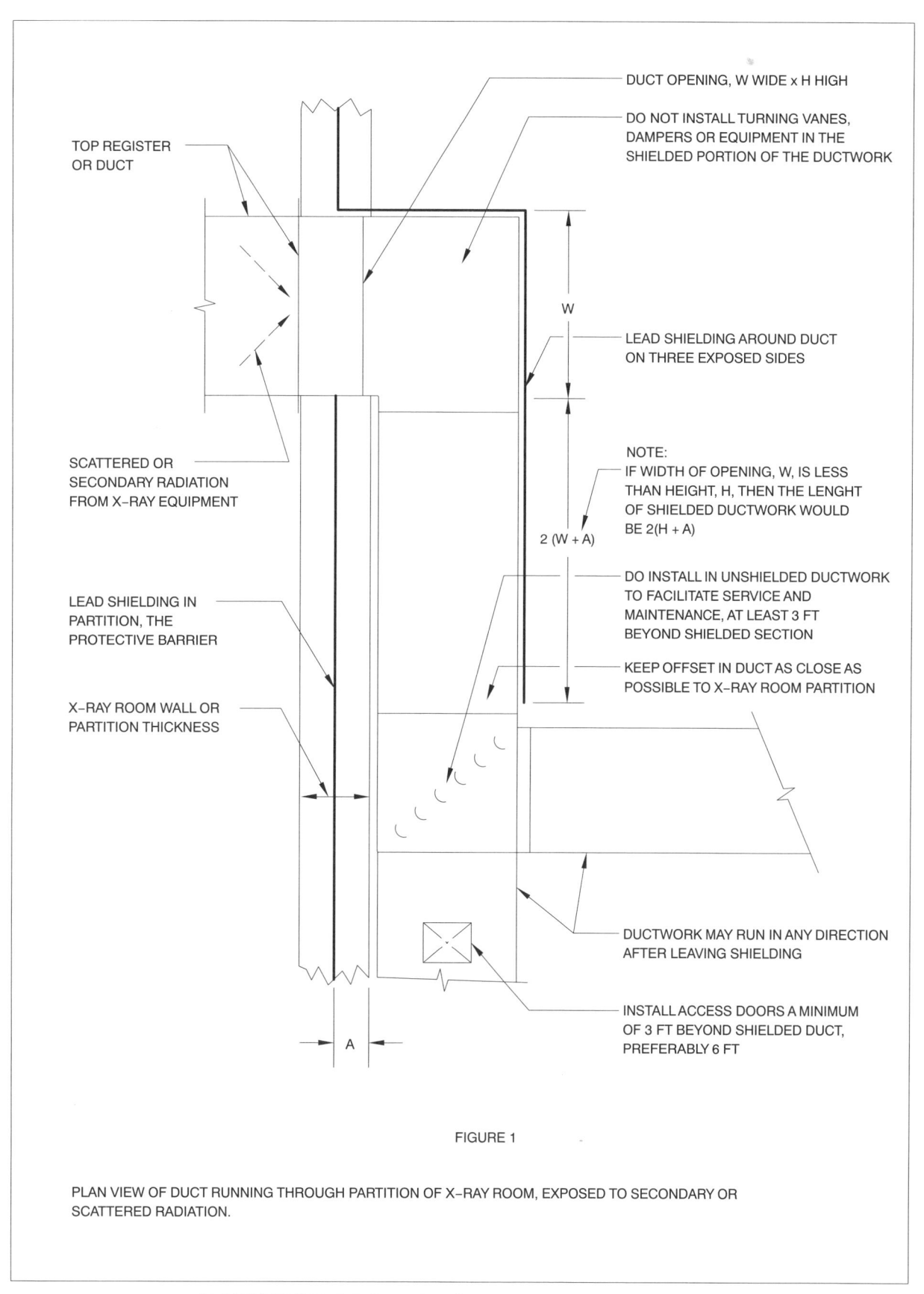

- TOP REGISTER OR DUCT
- DUCT OPENING, W WIDE x H HIGH
- DO NOT INSTALL TURNING VANES, DAMPERS OR EQUIPMENT IN THE SHIELDED PORTION OF THE DUCTWORK
- LEAD SHIELDING AROUND DUCT ON THREE EXPOSED SIDES
- SCATTERED OR SECONDARY RADIATION FROM X-RAY EQUIPMENT
- NOTE: IF WIDTH OF OPENING, W, IS LESS THAN HEIGHT, H, THEN THE LENGHT OF SHIELDED DUCTWORK WOULD BE 2(H + A)
- 2 (W + A)
- DO INSTALL IN UNSHIELDED DUCTWORK TO FACILITATE SERVICE AND MAINTENANCE, AT LEAST 3 FT BEYOND SHIELDED SECTION
- LEAD SHIELDING IN PARTITION, THE PROTECTIVE BARRIER
- KEEP OFFSET IN DUCT AS CLOSE AS POSSIBLE TO X-RAY ROOM PARTITION
- X-RAY ROOM WALL OR PARTITION THICKNESS
- DUCTWORK MAY RUN IN ANY DIRECTION AFTER LEAVING SHIELDING
- INSTALL ACCESS DOORS A MINIMUM OF 3 FT BEYOND SHIELDED DUCT, PREFERABLY 6 FT

FIGURE 1

PLAN VIEW OF DUCT RUNNING THROUGH PARTITION OF X-RAY ROOM, EXPOSED TO SECONDARY OR SCATTERED RADIATION.

RADIATION PROTECTION AT WALL OPENINGS

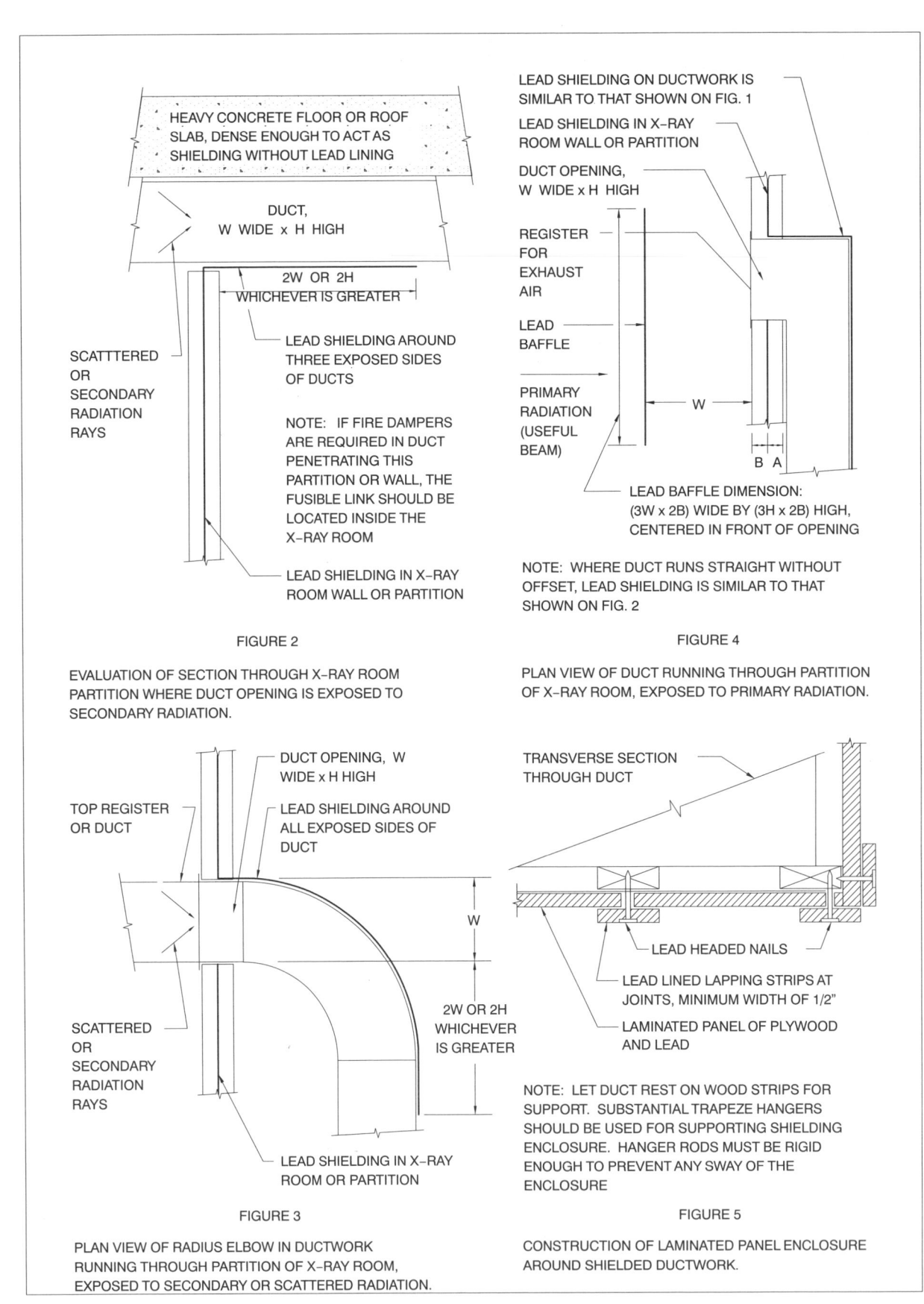

FIGURE 2

EVALUATION OF SECTION THROUGH X-RAY ROOM PARTITION WHERE DUCT OPENING IS EXPOSED TO SECONDARY RADIATION.

FIGURE 4

PLAN VIEW OF DUCT RUNNING THROUGH PARTITION OF X-RAY ROOM, EXPOSED TO PRIMARY RADIATION.

FIGURE 3

PLAN VIEW OF RADIUS ELBOW IN DUCTWORK RUNNING THROUGH PARTITION OF X-RAY ROOM, EXPOSED TO SECONDARY OR SCATTERED RADIATION.

FIGURE 5

CONSTRUCTION OF LAMINATED PANEL ENCLOSURE AROUND SHIELDED DUCTWORK.

RADIATION PROTECTION AT WALL OPENINGS

STRAIGHT   CANTED   RAISED - CANT'

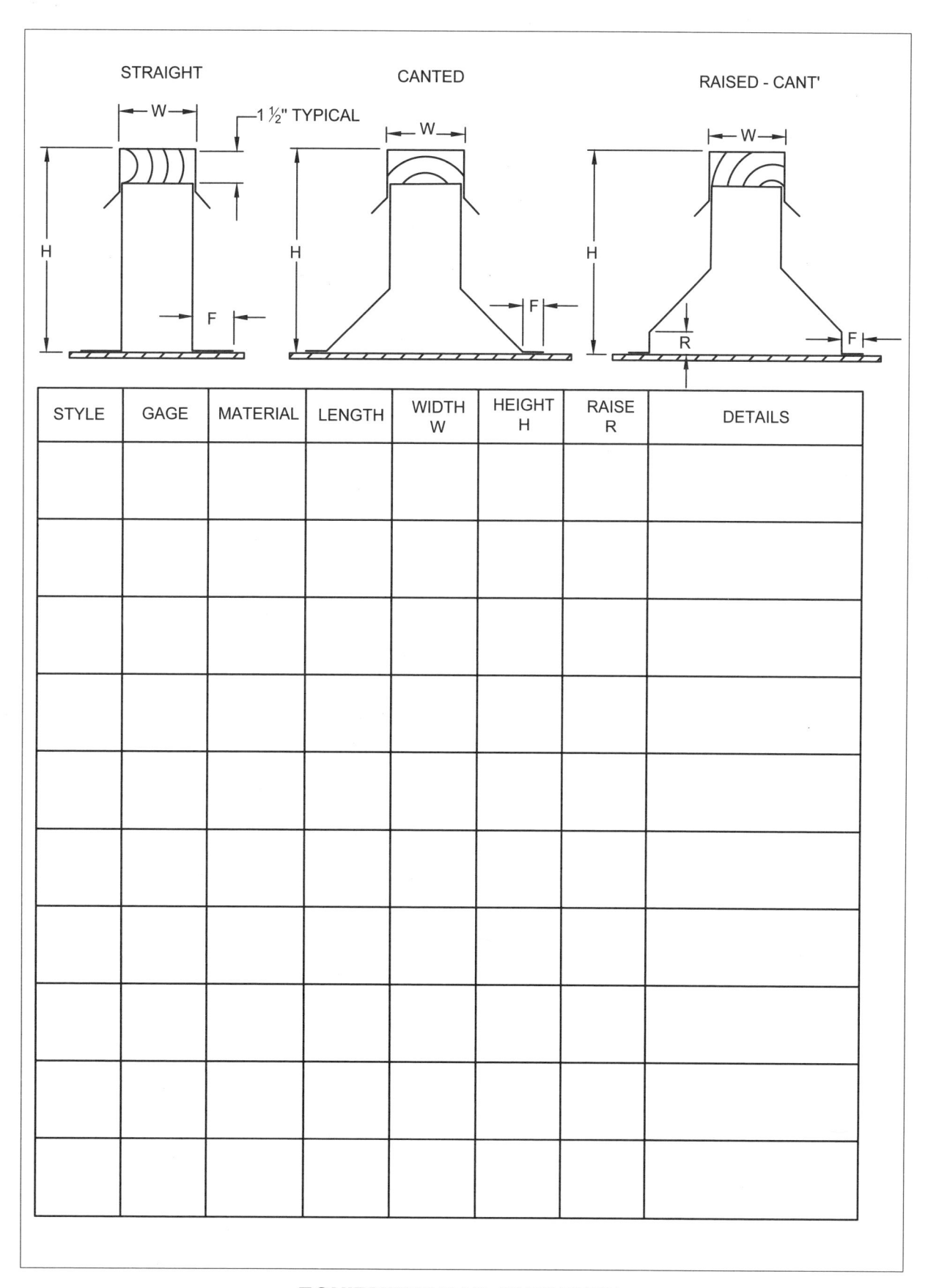

— 1½" TYPICAL

STYLE	GAGE	MATERIAL	LENGTH	WIDTH W	HEIGHT H	RAISE R	DETAILS

EQUIPMENT RAIL SUBMITTAL

CONTRIBUTORS TO THE FOURTH EDITION

Ralph Koerber, Fort Worth, TX
Norman Grusnick, British Columbia, Canada
Brennan Hall, Denver, CO

Air Duct Council
Ecco Manufacturing
Johns Manville
SPIDA

OTHER CONTRIBUTORS TO PREVIOUS EDITIONS

John Aimonette, Ft. Lauderdale, FL
Burton H. Anderson, San Leandro, CA
Pat Bentz, Vienna, VA
Robert W. Boltz, Arlington, VA
Ernest Boniface, Wayne, NJ
Thomas J. Boniface, Wayne, NJ
Arnold N. Brodie, Oak Park, Ml
Earl Burmeister, W. Des Moine, IA
John Burnett, Phoenix, AZ
Dick Cramer, Flint, MI
John Creegan, Hawthorn, NJ
G. E. Daniel, St. Petersburg, FL
Floyd W. Deeds, Salt Lake City, UT
Robert S. Deeds, Salt Lake City, UT
Herbert Delasco, South Windsor, CT
Gilbert G. Dorsett, Dallas, TX
Daniel J. Driscoll, Philadelphia, PA
Gene Van Dyke, Denver, CO
Frank D. Ellis, Sparks, NV
Wallace E. Fizer, Lexington, KY
Richard Friedman, Richmond, CA
Robert Gawne, Washington, DC
John Gruss, Kansas City, MO
John J. Gruss, Shawnee Mission, KS
Warren Hanna, Farmingham, MA
William M. Harmon, Columbus, OH
Norman T. R. Heathorn, Oakland, CA
Fred Hershman, Philadelphia, PA
John Higgins, St. Louis, MO
Angelo Hoffman, Milwaukee, WI
Joe Hunter, Falls Church, VA
Joe Ibsen, San Bernardino, CA
Isidore Jacobson, Cincinnati, OH
Charles H. Johnson, East Moline, IL
Ron Keeler, Edmonton, Alberta, Canada

William J. Knecht, Camden, NJ
Gerard Iacouzze, Vienna, VA
D. C. Lee, Birminghan, AL
D. E. Mannen, Cleveland, OH
Donal J. Mosshart Jr., Pittsburgh, PA
Harold Nepereny, Vienna, VA
Bill Orchard, North Brunswick, NJ
John Paoluccio, Modesto, CA
J. Frank Park, Compton, CA
Wayne Parriot, St. Paul, MN
Donald Partney, Granite City, IL
Lawrence Paul, Chicago, IL
Richard Peabody, Philadelphia, PA
Keith Pierson, Sacramento, CA
M. A. Punchard, Fort Worth, TX
James Ray, Atlanta, GA
Gordon Root, Burlington, VT
Jerome C. Ross, New York, NY
Robert G. Sandvik, Arlington, VA
Robert Schomann, Milwaukee, WI
Robert Segal, Farmington, Ml
Daniel Steimer, Portland, OR
Harold C. Stevens, Chicago, IL
John H. Stratton, Vienna, VA
Paul Stromberg, Washington, DC
Bill R. Svejkovsky, Oklahoma City, OK
Frank Swanda, Oklahoma City, OK
Robert E. Taylor, Salt Lake City, UT
Robert Tumberger, Kansas City, MO
Bowman Turner, Columbus, OH
Joseph B. Whatley, Tampa, FL
Claude Wilson, Bozeman, MT
Gilbert Wood, Houston, TX

National Insulation Manufacturers Association
Adhesive And Sealant Council, Inc.
Duro-Dyne Corporation

Gripnail Corporation
Stic-Klip Company
Thermal Insulation Manufacturers Association

SHEET METAL AND AIR CONDITIONING CONTRACTORS'
NATIONAL ASSOCIATION, INC.